P9-CFV-526

N

1981 Don Hanwart

With special
best wishes,

Perry A. Klopfenstein
9-10-87

Marching To Zion

A HISTORY OF THE APOSTOLIC CHRISTIAN CHURCH OF AMERICA
1847-1982

by Perry A. Klopfenstein

Copyright © 1984 by
The Apostolic Christian Church
of America

ISBN: 0-9611836-0-8
Library of Congress Number
83-071702

First Edition

1 2 3 4 5 6 7 8 9

Printed in the United States of America

SEKAN

SEKAN PRINTING COMPANY
2210 SOUTH MAIN STREET
FORT SCOTT, KS 66701

TABLE OF CONTENTS

INDEX OF CONGREGATIONS

Satellite Churches

INTRODUCTION

"Thy word is a lamp unto my feet, and a light unto my path."

By 1982 the Apostolic Christian Church of America had marked its 135th year in America. From an inauspicious beginning in a remote section of upstate New York in 1847, the church had grown to include more than seventy-six congregations in nineteen states along with two in Japan and one in Canada. In addition, in the early 1980's churches were being established in a few large metropolitan areas in the United States. Total membership exceeded eleven thousand, and a steady growth rate had prevailed over the years, especially since the English language replaced German in worship services during the 1920's and 1930's.

In all, counting churches that no longer exist, the faith had been promulgated in well over one hundred locations in the United States of America over the years.

Although many of the church's forefathers left their European homesteads with a sense of apprehension and uncertainty, the subsequent successes—both spiritual and material—of their descendants totally vindicated their decision to leave their homelands and emigrate to America, the land of freedom and opportunity.

As the church entered the decade of 1980, it was distinguished by two significant factors. First, it was enjoying the benefit of total religious toleration from civil authorities. Instead of experiencing discouragement and oppression, the church—as well as all religious faiths—worshipped freely under the mandates of the First Amendment protected by a government that encouraged freedom of conscience and the worship of a personal deity.

Second, a free enterprise economy which fostered the precepts of incentive, ambition, ingenuity, and hard work proved a real blessing to members of the church whose entire heritage was enshrouded in the work ethic.

1

In the mid-to-latter stages of the twentieth century, the brotherhood was enjoying a "golden age of prosperity." The three decades from 1950 to 1980 will be especially remembered in the church's history as a time when the brotherhood (in the true spirit of I Chronicles 29:14,15,16) gave willingly and joyfully for the construction of new churches, church remodeling, and new fellowship halls. Total appropriations, especially if allowed to account for the double-digit inflation rates of the late 1970's, would be considered noteworthy for a denomination of just over eleven thousand members.

While a rise in personal income resulted in a higher standard of living, the blessings of God were able to be channeled to charitable causes on a much larger scale than that in earlier generations. By 1982 the church operated nine nursing homes, a children's home, and a large home for handicapped persons. World Relief efforts to aid the poor and needy increased sharply.

As the church entered the 1980's, it reflected a remarkable degree of doctrinal unity, although, in a traditional sense, it was not unaffected by the extreme pluralism of American society. Even so, the basic tenets of the faith—for decades promoted and defended by the forefathers—were deeply rooted and found a warm reception among the churches.

This body, unique in its solid devotion to literal Biblical precepts and profound in its sense of brotherhood and oneness, seemed to stand out among the large number of protestant faiths in America. Paramount in its uniqueness was the unshakable and sincere devotion of its members to the Lord, to the "new birth" teaching, and to the ways and doctrine of the church based on solid Biblical precepts. Such a deep and loyal sense of spiritual kinship—centered in and because of Christ—could only be fully understood by those who were members of His body—those who had humbly knelt at the foot of the Cross in true repentance, had become converted, and subsequently arm in arm with Jesus Christ had begun marching to Zion.

How did it all begin? Where did a God-fearing denomination with such a deep devotion to Scriptures, to spiritual unity and oneness, and to true brotherhood find its origin? How did the Apostolic Christian Church come to be? This book was written to help provide an answer.

PROLOGUE

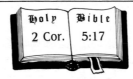

"Therefore if any man be in Christ, he is a new creature: old things are passed away; behold, all things are become new."

The German phrase *"Aller Anfang ist schwer"* best describes the feelings associated with taking on the awesome responsibility of writing the history of the Apostolic Christian Church. The phrase, which means "All beginning is difficult," aptly reflects an author's dilemma in trying to incorporate more than one hundred local histories into a coherent manuscript that explains the essence of church life—from the time of Samuel Froehlich in nineteenth-century Switzerland to the latter stages of the twentieth century.

Adding to the challenge is the fact that the Apostolic Christian Church is not just another typical American denomination. Rather, it is a fellowship of Christians where religious conviction and devotion to Christ run very deep—so deep that those who would become members must be willing to humble themselves before Almighty God and to take for their primary and all-encompassing motive in life the conforming to the image of Christ and the following of His ways as outlined in Holy Writ. Adjunct to these noble motives is the fact that church life and thought are deeply woven within the framework of brotherhood. Each member seeks to be submissive to the other "in the fear of God."

In this general context it is pertinent to state that each local congregation, perhaps often misunderstood by their local communities because of the devout lifestyle of its members, is a part of a larger, national body. This entire brotherhood, in which all members enjoy a common understanding of faith as well as a very warm and mutually engaging sense of fellowship, is something very precious to an Apostolic Christian.

Central to the unique bond of fellowship that exists between Apostolic Christians, both individually and corporately, is a common experience of faith, not only in the redemptive work of Christ, but in the deep experience of repentance and conversion—that crisis period of one's life when he or she turned from sin and a life centered on self-gratification to a life of faith and righteousness with one's life centered on the Saviour and His ways.

Another aspect of faith closely related with fellowship among the members is the ongoing common experience of daily seeking to overcome the flesh and living in obedience to God's word. Often, due to worldly enticements, this is not easy to do, and can only be accomplished with God's help. This daily battle against evil results in a great bond of fellowship as brethren, based on Scriptures, seek to encourage and assist one another to walk humbly on the narrow path which ultimately leads to everlasting life in Heaven.

For the reasons just stated, members of the church hold a deep sense of denominational loyalty. Thus, to list on paper the essence of all that is rich and meaningful to Apostolic Christians is not necessarily an easy task.

Generally, the objective of this book is to record the church's initial efforts in Europe and its establishment and growth in America. Much like the nation itself, which was officially formed more than seven decades before the first Apostolic Christian Church was established in upstate New York, the Latin phrase *"e pluribus unum"* (out of many one) clearly depicts this fellowship in that its people emanated from a variety of religious and cultural backgrounds into one common doctrine.

The history of the church, its deeply held doctrine, and the project of writing it all transcend the feeble efforts of the author. The true history of anything is only recorded accurately in the mind of God. Man's scope of history, especially when compared to God's, is both minuscule and microscopic. With these limitations the author has attempted to record data pertaining to the church that seems important and significant. In doing so, it is obvious, particularly to Almighty God, that the manuscript is imperfect, and much has probably been left out that will fade forever into oblivion, known only to God. The objective, then, has been to record the church history "not verbatim, but in essence."

To weave the histories of more than one hundred local congregations into one coherent account has been a major challenge. At the outset, it was decided to include all the local histories because the brotherhood exists with such a deep sense of spiritual kinship. To have omitted local histories would have been to miss an important aspect of church life.

It was difficult to know where to include each congregation in the manuscript. Eventually, it seemed the most appropriate to place each church in the time frame it was established and then carry its history through to the present time. Deciding when a local fellowship was "established" complicated matters further. Did it occur (1) when a few members assembled for the first time, (2) when they "officially" organized, or (3) when a church building was constructed? The author decided that the first choice was the best indicator, although listing the specific years in which local congregations were established is somewhat arbitrary because record-keeping has never been a high priority (particularly in the early days).

Information regarding this history came largely from local church historians who submitted general information. In addition, virtually every issue of the *Silver Lining* was perused. To augment these resources, the author also drew from numerous interviews as well as from diaries, family genealogies, and related documents.

In presenting these histories, it is obvious that some of the local church histories are longer than others due to the fact that some local historians submitted more information than others. There was certainly no intention to slight any church.

Also, there is information in some of the local histories which might seem to be somewhat irrelevant when considered from a local standpoint. Yet, it is deemed important when considered from a denominational viewpoint in that it reflects conditions that existed in nearly all the churches. Such information was also included in an attempt to keep the book interesting. Further, because in the mid-to-late twentieth-century Apostolic Christians traveled extensively among the various congregations, the author occasionally inserted interesting information about these areas.

Most of the book's footnotes are concentrated in the beginning portions of the manuscript which describe the church's place within the broader scope of ecclesiastical history. The author drew heavily from historical accounts describing factors which later influenced Samuel Froehlich and subsequently the church in America. On the other hand, data from local histories was not footnoted to such an extent. Supportive information, however, remains in the author's files.

There are two items regarding the book's style that should be mentioned. First, in referring to names of people, the title of "brother" or "sister" is omitted. This was done to avoid repetition and also because uncertainty exists in some instances whether various persons referred to were actually members of the church. Too, some who were members at one time may have later departed from the fellowship. To be consistent and to avoid misreference, these titles were omitted.

Second, in most instances, only ministers who served as Elders or Bishops are mentioned, with exceptions being made for those ministers who were associated with unusual historical circumstances or who served alone for several years in the ministry. This policy of referring mostly to Elders was adopted because sketchy historical records made it nearly impossible to make an accurate listing of all church ministers since 1847. This in no way was meant to slight those many humble and devoted men of God who have labored in the ministry. To someday compile an accurate list of all Apostolic Christian ministers would be a worthy project.

The reader should be aware that when the church first came to America, it was generally known as the Evangelical Baptist Church; but soon the brethren began using various derivatives of the name—Apostolic Christian Church—until an official name was adopted during the United States' entry into World War I. On occasion (in this history) the two denominational names—Evangelical Baptist and Apostolic Christian— have been used interchangeably, but are intended to mean Apostolic Christian.

The book's overall style and presentation is patterned after most conventional histories written about other denominations. Chapter titles are intended to reflect the various time frames of the church's history.

The pictures selected for inclusion in this work are mostly of buildings and occasionally of cemetery markers. Because Samuel Froehlich (who believed photographs were "graven images") and other forefathers had strong convictions regarding photography, it was felt widespread use of pictures of individuals would be disrespectful to their memory and also draw too much attention to men. For this reason, the author felt it would be inconsistent, in a denomination which emphasizes the Scriptural principle to "seek to be the least," to draw attention to church officials through the use of photography. Also, in this general context, an effort has been made not to give extraordinary attention to any one church official or leader. It is a generally held mandate within the church that any significant contributions men make on behalf of the church are manifestations of the power of God.

Although to many it might have been interesting, the book does not delve into the history of the church's theology with respect to standards of personal decorum and overall conduct. While the brotherhood has always encouraged high ideals in this regard, this subject itself would have required substantial additional study and would largely have been based on assumptions because no one has written extensively on this topic since the church began in America in 1847.

This book is not a sequel to *Apostolic Christian Church History, Volume I* written by Herman Ruegger of Goldbach, Zurich, Switzerland, in 1947.

It is well to state, too, that the information contained in this volume does not necessarily represent an "official" view of the church and its history, although a committee of Elders advised the author in writing various aspects of the history.

The author wishes to thank the scores of people who assisted in this project, both by providing historical data and lending sincere encouragement as the months of writing wore on. The Elder History Committee was of enormous help and support. Eleanor Yackley, Taylor, Missouri, should be commended for her excellent proofreading efforts.

This book is not intended to be a complete analysis of all that took place over the years. It does contain some analyses, particularly with respect to the church's origin and early influences, of several points of doctrine and practice and the cause for the first and second divisions; but largely it is a methodical recording of what actually transpired over the years in America. Admittedly, it is a little less than objective at times, and the author's deep affection for the church probably shows through then. In any case, the intent of the book was to make a historical record that will serve to inspire and delight present and future generations. Also, it was thought that if a history project of this magnitude was not begun during this decade, much of the early history of the fellowship would be lost.

It is also the author's sincere wish that this church history will in some way help to articulate both the origins and essentials of the faith, particularly to generations of "friends" who, for one reason or another, have never become a part of the church. As such, it is hoped this book will help to erase, if necessary, any misconceptions held by those outside the church.

It is both interesting and appropriate to note that this manuscript went to the printer in 1982, a year marking the sesquicentennial observance of the beginning of the "Froehlich movement." It was in 1832 that young, twenty-eight-year-old Samuel Froehlich was baptized and began in earnest to preach the true doctrine of salvation. Perhaps this book, in some small way, can serve as a fitting memorial not only to Samuel Froehlich but to all our forefathers in faith to whom we owe so much.

The author is not so vain as to think there are no mistakes in this book. Its scope and length certainly allow for this possibility. It is hoped that errors of fact or misspelled words will be directed to the author's attention. Subsequent editions will contain corrections as well as updated material, if God wills.

The author's fondest dream is that this book, hopefully written "without offense," can serve a twofold purpose. First, that it will be pleasing to God; and second, that it will help to generate in all of us a deeper understanding of our precious spiritual heritage without which our lives would be both unimaginable and immeasurably barren.

Perry A. Klopfenstein
Gridley, Illinois
October 12, 1983

"For thou, O God hast heard my vows: thou hast given me the heritage of those that fear thy name."   Psalms 61:5

"Then Peter said unto them, Repent, and be baptized every one of you in the name of Jesus Christ for the remission of sins, and ye shall receive the gift of the Holy Ghost."

CROGHAN AND NAUMBURG, NEW YORK

Two dates, seemingly unrelated, figure very prominently in the history of the Apostolic Christian Church of America. The first—widely acclaimed and heard around the world— occurred on July 4, 1776, when fifty-six men gathered in Independence Hall to sign the Declaration of Independence, a document which asserted unequivocally "that all men are created equal; that they are endowed by their Creator with certain unalienable rights; that among these are life, liberty, and the pursuit of happiness." Adjunct to this was the First Amendment to the Constitution which said, "Congress shall make no law respecting an establishment of a religion, or prohibiting the exercise thereof." This great event occurred with much fanfare and acclaim!

The second date was July 4, 1803, exactly twenty-seven years later. A boy, Samuel Heinrich Froehlich, was born in the city of Brugg of canton Aargau in Switzerland. In time he would grow up to lead a religious awakening which would erupt in Switzerland and spread to several other countries, including America. This event, while a joy for the Froehlich family, occurred without fanfare.

With the birth of Samuel Froehlich, the stage was set for the doctrines of repentance and conversion, particularly as understood by Apostolic Christians, to ultimately find their way to America. Religious liberty, America's grandest of freedoms, was instituted by the country's founding fathers in 1776. A few years later God raised up a man of unusual devotion and vision whose energies and zeal awoke multitudes to the One who could give them eternal life. As emigration from Europe to America began in great volume, it was inevitable that the faith of our fathers on that continent would gravitate to America, the land of religious toleration.

Yet, in a broader and more accurate sense, the true roots of the church date back to events associated at Mount Calvary when Jesus Christ of Nazareth, the Son of God, bled and died on the cruel Cross for the remission of sin.

The movement which Samuel Froehlich began in 1831-1832 found a presence in America in 1847. It was during this year that twenty-eight-year-old Benedict Weyeneth, having just recently been ordained an Elder in the Evangelical Baptist Church in Switzerland and personally consecrated by Samuel Froehlich, landed on American soil.[1]

Young Weyeneth, diligent in spirit and obviously feeling led of God because he was ordained specifically to come to America, patiently checked through customs and soon found the boat that would take him up the Hudson River to Albany, then by canal to Utica. From there he may have walked the twenty or so miles to the Black River and then taken some type of water conveyance (or he may have walked) the entire sixty miles to Lewis County, New York. This is the site of the two Apostolic Christian Churches which exist today at Croghan and Naumburg.

He was on a mission of profound importance. Rather than attempting to initiate a broadly based program of evangelism for America—which already had many Christian denominations—he instead was responding to a request from Joseph Virkler, a Lewis County Amish Mennonite farmer, to Samuel Froehlich for help in alleviating some spiritual problems which were besetting his group of believers in that area.[2]

It was during a previous meeting of Virkler's group that one of them, a former member of Froehlich's Evangelical Baptist Church in Europe, had recommended the group write to Froehlich to see if he could either adjudicate their differences or make other spiritual recommendations which might resolve the situation. It was their hope that Froehlich would come to America.

Because Froehlich was a strong, dynamic and very persuasive leader, no doubt this man, while separated from Froehlich's church, continued to retain a deep respect for his ability and talent in helping those who needed spiritual guidance.

Although he remains unknown, the man who recommended Froehlich played a very significant part in the history of the Apostolic Christian Church of America. Had he not suggested that Froehlich or one of his followers be summoned to America, the church might never have crossed the Atlantic at that particular time, and the history of the church in America might have been markedly different.

Research concerning the man who recommended that Joseph Virkler write to Samuel Froehlich fails to reveal any definite clues to his identity. In 1939 at Roanoke, Illinois, Fred Herbst, a local history enthusiast interviewed Priscilla Weyeneth Liebig, a daughter of Benedict Weyeneth. His notes of this interview, while somewhat difficult to read, contain the phrase, "Benhart Ben sent word to Europe." Whether she is referring to the name "Benhart" is unknown. At this time there is no known family in the church by the name of Benhart. Thus, the man's identity is a mystery that will likely remain unresolved. There is conjecture, however, that the man might have been John Keiffer, an early arrival in America who persuaded many Mennonites to move from Europe to Lewis County. This cannot be totally confirmed.

It is not altogether certain whether Benedict Weyeneth came to America alone or with a male companion. It is certain he was the only Elder to come over to help the Amish Mennonite colony in Lewis County, New York.

Joseph Farney and Rudolph Virkler served the Lewis County church as bishops and were probably the leaders who had previously brought the group to America.[3]

Arletha Zehr Bender,[4] in *A History of The Mennonites in Lewis County, New York,* describes Weyeneth as an "invited" Elder and says:

> Some have said that two men came at this time, both from Switzerland, who were of a sect popularly known as "die Frohlich." A little different teaching unfamiliar to the Amish Mennonite people was introduced by them. A writer indicated that one change pertained to the new birth experience by placing emphasis on feeling, impulse, or emotion. They also subscribed to the doctrine of baptism by immersion rather than pouring water on an applicant's head for this outward expression of an inner cleansing from sin.

Attending the regular Sunday morning worship service, Benedict Weyeneth was granted permission from Rudolph Virkler to read a song from a book. The song being read after the conclusion of the regular meeting indicated the teaching of immersion, it is thought. He presented to the congregation the importance of these doctrines and visited their homes reviewing to them the changes necessary for them to adopt.

His views were favored by Rudolph Virkler who became willing to leave his church to associate and affiliate with him. Soon his family and many relatives left the Amish Mennonite Church and started a new church of their own. They taught it was necessary for everyone to accept this teaching, and those who joined the new faith were rebaptized by being immersed. The first minister ordained for this new group was Joseph Virkler, son of Rudolph Virkler. After many of the Virkler family left the Amish Mennonite Church, other members gradually left and took the same step. Joseph Farney, our first bishop, was also influenced by the doctrine. He left two years after Rudolph Virkler and united with their group, which was then called the New Amish Church.

Members of the church continued to leave over a period of twenty-five years. Three out of every four were evangelized and left the old church to unite with the new group.

Later in her book, Bender again refers to the Weyeneth incident:[5]

Here they were known as the "New Amish." They claim for themselves the name of Evangelical Baptists. They were present at the usual meeting for worship and preaching services, and after the conclusion of the meeting, they asked to read a song out of a book. Some church officials would not allow such liberty, but Bishop Virkler granted them the liberty. Whether he talked the matter over with them before is not known, but it looks that way. Anyhow, he favored their views and doctrine and associated and affiliated with them without much discussion. His relatives took the same course and went with him; and others followed. Of the teachings of these people, one prominent feature was that of baptism, which they insisted must be by immersion, and all who united with them had to be baptized again, even though baptized upon confession of faith previously.

Second, no one was considered saved unless belonging to their church. [Author's note: This is not a tenet of the church today.]

Third, their new birth had to come to pass in a particular manner, and the main emphasis was laid upon feeling, impulse, or emotion. Many went over to the new organization in the first rush, and this continued until but a small number of members were left in the original congregation. Two years later, Bishop Farney also deserted his former church connection.

The above provides an interesting perspective written by a descendant of the original Amish Mennonite group. Obviously the mass exodus from that group to follow the faith and doctrine of the Evangelical Baptists as outlined to them by Benedict Weyeneth proved to be a devastating experience for the Amish Mennonite colony in Lewis County and left them struggling for several decades.

From Weyeneth's perspective, the first foray into America was a success. By introducing the important doctrines of repentance and conversion, a sanctified life, and a true inner peace of heart and mind, he found a willing audience and many followers.

As a young man of only twenty-eight, he likely felt the heavy brunt of awesome responsibility. First, he was not only entering a new land but also going among people with a different religious persuasion who were having various disputes about their beliefs. Second, he was dealing with two experienced bishops, Rudolph Virkler, age fifty-five, and Joseph Farney, age fifty-two, both many years his senior.

Among his first acts upon obtaining a following in America was the selection of Joseph Virkler as minister. Born in 1816 in Alsace-Lorraine, he was the eldest of eight sons of Rudolph Virkler.

Soon after the beginning of our nation in 1776, pioneers began viewing the vast expanse of land within its frontiers, and New York State was no exception. It, too, contained enormous acreage. The upper portions of the state, particularly the Black River Valley, awaited development.

For centuries this lush, virgin land lay placid and undeveloped, inhabited only by Indians. This scenic and spectacular valley was enclosed on one side by the steep ridges of Tug Hill on the west and the Adirondacks on the east. It was an untouched wilderness consisting of the bounty only a primeval forest can offer. Through the middle of this untamed area ran the patient and quiet Black River.

It was only a matter of time until this beautiful area would give way to "progress" and become inhabited by the white man. Such opportunity caught the eye of wealthy financiers from the courts of Europe. One of these was a Frenchman, Count James Donatien LeRay DeChaumont, whose family was on friendly terms with the Bonaparte family. DeChaumont eventually owned 100,000 acres in Lewis County.[6]

By 1810 DeChaumont's son Vincent began to manage his father's affairs in this country.[7] As he formulated plans to develop these virgin lands, his thoughts turned to Europe, and he began seeking colonists from the French provinces of Alsace and Lorraine. These were diligent and thrifty peasant farmers, mostly of Mennonite and Anabaptist faith, who had distinguished themselves as efficient husbandmen in that area. DeChaumont thought such farmers would be ideal for clearing the thick forests of Lewis County and converting them into tillable acreage.

To implement his plan the younger DeChaumont hired John Keiffer, a native Alsatian, to encourage persons to come and settle in Lewis County. Keiffer made his first voyage to America in 1830. He entered through a Canadian port, not an American port. In 1833 he was back in Europe trying to persuade Amish and Mennonite families in Alsace and Lorraine to emigrate to America and establish themselves on the lands being sold by LeRay DeChaumont.[8]

In order to entice these possible settlers to come to America, Keiffer distributed a flyer which DeChaumont instructed him to hand out:[9]

> This is mainly addressed to the people who wish to emigrate and settle on my land in the county of Lewis, state of New York.
>
> Upon arriving in New York City, the best thing for the emigrants to do is go immediately to the steamer that leaves for Albany every day at five o'clock in the afternoon. It will cost them fifty sous per cart to transport their luggage, from the place of landing to the steamer, where they will be asked for fifty sous per person to take them to Albany. Half fare for children; no fare, or else very little, will be asked for infants. They will arrive in Albany at five o'clock in the morning; at seven o'clock they will leave Albany, by train, for Rome, where they will arrive at two o'clock in the afternoon. It will cost $2.44, which permits each passenger to take along, without charge, 150 pounds of baggage. From Rome they will go to New Bremen, by way of Lowville, traveling by carriage, on a road made of boards; if they leave Rome early in the morning, they will arrive in New Bremen the same evening; and also, the hiring of a two-horse carriage will vary from three to five piastres depending on the circumstances involved.
>
> If, upon arriving in New York, they prefer to stop at an inn, it will cost fifty sous per day, or twenty-five sous per meal; the transporting of baggage, from the place of landing to the inn, or from the inn to the steamer, is set at fifty sous per carriage.

In cases where three families or less would want to settle on my land, they have only to find out, as mentioned above, the name of the ship, the time and place of its departure, and an authorized person will be waiting for them when they land in New York and will escort them to my properties.

There are already several hundred French, Swiss, and Dutch families on my properties. The land is sound and fertile. It is infinitely better to stop here, rather than to go fifteen hundred miles farther West, into a country that is still uncertain, at least with regard to conduciveness to health, and to take a risk on the great lakes of North America, with a navigation that is much more dangerous than that of the ocean itself. Several families have already returned from the West and have settled on my properties. Furthermore, if these properties are not suitable, there is nothing easier than moving elsewhere, since they are only one day from the train to Rome.

Many of these families who came to upstate New York to the area known as "French Settlement" later were those who left the Amish Mennonite Church and established the first Evangelical Baptist Church in America under the guidance of Benedict Weyeneth.

Arletha Zehr Bender describes the conditions facing these brave pioneers:[10]

Arriving at French Settlement, they faced the darkened depth of the thick forest with countless maple, hemlock, and birch trees with their thick, dense foliage veiling the sunlight from sending its rays on the well-moistened ground beneath. It was here they realized their need to purchase land on which to establish home life. The land was cheap, selling anywhere from $1.50 to $3.00 per acre. Mr. Keiffer, representing DeChaumont, pointed out the land for sale.

Among these first Mennonite settlers who made the voyage of forty-two days in a small sailboat were Bishop Rudolph Virkler and family and Bishop Joseph Farney and family.[11] Some of the conditions they faced are vividly described:[12]

Until the log cabins were built, the early settlers were forced of necessity to sometimes sleep under the trees among the wild animals and the friendly Indians. A mere shack, close to the banks of the Beaver River belonging to the Indians and wherein they were living, welcomed some of the night lodgers and gave a place of shelter for them. Some mothers with their babies and small children stayed in this Indian hut until a home of their own was built. When cold weather prevailed, a nearby inn served as a lodging center. However, shortly after the arrival of the Farney and Virkler families, a snowstorm greatly discouraged them, but nevertheless they continued on in building from the forest a new home.

Many large and small trees felled by storm or dead by age lay numberless on the ground, so trails had to be cut before the invaders could proceed with their tasks. On all sides was the forest with its shadows broken only by the wild animals and Indians close by. Panthers made the night hideous with their blood-curdling screams, or else the growl of the bear was heard, and some wolves inhabited the woods.

The first Mennonite homes built in and near French Settlement were simple one-story log cabins with a kitchen, living room, and bedroom. Overhead was a loft or attic which was used as sleeping quarters. There was no foundation under the cabins, the logs being laid directly on the ground. The chinks between the logs were well plastered to keep out the cold. In the fall, dirt was banked around cabins to make it warmer throughout the winter months.

A large fireplace was used to supply heat and used for cooking purposes. It had an iron bar inside where iron kettles hung on chains, and small brass pots on high legs were set in the fireplace to prepare foods. The nearby Indians often made themselves at home among the new neighbors by lying on the floor rolled in a coat or a blanket in front of the fireplace.

The Rev. Rudolph Virkler, who left the Amish Mennonite Church to join Weyeneth's Evangelical Baptist Church, was born in Alsace-Lorraine December 4, 1792, and died May 4, 1876. In 1814 he married Anna Breckbeil, also of France. They arrived in America in 1834 with their seven sons, Joseph, Christian, John, Andrew, Nicholas, Jacob, and Peter. The eighth son, Michael, was born in French Settlement, being one of the first three Caucasian children born there. Another son, Nicholas Virkler, died soon after arrival in French Settlement.[13]

Rudolph Virkler was the grandson of Peter Virkler, who was born about 1698 in the Emmental near Bern, Switzerland. About 1730 he migrated to Alsace-Lorraine near Avincourt in order to flee religious persecution for refusal to bear arms and swear oaths. Peter Virkler had one son, John, who had fifteen children of whom Rudolph Virkler was the youngest.[14]

Along with economic opportunity and cheap land in America, one of the major reasons the Virkler, Farney, and other Amish Mennonite families emigrated to America was the ongoing militarism among the governments of Europe which subjected the peace-loving Mennonites to conscription and military service.

Having long supported the Scriptural directive and Anabaptist tradition of not bearing arms in war, they were particularly offended when their young boys were involuntarily drafted into the military. The annoyance of this ever-present possibility undoubtedly caused these families to take a long, hard look at the possibility of moving to America, and subsequently many did.

Several of John Virkler's sons were conscripted into the Grand Army of Napoleon Bonaparte and served during the Napoleonic Wars of 1799-1815.[15] Some of these boys served during Napoleon's ill-fated invasion of Russia in 1812. An army of 400,000-500,000 men invaded Russia during the winter and, in the most horrible winter conditions imaginable, were forced to retreat with only 50,000 survivors, among them the Virklers.

Napoleon lingered nearly a month among the blackened ruins of Moscow in hopes of making peace with Tsar Alexander. This hoped-for peace never materialized, and Napoleon was forced to retreat amid impossible conditions:[16]

> The roads were soon churned to liquid mud, rain alternated with snow and ice, the horses that drew the cannon and baggage perished, disease multiplied, food failed. To all these miseries were added the incessant raids of swift-moving Cossacks, who harried the outposts, and killed the stragglers.
>
> Late in December, a few thousand starved, broken, and half-crazed men, the miserable remnant of what had been called the Grand Army, tottered across the Russian boundary into the comparative safety of a German area held by French reserves.

Among these survivors were some of the older brothers of Rudolph Virkler. In his later years Rudolph told many stories of his older brothers' experiences under Napoleon.[17]

To fully understand why the ancestors of the Apostolic Christian Church came to America, it serves a very useful purpose to review some of the terrible military encounters as those just described. It was because of such pathetic situations associated with war and killing that followers of Christ wanted to flee to a land where they would be relatively free of forced military service and not be subject to the arbitrary whims of the military adventurers that ruled European governments.

The Rev. Joseph Farney, like Rudolph Virkler, was a Mennonite Bishop and an influential family head who was largely responsible for several families coming to America.[18]

He was born April 26, 1795, in Alsace-Lorraine, France, and died April 18, 1873, in New Bremen, New York. His wife, Catherine Gerber, was born February 12, 1796, in the same area and died March 25, 1849, at New Bremen. They were married about 1815 in Alsace-Lorraine. He later married Mrs. Barbara Zehr.[19]

Joseph and Catherine Gerber Farney came to America with their family of four sons and two daughters. A daughter, Catherine, and a son, Andrew, were born in America. The son died in infancy.

Soon after their arrival, they were faced with a devastating snowstorm which severely disrupted their routine and greatly discouraged them. Nevertheless, in true pioneer form, and by seeking a comforting refuge in their God, they plunged ahead undaunted, and eventually their situation improved.[20]

In 1847 many of these families united together and formed the first Evangelical Baptist Church in America. The exact year this memorable event occurred varies slightly from author to author, but two reliable sources indicate the year was 1847.

In *Apostolic Christian Church History, Volume I,* Herman Ruegger discusses in detail the year Benedict Weyeneth was ordained as an Elder in Switzerland for the specific purpose of coming to America, and he identifies the year as 1847.[21]

Priscilla Weyeneth Liebig, the eldest daughter of Benedict Weyeneth, confirmed in an interview that the year was 1847. She further recalled that when the letter was received from the Lewis County Mennonites to send someone from Switzerland to America, a meeting of the Swiss Elders was quickly convened. It was at this meeting that young Benedict Weyeneth volunteered to go to America and was ordained an Elder specifically for this purpose.[22]

Both Priscilla Weyeneth Liebig and Herman Ruegger further state that Joseph Virkler, the eldest son of Rudolph Virkler, was appointed the first Elder in America by Benedict Weyeneth in 1847. Weyeneth then returned to Europe for a short period.[23]

Record keeping in the early days of French Settlement was not a high priority. Thus, it is somewhat difficult to establish specific dates, places, and important historical events. They did not keep any records of significance because they had often been persecuted for their faith in Europe and were still somewhat fearful of government. Also, there was very little record keeping because it was considered to be evidence of pride.

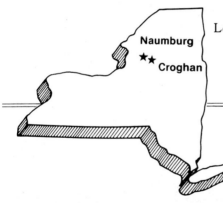

CROGHAN, NEW YORK
Lowville, New York   2 miles south of Croghan on Route 812

NAUMBURG, NEW YORK
R.R. 1, Castorland, New York
In Naumburg on Van Amber Road

While the Mennonite families united with Weyeneth in 1847 and likely met together as a group for an undetermined period of time, records indicate they did not "officially" establish a congregation until about 1850.[24] They did so at "French Settlement" which today is called Croghan. A few years later some of those families attending the Croghan church, but who lived in the Naumburg area, established a church at Naumburg,[25] for the sake of convenience. Thus, these two churches together claim the distinction of being the "first" church of the Apostolic Christian faith to be established in America.

The first church in Croghan was a small frame building. It had low wooden benches; kerosene lamps hanging from the ceiling lighted the assembly room. There was no center aisle, but rather a shoulder-high partition down the center divided the men and women.[26] Separated seating of the sexes during worship services was a normal custom of those times, not only in that particular church but in Christian churches generally. This was an old tradition practiced in the first century church and continued through the centuries.

Heat was furnished by large boxwood stoves, one in the church proper, one in the hall, and one in the basement.

The first building was erected in 1855 across the street from today's church. A church cemetery now exists next to the old location. In 1866 a new church was built on the present location; remodeling was done in 1901, 1929, and 1960.[27]

The church today is located two miles south of Croghan on Route 812.[28] Croghan, a hamlet of 765, was named for George Croghan, a distinguished military man. His mother was a sister of William Clark who, with Captain Meriweather Lewis, explored the Missouri Country in 1805-1807.[29]

The first church at Naumburg, New York, was organized with eighteen members in 1859. The first church edifice was located a few miles northwest of Naumburg where the church's cemetery is situated today.

In 1891-1892 a new church was built in the village of Naumburg on the present site. In 1903 the building was raised and a basement put in. In 1947 the horse sheds were removed, and the basement was remodeled, with rest rooms and cloak rooms being added.

By 1961 the basement and kitchen were remodeled, and the baptistery was moved upstairs behind the pulpit in keeping with a more modern and efficient baptismal liturgy. The enclosed front porch was removed, and a new entrance and fellowship hall were added.

Joseph Virkler was ordained as Elder and served until his death on October 2, 1866. His funeral service was conducted by Andrew J. Braun of Toledo, Ohio.[30] Joseph Virkler was a man of deep conviction and considerable energy. He visited New York City and several other cities to preach the gospel and was highly regarded in his time.

He was succeeded as Elder of the New York churches by his younger brother of thirteen years, Peter Virkler. Peter was born July 23, 1829, in Alsace-Lorraine and was presumably named for his great-grandfather.[31]

Peter Virkler was the next to youngest of seven surviving sons of Rudolph Virkler, and was five years old when the family emigrated to America. He was just a lad of eighteen when his father led a group of Mennonites out of their church of many generations into the Evangelical Baptist Church.

As a young boy he, no doubt, fell under the positive religious influence of his patriarch-like father, Rudolph, who on becoming disenchanted with his Mennonite faith, had the strength of conviction to go the way his conscience led him. Obviously, Peter was deeply impressed with this.

Thus, with a strong father and an older brother who was ordained as the first Elder of the new group in America, young Peter had two role-models to observe and follow. He deeply admired both his father and oldest brother and was obviously impressed by them as only a younger, more moldable brother can be. Thus, a strong religious conviction together with a bent for evangelism took root in this young man as it had earlier in both Rudolph and Joseph Virkler.

Peter was physically a large man and gifted in the art of persuasion. A vigorous and forceful preacher, he traveled extensively to preach the good news of eternal salvation.[32] He is remembered as a very dedicated and energetic man who would walk several miles to church to spare the horses who had worked so hard previously.[33]

During the Eldership of Peter Virkler, one of the greatest "in-gatherings" of converts in the history of the church occurred. During the summer of 1881, 140 converts were baptized. On thirteen successive Sundays beginning June 5 and ending August 28, 139 baptisms were performed; and a few weeks later on September 18, one more soul was baptized.[34]

It was a time of great joy for the church. The community and surrounding area took note of this overwhelming manifestation of the Spirit. An article entitled "Great Revival in New Bremen" appeared in a local newspaper. It refers to a Rev. Benedict Veianat who came from Illinois. The last name was misspelled from the German to English, and should have been Benedict Weyeneth.[35]

Great Revival in New Bremen.

Early last June Rev. Benedict Veianat, a minister of the German Evangelical Baptists, from Illinois, began a series of extra meetings at the church of this sect in New Bremen. Meetings have been held daily at the churches either at Naumburg or New Bremen, and as the fruit of this labor 127 persons, mostly between the ages of 15 and 30 years, have been converted and baptised into the church by immersion and the work still continues. The work is quiet, deep and thorough. The church is very particular in receiving members and before baptism there must be evidence of sincere repentance and conversion. As a result of this work the people all through the section over the river have been deeply interested and the meetings have been crowded. Mr. Veianat has been very successful as a revivalist among the Germans, which language he uses fluently.

Local newspaper article describing the great religious revival in Lewis County, New York during 1881. This article was found in the Bible of Priscilla Farney.

Mary Keiffer Rauhe Yousey, who was interviewed for the November, 1961, issue of the *Silver Lining* remembered the events of that summer. She recalled that on Sunday, July 3, twenty-four persons were taken into the church. That Sunday had such a profound effect on her that she answered the Lord's calling and was baptized by Peter Virkler on August 14, 1881, at Croghan at Black Creek.

One can only speculate on the reasons for such a massive spiritual harvest. No doubt Peter Virkler's God-given talents in preaching helped stir an awakening. Too, the Mennonite infusion into the church twenty years earlier was still in force, and it is likely a good number of the 1881 converts were those who decided to leave the Mennonite faith, repent, and join with the Evangelical Baptists.

Also, an event on the national scene may have prompted this revival. On July 2, 1881, President James A. Garfield was shot while waiting for a train in Washington, D.C. He lingered until September 19, finally dying of blood poisoning. The mood of the nation was gloomy, and this may have prompted many to seek the Lord.[36]

Peter Virkler's travels took him to the central part of the nation (Ohio, Indiana, Illinois, and Iowa) and all the way to Oregon. He is credited with helping organize the church in Portland, Oregon, in approximately 1879.

In 1871 he had traveled to Europe and toured widely.[37] He was accompanied by his wife, Anna Farney, whom he had married in 1853. The couple had no children, but were foster parents to many. He entered the ministry in 1853 and died at age sixty. His funeral was preached by Elder Michael Zimmerman of Congerville, Illinois.

A few years after the death of Peter Virkler, his nephew, Solomon Virkler, was ordained as Elder. This occurred in 1891 when he was thirty-six years old. He is recognized as the first minister in the New York churches to preach in the English language,[38] although he also preached in German. He served until his death in 1897.

Alpheus J. Virkler, Sr., born in 1853, and two years older than his brother Solomon, was ordained as the next Elder in 1903. In addition to being a farmer, he was also a carpenter.[39]

The next resident Elder was not ordained for another twenty years as the congregations were served by Elders from other states.

Philip A. Beyer, a great-grandson of Rudolph Virkler, was given the mantle of leadership of the churches in 1938 and served until 1958.

John Widrick was ordained Elder in 1962 and served for six years.

September 3, 1978, was a historic day for the Lewis County churches. Two great-great-grandsons of patriarch Rudolph Virkler were ordained Elders. Robert G. Beyer, son of Philip A. Beyer, was ordained at Naumburg, and Norbert V. Steiner was ordained at Croghan.

A newspaper article entitled "French Settlement In The Early Days," which appeared in the Black River *Democrat* at Lowville, New York, in 1913, described the Evangelical Baptists. With few exceptions, the article accurately reveals what the church was like:

When Elder Weyeneth began to preach the Evangelical faith, the meetings were held in the homes of the settlers. The message that came to the little world at the settlement was taken from Peter who said, "Repent, and be baptized every one of you." Repentance was not quite so easy as at first supposed. It must come not from the lips but from the heart; it had to be openly manifest before such repentance was accepted. The first Elder ordained by the missionary Elder Weyeneth was Joseph Virkler, one of seven sons who came with his parents from the province of Alsace-Lorraine. Mr. Virkler was an eloquent preacher and immediately drew a large number of the settlers to the Evangelical Baptist belief, which while it retained many of the features of the Ammanites, and also the Mennonites, was withal distinctive in itself. The fundamental principle of the Evangelical belief rested absolutely on the gospels. There was and is no creed, nor dogma, no confession of faith, nothing but repentance and adoption of the rules of the society.

The primary rule is the subjection of the flesh and the elimination of all carnal thought and desire. Not quite so simple when we come to it. Only the strongest system of discipline could effect this subordination of the flesh, and the highest conception of morality makes it lasting.

First, and foremost, to get a better understanding it may be well to mention that the Evangelical Baptist society was not a church, but a brotherhood only. The various congregations distributed over the earth in little clusters had no organization. Each congregation, like the Ammanites was entirely independent of the other. They were held together in brotherly fellowship only; there were no ties except the "rules" to hold them together, and whosoever followed these rules and was baptized in the faith was a brother and must be treated as a brother, whether white, yellow, or black. The idea of brotherhood reigned supreme in their hearts; there was no higher or lower brotherhood; there were none in authority. There was but one Master and that was Jesus Christ. The only title they tolerate is that of "learner" or teacher; there is no other between them and the Master.

A brother was selected by the congregation to be a learner for no other reason than that he might possess the gift of speech in greater degree than the other brothers. He was then ordained as a learner, not to elevate him above his brothers, but to qualify him before the law to perform the legal functions of a minister, which was mainly to legalize the marriage rite between brothers and sisters of the society. There were no professional learners; each must work at his own trade or other occupation, the same as the rest. No preparation of sermon was permitted, no selection of text. The Bible was opened at random and from the chapter appearing on such page, the exhortation was made. In the meeting house, which had no adornment whatever either on the outer or inner side, the learner sat between two brothers who could also preach, on a slightly elevated platform, in front of which was a pedestal (no pulpit) to hold the Bible and hymn books. The platform was constructed not to elevate the learner, but that the congregation might hear to better advantage.

The meeting room was filled with wooden benches entirely bare, no cushions of any sort allowed. In the center running lengthwise with the room, was a partition which divided the brothers from the sisters. No man had a pew of his own, nor did he sit with his wife or daughters. The men sat at the right hand of the learner, facing him, and the women on the left. The meetings opened with the singing of a hymn by the entire congregation. No music was allowed. The singing took on the tone of a chant, and as each of the members were thoroughly trained in vocal music, the singing was usually fine and touching.

During prayer, the brothers and sisters would kneel on the floor with their eyes covered by their hands, and elbows resting on the benches. The meetings, whether in the home or meeting house, consisted of singing, prayer and exhortation. It was social democracy pure and simple. No government was recognized, neither any church. These were of the world, in fact, held to be "the world," and had no place in the brotherhood. The salutation among the brothers involved considerable ceremony. When a brother met another brother, no matter where, the brothers clasped hands with the right hand, at the same time raising the hat with the left, they then kissed each other on the lips, after which they said, "God greet thee brother." It was then only that conversation took place. On parting the brothers observed the same ceremony, saying, "God care for thee, brother."

The churches in Croghan and Naumburg have retained the traditional name "Evangelical Baptist" even though they are indeed Apostolic Christian. On the front of each church is the name Evangelical Baptist, and then the clarifying phrase, "Affiliated with the Apostolic Christian Church."

FIRST AMENDMENT TO THE CONSTITUTION

"CONGRESS SHALL MAKE NO LAW RESPECTING AN ESTABLISHMENT OF RELIGION, OR PROHIBITING THE FREE EXERCISE THEREOF; or abridging the freedom of speech, or of the press; or the right of the people to assemble, and to petition the government for redress of grievances."

SARDIS, OHIO

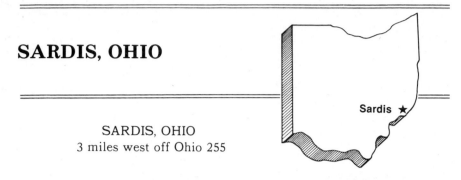

SARDIS, OHIO
3 miles west off Ohio 255

    The next area of church activity occurred in the hills of the Ohio Valley in the southeastern portion of Ohio. Tucked almost unnoticed between the banks of the Ohio River and the hills to the immediate west is the hamlet of Sardis, Ohio. It was founded by James Patton in 1843, only five years prior to being inhabited by ancestors of the Apostolic Christian Church.[40] In 1848, several families of Swiss origin landed near Sardis, Ohio.

    These brave pioneers—among them the Aeschlimans, Gehrings, and Gerbers—contained within themselves the priceless and comforting hope of eternal life found in surrendering to Jesus Christ. They had turned for one last look at their beloved Switzerland prior to leaving for America, a land they counted on to provide, in this order, more religious freedom and greater economic opportunity.[41]

    Arriving first in New York and then in Pittsburgh, they boarded a flat boat for the trip down the Ohio River. This river, named by the "Senecas" and meaning "great river," was known as a throughway "for the West."[42]

As this European party approached the area near Sardis, they very likely marveled at the hills and valleys to the west which reminded them to some extent of their native Switzerland. They might have decided to stop at Sardis and make this their home. Or, as suggested by Isaac Gehring, great-grandson of original pioneer Isaac Gehring, they could very possibly have hit a sand bar at the area called Duffy, which is just down the hill from the current church, and were forced to stop. Or perhaps being weary from weeks of travel on the ocean and then a spartan trip on a flat boat, they made a decision, with lifelong implications, to settle in the Duffy-Sardis area. In any case, they actually did settle in the hills near Sardis, and immediately a church was founded.

When they came to Sardis in 1848, the Ohio River was not navigable to the extent it is today due to the absence of a system of dams. In rainy weather the river would rise, making transportation easier; but in dry weather the river became narrow and shallow.

Stories are often told how sometimes river traffic would run onto a sand bar, be forced to stop, and subsequently the travelers would go ashore and establish a settlement. The earliest members of the faith may have experienced this and accepted it as a sign of God's leading.

A local resident has described the Sardis area: "The valley is one-half to one mile wide. The hills which form the valley are from 600-800 feet higher in elevation than the river level. The land between the river and the hills has always been very valuable. The bottom land provides excellent farmland, and records show that some of this land was owned and farmed by church people. The threat of floods, of course, was a great problem. In faith, these men planted their crops hoping they could be harvested before the floods would destroy them."[43]

Isaac Gehring is thought to have been the leader of the small band of believers who came to Sardis. Born in 1819 in Switzerland, he was only twenty-nine years old when he came to America.[44] He was an early minister and later ordained Elder in 1868, but the date he was selected as a minister is not known.

Having grown into adulthood by 1840, he is assumed to have associated with Samuel Froehlich and to have been under his direction and influence with respect to matters of faith. John H. Baumgartner, in *The First Hundred Years,* wrote, "Brother Gehring was a kind man—his friendly, loving ways were helpful in drawing many souls to salvation."[45]

There is a very interesting incident concerning Isaac Gehring:[46]

> Older brethren tell of hearing their parents tell of the kind and loving nature of Elder Gehring. A woman who had known him in Switzerland came to America and settled in a community near Sardis. When she learned of his whereabouts, she decided to visit him.
>
> As she approached his community, she made it known to others of her intentions whereupon they warned her of tales they supposedly heard of him. Their feeling was that Elder Gehring would immediately disapprove of her life style and insist that she make a change. Indeed, when they observed the flowers on her hat, they firmly advised her not to go as they were convinced he would rebuke her for her vanity and pride. But her heart was set. She would go and see for herself.
>
> Her visit turned out to be one of great blessing. They visited peacefully for hours, and not once did he reproach her. Further, when she left, they parted with a handshake, and he pressed a five-dollar goldpiece into her hand. She was so touched by his loving ways that she became crushed and soon sought his advice for her salvation. She later became a member of the church.

Another instrumental leader of the Sardis congregation was Joseph Bella, a single man who was their first Elder. He lived initially in the Sardis area, but spent a lot of time traveling around to newly established churches nurturing, counseling, and giving support and direction.

While in the Sardis area, he lived in a small house next to Isaac Gehring's home. Apparently the two men shared a common purpose and got along very well.

In 1980 the old Gehring homestead was still standing and was inhabited by Emma Riggenbach (a sister in the church) and her two daughters, Mildred and Marie. The homestead is located one-half mile from the Ohio River at Duffy (called Texas prior to 1900). Duffy is located four miles northeast of Sardis, so the Gehring homestead is four and one-half miles northeast of Sardis and two miles southeast of the present church building.

The small Bella dwelling consisted of a woodshed "lean-to" on one side and a two-room, two-story section on the other. Bella repaired watches for his livelihood in one room and slept in the other. A large portion of his time was devoted to the Lord's work, in shepherding the small flock at Sardis as well as traveling to other churches.

The early believers at Sardis built their first church in approximately 1850.[47] Prior to that they assembled in homes. Misfortune struck the small group in the early 1850's when their log church caught fire and was completely destroyed. A rail fence near the church apparently caught fire, and the flames eventually spread to the church. This occurred at night or at a time when no one was in the area. The next time the group assembled for worship, they arrived to find their church in ashes. One can hardly imagine the near-despair these settlers experienced, when already having endured much struggle, hardship, and confusion associated with adapting to a new country, they lost one of the things most precious to them—their house of worship.

But being men and women of faith, they realized that the true church is within their hearts, and consequently they did not totally despair. This temporary setback only filled them with a stronger zeal to endure and push ahead, trusting that God would provide for every need. The disaster of their church burning tended to bind them even closer together.

The old Isaac Gehring homestead as it looked in 1980. It sits approximately one-half mile from the Ohio River at Duffy. Church services were formerly held in the living room.

Isaac Gehring added a room to his home, and services were held in this stalwart's residence for several years. By 1875 a new one-story building (without a basement) was constructed on the present site. In 1890 this building was lifted and a first story built underneath to house a kitchen, dining room, and Sunday School.[48]

In 1964 a well was dug for the church. For over a hundred years, members of the church had to carry water in milk cans to provide for drinking, for making coffee for the noon lunch, and for washing dishes afterwards.[49]

In 1966 a major renovation and modernization of the church was initiated, including the installation of toilets, a more modern kitchen, and a new attractive brick entrance and foyer. A great deal of voluntary labor was donated to this project. Over ninety-nine volunteers pitched in and helped complete this task, and $18,000 of materials and labor were given. One man put in nearly eight hundred hours of volunteer work on this job.

The little church sits atop a hill which overlooks a beautiful valley as well as a variety of ridges and smaller hills. In the Sardis area one often hears that the church was built on a hill in order that the assembly would be "as near as possible to God."[50]

Just a few feet from the church building is a cemetery plot which was sold to the church for $3 in 1854 by Ulrich and Elizabeth Gerber. Some of the pioneer brethren buried there bear names such as Riggenbach, Ruesser, Gehring, Grossenbacher, Ingold, Gasser, Schmid, Knutty, Hinderlong, Ischy, Klotzle, Eisenbarth, Zink, Rist, Bucher, Ramsier, Schar, Baumgartner, Black, Dierks, and Marty. Today, many of these family names are found in several other Apostolic Christian Churches across America.

The Sardis church is located three and one-half miles from the village of Sardis, and eleven miles (by road) from the former New Martinsville, West Virginia, church (but only five miles by air). These two churches, as they sit on clearly-seen pinnacles, serve as citadels of a deep faith in God.

Isaac Gehring served as Elder at Sardis from about 1868 until his death in 1896 at age seventy-seven.[51] Prior to this time it is believed that Joseph Bella had oversight of the Sardis church.

Succeeding Gehring as Elder was Joseph Ingold who was born in Switzerland in 1847, the same year Benedict Weyeneth came to America. He was the youngest of nine children of Jacob and Barbara Baumgartner Ingold. This family came to the United States in 1844 and arrived in Monroe County in 1845. It is not known if they were associated with the church while in Europe, but it is known that after their arrival, Jacob and Anna and at least four of their children were converted. It is very likely that at one time they were Mennonites, as Ingold and Baumgartner were common Mennonite family names during that period. A son, Jacob, was born to this couple as they crossed the ocean coming to America.[52]

Joseph Ingold was married to Elizabeth Witschey and the couple bore no children. He served as an Elder until his death in 1932.

In 1868 Benedict Maibach, Sr., and family from canton Bern, Switzerland, came to live with Mrs. Maibach's brother, Fred Schupbach and family, who lived between Sardis and Duffy. They later moved to the Neinschwander farm which today is called the John Isaly farm. Benedict had six children, three boys and three girls. One son, Gottlieb, born in Bern, Switzerland, March 12, 1853, was later ordained an Elder at Pulaski, Iowa, in 1895.[53]

He was converted as a young man while in Sardis. He later moved to Mansfield, Ohio, where he learned the blacksmith trade even though he was slight of build. He moved from there to Tremont, Illinois, where he was placed into the ministry prior to his marriage to Lydia Kaufman of Morton, Illinois, on January 7, 1883. He moved to Pulaski, Iowa, in about 1890, and again to the Bay City, Michigan, area in 1905.[54]

Sardis is often referred to as the "Mother church" of many of the present Apostolic Christian congregations because many of the brethren settled here briefly before moving on to other newly established churches.

In the early phases of church growth prior to the development of commercial rail travel, Sardis was ideally located along a major mode of travel—the Ohio River. Travel down the Ohio, and then up the Mississippi (and on the Illinois River) was a prominent route to the West, and particularly to Iowa and Illinois where many Europeans sought to reside on farms.

U.S. INLAND WATERWAYS

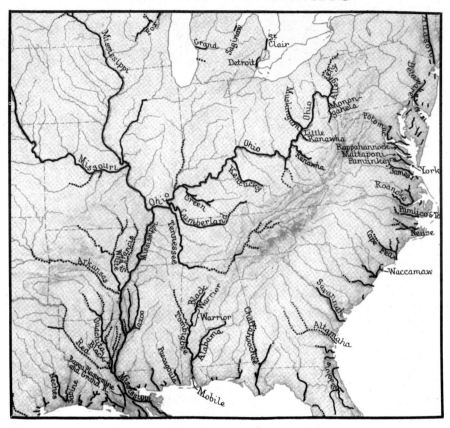

During the mid-to-late 1800's, the nation's inland waterway system pro-vided transportation for immigrants who were headed for farms in the Mississippi Valley and Great Plains areas. Apostolic Christians traveled on flat boats down the Ohio River and up the Mississippi and Illinois Rivers to their destinations.

Under the direction of Elders Bella, Gehring, and Ingold, the church prospered to the extent that by 1900 the church listed approximately one hundred members. This was not a small number for an area with comparatively marginal farm-land. The lure of financial gain, however, eventually prompted many to move to Wayne County, Ohio.

While the move away from Sardis may have been profit-able for many brethren, it was nearly devastating for the little "hilltop" church which dwindled to only a handful of members for many years. During this same span of time, many members from the New Martinsville church across the river moved to the Rittman, Ohio, area as well.

The church at Sardis struggled for many years. Virtually isolated in an area of southeastern Ohio with hilly and less productive farmland, and separated at least three and one-half hours by automobile from the nearest Apostolic Christian Church, their situation looked bleak for several decades.

With so many brethren moving away and the extinction of the church a distinct possibility, young Delbert Indermuhle decided he had better stay in the Sardis area. In 1942 he was baptized and in 1948 became a minister.[55] From 1961 to 1973 he served alone in the ministry. Often, with no other brothers present, he would offer all the prayers during the day—at the morning service, noon lunch, and at the afternoon service. But prospects began to brighten when in 1973 his son, Kenneth, was placed in the ministry and in 1979 William Brake became a minister.

During the decade of the 1950's, the general area became somewhat industrialized. This gave an economic lift to the area and was a good omen for the growth of the Sardis church.

During the years of low membership, there were often no brothers present at worship services who were able to lead the singing. When this occurred, Wiletta Indermuhle, mother of Delbert Indermuhle, assumed this task. Previously her mother, Rosina Walters, also led singing.[56]

Wiletta remembered in her early teens, while spending some time in Wayne County and attending the Rittman church, Fred Maibach had given her a copy of the *Zion's Harp* hymnal (in the German language) and encouraged her to sing. From this she developed a great love for music, especially the *Zion's Harp* hymns.

In about 1875, services were held on occasion in Switzer Township, located about twenty miles north of Sardis. Several brethren lived in that area, and services were held in homes. These members at Switzer also went to Sardis for services when it was convenient.

Also, in the late 1870's Joseph Ingold moved to Louisville, Kentucky, and several members of the church followed him. After a few years, he moved back to Sardis.[57] In 1896, following the death of Elder Isaac Gehring, Ingold was selected as the group's Elder.

NEW MARTINSVILLE, WEST VIRGINIA

NEW MARTINSVILLE,
WEST VIRGINIA
6 miles east, off Doolin Road

Early 1850's to late 1950's.

Limestone Ridge in the hills of West Virginia used to be the site of an active Apostolic Christian Church. Located eight miles east of New Martinsville, it sat atop a steep knoll in the hills of Wetzel County. Once a thriving congregation, its demise began shortly after the turn of the century when economic conditions motivated many members to seek "greener pastures" in other areas, primarily Wayne County, Ohio.

The church likely began early in the 1850's when immigrants came down the Ohio River on flat boats and settled in the area (some on the Ohio side near Sardis and others on the West Virginia side near New Martinsville). It reached its end in the late 1950's when periodic worship services were terminated.

Emma Riggenbach Barth, a daughter of Sebastian and Elizabeth Widmer Riggenbach who were early settlers in the area, wrote in her diary (April 4, 1958) of the "Limestone Ridge" church's closing days:

> One of the saddest things in my life is that our church has de-
> creased in place of increased like the churches in other places; there is
> where my mother carried me in her arms; there is where I went to
> Sunday School and Church all my life; there is where I found peace

with my God and where my husband and I took our children every Sunday morning. To me it is the dearest spot on earth. I still love to go, even though there are only four widows left, one sister is ninety years of age, one sister is eighty-eight, one is eighty-four and I was eighty-two my last birthday. One of the sisters is very sick now, has been bedfast for several weeks. It grieves me very much to know the door of that dear little old church will soon be closed. I have had many happy days there. The church used to be filled every Sunday. Those were the happy days and I will always love the little humble church on the West Virginia hills.

She wrote also of attending church in the late 1890's with her husband John Barth:

One Sunday morning Isaac Emch, who was one of the ministers at that time, was preaching. My eyes were opened while he was preaching, God touched my heart, I felt I was a sinner, and the tears flowed freely. I repented; and on April 4, 1897, I was baptized. When we got home that evening my husband started to repent, and it wasn't long until he was baptized. That was the happiest day of my life.

Nearly twenty persons were baptized during 1897 at this country church.[58]

Taking their children to church on Limestone Ridge was a special occasion for John and Emma Barth:

We looked forward to those blessed Sunday mornings. We had a hill to climb and dirt roads to travel. If it rained on Saturday night or on Sunday morning, the girls would walk to church in their bare feet and carry their shoes and stockings. We always kept a basin under the church and we would take rags with us and they would wash their feet and put their stockings and shoes on. When we started home they took them off again and went home barefooted. We always took our lunch and stayed for the afternoon service.

The exact date of the formation of a church on Limestone Ridge (near Green Hill, West Virginia) is unknown. It is surmised, however, that early immigrants traveling down the Ohio River settled on both sides of the river near Sardis and New Martinsville. While it is generally thought the Sardis congregation was established first, it is likely that worship services across the river were initiated a few years later.

Members met in homes prior to building a church. The church on the ridge was built sometime in the 1870's. Mary Heflinger Witchey died in 1874 and was buried in a cemetery close to where the church and cemetery are located today. Approximately one year later, her remains were transferred to the Apostolic Christian Church Cemetery next to the church on Limestone Ridge. Thus, that establishes the date of the church building as approximately 1875.

Files of the New Martinsville Cemetery Association (the group that administers the church cemetery) indicate that a deed to the church and cemetery was recorded in the Wetzel County Court House on March 1, 1877. The church was likely built in the early 1870's and later recorded with the county. Emma Riggenbach Barth related to her daughter Minnie Barth Welz that as a baby she was carried in her mother's arms to the Limestone Ridge church. She was born January 15, 1876.[59]

Among the early settlers east of New Martinsville was Sebastian Riggenbach, a brother of John Riggenbach whose descendants comprise a majority of the church at Sardis. The former moved from the Clarington, Ohio, area (north of Sardis) to West Virginia in 1863. He was the father of Emma Riggenbach Barth whose diary recorded many incidents of the West Virginia church.

Another early parishioner was John Kaufman. A native of Thun, Switzerland, he came to America with his parents in 1847. They settled on the Ohio side of the river at Hannibal. Shortly after his marriage to Wilhelmina Luekhart on January 7, 1869, he moved to a spot six miles east of New Martinsville. His obituary, which appeared in a West Virginia newspaper on February 20, 1925, included the paragraph, "He joined the German Baptist church many years ago and remained a consistent member to the time of his death, a well worn German Bible being mute evidence of his devotion and being the last book he read.

"Funeral services were conducted at the home of his daughter, Elizabeth Farmer, and concluded at the German Baptist Church at Green Hill, the church he has attended for over forty years." Reference to the "German Baptist Church" is erroneous, being simply a colloquial expression for the Apostolic Christian Church.

The cemetery next to the church contains grave markers bearing the following names: Blair, Lohr, Durig, Kaufman, Riggenbach, Kocher, Hassig, Barth, Williams, Hafely, Black, Widmer, Froelich, Rist, Knochel, Bleuer, Emch, and Zohnd.

At the turn of the century, the church (on Limestone Ridge) had at least thirty-five to forty members. This was considerably less than the Sardis congregation which numbered approximately one hundred.[60]

It is surmised that Joseph Bella and Isaac Gehring (both Elders at Sardis) were instrumental in nurturing and shepherding the New Martinsville flock. Bella traveled extensively in establishing the early congregations. Gehring died in 1896 and was succeeded as Elder at Sardis and New Martinsville by Joseph Ingold, who served until his death in 1932.

There was a close fellowship between the two churches, at least as much as the modes of transportation would allow. There are some names such as Emch and Riggenbach appearing in both cemeteries. No doubt funerals and other special occasions brought members of both churches together.

Their principal occupation was farming, which was made difficult by the hilly and rugged terrain. The desire for flat and more productive land was undoubtedly prominent among the many factors that led to their gradual exodus from the area during the early part of this century. Nearly all the brethren eventually left the area, a good many of them going up to Wayne County, Ohio, to till the more level and responsive land. It is interesting to note that while the first generation of families chose the area because of its similarity to Switzerland (the hills and valleys, etc.), the second generation was less interested in the sentimental aspects of the terrain, but more interested in better income that could be realized from more productive farmland.

As the church decreased to consist of only a few members, regular services were replaced by periodic gatherings. The few remaining members who were able to travel worshipped at the Sardis church. However, the journey across the Ohio River and up the hills on narrow, winding dirt roads to the Sardis church was a difficult one, and only the very faithful made such a sacrifice. Consequently, many of the young people (in the 1920's) who were not members began attending other protestant churches in New Martinsville. Essentially, when the country church was vacated by so many members over the years, the "friends of the truth" were left without a church. Today the First Baptist Church in New Martinsville contains families with names familiar to Apostolic Christians—names such as Fankhauser, Schupbach, Schwing, Witschey, Berger, Riggenbach, Durig, Hafely, and Frei.

Ministers who labored at New Martinsville were Fred Thomas, Isaac Emch, and Joseph Widmer. Isaac Emch moved to Girard, Ohio, in approximately 1910. Joseph Widmer moved to Rittman, Ohio, in about 1920.

The church in the New Martinsville area still stands and is not forgotten. An annual memorial service was started in 1966. Friends in the area with historical roots to the church, along with many visitors from other Apostolic Christian Churches in the United States, gather for worship services once each year, usually in June. The Sardis congregation assists in hosting this annual event. It is always a special day of warm friendship and renewed appreciation of a common heritage.

The annual service in June, 1979, was quite memorable. An overflow crowd attending the service caused the floor to give way and drop approximately three inches. Services continued. The crowd that day was estimated at 250.

Church at New Martinsville shown during annual memorial service. Annual services (begun in 1966) commemorate bygone days at "Limestone Ridge." An overflow crowd in 1979 caused the sanctuary floor to drop nearly three inches.

The closing of the church was a sad occasion, and the few remaining members were burdened to see it shut down. Emma Riggenbach Barth, a member since 1897, said, "It broke my heart."

The quaint little church on Limestone Ridge, adjacent to the small cemetery whose markers bear the names of faithful pilgrims, serves as a silent symbol of the deep and abiding faith which carried these early settlers through the hardships and privations they encountered late in the nineteenth century, and which will one day carry the true and faithful into the portals of heaven.

"And ye shall seek me, and find me, when ye shall search for me with all your heart."

In order to obtain a clearer perspective of the Apostolic Christian Church of America, it is essential to review events in Europe in the early nineteenth century, particularly as they relate to Samuel Heinrich Froehlich.

By the time Froehlich was born in 1803, Europe was still in a state of religious unrest, although less so than three centuries previously when religious reform was beginning to manifest itself.

In 1803 religious toleration existed to a limited degree, but those who led or belonged to a religious group outside the established state church usually did so at their own peril.

The year 1803 was a memorable one: the Louisiana Purchase more than doubled the size of the United States as the western border was extended to the Rocky Mountains; Ohio was admitted to the Union as the seventeenth state, and Thomas Jefferson served as the third President of the United States.

On July 4, 1803, in Brugg, canton Aargau, Switzerland, a son, Samuel Heinrich Froehlich, was born to Samuel Froehlich and Gottliebin Berger Froehlich. He was the sixth and youngest child of this union. In a historical sense, this was six years before the birth of Abraham Lincoln.

The Froehlich family came from a long line of ancestors associated with protestantism. Originally the family hailed from France and for many years was involved in the Hugenot movement in that country. While in France the family name was De Joyeux, which translated means "joyous." When the family moved to Switzerland, they changed their name to Froehlich.

French Calvinists were nicknamed Hugenots. Under the tutelage of John Calvin, this movement spread rapidly during

The above sketch of a neighborhood in Brugg, Switzerland, reflects the type of place Samuel Froehlich was born.

the decade of the 1540's, despite increased repression by the French monarchy, which was primarily Catholic.

Continued tension and eventually civil war with the state (which represented Catholicism) ensued until 1598 when Henry IV of Navarre, the Hugenot leader, ascended to the throne of France. He immediately issued the Edict of Nantes which granted the Hugenots full toleration and civil rights.

Hugenots were found among all classes of society: nobles, gentry, craftsmen, professional men, and farmers. Their meeting places were plain, though large, with some having seating capacities of up to eight thousand. Strict church discipline was instituted in true Calvinistic tradition. Sabbath desecration and frivolous conduct were severely discouraged. By 1685 there were about one million Hugenots in France, with eight hundred churches.[1]

The plight of the Hugenots remained on shaky ground over the years. Finally in 1685, when Louis XIV was firmly entrenched in power, the Edict of Nantes was revoked, which spelled terrible doom for the Hugenots. Persecution flared, and hundreds of thousands of Hugenots fled to other countries. This king was determined to make France the most powerful state in Europe; in his view, this involved ruling a state committed to one religion.

This was a time of suffering and persecution for the Hugenots. Previous to this, in 1672, several thousand Hugenot leaders were massacred on St. Bartholomew's Day when they had been invited to Paris to attend the wedding of Henry of Bourbon and Margaret, the sister of Charles IX. Instead, as church bells rang early on the morning of August 24, many leading Hugenots were killed by the authorities.

The De Joyeux family (later Froehlich) was very likely among the thousands who fled this deadly turmoil and sought refuge in neighboring Switzerland. It was not wise for any protestants to stay in France.

The Froehlich family continued their protestant ties and became a part of the Swiss Protestant State Church. This church was founded in 1519 by Ulrich Zwingli, the Swiss counterpart of Martin Luther.

Samuel Froehlich (the father) served as a sexton of the state church located in Brugg. As sexton, he was in charge of the

maintenance of church property, often ringing the church
bells, and sometimes digging graves in the church cemetery.

It was a tradition in the Froehlich family, as in many European families, to give one of their sons to the ministry. This
was decided by the parents of young Samuel Froehlich long
before he was able to understand its significance. As he grew
into manhood, he gave little thought to someday becoming a
minister. In his autobiography, Froehlich writes:[2]

> I did not know or feel in the least the responsibility of the high
> and weighty position of preaching redemption, but was supposed to
> learn it as a trade and profession. Thus, I went to school in my home
> town until I was seventeen years of age.

On January 1, 1820, Samuel Heinrich Froehlich entered the
University at Zurich to study humanities. During this time he
was exposed to many liberal philosophies which confronted
the beliefs instilled in him as a young boy. An assault was
made on his concepts of God and Christ by a professor, Dr.
Schulthess. The theory of rationalism was very prevalent at
this time, particularly in the school of theology. The young,
naive mind of Samuel Froehlich fell prey to these teachings,
and he entered into a state that bordered on unbelief. He
writes, "My God-fearing mother shed a thousand tears when I
would come home and boldly expose her to my imagination
and shamelessly tell her that 'there was no devil and no hell.'"

He finished his four-year course at Zurich and went on to
study theology at the University of Basel. It was here that he
came under the profound influence of Wilhelm Martin
DeWette, a German Biblical scholar, who was regarded as one
of the most influential theologians of the nineteenth century.
He wrote many books and was considered a "thoroughgoing
nonsupernaturalist. [3]

Froehlich writes:[4]

> What Schulthess had begun in Zurich, was completed by
> DeWette in Basel. I became utterly carried away by the idealism with
> which he treated the Scriptures. I thought this was the true way and
> was only sorry I did not have the wings to follow him in his flight. I
> honored him almost as a god. I felt no need of the living God and had
> no thought of conversion from my sins.

Accordingly, his lifestyle reflected the philosophy which so
completely enraptured his mind, and he fell into sin. His

attitude became hardened to the extent that he said to himself, "that which I am doing is not sin."[5]

While in this sinful condition, he preached his first sermon. It was on Psalm 51:10, "Create in me a clean heart, O God." This was his first and last sermon while in a state of spiritual ignorance.

During his stay in Basel, Froehlich met a sincere pastor who was recommended to him by the state vicar residing in his native city of Brugg. Froehlich referred to him as Reverend Lord Passavant. Apparently a sincere man in his devotion to God, he had a way with Froehlich and could visit with him about spiritual matters. The two had many frank discussions on the topic of religion. Often, he would ask Froehlich, "Well, how are things going in the most important matter of all?"[6] This would inwardly intimidate Froehlich and set him to thinking about his soul and its eternal destination.

It was also during this time in Basel that Froehlich met every Thursday evening with other young students to read and discuss the Greek New Testament. Many of these students were of the Community of Brethren, who were likely Anabaptist in their theology, and quite devoted to God. During these sessions Froehlich became a strident opponent. He writes, "When they finally decided to begin and close the hour with song and prayer, I became angry and stayed away and also made others desert them, so that gradually the class almost disbanded, until after my conversion it was again brought to renewed life and blessing."[7]

Already in his young life, he was entwined in a state of controversy. This was to be his lot almost entirely during the course of his life. The Christian beliefs instilled in him by his parents were challenged by his university professors. Now convinced by them in this hotbed of rationalism, he began challenging the views of his peers. His mind was obviously unsettled as he became hardened in his sins, and peace of heart and mind escaped him. During this time the words of his minister friend would frequently come back to haunt him, "How are things going in the most important matter of all?"

It was in 1825 during Easter vacation in Brugg, when he was twenty-one years of age, that Samuel Froehlich responded to the call of the Lord. He wrote:[8]

> A very soft voice, which was neither terrifying or depressing, but nevertheless very convincing and penetrating, spoke in the depth of my soul, 'It cannot remain thus with thee. Thou must change'—and at the same time it drew me irresistably onward. I knelt for the first time before the hidden God and with uplifted hands solemnly made an oath of fidelity, that from now on it would be different with me.

It was at this time that Froehlich, weak in true spiritual understanding but resolved to serve God, broke without reservation from his former life of sin and pointed his life toward Almighty God—he thus began a true repentance!

Froehlich describes his experience:[9]

> I went out into the mountain and forest, knelt and prayed and cried out in lonesome places. My whole being was longing, sorrowfulness, and anxiety. I sought the Lord Jesus Christ with ardent fervor and many tears.

He returned to school in Basel at the end of April, still searching diligently for the things of God. All theological or rationalistic lectures became an abomination to him, for as he said, "I was now in another school." The school of the Cross had now become the one of greatest importance.

For several months Froehlich existed in a somewhat suspended state—he sought God, but could not receive peace of mind. As an inexperienced babe in Christ, with no significant direction, he struggled in a lowly and burdened state for several months until finally the glorious peace of God filled his heart. Regarding this special event in his life, he writes, "For a long time I remained in this fiery furnace until at length faith in Jesus Christ, the Crucified, brought me rest, peace and light, and made place within me for a new creation. From then on Jesus Christ was the center of my whole life and sphere of activity."

Later that same fall, after spending two years in Basel, he left the university for economic reasons and returned to Brugg to live with his parents. By this time he had turned twenty-two and yet was mostly undecided as to what direction his life would take. Having experienced a true conversion and now living close to the Lord, he faced the very serious dilemma of no longer being in harmony with his training in the theology and doctrine of the state church.

While living at home, he began to prepare for the exams he must take to enter the ministry. From Christmas, 1825, until Good Friday, 1826, he studied for those exams. During his stay in Brugg, his parents requested that he preach a sermon in their local congregation (the state church). The Sunday before Christmas, 1825, he preached in Brugg on John 8:31-36. His sermon was well received. He did not preach again until Good Friday, 1826; but this time ridicule and scorn were heaped upon him, much to his dismay.[10]

In May of 1826, Froehlich began his examination for the ministry. As part of the requirements, he had to write a thesis on the Latin phrase, *"De Verbo Dei tamquam medio gratiae."* In essence this means, "What you get from the Word is equal to being in the middle of God's grace." He also had to write a sermon on St. John 17:16-17.[11] In the latter instance he made an unfavorable impression. He failed the examination and had to wait a year to take it again. His new religious principles were reflected in his exams, which generated a negative response from those who tested him. He took the news of his failure philosophically, feeling that the Lord's will was being done for his purification and further testing.

In May of 1827, he was called again to take the ministerial exams. This time he passed and was ordained into the ministry of the Swiss Protestant State Church at age twenty-three, approximately two months short of his twenty-fourth birthday.

His first request for service after being ordained came from the Girtannin family in Feuerthalen, near Schaffhausen, and he became their tutor. In August, 1828, he was assigned to the office of vicar in the district of Wagenhausen in canton Thurgau. It was here that he was relaxed in feeling very much at home and felt the nearness of the Lord. He was not to remain there long, however; in November his superior died, and the consistory of Aargau summoned him to go to the congregation at Leutwil as vicar. He accepted this without delay and began his new duties in the first part of December, 1828, when he was twenty-five years old.[12]

When he went to the Leutwil congregation and reviewed its spiritual condition, he was not impressed. He was undaunted, however, and accepted the challenge to minister to these people. Despite the apparent apostate condition of this local congregation, Froehlich began preaching with deep conviction and later wrote that God "gave such strength unto His Word that the testimony of the crucified Christ cut like a two-edged sword through their hearts and overthrew one proud fortress of Satan after the other."[13]

A great awakening took place in that congregation of eighteen hundred when Froehlich began preaching. One soul after another humbled himself at the feet of the Lord. Many souls from surrounding congregations began to attend Froehlich's services, much to the chagrin of their local pastors. Thus, criticism of his preaching became nearly rampant.

Froehlich described these sermons as being "in particular the chief teachings of the Gospel: That by our very nature we were all dead in transgression and sin and are children of wrath; that we are made righteous through Jesus Christ alone, through belief in the atonement which He brought about; that through this belief in Christ we must be born anew and receive into our hearts the new living law of the Holy Spirit in place of the deadening and damning law."[14]

The convicting, spirit-filled preaching of Samuel Froehlich posed a significant threat to the state church. Accordingly, he was recalled from his pastorate in Leutwil on October 25, 1829. This constituted a severe reprimand, and he was suspended from preaching.

For approximately one year he resided at his father's home in Brugg, apparently awaiting word from the church council as to the final disposition of his situation.[15]

About this time the council introduced a new program of rationalistic instruction for young children to replace the old Heidelberg Catechism which the church had used for many years.[16] This was written in 1563 by Kaspar Olevianus and Zacharias Ursinus, two prominent theologians.[17] While Froehlich was probably lukewarm toward the Heidelberg Catechism, he simply could not tolerate the new catechism "because in it, instead of a positive faith in Christ, its chief tendency is to lay a foundation of nature or reason-religion."[18]

In addition to the new rationalistic catechism, another point of severe contention between Froehlich and the state church involved the issue of infant baptism. This was a practice Froehlich could no longer accept. According to the baptismal liturgy of the state church, the infant's sponsors were asked five questions regarding the infant's beliefs and intentions.

Froehlich's reaction to this was without compromise: "This play with holy things I could no longer carry on, in my conviction."[19] Thus, he became a proponent of believer's baptism based on the candidate's faith, rather than as an infant or at the age of confirmation.

The confrontations between Froehlich and the state church culminated with his dismissal from the church on June 4, 1831, just a month short of his twenty-eighth birthday.

Samuel Froehlich had stood resolutely by his convictions. He dared to preach the truth, even if it displeased the church council or his peers in the clergy. The storm clouds of conflict and controversy continued to hover about him.

Being close to God but without a church affiliation, Froehlich awaited further direction from God. His first opportunity for Christian service came from a congregation in Wilhelmsdorf in Wurttemberg, Germany, that had separated from the state church. However, this church was not entirely receptive to his doctrine because it adhered to the practice of infant baptism.[20]

During this time Froehlich served several families as a tutor. Being highly educated and fluent in several languages, as well as possessing a brilliant mind, Froehlich was ideally suited for tutoring. It was also at this time that he met with and preached among groups of Mennonites in the area.[21]

Because of his interest in missionary work, Froehlich soon came in contact with the Continental Society of London, a group which supported missionaries on the continent. He learned to know a preacher from this group, Ami Bost, who like Froehlich had departed from the state church in Switzerland.[22]

In February, 1832, (at age twenty-eight) Froehlich was baptized by sprinkling at the hands of Pastor Ami Bost in Geneva. Although baptized by sprinkling, Froehlich later came to endorse the practice of baptism by immersion. He never allowed himself to subsequently be baptized by immersion as he thought the Scripture, "One Lord, one faith, one baptism" had great relevance.[23] He especially thought this since he had undergone a true and sincere conversion. He did demand, however, that persons baptized as infants, or who had been baptized by sprinkling without ever being truly converted, be rebaptized by immersion.

Even before he was baptized, Froehlich was in a quandary as to what to do regarding his service for the Lord. Beginning in April, 1831, he set out to "test the waters" in various areas of Switzerland in an effort to measure the potential reaction to his preaching. He thus traveled extensively, preaching in areas where he was welcome.

Ruegger, in *Apostolic Christian Church History, Volume I,* refers to these as "missionary journeys." The first missionary journey was made into canton Thurgau in April, 1831. It was at Leutwil in late April, 1831, that he baptized thirty-eight souls from his former congregation. These were people to whom he had preached previously, and they had responded to the gospel and had begun to walk anew in faith. During this visit in 1831, they requested to be baptized; and after carefully examining them pursuant to their readiness for this holy act, he fulfilled their request.[24]

The mode of baptism Froehlich used is not known, but it was probably by sprinkling. The church he was to found was not as yet established, and Froehlich had many doctrinal points to settle within his own mind. Without a doubt, he was still uncertain as to the proper mode of baptism, and he likely used sprinkling as did some of the Anabaptist groups in the area. In time, however, he came to strongly emphasize baptism by immersion, citing Biblical examples.

It is somewhat surprising that Froehlich conducted baptisms in 1831, yet was not baptized himself until 1832. This can be explained by the fact that Froehlich was a product of the state church. As a young man he was likely groping in matters of faith, and he had never before encountered a strong brotherhood order of the kind that he would later come to understand and zealously promote.

The second journey in 1832 took him into the canton Bern at Geneva. The third, in August, 1832, took him to the Emmental; and the fourth in October of the same year to Zurich and east Switzerland. Also during this time, he associated with Mennonites as well as other believers who had previously departed from the state church.[25]

It was during this third missionary journey to the Giebel (near Langnau) that he met Christian Gerber, with whom he had corresponded previously by letter.[26] Gerber was a minister

A building at "The Giebel" near Langnau, Switzerland, where Samuel Froehlich formerly preached. Sometimes as many as four or five hundred gathered to hear him deliver his sermons.

of the Mennonite Church in this area. Today, the oldest Mennonite congregation in the world is in Langnau.[27] In 1832 Gerber was nearly seventy years old; he had been ordained in 1821. He had become rather disenchanted with his church constituency and later came under the influence of Samuel Froehlich.

Ruegger writes, "Christian Gerber sought to instill new life into the congregation because he saw how lukewarm conditions were in the old Mennonite churches. The old outward form remained, but there was little inner and spiritual life. There was a lack of Elders and teachers. Since the persecutions, members lived widely scattered on solitary mountain heights, so that meetings could be held only monthly, later every three weeks, alternately in homes and barns.

"There was no growth because the missionary spirit was lacking. In places there was no preaching about repentance and regeneration."[28]

When Froehlich arrived at Langnau, a place ripe for reform and renewed leadership, he laid before them a copy of his letter of May 14, 1832, to the English Continental Society in which he had answered six questions outlining his religious views.[29]

Christian Gerber, almost seventy years old and obviously fascinated with this young energetic preacher of twenty-eight, called to his attention the fact that his written statement did not cover his views on military service. Because of this, Froehlich developed a position in which his followers would serve in the military, but only in a non-combatant role. Thus, the firmly held Mennonite belief of non-resistance, upheld through much tribulation and at times great loss over the years, had a significant influence on Samuel Froehlich.

Scholars have recorded the events which took place in Langnau from 1832 on. J. C. Wenger writes, "In 1832 Froehlich came to Langnau and created somewhat of a sensation with his earnestness and oratory. Soon a group of brethren withdrew from the others and met separately to hear Froehlich. The Froehlich group demanded that communion services be held almost every week in an effort to return to the apostolic pattern. About Christmas, 1834, Gerber and Christian Baumgartner, two Froehlich disciples, began to hold communion services separately with their own followers only."[30]

In January, 1835, the Mennonite Church sent four of their leaders to Langnau from the Jura to address the problems that had arisen, but they were unsuccessful in resolving the situation.

Froehlich, who had been forced to leave the Emme Valley, sent a young man, twenty-one-year-old George Steiger to Langnau. Steiger pronounced as "dead" all who remained in the old church and refused baptism by immersion.

About sixty members left the Mennonite Church, and together with a similar number who left the Reformed Church they organized a new congregation of some 120 members. This newly established church constituted a significant beginning of the Froehlich movement in Europe.[31]

The *Mennonite Encyclopedia* reviews Froehlich's life briefly from 1832 on: [32]

> In October and November, 1832, his fourth missionary journey took him to Zurich and eastern Switzerland. Here he met Susette Brunschweiler of Hauptwil, canton of Thurgau, whom he married in 1836. In January, 1833, upon the invitation of the Continental Society of London, he went to England for five months. He then returned to the cantons of Aargau and Zurich where he preached and taught in the face of growing persecution from state church authorities. In

March, 1843, he was expelled from Zurich as a sectarian. His marriage was not recognized by the Swiss authorities because it was not performed by a minister of the state church. Froehlich moved to Strasbourg in June, 1844, where he continued his activities of directing the work in Switzerland by letter and also by infrequent visits. He suffered much from sickness. He died on January 15, 1857. He held up to 450 meetings per year. Though he was often so weak he had to be led to the pulpit, his strength always returned to him as he began to preach. He wrote annually between 200 and 300 letters in duplicate besides keeping a diary. The grave of Samuel Heinrich Froehlich is marked to this day by a plain gravestone in the St. Helena Cemetery in Strasbourg.

A simple grave in Strasbourg, France, marks the final resting place of Samuel Froehlich 1803-1857.

Froehlich was slight of build and suffered early in life from lung troubles. The many religious conflicts and persecutions he endured gradually wore down his health. His early death at age fifty-three was largely due to the strain of his missionary activity and the battles he encountered with Swiss authorities.

As the doctrines of repentance and conversion grew in Switzerland, France, Germany, and eventually in the Balkan states, Froehlich became a well-known figure, and one despised by Swiss authorities. He was regarded as a dangerous sectarian because his preaching, although centered on Scripture, differed from the rationalistic doctrines of the state church. Often he was hailed before the magistrates to answer for his preaching. Once, when visiting Hauptwil to visit his newborn son, he was jailed. Always, at these times of confrontation, he confessed Christ and stood firmly on his religious principles.

Building at the end of narrow street in Strasbourg, France, where Samuel Froehlich conducted worship services.

As he matured and became more settled in his faith, Froehlich became very methodical and careful in the administration of his many new congregations. "Bitter experiences have taught me not to be too hasty," he wrote regarding baptism. Of those desiring baptism he said, "They must be ready, not alone to receive the blessings of Christ, but also to take up the Cross of Christ." Some of the early converts had apostasized when persecution became more severe, and subsequently Froehlich was more cautious that he baptize only those who were totally committed to their new life.

On August 28, 1836, he married Susette Brunschweiler of Hauptwil. Although their marriage was blessed by the united prayer of Froehlich's congregation in Hauptwil, it was not sanctioned by the state church because it had not been performed by one of their ministers.[33] This caused terrible problems for Froehlich and his bride. For almost seven years he was intermittently separated from his wife. Froehlich sought refuge in Strasbourg, France. His wife later joined him there, and their marriage was finally recognized and registered in the Strasbourg City Hall under the Napoleonic Code of Law.[34]

Froehlich's retreat to Strasbourg because of religious persecution was similar to a pattern established a few centuries earlier when many Anabaptists fled persecution in Germany and Switzerland and came to Strasbourg. Anabaptists, appreciative of this tolerant haven, termed it the "City of Hope," and the "Refuge of Righteousness."

Froehlich was so upset with the state church's unfair attitude toward his marriage that he wrote a lengthy treatise, "Matrimony According to the Word of God."

Susette Brunschweiler was born in 1803 in Hauptwil, the daughter of Johann Joachim Brunschweiler. The well-to-do Brunschweiler family was a major source of financial support for the Froehlich family during his many years of preaching.

The Froehlich union bore three children: Theophanie, the first born, died on July 3, 1841, at age two and one-half. Her father was not permitted to be present at her death. Eugenie Salome was born in Hauptwil on January 12, 1840, and died in 1917. She never married. A son, Samuel Gershom, was born in Hauptwil on April 12, 1842, (the name Gershom was taken from Exodus 2:22). He had a total of twenty-one children from two wives.

When Samuel Froehlich died in 1857, Samuel Gershom Froehlich, along with his mother and sister, returned to their native Hauptwil. He later was instrumental in founding the Free Church in Switzerland, which today has some ten thousand members.[35] He did not join his father's church. Thus, in America, very little is known today of the Froehlich family.

As Froehlich lay on his death bed, his last words were, "I shall die, Lord my God. May Thou keep Thy holy ones from temptation which is in the world, that they may not perish, but abide in Thee, and give them eternal life. For the prince of this world is prepared with his whole power of darkness, and preachers of unrighteousness, who seek to destroy Thy work, and to mislead Thy elect. Thou knowest that I have not sought glory before men, but only sought to further Thy glory and have declared Thy name before all and have not been ashamed of Thee and have fought until this hour."[36]

He then rasped at last, "My soul is saved and I am comforted in the Lord." He expired on January 15, 1857, at the age of fifty three and one-half years. His was a life of constant activity and diligence. At the end of six years of his ministry, he had established 14 churches; after fifteen years there were 55 congregations, and eventually there were 110 congregations. The movement also spread into the Balkan states and finally to America in 1847.

Significant to learning about the work of Froehlich is to understand how he proceeded to establish so many churches. Often he would go into a town, as led by the Spirit, and inquire if there were any persons who were dissatisfied with the state church. He would meet with them and later hold meetings, and usually there was a favorable response to his preaching and teaching.

Because so many of his early followers had Catholic, Lutheran, or Reformed backgrounds and were rooted in the doctrine of infant baptism and other questionable doctrines, Froehlich published two booklets: *Baptism: Who Shall and Who Shall Not Be Baptized?* and *The Mystery of Godliness and The Mystery of Ungodliness.* The former dealt with baptism and the matter with Scriptural truth as Froehlich perceived it. These two booklets were very helpful in giving people a better understanding of the doctrine which Froehlich promoted.

Those who followed the doctrines advocated by Samuel Froehlich realized they faced the possibility of persecution and harassment by state authorities. Often his followers were forced to appear before magistrates or to petition authorities on behalf of practicing their faith. The lack of religious freedom forced them into a deeper understanding of their faith which in turn gave them the necessary courage to stand firm and true when challenges by authorities (or even by friends and neighbors) came to haunt them. Sometimes they were required to offer a written statement of "confession" of their faith.

In the early days of the Froehlich movement, when new churches were being established, civil authorities harassed the brethren mercilessly. Ruegger describes "trouble" at Zurich in 1837: "At Zurich, on February 26, 1837, there was to be a vote on the revised constitution which aimed at removing the article on freedom of faith of 1831, and thereby put an end to the meetings. Everywhere fines were imposed. In Bern a meeting was stormed and the teaching-brothers severely abused. Teacher Marti, after his conversion, was removed from office and banned from the canton. In Thurgau newly baptized persons were beaten with staves and almost drowned in watering-troughs."[37]

Religious toleration in Switzerland had received a setback in 1803 with the repeal of the Helvetic Constitution of 1798 which guaranteed freedom of faith and conscience. Mass baptisms were forced on young children who had not been baptized as infants. As late as 1839 in canton Zurich, some believers had to leave their homes because they would not allow their children to be baptized.[38] They believed baptism should only be administered after a soul was accountable before God and fully able to understand the meaning of conversion and its serious implications.

Persecutions largely ended with the enforcement of Article 49 in the Constitution of 1874 which guaranteed freedom of faith and conscience.

This was true when the brethren in Schweinfurt, Germany, in 1850 petitioned the King of Bavaria for permission to practice their faith. This brilliant document follows on pages 56-57.

Civil harassment of believers in Schweinfurt, Bavaria in 1850 resulted in the writing of a marvelous "Confession of Faith."

Confession of faith and Constitution
of a Christian Congregation in
Bavaria and above all in Schweinfurt
as a communication of the highly-
honored and respected Government.

The undersigned members of the most holy faith of our Lord Jesus Christ, the Lord of Majesty—(who according to Ja. 2, 1 and 1 Cor. 5, 16, 17 is no respector of persons, but values and judges every person according to his inner worthiness before God)—follow this summons on the part of the honorable Government, to talk about ourselves and to tell what we are (Acts 26, 1 and the following)

To be sure, we are well known in respect to our outward station and life; but we are less known in respect to our inward stand and faith before God, and therefore bound to give account of the hope that is in us (Peter 3, 15-16) to everyone who asks us for the reason; most of all to the Government which should judge whether the citizens are beginning something which is disadvantageous to the welfare of the state. We gladly submit to such impartial examination since we are convinced that we are neither detrimental nor harmful to human society, but rather a blessing as children of the faith of Abraham. (1 Moses 12, 2-3; Gal. 3, 7-5.29.)

Now in regard to our faith we say wholeheartedly with the Apostle Paul: "We confess that according to the way which is called a sect, we thus serve the God of the fathers, that we believe all that is written in the Law and in the Prophets, casting our hope on God, which they also await, that the resurrection of the dead, the just and the unjust, will take place. But in this expectation we strive and practice to have a clear conscience toward God and men." (Acts 24, 14-16.)

The characteristic feature of our faith in Jesus Christ, the Lord of Majesty, therefore consists in this that this faith of ours is not a mere matter of form, not mere learning, not mere confession before men, but permeates our whole heart, sanctifies our whole life as divine strength. We leave it to each and everyone to judge whether our faith in Jesus Christ should be considered less (or inferior) than the usual faith of men just because our faith passes into our lives as a power of sanctification, in love to God and to man. The reason for our separation from the established church is also founded on this difference, not by our human volition, but through God's grace and summons, because the faith which does not produce a new life through Christ is a different faith from the one which the Apostles of the Lord had taught. (Ephes. 4, 1 and the following) The strength of faith has been lost as well as the light of faith. Matth. 5, 13-16.)

But when we are asked whence our faith in Jesus Christ received this light and this strength, we answer briefly and truly; from the baptism in Jesus Christ in which the promise of God to us was fulfilled, that He would give to those who believe in Jesus Christ and let themselves be baptised in His death His Holy Spirit, who makes it not only possible, but also easy to lead a new life according to Christ's image (Rom. 6) a thing which is not possible to human endeavor. That is then no longer a barren command and a moral-patch-work, but the product of God's power; and thus all should be who call themselves after Christ and confess Him by word of mouth. (Timothy, 2-19.)

Now just as we are considered a sect on account of our baptism in Jesus Christ, and are despised and cast off by men as if by that we had invented something strange and new, when we merely obeyed the command and order of the Lord with all our heart (Rom. 6-17); thus we on our part also can no longer have any spiritual (or church) communion with those who despise us because of the truth of Jesus Christ and who cast us off as a sect (Timothy, 3-5), and whose faith is death and unproductive for bringing forth a holy, godly life, such as was in Christ Jesus and was made manifest. (Ja. 2-20 and the following, 1 John 1, 2-7). He who does not have the life of Jesus Christ, denies Christ Himself as the One who gained and brought back life from death. (John 2-22 and the following.)

The true baptism in Christ, of which there is only one just as there is only one true faith for salvation, therefore stands between two types or manifestations of belief; for in order to become partakers of Christ (Heb. 3-14) one must proceed from faith to faith, as the apostle says, (Rom. 1-17) "For therein is the righteousness of God revealed from faith to faith"; and still there is only *one faith*, just as the Father and the Son are One God. The first deed of faith, which must precede baptism and proceeds from the preaching of the Word of God, avails for the justification of the wicked sinner in the eyes of God (Rom. 3-22 and the following, 5-1; 10-4 and the following.) The other faith flows and results from the baptism of him who first believed, and gives the baptised one strength in Christ to do the will of God, and to overcome the world to sanctification for the day of deliverance. (Gal. 2-20; 5-6; 6-15; 1 Cor. 7-19; 1 John. 5-4 and the following.)

We have and embrace absolutely no other faith than the one which God's Word teaches and gives us, in which we also find both the best precept and safest rule for establishing a *congregation* of such called believers, as was done at the time of the Apostles.

To be sure, in Schweinfurt and in general in Bavaria, there are as yet not many of us of that faith, nor do we use human means to persuade anyone thereto, but on the contrary we restrain those in whom we do not find divine manifestations of preceeding grace, repentance in God and faith in Jesus, and we exclude those who do not live according to their confession and in a way worthy of the Gospel; but we are united in one body and spirit of Christ with all the consecrated in the whole world, and not only with those who really live on earth, but also with those who have already preceded us beyond the grave to await with us the future revelation and glorification of the children of God. (Rom. 8-14-19.)

That is our confession of faith, whereby we are not concerned with art and wisdom but only with truth and conformity with God's Holy Word and Will, and whence it also follows that we have adopted neither a new faith nor a new baptism (i.e. are neither sectarians nor anabaptists) but the age-old, original command which *from the beginning* we have had and received from God to obey. (John 2-7.24; 2 John. 6-10.)

We appeal to the toleration and public protection on the part of our highly respected Government which has been ordained by God, with the greater assurance since we are loyal and obedient subjects, having the honor to remain,

Respectfully,

Schweinfurt
Sept. 9, 1850.

Johann Andreas Braun
John Kasper Koch
Konrad Belz
Marie Susanna Braun, Widow
Ursula Margaretha Braun
Marie Schmidt, Widow
Katharina Schmidt
Sabina Dorothea Schmidt
Margaretha Goebel, Widow

As such who, to be sure, have not yet been accepted into this congregation, but who, after having come to a realization for the most part of the genuine evangelical and apostolic principles, intend to shortly join the same if it be God's gracious will, the following also sign

Respectfully,

Johann Michael Reuter, Jr.
Magdalena Reuter
Friedrich Buettner
George Schmidt

During the periods of harsh treatment by the state, church meetings were prohibited and meeting places were locked. In 1837, Froehlich once held a meeting from 2:30 a.m. to 6 a.m. in order not to attract the attention of authorities. In 1841, a meeting in Teufenthal convened at midnight and lasted until 5 a.m.[39]

Ruegger comments on persecutions at Aargau in 1850, "Brothers Geistlich, Guenthard, and Leuthold, in connection with a visit in Aargau, 1850, were captured, shackled, and deported to canton Zurich. Only in isolated places and at night between 2 and 5 a.m. were meetings possible.[40]

Ruegger writes of a rock-throwing incident in Bachenbuelach: "When on May 23, 1850, as Froehlich was traveling through, a large audience listened to the Word, young people appeared at the door to speak abuse. A huge stone came flying through a window, but Froehlich calmly preached on."[41]

At his last evening meeting prior to his death, Froehlich concluded with the verse, "Therefore, I take pleasure in infirmities, in reproaches, in necessities, in persecutions, in distresses for Christ's sake; for when I am weak, then am I strong." This meeting was held in Basel on October 20, 1856.[42]

* * * * *

As the roots of faith in most churches reach deeply into the past, so those of the Apostolic Christian Church obviously go much deeper than the Froehlich movement of the nineteenth century.

Naturally, many churches attempt to link their history directly to the events of the first century, A.D. The Apostolic Christian Church, however, not being a liturgical church, makes no direct claim to organized apostolic succession. The church has believed over the years that man's calling is directly from God, and that a true Church (holy and pure) has existed since Christ's ascension, even if men have not recognized or known about it. The Apostolic Christian Church (Evangelical Baptist Church in Europe) began when God raised up a man and a people in the midst of religious apostasy and directed them by His Spirit along the pathways outlined by Holy Writ.

* * * * *

Over the years, since the greatest historical event of all time—Christ's death on Mount Calvary—there has existed a true remnant of faith. Along with this remnant there have existed many visible churches—some very large denominations—in a somewhat apostate condition, considering their doctrine and the lives of their members.

The Apostolic Christian Church considers itself to be raised up in the tradition of the "free church." This is a term given to bodies of believers who, over the years, have distinguished themselves by their devotion and attention to the literal ways of the New Testament. In so doing, they have usually suffered some type of persecution.

More specifically, the Apostolic Christian Church is a product of the Radical Reformation of the sixteenth century, and was particularly influenced by the Anabaptist movement that sprang up in Switzerland in 1525, approximately three hundred years before Samuel Froehlich began his work. As a young divinity student at Basel, Froehlich became exposed to, and later influenced by, the Swiss Brethren, and still later by other Mennonites. Thus, he had a distinct Anabaptist influence.

In 1569 Dirk Willems, a Dutch Anabaptist, saves his captor's life. Willems was later burned at the stake. The above sketch and subsequent injustice reflects the harsh treatment accorded Anabaptists.

The decade of 1517-1527 in Europe was one which ushered in both the Reformation and the Radical Reformation. Martin Luther, a Roman Catholic priest in Germany, engaged in perhaps the most symbolic act of what was later to become the Reformation when, on October 31, 1517, he posted his ninety-five theses on the door of the Castle Church in Wittenberg. These were strong complaints against abuses in the Catholic Church.[43]

In Switzerland, Ulrich Zwingli began to openly attack the Catholic Church in 1518 concerning the selling of indulgences. Eventually, a protestant state church was established in Switzerland. The church and the state were one entity.

By 1525, a group of Zwingli's disciples had broken ranks with him. Among the leaders of this group were Conrad Grebel and Felix Manz. For several months they attempted a reconciliation with the views of Zwingli, particularly on baptism. But after much prayer, they realized that it was hopeless to try to win Zwingli and the Zurich government for a re-establishment of the apostolic church, and the final division came.

Four men, Conrad Grebel, Felix Manz, Johannes Brotli, and Georg Blaurock—in a historic move—gathered together for the purpose of re-baptizing themselves. Fritz Blanke, in *Brothers in Christ,* writes, "The few believers gathered, probably on the evening of January 21, 1525, supposedly in the house of Felix Manz in Zurich. They prayed together, and then Georg Blaurock arose and asked Grebel to baptize him. Grebel baptized him, and afterwards Blaurock baptized the other participants in the meeting. That is the hour of the birth of the Anabaptist movement."[44]

The term "anabaptist" means "re-baptized." Most of those who joined this movement had been baptized as infants, and when later requesting baptism based on their living faith, they were actually baptized again, or "re-baptized." This was the name their opponents gave them. A long period of vicious and intense persecution took place as authorities tried to stamp out this new movement. But the heavier the heel of oppression, the greater their devotion grew, and the Anabaptist movement flourished.

The Anabaptists made the most radical attempt of the Reformation era to renew the church. They rejected infant baptism and practiced the baptism of adults upon confession of their faith. Authorities pursued them relentlessly. Many converts had second thoughts when they learned the cost of discipleship was so high. Drownings, hangings, and burnings were common for those confessing to be Anabaptist. Because they refused to baptize their infant children, they were called "soul murderers," and were hated by the general populace.[45]

The movement grew and became quite widespread as persons from many countries accepted this faith. There was little central administration or cohesion. A meeting was called at Schleitheim on February 24, 1527, to discuss their major beliefs and list the important tenets of their faith. Michael Sattler, an ex-monk and a leading advocate of the movement, wrote a document outlining their main beliefs which was adopted by the meeting.[46] Only a few months later on May 20 of the same year, Sattler was brutally tortured (his tongue was cut out) and later burned at the stake.[47]

The seven articles of faith (known as the Schleitheim Confession) adopted by the group in 1527 dealt with the matters of (1) baptism, (2) the ban, (3) holy communion, (4) separation from the world, (5) duties of Elders or Shepherds, (6) non-resistance, and (7) oath-taking.

The articles, when read in full, would find great support in today's Apostolic Christian Church. Also, the Dordrecht Confession of Faith, adopted April 21, 1632, in the Dutch city of Dordrecht, contains beliefs that have found their way into the Apostolic Christian Church.

Mirror of the Soul

Humility makes a man peaceable among the brethren, fruitful in doing good, joyful in suffering, and constant in holy living. Humility makes us fit for the highest service that we owe to Christ and at the same time is not negligent of the lowliest service to the humblest saint. Humility can be content with the most modest table and yet will enjoy the most precious delicacies as with God, with Christ, and in glory. Humility makes a man willing and ready to bless him who curses him and to pray for him who persecutes him; a humble heart is an abode of God, a disciple of Christ, a companion of angels, a preserving-vessel for grace, and is prepared for glory. Humility is the faithful nurse of our graces and gifts and the mighty impulse to sacred exercises in duty.

Samuel H. Froehlich

Froehlich's *Mirror of the Soul* illustrates, the importance he placed on the Biblical doctrine of humility. Anabaptists placed a great emphasis on *Demut, Einfacheit,* and *Gelassenheit,* or in English, humility, simplicity, and yieldedness.

Anabaptist beliefs about the church were very distinctive. They were not interested in reforming the church, but in restoring it to the vigor and faithfulness of its earliest centuries. While earlier reformers had stressed the concept of "faith," the Anabaptists stressed both "faith and life." It became very important, in addition to having faith in God, that one live according to His Word. As one Anabaptist put it, "No one can truly know Christ except he follow Him in life."

Anabaptism brought renewal to the concepts of brotherhood and church order which are so clearly stated in the Scriptures. In some places the opposite tendency appeared in which the place of the church was minimized and heavy emphasis was placed on the individual and his autonomy within the brotherhood, but generally among Anabaptism the concept of brotherhood prevailed.[48]

The *Mennonite Encyclopedia* describes the Anabaptist concept of the church:[49]

> Since the Anabaptist conception of the church is ultimately derivative from its concept of Christianity as discipleship, i.e., complete obedience by the individual to Christ and the living of a holy life patterned after His example and teachings, an essential idea in it is that the church must be holy, composed exclusively of practicing disciples, and kept pure. It is a church of order, in which the body determines the pattern for its members, and therefore has authority over the individual's behavior. It controls admission of new members, requiring evidence of repentance, the new birth, and a holy life, and maintains the purity of the church through discipline using the ban or excommunication. Adopting the program of Christ for the church (Eph. 5:27) as their aim, the Anabaptists sincerely sought to achieve a church "not having spot or wrinkle or any such thing; but that it should be holy and without blemish." They cannot, however, rightly be charged on this account with perfectionism, for their position expressedly provided for discipline for sinning church members.

Three centuries later Samuel Froehlich fell under partial influence of Anabaptism, and the churches he founded eventually resembled their counterparts of three hundred years earlier. Although the Bible was Froehlich's major influence, his association with the Swiss Brethren caused him to adopt many of their practices and church procedures which proved beneficial to his followers. Also, many of the first members of the church in America had an Anabaptist background (Mennonite, Amish), and this influence was manifested both in their church order and liturgy and even in the simplicity of their outward appearance and manner of life.

CHAPTER III   TOWARD A BETTER LAND

"...and, lo, I am with you always, even unto the end of the world. Amen."

That majestic lady, her arm raised high above her head holding the torch of liberty, stood in mute silence as millions of European emigrants gazed up in awe and anticipation.

Men, women, and children who were tired, anxious, and uncertain after a long ocean voyage glanced up at the famous symbol of freedom and goodwill—the Statue of Liberty. Rumpled and bone-weary, they clutched their meager possessions, and, packed tightly among others whose hearts were emblazoned with the hope of liberty, they realized that "America" was just ahead, and that perhaps in a few days or weeks their eventual American destination would be reached.

Had they been closer to the great lady and been able to read English, they might have broken down in tears as they read (after 1903) the words of poet Emma Lazarus who wrote in "The New Colossus":

> *"Give me your tired, your poor,*
> *Your huddled masses yearning to breathe free,*
> *The wretched refuse of your teeming shore,*
> *Send these, the homeless, tempest-tost to me,*
> *I lift my lamp beside the golden door."*

They came and they came, boatload after boatload, to the grand "America." They came through the golden door to the "utopia" they had heard so much about in Europe, the "pot of gold" at the end of the rainbow. It had taken virtually all their inner resources to pursue and endure this great new adventure. When they left their homelands in Europe, they essentially "burned their bridges behind them." Almost everyone gave up their homes, their lands, their possessions, and even their loved ones. Most who left never returned again, and many who left loved ones never saw them again. Going to America was a powerful commitment, but millions were up to doing it.

The "America fever," which spread like a contagion in late nineteenth-century Europe, was based on many factors. A major one was the significant population growth which had taken place in Europe during the previous few centuries. The population of all of Europe in 1650 was 100 million persons. By 1850 that had swelled to 500 million.[1] Thus, the upward trend was well established in the mid-nineteenth century. With conditions more crowded, economic opportunity correspondingly lessened.

The statistics of European-American migration dramatically illustrate how the coincidence of bad economic conditions in Europe and demand for cheaper labor in the United States raised emigration figures to high peaks, and also how good times in Europe and depression in the United States later brought an abrupt halt to this process.

Aside from economic considerations, there were other reasons why persons came to the United States in such great numbers. Among them were unfavorable taxing policies, a rigid class structure, forced military service, and religious persecution. The last two in particular were major reasons why the forefathers of Apostolic Christians came to America. Religious persecution was not as severe as it had been two or three hundred years earlier, but nonetheless it was enough of an annoyance to induce many to seek religious asylum in America. Adjunct to this concern was the mandatory conscription, in many cases, of the young sons of believers who had to serve in the military and were subsequently subject to the whims and excesses of adventurous princes and generals. This was particularly troublesome and sharply conflicted with the faith of those who believed deeply in the Scriptural mandates of "thou shalt not kill" and "do violence to no man."

America offered fertile pastures of opportunity to millions of Europeans. An open policy existed with respect to emigration, at least until 1924. The rise of maritime nations whose fleets allowed for widespread ocean travel was a significant factor in waves of emigrants coming to America. If this had not occurred, emigration could well have been curbed, almost totally. Transportation to America was inexpensive, and in some instances European governments paid a portion of the passage.

The American industrial machine had shifted gears by mid-1800. Previously, owners would often work alongside workers, and the general mode of operations was more relaxed. As manufacturing plants later became larger, however, stockholders hired managers, and profits became very important. This encouraged the use of emigrants who were accustomed to a lower standard of living and who would work for less money.

Men, women, and even children could secure jobs in factories. Because of poor food and political conditions, about 1.5 million Germans came to America between 1840-1860.

The vast expanse of available and cheap farmland, especially fertile farmland in the Mississippi Valley, proved to be a significant incentive for industrious husbandmen to emigrate to America. For those willing to work long hours against terrific odds, to clear forests and drain swamps, and to endure crop failures and other hardships, the farmlands of Ohio, Indiana, Illinois, Iowa, and Kansas pulled like a magnet on the dreams and hopes that kindled endlessly in the bosoms of the potential emigrants.

E. Kay Kirkham writes in *Survey of American Church Records, Volume II,* "Of course good soil and productive land has always been an incentive to migrate to America. Mother Earth offered special attraction to those who had the faith and courage to look to the horizons, whether north, south, and especially westward in America."[2]

Also, "In Europe there was a scarcity of land; social conditions were oppressive to many; and there were famine and wars, too many wars."[3]

Previous to coming to America, many European forebears were forced to make decisions of enormous, lifelong implications. When they decided to emigrate, it meant leaving their homesteads and loved ones once and for all time. If a young man decided, due to reasons of conscience, not to serve in his country's military units, he left for America knowing he could probably never return to his native land. The enormity of their willingness to leave their European homelands is difficult to comprehend.

The ancestors of Apostolic Christians came in great numbers to participate in the promises of America. Many became farmers, and from the most meager of circumstances, many descendants of these families ascended, one hundred years later, to a prosperity unprecedented in the annals of agrarian history.

Significant to immigration and the development of the nation was the development in the mid-nineteenth century of travel by canals, roads, and railroads. This hastened the travel capabilities between the eastern seaboard and the Mississippi Valley. The Erie Canal tied the Hudson River to the Great Lakes.

By 1850, the federal government began aiding western railroads with grants of public lands which the railroads could mortgage or sell to raise money. Native Americans and emigrants then headed west to occupy this farmland.

The Homestead Act of 1862 also promoted the development of western lands. Any citizen or alien might acquire 160 acres by residing on it for five years and paying a small fee. By 1880, almost twenty million acres were claimed by "homesteaders."[4]

Evangelical Baptists in Europe, like many others, suffered economic hardship. They, however, suffered religious persecution as well. More and more, from the 1850's on, it became clear that emigration to America was a viable alternative.

Already in 1847 Samuel Froehlich had commissioned Benedict Weyeneth to go to America. In 1848, more Froehlich followers settled near Sardis, Ohio. Froehlich, in his diary entry of February 28, 1855, writes, "This morning in Basel, Sister Barbara Ingold of Niederwil came to me. She and her husband and five small children are emigrating to America together with thirty-three other persons. Because they are so poor, the civil community must support them. The goal of their journey is Illinois. I gave her the address of the brethren."[5]

Andrew J. Braun of Schweinfurt emigrated to America along with his family and the entire congregation on July 2, 1854. They landed at Peoria, Illinois. This was on the advice of Froehlich who wrote, "If it is no longer possible for you to live your faith where you are, then emigrate to America." Braun had been forbidden to hold meetings and spent Christmas Day, 1850, in jail. He was finally told by authorities that his congregation had the choice of giving up their faith or emigrating.[6]

Phillip Braun, a descendant of Andrew J. Braun and for many years an Elder in the Apostolic Christian Church (Nazarene) at Syracuse, New York, said that Samuel Froehlich was dubious about his followers going to America because he feared that prosperity might lead to spiritual leanness and this could harm the church.

The travel route in Europe for those emigrating usually culminated at Le Havre, France, the English Channel port some seventy-five miles east of the British border, and the same distance from the city of Paris. Emigrants from Switzerland, Germany, and France mostly traveled this route, often stopping overnight in Paris, and then boarding the ocean-going vessels at Le Havre.

Frederick Guth, who came to America in 1882 with his parents, wrote a vivid account of his family's experience in leaving their German homeland and making the trip to America. He was only seven years old at the time, but later recorded his recollections:

> I personally remember when in 1882 in late summer our parents with eight children left Lorraine, Germany, for America. Although I was only seven years old, the high-spirited enthusiasm which permeated us all is still fresh in my memory.
>
> When in the evening hours the family circle would gather in the large living room in that massive stone house known as *"Baersitter Hof,"* we delighted in hearing father read the glowing reports out of American Land Company literature of the great success of those immigrants who had already preceded us.
>
> Finally the day of departure for the far-away new world was at hand. It was early in the morning and still dark, when all of us were securely placed on the wagon and a final look at the old home and good byes were said to those servants, neighbors, and friends forever.
>
> The trip to France where the Reebs lived was over an ancient and rough road. Arriving there we all had the assurance that now we were on our way to the promised land of opportunity. After a day's rest there, we entrained for Paris and then to Le Havre where we embarked for New York. The long ocean voyage was mingled with fear and hope. All of us eight young children were seasick most of the way.
>
> All of these memories still haunt me because of my intimate sympathy for the hopes and aspirations of our mutual desire to go forward and pioneer for a more full life in America. What a sense of relief and joy overcame us all when early in the morning the word was given—we are here, there is New York.

The family of John Adam Meiss left the village of Voiller-dingen in Alsace-Lorraine for the great trip to America.[7] They traveled to Paris and then on to Le Havre where they stayed overnight at a hotel. The next morning they arose and boarded the new ship, "The Normandy." It was a beautiful day when they began their ocean voyage, and good weather lingered the entire trip with the exception of only one day when stormy weather caused some of them to experience sea-sickness. The children played, sang songs, and ran around on the deck. There were fifteen persons in their party, and they traveled second class. As one of their descendants wrote, "One particular memory of the voyage was about the French waiters, young boys, who wanted to be friendly with them, but with whom they could not exchange many words since they could not speak each other's language."

There were a variety of other experiences by many of the stalwarts of faith who came to America. Two men who later served as Elders at Cissna Park, Illinois, had unusual experiences when they crossed the Atlantic Ocean en route to America. The ship carrying the John Adam Eisenmann family encountered a severe storm. Many passengers had given up hope and resigned themselves that the ship would sink. Amid the despair, one of the Eisenmann children became very sick, and Grandmother Eisenmann held it in her arms, expecting it to die. The unwavering faith of Elder Eisenmann kept him on his knees praying for the poor little child. Suddenly, someone appeared and gave the child some medicine. The child immediately responded and began to show improvement, and at the same time the storm abated. Grandmother Eisenmann was convinced that God sent an angel to minister to them because during the remainder of the trip she never could find anyone on the ship who resembled the man who gave the medicine to her sick child.

In 1889, Elder John Adam Reeb and other families left Alsace-Lorraine and crossed the ocean on the ship "La Lorraine." Some were skeptical that the huge vessel might sink, but one faithful soul said, "Oh no, Minister Reeb is with us, and I know God will not let anything happen to us."

Often, in the evening, whoever was able (and wasn't sea-sick) would go on the deck and sing hymns from the *Zion's*

Harp hymnal. Elder Reeb liked to sing the song, "God Is Still With Me" (No. 148).

Conditions on the trip were often rugged. Seasickness was a constant problem for many emigrants. John Wernli, a native of Switzerland who settled near Lamont, Kansas, became so seasick during the ocean trip that he was nearly tempted to jump overboard.[8]

In 1883, Jacob H. Schlipf, 18, (who later settled on a farm southwest of Gridley, Illinois) came to America. After working in America for six years, he returned to Germany to bring his parents, Elder Johan and Katherine Schlipf, to this country for a visit. A total of thirty-four persons made up the party that traveled together to America. An account of their trip is recorded in the *Genealogy of the Georg Leonard Schlipf Family, 1790-1960:*[9]

> The first evening on their return to America, as they were singing the evening hymn No. 49, "Thou art still our shield and Saviour, Our good sentinel at night, etc.," a sailboat ran directly into their ship, tearing about a three-square-foot hole into it. Life boats were sent out, the people in the other boat were all saved, and within two hours the other boat sank. Their group clung together pleading and calling to God for protection in great need and distress, wondering "Oh Lord must we die here," all their friends had wished them so much luck and God's blessings on their journey.
>
> Father, mother, and Jacob went into their room and on their knees prayed that God, their Lord, would hear their prayers, and grant the wishes of their many friends. As they prayed, it became quiet and the people were sent from the deck to their cabins, as many would have gone over the deck so great was their fear. They said good-night together, and trusting in the Lord, they had a restful night.
>
> They sailed to South Hampton, England, to have the ship repaired and were there for three days for repairs before they could continue on their journey. They put their trust in God and had a safe trip the rest of the way.
>
> When they arrived in New York, Grandfather said *"So kinder yetz sind ihr in ein fremdes land"* (trans. "Now, children, you are in a strange land.") He went on to tell them to do as they do in America and be good citizens.

John H. Baumgartner, in *The First One Hundred Years, 1870-1970,* describes travel conditions as emigrants crossed the "stormy" Atlantic in sail boats:[10]

> The voyage across the Atlantic was especially hard on children. The Aeschlimans, Ballers, Gerbers and Strahms all had children die while crossing the ocean and were buried at sea. Sometimes the wind

would be contrary, and they would drift back, waiting for favorable wind again, and then they would come forward toward America. The captain of these ships, his skill in handling the sails made several days' difference in crossing the Atlantic. The ships generally had three masts. Sails were made of linen. The French ship, "Persistent," sailed from Le Havre, France, where many of our fore-parents sailed from. Had the emigrants sailed from New York to Le Havre, it would have taken much less time as the winds were more favorable to sail from America to Europe. The sailboats had severe competition with the steam ships from 1840 to 1860, and they had to have very cheap rates from Le Havre, France, to New York for the emigrants. They lined the docks by the thousands, clutching their pathetic bundles, their children, but also their hope of a new life in a new land. Rates were low, service was poor. They had water and sometimes a fire to cook by. Each passenger got a space of two by seven feet between decks. Bad weather pushed them below closed hatches. Disease and hardship took their toll. The Havre Packet Empire saw 75 of her 675 emigrants die and the Constellation saw 100 of her 922 passengers buried at sea.

With moistened eyes, millions of European emigrants gazed up at the Statue of Liberty from their New York Harbor vantage point. Apostolic Christian forefather were among them.

In 1851 Jacob Wittmer, twenty-eight, and his wife Mary, twenty-one, along with their two small children, Mary, twenty-one months, and Jacob, six months, left their home in Bern, Switzerland, to emigrate to America. They spent thirty-six days on their boat.

Both Jacob and Mary Wittmer were good sailors as neither became seasick. Their children became quite sick, but survived the trip. These two children, along with another child, were the only three of thirteen children on the boat who survived to reach American shores.

When this family reached a hotel in New York City, they found it was completely filled. The proprietor of the hotel, noticing their crestfallen countenance, very kindly offered them his personal quarters for the night. The bone-weary Wittmers were very grateful for this deed of kindness.

They eventually found their way to Monroe County, Ohio, (Sardis) where they lived for one year before moving to Elgin, Iowa. The route they took was down the Ohio River and up the Mississippi River until they reached McGregor, Iowa. They chose to settle near Elgin because of the plentiful supply of water and trees.

Along with a Rothlisberger family, whom they met in Ohio, they built a log cabin where both families lived for two years. This home had two rooms—one upstairs and one downstairs, with only a ladder to reach the upstairs room. The two families also purchased a horse and a cow during the time they lived together.[11]

Samuel Aeschliman, who served many years as Elder of the church's largest congregation at Bluffton, Indiana, recalled how his grandparents came to America in 1853 and settled initially in Monroe County, Ohio. The ocean trip took forty-nine days on a sailing vessel. During the Atlantic crossing, one of their children died and was buried at sea.[12]

Ellis Island as viewed from New York Harbor boat. Known as the "Gateway to the New World," it served as a processing station for more than twelve million aliens. It opened in 1892.

On arriving in the New York harbor, the newly-arrived settlers were hastened to the large registry hall on Ellis Island
(after 1892). This was a place of great fear for the new arrivals
because, in addition to facing all the uncertainties that might
lie ahead in America, each emigrant faced the possibility,
however remote, of rejection—of being sent back to their
homeland—because of improper papers, because of poor
health, or for other reasons.

The low-slung main building of Ellis Island consisted of
warm red brick with limestone trim. It indeed looked forebod-
ing to each newcomer. Close to five thousand emigrants per
day were processed here. One writer wrote, "A constant bab-
ble of incomprehensible tongues rose like flocks of starlings to
the ceiling." One can readily imagine the commotion and
general hectic atmosphere of such a situation.

Interrogation and inspection were quite impersonal. There
was a rapid legal examination. In two minutes inspectors, aided by interpreters, fired twenty-nine questions at a newcomer.
Among them: "Are you an anarchist?" And the trick question:
"Do you have a job?"

The medical examination took place before emigrants
were even aware of it. Doctors stationed in the hall simply observed newcomers as they walked by. In six seconds physi-
cians checked off fifteen diseases. They placed chalk marks on
the lapels of those who needed closer scrutiny: "H" for heart,
"L" for limp, and "X" for mental defect. After this, a doctor
dipped a buttonhook into an antiseptic solution and used it to
flip back the eyelid. The reason: to check for trachoma, a blind-
ing disease that would leave the emigrant an unwanted public charge. Trachoma was the most common medical reason
for sending emigrants back to their native country.

For an emigrant, the first days in Manhattan were nearly
overwhelming. Naive, mostly uneducated, and often from
rural areas, they faced not only a new country, but a new
language as well. Those who came during the early 1900's had
likely never seen subways, trolley cars, or coal stoves. Also,
they had never seen such hordes of people.[13]

New York City was a key place to the new emigrants, especially to the Apostolic Christians (then still known as
Evangelical Baptists). It was here they arranged for transportation, first by water conveyance and later by rail as they fanned

out onto the great expanse that was America. Most of those associated with the church had previously scheduled their destinations with friends and relatives, and when arriving in New York City, they sought to make connections to reach these local areas.

Elder Rudolph Witzig, who served as Elder at Gridley, Illinois, for many years did his utmost to aid his acquaintances to their destination in Gridley. J. Earl Taylor, in *The Old Timer* writes, "Dr. J. A. Taylor of Gridley and Dr. S. A. Dunham of Kansas City took a post graduate course at Bellevue Hospital in New York in 1885. On a visit to the wharf at the Port of Entry, they observed a large black sign about three by twenty feet. On it was painted in white a large hand followed by these words, 'This Way To Gridley, Illinois.'"[14]

Travel conditions to the hinterland were not very comfortable to those given to a proud nature. Nicholas Bach, for many years a resident of Fairbury, Illinois, until his death in 1951, recalled as a young lad of eight when he traveled as an immigrant with his family from New York to Chicago and on to Nebraska. Coming across the wide ocean, his heart had blazed with fervor as he anticipated this great place—"America!"

After clearing customs, emigration channels, and finally bording a train en route to the West, he was terribly anxious to witness this great land. For a long time his hopes were dashed because the rail passenger car in which he and his family were traveling was so cold the windows were frosted on the inside, and young, curious Nicholas could not see outside. To do so, he had to try, with his fingernails, to scratch the frost off the inside of the windows.

On arriving in Chicago for an overnight stay before changing trains for Nebraska, the Bach family stayed at a hotel in downtown Chicago. Their quarters were on the third floor—the immigrant floor—which was one huge hall where immigrants slept on the floor with straw for a mattress. Apparently this mattered little to the immigrants. They were in America. This was the land of the free and the home of the brave. A little discomfort was readily tolerated.

The Stormy Atlantic in 1850

As I sit on the sand by the deep blue ocean
Thoughts come to me and I'm filled with emotion.
As I think of the time many years ago
Probably one hundred and thirty or so
When my grandparents sailed in a boat so small,
From the land of the Alps through storm and squall.

The sails were up and westward they came
Day and night they sailed sometimes the same!
No progress they made but lifted their eyes
To Him who is ruler of the sea and skies
And again forward they came brave and strong
A prayer in heart and on their lips a song.

As I see the waves dashing on the shore
The emotion rises in me more and more
As my thoughts go back many years ago—
How grandmother was rocking me to and fro
In her rocking chair by the fire so red
Telling me of the voyage before going to bed.

As she rocked me gently she would say to me
That is how the boat rocked while crossing the sea
Since then I have heard how others did fare
How storms would arise had nothing to spare,
Few earthly possessions little money on hand,
How so many survived is hard to understand.

Many children became sick, suffered and died
People spoke in low tones; parents sobbed and cried—
As their little one was prepared, wrapped all alone
On a board tied safely and at its feet a stone
A prayer was then offered and it slipped away
In the depth of the ocean—at the close of day.

And then, Oh then, what a wonderful sight!
When day after day and night after night—
In the distance they saw (as the promised land)
Birds, hills, and trees—they all looked so grand
They were nearing the land for here they found
Freedom of worship as their feet touched the ground.

The love and the smile of her face I still see
The nice cakes she fried specially for me
How good the taste of a sweet lump or two
Of brown sugar she had in a white jar for you
The apron strings I pulled (this I shouldn't have done)
But she tied them again neatly, and took it for fun.

Her brothers and sisters all left as she did
Her children passed on at their Maker's stern bid
The lines of time now appear on our face
It's something you and I just can't erase
So time is fleeting on, what can we say more?
Like surge upon surge of the waves on the shore.

This life here below often seems to me
Very much like the voyage crossing the sea.
The storms of life as they assail us here—
Bring us close to the Master and often a tear.
But if we do what He tells us and all do our best
He promises to guide us to the haven of rest.

Written in Fort Lauderdale, Florida, in 1965
John H. Baumgartner

148. GOD IS STILL WITH ME

Zion's Harp.

1. No-ah's ark long drift-ed On the surg-ing flood, But with eyes up-lift-ed, Trust-ed he in God. When through-out life's jour-ney Rag-ing storms I see, This shall be my com-fort: God is still with me.

2. Moses, brave and dauntless,
Crossed the sea to land,
Leading with him fearless
Hosts of covenant;
Thus resigned I'll travel
Through the desert sea,
Trust my soul to Jesus;
God is still with me.

3. Jonah's hour of trial
Led through night and fear;
Yet God showed with power
That His help was near.
Thus in all distresses
When by fear I'm tried,
Hope my heart posesses:
God is at my side!

4. Daniel's den of lions
Teaches true and sure,
When on God depending,
We can feel secure.
So in all distresses
I can pray to Thee;
Faith my heart possesses;
God is still with me.

5. Three men in the furnace
Praised their God on high,
Stood their foes confounded
Silenced scorn and lie.
In reproach and censure
I rest calm and free
On this blessed promise:
God is still with me.

6. Jesus' death arena
And His cross and grave
Teach me wait serenely
God's will sure and safe;
My support and pillar
And my gain is He,
My strong fort in terror;
God is still with me.

7. He broke Peter's fetters
Opened doors for Paul;
He will those deliver
Who trust Him in all.
So I'll wander gladly,
Till my home I see,
And in Zion's mansion,
God is still with me.

In 1889, on the ocean vessel, "La Lorraine", Apostolic Christian fore-fathers found great solace in singing the hymn, "God Is Still With Me."

"Go ye therefore, and teach all nations, baptizing them in the name of the Father, and of the Son, and of the Holy Ghost."

By mid-nineteenth century the United States was well on its way to establishing itself as a great nation. The strong ideals that had formed the nation were becoming firmly embedded in the minds and laws of its people, and consequently these strengths gave an enduring quality to the fledgling country.

Also, by this time many religious denominations had been established. Christianity, in one form or another, had come to America long before anyone from the Apostolic Christian Church had stepped ashore. Men of faith, often with zeal and elaborate plans to "evangelize" this new frontier nation, had traveled to America, and by the time Benedict Weyeneth had arrived, there were many church denominations preaching various interpretations of the truth.

These many religious groups, which flourished under the new nation's tradition of religious liberty, mushroomed into over twelve hundred denominations by 1978.

Because the church and the state were not one entity (as was the case in many European countries), full religious toleration resulted in a flood of thought and interpretation, and people were thus free to believe as they wished. The state did not dominate the church, but conversely encouraged its citizens to follow their own conscience.

Thus, by the time the Apostolic Christian Church's forefathers began to preach and establish a foothold in America, the nation was already dotted with many churches and many church denominations.

In the Apostolic Christian Church, growth initially was slow. Their outreach was generally limited (due to language and culture) to persons of Swiss or German background, and particularly of Anabaptist background. As time unfolded, however, and as more and more emigrants poured in from

Germany, Switzerland, and to a lesser degree from the Balkan countries, the fledgling church denomination began to take root.

If there was a spark that set off the process of growth, it was the willingness of the brethren in Europe, under the guidance of leader Samuel Froehlich, to send young Benedict Weyeneth to America. In 1847 the church in Europe was only fifteen years old, and in a mixture of courage and faith, they ordained their first Elder for service in America.

It is quite interesting to note that Weyeneth's trip to America was not to institute a "plan" to evangelize America or to start several churches. Instead, his efforts were made in response to a request from a group of Mennonites in upstate New York to help resolve some religious disputes within their group. Being ordained specifically for this purpose, Weyeneth made the trip solemnly and perhaps with little thought what might unfold beyond his special mission to Lewis County, New York.

There emerged in the American church a few leaders whose efforts and inspiration won a following and whose untiring devotion to the church was blessed by God to the extent that churches began to form as more and more hungry souls responded to the call of the gospel.

It is very significant, however, that the early Elders and leaders of the church, while endowed with the grace and zeal of God, laid out no plan of action to proselytize America. There was no grand strategy for evangelism, no objective regarding the number of converts they hoped to achieve, and no series of meetings to decide how to proceed. Rather, they were humble and devoted men of God who used whatever talents were given them to preach God's word as the way was "opened up."

They were zealous to the ideal that it was God who would lead the way, open opportunities, and show them which direction to take. Only He, and not man, could bless and guide their efforts, and they were very careful not to "run ahead of the Lord." It is noteworthy that this same concept of spreading God's message is still followed in the church today. The church is quite concerned in modern times that any efforts to grow and "spread out" be based not on the ingenuity and imagination of men but only in response to God's calling and according to His holy will.

It has always been a firmly held concept that it is the church that sends people out to work in the preaching vineyards. Brethren do not go out arbitrarily to evangelize, but God's will is instituted in this regard through the church in order to gain the support of the brethren.

In the early stages of church development, there emerged five leaders whose zeal and untiring efforts benefited the young church. Obviously, there were other leaders of note, as well as countless unknown brothers and sisters who without fanfare supported the ministry in prayer, but these five leaders were ones who history has remembered in that research yields significant information on their lives and activities.

They were Benedict Weyeneth, Peter Virkler, Joseph Bella, Isaac Gehring, and John Kreinbill. All except Virkler and Kreinbill were acquainted personally with Samuel Froehlich, it is assumed, and were deeply influenced by him. All five men were very devoted to the pure gospel of salvation and to the church order and brotherhood concepts which were so deeply rooted and embedded in the European brethren as led by Froehlich.

Thus, the doctrine of the Evangelical Baptist Church in Europe was brought to America, both with diligence and a sense of stewardship. The church today is the benefactor of the forefathers in general and these five brothers in particular for their efforts in "preserving the faith." Although they did not visualize themselves as such, these men, as a result of their extensive travels and nurturing of the first American churches, were truly "evangelists." They served, perhaps unknowingly, in the finest tradition of the spirit of Ephesians 4:11, "And he gave some, apostles; and some, prophets; and *some, evangelists;* and some, pastors and teachers."

They literally did the early "legwork" in getting the first churches started. They were not hesitant in walking, if that was what was required, for days at a time if need be, to minister to those who were hungry for God's word.

A biographical summary of each of these five leaders follows.

Benedict Weyeneth	Joseph Bella
John Kreinbill	Isaac Gehring
Peter Virkler	

BENEDICT WEYENETH

This energetic leader was born in canton Solothurn, Switzerland, on June 2, 1819.[1] He died December 11, 1887, and is buried in the church cemetery east of the church at Roanoke, Illinois. He was from the Weyeneth family that lived at (or came from) Luterkofen, canton Solothurn, Switzerland.

At age twenty-eight, he was the first Elder to come to America, having been ordained specifically to travel to Lewis County, New York. After establishing the first church of the faith in America among a group of Mennonites in 1847, he returned to Europe for a period of time. On November 20, 1850, he married Elizabeth Blunier, daughter of Casper and Elizabeth Schoental Blunier of Trub, Bern, Switzerland.[2]

Weyeneth came from fairly devout religious parentage as evidenced by the inscription on the Weyeneth home in Luterkofen:

> In hope and trust in God did Jakob and Daniel Weyeneth have this house built in 1812. It was erected the 17th of April. O, Lord, watch over this house and those that go in and out, the housewife and the children of mine and all that is therein, let to Thee, O Lord, be committed.

The old Weyeneth family home in Luterkofen, canton Solothurn, Switzerland, as it looked in 1981. It was built in 1812 for Daniel and Jacob Weyeneth by Johannes Kohler, a master carpenter.

Weyeneth and his young bride returned to settle in America in 1851, first going to New York (possibly to visit the church there). From there they moved to Ohio where he was employed as a tailor.

Farming opportunities soon unfolded, and in time Weyeneth moved to Elgin, Iowa, an area similar in terrain to Switzerland. Because he was very active in the promotion of the gospel, it is likely he held meetings in this area which laid the foundation for an eventual congregation at Elgin. His stay in Elgin was short as he moved to the vicinity of Peoria, Illinois, in 1853.[3]

The exact sequence of Weyeneth's life in the early 1850's is rather sketchy. Whether he actually became a permanent resident in the Elgin, Iowa, area is difficult to establish. In a letter to Christian Steffen of Switzerland, dated January 25, 1853, he indicates that he was staying in Peoria with John Kreinbill and that he planned to become an Iowan "as I have bought land in that area." He also states that "my wife is still in Ohio with her parents. They urged me to leave her with them and promised to bring her to me last autumn, but it did not come to pass, but I hope that someone will bring her next spring."

A check of court records in the Elgin, Iowa, area yields no information that Benedict Weyeneth ever owned land in that area. Thus, it is possible he went to Elgin in either 1851 or 1852 and spent some time there. He returned to Peoria early in 1853 for a visit (he came by boat) with the intention of establishing a residence in Iowa. He probably went back to Elgin, changed his mind about settling there, and moved to the Peoria area later in 1853.

His residence was later established near Dillon, Illinois. He continued farming and reportedly raised soybeans, hoeing the soil by hand. He thought his calling was more as a minister than as a farmer.[4]

After harvesting his crops in the fall, he would set out during the winter to preach the gospel. He flung himself vigorously into an extraordinary amount of activity in the Lord's vineyard. He would continue this activity until spring.

One spring his schedule was so busy he hardly had time to return to his home. In fact, his wife exclaimed, "Benedict, it is high time you come home."[5] During the winter he would hold meetings every evening except Saturday. In the winter of 1879, there was a great awakening, and he baptized 159 souls.

He moved from the Dillon area and located permanently at Roanoke in 1857, acquiring land from the railroad. He had heard a railroad was being built from Pekin to Streator and thought this would be a good place to purchase a farm.[6] He was also aware of a settlement of Swiss people in nearby Partridge Prairie.

He probably viewed this group as likely prospects for evangelization. These were people of Mennonite persuasion, and several later became a part of Weyeneth's group. This followed a pattern that had been established in New York, Ohio, Indiana, and Iowa.

In 1869, thirty-four souls were taken into the Roanoke church. Then, for an extended period of time, no baptisms occurred, and Weyeneth became anxious and concerned to the extent he sold his farm and prepared to move to Kansas where he thought the spiritual soil might be more fertile. He thought the Roanoke area had become spiritually barren with respect to adding more souls into the church. Then, he suddenly changed his mind, bought another tract of land, and remained at Roanoke.[7] It was a wise decision. Of the 159 souls he baptized in 1879, 94 were at the Roanoke church.

He was a man of great persuasion. One time he had to reprimand some young non-members who were out of order. The young boys decided to get even with him. The next time they were gathered at his place they planned to treat him coldly and stay out in the barn. When Weyeneth learned this, he headed for the barn, and with his gracious and winning personality said, "Come on boys and have some lunch." At this, the boys simply melted and yielded to his request. He had an excellent manner with people. He is remembered as one who, when his children quarreled among themselves, always instructed them to "make-up" before the sun went down.

Benedict Weyeneth was an extraordinarily gifted speaker and effective in God's work of persuading souls to embrace the faith. He, with God's grace, could point men to Christ. He was particularly successful in drawing people of Mennonite and Anabaptist background to his doctrinal precepts of salvation.

Weyeneth's zeal knew no bounds when it came to caring for his church and preaching the gospel of salvation. Not only did he seek to win lost souls for the Saviour, but he was diligent as an Elder in traveling to and fro in an attempt to care for them spiritually. He took the lead in attempting to keep the churches he established spiritually strong and pure.

It is reported that one time he and Nicholas Baumgartner walked from Elgin, Iowa, to Illinois (probably the Morton/Peoria/Roanoke area) in the winter. When they arrived in Illinois, their leather boots were frozen to their feet and they had to open the seams to take them off. As one author wrote, "This they did in the service of the Lord."[8]

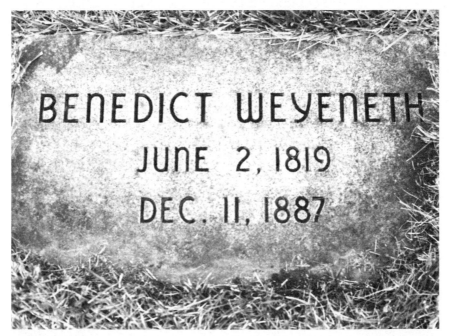

Benedict Weyeneth, after spending forty years laboring for the gospel in America, was buried near the church at Roanoke, Illinois.

JOSEPH BELLA

Joseph Bella, who was born in 1812 and died in 1902, was an early proponent of the faith who emigrated to America sometime between 1855 and 1861.[9] He was a native of Hungary who, after languishing in several prisons in that nation, was finally allowed to come to America. Bella never married, so consequently had no descendants, and today he is virtually unknown among the Apostolic Christian Church brethren. Historical evidence suggests that his untiring zeal and limitless contributions to the early American churches were quite impressive.

When Bella came to America, his first "base of operation" was at Sardis, Ohio, where he served as their first Elder. He was instrumental, particularly, in helping to establish churches at Bluffton, Indiana, and Mansfield, Ohio. In addition, he traveled extensively among the churches, and his ministry served to be very beneficial to the brethren.

Because he never married, he was free to travel almost at will, and he became known as the "traveling preacher."

After his initial efforts at Sardis, where he lived in a small dwelling on the property of Isaac Gehring, his traveling schedule was such that he never "settled" at any one place. The entire church was his domain, and wherever he was, he considered it "home."

He lived to be eighty-nine years old. In his declining years he became quite feeble due to a stroke and could not walk without aid. He was graciously taken into the home of Christian Gerber, who served as Elder of the "South Side" country church near Fairbury, Illinois. He is buried in the "South Side" cemetery where a simple marker reads: "Elder Joseph Bella, Feb. 13, 1812; Jan. 31, 1902."[10]

Cemetery marker of Elder Joseph Bella. He rests in the "South Side" cemetery.

Bella's life was a legacy of faith and courage. He survived many fierce storms, particularly in the form of persecution for his faith while in Europe. America proved to be a safe haven of religious freedom for this man who had suffered so terribly for the Lord.

Bella learned of the Biblical doctrines taught by Samuel Froehlich in a rather roundabout way. In the summer of 1839, two Hungarian journeymen-locksmiths named John Denkel and John Kropatschek were traveling in Switzerland. Through an act of Providence they came in contact with Samuel Froehlich, accepted his teachings, and were eventually baptized. They returned to their native land and were zealous in expounding the message of salvation.

In the spring of 1840, Bella was present when Denkel conducted a meeting in Budapest at the lock factory of his employer. Denkel preached and later baptized Ludwig Henscey who was to become an effective proponent of the faith. Although Bella was present at this meeting, he had not yet been received into their group. He was, however, associated with, and under the influence of, the strong-minded brothers Denkel, Kropatschek, and Henscey.[11] It is very likely that after Bella was subsequently baptized, he soon became a devoted man of deep convictions. At this time he was a journeyman-artisan of twenty-eight.

In Hungary, authorities did not take kindly to those who refused military service or to those who refused to swear an oath of allegiance. Bella, a man not given to bending when his religious convictions were at stake, fell under the harsh treatment of the government. He was transferred from one prison to another because of his faith, and prison officials finally concluded he could not be broken.

In one prison, his hands and feet were bound together, and they hung him up on a ring on the wall so he could not sit, stand, or lie down. This was a deplorable form of torture. His indomitable will, however, with God's grace, did not bend, and finally his jailors exclaimed, "We cannot watch this any more; something has to be done."[12]

The Hungarian authorities, realizing nothing could persuade Joseph Bella to alter his religious convictions, and that he was strong enough to both spiritually and physically to endure all the torture they could administer, permitted a passport for him so he could emigrate to America.

Just prior to his release from the prison in Pest, the warden, his wife, and sister became converted through the testimony of Joseph Bella.[13]

His release from prison was intended by authorities as a public relations gesture. Devious plans were laid to kill him when he reached Bremen. On the way, by the inspiration of God, Bella changed his route and boarded a ship to America at Hamburg. His life was spared, and he escaped from his detractors.

His journey to America saw him plunge into an eventual lifetime of energetic devotion to his beloved church. The zeal and dedication he witnessed among the brethren in Europe was conveyed to America as he spent himself tirelessly in pursuit of spreading the wonderful gospel.

When Elder Henry Geistlich of Meilen, Switzerland, visited all the Apostolic Christian Churches in America in 1866, Joseph Bella accompanied him most of the way.

On Sunday, June 17, 1866, Geistlich visited the church in Mansfield, Ohio. He writes, "Today I am in Mansfield. Dear brother Joseph Bella was here in Mansfield by the brethren Sorg. He met us Saturday evening at the depot. I had to weep as I saw him; I was so stricken."

One time when Bella was living in Hungary, he was overcome with a burden that weighed heavily on him. For some reason, he vowed to God that if he could be subsequently spared of this burden, he would never marry. In time, the burden was lifted. Later, young Bella fell in love with a sister in faith, and he fully intended to marry her. Either his mother or some of the brethren reminded him of his earlier promise to God regarding marriage. He thus relinquished his plans to marry and remained single for the rest of his life. Later, when he was in America, he sent alms to this sister.[14]

Bella's trade in America was that of a watch repairman, but his major vocation, and one that continuously consumed him, was that of preaching and teaching.

JOHN KREINBILL

Another significant church leader who was very active in the 1850's and 1860's, but who is virtually unknown because none of his descendants are in the church today, was John Kreinbill. This name has several variant spellings such as Graybill, Krayenbuhl, and Grabill, etc.

He was born in 1803 and died August 14, 1887, at the age of eighty-four. It is interesting to note that he was born in Strasbourg, the city that Froehlich adopted after being deported as a sectarian from Switzerland. By the time Kreinbill left Europe in approximately 1836 (at age thirty-three), the Froehlich movement was in its initial stages. There is no known evidence that suggests these two men were acquainted, although Kreinbill may have known of Froehlich since the latter's reputation as a minister was widely known in various Swiss and German areas.

He was married to Jacobena Gehring who was born in approximately 1807 in Alsace, France. She died of a blood clot in 1885.

Kreinbill emigrated to America in 1836. He was from a well-known Mennonite family. He and his family first settled in Titusville, Pennsylvania. He later lived in Ohio, and subsequently moved to Illinois.

His first home in Peoria, which he purchased June 11, 1847, was a log cabin at the foot of Munson and Sanford Streets.[15] There was a cluster of log cabins at this site, and Kreinbill occupied one of them. He would take his cow up on the hill to graze (possibly in the area between Main and High Streets).

John Kreinbill is thought to be the first convert of the Apostolic Christian Church in Illinois.[16] His conversion was apparently due to the efforts of Benedict Weyeneth. Kreinbill was soon selected as a minister, and by 1852 he held services in the Sommer home across the Illinois River from Peoria on Metamora Road.[17] Although considered for the Eldership, he was never ordained as Elder.

He was very active in helping to establish the new church denomination in America. He traveled by buggy to many areas to spread the gospel.[18] His improvised suitcase was a large handkerchief tied to a stick.

He also traveled to Canada to preach and seek converts. A diary entry by his daughter, Catherine Hofstetter, on November 15, 1876, states, "Father starts for Canada from Gridley." An entry of May 5, 1877, says, "Father came home." Thus, it appears the trip to Canada lasted from November to May.

Kreinbill is noted, too, for traveling to the east coast and picking up newly-arrived emigrants who had just come from Europe. He helped them adjust to their new country. No doubt this made them more dependent on him, and he then felt inclined to tell them about this new church of which he was a part.

From Peoria, he later moved to Partridge Prairie near Metamora.[19] His daughter's diary indicates he worked diligently in central Illinois, preaching in all of the churches which existed at that time.

Henry Geistlich, when visiting America in 1866, mentioned in his diary on June 10 (at New Bremen, New York), that he met John Kreinbill from Illinois: "He was on his way to Canada. Earlier he was born in Alsace, but this has been his country for about thirty years. He is now a minister in our church. He is a lovable brother, being a real example to the unbelievers and unfaithful. He offers almost his entire life to the work of the Lord."[20]

Kreinbill was instrumental in the formation of the Apostolic Christian Church in Pulaski, Iowa. In the winter of 1864-1865 he traveled from the Peoria, Illinois, area to Pulaski. Local history has it that he traveled by train to Ottumwa, Iowa, and then walked the remaining twenty-five miles to Pulaski.[21]

He went to the Mennonite Church located about two miles southwest of Pulaski where he conducted a series of meetings. The mode of baptism was a major point of discussion. The Mennonites had always baptized by pouring instead of by immersion. Kreinbill emphasized this was inadequate and not patterned after the New Testament example. About half the membership of the Mennonite Church were convinced he was right and followed him.[22] This was the beginning of the Apostolic Christian Church in Pulaski.

His activity symbolized the willingness of early church fathers to respond when called upon by the Lord to travel far and wide to attend to the duties of the church, even to the extent of going into the midst of a perhaps "skeptical" crowd and standing up for the truth.

Two years earlier, Kreinbill had traveled to the Leo, Indiana, area where he preached the first sermon in the Apostolic Christian Church in that area.[23]

The May, 1968, issue of the *Silver Lining* indicates that along with Elder Benedict Weyeneth, Kreinbill helped to establish the Mansfield, Ohio, church early in the decade of 1850.

Some historical sources indicate that in 1862 Kreinbill traveled to Butler County, Ohio, and founded a church. This is the area north of Cincinnati. Today, there is no Apostolic Christian Church in that area. There was, however, an Amish settlement in Butler County as early as the decade of 1830, and perhaps Kreinbill, in his far-flung travels, visited some of his former Amish friends in that area and attempted to establish a church.

In 1877 Kreinbill published a pamphlet concerning the condition of the church entitled, *From the Beginning to the Present as a Voice of Warning and Judgment.*[24] It is written in German and is difficult to understand. At the time it was published, he lived at Metamora, Illinois.

In later years he lost his eyesight but continued preaching. He was well versed in the Scriptures and was able to correctly refer to many passages. Those who followed the reading with their own Bibles would testify that his references or quotations were correct. His grandchildren used to lead him around the barnyard and to the well after he lost his sight.

ISAAC GEHRING

Isaac Gehring was only twenty-nine years old when he arrived in America. In typical emigrant fashion, he cleared customs and headed westward traveling via the primitive conveyances existing at that time. He and his party headed down the Ohio River in a flatboat and eventually settled in the Sardis, Ohio, area.

Despite the hardships and privations that faced them— including the loss of their first house of worship to fire— Gehring and his followers continued on. This band of believers, under the leadership of Isaac Gehring, formed the second church in the United States.

For the twenty or so years after Gehring arrived in Sardis (1848), the Sardis church was a haven for newcomers. Sardis was strategically located on the Ohio River, so the church became a "passing through" and a "feeder" church; many European emigrants spent time in Sardis before settling in other areas where congregations were formed. Gehring, as a minister and later as an Elder, made a significant contribution by ministering to these many newcomers.

He worked closely with Elder Joseph Bella. Because Sardis was a hub of church activity, these two men exerted a wide influence in establishing the faith in America. Gehring was ordained Elder in approximately 1868 and served until his death in 1896.

Gehring is remembered for his kind and gentle disposition. He is remembered as a brother who had a sincere love for everyone and once said, "One cannot catch fish by striking in the water."[25] One is more successful by luring the fish and furnishing an appeal to them. In the realm of salvation, this is true because people cannot be coerced into repentance, but instead will respond more readily to the gentle and appealing message of love, and also to the radiant example of a believer.

He was very influential in the conversion of Matthias Strahm and Ulrich Kipfer, two young men formerly of Bern, Switzerland, who settled near Bluffton, Indiana. As young Mennonites, they had heard of Samuel Froehlich while living back in Switzerland, and when they came to America, they had a desire to learn more of his movement.

They set out from the Bluffton, Indiana, area to Sardis, Ohio, to talk with church officials and to inquire into the essentials of the faith. They walked the entire way to Sardis.[26] After spending an evening discussing salvation with Isaac Gehring and Joseph Bella, these two young men were satisfied that this faith was what they had sought, and they took the steps necessary to later be baptized. Thus, the persuasive testimony of Gehring proved beneficial in helping to convince these two men to embrace the faith.

In 1855 Gehring learned there were individuals in the Rittman, Ohio, area who were interested in their soul's welfare.[27] The matter of providing a ministry to the Rittman area was of no small consequence since it was nearly 140 miles from Sardis. Gehring, full of youth, vigor, and zeal, set out walking to Rittman. In 1928 John Ott of Lamont, Kansas, recalled an incident that he, along with Andy Yost and Isaac Gehring, experienced during Gehring's first walk to Rittman. The account was told to Rudolph Graf who recorded it:

> He then told me a long story. At seventeen years he with a young man named Yost were baptized by Elder Isaac Gehring. The next day on Monday he joined this Elder Gehring who started for what is now the Rittman area. This trip they made on foot taking six days. Father Gehring made this long trip three times during his life. Must have been his first trip for near New Philadelphia they made inquiry as the shortest way to their destination. This they said was along a new laid railway. About two miles further on they met a woman with a bag of groceries on her arm. They bid her the time of day in their Swiss dialect, walked on but soon were called back by this woman, also speaking Swiss. The conversation was pleasant. The woman asked their destination and reason for such a long walk. Then Bro. Gehring revealed the whole matter. There were seeking souls where they wished to visit. This woman then asked about the faith and doctrine Bro. Gehring preached. Then she also related to them of a deep soul's conviction which she made eight years before. Repentance and a heart's conversion followed by peace of heart, which she had never experienced before though baptized as a babe and confirmed in the state church in Switzerland. She lived nearby and asked these brothers to stop on their return way. She said her name was Katherine Wingeier and that she had four children then, all boys.
>
> The visit to Rittman area was blessed by the Lord. It was the beginning of the large assembly there at this time. The brothers returned during the week following. They were heartily received by this Katherine Wingeier. In the eight years this woman said she had never found anyone of like experience as was her conversion. The Wingeier home was near Stone Creek. About a year later a second walk was made to the Rittman area, Bro. Ott again accompanying Bro. Gehring. They called at the Wingeier house. It was empty, also none of the neighbors had any idea where this family had gone. One said it had been rumored that they had left for Michigan. It was a grave disappointment. This was Bro. Ott's story. He had never heard any more for his family soon moved to Kansas. Also mentioned that after the baptism of he and Andy Yost, he had not seen nor heard anything of this Yost.

On December 9, 1892, when he was seventy-three years old and growing obviously older, Isaac Gehring wrote a letter to a family in Wayne County, Ohio. He made reference to these long walks to the Rittman area:

> Last year I had a faint hope that I could visit you dear ones, but this hope soon faded; my leg got worse all the time, besides other ailments. I know we could enjoy each other in the Lord and I would be

heartily welcome. Thirty-five, thirty-six, thirty-seven years ago, I used to walk when there were no trains, but those times were also blessed times. The Lord gave me strength and inspiration and I am glad I did go, and so it always fills my heart with joy when I can hear that it is well with all the dear ones in Wayne County and that there are still souls that come to the Lord.

In regard to growing weaker in the body he said, "I was young and could walk good, and now I am like an old horse which at any time might break down. But if I can only receive a house not made with hands from God eternally, which from all my heart I wish for myself and all the true and faithful." He finished his letter by writing three verses of Hymn 145 from the *Zion's Harp,* "Our Happy Lot."

During one of his early trips to the Rittman area, he was visiting a home of prospective believers. A young son in the home where he was visiting sat with his feet perched up on the dining room table. He somewhat casually or disrespectfully asked Gehring, "Where are you staying tonight?" To which Gehring replied, "Wherever the Lord opens the door." Such a forthright statement tends to symbolize the faith and trust exemplified, not only by Gehring, but by other forefathers of the faith. The Lord and the church were first in their lives, and they served both with all diligence.

The young lad who irreverently asked Gehring this question, and had previously scoffed at his preaching, was Daniel M. Steiner who soon became converted and was the first minister of the Rittman congregation.

While Gehring experienced many wonderful times preaching the gospel, he also had his share of setbacks and danger. One of these incidents occurred on August 30, 1866, when he and Elder Henry Geistlich of Switzerland were driving home from a church service at Sardis, Ohio. Geistlich recounts the incident in his diary, "Gehring and myself were driving home. The horses became frightened and ran away, throwing us both out of the wagon. I was slightly injured."[28]

PETER VIRKLER

Peter Virkler served as the second Elder of the New York churches. He was born in Alsace-Lorraine July 23, 1829, and died in New Bremen, New York, December 14,

1889.[29] He was the younger brother of that church's first Elder, Joseph Virkler.

He was the son of Rudolph Virkler, a former Mennonite bishop, and came to America when he was a small boy of five. His early upbringing was rooted in an old order Mennonite lifestyle which, with modifications, was an influence he and his family (and others) brought into early church life here in America.

In 1853 he married Anna Farney, daughter of Peter and Mary Schertz Farney. She was born September 19, 1829, in Alsace-Lorraine.[30] This union bore no offspring. This couple, however, acted as foster parents to many children. They took both the young and the old into their home. Not having children of their own allowed them to devote a great deal of time to activities associated with the church, and he as a minister did not hesitate when the Lord called him to do special tasks for the church.

Peter Virkler was ordained Elder in 1867, thirteen years after being installed as minister.[31] He traveled widely in the furtherance of the gospel. He traveled to the midwestern states and eventually to Oregon and is credited with assisting the formation of the first church in that state. He and his wife traveled extensively in Europe in 1871, probably visiting their ancestral homeland and relatives they had heard their parents mention.

Virkler presided over one of the greatest "in-gatherings" in the church's history in the summer of 1881 when 139 persons were baptized during thirteen successive Sundays and one three weeks later for a total of 140 converts. God worked miraculously in the hearts of these souls, and also through Peter Virkler who was noted for his powerful oratory on behalf of the Lord. He was a large man physically and had a forceful personality.

In 1879 Peter Virkler traveled to Oregon at the request of Swiss immigrants who were living in that area. Some were originally from New York. Included in this group was the Mathys family from Beaver Falls, New York.

Friends and believers in the Portland and Silverton area were typical of the many persons of German and Swiss Anabaptist background in the nineteenth century who had come to America and were unfulfilled (in a religious sense) and were seeking a more secure spiritual habitation. Visiting ministers and pastors were usually enthusiastically welcomed in these places. These people were not exposed, as society is today, to the mass media and did not have vast amounts of leisure time to occupy themselves. Their lives were often lonely and somewhat barren. Thus, they were extremely receptive to forceful and gifted speakers who brought the truth to them.

Many of these immigrants, scattered in remote outposts, had heard of Samuel Froehlich and his movement in Europe and were glad to hear and receive pastors bearing such truth-laden messages. This is why Peter Virkler and others had continuing successes in preaching the gospel. It was in such a context that Peter Virkler helped to establish a beginning in Oregon.

CHAPTER V   DECADES OF PROMISE 1850-1870

"...Lift up your eyes, and look on the fields; for they are white already to harvest."

Opportunities for faithful men of God to reach out and promote the gospel were very inviting at the beginning of the 1850's. Emigration laws encouraged waves of Europeans to come to America, and vast prairies quietly awaited enthusiastic husbandmen to come and care for them.

As followers of Samuel Froehlich left their European homelands and arrived in America, they settled mostly on farms and partially in cities. They were in need of persons to minister the Word of God to them. In connection with this, particularly in rural areas, many Amish Mennonite families were looking for a deeper and more enduring spiritual kinship.

During the early portion of the decade of 1850, the stage was set for the growth of a new religious denomination. By 1850, the population of the United States was twenty-three million, up nearly thirty-six percent from the previous decade.[1] Slavery was causing sectional controversies, and Millard Fillmore took office as the thirteenth president.

Benedict Weyeneth and his bride had just returned from Europe to live permanently in America. The church in upstate New York had been established with Joseph Virkler as Elder. The new church in Sardis, Ohio, had several parishioners and two men of profound energy and religious conviction in Isaac Gehring and Joseph Bella. The new denomination was beginning to take shape. The early leaders had no grand strategy for development. Their only intent was to be true to God's Word and to be responsive to any doors He opened for the furtherance of the gospel.

MANSFIELD, OHIO

MANSFIELD, OHIO
60 North Illinois Avenue

The next area of development occurred at Mansfield, Ohio, a town in north central Ohio situated near the western slopes of the Appalachian foothills. It is a pleasant green valley marked with spring-fed lakes, wooded areas, and rugged hills.

A city brochure refers to Mansfield as "the city of churches." It was named for Jared Mansfield, Survey General of the United States in 1808. Johnny Appleseed made Mansfield his headquarters for many years. Senator John Sherman, who wrote the Sherman Anti-Trust Act, hailed from Mansfield.

In 1850, a small group of people formed a church known at that time as "Believers in Christ." It consisted of Irene "Mimm" Yoder, Fred Matthes and his wife, and Anna Matthes Brehm. The church had no resident minister until 1854 when Frederick Lantz and family moved here from Monroe County (Sardis), Ohio.

There is speculation, although unconfirmed, that perhaps in 1850 Benedict Weyeneth and John Kreinbill, as missionaries, helped to initiate the Mansfield congregation.[2]

Joseph Bella served as the church's first Elder, but as a traveling man, never resided permanently in Mansfield.

The early preaching in Mansfield soon began to bear fruit. By 1860 the first baptisms were held. The first converts were Rosina Leuthner and Elizabeth Imthurn Rehklau. They were baptized by immersion in a creek which flows into the Rocky Fork east of Mansfield. This was the customary site for baptisms, and often during the winter months holes were broken in the ice to accomplish this rite.

The sacrament of baptism must have been enormously impressive under these primitive circumstances. The broken ice, freezing temperatures, and spectators and participants huddling together amid the chilling winds would leave an indelible imprint in one's memory, and the zeal with which they yielded to these conditions provided a shining witness to those who remained unconverted.

As the small gathering at Mansfield began to grow in number, it soon became necessary to construct a building to accommodate the increased attendance of brethren and friends. Previously, members met in homes. Christine Engwiller, wife of Elder Samuel Engwiller, related memories of her early days:

> Brother Bella made his home with Sister Mimm Yoder. I attended meetings there. They had benches without backs, and mother gave me candy to amuse me. I must have been very young but remember plainly. She lived on North Adams Street, the second house from Sixth Street. I remember meetings at Lantz's where Brother Miller chided us for being so noisy playing out of doors during services.

In 1863, a small church was built on East Market Street (now Park Avenue East). It cost $1,500. In 1868, a Sunday School was organized with twenty-five children. It was held in the basement of the church, and a Brother Miller served as teacher. He used to give lead pencils as prizes to stimulate the learning of Bible verses.

It took approximately two decades to outgrow the little church on East Market Street. A new church was subsequently built in 1886 at Diamond and East Second Street. The first service was held June 12, 1887.

Serving as Elders were Henry Schwier (1834-1905), who came from Hanover, Germany, and Sigmund Sorg (1840-1893), a native of Hungary. Schwier was a tailor and Sorg a jeweler. Schwier was installed as Elder in 1881 and Sorg in 1887.

Wilhelm Matthes, Sr., was later ordained Elder, and for a period of time, the Mansfield congregation had three resident Elders at the same time. In 1901, Samuel Engwiller was ordained Elder.

The church on Diamond Street served the congregation until April 4, 1965, when a new house of worship was completed with the first services held April 11, 1965. The new church was built at a cost of $200,000. Open House was held August 29, 1965, and dedication September 5, 1965. The church seats 280 in the sanctuary and 120 in the balcony.

One summer, several years after the Diamond Street church was built, the time came when redecoration and repairs were needed. Consequently, the church was closed for two Sundays. At this time the church assembled in large dairy barns. The first Sunday services were held at the farm of Karl and Tillie Oesch, and the second at Robert and Katherine Beer's farm.

One person who attended those two meetings as a child later wrote:[3]

> The sweet smell of the new mown hay that had earlier in the week been brought into the barn and the beautiful singing seemed to blend into a majestic atmosphere.
>
> The noon meal was not the usual menu of bread, jelly and coffee, but instead a tremendous feast spread out on a hay wagon for all to partake.

Although baptisms were conducted in a creek in the early days, at the Diamond Street church they were held indoors. Before the days of running water, the sequence of preparing the tub for baptizing was quite interesting. Following the morning church service, the baptismal tank (a horse trough) would be carried from the baby room to the second floor. Bucket after bucket of water would be carried upstairs to fill the tub. In those days, the water was not as warm as today because it was taken directly from the tap.

Also, at that time the baptismal tub served two purposes. On normal Sundays it was placed upside down in the baby room with a coverlet on it and was used as a bench because space was limited. Then, on Sundays when baptisms were held, it served the purpose for which it was intended.

When the congregation moved into their third (and present) house of worship in April, 1965, five persons had the unique distinction of having attended services in all three churches: Katherine Matthes Houston, Jesse Beer, Simon Beer, Bertha Matthes, and Anna Engwiller.

There were many stalwarts of the faith in those early, pioneer days at the Mansfield Church. Some who are listed in local historical accounts are Mimm Yoder, Katie Feldie, a Grandmother Hoffman (her first name may have been Rosina), Rosina Leuthner, George and Eve German, Judith Hazzenzahl, Rosina Isley, and Jacob John Miller, to name only a few. Their deeds and firm support of the early congregation are forever etched in the portals of time and eternity and serve as an inspiration for their descendants.

An interesting story is told of John Fuhrer who served for thirty-seven years as minister. He was born in 1860 at canton Bern, Switzerland. His family was very poor, and as a young boy he had to beg for food. One day a nice lady gave John and his brother each a large piece of bread. His older brother quickly ate his piece and then deftly grabbed John's piece and ate it. Poor John had no bread to eat. Approximately thirty years later, when he was living in the United States, John received a letter from his brother who wrote to ask forgiveness for taking that piece of bread. It had bothered his conscience for many, many years. When John received the letter it touched his heart immensely and made him weep. His mind was impressed with his brother's humility in asking forgiveness, and it also reminded him how poor his family had been when he was a young boy in Europe.

The church's second Elder, Henry Schwier, was ordained January 26, 1881. This occurred on a Wednesday afternoon. Holding church services on Wednesday afternoon was in keeping with a rural tradition in that era of holding midweek services in the afternoon, especially during the winter months.

Elder Schwier died October 12, 1905, and his obituary reads:

> The Rev. Henry Schwier died at his home, 200 East Second Street, Thursday afternoon at 2:30 o'clock, at the age of 71 years, 7 months and 10 days. In August of last year (1904) the deceased suffered an attack of paralysis, since which time he has been practically confined to his bed and after a later attack, he constantly grew weaker until death finally came to his relief on October 12, 1905. Until that time, and for

many years past, the reverend gentleman had been pastor of the denomination known as the Believers in Christ, whose church is on South Diamond Street.

The Rev. Schwier was born in Hanover, Germany, March 3, 1834, and came to this country at the age of 18 years, almost immediately located in Mansfield, where he has resided ever since. He learned the tailor's trade and continued in this line of work in connection with the ministry, into which he was later ordained.

A few years after coming to this country, he was united in marriage with Miss Mary Mentzer, whose death occurred some years ago.

Five children survive—Catherine Schwier, Christian and Sigmond Schwier, residing in this city; Mrs. Mary Hafley of Cleveland, and Henry Schwier, Jr., of Springfield, Missouri.

The funeral services will be conducted at the home on East Second Street, Sunday afternoon at 1 o'clock, the Rev. Samuel Engwiller of the church of the Believers in Christ will officiate.

The obituary of Elder Samuel Engwiller, who presided over the church from 1901 to 1922, is below:

Mr. Engwiller was married to Miss Christina Leuthner in 1884, who with three daughters, Anna, Mary, and Christine, survive him; also one foster daughter, Martha Lowe. Funeral services will be held from the home Saturday afternoon at 2 o'clock. Please omit flowers.

Samuel Engwiller, aged 66 years, died last evening, Feb. 16, 1922, at 10 o'clock at his home, 670 Park Avenue West, the result of a stroke which he sustained on February 5 at Rittman where he had gone to conduct services for the Believers in Christ Church, in which he had been presiding Elder for the past twenty years.

Mr. Engwiller was born May 30, 1855, in Philadelphia, Pennsylvania, near the corner of Second and Arch Streets. His father died in 1871, and in 1874 he and his mother moved to Mansfield. Mr. Engwiller entered the employ of Sigmund Sorg, jeweler and optician. He has been in business in his present location, 98 North Main Street, continuously for the past 47 years, first in Mr. Sorg's employ, then as his partner, later buying Mr. Sorg's interest, and since 1915 in partnership with his daughter Anna.

When Samuel Engwiller died, several men from other churches served the congregation as Elder. They were: Ernest Graf, Sr., Akron, Ohio; Noah Hartzler, Rittman, Ohio; Samuel Aeschliman, Bluffton, Indiana; and Rudolph Graf, Akron, Ohio.

In addition to the Elders who have served the church, fourteen other men have served as ministers.

PARTRIDGE PRAIRIE, ILLINOIS

South of Metamora

Early 1850's—1870's

In the early 1850's, church services were held in the Metamora, Illinois, area in Partridge Prairie.

Partridge Township has the distinction of being the home of the first white settler in Woodford County. The township was named for the Indian chief, Black Partridge.[4] The area at that time was heavily wooded. This attracted early settlers because the timber provided lumber for their homes and barns.

Early settlers came to the area in 1831. Joseph Belsley, known as "Red Joe," came to Partridge from France in 1831. By 1833, an Amish Mennonite settlement was organized near Metamora (formerly known as Hanover).[5] The first minister of this group was Christian Engel. Some of these people later became Apostolic Christians.

These people had arrived in Partridge Township after traveling down the Ohio River and up the Mississippi and Illinois Rivers to Peoria.

Approximately two decades later, religious proselytizing was begun in the general area, perhaps by Benedict Weyeneth. The first converts were John Kreinbill, who became the first minister of the faith in Illinois, and Peter Engel, who was one of the first settlers in Woodford County. Both were former Mennonites. Kreinbill was a zealous devotee of the new faith and traveled widely on its behalf. Others also left the Amish faith and united with this new group. They were referred to as the "New Amish," but among themselves as *"Glaubige"* (the believers).

The Amish Mennonites in this general area consisted of family names which are today well known in the Apostolic Christian Church: Schrock, Gerber, Wagler, Rocke, Ramsier, Belsley, Gingerich, Kinsinger, Klopfenstein, Maurer, Roth, Slagel, Verkler, and Zehr.

There was never a church building on Partridge Prairie. Instead, brethren met in homes and often gathered in the barn of Peter Engel.

When Elder Henry Geistlich visited Partridge in 1866, he noted in his diary:[6]

> Today there was church here at Peter Engels. A large barn was our place of assembly, there being a large number of people assembled. In the forenoon there were fifty-three rigs in the yard, and in the afternoon still more. It looked as if a party of artillery had camped, there being many unbelievers with us.

Services were held at Partridge until sometime in the decade of 1870. The church in Roanoke was begun in the late 1850's, so two churches existed simultaneously approximately ten to twelve miles apart. This was a great distance in those days. Kreinbill, although not an Elder, was the leader of that church while Elder Benedict Weyeneth was head of the church "on the prairie" south of Roanoke.

There are two possible reasons why the church in Roanoke flourished and the one at Partridge eventually disappeared. First, the more fertile open prairies to the east provided a lure to farmers that could not be easily resisted. Second, Benedict Weyeneth, the influential Elder and unofficial titular head of the new denomination (by virtue of being the first Elder in America) settled near Roanoke. It is likely his enormous strength of personality was partially responsible for the early successes of the church at Roanoke.

Conditions at the early Partridge church were primitive, and those who endured such hardships without complaint reflected an inner zeal and love for God that serves as both an inspiration and an admonishment to today's brethren who are allowed to assemble with little effort and with complete ease and comfort.

Meetings were usually held in homes, but when there were a lot of visitors—or guest ministers—they would conduct services in barns in order to provide a larger capacity for seating.

Worship services were sometimes held in the Engel Barn on Partridge Prairie, Illinois (near Metamora). Benedict Weyeneth and John Kreinbill were among early ministers who preached here.

The barns were thoroughly swept and cleaned including walls and rafters. Benches consisted of planks that were laid across logs. Chickens would sometimes wander in, but if they became too noisy, someone would "shoo" them out.

Attending church in those days required diligence and dedication. Only those who "hungered and thirsted" for righteousness would arrive for services. Brethren and friends who worked across the Illinois River in Peoria crossed the river on a ferry and walked the remaining ten miles to church. Others, from the Morton and Dillon areas (a distance of twenty-five miles), walked to Partridge. This required leaving home at 2 a.m. on Sunday morning in order to arrive in time for services. After services, they began the arduous trek back to their homes.

One family who lived at Crow Creek (near Lacon) drove to Partridge early on Sunday morning with their log wagon.

Baptisms were held in nearby creeks. Sometimes, when the water was low, those being baptized would emerge with their clothes soiled by the mud. Other times, the ice had to be broken to perform the rite of baptism.

John Kreinbill, an early minister in Peoria and Partridge Prairie, purchased land in Worth Township as early as September 2, 1854, and it is likely that church activity in this area increased when he moved here.

ELGIN, IOWA

ELGIN, IOWA
507 Mill Street

As one nears the small village of Elgin, nestled securely in the hills of northeastern Iowa, he is immediately struck by a sign which heralds the area as "The Switzerland of Iowa."

Perhaps such a poignant sign is not needed to remind visitors that this scenic area is similar to Switzerland. The resemblance is striking as evidenced by the rolling hills and the beautiful trees surrounding the scenic Turkey River. In fact, in 1937 a reporter for the Des Moines *Register* referred to Elgin as, "Little Switzerland located in a valley between hills typical of the Swiss Alps."[7]

Eleanor Butikofer, *Silver Lining* reporter, described the fall of the year in beautiful Elgin: "The brilliant fall colors as displayed by the trees have been awe-inspiring: the vivid oranges, reds, yellows, and rusts as seen on the rolling hillsides of Iowa have been beautiful. We might name this the 'golden season' after this area with its golden corn, golden leaves, and golden sunshining days."

It was only natural as time unfolded that people of Swiss descent would eventually find their way, somehow, to Elgin, Iowa. Many immigrants who first settled in Sardis, Ohio, (an area also similar to Switzerland) later came to settle in this Iowa beauty spot.

Many years before white men arrived in the Elgin area, it was known to the Indians as "Sac Bottom," an Indian burial ground. The Indians were often indifferent to the depths of the graves they dug, and over the years soil erosion disrupted the graves, and human bones became exposed in great number. Hence, the area also became known as "Shin Bone Valley."[8]

In the fall and winter of 1851-1852, a town was laid out by M. V. Burdick, a surveyor. Because he hailed from Elgin, Illinois, he honored his home town by naming this new village Elgin.[9] This was an ironic act because eventually Apostolic Christian Churches were established at both Elgin, Iowa, and Elgin, Illinois. The only other towns within the denomination that have the same name are Gridley, Illinois, and Gridley, Kansas.

Both economic opportunity and the natural beauty of the area drew Apostolic Christians to the area. In the early 1850's, when Indians were still returning annually to their burial grounds for festivals and dances, Benedict Weyeneth and others were moving here to get established, both with respect to farming and religion. This was less than a decade after Iowa (named for an Indian tribe of the Siouan stock) achieved statehood in 1846. It is both ironic and fortuitous that they settled less than twenty miles west of a village named Froehlich (which had no known relationship to the Froehlich sect in Europe).

It is believed the first Apostolic Christian minister to visit Elgin was Benedict Weyeneth who came to the vicinity in late 1851 or sometime in 1852. Worship services were held in homes, and he was very instrumental in establishing a following prior to his departure to the vicinity of Peoria, Illinois, in 1853.[10]

The first service of the group was held in the home of Michael Gerber in the northeast quarter of Section 30 in Marion Township, although the exact date is not known.[11]

From this inauspicious beginning, others were soon added to the group. Benedict Frieden, Sr. (1827-1893), one of the first to immigrate to Iowa and who eventually acquired one thousand acres of land, was typical of many Swiss immigrants who passed through the Apostolic Christian settlement in Sardis, Ohio, before moving to Iowa. In 1848, Frieden had emigrated to the United States. In 1849, he married Anna Baumgartner in Sardis, and in 1851, they moved to Marion Township, Clayton County, Iowa.[12]

To get to Elgin, Iowa, from Sardis, Ohio, these brave immigrants traveled down the Ohio River, then up the Mississippi River to McGregor, Iowa, where they disembarked. From here they traveled, either by oxen or on foot, across the frigid and rugged hills of northeastern Iowa to their "New Switzerland." This area had the basic staples needed by these pioneers— wood and water.

Early migration to the Elgin area included the families of Jacob Butikofer, Sr., Christian Lederman, John Ulrich Banwart, Nicholas Pfarrer, Christian Beer, Sr., John Isch, and John Wenger in 1854. Joseph Schneider came in 1855. Other early family names included those of Braker, Sutter, Aeschliman, Etter, and Gehring.

In 1854, Jacob and Anna Martie arrived near Elgin. Their daughter Anna, age three, became ill while on the ocean and died at Dubuque, Iowa, on November 5, 1854. Her body was brought to Elgin and laid to rest in what is now the Apostolic Christian Church Cemetery.

When Benedict Weyeneth left for Illinois, the group was without a minister. In 1854, Christian Baumann came from Switzerland and ministered to the group until his death in January, 1870. The next senior minister of the church was Jacob Reugg.

In 1862, Christian Lederman built a two-story home which contained a very large room where church services were held. This was adequate for approximately four years until 1866 when a white, stone church was built approximately two and one-half miles east of Elgin. It cost $1,600. Worship services also had been held in the homes of Samuel Rinehart and Michael Gerber, Jr.

Uriel Gehring wrote in 1956, "Many early church-goers walked as far as ten miles and drove horse and buggy fifteen miles to attend church. As a result of the great distance traveled to church, the members brought their lunch and ate dinner in a section of the church used for a dining room. Services were held in the forenoon and afternoon. This custom still prevails."[13]

Baptisms in those early days were held in the Turkey River. In the winter it was often necessary to cut a hole in the ice. Following baptism the converts, shuddering and shivering, were loaded in a buggy and driven to the Alexander Baumgartner home, one-quarter mile away, where they changed clothes. Sometimes it was so cold their clothes nearly froze to their skin.

About 1900 a wooden frame section was added to the original stone structure. The church was heated with wood furnaces and was lighted for the evening services with kerosene lamps until 1939 when the Rural Electric Administration paved the way for electric lights.

In 1955 the wooden section of the church was moved to a knoll on the southern edge of Elgin. In 1972 a new brick front and entrance were added. The first service in the town church was held Easter Sunday, 1956. Dedication of the church was held July 8, 1956, with Elder Ben C. Maibach, Jr., Detroit, Michigan, conducting the services.

Fred Schupbach served as minister at Elgin for twenty-eight years until his death in 1915 at age eighty-nine. He was remembered in his obituary as one who "never gained a large amount of earthly wealth. His hands were always open to the poor and needy. None were ever turned away empty from his door."

Jacob Gehring, Sr., also served as a minister for many years. He became blind at age ninety, but continued to preach. He let other ministers read the text from Scriptures, and then he would meditate on it. He lived approximately one mile from the country church and would walk, although blind, to church using a cane to feel his direction. He is remembered as one who never complained of his blindness.

Gehring was a nephew of Elder Isaac Gehring of Sardis, Ohio, for whom he worked prior to moving to Elgin, Iowa. When he turned to the Lord, he found it necessary to travel back to Sardis to make restitution for past wrongs.

An interview with Marie Butikofer, a lifelong resident of Elgin, yielded many interesting historical points:[14]

—The practice of footwashing sometimes took place at Elgin. Men performed this rite in the assembly room and the women in a downstairs room. This occurred in approximately 1906.

—The church in Elgin was often erroneously referred to as the "Dunkard Church" by those in the community. Records at the local mortuary list burials of persons who were from the Dunkard Church.

—Members formerly carried their personal songbooks to church. These hymnals had the owners' names engraved on them. This was a common practice among all the Apostolic Christian Churches.

—Changing the worship language from German to English was not without difficulty in Elgin. The church was evenly divided, either pro or con, on this issue. Edward Grimm, who later moved to Taylor, Missouri, was the first to preach in English. Alfred Imhoff was one who favored retaining the German language.

—The common church term "taken up" (referring to a convert being proved, baptized, and received into the church) stems from the Swiss word *Aufgenommen.* It means "taken in."

—Membership in Elgin peaked in 1904 when the church had approximately eighty to ninety members. During this year twenty-two persons were baptized on two successive days by Elder Gottlieb Maibach (then of Pulaski, Iowa).

The church has had one resident Elder. Paul Butikofer was ordained December 15, 1968. Non-resident Elders who have had charge over Elgin were Gottlieb Maibach, Pulaski, Iowa; Christian Gerber, Fairbury, Illinois (who once walked the thirty miles from McGregor, Iowa, to Elgin); Michael and David Mangold, Roanoke, Illinois; Jacob Stettner, Elgin, Illinois; Paul Banwart, West Bend, Iowa; Noah Schrock, Oakville, Iowa; and Leo Moser, Lester, Iowa.

TREMONT, ILLINOIS

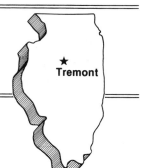

TREMONT, ILLINOIS
601 South Chestnut Street

"This is a beautiful region, being very fertile. Here grapes grow in abundance. This place would suit me the best of any place I have seen so far, if I had to live here (in America)." Such were the thoughts of Elder Henry Geistlich of Switzerland when he visited this area in 1866. The grapes have long since been replaced by vast acreage—section after section—of corn and soybeans. The Apostolic Christian Church at Tremont, Illinois, has grown from a handful of brave pioneers to a large congregation of over 265 persons.

The hamlets of Dillon and Tremont were convenient places for forefathers of faith to immigrate and settle. Both are only a few miles from the Illinois River. Both Pekin and Peoria (now fairly large cities) were early disembarking points for these immigrants. Also, the fertile land in this area offered unlimited challenges and opportunities to these hard-working, freedom-seeking people.

The congregation in this area forms the southern flank of a hub of Apostolic Christian Churches which exist in central Illinois today. They extend as far east as Cissna Park and Forrest and north and west to Princeville and Bradford. This cluster of churches totals sixteen with an approximate membership in 1981 of over 4,300—more than forty percent of the denominational total.

The activity of the church at Dillon and Tremont dates back to the early portions of the 1850's. Benedict Weyeneth had moved to Illinois from Elgin, Iowa, and (according to the author Herman Ruegger) lived for awhile in or near Tremont. He did not live here very long, but due to his evangelistic tendencies, took the initial steps to pastor the growing number of Swiss and German immigrants who had previously been associated with the Evangelical Baptist Church in Europe.[15]

One of the first settlers of the faith was Kasper Koch. Hanna Koch, in *Genealogies of the Getz-Koch-Wick Families,* writes of the persecution suffered in Germany which prompted several families of believers to emigrate to America.[16]

> Thus, denied freedom of worship in the Kingdom of Bavaria, Kasper Koch with his sister Magdalena Reuter, her husband Michael Reuter, Jr., and his friend Johann Andreas Braun (also known as Andrew J. Braun) immigrated to America in the year 1854, settling near Dillon, Illinois.
>
> In the year 1855, Kasper Koch sent for his financee, Katherine Getz. She arrived at Tremont January 2, 1856. They were married January 10, 1856, at Tremont.

Kasper Koch was born in Schweinfurt, Bavaria, Germany, on July 25, 1825. He was a young man of only twenty-nine years when he ventured to America. He was the son of Andrew Koch, a stagecoach driver. In this capacity the elder Koch used eight horses, riding on one of the first two. One day Andrew Koch had Napoleon Bonaparte as a passenger. His orders were to drive as rapidly as possible and to maintain this speed despite the dangerous curves and hills. In doing so, great peril and risk were faced, but their destination was met without accident.

Kasper Koch had intended as a young lad to study the violin. Events proved otherwise. One day after a long absence, he met his good friend, Andrew J. Braun, whom he heard had embraced a new religious faith. After discussing this matter with him, Koch, too, embraced the doctrines of repentance and conversion, became a "new creature in Christ," and was baptized by Samuel Froehlich in Strasbourg, France.[17]

Andrew J. Braun was a faithful confessor of the new faith in America. He later left the central Illinois area and moved to Wauseon, Ohio. He was very active in nurturing early phases of church growth in this new country.

The first Elder of the congregation was Michael Reuter, a brother-in-law of Kasper Koch. He was ordained in 1854.

The early church activity in this area likely centered around worship services in the homes of various members and occasional travel to Partridge Prairie for services there.

The first church building was constructed in 1870, near the home of Michael Reuter. This was just north of Dillon Cemetery, about one mile north of Dillon. The "Dillon" Church was a small rectangular building which soon became outdated due to the growing number of immigrants coming to the area. Going to church in those pioneer days was no casual matter. Many walked several miles. Caroline Wick Koch used to tell how she would sometimes fall asleep in church because of the fatigue associated with walking so far to church.

Baptisms were conducted in Dillon Creek, and many persons were baptized there. After being baptized, the converts would be wrapped in a blanket to protect them from the elements, and then the entire entourage would walk the one-half mile or so back to the church. There was no road available for buggies to carry them.

In 1881, a larger church was built on the Kasper Koch farm one and one-half miles south of Tremont. At its peak this church had approximately two hundred members. A board walk from the village of Tremont to the church was constructed, and many persons walked this route to church. The congregation had previously decided to locate the church building just south of Tremont because a majority of the members lived in this region with a lesser number in Dillon. Thus, Tremont became the focus of the congregation's existence rather than Dillon. Also, Tremont thrived more as a community because it was located on stagecoach lines. Earlier, Tremont was the county seat of Tazewell County until it was moved to Pekin in 1848.

In approximately 1908 a group separated from the congregation and established their own building and services. In 1910, the remaining brethren built a large, two-story wood frame church on Chestnut Street. A cemetery was located east of this church.

In 1962, a new brick building was built with a seating capacity of 550. A large fellowship hall was added south of the new church in July, 1977.

Karl Knapp served as Elder from 1876 until his death in 1894. For a short period of time, he served as Elder concurrently with Ludwig Getz because he did not want the responsibility all by himself. Both men were farmers. Getz was an Elder from 1881 to 1898.

Ludwig Getz, a son of Peter and Katherine Gress Getz, was born January 26, 1830, in Wurttemberg, Germany. He came to America with his youngest brother, John, and six other boys in 1857. He was only twenty-seven years old. They traveled west by train as far as the Ohio River, then by boat down the Ohio, then up the Mississippi and Illinois Rivers to Pekin, Illinois.

For five years (approximately 1860-1865), the Ludwig Getz family shared a home with the George Welk family. Welk later served as Elder at the neighboring Morton, Illinois, congregation.

Elias Winzeler, who was born in Wauseon, Ohio, on April 8, 1858, and died April 11, 1939, served as Elder from 1911 to 1939.

There was no resident Elder at Tremont from 1939 until December 11, 1966, when Daniel Koch was ordained.

UNION CITY, NEW JERSEY

Formerly
Williamsburg (Brooklyn), New York
West Hoboken, New Jersey

UNION CITY, NEW JERSEY
2410 West Street

Prior to the establishment of a church in Union City, New Jersey, members of the faith lived in the Williamsburg section of Brooklyn, a borough of New York City. The time of their arrival from Europe is uncertain—but it was very early as viewed from an overall church perspective. Union City church records indicate that brethren bought a section of cemetery lots in Queens as early as 1854, only seven years after the first Apostolic Christian Church was established in up-state New York. Two years later, still more lots were purchased by the church. This indicates that at least a few brethren were living in the area during that time.

Gate to church cemetary plot in the Queens section of New York City.

The extent of their church activity and the exact number of members is not known. A church building was never built in Williamsburg, but members did meet in a house. Whether this was a special house purchased for worship or it simply belonged to a member of the church—or if they alternated meeting in homes—is not known for certain. Whatever did exist at Williamsburg—both with respect to numbers and facilities— was later absorbed into the church that was established in West Hoboken (now Union City), New Jersey. This lies across the Hudson River from Williamsburg.

Nicholas Ludwig, who was later the first minister at the church in Rockville, Connecticut, stopped at the Williamsburg assembly when he first arrived in America in 1872. Ludwig and his family were en route to Rockville. After landing on American shores, they went directly to Williamsburg to find fellow believers in Christ. While still in Europe, they had been informed they could find persons of like mind and faith in Williamsburg. After spending several hours looking for the correct address, they finally found the house where brethren were assembled. The meeting was nearly over when they arrived. Ludwig introduced himself and was accepted as a brother. After a long ocean voyage, and an uncertain future in a new land, meeting with precious brethren must have been a welcome balm for his travel-weary soul.

There were approximately twelve to fifteen families living in Williamsburg. Most of them came from Vienna, Austria. They included Mrs. Christian Burkert, and the Rehbein and Swibold families.

Also, during this time members from Rockville, Connecticut, assembled periodically at the house in Williamsburg because a church had not yet been established in Rockville.

In 1982, the old cemetery section, located in the Lutheran Cemetery, 67-29 Metropolitan Avenue, Middle Village, New York (in the borough of Queens) seemed somewhat deserted, but it still existed. Although in a "run-down" condition, it consisted of approximately twenty graves, the last burial (from the church) having taken place in 1953. Only about four or five burial stones were legible, with some no longer standing upright. Until 1980, the church at Union City paid the cemetery association a yearly fee of $65 to provide upkeep for the cemetery section.

After services were held for many years at Williamsburg, they were moved to West Hoboken, New Jersey, a town located in the urban sprawl across the Hudson River from New York City. The Jacob Ringger family was one that hosted the meetings in their home.

In 1892 a church was built a few blocks from the Hudson River in the eastern section of West Hoboken. Jacob Ringger and a Brother Friedinger were instrumental in building the new church at 2410 West Street. The town's name was changed to Union City in the early 1920's.

The church here thrived, and in the early 1900's had in excess of two hundred members.[18] The first denominational schism affected the Union City Church in 1906-1907. Those who departed included a minister, leaving only Walter Wartman in the pulpit. He was alone in the ministry for several years, and following the schism, performed the duties of song leader in addition to preaching. He served in the ministry for fifty-four years, from 1892 to 1946.

August Mueller, who was a member of the Union City congregation for many years and also a local reporter for the *Silver Lining,* wrote of Walter Wartman, "I cannot think of anyone that did as much for a church as Brother Wartman did. Many years he fired the coal furnace heating the church. There was no electricity in the church—he had to light the church with gas lights. He also made all the repairs, without pay.

"His heart was filled with love for his God and for the members and friends. Many times he told me his only concern was the congregation."[19]

Walter Wartman died in January, 1951, at age ninety-one. John Bahler, Elder at Rockville, Connecticut, conducted the funeral services.

Other than John Trittenbach of Rockville, Connecticut, who served as Elder here prior to 1917, the record is sketchy regarding who served as Shepherds in the church's early years. Christian Gerber, Rockville, Connecticut, was ordained Elder over the Rockville and Union City Churches in 1917. He served until 1953 when he passed away at age eighty-three. He was succeeded by Philip Beyer of Naumburg, New York, who served as Elder until his death in 1958. John Bahler, Rockville, then assumed the duties of Shepherd. His son Corbin succeeded him in 1981.

In the early 1870's, a man by the name of Heinrich Arlt served as minister at the Williamsburg meeting. Little is known of him. Ruegger, in *Apostolic Christian Church History, Volume I,* refers to the early meetings held in Williamsburg, "The Elder Arlt proclaimed the gospel, while at that time there was, as yet, no meeting at Rockville."[20] Although Ruegger refers to him as an Elder, his holding this office cannot be totally confirmed. Elder John Bahler indicated in 1982 that he felt Arlt was an Elder.

A very memorable year for the church at Union City was 1917. A few years earlier new families began attending church here because members and friends arrived from Europe and a few returned to church who had left the fellowship in 1906-1907. In 1917, twenty-one souls were baptized. Because John Trittenbach had died and the church was without a local Elder, the converts were "taken up" by Elders Michael Mangold, Roanoke, and Barthol Rapp, Morton, Illinois, who traveled to New Jersey specifically for this purpose.

Among the 1917 converts was young John Diggleman, twenty-three, who was later placed in the ministry in 1954 at age sixty. In the early 1980's, during the sunset years of his life, he remained in the ministry, leading a small flock of approximately twelve members.

In the early days, many of the members attending church in Union City worked at the Schwartzenbach and Huber Company, a silk mill in Union City. It was a large plant that covered nearly two square blocks and employed over two thousand persons in the 1920's. The firm went broke during the Great Depression. Its collapse was probably one of the major reasons the Union City church began to decline in numbers.

During World War I, several young men of the church, who were either in training at nearby Camp Mills or otherwise en route to Germany, attended church at Union City. Shortly before her death in 1980, Frieda Wartman, daughter of minister Walter Wartman, recalled the church's many good times of spiritual fellowship with the young soldiers who visited the Union City church. An example of one such serviceman was Elmer J. Klopfenstein, Sr., Gridley, Illinois, who was baptized in Union City prior to shipment overseas to engage in World War I as a non-combatant.

Louise Mueller Akel, North Lauderdale, Florida, who attended the Union City church for many years, recalls that at one time the attendance at the church was so large there was talk of removing the back walls to make more room. She also remembers hearing that the church's stained-glass windows were once a great point of controversy.[21]

She also remembered when she was a little girl attending the church, "There was a large furnace for heating the building in the basement. After lunch, when it was time to go upstairs, Walter Wartman would call, 'All aboard.'"

RITTMAN, OHIO

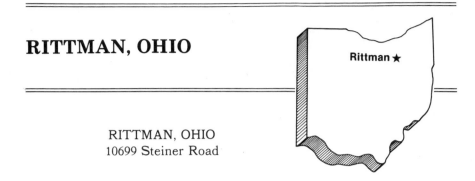

Rittman ★

RITTMAN, OHIO
10699 Steiner Road

In 1855, the issue of slavery burned deep in the hearts of Americans on a national basis. In Wayne County, Ohio, among a few persons of the Amish Mennonite faith, the matter of religious unrest also seemed to burn deeply. Their dissatisfaction continued to the point where Isaac Gehring of the newly-established church in Sardis (Monroe County) came and held meetings for those who were interested. It was Gehring "who had a feeling some fellow believers could be found." He walked the 140 miles up to Wayne County where he was "able to find souls that were interested in their souls' salvation."

In an incredible turn of events, the first person to respond to Gehring's preaching and embrace the new faith was Anna Steiner, wife of John Steiner, bishop of the Chippewa Mennonite Church in that area. The other convert was her sister Elizabeth. Both women were daughters of Bishop Daniel Steiner of the Mennonite faith. Elizabeth was the wife of Ulrich Steiner, brother of Bishop John.[22]

Shortly after these two women turned to the new faith, Anna's oldest daughter, Barbara, also embraced the new beliefs.

Because of her departure from the Mennonite Church, despite the fact her husband held the office of bishop, Anna Steiner very likely experienced much social and religious hardship. Not being in accord with her husband obviously caused some difficulty. Nonetheless, she remained deeply devoted to her newly-found faith. Sometimes she would walk as far as five or six miles to church. Often she would carry a young child, with other children following behind her.

Sometimes, when she would return home from church, it would be dark, the door locked, and she would have to spend the night outside. This is mentioned, not to cast aspersions on her husband, but to call attention to the zeal with which she served God and her new church.

She and her husband had thirteen children, and nearly all of them eventually united with the Apostolic Christian Church.

The number of dissident Mennonites who joined the new church—called the *Neutaufer* or "poor Chippewa" Church— totaled approximately eighteen in the initial stages. What caused these Mennonites to seek a new faith? No one knows for sure, but it is likely that the Mennonites—having existed for over three centuries—had evolved into a stagnant spiritual state with heavy emphasis on tradition and form to the exclusion (in many instances) of the new birth and regeneration in Christ Jesus. When Isaac Gehring and others came with a ringing gospel message preaching repentance and conversion, these people obviously felt touched by the Holy Spirit and could do nothing other than respond to their convictions.

The actions of these Mennonites in Wayne County was a pattern that began earlier in Lewis County, New York, and continued in many areas where Apostolic Christian Churches were established. These new Apostolic Christian Churches in the mid-to-latter nineteenth century drew many converts from the Mennonite Church, particularly in the following areas: Lewis County, New York; Leo and Bluffton, Indiana; Partridge Prairie, Roanoke, and Congerville, Illinois; and Elgin and Pulaski, Iowa.

In the very early days, the Rittman church was served by Isaac Gehring of Sardis (often called the "mother" church of Rittman) and by Joseph Bella who traveled most of the time from church to church and had no permanent home.

Bella often stayed in the Daniel M. Steiner home when he was at Rittman. The family had a special bedroom always ready for him. It was called the *Bella stubbe*.

One time Bella and Barbara Horn were going to take a train from Marshallville to Akron. As they walked from the Horn home along the railroad to the Marshallville depot, Bella wanted to sit on a stump and read some Scriptures. Barbara Horn was worried they might miss the train, but Bella did not seem too concerned. Before they reached the depot, the train came and Bella waved his hat. The train stopped, and they got on and rode away to Akron.

Although many families have contributed to the well-being of the Rittman church, the Hartzler family by virture of its ancestry proves to be quite interesting.

The first Hartzler to arrive in America was Jacob Hertzler (1703-1786) who came to Philadelphia on September 9, 1750. He was an Amish Mennonite bishop with a reputation as a conscientious, untiring Christian leader, teacher, preacher, and disciplinarian. For many years he was bishop of a prosperous Amish Mennonite congregation at Malvern, Pennsylvania, where the first Amish meetinghouse in America was supposedly built.[23] Five generations later, Solomon Hartzler, a direct descendant of Jacob Hertzler, married Martha Lanz, and all the Hartzlers of the Rittman area stem from this union.

Solomon Hartzler had two sons who ascended to leadership positions in the Rittman Apostolic Christian congregation. Noah Hartzler (1864-1947) served as the first resident Elder of the church from approximately 1925 until his death in August, 1947.[24] His brother Amos served in the ministry for many years and was instrumental in beginning the church's missionary activities in northern Alabama. Noah became a minister as early as 1912, and Amos in 1916.[25] They were both helpful in preaching in the English language. They were installed at a time when the language of worship was changing from German to English.

The first resident minister at Rittman was Daniel M. Steiner who, as a young Mennonite boy, scoffed at the preaching of Isaac Gehring when services were held in the Steiner home.

Other early ministers were Dave Steiner and Fred Domnick; Ben Maibach, Sr., and Robert Bauman moved to Rittman from Sardis in 1899 and 1902 respectively and served as ministers. Other ministers who moved from the Sardis area were Alex Bachman in 1919 and Joseph Widmer (from West Virginia) in 1920.

Noah Bauman was elected Elder on January 11, 1948, and served until his semi-retirement because of ill health in 1973. He died January 24, 1974. He was succeeded by Joseph Ramsier, a great-grandson of Isaac Gehring, who was ordained September 23, 1973.

Much activity regarding church structures has transpired at Rittman. In 1874, the first church was built on land donated by Daniel M. Steiner, father-in-law of Noah Hartzler. It was a little white frame building that was eventually enlarged and remodeled in 1902. This building was moved to its present location north of the present Rittman Church. By 1982 it was used as a tool shed and storage facility.

Rittman's first church building located near the current church. Constructed in 1874, it was still used as a storage shed in 1983.

In 1918, a red brick, two-story church was built at a cost of $7,000. In 1948, a 40-foot by 60-foot addition was annexed to the church at a cost of $90,000. In 1963 a new 80-foot by 154-foot sanctuary was added at a cost of $250,000. It had a seating capacity of 1,000 plus a balcony.

In 1971, a 50-foot by 100-foot fellowship hall was built about one-half mile east of the church. It is used for wedding receptions, suppers, singings, and various meetings.

A beautiful new nursing home was built in 1974 across the road from the church. This spacious unit reflects the prosperity of the congregation, both spiritually and materially. This home for the aged indicates the church's concern for the elderly as stated in a brochure: "In the fear of the Lord is strong confidence: and his children shall have a place of refuge." Proverbs 14:26.

By 1981, the Rittman congregation was the fifth largest in the Apostolic Christian denomination with approximately 470 members.

A vivid description of "yesteryear" at Rittman appeared in the *Silver Lining* periodical:[26]

TIMES PAST AT RITTMAN

It is not possible to turn back the hands of time. Yet, how often do we wish we could walk the path as our forefathers walked it, if even but for one day. Change is inevitable. And so it is with interest that we try to catch glimpses of things as they were "in times past."

If you were to look in on the Rittman congregation as it was, in the late 19th century, you would find everything breathing simplicity and conservatism. A small, modest, white frame building adorned the ground where our present church stands.

No comfortable, factory benches were found for seating, but rather a cruder, homemade type. There was no electricity. Coal oil was used in the stove—for cooking—and in the lamps for lighting. The wood or coal-fed stoves provided heat for the assembly room. A baby room was unheard of. An inside baptistry—no; baptism was either performed in a trough or a creek. German was the predominant language spoken from the pulpit. The noon lunch consisted of bread, butter, spread, coffee and milk. Church cleaning was done by families, each taking their turn.

Outside the frame church were two wooden sheds. Here, the buggies and horses were kept during the services.

Simplicity was the vogue, in dress, of this period. Clothes were usually dark, dress length to the ankle, sleeve length to the wrist, neckline high, and skirts full. Men wore no ties. Beards were common. Black or other dark colored veils were worn by the women.

With all the above differences, there were similarities between the past and now. The greeting was practiced, men and women's seating segregated, women veiled, provings closed, noon lunch served, conduct of services and messages of the ministers much the same.

From a spiritual standpoint, much good must be said for times past. The enticement of worldly entertainment seemed not as great. There was not as much, nor was it as easily available. The slow pace seemed to offer more time for meditation, and "Time for God." There were no newspapers; reading of the Bible and Sunday School books predominated. Because of the slow mode of transportation, living centered about the home. There seems to have been much fellowshipping among the church families.

We are thankful that, during these past years, our flock could grow. A new brick building (seating capacity for 1,000-plus) proved a necessity.

Today, all manner of modern conveniences are at our fingertips. Satan, in his cunningness, works through the prosperity of this time. We must constantly be on guard to retain the simplicity and moderate living that is so strongly stressed.

Our heritage is great. Our faith has been handed down so unadulterated. Just as our forefathers were concerned about a place and mode of worship, a true and simple worship, so must we be sure that those who seek aright can be guided to the right by us. Our forefathers are gone, their earthly life o'er. They await for us and future generations to join them in eternal bliss on yonder shore. With fondest expectations, we wait this last great change.

ARCHBOLD, OHIO

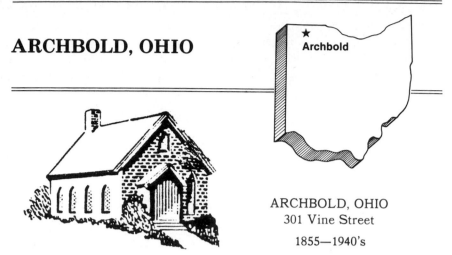

ARCHBOLD, OHIO
301 Vine Street

1855—1940's

An Apostolic Christian Church was formerly located in the village of Archbold on the corner of Vine and Williams Streets. It was established in 1855, and in the early days was known as the "Froehlic Church." The congregation consisted of emigrants who came from Germany and Switzerland. Archbold is located in German Township. Adam Imthurn, the Elder of the church, assisted in providing transportation for many of these people who came to America.

They settled in this area because the rich farmland was similar to that found in the Black Forest of their homeland. The productive soil here was covered with acres and acres of hardwood timber which had to be cleared before crops could be planted. There were also numerous wolves that had to be dealt with, and mosquitoes were in abundance. This part of Fulton County was known as the Black Swamp area. It was also a part of the Northwest Indian Territory.

An important factor leading to the development of this prosperous little village was the railroad. In 1851, engineers and surveying crews started making trails through the virgin hardwood timber of Lucas, Fulton, and Williams Counties. There was a demand for land, and new villages and towns were started. In 1853, the railroad was completed to Archbold, and a year later it was extended to Bryan.

The building of this railroad system provided employment for many area men. One was John Rehklau who boarded at the Imthurn home and became a member of the *Gemeinde* (the church in Archbold). He later married Elizabeth Imthurn, a sister of Adam Imthurn.

Adam Imthurn was one of the first settlers in Archbold. He established a tailor shop and residence on the corner of Defiance and Williams Streets. He was one of the most honorable and respected citizens in the village and was a petitioner to incorporate the village of Archbold. He was known as one who always had an encouraging and kind word for everyone. Even though he was crippled, he never failed to smile at all who passed by his window as he sat upon his work table with his deformed legs under him.

Adam Imthurn was the victim of an accident in his youth. He fell from a tree when he was a boy, and his injuries were never properly treated. His back was left in a somewhat hunched position. He found it necessary to walk with crutches, and his height for the rest of his life was about that of a twelve year old child.[27]

When Adam Imthurn's father, mother, brothers, and sisters were ready to leave Europe for America, his father became very ill and was unable to make the trip. This was a sudden crisis, but arrangements were made for the mother and children to journey alone to their future destination. The father was to come later, but they never heard from him again.

Since Adam Imthurn was a cripple, how did he manage to clear customs in New York? The story is told locally that when he was confronted by authorities, his stronger, huskier brothers offered to sign any necessary papers to insure their brother would never appear on any relief rolls.

Elder Imthurn and his wife, Margaret, lived near the church in Archbold. He was often taken to church in a wheelchair. At church he had a chair of suitable height which was used for pulpit services.

Two services in the German language were held, one in the morning and one in the afternoon with an intermission between. During this time a lunch was served which consisted of homemade bread, butter, sugar, milk, and coffee. Since there were no screens on the doors and windows, the food drew many flies to the dining room during hot weather. They were dispersed by the use of fly swishers.

The church was a white rectangular building about 40 feet by 60 feet. The building was heated with wood burning stoves. Kerosene lamps were used for lighting the interior. There were numerous sheds at the rear of the church property for horses since the mode of transportation was horse-drawn buggies. Surreys and sleds were used for transportation in the winter.

Residence at 301 Vine Street in Archbold was formerly a church building used by Apostolic Christians.

The Manz, Imthurn, Rauber, Storrer, Rehklau, Schlatter, Schrenk, Schnider, Weiderkher, Meister, and Miller families attended church in Archbold. Their ministers were Elder Adam Imthurn, Jacob Storrer, and Carl Baer.

About 1879, a westward movement developed, and many of the congregation left Archbold for Kansas, Iowa, and Utah. The church building was sold around 1930. For those who remained, services were held in homes. The last family moved to Paulding, Ohio, in the late 1940's.

When Adam Imthurn died on February 12, 1921, the Mayor of Archbold issued the following proclamation:

> Rev. Adam Imthurn, one of the last resident survivors of the petitioners to incorporate the Village of Archbold, has been called to the great beyond. Rev. Imthurn, besides being a minister of the Gospel,

has been one of our most energetic, upright, and progressive citizens of the Village of Archbold for the past sixty years. What Rev. Imthurn was and has done as a citizen and businessman of the Village of Archbold is now history. As a mark of esteem and respect, I request that all business houses in the Village of Archbold be closed from 10:30 a.m. to 12 noon on Wednesday, February 16th, during the hours of his funeral.

Residence at 305 Vine Street in Archbold where Elder Adam Imthurn lived and worked as a tailor. Crippled, he sat on a table next to the picture window and did his stitching. He often waved to passers-by.

There were actually two Apostolic Christian Churches in Fulton County. One was in Archbold and the other three miles north and two miles east of Archbold. The church in the country was located on the southwest corner of the Lue property on County Road 21 near what is now known as Alternate U.S. 20 (called the Lauber Hill area). The church in this vicinity was called the "Apostolic Evangelical" or "Froehlic Church." Some came from a considerable distance week after week when the roads were passable. Nothing short of a severe illness would keep the families from the *Versamlung.*

Andrew J. Braun, a minister who lived in Toledo, came at intervals to visit the church. His services were enjoyed by the many who gathered to hear him.

Due to a significant increase in population, timberlands were converted into farmland. Yet, many felt that greater economic opportunity existed in the West. Consequently, many people from the congregation left to earn their livelihood elsewhere.

The Lue, Britch, Meister, Bruehlman, Henderer, Miller, Kutzli, and Wintzler families were among those who attended church in the country.

CONGERVILLE, ILLINOIS

CONGERVILLE, ILLINOIS
2 miles west on U.S. 150

The Mackinaw Dells area was settled in the decade of 1830. In 1834, many Mennonite families from Ohio and Pennsylvania came to the area and settled along the Mackinaw River.[28] They came to the area to advance themselves economically and to take advantage of the cheap land. Some of the earliest settlers in the area were the Farney, Zehr, Yoder, Klopfenstein, Ehresman, and Schertz families. Later, family names included Holderly, Zimmerman, Rinkenberger, Ramsier, Miller, Hotel (forebears of Cissna Park Hodels), Schrock, and Hohulin.

Early settlers came here because there was plenty of wood for building and the hills drained naturally. The prairie or flat land at that time was considered undesirable because it was swampy, wet, and had no drainage. Prairie fires were a constant threat, and malaria often resulted from damp and swampy conditions. The broad, unsettled prairies gave an uninterrupted sweep to the many snow storms that swept across them with a terrible fury. With few landmarks, travel was difficult in bad weather. Thus, the early settler preferred the security of the river and woods to the "wild" prairies.

It was into this general setting that Joseph Virkler, Benedict Weyeneth, and others presented the views of the Apostolic Christian Church, (then known as the Evangelical Baptist Church). As in several other areas, many Mennonites willingly embraced this new faith. These families of Mennonite background constituted the nucleus of the new group which later grew into a sizable assembly near what was later Congerville.

The first meetings were held in 1857. The people met in barns, homes, and outdoors. Some of the early meetings were held in a barn owned by Peter A. Klopfenstein, grandfather of Joseph M. Klopfenstein, who served for many years as Elder of the Gridley, Illinois, congregation. This old barn was still standing in 1982. Peter A. Klopfenstein, a Mennonite, was apparently impressed by this new faith. He died at a young age, and it is not known if he ever was a member of the new church group. He was married briefly to Mary Sommer, daughter of Peter Sommer, another Mennonite. When Peter Klopfenstein died, his widow and infant son, Peter, along with her father, Peter Sommer, moved to Gridley where the former was instrumental in helping to establish the Gridley Church in 1870. Mary Sommer Klopfenstein often referred to the dynamic preaching of Benedict Weyeneth and traveled often to Roanoke from Gridley (before 1870) to hear him preach.

It is very likely Benedict Weyeneth, as a leading proponent of the faith, conducted meetings at the Klopfenstein barn near Mackinaw Dells.

In the early days worship services were held in the loft of the "Klopfenstein barn" owned by young Peter Klopfenstein. By 1983 the barn was still standing.

One of the brethren who introduced the faith to the Mackinaw Dells area in the 1850's was Elder Joseph Virkler of Lewis County, New York. He was the first Elder ordained in the United States. He was visiting in the Fairbury area and met a man named John Zimmerman. Zimmerman apparently took a liking to Virkler and suggested they go to "Slabtown" (near what was later Congerville) and visit Zimmerman's brother, Michael, who lived in that area. So they walked from Fairbury to Congerville, a distance of forty miles.[29]

They arrived at Michael Zimmerman's place in the evening, and John introduced Virkler, "Here is a preacher from New York State." Michael rather gruffly replied, "I suppose you picked up some tramp and brought him down here." Such was the reception given to this man of God.

Although Michael Zimmerman paid little heed to Joseph Virkler on this occasion, he later succumbed to his views and was converted and baptized. He became the first resident Elder of the Mackinaw Dells-Slabtown church. He served the assembly in this capacity until 1907.

In *The Past and Present of Woodford County, Illinois,* reference is made to Michael Zimmerman:[30]

> He was born in Baden, Germany, September 19, 1820, the son of Andrew and Annie Miller Zimmerman. He immigrated to America in 1839 with his father and family. He was on the sea thirty-one days. The family settled in Butler County, Ohio. His father died there. In 1848, he left Ohio and came to Illinois and settled in Tazewell County; thence to Woodford County. He first purchased 100 acres of land, and today he owns 330 acres of fine farming land. He married Miss Catharine Noffzinger, born on the Atlantic Ocean, in 1845, and they have nine children. He is a member of the Christian Church for nineteen years. He is Elder of that church

Local records indicate (1) he was married to Catharine Naffzinger (Noffzinger appears on her tombstone) and (2) he was a member of the Apostolic Christian Church.

Following this unsuccessful first meeting with Michael Zimmerman, Joseph Virkler remained in the area for awhile. On June 8, 1852, he attended the wedding supper held in honor of Joseph Schrock and Magdalena Guingrich south of Deer Creek, Illinois. This was a gathering of Mennonites, and Virkler was invited to attend. After the wedding supper a game of dominoes was brought into the parlor for all the guests to enjoy. Joseph Virkler was invited to participate.

To their exasperation he politely said, "No, that's not for me." He, as a man of God solely devoted to his faith, was resolute not to engage in frivolity that did not bear fruit for the Lord. While it seemed quite unusual in the minds of the other guests, and they probably misunderstood his spiritual intent (his non-participation), his action was not much different from today's brethren who refrain from engaging in frivolity, competitive sports, worldly entertainment, and other unfruitful works of darkness which bear no fruit in the Lord's vineyard, and who are consequently often misunderstood by their peers and associates.

The young bride, Magdalena Schrock, in a very demure way, witnessed Virkler take a stand for his religious beliefs and refuse to bend temporarily to satisfy his peers. Such devout principle kindled a flame in her heart. She said nothing about it then, but for a period of time she pondered this incident in her heart and inwardly wondered, "What does he have that I don't have?" Spiritually, she was not satisfied with her Mennonite faith which she had embraced at about the age of twelve after being able to recite from memory some pre-assigned Scriptural passages. She was then sprinkled (a form of baptism), adorned in the plain Mennonite garb, and was considered a member.

As time unfolded, Joseph and Magdalena Schrock heard the preaching of Elder Benedict Weyeneth and accepted the Apostolic Christian faith. They became devout members of the church and were among the first persons to be baptized in Illinois among the Apostolic Christians. Before the Congerville church was established, this couple attended church either at Dillon (southwest of Tremont) or at Partridge Prairie (south of Metamora). Each location was twenty-two miles from their home. They could hardly wait for Sunday morning to come so they could attend worship services.

On Sunday morning they hitched a team of horses to an old wagon bedded down with straw on which they placed their new baby for the trip to church. Rising early, they prepared themselves for a 4 a.m. departure. They traveled at approximately four miles per hour. They forded the Mackinaw River and traveled on the most meager of roads. This they willingly did, in all kinds of weather, in devotion to their God.

Living conditions in these early days were indeed primitive. In *The Genealogy of Peter Rinkenberger II* the author describes conditions in the Mackinaw Dells area:[31]

Homes were generally log houses, and had ground floors. If there was an upstairs and especially in winter, it was rather uncomfortable as snow would sift through the poor clapboard roof. Sometimes the bed covers had snow on them.

Wild animals were quite abundant and some were good for food. There was no shortage of wild game. It was a common thing to see deer running near their homes. Snakes also were plentiful, sometimes curling up on crocks of milk which was not very nice.

On Sunday people would gather in homes, sometimes even in barns, for worship services, and usually the whole family would attend. When weather was fair, services were sometimes held outside. Benches were used but were not the most convenient. Sometimes services would continue for two hours. Some would attend by walking a long distance, some on horseback, and others on a lumber wagon. Peter Rinkenberger I walked to church services from Farmdale to Slabtown, a distance of about twenty miles.

The first church building of note was constructed in either 1874 or 1875. Some type of meeting place was apparently being prepared during 1866, but the details are unknown. Elder Henry Geistlich refers to his visit there on August 5, 1866:[32]

Today we had church at Mackinaw. The brethren here are rebuilding their church, so we had to have our assembly out in the open. About twelve rigs drove over from Partridge Prairie.

In the middle of the nineteenth century near Mackinaw Dells, a promising village emerged called Slabtown. It was called Slabtown because the houses were shanties built from slabs. Slabtown enjoyed a flourishing economy, but was doomed to extinction when new railroads were routed through other towns. Across the river was another settlement called Farnisville, which eventually died out as well.

The first remodeling of the new church was done during 1898-1900 when the assembly room was enlarged. Other minor changes were also made at that time. In 1936, a second major remodeling took place when the church was raised, a basement put under it, a combined balcony and Sunday School room added, and a furnace and plumbing installed. Another major addition was initiated in 1958 when a new assembly room was added.

While Michael Zimmerman was the first man to serve the Congerville church as a resident Elder, Robert Walder, formerly of the Cissna Park congregation, was ordained as the second resident Elder on September 6, 1981. Non-resident Elders who have presided over the congregation were Andrew and Barthol Rapp, Morton; Michael and David Mangold, Roanoke; Frank Woertz, Goodfield; Leroy Huber, Eureka; and Joshua Broquard, Fairbury, Illinois.

An interesting incident is recalled concerning the first Elder, Michael Zimmerman. On July 4, 1906, a large number of converts were "taken up" at the Roanoke, Illinois, congregation. Elder Zimmerman was present. One of the converts, Elizabeth Gudeman Pfister, granddaughter of Elder Benedict Weyeneth, remembered him saying to her during her "proving," *"Obwohl sie so viele waren, zerrte doch das Netz nicht."* Translated, it means, "Although there was such a large number of converts, nevertheless the net did not tear."[33]

Joseph B. Schrock, a minister for many years at Congerville, wrote a book on prophecy entitled, *Daniel—Revelation and Prophecy of the End Times.*

ROANOKE, ILLINOIS

★
Roanoke

ROANOKE, ILLINOIS
2 miles west, 1 mile south, ½ mile west

It is certain that when young Benedict Weyeneth was consecrated by the brethren in Europe specifically to travel to
America and preach the gospel (he was the youngest Elder in
the European church at that time), he accepted the assignment
with unswerving diligence and dedication. In all aspects of his
life, his ministerial and pastoral duties had first priority.

He worked very hard in the Lord's vineyard. His efforts in
America were concentrated particularly in the central Illinois
areas east of Peoria. His labors bore noticeable fruit as his
work among German-speaking people of European descent
drew many converts. In 1879 he baptized approximately 159
persons with ninety-six baptisms taking place at his home
church in Roanoke.[34]

It was Weyeneth who once said, "Dear ones—we should
choose the better part—to follow the Lord and to love Him as
He commanded." Also, he stated, "Therefore, it is so important that we are submissive to our Lord, so that He can mold us
as He would have us."

With such thoughts deeply imprinted on his heart—and his
faith firmly grounded on the Word of God—Benedict
Weyeneth settled in Roanoke in approximately 1857, only ten
years after his first visit to America in Lewis County, New
York. In these few years since coming to America to live permanently, he had spread his influence in such places as Lewis
County, New York; Sardis, Ohio; Elgin, Iowa; Peoria, Illinois;
and the areas tributary to the eastern side of Peoria (Morton,
Dillon, Tremont, and Congerville).

When he came to Roanoke Township, he first lived in the
southwest quarter of Section 20 about one-half mile west of the
present church in a log cabin built by Joseph Virkler of New
York State. (When Virkler finished the log cabin, he left for
Chicago to preach the gospel.) Weyeneth later moved to a farm
one mile west and one mile south of Roanoke in the southwest
quarter of Section 22. Both locations contained small cemeteries (three graves are at the first site and approximately
eleven at the second). It was the custom at that time to bury the
deceased on the Elder's property. The congregation had no
building or property, and these European emigrants were
reluctant to bury their dead in community cemeteries. Thus,

an alternative was to bury them on a plot owned by the Elder. Today, the church has a cemetery east and north of the present church (where Weyeneth is buried).

Later, Elder Weyeneth moved a quarter-mile east of the present church in the northwest quarter of Section 28. This residence was known as the "Weyeneth Homestead." It was here that many visitors from surrounding churches, and others, were received and cared for by Weyeneth and his family.

In *The Past and Present of Woodford County, Illinois,* reference is made to the Apostolic Christian Church:[35]

> The Apostolic Christian Church is a society of Christian German people who came to this township originally from Germany, Switzerland, and France. Their location is in the south part of the township. Twenty-eight years ago, B. Wyaneth, a minister of this denomination came to this place, and began preaching to the few of this faith who had preceded him. He soon succeeded in gathering about him quite a little band of his people; and from that time to the present, the society has been receiving additions, mostly, however, from immigration, until it numbers, including the branch churches in Livingston, McLean, Tazewell, and Peoria Counties, more than four hundred.
>
> The people who worship here are very simple in their customs, dress, and religious views. They take the Bible for their only rule and guide of faith.

Weyeneth had chosen to settle near Roanoke because he learned a new railroad was to be built through the area. He thought this would yield economic dividends. He foresaw the rush of immigration, the development of the land, and future commercial progress. As events would unfold, he reasoned, population would increase and spiritual opportunity would ensue. While the fields of the prairie yielded golden harvests of grain, the church, too, became "white unto harvest" in a spiritual sense, and Weyeneth's timely arrival in the area, together with his and others' diligent preaching, bore fruit in the Lord's vineyard. There were several years when the number of baptisms was quite high. The list below, giving approximate numbers, shows years when baptisms were especially high:

1893	43	1916	78	1937	76
1896	59	1920	50	1940	43
1906	106	1926	86	1947	51

During the time Weyeneth was active in organizing the local Roanoke congregation, he also was busy with preaching and nurturing the assemblies of other believers in areas at Dillon, Peoria, and Partridge Prairie. (In fact, when the Roanoke church was organized, the Partridge assembly continued to meet into the decade of 1870.) His efforts were Herculean. His position was truly one of leadership, and by virtue of his being an associate of Samuel Froehlich in Europe, the growing number of immigrants looked to him to guide them in their spiritual endeavors. In giving counsel to his flock, he once said, "May the Heavenly Father grant us grace in this evil time that we can stand fast and not be carried away with the temptations of the times."

The generation preceding Weyeneth's arrival in the Roanoke area saw a vast prairie covered with tall grass as far as the eye could see. The area was poorly drained. Ponds, sloughs, and swamps were common. In these wet places swarms of mosquitoes thrived, and the prairie was thought to be unhealthy by early settlers who preferred to dwell either near rivers or in forests.

Decades later, the area became more agriculturally inhabitable when men dug ditches, straightened channels, and laid expensive drain tile so corn could be grown. This, together with the development and mass production of the plow, raised the farming potential of the area.

As immigrants moved to the "prairie," progress hastened very rapidly.

While much of the prairie grass was broken up by the plow, some of it was removed by grazing and burning. When prairie grass was grazed below twelve inches, it began to dry out and die. It was then burned, and the soil was ready for plowing with teams of oxen.

The plowing of prairie sod was not always the most hospitable occupation. Often snakes were encountered when disturbed by the plow. Elder Henry Geistlich, while visiting Roanoke in 1866, wrote, "Because they live on the prairie, the people here are troubled with snakes and other pests. One brother told me that in the breaking up of prairie sod he killed thirty snakes and that such uncomfortable work taught him to call on God."[36]

Deer also visited the area in those days. The Xavier Martin family once counted fourteen in one herd. Buffalo, too, roamed on the prairie. Priscilla Liebig told the story of buffalo that used to destroy gardens and fences. One time two farmers named Sauder used axes as weapons and killed one of them. They buried it near the Weyeneth homestead.[37]

It is believed the first church building was built in 1861 on the site of the present church.[38] This frame building was enlarged in 1864 and again in the 1870's. Along with the church building, structures were provided for horses and buggies. In 1929, the church was extensively remodeled to include brick veneer and modern facilities. Additions were again made in 1955 and 1958.

In the early days, there were many who walked to the church on the prairie from Eureka and Roanoke. In a *Silver Lining* article, this account was described:[39]

> From Roanoke the first mile was along the railroad, and from there a board walk was laid to the church, consisting of 2" x 12" planks, laid end to end, a distance of approximately one and one-quarter miles.
> There were occasions when visitors came from Morton and Peoria on the train. The train would stop at the crossing, about one and one-half miles east of the church, and the visitors would get off the train. They were met by some of our congregation, who would escort them to the church, either on the boardwalk or with horse and buggy.

In 1884, a small church was built in the 400 block of West Davidson in Roanoke to accommodate the congregation for mid-week services. A small room in the back of this building was used for German school. The church made an effort at that time to preserve its German culture and was not unlike other ethnic groups who did likewise. When the war with Germany occurred, however, church leaders quickly learned it was wise to refrain from strengthening their German culture, and all trends toward preserving a German heritage began to reverse.

With improved transportation the old church in town was no longer needed by mid-century. Accordingly, it was sold on June 28, 1952. Persons attending the "Night" church remember many enjoyable times of worship at that location.

The old "town church" on West Davidson in Roanoke. A small room in the back was used to teach the German language.

Following Benedict Weyeneth, the second Elder at Roanoke was Conrad Fehr who was born October 31, 1831, in Eglisau, Switzerland. During the 1870's he had held the teaching office in the church at Toessriedern, Switzerland. In 1877, he emigrated to America with his family and some neighbors, a total of fifteen persons in their party.[40] He became an Elder in 1887 and served for a time until 1902. During his tenure, he crossed the Atlantic Ocean five times to preach in different European countries. During his absence, other Elders watched over the Roanoke flock.

The third resident Elder was Michael Mangold who was born in Alsace-Lorraine, April 6, 1859. He was the son of G. M. Mangold who was appointed Elder at a brother meeting in Switzerland, January 1, 1847. G. M. Mangold later emigrated to America in approximately 1878 but did not serve very long as an Elder here. He is noted more for his work in assembling and writing hymns for the *Zion's Harp* hymnal. He wrote twenty-six songs for this book including number 191, entitled "Now and Then," which was written on the prison wall in Mosbach, Germany, where he was detained for his faith.

He also wrote a scholarly book on prophecy entitled *Meditations of the Past, Present, and Future*. This book was translated from German to the English language by Elder Ernest Graf, Sr., Akron, Ohio.

Michael Mangold was ordained in 1902 and served as Elder until his death April 19, 1930. A farmer, he came to this country in 1878 while a teenager. At his death a newspaper obituary included these remarks:

> Rev. Mangold had been pastor, preacher, and minister unto his congregation for nearly a half century. His salary for this was nothing more than to serve his calling. He had attended the sick beds of hundreds. He had united scores in the holy bonds of wedlock. His services had been spoken o'er and o'er again for years and years.

His son, David Mangold, succeeded him in the Eldership. He was born April 27, 1892, in Roanoke and ordained Elder October 16, 1934. He died December 4, 1964, having served as Elder for thirty years.

A man who served many years as an Assistant Elder was John W. Schmidt. He was born June 5, 1844, in Hessen Darmstadt, Germany. He was a tailor who moved first to Peoria and later lived in Eureka. He was an early forefather in America, having preached occasionally at the Partridge Prairie church. From 1929 to 1934, when various Elders from other congregations had the oversight at Roanoke, John W. Schmidt had the title of Assistant Elder. In the German language this translates to *Miteldister,* meaning "with the Elder." He died October 7, 1939, at age ninety-five after having served in the ministry for seventy-two years.[41]

On November 20, 1966, Eugene Bertschi assumed the mantle of leadership. Born April 12, 1918, he was the first of seventy-six souls who answered the call of the Lord in the memorable year of 1937. He was baptized December 5, 1937.

In 1977, Elder Bertschi suffered ill health which necessitated relinquishing his leadership duties. He was succeeded by Donald F. Sauder who was ordained Elder October 2, 1977.

In a stunning event which few congregations experience, the Roanoke brethren saw their large church go up in flames and burn to the ground early on the morning of June 20, 1964. Late in the night of June 19, the church was struck by lightning and was engulfed in flames shortly before midnight. Although

140

the tragic event was devastating to the membership, they listened to the wise counsel of their Elder David Mangold who reminded them that the true church of Christ does not consist of bricks and mortar, but is "within" the hearts and minds of the believers.

A spectacular fire completely destroyed the Roanoke church building in 1964. Six area fire departments were summoned to subdue the blaze.

Irene Hodel Legel wrote: "We shall never forget that night. So many of us stood there with heavy hearts watching so help-lessly, not being able to do anything about it, knowing our be-loved house of worship and everything in it was being destroyed.

"It made one think how terrible it will be when the whole earth will be a roaring fire, and if we can't prepare ourselves now, it will be too late, then, to do anything about it."

Our Church

Our church was just a building—
composed of brick and wood.
To many of us, our church, a
cherished haven stood.

As children we were carried to
church in arms of love.
We learned to sing and pray, and
think of the home above.

When we grew older still, we chose
the way of the cross,
And found the Holy Spirit a
comfort for each loss.

Yes, our church was just a building,
and now it stands no more,
But our church goes right on living,
in the hearts for evermore.

Written by a Roanoke sister

Excerpts from the *Roanoke Review* on June 23, 1964, read:

A roaring fire completely destroyed the large Roanoke Apostolic
Christian Church late Friday night and early Saturday morning.
Lightning apparently caused the fire, which started in the east gable.

The six fire departments of Roanoke, Eureka, Metamora, Benson,
Secor, and Washburn responded. Despite their efforts and a heavy
rain, the building was completely lost. The loss, partially covered by
insurance, was estimated at approximately $500,000. Firemen re-
mained at the scene all night.

The ministers and trustees of the church met Saturday afternoon
to make arrangements for services. Sunday they joined the Eureka
Apostolic Christian congregation.

The membership remained undaunted in the face of this
major setback. Gathering themselves, they realized that "all
things work together for good to them who love the Lord." A
week later, on June 30, 1964, the *Roanoke Review* reported:

Members of the Roanoke Apostolic Christian Church are actively
co-operating to replace their church building which was destroyed by
fire last week. A conference room has been set up at Prairie
Dehydrating plant, and committees and sub-committees meet almost
continually.

The work of demolition and clean-up of the burned out building
was undertaken and finished in one day from 7:30 a.m. to 6:00 p.m.
Tuesday. More than one hundred members with willing hands and
shovels, thirty trucks, nearly a dozen tractors equipped with scoopers,
bulldozers and crane hoists co-operated with almost unbelievable results. All work was volunteered.

The new church, which is a massive structure of contemporary design with light red brick and smooth Indiana limestone on the exterior, stands solemnly on a quiet prairie. It was dedicated October 30, 1966. While both their building and Elder were lost in the same year (David Mangold expired in December that same year), the Lord's blessings again shone on the congregation as the beautiful new church attested.

The Roanoke congregation built a fellowship hall a few hundred feet northwest of the church in 1977. It was dedicated July 20, 1977.

In 1974, the church purchased the Roanoke Manor nursing home and continues to operate it under the name Apostolic Christian Home of Roanoke.

The Roanoke assembly, often called the "prairie church," continues to flourish in the lush and rich prairie soil south of Roanoke. Yet, their hearts are not set on this present world, but on that home across the river Jordan referred to by Elder David Mangold a short time before his death, "That home in heaven, that is the one I am looking for."

O, Tree of Life

O, Tree of Life, O, Tree of Life
That flourished there in Eden;
Then, barred by sin that entered in,
Man's curse from God was given.
And pain and sweat was the reward;
From dust to dust God's voice was heard,
The flaming sword was placed to guard
So Man could not re-enter.

A ray of light to this Tree of Life
To Adam then was given;
The Woman's seed would crush the head
Of the deceiving serpent.
And when the dawn of grace drew near
Our Lord and Saviour did appear
And brought God's love and peace so dear
For healing of the nations.

At Calvary, dark Calvary,
The sacrifice was given,
Christ's blood alone could e'er atone
And pardon every sinner;
Man's curse of sin was on Him laid,
In pain and torture, sore afraid,
My God, My God, aloud he prayed,
Why hast Thou me forsaken?

O dismal tomb, from rock newhewn
And readied there for mortal,
All hope now gone that anyone
Would open Heaven's portals.
But Lo, the stone was rolled away!
And Christ arose on the third day;
His Word now calls, repent, obey—
O hear Him all ye nations.

Written by a Roanoke brother

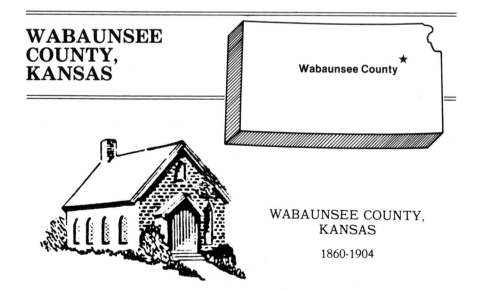

WABAUNSEE COUNTY, KANSAS

Wabaunsee County

WABAUNSEE COUNTY,
KANSAS

1860-1904

As early as 1860, services were held in the homes of a few believers who lived in Wabaunsee County, Kansas, an area approximately eighty miles northwest of Gridley and Lamont and forty miles southwest of Topeka. This is a hilly area with lots of valleys suitable for grazing.

One of the first settlers of the faith to live here was Henry Grimm who emigrated from Germany in 1851 or 1852. He was apparently quite endeared to the American frontier. Before coming to Wabaunsee County, he had lived in Kansas City, Missouri, and at one time, prior to becoming a member of the church, had served as a corporal in the U.S. Army during Indian wars in Wyoming.

Also residing there were the Henry Fechter and Albert Young families. A Schuch family resided there as well. Eventually, the Fechter and Young families moved to Lamont.

One time a young man from the group, Adolph Krolick (a brother to Lizzie Young), was returning home after selling his furs. He was shot and robbed of the cash. The robber was never found.

Worship services were held, primarily, in the home of Henry Grimm near Volland, Kansas, from 1860 to 1904. There were never more than a few believers in this area. He managed to accumulate over two thousand acres of land before he died. When he passed away, his children sold the land and moved to other areas. His death apparently contributed to the demise of the small church.

BLUFFTON, INDIANA

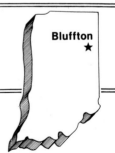

BLUFFTON, INDIANA
Five miles east, two miles south
of Bluffton

The roots of the Apostolic Christian Church at Bluffton, Indiana, can be traced directly to the emigration to America of several Swiss Mennonite families.[42] This sect of people left their homeland in Europe to pursue greater freedom, both economically and spiritually, on this side of the Atlantic.

It is interesting to note that the pattern which was earlier established in Lewis County, New York; Rittman, Ohio; Congerville and Partridge Prairie, Illinois, also took place in the Bluffton area. Namely, many of the church's first converts were of Mennonite background.

Specifically, the Bluffton church evolved from early Swiss Mennonite settlers who first migrated to Wayne County, Ohio. Some of these people later moved to Adams County, Indiana. Other Mennonite settlers moved to the Adams and Wells County area directly from Switzerland.[43]

Delbert Gratz, in *Bernese Anabaptists,* refers to the "Baumgartner Settlement" in Indiana in these words:[44]

> On September 15, 1838, Christian Baumgartner and his bride settled near Vera Cruz in Adams County, Indiana. With them came his brother, Peter. In August of the following year, their father, David, who was a minister, together with several other families, joined them. Under the guidance of David Baumgartner, meetings were held in the various homes.
>
> In March, 1852, a number of Bernese Anabaptists from the Emmental region located near Vera Cruz and joined the Baumgartner group. Among them were two ministers, Ulrich Kipfer and Matthias Strahm.

The Strahm and Kipfer families came from a long line of Mennonite families. The Strahms were of Swiss origin, but many later moved to Germany to avoid religious persecution. Johannes Strohm (1771-1852), a preacher of Schway, Bavaria, 1821-1847, emigrated to America with some children and many grandchildren.[45] One of these was the preacher Matthias Strahm.

Matthias Strahm was born in 1813 at Oberamt Langnau, canton Bern, Switzerland. He and his family were among a group of forty-two who sailed on Easter Sunday, 1851, and arrived in America after an ocean trip of thirty-three days. During this trip, his five year old daughter died. A short funeral service was held, and the hymn *"Meine Lebenszeit Verstreicht"* (No. 253 in the *Zion's Harp*) was sung. Following a prayer, a stone was tied to her feet, and she was lowered into the ocean.

The Kipfers, too, had deep roots in the Mennonite faith with several serving as Elders and deacons. One ancestor, Ulrich Kipfer (born in 1772 and the father and grandfather of the two Ulrich Kipfers who emigrated to America), was a deacon in the Emmental and wrote a detailed account of the division in 1835 at Langnau, Switzerland, when Samuel Froehlich drew over sixty members from the Mennonite Church, creating what became known as the *Neutaufer* movement.[46]

It is evident that the Strahm and Kipfer families, along with many others, were familiar with the *Neutaufer* movement in Switzerland, and many were sympathetic to its views. There was much religious dissension at Langnau in the early 1830's. When these families later emigrated to America in 1852, they joined the "Baumgartner" Mennonite Church Community in Adams County, Indiana. In the same year, the aged leader, David Baumgartner, passed away. This resulted in much confusion and dissension in the church community during the ensuing years. In 1858, remembering the Froehlich movement, Matthias Strahm and Ulrich Kipfer's son, also named Ulrich, decided to search out this faith in America.

So determined were these two men to find a "true" religious faith, that in March, 1858, approximately seven years after arriving in eastern Indiana, they set out on foot for Sardis, Ohio, a distance of 260 miles. It was a long and strenuous journey. Often they would become discouraged and occasionally would hitch rides on wagons. Although walking had been a chief mode of transportation in their native Switzerland, it hardly prepared them for the rigors of walking to and from Sardis.

Their objective was to visit with Isaac Gehring and Joseph Bella, ministers of the Apostolic Christian Church (or at that time called *Neutaufer*) at Sardis, Ohio, and to discuss the basic principles of the religious faith these two men espoused.

Kipfer and Strahm, being familiar with the Froehlich movement in Europe, desired to apply these beliefs to their own lives and community.

It took only one evening of talking with Gehring and Bella to ignite a flame in their hearts. They stayed a few days in the Sardis area and became fully convinced they had truly found the "firm foundation" in Christ Jesus. Subsequently, they fully committed their lives to the Lord in repentance and embraced the new church.

When these two men arrived back in the Newville community (a small town near the Adams-Wells County border, later named Vera Cruz), they enthusiastically told their relatives and friends of the new faith they had acquired. It was with joy and conviction that they related the "new birth" experience and how God, in mercy, will grant peace of heart and mind to all who will surrender to the Lord and humbly follow His teachings.

There was an immediate response to the gospel, resulting in the beginning of what is now known as the Bluffton Apostolic Christian Church. A total of eighteen souls were ready for baptism when Elder Joseph Bella later came to the Newville area. When he arrived, there arose a lengthy discussion about where to conduct the baptisms. Although the Wabash River was close by, a heavy rain the previous evening had filled a pond in a nearby meadow and this was thought to be a more convenient spot. Ulrich Kipfer was the first of eighteen to be baptized in the pond. Later, many souls were baptized in the Wabash River about one-quarter mile west of the steel bridge spanning the Wabash River at Vera Cruz (formerly Newville).[47]

Thus, the fateful trip made by Matthias Strahm and Ulrich Kipfer to Sardis, Ohio, in 1858 proved to be of enormous importance. Little did they realize when they accepted the Biblical views of Isaac Gehring and Joseph Bella that their action would subsequently affect countless souls over many generations. The action of these two, sincere men of God precipitated a following that by 1981 had grown into a church with approximately 1,100 members and over 485 families. Thousands, over the years, have heard the glorious, pure, and unadulterated gospel sounded from the pulpit of the Bluffton, Indiana, church.

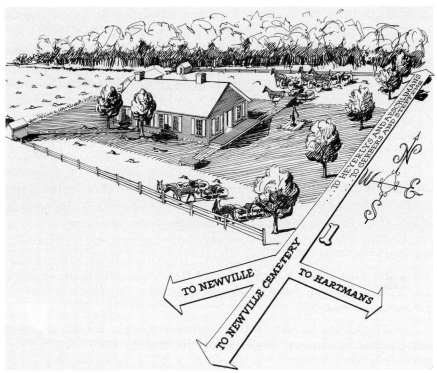

An artist's sketch of the early days at the Bluffton congregation.

In addition to working out their souls' salvation, these early settlers faced great hardship and privation as they attempted to carve an existence out of virgin land. It was often necessary to clear the land of forest in order to begin planting. Also, it was necessary to deal with the soil which is of the heavy impermeable variety. It was with the will and courage of their Swiss heritage that they overcame the obstacles of the Adams and Wells County soil, just as they had conquered the unyielding soil of the Jura Mountains of their native Switzerland.

Significant to their success, but second, of course, to the benevolence of Divine Providence (the foundation of their spiritual well-being), were the ideals deeply imbedded in their hearts: the fear and love of God, obedience to His Word, brotherly love, faith, charity, honesty, hard work, and an unceasing persistence in His truth.

By 1867, the church community grew to the extent that a church building was required. A 2,040-square-foot structure was built in the area of Newville. Elder Joseph Bella watched over the new congregation. Matthias Strahm was chosen as the first minister. In 1865, Nicholas Baumgartner (1831-1901), son of Benedict Baumgartner, moved with his family from Elgin, Iowa, to Newville, Indiana, and became the second minister. Jacob Schar, who later moved to Oregon in 1879, was chosen as the third minister. The fourth minister, Adam Hartman (1838-1888), was elected the first resident Elder in 1887 and served for approximately one year until his death in 1888. In 1897, church membership had grown to 130, and new accommodations were needed. A new building, erected on the same site, seated 450 people. It was approximately three times larger than the first building. Skilled carpenters worked eleven-hour days at $1.40 per day during this construction period.

During these days, the church was known as the Newville Apostolic Christian congregation. In about 1900, when many families moved to Bluffton, and Newville faded as a settlement, the church became known as the Bluffton Apostolic Christian Church.

Construction of the third (existing) church, which replaced the structure built in 1897, began in March, 1949. It is a large structure of 27,800 square feet, with a seating capacity of approximately fifteen hundred. A fellowship hall was built in 1969 to accommodate various church functions. In 1976, an addition to the church was constructed to provide additional Sunday School facilities. The existing Sunday School area was used to expand the dining area. In 1980, due to crowded conditions and difficulties associated with enlarging the existing assembly room, the church decided to build a second church, with a seating capacity of six hundred, on the northeast edge of Bluffton. Construction began in November, 1981.

The present church stands in the middle of a peaceful farming area. This large cathedral-like building stands as both a majestic milestone and ringing monument to the work God has wrought in the hearts of all who have sat under the sound of the gospel message since 1858 when eighteen humble souls submitted to baptism in a nearby pond.

The church has been faithfully served by several Elders over the years:

Joseph Bella	Sardis, Ohio	————
Adam Hartman	Resident	————
Henry Dotterer	Latty, Ohio	————

Henry Souder	Leo, Indiana	————
Adam Imthurn	Archbold, Ohio	————
Elias Dotterer	Junction, Ohio	————
Godfrey Rauch	Resident	1913-1935
Samuel Aeschliman	Resident	1941-1975
John Yergler	Resident	1966-1977
Orville Ringger	Resident	1975-

The church has experienced many large "in-gatherings." These are times when the Spirit of God seems to sweep over the congregation with a vigorous force, prompting many into repentance and a firm commitment to God. In the early days, when a soul turned to the Lord in repentance, he or she would sit on the *schamelie bonk* or "mourners bench" until peace with God was acquired. A special section in the church was reserved for those seeking souls. Although the *schamelie bonk* is gone, the doctrine of a born-again conversion, through repentance, remains strong in the church. Great emphasis is placed upon the price Christ paid in His sacrifice for sin and the ensuing responsibility of converted souls to live their lives in harmony with the teachings of the Scripture.

BLUFFTON NORTH
(Bluffton, Indiana)

Bluffton North

BLUFFTON NORTH
North edge of Bluffton, Indiana

In 1981 construction began on a 25,000-square-foot church building at 602 East Dustman Road on the north edge of Bluffton. This church was built to relieve the large attendance at the country church east of Bluffton.

First worship services were held here on Thanksgiving Day, 1982.

The sanctuary at this church, although smaller, resembles the one at the larger church east of Bluffton. The two congregations maintain a warm fellowship and special closeness.

Thanksgiving Day, 1982, marked the first worship services at the Apostolic Christian Church on the north edge of Bluffton. To distinguish it from the large country church, it is referred to as Bluffton North.

The following poem was written when the large country Church was divided into two loving congregations.

ONE CHURCH IS TWO
TWO CHURCHES ARE ONE

Our church has prospered
Throughout growing years,
Joys have been many
Along with some tears.

The peace we enjoy
In our brotherhood,
Is given from God,
And it is so good.

Our love and concern
Each for the other,
Reaches to each friend,
Sister and brother.

We give God all praise
For this precious love,
It's not of ourselves
It comes from Above.

The Gospel is preached,
The good seed is sown,
And it has been blest
For our church has grown.

It has come to this;
We need to divide
And start a new church.
The Lord is our guide.

We love each other
We are glad to say,
And it's hard to part
And go separate ways.

But our Jesus left
To go His blest way.
Leaving His loved ones
On this earth that day.

So He understands
And He knows each heart,
And He will help us
As we now must part.

Unity and love
Prevailed in the past.
We now become two;
May this oneness last.

Yes, we're divided
But our path is the same.
Our worship is still
In His holy name.

One church becomes two,
Two churches are one.
We all love our God
Who gave us His Son.

— Eunice Fiechter

PEORIA, ILLINOIS

PEORIA, ILLINOIS
3420 North Sheridan Road

The church at Peoria has followed the growth of the city itself and has become a large congregation. Peoria was only a village of 550 in 1835 and has since grown to include over 130,000 residents. The church here has correspondingly grown from a handful of persons in the decade of 1850 to a sizable assembly of over 515 members in 1980.

In a little over a century, the church in Peoria has made tremendous advances. The few immigrant believers who used to meet in homes and when minister John Kreinbill's cows lazily grazed on a tranquil hill overlooking the Illinois River have since progressed to an active and large assembly.

Instead of meeting in a private home "parlor" as in former days, the church assembles in a large structure on Sheridan Road which seats nearly one thousand persons and is designed to handle large crowds of the faithful. While the church in 1860 existed amid the peaceful confines of a rural environment, today the brethren dwell in a bustling, industrialized, metropolitan area.

Peoria was a small and tranquil village in the early 1830's.

It all began in Peoria during the decade of 1850. During the early phases of this very significant decade (for Apostolic Christians, that is), Elder Benedict Weyeneth was seeking converts in the general area by virtue of his preaching in the settlements at Dillon, Congerville, Partridge Prairie, and Peoria. One of the earliest converts in Illinois was John Kreinbill, a former Mennonite. He became a minister in the general area and served at both Peoria and Partridge Prairie. His conversion was significant to the church in that he was very zealous in traveling to various churches, preaching the gospel, and assisting new immigrants in acclimating themselves to the privations and challenges of rural life in pioneer America. His zeal and love was of great benefit to the early believers in Peoria.

Although no church was established at this time, a church meeting was held in Peoria as early as 1850 by Elder Joseph Virkler of New York State who had been ordained as the first American Elder a few years previously.[48] Later, in 1852, services were held at the home of a Sister Sommer just across the Illinois River on Metamora Road. John Kreinbill conducted these services.[49]

Although John Hartman came to Peoria in 1851, it was not until 1859 that the church got its official start. He was ordained as minister, and services were held regularly in his home at 1507 North Monroe Street.

Worship services were held in the late 1850's at the home of John Hartman, 1507 North Monroe. In 1983 this house was still standing.

Although known as John (Johann) Hartman after he arrived in the United States, he was born Ludwig Johannes Hartman on May 15, 1815, in Rothekuhle, Sommersell, near Barntrup, Germany. It is not known for sure what his religious faith was when he came to Peoria, but research of the Hartman and collateral families back to 1500 A.D. indicates all were members of the Catholic Church. They lived in a small area about fifty miles southwest of Hanover, most inhabiting the area around Detmold, Lippe.

John Hartman was married to Anna Marie Uckermann October 17, 1841, in Brake, Germany. They arrived in 1847 at the Port of New Orleans, proceeding from there to East St. Louis.[50] In 1851, they came to Peoria. He was a tailor.

A chance encounter with Benedict Weyeneth resulted in Hartman's eventual membership in the Apostolic Christian Church. He, along with John Huette, was walking down the street to his home in Peoria one day when they ran into Benedict Weyeneth who was a total stranger to them. Likely because they all spoke German, they struck up a conversation and a sense of camaraderie resulted. Knowing Weyeneth, it is very possible the conversation turned to religion. Perhaps Weyeneth invited them to church.[51] In any case, Hartman became converted and was soon placed into the ministry.

Another early arrival in Peoria was Andrew J. Braun. He and several members of the congregation at Schweinfurt, Germany, came to Peoria in 1854. As leader of the group, and having been jailed and subject to persecution by civil authorities in Europe, Braun led his followers to America where protection under the First Amendment guaranteed freedom of religion. The record of Braun's time in Peoria is sketchy. He eventually moved to Morton, Illinois, and then to Wauseon and later Toledo, Ohio.[52]

On May 10, 1874, a frame church was built at 511 Green Street at a cost of $1,000. This was the group's first house of worship. At this time the church's official name (in Peoria) was the "Apostolic Church of Peoria, Illinois." Legal papers reflect that on February 20, 1897, the church adopted the new corporate name of "Apostolic Christian Church of Peoria, Illinois." The signatory to this document was John Schneider.

Less than twenty-five years later, the church had blossomed to the extent that a larger church building was needed. The frame church was torn down, and a brick building costing $7,500 was built on the same site. The "Green Street" church served the congregation until 1949 when a large, impressive Gothic-style church was constructed at 3420 North Sheridan Road. The building cost $350,000 (or forty-six times more than the previous church) and was dedicated to the Lord on December 10, 1950. An addition to this structure, consisting of a dining room, additional Sunday School rooms, kitchen, rest rooms, baby room, fellowship area, and other improvements to the original building was completed in 1978.[53]

As early as 1912, a senior citizen facility was built for "the old sisters." Care for the elderly has continued, and today the church maintains a beautiful facility for the aged at 7023 North Skyline Drive.

In 1969 a fellowship hall was built on Route 150 West in a beautiful and scenic area. An addition was made in 1974. This place is distinguished by a placid setting including a lake and gorgeous landscaping.

Rudolph Witzig was appointed Elder of the church in 1894. Residing in Gridley, he traveled via train to Peoria approximately once per month to care for the church. He died in 1912. Assisting Witzig in this capacity for many years was Elder Andrew Rapp of Morton.

The first resident Elder was Emil Schubert who was ordained by Michael Mangold in January, 1929. He served until his death on August 14, 1950. The respected and gentlemanly Schubert—stately in manner, yet humble of mind—was often mentioned in sermons and discussions many years after his death. References to "Father Schubert" always engendered a warm feeling in the hearts of older hearers as they remembered the many deeds of kindness and wise counsel of this church official.

Emil Schubert was born September 22, 1874, in Rodlitz, Saxony, Germany, the son of Anton Schubert. He was baptized in the Evangelical Baptist Church in Germany and received his schooling in that country. He spoke "high German" and used excellent grammar.

In 1895, he married Anna Sieber. In 1906, they emigrated to America, arriving in Philadelphia where he secured a job with Larkin and Co. For two years they lived in Philadelphia and met with another Schubert family (no relation) for "church" services. At the end of two years, they moved to Peoria.

He is remembered in the *Silver Lining:*

> For forty years or more he lived and preached God's gospel—traveling far and wide to expound the living words. His heart was always with those less fortunate, and with the Lord's help, he wept with those that wept and rejoiced with those that rejoiced. Never forgetting his loved ones in the old country, he was blessed with the opportunity to return in 1923, to reaffirm convictions with fellow pilgrims in faith.

He began preaching in the English language in 1932. He died of heart trouble in 1950 at age seventy-five.

Although official church records were not kept during his tenure as Elder, it is believed that during one brief period he had the oversight of all the "western" churches in the United States.

Elder Schubert is remembered for his regal bearing and precise manner of speaking. He partially attributed this to his service as a sergeant in the Prussian army prior to his conversion.

The second resident Elder selected to lead the Peoria flock was Roy Sauder who was ordained January 3, 1965. Others who have served as Elder were Michael Mangold, Roanoke; Joe A. Getz, Morton; David Mangold, Roanoke; and Silas Leuthold, Princeville, Illinois.

MORTON, ILLINOIS

MORTON, ILLINOIS
225 East Jefferson Street

Almost from the beginning, the Morton church was destined to eventually become a large one. Located in an area flanked by Dillon and Tremont to the south, Congerville to the east, and Roanoke and Peoria to the northeast and northwest respectively, Morton could draw—in the early days—on the vast number of farmers in adjacent areas who had Evangelical Baptist and Mennonite backgrounds. This, coupled with the fact that Morton became semi-industrialized early in its history, led to the swelling of membership as the decades unfolded. By 1980, the church had grown to include more than 650 members and 370 families making it the largest Apostolic Christian Church in Illinois, and the second largest in the denomination nationally.[54]

Big numbers seem quite common to the Morton Apostolic Christian Church. Already in 1894, the church enjoyed a tremendous "in-gathering" with 119 persons baptized during that year. In subsequent years, waves of conversions transpired totaling

65 in 1906
109 in 1922
49 in 1947
31 in 1970
44 in 1974
39 in 1975

From 1894 through 1976, the Morton church baptized 1,192 persons.[55]

The first settlers came to the Morton area as early as 1826, and primitive log cabins soon began to dot the area. From 1830 to 1836, a steady stream of immigrants arrived in Morton. By 1837, names like Ackerman, Belsley, and Hartman began showing up in the general vicinity.

Christian Ackerman, who was born on Christmas Day in 1913, in Bavaria, Germany, was the first person who eventually became associated with the Apostolic Christian Church in Morton. It is likely that he was of Mennonite extraction. At age twenty-four, he arrived in New York City. He started his trip west on foot and by wagon train and settled on a farm in Ohio for approximately six months while accumulating enough money to continue pushing west.

Ackerman eventually traveled by riverboat to Spring Bay, Illinois, where he found work as a farm laborer. It was here he married Anna Belsley who had just arrived in America. After two years, the couple moved to a farm between Morton and Pekin, Illinois. Later they moved to a spot north of Morton where they built a two-room log cabin.

The early development of the Apostolic Christian Church in central Illinois seemed to center on areas such as Dillon, Congerville, Peoria, and Partridge Prairie (Metamora). Several persons of this faith resided in the Morton vicinity but attended church in the early days at these villages. The trip to Partridge Township was quite tiring, but nonetheless, many made the trip either walking or by wagon.

Benedict Weyeneth was instrumental in guiding the early church in central Illinois. He was active in the Morton area as early as 1853, but a church was not built until 1867.[56] The precise extent of his initial labors in Morton remain unknown. It is surmised that the few early church families residing in Morton attended services at churches in the villages already mentioned.

Church families who were among those to come to Morton in the late 1850's and early 1860's were names such as Voelpel, Welk, Rapp, Beyer, Getz, Hauter, Frank, Miller, Balzer, Dauchert, Reuter, and Freidinger.

In 1866, when Elder Henry Geistlich of Switzerland visited Morton, there was no church building. Instead, brethren met in the woods on the Ackerman farm. Geistlich said:[57]

> As I saw this place, I thought of the plains of Mamre, as we find in the Scriptures, where Abraham lived. Also, I had a real feeling of love toward the Ackermans who were very hospitable.

The momentum of the early assembly at Morton had advanced to the point of building a small church in 1867. A small white frame building was built on the corner of what now is Jefferson and Third Streets. The church was lighted by kerosene lamps that hung from the ceiling. Interestingly, this little church contained two dining rooms—one for men and one for women. There were no screens on the windows, and in the summertime, during the lunch hour, some of the sisters would go up and down the aisles using fly chasers to chase the flies away from the tables. The fly chasers consisted of paper streamers attached to long pieces of wood.

George Welk became the first resident Elder of the Morton church. He was born December 29, 1829, in Germany, the son of Daniel and Juliana Herbolt Welk. He and his wife, the former Hanna Getz, along with their infant daughter Katherine, and his wife's parents, Peter and Katherine Gress Getz, emigrated to America in 1859.

The Welks lived with Ludwig Getz and family near Dillon, Illinois, for five years. Ludwig Getz, who later became Elder at Tremont in 1881, then purchased a farm northeast of Tremont and sold his farm to George Welk. In 1871 or 1872, Welk was persuaded by the Morton brethren to purchase some choice, well-drained land two miles east of Morton. He purchased the land and sold his Dillon farm to Kasper Koch.

George Welk, after serving as Elder for almost three decades, met an untimely death on March 17, 1895. A few days previous to this, he was standing beside his buggy when the horses inadvertently backed up and pinned him between the buggy and the wheel, leaving him badly crushed. Somehow, he managed to walk one block to the residence of his daughter, Mrs. Julia Rapp, wife of Barthol Rapp. He lived for a few days, but the injuries he sustained were so severe he soon expired.

The mantle of church leadership subsequently fell on Andrew Rapp, who was the husband of Welk's other daughter, Katherine.

A significant part of the Morton Apostolic Christian Church's history reaches back to Burgberg, Baden, Germany, a small village in the beautiful Black Forest region. It was here that fifteen children were born to the union of Christian and Mary Weisser Rapp. Two of their sons, Andrew and Barthol, would later perform significant leadership roles in the Morton congregation. Also, their family business venture would grow—for a time—into one of Morton's leading industries.

The Rapps came to America to avoid compulsory military service. Andrew, the family's oldest boy, had served in the German Army during the War of 1870, and his military experience was made difficult due to his religious convictions.[58] In 1874, his commander suggested he leave the country (perhaps not believing he would actually do so).

As fate would have it, that evening a farmer with a load of hay came along and suggested that Andrew crawl under the hay, and he would take him to the French border. That very evening, after reaching the border, Andrew met a group going to America who invited him along and financed his ocean trip as well as the overland trip to Forrest, Illinois.[59]

His parents were unaware of his desertion from the armed forces and were later questioned sharply by military authorities.

His younger brothers, Barthol and Christian, who also faced military conscription, soon made the trip to America. Their ocean voyage was quite hazardous. Their ship sank in mid-ocean, and they spent several days and nights in life boats prior to being rescued. They arrived in America with no personal possessions.

In 1875, the father and mother and the rest of the Rapp family emigrated to America to join their three sons. They settled in Forrest, Illinois.

When Andrew Rapp was a lad of fifteen in Germany, he took courses in stone masonry and architecture. Arriving in Forrest, Illinois, he sought employment in this realm only to be directed to Morton, a booming town. Brick and tile were in great demand, so he traveled there to seek economic opportunity. So brisk was the demand for brick that in 1875 he summoned his two brothers, Barthol and Christian, to Morton to help him. Eventually, all six Rapp brothers came to Morton.

From this beginning, the Rapp Brick and Tile Company realized rapid growth. Tile was used to drain the swampy, prairie grassland, making it more suitable for tillage. When land was properly tiled, it added to the value. Thus, demand for tile was strong.

The firm also made pottery, and by 1916 the sons of Andrew Rapp started the Morton Pottery, a firm which shipped its products nationwide. The firm became quite well known.

Thus, the size of the large Rapp family, together with the jobs their enterprises offered, gave a significant boost to the Morton church. Also, the Interlocking Fence Company, operated by the Getz family, was beneficial to church growth by providing jobs.

Andrew Rapp, who fathered fifteen children, was ordained Elder in 1895. He served until his death on May 2, 1911, and was succeeded by his younger brother (by two years), Barthol. Barthol was ordained in 1911 and served until he died on January 24, 1924. Barthol was born August 15, 1854, in Konigsfeld, Germany.[60]

By 1891, the first little church building became too small, so a larger one was built on the same site. To the rear of the building was a row of stalls which accommodated the horses as well as the hearse used for funerals. John Zobrist usually furnished a team of stately black horses to pull the hearse.

Because the roads and yards were quite muddy in those days, a planked platform was constructed on the west side of the church. It was here buggies would unload and pick up their passengers.

The twelfth day of the twelfth month of the twelfth year—December 12, 1912—bode ill for the Morton congregation. On this fateful day, the church—now twenty-one years old—burned to the ground. The fire was set by an arsonist. It was the second Morton institution to succumb to an arsonist's flare. In 1868, the Morton Library had also fallen victim to arson.[61]

The church fire broke out at 4 a.m. on a Thursday morning, and its intensity caused a great commotion. Mary Getz, who lived with her parents four blocks from the church, recalls that sparks from the blaze blew on the snow in their yard. People living near the church were terrified the fire would spread and consume their homes. Accordingly, they began gathering their clothes and personal belongings in order to flee the area, if necessary.[62]

Ringing fire bells and a huge crowd at the scene provided an unusual atmosphere of excitment, but it eventually subsided as efforts to contain the blaze and protect surrounding homes proved successful.

Construction of a new church building began in 1913. A year later, at a cost of $50,000 and seating capacity of 750, this building was completed. J.C. Ackerman and Valentine Wick helped every day on the construction. This two-story building, with the sanctuary on the second floor, was still serving the church in 1982. Many physical improvements have been made over the years. A large remodeling project was initiated in 1957.

Carl Rassi, a native of Bavaria, Germany, was ordained as Elder in 1932. He died July 4, 1952. He was succeeded by Joe A. Getz who served from 1948 to 1966. He was the first American-born Elder to serve at Morton.

Russell Rapp, a descendant of the large Rapp family which came to Morton in the 1870's, was ordained Elder December 11, 1966. For health reasons he stepped down as Elder in 1974, although he remained a minister. In 1979 he resigned his membership in the Apostolic Christian Church.

Joe J. Braker was installed as Morton's seventh resident Elder on September 8, 1974.

Morton, Illinois, is the site of the Apostolic Christian Home for the Handicapped, a sprawling and beautiful complex on Veteran's Road.

Restmor Nursing Home on the southeast edge of Morton is operated by the local Morton congregation.

A fellowship hall was built north of the Home for the Handicapped in 1975.

The church at Morton is symbolic of the change in church membership from basically rural to urban. In the early decades, the occupational composite of the membership was decidedly farming, but over the years as farms filled up with settlers and technology reduced the number of farms and farm laborers, members of the church became more urban oriented. Consequently, the Morton church—as well as many Apostolic Christian Churches across the land—consisted of more and more non-farmers.

LEO, INDIANA

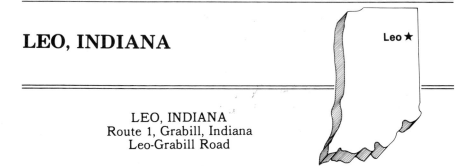

LEO, INDIANA
Route 1, Grabill, Indiana
Leo-Grabill Road

The year 1862 was a memorable one for Apostolic Christians in the Leo-Grabill area of northeastern Indiana. Not only was the Homestead Act signed into law by President Abraham Lincoln on May 20 while the nation was in the second year of Civil War, but the flame of faith that had burned so fiercely among followers of Samuel Froehlich in Switzerland and Germany—and later found its way to fifteen locations in the United States—had now come to Allen County, Indiana.

The faith came to the area one day in 1862 when a stranger came to Cedar Creek Township near Leo, Indiana. His team of horses was hitched to a wagon, and he stopped at the residence of Jacob Schwartz. He was received cordially into the Schwartz home. They offered him a meal. Following supper he read from the Scriptures and meditated on the words of life. This man was Benedict Weyeneth, who had come to the Leo area from Bluffton, Indiana, a distance of approximately forty miles.

The meeting between Weyeneth, forty-three, and Schwartz, thirty-five, left a deep impression on the younger Schwartz, and the results of the meeting had lasting implications for the spiritual aspects of the area.

Until this time, Jacob Schwartz had been an Amish Mennonite. For generations his ancestors had been steeped in the Anabaptist tradition. The Schwartz name today is prominent in both Mennonite and Old Order Amish circles particularly in northern Indiana.[63] Yet, in 1862, Jacob Schwartz was not at peace concerning his spiritual outlook. The words of Benedict Weyeneth spoke to his heart. So great was this influence that he became the first member of this new religious group in the Leo, Indiana, area.

The church organized with only two converts—Jacob Schwartz and Jacob Conrad. Both were former Amishmen. From this token beginning in 1862, the church at Leo—the second congregation of the denomination in Indiana—grew from only a few members to a church consisting of over fifty families and approximately 125 members in 1982.

Jacob Schwartz was apparently a man of great courage and always ready to challenge the unknown despite uncertainty and privation. His willingness to leave his native Europe and embark toward the uncertainties associated with emigrant life in America reflect such a spirit. In this realm, however, he endured bitter disappointment. While crossing the Atlantic in 1854, his little daughter, Anna (not yet two), fell ill and died and was buried at sea. This, no doubt, crushed his spirit, and his religious faith could not sustain him. By 1862, the promises of regeneration and sanctification in Christ became as balm to his aching heart, and after turning his all to God in repentance, he found the "peace that passeth all understanding." True to his willingness to face the unknown, he was not afraid to pursue this new and more enriching faith.

The early history of the Leo-Grabill-Cedarville area essentially follows the pattern of most areas settled by descendants of European Anabaptists. Like the Bluffton, Indiana, area—but not to such an extent—Mennonites of various persuasions engulfed the area, and the Apostolic Christian Church was born out of persons from this background. William C. Ringenberg writes:[64]

> The Allen County Mennonites developed from the Swiss Anabaptist branch of the sixteenth century Reformation. The Swiss Brethren, as they called themselves, were led by Conrad Grebel (1498-1526) and others; they emphasized the importance of personal conversion, believer's baptism, a voluntary church, a strong sense of social concern for the brotherhood, high moral living, separation from worldly culture, and a literal interpretation of the Sermon on the Mount with its emphasis on nonresistance and against oath taking.
>
> No religious group suffered more than did the Anabaptists, five thousand of whom became martyrs."

Many who fled the harsh persecution encountered in Switzerland were the ancestors of the nineteenth-century emigrants who came to Allen County. Many of them continued to espouse, in varying degrees, the solid principles their ancestors died for. Early arrivals to Allen County in 1852 and 1853 included names familiar today to Apostolic Christians: Conrad, Miller, Klopfenstein, Ramseyer, Schrock, Sauder, Schwartz, Steiner, and Bertsch.

Ringenberg describes the situation which saw some of the Amish embrace the Apostolic Christian Church:[65]

> The troublesome decade of the 1860's witnessed still another division when the Leo Apostolic Christian Church came into existence in 1862. The Amish who joined this church stated many of the criticisms that the Defenseless Mennonites were making against the Old Amish Church, namely, that it was too formal and that it placed insufficient

emphasis on experimental religion. But the Apostolic Christian Church differed from the Defenseless Mennonites in that it greatly stressed sanctification theology and the importance of separation from churches of other denominations.

Significant to the subsequent development of the Leo church was the arrival in Cedar Creek Township of the Jacob Sauder family in 1848. He was born May 7, 1828, in Ohio, the son of Henry and Elizabeth (Schrock) Sauder, natives of Pennsylvania. His second wife, Mary Eicher, bore him four children, one of whom was Henry, who later was to become an Elder of the Leo congregation. The name was eventually changed from "Sauder" to "Souder," apparently for easier pronunciation.[66]

Henry Souder, Sr., (1846-1924) was born August 17, 1846, in Wayne County, Ohio. He moved to Indiana with his parents at age two and grew into manhood. As a young adult, he became dissatisfied with his family's religious faith and began to seek another. He sought a faith which complied more closely with the Word of God.

Reference is made to Souder's search for a more enduring faith in *History of American Elders:*[67]

> In the meantime he repented and received peace with God; then he prayed that God should lead him to the church where he would find the True Light. Brother Souder was a kind and loving Shepherd. He was loved and esteemed by young and old."

The first church service at Leo was held in the home of Jacob Schwartz in 1862. Preaching the first sermon was John Kreinbill of Peoria, Illinois.[68] Kreinbill was very instrumental in helping to nurture the early churches in America. He traveled at length to this end.

The newly organized Leo church met in homes from 1862 to 1878 with Jacob Schwartz and Joseph Conrad as ministers. In 1878, Jacob and Elizabeth Conrad, parents of Joseph, deeded half of their land to the church for $1 to build a house of worship. The building was dedicated by Henry Souder and Joseph Conrad, who were ministers at that time.

On August 20, 1866, the Leo brethren hosted a "brother meeting" which was described by Elder Henry Geistlich as, "A very blessed day." Participating in the meeting were Elders

Benedict Weyeneth and Joseph Bella and church leaders from other states.[69] Geistlich deeply appreciated his visit to Leo and wrote:

> The hospitality of these brethren reminded me of Abraham, how he said to Sarah to go and make ready three measures of fine meal and knead it and bake, and dress a tender calf and prepare it, and then they gave it to the men or angels.

The first church building was a small, wood-frame structure, spartan in design, and in accord with the plain architecture of that era. In 1910, this building was moved, and a new two-story brick building was erected. It has been remodeled and expanded over the years to meet the needs of the times. On June 26, 1968, ground was broken for an addition to the main building. This 80-foot by 40-foot addition provided expanded Sunday School space. Also, at this time the dining room and mothers' room were remodeled. The new quarters were dedicated on October 12, 1969.

In 1961, the church built a fellowship hall at Cedarville, a short drive from the church. This rustic dwelling sits next to a tranquil lake, and the setting is very peaceful.

Leo was chosen as the site of the denomination's orphanage, and on October 24, 1976, the Apostolic Christian Children's Home was dedicated to the Lord.

The Leo area has further distinguished itself by being the "home" of the *Silver Lining,* the denomination's monthly news bulletin. For many years Henry Souder, grandson of Elder Henry Souder, served diligently and single-mindedly as editor. Following an abrupt death, he was succeeded by his brother Ed Souder, who, too, died suddenly after serving awhile as editor.

On April 25, 1925, Henry Souder, Sr., the first resident Elder of the congregation, died. This ended many years of service to the church, both as a minister and Elder. He was already a minister when the first church was built in 1878. He was ordained Elder in 1902.

The second resident Elder was David Bertsch, born March 5, 1920, at Grabill. The Bersch family came to the area in 1868.[70] He was ordained Elder February 13, 1966.

Others who have served as Elder at Leo were Benedict Weyeneth, Roanoke, Illinois; Joseph Bella, Sardis, Ohio; Elias Dotterer, Junction, Ohio; and Samuel Aeschliman, Bluffton, Indiana.

Otto Norr, who was born February 28, 1882, served as a minister for forty-six years. Raised a Lutheran, he began attending Apostolic Christian services and eventually joined the church, being baptized by Elder Henry Souder. It was Norr who once said, "In our pathway, which is always growing shorter, we want to be kind, a light to all. We shall not pass this way again, ever."[71]

GIRARD, OHIO

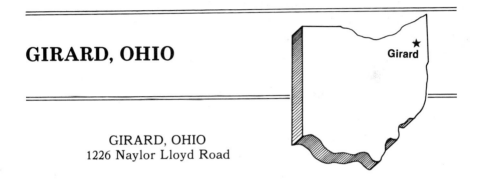

GIRARD, OHIO
1226 Naylor Lloyd Road

The small church at Girard, Ohio, located only fifteen miles from the Pennsylvania state line midway between Warren and Youngstown, is symbolic of the few extremely small churches in the Apostolic Christian denomination that, despite disappointment and small numbers, continue on year after year faithful to the stewardship placed on them. It is a credit to the worthy concepts of diligence and obedience that these stalwart churches continue on and remain devoted to the Lord and to the rich heritage of the Apostolic Christian Church. By 1981, the Girard congregation consisted of less than five families and thirteen members.

Church activity began here in 1864 when a few believers gathered together for worship services. These services were held infrequently and were conducted by Isaac Gehring of Sardis, Ohio, and John Kreinbill of Illinois.[72] The fact that the latter helped in establishing the Girard church bears testimony to his far-flung travels on behalf of the fledgling denomination.

Included in the original group were the William Ludt and Charles Schoenfeld families along with Mary Thatchfield. The Girard-Youngstown area has traditionally been one of heavy industry, and this is one of the reasons brethren came to the area.

The first resident minister was John Bakody. In 1874, the group was officially organized by Jacob Bollinger who served as minister. In 1878, the assembly had grown to the point where a permanent place of worship was required. A one-story frame church was built at 29 West Wilson Avenue in Girard at a cost of $1,600. In 1905, the church building was raised and a basement placed underneath. Isaac Emch, who had moved to Girard from Sardis, engineered the project. With some additions and remodeling, this building served the congregation until 1966. During this time Karl Schladenhauffen was the senior minister. He had emigrated from Germany and served as minister from 1896-1925.

Some of the early brethren at Girard came from the church at Sardis, Ohio, which was a "stopping-off" place for early immigrants of the faith. Abraham Emch, who attended church at

New Martinsville, West Virginia (located across the Ohio River from Sardis), was another example of one who moved from that area to the Girard-Youngstown area. He ministered for many years at Girard and was the father of Jesse Emch and Lorenz Emch who also served as ministers.

The Hafely and Klotzle families also hailed from Sardis. Lydia Klotzle, daughter of Jacob and Elizabeth Hafely, recalled how her parents, along with the Benedict Emch family and a Brother Schupbach, left Aargau, Switzerland, on March 17, 1874, and later arrived in Sardis, Ohio.

They were on an America-bound ship for several days. On the seventh day they were shipwrecked and forced to transfer to another ship.

On January 16, 1896, Lydia Hafely was married to John Klotzle, and the next day they moved to a farm near Girard. This union bore six children, among them a son, Joseph, who served as a minister at Girard. He later moved to Altadena, California, where he also served as minister.

When the congregation moved into its new church on January 16, 1966, they had fifty members. Groundbreaking for the new church took place on Sunday, June 20, 1965, at 1226 Naylor-Lloyd Road, about three miles northeast of the old location. The new building was comprised of brick, concrete block, and exposed laminated wood arches. It cost $104,000. The sanctuary seats 175.

Declining membership has resulted from a separation in 1972 which took several members including all the young people of the church. This, along with the death of several older members, left the church with only thirteen members in 1981. Average age was seventy-six with only three members under seventy-five. Harold L. Emch served alone in the ministry.

Over the years Girard has been served by Elders Joseph Bella and Isaac Gehring of Sardis; Sigmund Sorg, Henry Schwier, and Samuel Engwiller of Mansfield; and Ernest Graf, Sr., and Rudolph Graf of Akron, Ohio.

NORTH SIDE
(Forrest, Illinois)

North Side ★ Forrest

NORTH SIDE

North of Forrest, Illinois

1867—1949

In 1864, a church was established when the Joseph Verkler family (originally from Strasbourg, Alsace, France, and who later lived in Lancaster County, Pennsylvania; Butler County, Ohio; and Peoria and Metamora, Illinois) moved to a farm in Pleasant Ridge Township north of Forrest, Illinois.

Joseph Verkler is not to be confused with Elder Joseph Virkler who was the Elder of the Lewis County, New York, church, having been ordained by Benedict Weyeneth in 1847. Elder Joseph Virkler did, however, visit in the area and once walked, along with John Zimmerman, to Mackinaw Dells to visit Zimmerman's brother, Michael.

The Verkler family, along with a few other families, met in homes for four years. In 1867 the Jacob Honegger family from Zurich, Switzerland, came to the area to live (after spending a year in Morton), and in 1868 the Rudolph Leuthold family arrived in the township. These families consequently formed the nucleus of a group that would later flourish and lay part of the foundation of a church that exists today at Forrest, Illinois. In fact, this infant church grew and maintained itself for eighty years. Then, due to improved means of transportation, it united with a similar church south of Forrest—the "South Side" church—in a new building located in Forrest.

The life of Joseph Verkler seems to be one of adventure and bravery. As a young Mennonite in Europe, he found himself serving in the military. After serving two and one-half years, he came home on furlough. At this time his mother encouraged him to follow them to America. In a brave and risky act, he took her advice. He did not return to his military unit, and as he fled to Le Havre to board a ship, he did so at great peril. If the authorities would have found him, he would have been executed. Nonetheless, he pressed on and—using the name of Joseph Guingrich—set sail for America. This was in 1829 when an early period of emigration began.

Arriving in New York City, he walked to Lancaster County, Pennsylvania, where he worked for seven dollars per month. Eighteen months later he crossed the Allegheny Mountains on foot, averaging an astounding fifty miles per day, until he arrived in Butler County, Ohio. Six months later he took a boat down the Ohio River and then up the Mississippi and Illinois Rivers to Peoria (then called Ft. Clark).[73]

On December 27, 1832, he was married to Jacobena Engel of Metamora, daughter of Christian Engel, a Mennonite minister. Their first home was a one-room log cabin at Aiken's Mill on Kickapoo Creek west of Peoria. In 1834, the couple moved near Metamora where they cleared several timber farms. It is likely that while living near Metamora they encountered John Kreinbill and Peter Engel (perhaps a relative), two early converts and promoters of the Apostolic Christian faith in the Peoria and Metamora areas. In 1864, the Verklers moved to Pleasant Ridge Township where they purchased eight hundred acres of farmland.

The first church building in Pleasant Ridge Township was erected in 1868 on a plot of ground in the southwest corner of the Verkler farm. Families attending the new congregation had the following names: Keller, Ramseyer, Schwartzentraub, Metz, Huber, Abersol, Scharlach, Stoller, and a few others.[74]

In 1875, a larger church was built on Verkler land one-half mile farther east. Many new families soon arrived during the waves of immigration that were so prevalent in the 1870's. Family names at this time included: Bach, Bollinger, Detweiler, Ebach, Fehr, Fortna, Geiger, Haab, Hess, Herstein, Lear, Mauler, Moser, Munz, Nussbaum, Schneider, Stortz, Yackley, and Yoder.

In 1893, a 32-foot by 44-foot assembly room was added to the south side of the church, and the old assembly room became a dining room. The old dining room became a Sunday School. Also at this time, additional land was purchased from Andrew Abersol to build stables for the teams of horses that pulled the buggies and wagons over the mud roads to church.

The old "North Side" church building.

Rudolph Leuthold, who came to America from Zurich, Switzerland, where he was born in August, 1813, emerged as the group's first Elder. He died March 27, 1892, and is buried in the North Side Cemetery.

Jacob Honegger (1832-1920), also of Zurich, succeeded Leuthold as Elder. He preached for many years. As he grew older, failing health inhibited his style in that he could not stand for long periods of time. To overcome this obstacle, John Maurer, Sr., built a small table between the pulpit and the minister's bench which held a Bible. This allowed Honegger to read Scripture and deliver a sermon while in a sitting position.

Peter Bach (1873-1946), a native of Alsace, France, served as Elder from 1932 to 1946. He was succeeded by Henry Kilgus who served from 1946 until the congregation's merger with the South Side church. Kilgus continued as Elder of the merged churches.[75]

In 1948, the church voted to join the South Side church in building a new, larger church in Forrest. Final services in the North Side church were held December 11, 1949. In a fitting farewell to the old church on the ridge, Lena Bach, widow of the late Elder Peter Bach, served the noon lunch. The final sermon was spoken by Elder Henry Kilgus—and the old era was ushered out.

For several years in the early days of the church, transportation to church was provided for Forrest residents who needed a ride. This was a three and one-half mile ride each way in a horse-drawn hack purchased from buggy-maker Wilhelm Schlipf. The family responsible for serving the Sunday lunch was also obligated to furnish a team and driver.

The church attempted, eventually in vain, to perpetuate their German heritage. Winter classes teaching the German language were held in the church dining room until after 1900. The sessions began after "corn shucking" and lasted until the spring field work began. Two teachers were Will Yoder and Conrad Munz, Sr.

The North Side church was distinguished by its unity in 1932 when a troublesome separation took place in the South Side and Fairbury churches. Ben Nussbaum, in *100 Years of North Side History*, wrote:[76]

> Some members of the other area churches insisted that the 'old ways' be retained. In 1932, they elected to withdraw and re-establish under another name. It was a time of great turmoil, and one must admire the unity displayed by the North Side—not only through this schism, but also the previous one in 1907.

The old North Side church is now gone, never to return. The gallant and sincere efforts of those who attended this country church will fade from memory as the years pass on; yet their deeds of goodness and charity will live on forever in the mind of God.

JUNCTION, OHIO

★ Junction

JUNCTION, OHIO
1½ miles south, ½ mile east of
Junction 111 and 637

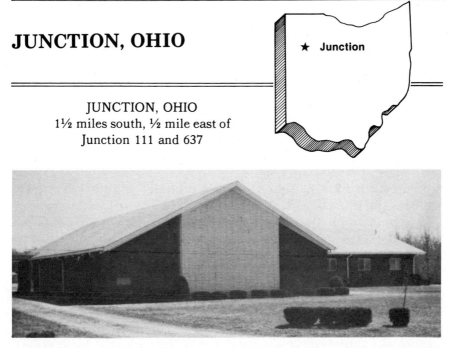

Early development of the church at Junction, Ohio, was partially due to the activities of the Dotterer family. In 1849, Christopher Henry Dotterer and his family came to America from their native Baden, Germany. They lived in Morrow County, Ohio, but later moved to Paulding County in 1851.

In 1864, Christopher Henry Dotterer returned to Germany for a visit and encountered representatives of Samuel Froehlich's Evangelical Baptist faith who witnessed the truth of God's Word to him. On parting, he was advised that churches of this faith existed in his home area at Archbold, Ohio, and Leo, Indiana.

When he returned home, he asked his son, Henry C. Dotterer, twenty-eight, to accompany him to church services at Leo, Indiana. Henry complied, and it was here that they became familiar with the doctrinal basics of the church. Soon both men united with this faith.

Christopher and Henry Dotterer later bore witness to their faith as they visited with friends and neighbors of German descent in the Junction area. One day Henry Dotterer was at a feed mill in Defiance, Ohio, when he overheard two men discussing some of their church's problems. Henry approached the men, talked to them, and invited them to his church in Junction. Both men came to visit the church, although one of them never returned. The other man, Gottlieb Wahl, returned again and brought his family. In time, Wahl, a former Methodist, and his entire family joined the church.

One time Charlie Dotterer, a brother to Henry, met Joseph Reineck of Fremont, Ohio, at the livery stable in Defiance. Charlie arranged for Joseph to work on the farm of his brother Henry. In this way Joseph Reineck was introduced to the faith. He formerly was a Lutheran, and his wife, a Catholic. He later became a minister in 1905.

The church is named after the hamlet "Junction," a name derived from its location at the junction of the old Miami and Erie Canal with the Wabash Canal. These were barge canals and were formerly traveled by flat boats drawn by mules on a side of the bank.

The church is located approximately eight miles northeast of Paulding or eleven miles southwest of Defiance. It sits one-half mile west of the former aqueduct over the Miami and Erie Canal and the Flat Rock Creek, a historic spot.

Traditionally, the members in this church have been farmers or retired farmers. In later years, however, economic reality has fostered more non-farming occupations.

Henry C. Dotterer was the first minister of the church, being installed in 1870. He was later ordained as the first Elder in 1893 and served until his death in 1905. A very interesting story is told about Elder Dotterer. Back in the 1890's, land speculation was sweeping the Midwest. Some of the brethren were involving themselves in undue speculation. The practice multiplied to the extent that, in approximately 1902, the Elders of the church convened a meeting in Morton, Illinois, to address the problem.

At this meeting, a number of brothers arose and contritely acknowledged their involvement. There was a lengthy discussion. Finally, Elder Henry Dotterer arose and in his soft, gentle manner said:[77]

> Brothers, I also bought some land, and I will explain how I went about it. I had a small farm, and my boys were growing up, so I felt if I could buy a piece of land next to my farm, I would have work for them and be able to keep them at home. Now, this is the way I went at it. I took my concern to God in prayer and asked the Lord for a token if it could be His will that I buy that land. I prayed that when I go out on the road, the owner of that land should meet me on the road. So, when I went on the road, here came the owner of that land. We spoke with each other about me buying his land. We came to a peaceful agreement and made a satisfactory deal.

He then sat down. It was stated from the podium that the other brothers who bought and sold land should compare their dealings with those of Henry Dotterer.

The second resident Elder of the Junction church was Elias Dotterer (1881-1952). He served from 1923 until his death on February 14, 1952.

After nearly three decades, the Junction brethren built their first house of worship in 1892. It was extensively remodeled in 1913. This structure, with additions and proper maintenance over the years, served the congregation until June 9, 1968, when services were held in a new brick structure for the first time.

THE OLD AND THE NEW

Our old church house, it stands no more
high upon the hill;
but in our hearts its memory
lingers with us still.

In it we spent many days,
some happy, sad, and blessed;
we recall the days of baptisms,
of loved ones laid to rest.

In it many passed their life,
and others there were wed;
and some their hearts to Christ did give,
and unto sin were dead.

For our new church we are
so thankful to the Lord,
and may we always worship there
in love and one accord.

Oh may our children herein find
the things that we have found,
and may the love and grace of God
forever here abound.

Carolyn Manz

During 1911 to 1915, a number of families came to Paulding County from Illinois. They settled in the southern part of the county and traveled by horse and buggy to Junction for worship services. In 1915, these people purchased a church in their area, and this was the beginning of the Latty, Ohio, church. These two churches have maintained close ties; two Latty Elders, George Sinn and Loren Stoller, have also served the Junction congregation.

PULASKI, IOWA

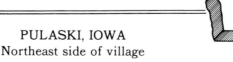

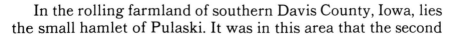

PULASKI, IOWA
Northeast side of village

In the rolling farmland of southern Davis County, Iowa, lies the small hamlet of Pulaski. It was in this area that the second

Apostolic Christian Church was formed in Iowa during the winter of 1864-1865.

At this time, the indefatigable John Kreinbill, a minister of the Apostolic Christian Church in Peoria, Illinois, and one who traveled widely on behalf of the church, came to Davis County. Why he came to such a remote place is not known for certain. He may have had relatives in Iowa because a Kreinbill family lived in Lee County in the late 1860's.[78] Or, more probably, he had developed quite a reputation both as a minister and as a proselytizer among people of Amish and Mennonite extraction. He quickly responded when asked to visit the area.

When he came to Pulaski, he very likely traveled by train to Ottumwa. He walked from Ottumwa to Pulaski, a distance of approximately twenty-five miles.

Ten years earlier an Amish settlement had taken root in the area, and a church was eventually established. By 1864, the unity of this group was apparently on shaky ground. It was into this environment that John Kreinbill came. He held several meetings with them. He presented a powerful message on the need for every soul to repent before God and experience a life-changing conversion. Melvin Guingerich, in *The Mennonites in Iowa,* indicates that the chief point emphasized by Kreinbill was the inadequacy of any form of baptism aside from immersion.[79] As the Amish practiced pouring instead of immersion, it was possible for him to make an attractive appeal in this community.

179

Kreinbill's appeal was so strong that one-half the congregation, including their two ministers, Christian Kropf and Christian Sharp (who had previously been chosen by lot), left the Amish Church. The events associated with the cleavage that occurred in Pulaski are a virtual carbon copy of the events which occurred in 1847 among the Amish in Lewis County, New York, when young Benedict Weyeneth won over a number of Amish Mennonites by emphasizing the "new birth" experience and baptism by immersion.

Those who left the Amish Church formed the second Apostolic Christian Church in Iowa. They were referred to as the "New Lighters" by their neighbors, and especially by the remaining Amish, because they presented a "new light" on the Scriptures. Christian Kropf and Daniel Kinsinger were among the new group's first ministers. In time Kropf was chosen as Elder, but later relinquished this duty.[80] He died in 1905 at age eighty.

The new group built a church sixty rods south of the Amish Church on the west side of the road sometime between 1865 and 1870. This new church was built on land donated by Daniel Kinsinger.

Those who formed the new church had a deeply-rooted Amish background. Among the first of the Amish to settle in Davis County was the Peter Miller family from Ontario, Canada, who purchased land in 1854. He is thought to be an ancestor of the Miller family who had been a part of the Pulaski church for several years. Other Amish families who settled in Davis County in the 1850's included the Waglers, Conrads, Kinsingers, and Kropfs. These are family names that later appeared in the Apostolic Christian Church.

The decade of 1880 saw the church grow to its peak of eighty members. Several families had moved to the area and membership increased. Among them were the John Stollers from Switzerland; the Chris Waglers from Gridley, Kansas; the Gottlieb Maibachs from Sardis, Ohio; and the Fred Wuthrichs from Bern, Switzerland.

In 1904 the old country church—now nearly thirty-five years old—was moved to the southeastern edge of Pulaski on land donated by John Wuthrich. The church sat on a high cement block foundation. The assembly room was on the second floor; a dining room was in the "basement" section. Sunday School was held in the dining room.

At the church in town, they sometimes met together amid anxiety during the time of World War I when the United States was at war with Germany. Because most of the membership spoke the German language and was still largely accustomed to German ways (that appeared peculiar to civil authorities), their loyalty to the flag and the country was somewhat suspect.

Early one Sunday morning the brethren came to church and noticed a large United States flag hanging down from a horizontal pole attached perpendicular to the church by the front door. When the members came from the horse barn they had to either walk around the flag or under it. Authorities watched to see if they walked under it (which for some unknown reason would prove loyalty to the flag) or around it (which would indicate disloyalty). Fortunately, everyone walked under the flag and no incident developed.

So intimidated were these humble brethren by this test of their patriotism that no one dared remove the flag, and it remained in place for ten or twelve years, tattered and torn. Finally, Albert Wuthrich took it down.

In 1957, a new church was built in Pulaski on property donated by Keith Stevig. It is interesting to note that the Pulaski congregation has a tradition of brothers donating the lots where their churches have been built. All three of their churches sat on land donated to the assembly.

The Pulaski church's second resident Elder was Gottlieb Maibach who was ordained in 1895. He and his family had moved to Pulaski after living in Mansfield, Ohio, and Tremont, Illinois. He lived in Sardis, Ohio, as a boy and was converted there as a young adult.

The Pulaski church, for no significant reason, has a history of ministers moving on to other locations. Gottlieb Maibach moved to Bay City, Michigan, in 1905; Chris Wagler to Fairbury, Illinois, in 1919; Mike Miller to Winthrop, Minnesota, in 1924; Guy Miller to Gridley, Illinois, in 1936; and William Funk to Garden Grove, Iowa, in 1967 (although he continued to minister here until the early 1970's).

The membership of the church eventually declined over the years to approximately thirty-five. In 1980 it had a total of thirty-four. Albert Wuthrich served alone in the ministry from 1936 to 1952. He retired from the ministry in 1980.

In 1942, Noah Schrock of Oakville, Iowa, who served as Elder at Pulaski for many years, preached a funeral service at Pulaski. One of the men from the community was impressed with his remarks and told Albert Wuthrich he would like to hear him (Schrock) preach again. The next time Schrock came to Pulaski, the people of the community were notified beforehand. With appropriate permission, minister Albert Wuthrich placed signs in store windows and announced the upcoming services on the telephone party lines. The service, held on a night during the week, had an overflow crowd. Songs were sung from the *Heftli* hymnal, and the many townspeople and Mennonites in attendance sang vigorously.

Later, Schrock and Wuthrich went to visit many of those people to discuss their reaction to the service and their overall faith and belief. Although many liked the sermon and the church service, they did not want to leave their own churches where they felt they were already well established.

ROCKVILLE, CONNECTICUT

ROCKVILLE, CONNECTICUT
34 Middle Butcher Road

The year 1868 was a memorable one for Apostolic Christians who lived in the fertile Connecticut River Valley. It was during this year that a few members of Samuel Froehlich's Evangelical Baptist Church (in Switzerland) began to settle in and around Rockville, Connecticut. On the national scene many things were taking place as well. The Civil War had ended. Jefferson Davis, former President of the Confederacy, was charged with treason on March 26. Ulysses S. Grant won the Presidency by an electoral landslide on

November 3. On August 23, Louisa May Alcott had published *Little Women*. A sense of optimism seemed to exist in the nation.

The floodtide of emigration, which reached over 400,000 persons a year by 1854 (but declined to approximately 98,000 annually during the Civil War), was again on the upswing in 1869 with just under 400,000 coming to America. Among those who came in 1869 was Mrs. John Kloter of canton Zurich, Switzerland, who emigrated following the death of her husband. She was a member of the Evangelical Baptist Church. "Mother Kloter," as she was referred to, was accompanied to America by her two sons (Gottlieb and Henry) and three or four daughters (including Rose, Minnie, and Anna). They lived briefly at Warehouse Point, Connecticut, where they worked as silk weavers, an occupation they had pursued in their native Switzerland.

Mrs. John Kloter kept in touch with minister Heinrich Arlt in Williamsburg (Brooklyn) and visited there several times. It was at Williamsburg, approximately 125 miles away, that Rose and Minnie were taken into the church.

Fredrich Ludwig came to the area from Baden, Germany, in 1870. Two years later his father, Nicholas Ludwig, followed along with his wife and children (three sons and four daughters). After stopping in Williamsburg and meeting with brethren, the Nicholas Ludwig family traveled northeast to Rockville to be met by their son, Fredrich. Soon after their arrival, Fredrich showed them where a few members of the church lived. One of the first members they met was "Mother Kloter" who resided with her daughter, Anna.

Every Sunday these few members, along with their friends, met at either the Kloter or Ludwig homes for fellowship and hymn singing. In 1873, Nicholas Ludwig was placed into the ministry. Ludwig was a man of large physical stature but had a quiet nature and was loved by everyone.

The William Pfunder family arrived here in 1873 following some anxious moments on the Atlantic Ocean. Their ship was wrecked at sea, and they arrived in New York with virtually no possessions. Initially, they stayed with the Ludwig family before purchasing a home of their own.

Eventually, the group contacted Elder Peter Virkler of Lewis County, New York, and in 1875 he came to serve as the Elder of the new Rockville congregation.

William Heintz, a native of Alsace-Lorraine, came to America in 1881 and settled in Rockville. He was made a minister, much to the delight of Nicholas Ludwig who now had a co-worker in the ministry. The church met on Sundays and twice during the week, one evening at the Kloter's, the other at the Ludwig's. Nicholas Ludwig served in the ministry until his death in 1892, and William Heintz served until he died in 1924.

During the initial stages of the Rockville church, nearly all members were factory workers. Then, in 1886 Jacob Lanz, with five sons and two daughters, came from canton Bern, Switzerland. They were the first farmers to be a part of the church group. Also during this time, several young unmarried people came to the area. In time, they were converted, became married, and gave a numerical boost to the congregation.

To accommodate the growing flock, William Heintz had a wall removed to make a larger room, and church services were held in his home. This unselfish act took place in approximately 1888. Eventually this meeting room became inadequate, and the first church building was constructed in 1891 on "Fox Hill" in Rockville. It seated approximately one hundred persons.

Many families subsequently began moving into the general area. Among those who came during 1895 to 1905 were the families of Adolph and Gottfried Bahler (who had first settled in Fairbury, Illinois), Rudolph Gottier, Fred Hoffman, Fred Gerber, Christian Gerber, Sam Kupferschmid, Fred Luginbuhl, and Marianna Wuthrich.

It was not long before the little church building on Fox Hill became too small. Also, because so many members began to settle in the Ellington area, the church here lost its central location. Alfred Schneider, a minister who came to this country in 1893, donated a tract of land on Orchard Street to build a new church. It was completed in 1899. Membership at this time was approximately 150.

On Easter night, April 20, 1908, this new church was destroyed by fire. It was immediately rebuilt on the same location. While construction was in progress, services were held in the homes of John Lanz and Alfred Kupferschmid. During this time, Frank Ludwig and his daughter, Marie, taught Sunday School in the Cogswell School.

Only forty-five years later a new church—costing $200,000—was built at 34 Middle Butcher Road in Ellington, Connecticut. In 1961, educational facilities were added at a cost of $50,000. By 1980 membership had reached 365 with 300 Sunday School students.[81]

Elder Joseph Bella, a single man who traveled extensively assisting the early churches in establishing themselves, presided for many years over the congregation. Age finally forced him to relinquish his duties. In 1895 or 1896, Urs Isch (born in 1831) was ordained as Elder. He, along with Alfred Schneider (both ministers) had come to Rockville in 1893 from Switzerland (Isch was a native of Solothurn). Ill health befell Isch soon after he was ordained. He suffered from dropsy and died on May 6, 1898. His short tenure as Elder saddened the congregation, and they were disappointed that their first resident Elder could only serve for a few years. Alpheus Virkler of Croghan, New York, conducted his funeral service. Isch was the first to be buried in a church-acquired burial plot known as "God's Acre." After he was buried, a weeping willow tree was planted near his grave.

John Trittenbach (1843-1917) became the church's second resident Elder. He had been ordained as Elder while still living in Switzerland. When Elder Henry Geistlich (who in 1866 visited all the American churches) died in 1884, Trittenbach had been ordained as Elder at Zurich. He served with Jean Studer until the latter's death in 1894 and then served alone until his departure for America in 1898.[82]

John Trittenbach first lived in West Hoboken, New Jersey, and served as Elder of the West Hoboken (now Union City) congregation. In 1903, he took the responsibility of Elder at Rockville and moved there in 1904.[83]

Trittenbach was remembered by Clara Merz, Castorland, New York, as "a very neat person. He wore a small tie, and had a beard." He was regarded as one who had a deep spiritual intellect. He died unexpectedly on February 9, 1917. He had just finished eating his noon meal on that day when he suddenly slumped over and passed away. His death was a severe blow to the congregation.

Christian Gerber was ordained as the third resident Elder in 1917 and served until 1932. He is not to be confused with Christian Gerber, a minister who associated with Samuel Froehlich at Langnau, Switzerland, in the decade of 1830, or with Christian Gerber who served as Elder at Fairbury, Illinois (and at the South Side church).

From 1932 to 1943, Ernest Graf, Sr., of Akron, Ohio, served as the Elder at Rockville.

On June 6, 1943, John Bahler, forty-two, was selected as the fourth resident Shepherd. He was born March 27, 1901. He had previously entered the ministry in 1938. His son, Corbin Bahler, was ordained Elder September 26, 1981.

The church in the Rockville-Ellington area has had a wide impact on the community. Its image as a "separated" and "peculiar" people was underscored by a newspaper article which appeared in the *Hartford Times* in January, 1970. Written by Rudy Jordan and entitled "Swiss Youth Reject Instant Pleasures," it contrasted the sanctified life led by young members of the church with many young people of society who were involved in drugs, instant pleasure, and rebellion against authority.

Minister Roy Luginbuhl was quoted, "There's no way for a person outside the church to understand what happens to our young converts. There's a change in attitudes, moderation in hairdo and voice, and a change in words that come out of the mouth. Cursing is gone and smoking is over."

The article explained that about twenty percent of the six hundred students at Ellington High School are "Swiss." Principal Gordon C. Getchell said, "They are hard-working, industrious kids and no discipline problem." An English teacher said, "We have no discipline problems here, and I think it's because of the influence of the Swiss students and their respect for authority."

Jordan gave an accurate description of the congregation's sanctuary worship service: "Members enter the church on Sunday morning addressing each other as 'Brother' or 'Sister.' The women sit in pews on the right side of the church, and men sit on the left. Every member greets the person sitting next to him (or her) with the holy kiss or kiss of love, as instructed by Paul." (Author's note: Men kiss men, and women kiss women.)

The Rockville congregation's first church building was built in 1891 on Fox Hill. In 1983 the structure was still used as a residence.

The church at Rockville, and nationally, enjoys a modern miracle each time a young person repents, is converted, and is humbly willing to reject and renounce the hedonistic pleasures of society, and in the spirit of self-denial seek after righteousness as outlined by Christ and the Apostles.

Elder John Bahler made the following points concerning the history of the Rockville congregation:[84]

1. In the early years of the church, if visitors were present (in the winter), church services would be held on Saturday afternoon as well as on Sunday.

2. Mid-week services were discontinued during World War I due to gas rationing.

3. Early teaching in the Sunday School included instruction in the German language as well as music. When public schools began teaching music, this was discontinued in the Sunday School.

4. A man named Rudolph Zueg of New York City, who worked for a steamship company, used to welcome many church people as they arrived from Europe.

5. In 1925, the Rockville congregation had a total of forty-six converts.

6. At certain places in Switzerland, people used to refer to Evangelical Baptists as *Stundlers* because they spent so much time in church on Sunday.

Church records indicate that up to May 6, 1979, 421 baptisms had taken place at Rockville.

WEST BEND, IOWA

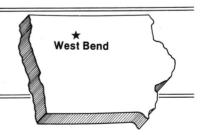

WEST BEND, IOWA
One mile east

On a vast prairie in northwestern Iowa a few miles east of the Des Moines River lies the small village of West Bend. A mile east stands the Apostolic Christian Church. This church, situated some forty miles north of Fort Dodge, stands "alone" when viewed in a denominational perspective with the nearest churches located at Lester, Iowa, 125 miles west, and Elgin,

Iowa, 165 miles east. Despite being somewhat "remote" in location, it, nonetheless, has grown and prospered over the years. In 1980, the West Bend, Iowa, congregation numbered approximately 170 members and 130 families.[85]

It was farmland that drew early settlers to the area. The soil was cheap in price and offered opportunity to those willing to submit to long hours of backbreaking labor and effort.

Beginning in 1868, several families of the Apostolic Christian faith accepted the challenges of hardship and uncertainty and set out on the long and arduous journey that took them to Kossuth and Palo Alto Counties in Iowa. Some of these early brethren came from Elgin, Iowa. Others came from various places including Ohio and Illinois. A few came from Switzerland. After they arrived and settled in their primitive places of abode, they quickly took steps to engage in the worship of God. As they gathered together for this purpose, they began the third Apostolic Christian Church west of the Mississippi River.

Aside from the opportunity to acquire land and to work out of doors, rural life in those early days offered very few of life's niceties. Everyday living was indeed rugged. In the area around West Bend, there were few trees except along waterways. Prairie grass blanketed the area, often growing over eight feet tall. Many families lived in log cabins, others in sod houses. The latter were made by stacking squares of sod for walls. Roofs were made of small willow limbs tied together with prairie grass. There were dirt floors in most of these "homes." Some families, if they were fortunate, had an animal skin for a rug. Open fireplaces were used both for cooking and warmth. There was little occasion, or adequate time, to seek to be "fancy" in those days.

Typical of pioneers who endured the rugged lifestyle of a century ago was the family of John Ulrich Banwart, father of Joel A. Banwart who later served as Elder at West Bend, and grandfather of Paul Banwart, Sr., also an Elder.

Born July 20, 1833, John Ulrich Banwart and his wife, Anna Mary Yost Banwart, departed for America from their native Bern, Switzerland, on September 4, 1852. After living in Ohio, Wisconsin, Illinois, and Elgin, Iowa, they embarked for West Bend in June, 1869, along with their nine children. They started out with three covered wagons. Two were pulled by yokes of oxen, and the third by a team of horses.

This family was schooled in pioneer life and had suffered bitter hardships. Foremost was the loss of their firstborn son, John U., who died of scarlet fever as they left Illinois. He was laid to rest in a little grave along the roadside. Such grief was probably a heavier burden than any difficult and hard work the frontier required of them.

Their three-wagon caravan arrived in Kossuth County near West Bend a number of days after departing Elgin. During the latter stages of 1869, the Banwart family bought eighty acres of land for $300, a mere $3.75 per acre. The first year they lived in a slab house. The next year they built a sod house. Finally, in 1873 they built a frame house.

The early families of West Bend met in homes for worship services. By 1878, growth required a permanent facility. John Ulrich Banwart and his wife donated a lot in Garfield Township (Kossuth County), and a small frame church was built for $600. Garfield Township was named for President James A. Garfield.

The first church consisted of a sanctuary and a kitchen. Near the west edge of the lot was a row of stables for the horses which drew the wagons, buggies, and sleds (in the winter) to church. Some of the men and boys arrived for church on horseback. It was not uncommon to see some men attend church in denim overalls. The women and some friends wore triangular head coverings of fine black·wool all year long.

During these early days two sisters of the church, Mary Zaugg and Louisa Habeger, lived in the church for a time. They used a small attic room above the kitchen for their bedroom. They also had a garden and a horse and buggy.

It is believed that John Gerber was the first minister of the church. John Anliker was later persuaded to come to West Bend (from Ohio) to serve as a minister. He was given a small plot of land as an inducement to come to the area. Eventually, he was ordained an Elder, but his tenure was short.

Among the first church families in the West Bend area and the year they purchased land in Kossuth County were:

Eugene Beechen	1872
Fred Minger	1875
John U. Banwart	1875
Henry Rinehart	1878
Christ Moser	1878
Jake Moser	1880
John Ramsier	1880
John Gerber	1882
John Isch	1883
Peter Habeger	1883
Christ Schupbach	1885
David Zimmerman	1885
John Anliker	1888
Christian Luthi	1888
Christ Streit	1892
August Traub	1893
Samuel Braker	1893
Frank Frieden	1894
Ida Messner	1897
Joshua Braker	1897
Theophil Zaugg	1899
Emil Bruellman	1899
Nicholas Marti	1901
Mathias Gerber	1902
Joseph Schneider	1908
August Fisher	1909
Jacob Wirtz	1911
Awalt Jurgens	1913
Albert Keller	1914
Louis Schafer	1917

It is likely that some of these families lived in the area for several years before they engaged in buying land.

Several men bought land in adjoining Palo Alto County: John Zaugg, Benjamin Rinehard, Benedict Mathys, Henry Fehr, Fred Falb, and John Benninger. Also the Schlupp, Ruch, Lanz, and Metzger families became land owners.

In 1896 a new auditorium (40 feet by 40 feet) was built, and the old one was used for a dining room and Sunday School.

The noon lunch at that time consisted of homemade bread and homemade butter. Coffee was made in a large wash boiler used exclusively for this purpose. The noon hour fellowship on Sunday (as now) was a time of friendliness and good will. The mode of travel was much slower than today, and people did not see each other as often, so the opportunity to visit at church was especially precious to them. In the Swiss language they referred to the noon lunch at church as *Tsimmies*.

The practice of serving coffee and lunch at church saw Apostolic Christians in the area referred to as the *Coffee Dutch*. Also, because they practiced baptism by immersion, they were called *Dunkards*.

In 1902, several families moved to Lamar, Missouri, where they were able to purchase cheaper land. In 1903, one family moved to Oklahoma, one to Morris, Minnesota, and another to Oakville, Iowa. The pioneer spirit still ran deep at this time, and many brethren were not hesitant to seek supposedly greener economic pastures in other areas. This was a severe blow to the West Bend congregation, and a few thought the church might eventually become extinct.

Instead, the church again began to grow. By 1919, a 10-foot by 40-foot addition was added to the existing building and used for a hallway and cloakroom. In 1947, a major remodeling of the church took place. In 1954, a Sunday School addition was made.

A building fund was established in 1956 to generate funds for any future expansion plans that might unfold. In the fall of 1964, many Sunday School students, their teachers, and other adults spent several Saturdays (and other days) picking up fallen corn in fields owned by members and friends. The corn was shelled and sold for $1,364—a tidy sum for the building fund.

In 1965, a new church was constructed on a one and one-half-acre plot donated by Elder Paul Banwart. His grandfather, John Ulrich Banwart, had donated land for the first church eighty-seven years earlier. The new building was built on land adjacent to the site of the old church. The old church was razed and the area landscaped. First services were held in the new building on April 17, 1966. The structure, comprising 14,000 square feet, cost $250,000.

Joel Alexander Banwart (who was always referred to as Joe A. Banwart) became the second resident Elder at West Bend. He was born June 19, 1864, in a log cabin at Elgin, Iowa, one of ten children born to John Ulrich and Anna Mary Yost Banwart, pioneers of the West Bend church. He was converted in 1883 at age nineteen and entered the ministry on his thirtieth birthday in 1894. He later became an Elder for a short time.

He married Mary Mathys of Elgin, Iowa, on April 29, 1888, and this union bore ten children. He preached in both the German and English languages. He enjoyed traveling and was known far and wide as "the old man with the beard." He kept his beard until past eighty when cataract surgery required it be shaved. He never grew it again. He died April 15, 1951.

His son, Paul Banwart, Sr., born in 1890, was ordained as Elder in 1949 and served until 1970 (at age eighty) when he retired from active duty.

Wayne Fehr was ordained as Elder in 1983.

SOUTH SIDE
(South of Fairbury, Illinois)

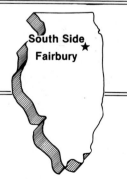

SOUTH SIDE
Three and one-half miles
southeast of Fairbury, Illinois

Late 1860's—1949

Mass production of the automobile, together with advanced technologies in agriculture, were among the factors that sealed the doom of the old "South Side" church three and one-half miles southeast of Fairbury, Illinois. Improved farming practices resulted in larger farms and fewer farmers. The automobile allowed faster travel and shorter travel time. Consequently, the need for a rural church located so close to

Fairbury and Forrest no longer existed, and in 1949 the structure was closed down.

The final worship service was held December 11, 1949. It was conducted by Herman Hueni of Bremen, Indiana, who attended the church as a boy. The last time Scriptures were opened and meditated upon marked seventy-four years of worship services at this tranquil spot deep in the heart of the Illinois prairie. An overflow crowd commemorated this sad occasion.

In 1950, the church buildings and property were dismantled and sold. The old church, where the spiritual hopes of many persons were nurtured for over seven decades, is remembered only by a small monument alongside the highway fence adjacent to the spot where the church formerly stood. The area, which today is visited only by the rain, sun, snow, wind, and seasonal whims of nature, is brought to mind by a marker which reads:

The history of the South Side church is tied directly to its "twin"—the country church that formerly existed north of Forrest called "North Side." Early settlers came first to the area north of Forrest, and services were held there as early as 1864.

In time, land south of Fairbury and Forrest was also occupied by Apostolic Christians. Many of these settlers went to church at the North Side, a long journey in those days. The eight- or ten-mile drive, made with horse and buggy, was often difficult and inconvenient. As a result, the many farmers located southeast of Fairbury decided to organize their own fellowship.

In the late 1860's and early 1870's, many families of Swiss and German descent—with an Evangelical Baptist background—began to inhabit southeastern Livingston County, Illinois, particularly in Indian Grove Township. Familiar names began to appear: Bittner, Farney, Gerber, Hari, Hartman, Nussbaum, Roth, Slagel, Sohn, Sommer, Steffen, Wenger, Yoder, Ziegenhorn, Zimmerman, and others.

Private homes served as the sanctuary for their early church meetings. Indian Creek was a convenient place to baptize converts.

Expanded membership eventually required a church building to house worship services and fellowship. The group officially incorporated in 1875 with Andrew Roth, Ulrich Steffen, and Rudolph Leuthold (Elder at the North Side) named as trustees.

Many brethren offered sites on which to locate the new building. Finally, a suitable choice was made in Section 36, Indian Grove Township. Joseph Hosterwitz donated the north half of the plot and Peter Sommer the south half. Sommer also donated land for a church cemetery.

The old "South Side" church building. Notice the stables in the background.

The original ministers of the South Side church were Rudolph Leuthold, Peter Sommer, Nick Wanner, Henry Ziegenhorn, and Christian Gerber.

Rudolph Leuthold, who served as Elder of the North Side church when the South Side was being formed, became the latter's first Elder. He served until shortly after the new church was built in 1875. It was only a few months until John Georg Steidinger emigrated from Germany and assumed the duties of Elder, both at the South Side and at Fairbury. Steidinger served as Elder for several years until Christian Gerber, his co-laborer in the ministry, took over as Elder, thus relieving Steidinger from making the long and tiring horse-and-buggy trips all the way from Fairbury. Gerber became the first and only resident Elder of the South Side church.

When Gerber died in 1910, Elder Jacob Honegger from the North Side and Elder Martin Steidinger of the Fairbury church served the South Side congregation. Honegger died in 1920 leaving Steidinger as the sole Elder. Steidinger continued in this capacity until withdrawing from the church on February 7, 1932, along with a sizable portion of other members.

Emil Schubert of Peoria became Elder of all three churches—North Side, South Side, and Fairbury—following the departure of Martin Steidinger. This was a time of great spiritual upheaval, and the overall schismatic environment caused a burden on the hearts of members and friends alike. It was a time, however, of "troubled waters," and soon more than seventy persons in the area sought the Lord in repentance. In view of this, it became obvious that a "local" Elder was badly needed. To meet this need, Peter Bach was installed as Elder at the North Side on November 20, 1932. He had jurisdiction over all three churches until he died on May 5, 1946.

When Peter Bach died, the three churches were left Shepherdless. Elders David Mangold, Roanoke, Illinois, and Noah Schrock, Oakville, Iowa, took the oversight of the congregations until Henry Kilgus and Joshua Broquard were ordained Elders on December 24, 1946. Henry Kilgus, Elder at the North Side, served the South Side until it closed in 1949.

The church gathering at the rural South Side location represented the best of farm life in an era that is long past. Its history clearly reflects a lifestyle that prevailed during the initial stages of the twentieth century. The church has been fortunate that the late Ben Nussbaum of Fairbury, who attended the South Side church as a youth, wrote a booklet entitled *South Side Church History* which graphically describes church life many years ago.

In describing the interior of the church, which included kerosene lamps suspended from the ceiling, as well as four-foot-high wainscoating around the bottom part of the walls, Nussbaum tells of the church benches:[86]

> The bench seats were not the most comfortable but were probably on a par with any of that era. The seat part was a wide board with a sturdy backrest, all of which was very solidly built. The carpenters that built the church were probably responsible for these seats. At any rate, they were not factory-built pews. The varnish used on the pews at that time lacked the quality of today's. I recall that in very hot weather it would become quite tacky and stick to clothing. It was once rumored that a man, after sitting for a considerable time, tore the seat from his trousers upon rising to his feet.

Nussbaum richly remembers "buggies" being driven to church in the early days:[87]

> I enjoy recalling those Sunday panoramas of converging vehicles—always a dozen or more in view—as they navigated the straight roads which bounded our flat, square-mile sections. They reminded one of small sailboats tacking and running to take advantage of the ninety degree roads. Dust clouds, during the dry season, revealed the positions of those intermittently hidden by hedge or crop. Remember how the horses would snort and whinny as they rhythmically clopped along the crusted roads? Or the muffled crunch of hoof and wheel on bitterly-cold snow? Even the thought of greasy mud squishing and splattering against the buckboard or clinging to the spokes brings forth a nostalgic sigh.
>
> Some of these teams were beautiful to behold: matched drivers that pranced ever so briskly; well-curried coats and oiled harnesses that glistened in the sunlight; taut leather traces hooked to doubletrees that scarcely wavered as the stylish black carriages wheeled majestically alongside the church "steps." Warm harness oil and the steam from the horses, both a result of their exertion, combined to permeate the surrounding air with a unique aroma that can only be recalled by those whose nostrils have sensed it firsthand. Occasionally a frisky colt, too young to leave at home, trailed closely behind. After the team was tied, the barn doors would be re-opened, permitting it to nurse or frolic amid the vehicles in the yard.

A very vivid account of the family leaving for church on Sunday morning is given:[88]

Hay and grain were put aboard the vehicle and fed to the horses at noon. Blankets and foot warmers helped ward off the bitter cold when winter was severe. Those warmers made of soapstone seemed to retain heat longer—no one remembers why. At Mother's urging, one of the girls would fill a jug with milk; a last minute ritual on those weeks that we were to assist with the "serving." This was the signal that starting time was fast approaching; awaiting only that final word from Father—"Giddap."

During one cold Wednesday morning in the winter of approximately 1930, Walter Steffen, who later served as minister for fifteen years, came to the church to fire the furnace for the upcoming afternoon church service. As he completed his task, he approached the door to leave. On opening the door, the scent of smoke stopped him. He soon realized the wainscoating surrounding the chimney in the dining room was on fire. Quickly he rushed to the basement to get a shovel and two pails of water. With the shovel he pried the smoldering boards away from the chimney, then threw water on the exposed area. His gallant efforts stopped the fire and saved the church. If he had left the premises only a few minutes earlier, the church might have burned to the ground.

When deaths occurred among the brethren, burial was made in the church cemetery located one-half mile south and one-half mile west of the church. At first all interments were in a single row and side by side irrespective of any family relationship. This practice was changed in 1910. Interestingly, when a body was brought to the cemetery for burial, the casket was re-opened for the song and prayer that followed.

In the 1890's, German language classes were held at the church. The idea of preserving the language of their native country ran deep among the brethren at the South Side, as well as among the brotherhood nationally. Many young men and women attended German school during the winter months. Robert Bahler was one of the instructors. By 1900, classes were no longer held.

The members and friends who comprised the South Side church enjoyed an era of life that people of today's modern, complex, industrialized society will never know too much about: continuous hard work, simplicity, separation from the mainstream of society, quietness, and a rich closeness to the soil.

"Preach the word; be instant in season, out of season; reprove, rebuke, exhort with all longsuffering and doctrine."

By 1870 many Apostolic Christian Churches had been formed in America. Even so, significant growth was still taking place, and the three decades from 1870-1900 would usher in the establishment of twenty-one more congregations in Ohio, Illinois, Missouri, Oklahoma, Kansas, Arkansas, Michigan, and Oregon. The preaching of God's Word, as taken directly from Scriptures, helped to ignite a flame that spread swiftly across the prairies for the eternal benefit of many hearers who found the grace to accept the divine messages of repentance, conversion, and the hope of eternal life.

PRINCEVILLE, ILLINOIS

PRINCEVILLE, ILLINOIS
710 East Main Street

The church at Princeville is tied directly to the congregation formerly located at the northern edge of Akron Township in Peoria County. For many years it was referred to as the "Streitmatter Prairie" church, and reference to the congregation as "Princeville" did not occur to any great extent until the church's second building was built in Princeville during 1920-1921.

It is interesting to note that when brethren from visiting churches would visit the prairie church in Akron Township, on returning to their home congregations, they would extend "greetings" from the "Streitmatter Prairie" church. During this era, the giving of greetings (following the morning worship service) was not as prevalent as today because travel was limited by slower modes of transportation.

The family name "Streitmatter" looms significantly in the history of the Princeville congregation. It was only by the most fortuitous of circumstances that this large family came to the area, that they learned of and embraced a new faith, and that eventually a church was born.

In the 1840's Michael and Catherine Streitmatter lived in Hegelberg, Baden, Germany, with their eight children, including six sons. Michael's trade was that of a *nagelschmidt,* or nailsmith, and a mechanic who could do any repairing in wood or iron work. He also made shoes and had many other talents.

In the latter stages of this decade, his sons faced the possibility of serving in the German military, a situation of which Michael did not approve. Consequently, he told his boys if they would help and support him when they arrived in America, he would take them there. They promised to do so, and plans were made to emigrate.

They arrived in America, probably in 1847, and landed in Eden, near Hamburg, about twelve miles southwest of Buffalo, New York. Little did they realize they were situated only about 250 miles from the first Apostolic Christian Church (known then, as well as now, as the Evangelical Baptist Church) that had begun to blossom in Lewis County, New York, during that same year.

Poor economic conditions resulted in Frederick Streitmatter, the eldest son, coming to Princeville in approximately 1849. He first worked for Thomas Black in Section 33,

Akron Township. Sometime later he sent for the remainder of the family.

Prior to leaving New York, Michael Streitmatter had a dream that some calamity might befall them on their westward journey. In his dream, the floor sank and was replaced by water. They traveled by boat on Lakes Erie, Huron, and Michigan, the Illinois and Michigan Canal, and the Illinois River. Their little steamer was accidentally rammed by a larger one near LaSalle, Illinois. The collision knocked a big hole in the smaller boat causing one end to sink. The passengers had to abandon their boat, and many personal possessions were lost. The sinking of the boat tended to vindicate Michael Streitmatter's earlier dream.

The passengers fled to the nearby timber, built fires, and stayed overnight. The next day it rained, and they took shelter in an old log cabin. Eventually, another steamer came along and took them to Peoria. By 1854, Michael Streitmatter had purchased eighty acres of land in Akron Township.

The church at Streitmatter Prairie was organized in 1870. In 1880 the above church was built on land donated by Jacob Streitmatter.

One of Michael's sons, Christian, found employment as a shoemaker in Peoria. It was here he learned of the Apostolic Christian faith. He soon became converted and was baptized at the church which had just recently been established in Peoria.

Christian, enthusiastic and sincere about his "new birth" experience, went and told his brothers about it. Several accepted his message. It was during this time that the flame of faith in the Princeville area was ignited.

It was not until 1870 that the church at Streitmatter Prairie was organized. The Streitmatter family and others who moved to the area held worship services in homes. Benches used during worship were moved to the house of the host family.

The first church building was constructed in 1880 on land donated by Jacob Streitmatter in the southwest corner of Section 3, Akron Township.[1] It was located just east of Christian Streitmatter's home. Located near the church were horse sheds which housed the horses that pulled the buggies to church. A few years after the church was built, Sunday School classes were held in a former schoolhouse across the road.

Christian Streitmatter, who was largely responsible for initiating a church in this area, served as the first minister. Karl Wirth and Louis Herbold were the only other ministers of record prior to 1900. Since then, thirteen ministers have proclaimed God's Word in the Princeville church.

The old country church generated memories that have been passed down through the generations. The physical aspects of the church included open-back benches, plain wooden floors with runners in the aisles, and four coal stoves that were often replenished during the worship service.

The sequence of preparing the noon lunch differed somewhat from today. Whoever served the lunch went to the kitchen prior to the end of the morning sermon to insure that everything was ready. The coffee was poured before the people were seated. When the ladies were ready to serve, someone went to the door of the assembly and announced in German, *Kommt zum essen* (in English, "Come to dinner"). They used white linen tablecloths which had to be ironed with sadirons heated on top of the range.

By the turn of the century, many of the older brethren began moving off their farms and into town. At the same time, many new converts came into the church. As a result of these two trends, the congregation decided to find "a town" in which to build a new church. Princeville was the most logical place. In 1920-1921, a large two-story brick church was built in Princeville at a cost of $60,000. Also, a place for a cemetery was provided in a five-acre plot nearby.

In 1939, and several times later, this church was remodeled and redecorated. Crowded conditions and the fact that several families lived in areas north of Princeville led to the establishment of the Bradford, Illinois, congregation in 1964. Approximately thirty-five families from the Princeville congregation began attending the new Bradford church.

Even so, continued growth at Princeville ultimately resulted in the construction of a new and larger church costing $511,000. Groundbreaking ceremonies took place on May 14, 1968. The first service in the new church was held, appropriately, on Thanksgiving Day, November 27, 1969. Twelve members who were baptized in the country church and also attended the church built in 1920-1921, were able to worship in the new church (their third).

The Streitmatter Prairie and Princeville church never had a resident Elder until 1949—seventy-nine years after it was formally organized—when Silas Leuthold (born September 8, 1891) was ordained. He and his wife, the former Mary Metz, were both born in Forrest, Illinois, and lived there until 1921. In 1928, they moved to a farm north of Peoria after living for a time in South Dakota before their conversion. In 1934, he was placed in the ministry at Peoria, Illinois. In 1937, the Leutholds moved to a farm just south of Princeville and became part of the Princeville church.

In 1937, the church at Princeville enjoyed a large ingathering of thirty-one souls. This was only five years after 1932 when forty souls sought the Lord in repentance.

At the time of the 1970 church dedication, Elder Silas Leuthold wrote, "It is our wish and sincere prayer that this house may ever be a haven where the truth will be proclaimed and sinful man may find eternal hope and salvation." Leuthold's grandparents, Rudolph Leuthold and Jacob Honegger of Forrest, were both Elders.

The congregation was struck by tragedy on September 20, 1965, when minister Lowell Stoller was fatally injured in a traffic accident. He had been placed in the ministry in 1957.

By 1982, David Kieser, ordained January 12, 1972, was serving as the second resident Elder.

Church records indicate that from 1883 to 1976 there had been a total of 437 baptisms—a firm testimony to God's power.

GRIDLEY, ILLINOIS

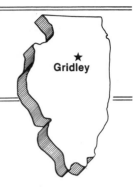

GRIDLEY, ILLINOIS
319 East Seventh Street

During more than 110 years, the congregation at Gridley, Illinois, has multiplied to include over 300 members and 150 families. Its fortunes have been tied closely to the development of the land in the area.

Initially, the area was swampy and covered with prairie grass. Featured on what is now Gridley's north side was a large pond which resulted from a lack of adequate drainage. By the middle of the 1850's, farming methods advanced to the point where the tall prairie grass was subdued and swamps and ponds were drained. Land was cheap, and a vast acreage of prairie awaited development.

The village of Gridley was formed in 1856 soon after it was learned that the Peoria and Oquakwa Railroad (now the Toledo, Peoria, and Western) would locate a station in this vicinity. Accordingly, agents of General Ashael Gridley bought Section 4, Township 26, Range 3 and proceeded to lay out the town.[2] Due to the availability of inexpensive farm land and the coming tide of European emigrants, the area was destined to succeed.

The time between the end of the Civil War and the beginning of World War I saw immigration (nationally) reach high levels, especially during the decades of 1880-1890, 1900-1910, and 1910-1920. The Gridley church benefited greatly by this process.

It was not only those who came directly from Europe that contributed to the growth of the Gridley area. Several settlers who had come to central Illinois during 1830 to 1840 and had previously settled near the Mackinaw River (at a time when it was thought the "prairie" was unproductive and unhealthy) began to move out on the prairie areas such as at Gridley and Waldo Townships. Gridley benefited, particularly, from farmers who moved here from the Congerville (Slabtown) area.

One of the first settlers of the faith to come to the Gridley area was Peter Sommer who, in 1864 or 1866, moved onto a 160-acre farm two miles west of Gridley adjacent to the road that is now U.S. Route 24. He bought land near Gridley because it was flat and offered brighter prospects for production. He was born near Strasbourg, Alsace, France, April 24, 1811, and emigrated to Mackinaw Dells in 1834 when Indians still occupied parts of the territory. He took his claim from the government, built his log cabin, and began to carve himself a home in the wilderness.

In *The History of McLean County,* his brief biography states:[3]

> He is a leading member of the Apostolic Christian Church, and was prominent in the building of the new church.

It is likely that during his first four years in Gridley Township, he and his family traveled to Roanoke to attend Apostolic Christian Church services there.

Peter Sommer was a former Mennonite. He became acquainted with the Apostolic Christian Church while living in the Congerville area. The first time he took his young widowed daughter, Mary Sommer Klopfenstein, to the church at Roanoke, she knew right away "this is the right church."

FAIRBURY, ILLINOIS

FAIRBURY, ILLINOIS
705 North Fourth Street

The church at Fairbury, Illinois, was the third of a cluster of three Apostolic Christian Churches which existed in the southeast portion of Livingston County prior to 1949. The others were the church north of Forrest (the North Side church) and the church southeast of Fairbury (the South Side church). These latter two churches were organized a few years previous to the one at Fairbury.

Some of the members who attended church at the North and South Side congregations eventually began attending the early meetings at Fairbury. They, along with an influx of people from the church in Europe, provided a nucleus from which a new church was born.

The village of Fairbury was organized seventeen years prior to the formation of the Apostolic Christian Church. Fairbury was laid out by Octave Chanute who was later to become a famous American aviation pioneer. Chanute Field in Rantoul, Illinois, a military installation of the U.S. Air Force, is named after him. His associate in the platting of the town was Caleb L. Patton, original owner of the site.[5]

The Kellers and Von Tobels were among the early church families instrumental in organizing the Fairbury congregation. Jacob Von Tobel in 1869 emigrated from Meilen, canton Zurich, Switzerland—the home of Elder Henry Geistlich who visited all the Apostolic Christian Churches in America in 1866—and sent for his fiancee, Katherine Keller, a year or so later. In 1871, they were married by Elder Rudolph Leuthold.

Nicholas Keller immigrated to Woodford County in 1863. He later moved to a farm near Wing, Illinois. Although it is not known for certain what year he moved to Wing, he was farming there by 1869. Ill health eventually forced him to quit farming. In 1874, he moved to Fairbury and became involved in business with his brother, Jacob Keller, and Jacob Von Tobel.

By the time these three men began their business venture, there had been some sporadic church activity in Fairbury. By March, 1874, the congregation had purchased a white frame building—the structure which had belonged to the First Presbyterian Church—for $1,100. It was located at 207 West Walnut Street. The brethren at that time might have been hard-pressed financially because they did not pay cash in full for the church building. Rather, they put $400 down and agreed to pay a total of $700 over a three-year period at eight percent interest (to be paid annually). The mortgage was signed by Jacob Keller, Gilgian Stoller, Jacob Von Tobel, Gottfried Eggli, and Nicholas and Anna Keller.

Jacob Von Tobel and Nicholas Keller very likely served as the first ministers at Fairbury. John Georg Steidinger came to Fairbury in 1875 when he was fifty years old and became the first Elder. He also had charge over the South Side congregation but eventually relinquished that duty to Christian Gerber. Steidinger was a native of Germany and was the father of Martin Steidinger who also served as Elder for a time at Fairbury and the South Side.

In 1884, a small house and lot adjacent to the church were acquired from Mr. and Mrs. Nathan Shepherd. The house was connected to the church to be used as a kitchen. A year later, the church purchased a plot of ground, 200 feet by 54 feet, from Albert Phelps in the Atkins Addition for use as a cemetery. This lot cost $50.

In the early 1890's—a time when immigration was progressing at high levels—the current church facilities became inadequate. In 1891, a lot was purchased from Gertrude Yakli Wagler and Christian Wagler. In 1892, $4,500 was raised to build a new church. A new building was erected on East Walnut Street with a seating capacity of 340. It was completed in 1893. John Schieler, one of the ministers of the church, supervised the construction.

The old church was moved from its original foundation. Two-thirds of it was moved to other locations, with one section later serving as a residence in Fairbury. The remaining section —approximately one-third of the old building—was transferred to the south edge of the church lot. It was used as a horse stable and to house a horse-drawn hearse.

The new church on East Walnut Street was a large, wood-frame, two-story structure. A large sanctuary occupied the second floor; dining facilities and a Sunday School were on the ground floor.

Fairbury historian Alma Lewis-James described the church:[6]

> Their church was a large, two story, white frame building on Paducah Avenue. In the rear, along three sides to form a courtyard, were the neat sheds for their horses and Klondike buggies. They were necessary for the protection of the animals in stormy weather because the services were day long meetings with bread and coffee served at noon.

This church was remodeled in 1950. It was sold to the Church of the Nazarene when the congregation moved into new quarters fifteen years later.

The congregation was the beneficiary of a beautiful new stone structure of Gothic styling which it occupied in 1965. Built at a cost of $308,177 and seating five hundred, it was built at 705 North Fourth Street on land donated by Katherine Roth. In 1978, more space was added for a hall and baby room. This project was completed in April, 1979.

In 1975, the church built a fellowship hall southwest of Fairbury on a plot of ground obtained from Duane Kilgus, a minister of the church. This picturesque area, complete with large playground facilities, was finished in the spring of 1976 at a cost of $181,000. It serves as a place for weddings of non-members, church suppers, "singings," and similar gatherings.

Resident Elders who have presided over the Fairbury church were John Georg Steidinger, Christian Gerber, Martin Steidinger, Peter Bach, Joshua Broquard, and Arthur Bahler. Joshua Broquard was ordained December 24, 1946, and was still serving in 1982. Arthur Bahler was ordained in 1980. David Mangold, Roanoke, Illinois; Emil Schubert, Peoria, Illinois; and Noah Schrock, Oakville, Iowa, served as Elders at Fairbury for interim periods.

The early 1930's was a difficult time in Fairbury as cleavage developed among the members primarily over the use of the English language (as opposed to the customary German) during the worship service. Auxiliary issues of controversy centered around how far the church should carry the Biblical themes of non-conformity to, and separation from, the world of sin. Those who were partial to the German language and who favored more exacting standards with respect to church order departed and formed what later became known as the German Apostolic Christian Church. The split was made final on February 7, 1932.

Although the church had suffered the effects of schism, it soon regrouped and growth again occurred. By 1980, nearly fifty years after the division, the church had progressed to a membership of over 250 with approximately 170 families. The church benefited in numbers when the South Side congregation closed down in 1949 and several members were absorbed into the Fairbury church. Also, by 1980 several families, whose heritage was associated with the German Apostolic Christian Church and subsequent splits, began to unite with the Apostolic Christian Church in Fairbury.

In November, 1962, the church built "Fairview Haven," a care center for elderly citizens. Originally, they cared for twenty-nine residents. By 1981 the home had forty-seven residents.

The worship of God at Fairbury has brought untold blessings to hundreds of people. An elderly couple, having been members of the church for fifty-five and sixty years respectively, was asked about their attitude concerning the Saviour and the church fellowship. They responded with the following testimony:[7]

> We think words cannot express the appreciation for the faith we found in our Saviour and Lord, and can enjoy fellowship with the Lord and with Christians of like faith, and as the years go on, we cherish it all more and more.

CISSNA PARK, ILLINOIS

Cissna Park ★

CISSNA PARK, ILLINOIS
One mile south,
two miles east

    The flame of faith that spread across the prairies with an unusual intensity during the decades of the 1870's and 1880's found its way into southern Iroquois County, Illinois. As families of German extraction came to this area, they brought with them a deep and abiding belief in God. Their primary goal in life was to serve the Lord. Such a noble motive subsequently resulted in the establishment of a large Apostolic Christian Church which today stands one mile south and two miles east of Cissna Park, Illinois.

    The first Apostolic Christian believers came to the area as early as 1863. Among them were the Richoz, Landes, and Cramotte families. In 1865, two more families arrived—those of Sam Kaufman and John Guingrich. The next fifteen years saw a large influx of families—mostly farmers—into this agriculture-rich settlement. They included the families of Karl Hurliman, John Hofer, Henry Ziegenhorn, Jacob Heineger, John Baumgartner, Jacob Brigger, John Zurlinden, and Peter Ramsier. The place to which these forefathers came was primarily the East Lynn community. The village of Cissna Park was not founded until the decade of 1880.

Heinrick "Henry" Ziegenhorn was the first minister of this group. However, he and his wife, the former Anna Guingrich, along with their large family (they eventually had thirteen children) moved to Weiner, Arkansas, in 1891 to make an attempt at farming in that area. Several church families from other areas went there as well, and church services were held in homes. The Ziegenhorns returned to Cissna Park a few years later.

An early leader significant to the growth of the church in Cissna Park was John Adam Eisenmann (1832-1888). He was a native of Newhutton, Germany, where he operated a grocery store. He was an Elder in the Evangelical Baptist Church in Germany. He emigrated to Tremont, Illinois, in 1880 and a year later purchased a farm near the Fountain Creek Station. This farm is still in the Eisenmann family today.

The Apostolic Christian community was increasing in number to where a church building was required. In 1881, the group purchased a building known as the Bethel Church. It was moved from east of Fountain Creek Station onto the Eisenmann farm. They dismantled the structure and re-assembled it on the west side of the farm between the road and a creek. The creek, which could be crossed by walking on a plank, was used by the Elders for baptizing converts.

A cemetery was started several rods southeast of the church. Previous to this, bodies were interred in private gardens or orchards. As the years passed, the cemetery markers became deteriorated, and it became impossible to read the names on them. In 1954, a large cement marker with the names of the twenty-nine bodies buried there was installed. These burials had been made during the period from 1881 to 1891.

John Adam Eisenmann gave some sage advice when he said, "It is very much worth your while to be a child of God, to be able to live in the millenium; not even to mention the heaven in all eternity." He also felt that on Sunday—a day of rest—a person should not read anything that did not pertain to the Bible or matters of faith.

Eisenmann's presence in the area was a boon to the fledgling church. The group now had a church building as well as a local Elder. This was an inducement for other families to locate here. In the 1880's, several more did. They included the families of Henry Miller, Charles Kaufmann, Jacob Moser, Ed Haab, Christ Grimm, Solomon Farney, and John Miller. Others who came were George Keidel, Christ Alt, Fred Stock, Adam Stoertzer, Nick Eberhart, George and John Hartter, Ludwig Dallinger, and Jacob Alt. Minister John Spiess, who later ministered at Gridley and Elgin, Illinois, came in 1884.

In 1889, John Adam Reeb and family emigrated to this country from Alsace, Lorraine. This was one year after Elder John Adam Eisenmann had passed away.

There was a large contingent accompanying the Reebs on their ocean voyage: The George Mangolds and Peter Bauers, Emil Feller, Charley Manshott, Sophia Hainel, and others by the name of Geyer, Froehlich, and Hager. The Bauers, Geyers, and Emil Feller all settled in this community. This group, much to their surprise, was met in New York by Michael Mangold and a Brother Leman of Roanoke.

John Adam Reeb was installed as the second Elder of the church in 1890. He was born of Lutheran parents in 1836 in Alsace-Lorraine. One day as a young adult he was encountered by a soldier who—ironically—was selling Bibles. Reeb told the soldier he was not satisfied with the Lutheran faith. In a miraculous twist of fate, the soldier told him of a certain religious group he might want to look into and learn more about. Accordingly, the soldier put him in touch with Samuel Froehlich's Evangelical Baptist Church.

When young Reeb heard his first sermon in this church, he said, "This is what I want." He soon repented for his sins, found peace with God, and was baptized. At age nineteen he was made a minister, and later ordained an Elder.[8]

By 1890, the thriving congregation in Cissna Park (often pronounced by old-timers as "Cis-nee") was pressed for more space during worship services. Rather than enlarging the church on its present site, the building was moved four miles northwest. It was doubled in size. The new location was closer to Cissna Park and more centralized for the membership. This location was across the road from today's present church.

In 1893, a group of eighty-one persons repented and were baptized. This "in-gathering" was second only to the one which occurred from October, 1911, to October, 1912, when one hundred persons were taken into the church.

The "olden days" at Cissna Park.

In 1894, only four years since the church building had been doubled in size, the congregation had realized such phenomenal growth that an addition was made to again double the size of the assembly room. Such rapid growth could conceivably be unmatched in church history—when a church building was doubled in size and four years later nearly doubled again.

The mushrooming growth of the Cissna Park church was tempered in 1900 by the loss of Elder John Adam Reeb. Estimates on the size of his funeral ranged from two thousand to three thousand. A special train was scheduled to bring mourners to his funeral. Reeb had been an engaging speaker and was widely appreciated in many states.

The next resident Elder was Eugene Schladenhauffen (1855-1926) who served the congregation from 1906 to 1926.

In the early 1900's, a church building was constructed in the village of Cissna Park. For several years it was used only for Wednesday evening services. As more and more people moved to Cissna Park, services were held on Sunday in both the town and country churches.

In the early 1930's, the church felt the frustrating pangs of schism which culminated in 1932 when the church's Elder, Martin Steidinger (of Fairbury, Illinois), and the rest of the ministers bade farewell to the congregation telling them they were unwilling to continue serving them. Approximately ten percent of the congregation followed, leaving the church in a state of bewilderment and disorientation with no ministers or leaders.

Reorganization of the stunned church occurred when Elders Ernest Graf, Sr., Akron, Ohio, and Elias Dotterer, Junction, Ohio, assumed Eldership duties at the church. Almost immediately new ministers were chosen: John Laubscher, Philemon Aeschliman, and Gust Meiss.

The remaining congregation then used only the country church and disposed of the building in town by moving it to La Crosse, Indiana, where the larger building was gladly welcomed by the brethren there.

John Laubscher became Elder in 1940 and served until he died in 1942. On October 14, 1942, Philemon Aeschliman was placed in the Eldership and served until May 2, 1954. It was during his tenure that a large, impressive new church—costing $320,000—was completed in 1949. The membership of the church peaked in 1956 at 460. Membership in 1980 was 290.[9] The decline was due to a serious split which occurred in the congregation in 1969.

In 1965 Ezra Feller and Emanuel Gudeman were elected as Co-Elders. During the ensuing four years, the church realized a sizable number of converts, but in time the ugly head of schism appeared which resulted in about twenty percent of the congregation departing. Elder Emanuel Gudeman was among those who chose to leave. Ezra Feller then continued alone as Elder. In January, 1980, Stephen C. Rinkenberger was ordained as Cissna Park's eighth resident Elder. Ezra Feller retired as Elder on September 27, 1981.

In 1970, the inside of the church was remodeled. A new pulpit was installed, and carpeting was placed throughout the assembly room, foyer, and steps. In 1972, a new front entrance was added.

The church at Cissna Park has been served by a host of non-resident Elders over the years. They include Christian Gerber, Fairbury, Illinois; Jacob Honegger, Forrest, Illinois; Martin Steidinger, Fairbury, Illinois; Robert Bahler, Remington, Indiana; Ernest Graf, Sr., Akron; Elias Dotterer, Junction, Ohio; George Yergler, La Crosse, Indiana; Joshua Broquard, Fairbury; Dave Mangold, Roanoke; and Joe A. Getz, Morton, Illinois.

DIAMOND, MISSOURI

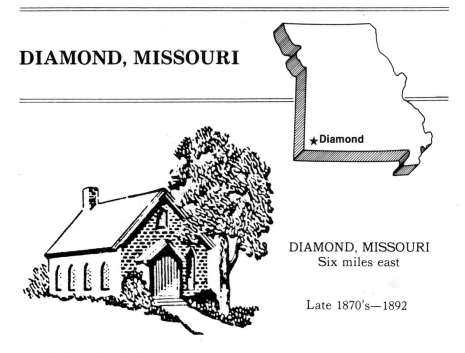

DIAMOND, MISSOURI
Six miles east

Late 1870's—1892

A church of the Apostolic Christian faith formerly existed in the area of Diamond, Missouri. Formerly known as Diamond Grove, this little village is located on Route 71 approximately thirty miles south of Lamar and ten miles south of Carthage, Missouri.

Several families who were associated with the Evangelical Baptist Church (the church name used in Europe and in the New York churches) in the Lewis County and Watertown, New York, area later migrated to Missouri. The first families came here in 1874. Most of them settled on farms in a triangular area formed by the small communities of Diamond, Park, and Ritchey.

One of the families was that of Martin Beyer and his wife, Elizabeth Schiffer Beyer. This couple arrived in 1874 with their children, one of which was a son, Martin N. Beyer, twenty-three. His marriage to Virginia Slane bore nine children. The youngest, Leamon Rex Beyer—known locally as "Rex" Beyer—was born in 1899 at Diamond where he was still residing in 1981.[10] Although not a member of the Apostolic Christian Church, he attended services as a young boy at Lamar.

When interviewed, he had a good knowledge concerning the early activities of the Apostolic Christian Church in the area. His credibility as a source of information is strengthened by the esteem he holds locally, with respect to both his business skills and his understanding of local history. In September, 1979, he was the subject of an article in *The Water Well Journal,* a trade publication. And on June 23, 1979, *The Carthage Press,* Carthage, Missouri, featured an article on Rex Beyer. Thus, his reputation in the area is without reproach, and he is considered somewhat of an authority on the area's early days.

According to Rex Beyer, the dozen or so families who came to the area initially held services in a two-story home located six miles east of what is now Diamond on the east edge of a now-defunct settlement called Park, Missouri.

In 1880, these families built a small church on the east bank of Jones Creek in Park. It was built with pine lumber hauled up from Eureka Springs, Arkansas. At that time it was the only church in the area.

Several years after the church was dissolved, the old building was moved to a farm, formerly owned by Joe Morgan, located midway between Diamond and Wentworth. A "lean-to"

The old church built in 1880 was still standing in 1983. It is located six miles east of Diamond, Missouri, on the east bank of Jones Creek.

was added, and it was used as a granary. In 1980, the old structure was still standing—weather-beaten, full of junk, and forgotten. It faintly resembled a church; three windows (complete with shutters) on each side of the building gave evidence it was once a house of worship.

The church was headed by "Old" Pete Farney. He is not to be confused with another Pete Farney who moved back to New York. Old Pete Farney was very likely the church's minister, or if not, he was considered the leader of the congregation. He was one of the best and most progressive farmers in the area.

As the church became established, it soon met with difficulty. Old Pete Farney lost his membership in the church for indiscretions unbecoming to a member. This was a severe blow to the congregation. Also, late in the decade of 1880, several heads of families were excommunicated from the church for disorderly behavior.[11] This resulted in the gradual demise of the congregation. With the exception of a couple of sisters who remained faithful until their deaths in the 1950's the flame of faith here was virtually extinguished by 1892. These sisters were visited occasionally by ministers from other Apostolic Christian Churches.

Rex Beyer's parents, following the closing of the Diamond church, began attending services at the Lamar church in Barton County. They were members of the church (having been baptized in 1879) who apparently escaped the discipline imposed on the Diamond church. Rex Beyer remembers the Lamar church (during 1910-1920) quite well—women dressed in black, men and women seated separately during worship, a big noon lunch and both morning and afternoon services with the latter often lasting until mid-afternoon. He remembered hearing preaching in the German language, but this stopped when World War I broke out. In 1921 his father, Martin Beyer, passed away, and the family no longer traveled to Barton County to attend services.

The old church cemetery, ramshackle and weedy, still exists three and one-half miles east and one mile north of Diamond. Sixty-five persons were buried in the cemetery; the most recent was Joseph Oyer in 1910. Legible family names on the tombstones in 1980 were Beyer, Farney, Oyer, Boehning, and Clapper. The tombstone of Peter Farney was very clear (Born April 28, 1822, died October 10, 1889).

Cemetery plot northeast of Diamond, Missouri, where former members of the Apostolic Christian Church are buried.

The small church in this area lasted a little more than a decade. Some of the families later moved to Kansas, while others quit going to church altogether.

Diamond, Missouri, is only a few miles from the birthplace and early home of George Washington Carver, noted agronomist and agricultural chemist. This historic site annually draws many tourists and sightseers.

ASHTABULA, OHIO

Early 1880's—1892

Early in the decade of 1880, several families of Swiss origin formed a settlement in Ashtabula County, Ohio. This is Ohio's most northeastern county and is located next to Lake Erie.

John Meyer, Sr., of Rittman, Ohio, led this migration. Among the early families in this area were those of Jacob Sommer, Sam Steiner, Albert Zollinger, and Jacob Kaufman. Other Swiss families eventually settled here, and several persons were converted in Ashtabula County. Among these families were Christ VonGunten, Sr., Jacob Rupp, Gottlieb VonGunten, Carl Tschantz, Christ Roth, Ernest Graf, Sr., and Samuel Baumgartner.

Ernest Graf, Sr., recalls his experience of turning to the Lord while living in the Ashtabula area with his sister Elizabeth and her husband Christ Roth:[12]

> I had always intended to become a member, but now something stirred and awakened in me which I recognized as a call from the Lord to repent and give Him my heart.

227

It took me a whole week to decide between this and a worldly career which opened up to me at the same time. I thank the Lord that I chose to endure the reproach of the world, rather than to enjoy the pleasures of sin for a season. I was led to repentance, spent several weeks in conflict with the evil one and in earnest prayer. Finally I won the victory, and grace and peace filled my heart. On Christmas Day, 1889, I was baptized by immersion in a brook by Elder Henry Schwier, who had come from Mansfield. I felt that in this new birth I had become a child of God, and still feel so.

It was after buying land in Ashtabula County that these farmers realized it was not as fertile as they had hoped. Consequently, material successes did not occur, and eventually they were forced to abandon the area. In 1892, the colony disbanded to the Akron and Rittman areas. Sam Steiner, however, remained until 1912 because his farm near town proved more successful.

John Meyer, Sr., served as minister and was later assisted by Christ VonGunten, Sr. Although, in a general sense, the farming areas did not yield satisfactorily, the spiritual fields bore fruit as eighteen souls were taken into the fold during the ten years of the church's existence. Because of this, the church in Ashtabula must be considered a success despite the fact that all the families eventually moved away.

ELGIN, ILLINOIS

ELGIN, ILLINOIS
651 Lillie Street

The beginning of the church at Elgin, Illinois, dates back to the early years of the 1880's. The roots of Elgin's history center essentially on the early activities of the Lindoerfer and Schambach families.

In the fall of 1880, Jacobena Schmitt Schambach, widow of John Schambach, together with her daughter Christina and two sons, John and George, moved from Germany to a farm

228

near Morton, Illinois. The two boys soon moved to a farm near Elgin, Illinois, where they found employment.

Jacobena Schmitt Schambach's daughter Frieda Ricka and her husband Christian Lindoerfer were still residing in Germany where they received word from her brothers, John and George, that employment as a stonecutter could be found in Elgin. A Mr. Trieber told them plenty of work was available and he would be willing to sponsor Christian and Frieda Ricka Lindoerfer's emigration. They came directly to Elgin to live, even though her mother lived in Morton.

Jacobena Schmitt Schambach, while living in Germany, was formerly of the Lutheran faith, and her husband, John, was supposedly a Lutheran minister. She had heard of Samuel Froehlich and his reputation of preaching about a "second baptism" (a baptism based on a conscious profession of faith and belief instead of infant baptism which was customary in almost all of Germany). She became curious about this doctrine and attended one of Froehlich's preaching services. He spoke of repentance, conversion, and the "new birth." When she came home after hearing Froehlich preach, she was so upset and in such a state of deep spiritual conviction and upheaval that her husband suggested she stay away from those meetings. In time, though, her husband also became curious and attended one of Froehlich's meetings. He, too, fell under the profound weight of spiritual conviction, and the two of them subsequently repented and experienced a true conversion. These incidents demonstrate how God worked through the preaching and persuasive skills He gave to Samuel Froehlich.

The following spring after arriving in America, Frieda Ricka Lindoerfer was brought under conviction and found grace to turn to the Lord in repentance. A few others in the area also sought the Lord. She wrote a letter to her mother in Morton who in turn told the Morton Elder, George Welk. He sent minister Gottlieb Maibach to the Elgin area with the instructions to preach "repentance." When he arrived in Elgin, he was directed to the home where several friends of the truth had assembled for preaching services.

When Maibach opened the Bible to find a text, it was not granted to him to preach "repentance." The Spirit prompted him to preach faith and peace instead. He was unaware that some of the friends in the audience, who had previously sought the Lord, had found forgiveness of their sins and peace with God. His sermon thus was very appropriate and served as an encouragement to those who were making progress in their new walk of life.

It so happened that a young Lutheran man, Gottlieb Huber, was in attendance during this sermon. When he came to this country from Germany, he was firmly resolved never to depart from the Lutheran doctrine. On hearing young Gottlieb Maibach preach with sincerity directly from the Scriptures, he fell under conviction and saw the Light.

Later in 1881 Elder George Welk of Morton traveled to Elgin and baptized Frieda Ricka Lindoerfer, Elgin's first convert, after her husband, Christian, had broken the ice on Willow Creek in Lord's Park. Soon after this a few others were spiritually awakened and baptized in the same place. Christian Lindoerfer was later baptized in 1894.[13]

Because of the awakening of souls in Elgin, it was decided to begin holding regular church services. Some of the brethren in Morton (the church which seemed to have an unofficial responsibility for the Elgin area) thought the few converts in Elgin ought to move to an area where a church already existed. Elder George Welk disagreed. He felt if souls in Elgin had turned to the Lord, it was God's will that a permanent church be established in that area. His advice proved wise because over the years the Elgin church blossomed to the extent that by 1980 it had 243 members and 197 families.[14]

First church services (on a regular basis) were held at the home of Frank Woertz at the corner of Chicago and North Liberty Streets. Woertz was a minister who had come to Elgin from Germany. His arrival was timely in that the young flock at Elgin needed a minister. He was the grandfather of Frank Woertz who served as Elder at Goodfield from 1948-1967.

Some of the first families of the church were the Lindoerfers, Burgers, Muellers, Traubs, Stettners, Spiesses, Schellenbergers, Stechers, Fehrmanns, Hubers, Grafs, and Schambachs. In August, 1882, Ernest Oettinger, Sr., and family moved to Elgin from Cissna Park. A short time later he met with a fatal accident, and the family moved back to Cissna Park.[15]

Worship services at Elgin, Illinois, were held in the above home from 1881 to 1886. As Apostolic Christian Churches were established across America, it was customary to initially meet in homes.

On July 15, 1887, a lot was purchased at the corner of Lillie Street and Preston Avenue for about $250, and a small frame church was erected. There were twenty-six members at this time. Worship services were held in the morning. Then everyone went home to eat lunch and returned for an afternoon worship service. By 1895, this facility became too small, and an east wing was built at a cost of $1,700 and used for a sanctuary. The old portion became a dining room and Sunday School.

At the turn of the century (and later) many more people of like faith came to Elgin to live. The Elgin National Watch Factory employed many people who were associated with the church. In 1912, another remodeling project was initiated at the church to better accommodate the growing congregation.

Crowding again posed a problem in 1930, and the church was torn down and a new, modern brick building erected. During this time the congregation met at the Lincoln Street Chapel. This new church building served very well until 1961 when further renovation made the overall accommodations more suitable. This cost $43,000, including furniture.

An early minister at Elgin was John Spiess who came here in the early 1880's. He had previously lived in Peoria, Cissna Park, and Gridley, Illinois. He was born October 21, 1850, near Stuttgart, Germany. Despite growing up in an atmosphere of militarism and having a father who was somewhat materialistic, his mind was bent toward sympathy, compassion, and tenderness for his fellow men.

Because the Lutheran faith failed to give solace to his spiritual longings, he sought God elsewhere, much to his father's displeasure. Finally, after much derision and criticism from his father, he fled Germany and came to America at age fifteen. He developed a deeply-rooted religious faith and sometimes walked as far as twenty-two miles to church and back (in central Illinois). Once a neighbor pitied the young Spiess so much he drove him to his place of worship and back. He never did it again. He said it was "too much even for a horse" to do in a day.[16]

Spiess married Rosa Christine Richt of his native Stuttgart, eight years his senior, at the church in Peoria. He was the father of Joseph Spiess, founder of a noted Elgin department store.

For several years the Elgin congregation was served by non-resident Elders: George Welk, Morton, Illinois, and Christian Gerber and Martin Steidinger, Fairbury, Illinois.

George Schambach served as Elder at Elgin, but his exact term of service is unknown. Marie Butikofer of Elgin, Iowa, remembered visiting at Elgin, Illinois, in 1909, and Schambach was the Elder at that time.[17] He later stepped down from his position as Elder. This happened sometime between 1912 and 1914. A few years later he was killed in a "runaway" involving a team of horses.[18]

Jacob Stettner served as Elder from 1928 until his death in 1955. He was born in Ohringen, Wurttemberg, Germany, and came to the United States in 1884; he worked on a farm in Morton for Frank Funk. He later came to Elgin and worked as a machinist at a watch factory. In 1897, he married Wilhelmine Spiess, daughter of John Spiess (she died December 29, 1926).[19]

He moved to Morris, Minnesota, in 1911 where his older brother, Louis, had moved two years previously. It was in Morris that he became a minister in 1913 and an Elder in 1921. In 1928, he returned to Elgin and resumed his work as a machinist until 1935 when he met with an accident which left him disabled. He married Frieda Ricka Lindoerfer in 1929. He died October 27, 1955, at age eighty-five and is buried in Bluff City Cemetery, Elgin.

Stettner, a man of resolute faith together with a lifestyle that reflected propriety and rectitude, is remembered as one who sought order in the church. Sometimes, during the noon lunch hour at church when conversation became too loud, or the young children too restless, as Elder he would pick up a bell and ring it. Immediately, this reminder quieted the assembly and a more suitable, calm atmosphere again prevailed.

His younger brother, William, born August 5, 1879, in Ohringen, Wurttemberg, Germany, came with his parents, Lui and Fredericka Schlipf Stettner, to America in May, 1884. With the exception of six months in 1894 when he worked for his cousin, William Schlipf, in Forrest, he lived the rest of his life in Elgin. He married Emma Spiess in 1910, became a minister in 1934, and was ordained as Elder in 1946. He served in the latter capacity concurrently with his brother, Jacob, for nine years. William Stettner died May 15, 1964.

On July 16, 1961, Herman Kellenberger, who was born January 27, 1902, at Fort Scott, Kansas, was ordained as Elgin's third resident Elder. Nathan Steffen was ordained Elder on October 23, 1977. Kellenberger died in 1983.

After a century of existence, the Elgin, Illinois, church is still hearing the message of hope and salvation. A respected church official once wrote:

> The same pure and holy gospel message is still being preached today as in the beginning, as Christ instructed His Apostles to preach repentance for the remission of sins, and all those who believe can then be baptized in the name of the Father, the Son, and the Holy Ghost.

AKRON, OHIO

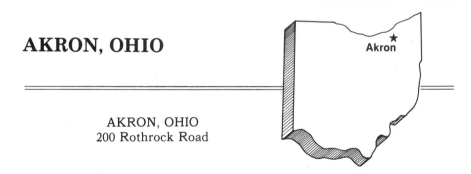

AKRON, OHIO
200 Rothrock Road

Brethren lived in Akron as early as 1866 but did not begin assembling together for worship until 1880. The first families of the faith to locate here were the Briggers, Blumensheins, and Schwings. There was no mass movement of church people to Akron as families generally came one at a time.

They were drawn to Akron because this industrialized city, built around the Ohio Canal which runs to Cleveland, offered jobs and economic opportunity. The economy initially centered around coal and grain. The latter was shipped to Cleveland via canal.

When worship services were begun in homes of members, ministers were provided by the Rittman, Ohio, congregation located twenty miles southwest of Akron. In the early phases of the church gathering, minister Daniel Steiner would ride horseback to Akron. This amounted to a full day's journey. Later, he took the train during these bi-monthly trips. Baptisms were performed in the Ohio Canal.

Brethren met in homes from 1880 until 1894 when a church was built. Jacob Rupp built the benches for these home services, and they were later transferred to the new church.

In the early 1890's, the church in Ashtabula County disbanded, and several families relocated in Akron. This included the families of Christ VonGunten, Gottlieb VonGunten, Carl Tschantz, and Jacob Rupp. Ernest Graf, Sr., who was to become the group's Elder thirty years later, also came to Akron.

The first church building was constructed at 425 West Thornton Street. It was a wooden building with an assembly room accommodating one hundred people.

An older member once recalled the early days at the Thornton Street church:[20]

> To the rear (of the church) were covered sheds with feed bins. At noon, the young boys fed the horses from the sacks of feed the families carried beneath the buggy seats. Between the services of German and English could be heard the ticking of the antique clock, and near noon was the aroma of freshly steeped coffee, as bread cut on a bread slicer was stacked high, to be served with butter and often apple-butter.
>
> Economic conditions being different then, there was a great dependence upon God, it seemed, for material as well as for spiritual needs, and a gratefulness to Him in return for what sometimes today we take for granted.

A touching story is recorded in Akron's history which reflects an immovable devotion to God on the part of a local housewife. Maria Strait had come into contact with the church through the Meyer family sometime in the early 1890's. After hearing the gospel, she came under conviction and wished to become a member of the church. Her husband opposed her in this endeavor and threatened her with extreme physical harm if she went ahead and was baptized.

She did not relent. After giving a testimony of faith to the satisfaction of the congregation, she was baptized. When she returned home, full of grace and completely trusting in the Lord, she encountered her husband. She forthrightly told him she had been baptized that afternoon. He reminded her of his previous threat and told her he intended to carry it out. She told him not to hurry because she wanted to make him some coffee and something to eat first. She did so, and after enjoying this snack, he no longer felt inclined to physically abuse her. Her faith, and the intervention of God, had carried her through this ordeal.

By 1925 a large lot was purchased at 545 Noble Avenue, and in 1927 a brick structure was erected. Both the lot and building cost $25,000.

Initially, the church was served by a non-resident Elder from Mansfield. On May 22, 1922, Ernest Graf, Sr., forty-eight, was named the first resident Elder of Akron. A humble man, he was called of God to perform seemingly endless missions on behalf of the church during his many years of service. He served as Elder at Akron until 1946. He traveled widely performing the duties of Elder. He assisted Elder Christian Gerber at Rockville, Connecticut. He was the counseling Elder of churches at Croghan and Naumburg, New York; Union City, New Jersey; Sardis, Rittman, Girard, and Mansfield, Ohio; and Maywood, California. He also traveled to Alabama to assist in the church's missionary activities there.

He began his tenure as Elder during the time when the church was facing the issue of changing worship service language from German to English. World War I had just ended, and the church's German heritage was not looked upon with favor among the people of the "world." He was one of the Elders who helped ease the English language into the church. Also, he was instrumental in registering the official name of the church—Apostolic Christian Church—with authorities in Washington, D.C., when it became necessary to do so to allow the church's young men to serve in the army as noncombatants.

Elder Graf is remembered, too, for translating George M. Mangold's *Meditations of the Past, Present, and Future* from the German language into English. He completed this task during the winter months when snow and cold weather prevented outside work on his farm.

He was one of the first church leaders to encourage young Henry Beer of Milford, Indiana, to translate songs in the *Zion's Harp* hymnal from German into English.

He was succeeded as Elder by his son, Rudolph, who was ordained December 1, 1946, six months after his father's death. Rudolph Graf had been placed in the ministry seven years earlier.

During one year in the early 1940's, the Akron church baptized ten or twelve converts during the entire year, making this the largest group to be baptized in a single year. Although the church at Akron has never achieved large numbers, it has maintained a solid base over the years. In 1980 the church had fifty-one families and ninety-six members.[21]

In 1968, a time of turmoil in American cities, the church was forced to seek a new location. Social unrest, precipitated by the Vietnam War and the assassination of several prominent national leaders, culminated in widespread rioting in many large cities. Akron was no exception, and the Apostolic Christian Church's close proximity to the areas of unrest dictated that a new location be secured so the church could assemble in an environment conducive to the proper worship of God. During this time the church had been both burglarized and vandalized. Cars were broken into, and one time a sister of the church had her purse snatched. Another time, local citizens set a bonfire at the church's rear door. Elmer Graf, the church janitor, happened to arrive on the scene just in time to extinguish the flames. If he hadn't arrived when he did, the church likely would have burned down.

During 1968, a four-acre plot was bought in northwest Copley Township, and a year later a new church, seating three hundred, was built at 200 Rothrock Road. On October 2, 1983, Eugene Pamer was ordained as Elder.

KANSAS
Gridley and Lamont

The faith that found a following in the eastern United States and then in the fertile prairies of the central Midwest soon found its way onto the broad expanse of the Great Plains.

The penetrating message of salvation and the hope of heaven, which had moved so many hearts to make a revolutionary change in their lives—from serving the prince of this world to serving the one true God—and which had previously taken place in the towns and villages of Switzerland and Germany as well as in the eastern half of the United States, also wrought change in the hearts of many who lived in the Sunflower state.

An example of one moved by the irresistible call of God was a second generation Kansan of Gridley, Kansas, who wrote a moving testimony typical of all the faithful, which appeared in the *Silver Lining* in February, 1971:

> When I came under conviction forty-seven years ago and felt my lost condition at age twenty-three, I knew I had to make a change in my walk of life. When I asked God to help me, I found the love He had for a sinner (but not for the sins he commits). How willing He was to help and forgive me when I came to Him with a broken heart asking for His help and guidance. Then, after I was converted and taken into the fold of His believing children, I could never forget how merciful the Lord was to me.

The Gridley and Lamont, Kansas, local histories are very much entwined because initially, in the 1870's, there was only one assembly of believers which later developed into two groups.

The first Apostolic Christian families came to Kansas in 1876. They included the Imthurn, Leu, Ott, and Sauder families. By the end of the decade, approximately forty-nine families had moved to acreage in Greenwood and Coffey Counties. The majority of these brethren settled in an area measuring about twenty miles from east to west on the eastern edge of Greenwood County and the western edge of Coffey County.

Two distinct settlements soon evolved. One was in the more productive Verdigris River Valley of Greenwood County (Lamont), the other in the southwest part of Coffey County (Gridley).

These families met to worship God at a point midway between their two general areas of abode—at a newly-organized school now known as the Erret District. Members would bring their noonday lunch with them and then spend the noon hour at the Moser home nearby where hot coffee awaited them.

The church met for a few years at the Erret School, but travel in wagons or open carriages became too difficult and inconvenient. Consequently, the members from the Verdigris Valley area (Lamont) built a church in 1881 approximately ten miles west of where initial services were held. The Coffey County brethren (Gridley) soon followed with a church eight miles northeast. Thus, two churches were established in the same year, each with its own separate autonomy. Both the Lamont and Gridley churches have maintained close ties of brotherhood over the years.

Living conditions among the Kansas brethren in the early days were sometimes harsh and often dangerous. These early settlers often had to travel several miles with teams and wagons into the timber to obtain logs and kindling wood. They generally drove in groups to protect each other from wolf and coyote packs.

One time two brethren living near Gridley, Kansas, went to a neighbor's home to butcher beef. When they were done slaughtering the beef, they loaded their half on a wagon and headed home. When they were about halfway home, a pack of coyotes, lured by the smell of beef, came out of the timber and attacked them. The brethren tried their best to escape, but when they got about one-half mile from home, another pack of coyotes joined the earlier pack. In such a state of peril, the two brothers began pitching the beef to the coyotes and, in this way, were able to safely reach home.[22]

GRIDLEY, KANSAS

Gridley ★

GRIDLEY, KANSAS
Third & Reed Streets

Early settlers came to this general area in the 1870's. The land was cheap because crops were difficult to grow due to drought, prairie fires, and grasshoppers. Many early pioneers worked long and brutal days only to see their crops fall prey to these uncontrollable adversaries.

Farming then was a far cry from today's modern and efficient operations. It was necessary to break up the virgin sod formed by the natural prairie grass. Farmers pulled fourteen-inch "sod plows" behind teams of oxen. In backbreaking fashion they were able to plow two or three acres per day. To make matters even more difficult, or at least uncertain, Indians were still in the area, and buffalo roamed as well. Some of the brethren eventually became discouraged with these conditions and returned east to where farming, while still hard work, was more bearable.

Typical of these hard-working farmers was Peter Kraft who came to America from Russia. He and his family emigrated in 1857 and landed in Rush County, a county in western Kansas inhabited by people with a Russian heritage. A homesteader at age twenty-nine, he built a sod house and a sod barn. One time he hauled a load of wheat from La Crosse, Kansas, to Wichita (a distance of about one hundred miles) with a team of horses. When the family moved to Gridley, they put all their possessions on a wagon and followed behind on foot. He eventually served as a minister at Gridley.

Some of the early Kansas brethren existed near the poverty level. Conditions were harsh, and annual crops were not always a certainty. An account is told of a Wagler family who lived in Ness City, Kansas, located nearly 150 miles west of Emporia. This family was destitute and near starvation. They appealed to church people to respond to their dilemma. Consequently, brethren traveled to Ness City to alleviate their suffering. After they departed from their train during the night, they walked through the streets of Ness City attempting to find the Waglers. As they were walking they heard a family singing in their house. The song was *Joyfully, Joyfully, Onward I Move,* a song from the *Heftli* (today's *Hymns of Zion*). This was the Wagler family who, despite their hunger, was still rejoicing in the Lord.

Several families comprised the early membership at Gridley: Birk, Dietrich, Huber, Kraft, Krepp, Kaufman, Kurth, Kurtz, Leibig, Metzger, Roth, Schneider, Selsman, Somerhalder, Steffen, Wagler, Walter, and Wietrich.

The first Gridley church was built in 1881 two miles north and one mile west of the village of Gridley. In 1895, it was destroyed by a tornado. In 1910, it was destroyed again—this time by fire. That same year a new church was built on the edge of Gridley.

Peak membership in the Gridley congregation occurred during 1910 to 1925 at approximately one hundred. During those early years, forty families were on the "dinner list" compared to nineteen in 1980.[23] Attendance at the church during the 1920's was so great it became necessary to place benches longways in the aisle to accommodate all the people. During 1949-1950, the church realized a harvest of nearly thirty souls who turned to the Lord in repentance.

The church in Gridley is unique in that the building and its surroundings comprise a most idyllic setting somewhat reminiscent of the Old West. The white, wood-frame structure sits on a slight incline on the edge of town. A tall tree shades a portion of the building. The tranquillity of the area—quietness on the vast, wide-open prairie—together with the shining hue of a brilliant sun and clear blue sky makes Gridley, Kansas, a special place.

The first ministers were Christian Wagler and Joseph Huber. The latter, born December 29, 1838, in Gutmadinger, Germany, was installed as Elder in 1881 by Elder Benedict Weyeneth, who lived at Roanoke, Illinois.[24] Huber had become a minister at age twenty-seven while still in Germany. He later served as Elder at Lamont and Fort Scott, Kansas, and Lamar, Missouri. He died August 7, 1917.

In 1921, Jacob Somerhalder, who was born November 29, 1853, in Rahage, canton Aargau, Switzerland, was ordained as the next resident Elder at Gridley. He passed away November 5, 1945.

Samuel Anliker assumed the duties of Elder in 1951 and was still serving in 1983.

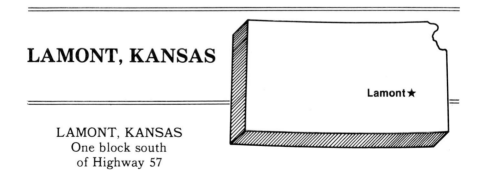

LAMONT, KANSAS

LAMONT, KANSAS
One block south
of Highway 57

The congregation at Lamont, like Gridley, existed before the town bearing the same name was founded. In 1881, Apostolic Christian farmers who tilled the more fertile soil of the Verdigris River Valley built a church on a plot of land donated by Jacob Leu three miles southeast of Lamont.

Lumber and supplies for the new building were secured at Burlington, Kansas, twenty-five miles northeast.[25] Brethren contributed so much labor that it was unnecessary to hire a

carpenter. While these humble, quiet, and diligent brethren busied themselves in building this small country church in 1881, shocking events were occurring elsewhere in America. President James Garfield was shot on July 2 while waiting for a train and died in September.[26] Sitting Bull, the Indian leader who had been a fugitive since the battle of Little Bighorn, surrendered to authorities in the Dakota Territory. The latter incident illustrates the frontier nature of the Lamont area in those formative years.

Early membership in the Lamont assembly included the following family names: Bahr, Beck, Blanck, Brandt, Brenkman, Britsch, Burkhart, Demler, Dreyer, Emch, Esslinger, Fankhauser, Fechter, Getz, Graff, Gruber, Imthurn, Isch, Kutzley, Kyburz, Leu, Luthi, Moser, Ott, Riggenbach, Sauder, Schwab, Schurter, Storrer, Streit, Schupbach, Sutter, Young, Wenger, Weyeneth, Winzeler, and Wernli.[27] As land prices increased in the fertile areas of Indiana, Illinois, and Iowa, settlers moved farther west in search of cheaper land. The Lamont church gained in membership by this development. By the turn of the century, membership peaked at eighty to one hundred members. Large attendance often made it necessary to bring kitchen benches into the sanctuary and place them sideways in the aisle during church services.

A gradual membership decline took place over several decades which lowered the total to approximately thirty-eight members and thirty-four friends in 1981. Despite the fact that a good many residents in Greenwood County have roots in the Apostolic Christian Church, the congregation did not prosper to the extent that would seem likely. Several factors coalesced to hinder growth at Lamont. Probably the most important factor was improved farming methods which no longer required large amounts of physical labor. As technology continued to improve, more and more young people moved to cities and other areas in pursuit of a living. Other factors include: (1) many children simply did not follow their parents and become members, (2) several families died out, (3) a few farmers moved to other areas, and (4) the division of the church nationally in 1906-1907 caused turmoil (although this did not occur in Lamont until 1911).[28] Despite many setbacks, however, the firm faith of stalwart brethren held fast over the years. Although Lamont's numbers have not been large, their brotherly love and peaceful contentment seem to transcend large numbers.

A brother who labored in the ministry at Lamont for several years—alone for thirteen years—was Pete Fankhauser. The son of John and Rosa Fankhauser (who came from Switzerland, through Sardis, Ohio, and to Lamont in 1880), he was born in 1881, the year the first church was built southeast of Lamont. He began in the ministry in 1931 and continued for thirty-two years. He is typical of many Apostolic Christian ministers who, without pay and sometimes amid discouraging circumstances, continue with diligence to preach the gospel of salvation. He was a quiet man, tilling the soil and feeding and pasturing cattle in the Flint Hills grasslands of Kansas. His daughter, Geraldine Fankhauser Beyer, remembers:

> My parents were one of the first to arrive at church and welcome the little flock of worshippers of our dear Christ and Lord.

Fankhauser often quoted Psalms 90:12, "So teach us to number our days, that we may apply our hearts unto wisdom." He died in 1975 at age ninety-three.[29]

Philip Wenger and Alf Weyeneth were the congregation's first two ministers, serving from 1876 to 1900. The Elders who served at Gridley—Joseph Huber and Jacob Somerhalder—also presided at Lamont. During one twenty-year interval, there was no "local" Elder, and until 1941 the church was served by Elders from the East. Noah Schrock of Oakville, Iowa, was Elder from 1941 to 1951. Samuel Anliker, who was born near Forrest, Illinois, on February 19, 1905, and moved to Kansas in

1931, assumed the duties of Elder in 1951 and by 1983 remained as the only resident Elder of the Lamont congregation. He also served as Elder at other churches.

The church in Lamont is often referred to as the "old German church" by townspeople. Elder Samuel Anliker said he always corrects them when people make this erroneous reference.

The old country church southeast of Lamont served the congregation until 1977 when a new structure was built in the hamlet of Lamont on property donated by the aged Fred Luthi. This beautiful, modern, one-floor structure, far different from the assemblies in the 1880's, is symbolic of the general prosperity that has been realized, not only at Lamont, but in the church nationwide.

While the church here has realized many blessings during its years of existence, it has also had its share of setbacks. One of the most severe blows to the church occurred in 1890 when two young sisters in the church, Emma and Della Burkhart, drowned while fording Long Creek on the way home from Sunday afternoon services. Their open-top buggy upset, and they were apparently pinned underneath. This was a terrible blow to the family and to the church.

OREGON

Families who eventually associated with the Apostolic Christian Church in Oregon may have lived there as early as 1870. Historical evidence, however, suggests that the first church here was not established until the latter stages of that decade.

One factor stands out regarding the history of the Apostolic Christian Church in Oregon. It was nearly devastated by schisms which occurred in 1906-1907 and 1932-1933. In the first division, the Portland church was left with only a "handful" of members, while Silverton had only a few members following the second division. The effects of those unfortunate schisms still exist today as evidenced by the relatively small churches at Portland and Silverton.

SILVERTON, OREGON

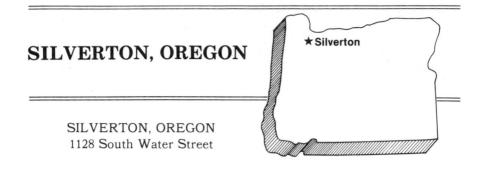

SILVERTON, OREGON
1128 South Water Street

With the completion of the Union Pacific Railroad in 1869, a new era in population and economic activity began in Oregon.

The extremely fertile Willamette Valley, noted for its fruit growing, dairying, and lumbering, awaited development. Located in an area flanked on the east by the Cascade Mountain Range and on the west by the Coast Range, the soil contained the fertility sought by many immigrants. These included persons of Swiss descent who came to initiate farming operations. Wheat, barley, and oats were among the crops grown in the Silverton and Salem areas.

Families of Mennonite background had previously settled in the Willamette Valley near Pratum, Oregon, and had established a church several years before anyone associated with the Apostolic Christian Church had come to the area.

In 1877, Christian C. Wenger, along with the John Lichty and Peter Steffen families (all Swiss Mennonites), came to Oregon and settled near Pratum. They apparently had some knowledge of the Evangelical Baptist Church while in Switzerland because, when they first began attending the Pratum Mennonite Church, discussion arose concerning the differences between the Mennonites' beliefs and those explained to them by Apostolic Christians whom they had previously met in the East and Midwest. C. C. Wenger (as he was called) was especially anxious to learn more about the Apostolic Christian Church. The others remained with the Mennonite faith.

C. C. Wenger (1845-1920) took a historic step when he wrote to Elders of the Apostolic Christian Church inquiring about their beliefs. In 1879 Elder Peter Virkler of Lewis County, New York, traveled three thousand miles to Oregon. He apparently was the Elder chosen to respond to the request of C. C. Wenger. Virkler's willingness to go all the way to Oregon, despite comparatively primitive travel conditions, illustrated the church's concern for even one soul.

Peter Virkler, it is believed, was accompanied to Oregon by young Gottlieb Maibach, twenty-six, who later served as Elder at Pulaski, Iowa, and Bay City, Michigan. It is likely, since the Union Pacific Railroad was completed ten years earlier, they traveled by rail to Portland and then made their way to the Pratum area as best they could. Oral history suggests they traveled the final phases of the trip by horseback led by an Indian guide. This is very logical because Oregon at that time was a veritable wilderness of fir trees, log cabins, and Indians.

C. C. Wenger, William Kaufman, and Fred Krug, Sr., (all Mennonites) were employed in the Pratum area cutting railroad ties. C. C. Wenger, along with his wife, was baptized by Elder Virkler, thus being the first of the Apostolic Christian faith to be baptized in Oregon.

Kaufman and Krug, although they later joined the church, did not do so during Virkler's 1879 trip. In fact, Kaufman was apparently not inclined to do so because the story is told that, during Virkler and Maibach's stay in Oregon, he sent young Gottlieb Maibach off to purchase some tobacco for him. Maibach, a member in the church, was taken aback, but procured the tobacco anyway because he was prompted by the

Scripture that says, "...servants to be obedient unto their own masters, and to please them well in all things; not answering again" (Titus 2:9).

Maibach's humble obedience touched William Kaufman's heart and shamed him. Finally, realizing the anguish he had caused Maibach, he did not use the tobacco.

The exact date when William Kaufman turned to the Lord is not known, but both Fred Krug, Sr., and he were baptized June 13, 1881, by Elder Benedict Weyeneth of Illinois. Kaufman became the first Oregon Elder on July 1, 1883, and served alone, through much turmoil and church strife, until his death on December 17, 1931.

The Kaufman family history goes back to Basel, Switzerland. In 1867, the father of William Kaufman brought his wife and ten children to America. William was thirteen years old at that time. Two children were left in Basel because the family could not afford passage. They planned to send for them later. The pain of leaving these two children was particularly excruciating for the parents. The family traveled on the boat *Cleopatra,* which on its next trip to America was lost at sea.

The family, consisting of the parents and ten children, arrived in New York Harbor with only $1.50. Fortunately, a Mennonite minister asked them what they were going to do. Father Kaufman replied, "I don't know." With this, the kindly minister took them back to his home area near Canton, Ohio, and helped them get established in America.

After several years, William Kaufman and his brother (either John or Fred) went to California to find work. They labored in the California harvest fields in 1878. William came to the Silverton area in late 1878 or early 1879. He lived in a log cabin. He was married on October 28, 1884, to Caroline Affolter at Morton, Illinois, by Elder Peter Virkler. She was born July 25, 1858, at Round Bottom, Monroe County, Ohio.

Kaufman and his wife purchased sixty acres of land in Oregon which consisted mostly of fir trees. They often said they had "fir and snakes." When they picked strawberries, they were always dubious of encountering snakes.

William Kaufman was a large, broad-shouldered man of six feet or more. He is remembered as a gifted speaker, especially in the German language. He was a kind and gentle man and thought sharpness served no useful purpose.

Bertha Kaufman Klopfenstein of Salem, Oregon, remembered her father as very "easy going," although to him "black was black and white was white." She said he used to travel to Portland to care for the church there. On the way back, he would change trains at Woodburn for the ride to Silverton. Sometimes he would miss his connection at Woodburn and walk the remaining seventeen miles to his home. Bertha Klopfenstein says he never complained.

Kaufman used to conduct baptisms in the Pudding River (called the *Ahantchuyuk* by the Indians). Members, friends, and even neighbors would gather on the banks of the river to witness this impressive act. Kaufman would roll up his pants above the knees during the baptismal rite.

One time Kaufman and Rudolph Diriwachter, a minister at the church in Portland, along with four others, were riding in a large buggy when their team of horses engaged in a "runaway." Something scared the horses and they took off running through fences and fields. The other four occupants were injured and taken to a hospital in Silverton. Later, the staff at the hospital was very impressed by several of the brethren coming to visit the injured and were additionally impressed when prayer was offered at their bedsides.

William Kaufman and Fred Krug, Sr., deeded property for a church building and cemetery in 1883. The church was probably built in 1884. It was located five miles southwest of Silverton. In 1910, this church was torn down and a new one built. Rose Steffen Miller, as a young adult, remembers the quaint country church at Silverton:

> I used to walk to the Silverton church for the Thursday night meeting. It was three miles to church. In the summer, I often walked through the fields on the way home from church, rejoicing in the Lord! How I loved our church and the brothers and sisters in faith!

From 1880 to 1900, the church grew and prospered with many families moving to the area. Jacob Schar of Bluffton, Indiana, formerly of Switzerland, came in 1880 and preached along with Kaufman until 1908 when his family and the Rudishauser family separated to join the Apostolic Christian Church (Nazarene).

The first major nationwide division in the Apostolic Christian Church occurred during approximately 1906-1907. While nearly all the members at Portland left to join what is now known as the Apostolic Christian Church (Nazarene), very few departed from the Silverton church. In 1932-1933, however, another split occurred, although to a much lesser extent (when considered on a national basis), and almost all the Silverton brethren departed. William Kaufman had died in 1931, and many say if he had lived, no schism would have developed at Silverton.

Martin Steidinger and Jacob Edelman, Elders and leaders of the group who departed from the Apostolic Christian Church, came to Oregon, and nearly all the Silverton church followed them. The division in Illinois occurred in 1932. Because Silverton was so far away, the church there remained intact until Steidinger came out a year later and, more or less, precipitated a decision by the Silverton members. They subsequently became known as the German Apostolic Christian Church, and they presently occupy the church built in 1910 southwest of Silverton. Emil Hari was ordained as Elder at Portland and Alfred Kuenzi at Silverton for this new group.

These circumstances nearly destroyed the Silverton Apostolic Christian Church, leaving only two members, William Maurer and Gottlieb Hari, twin brother to Emil Hari. Thus, the schism not only divided the church, but some families as well.

For several years the Silverton church limped along with only a few members. They would meet together in a Legion Hall or with the few members at Portland. In 1955, they purchased a house in Silverton where a sanctuary was arranged in a first floor room, and services were conducted here. In 1956, Elder Noah Schrock appointed Gottlieb Hari, then sixty-six, as a minister to serve only when no visiting minister was present. He served two years, returning to Illinois in 1958.

For many years, ministers from Portland served the few remaining brethren at Silverton, helping to keep the Silverton church alive. In 1970, the Clarence Dietrich family moved to Silverton from Elgin, Illinois. He was appointed a minister

February 17, 1971, and during the late 1970's and early 1980's, church growth was realized. The old church was torn down and a new church built in 1976.

NEEDY, OREGON

From 1884 to 1920, a few members and friends lived at Needy, Oregon, located east of Hubbard. They did not have a church building of their own. When possible, however, they attended services either at Portland or Silverton.

PORTLAND, OREGON

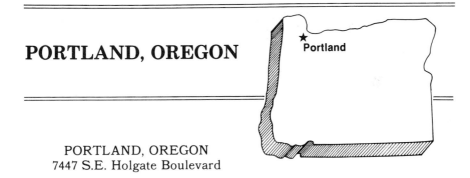

PORTLAND, OREGON
7447 S.E. Holgate Boulevard

Activity among Apostolic Christians in Portland, Oregon, began soon after a beginning was made at Silverton. It was probably less than a year later when brethren began to assemble together in Portland. The approximate year when Swiss immigrants began coming to the city was 1880.

Portland is known as "The Rose City" because of the great number of roses grown here. The International Rose Test Gardens of the American Rose Society are located in Washington Park, and over seven hundred varieties of roses are raised there. While virtually millions of persons over the years have viewed these beautiful roses that "bloom but for a season," brethren of the Apostolic Christian Church have met together to nurture a hope and faith that will one day take them into heaven's portals where, as a hymnwriter describes, "the roses never fade."

Portland, the state's largest city, is a bustling area regarded as the center of finance, trade, and industry in the Columbia River basin. The founders, Asa L. Lovejoy of Massachusetts and Francis W. Pettygrove of Maine, tossed a coin in 1845 to determine whether the settlement should be named Boston or Portland in honor of towns in their states. Pettygrove was the winner, and the settlement was named Portland.

The Portland congregation first met above the store of Max and Emma Otto on Southeast 16th Avenue and at the John "Pap" Meier residence at 16th and Southeast Morrison Streets. Meier may have preached for a short period, but George Schwartz from Switzerland was the first regular minister. Fred Feldman was also an early minister. The original membership consisted of the Meier, Stoller, Feldman, Otto, Kaufman, Krug, Mathys, Goss, Schwartz, Montandon, Bohren, and Kuenzi families.

Because Portland was a thriving community and offered economic opportunity, several families moved here from 1880 to 1900 including several unmarried young women who were able to find work as domestic "hired girls."

In 1894, property at 420 Southeast 22nd Avenue (at Stark Street) was deeded to the church, and in 1896 a two-story, wood-frame church was built. Around 1928, this building was remodeled to its present architecture. In 1981, it was occupied by the Grace and Truth Church (Pentecostal). At the time of the national schism in approximately 1906-1907, the vast majority of Portland's members went with the Apostolic Christian Church (Nazarene), so the church facility remained in their hands. It did so until 1953 when that congregation built a new church at 5101 Southeast Mitchell Street.

George Schwartz, who was one of the first ministers of the congregation, was remembered as a gifted preacher. Eventually, against the wishes of Elder William Kaufman, he visited Europe during the time controversy was simmering within the church in the United States in the early 1900's. When he returned, he and virtually the entire Portland church joined with the national group that came to be known as the Apostolic Christian Church (Nazarene), leaving only three known members remaining with the Apostolic Christian Church. They were, according to local sources, Anna Kuenzi, Emma Montandon, and Clara Kuenzi. They then met, on occasion, with brethren in Silverton until the situation in Portland normalized.

Rudolph Diriwachter, a tailor who left the church along with the Schwartz group, remained with them for approximately one year, and then returned to the Apostolic Christian Church where he served as a minister for many years.

During 1909-1910, a new church was built at 30th and Pine Streets. It was built under the supervision of Sam Ramseyer, a minister. In 1981, it was still occupied by the German Apostolic Christian Church.

In the decade of 1910 to 1920, a good labor market drew many families to Portland, and this gave added numbers to the small church. The Conrad and Hari families were two who arrived during this decade. Emil Hari served as a minister, but in 1933 he left to join the German Apostolic Christian Church of which he became an Elder. He served for many years in this capacity.

The church in Portland was wracked by controversy for the second time in 1932-1933 when many members left to form what later came to be known as the German Apostolic Christian Church. This group kept the church at 30th and Pine, so the remaining brethren were again without a church building —the second time in twenty-seven years this situation arose. But, in true Christian stride, they meekly and patiently accepted their plight. For nearly four years these families met in homes and were led by their loyal and respected leader,

Rudolph Diriwachter. They also met once per month at Silverton in the home of William Maurer. Fred Feucht also served as a minister at this time (from 1934-1937).

In 1937-1938, a small church building—which resembled a residential home—was built at a cost of $2,000 at 36th and Main Streets. It seated forty-five. Theo Conrad supervised the project and devoted an enormous amount of time toward the construction.

For the next ten years the church existed with little growth, and as Rudolph Diriwachter grew older, another minister was needed. In 1947, the Guy Miller family of Gridley, Illinois, (formerly of Pulaski, Iowa) was persuaded by Elder Noah Schrock, and others, to move to Portland and serve as minister. His five adult children followed him and gave new impetus to the church.

Rudolph Diriwachter died in 1952 and was greatly missed by the congregation. In his declining years he would have co-minister Guy Miller read the sermon text, and he would meditate on it.

A new church was built in 1955 at 7447 Southeast Holgate Boulevard on the city's southeast side. Theo Conrad, although in failing health, again took a great interest in the building project. Even while hospitalized, he assisted in preparing the building plans. He expired while the new church was only partially constructed. The church was dedicated March 18, 1956.

The church in Portland, despite its small numbers and various struggles, has been quite active and has served a very useful purpose over the years. In 1953, services were held at Fisher, Oregon, 140 miles southwest of Portland. Intended for Robert Bertsch, a friend living in that area, efforts were made to invite people of the community to attend services. The first worship services were conducted September 13, 1953, at a church building formerly occupied by the Free Methodist Church. Services were subsequently held every other week for ten months with the exception of the winter months when services were held once per month. The three ministers at Portland alternated driving to Fisher. The ten-month effort resulted in the conversions of Ray, Sr., and Anna Cooper, and two of their children.

The Portland church also sent ministers to Tacoma, Washington, once per month during 1963 to 1965 to conduct worship services in that area. Services were held the first Sunday of the month at Mountain View Chapel on Steilacoon Boulevard.

A major reason for holding services at Tacoma was to accommodate church boys stationed at Ft. Lewis, Washington, some eight miles away. Also, there were a few members and friends living in the area.

The Portland church has also been a haven for many young servicemen stationed at Ft. Lewis. Too, it has been a convenient "stopping-off" place for persons traveling to and from the church in Japan. In the past few years, due to economic prosperity, many brethren in the United States have been able to travel to Oregon on vacation. Portland thus became a favorite place to visit, and local brethren have been noted for their loving hospitality.

In 1976, brethren of the Portland and Silverton churches united to build a cabin situated on the Pacific Ocean at Yachats, Oregon. Members and friends from many churches traveled to Oregon to help in the construction of the cabin named *Restless Surf.* This three-story structure is snugly nestled in a heavily wooded area on the western edge of the Siuslaw National Forest. It features a grand and panoramic view of the Pacific Ocean. The cabin was built for use by the local brethren and also for church visitors within the denomination from other states.

Cabin at "Restless Surf," Yachats, Oregon.

For more than a century, the Apostolic Christian Church in Portland has stood firm amid many trials and disappointments. Twice it was nearly extinguished by schisms, but the flame of faith was never snuffed out, and by 1980 the church began its second hundred years.

Elders who have served at Portland have been William Kaufman, Silverton; Ernest Graf, Sr., Akron, Ohio; Noah Schrock, Oakville, Iowa; and Carl Kinsinger, Altadena, California.

TOLEDO, OHIO

TOLEDO, OHIO
3011 Marvin Avenue

Apostolic Christian Church services in Toledo were first held in the home of David and Ursala Meister Frautschi in 1880. They were emigrants who came from Switzerland and lived on 13th Street. A number of families frequently met here for worship.

Ursala Meister came from a family of believers who settled in an area near Archbold, Ohio. She came to Toledo for employment and worked in the home of a doctor. After meeting her husband, they attended the Methodist Church where they were married. In this faith they sought their souls' salvation. With the passing of time, they concluded that the Methodist faith did not meet their spiritual needs, and they began to assemble with the members and friends of the Evangelical Baptist Church (later known as Apostolic Christian). This church was located in the country near Archbold which is approximately fifty miles west of Toledo. They became members of the church in about 1876. At this time there was no Apostolic Christian Church in Toledo.

The decision of David and Ursala Meister Frautschi to become followers of the Lord in the Apostolic Christian faith demonstrates the personal significance of one's commitment to serve God. Had they rejected the call of God and neglected their subsequent repentance and conversion, a church of this faith in Toledo might not have been forthcoming. As a result of their decision, however, many people in Toledo were subsequently touched by the gospel and acquired the priceless pearl of salvation.

Toledo is situated on Maumee Bay at the southwest end of Lake Erie which is at the mouth of the Maumee River. In 1833, it united two smaller towns, Port Lawrence and Vistula. This city offered work in the industrial field to its population. Several families who earlier settled around Archbold and attended the Apostolic Christian Church later came to Toledo for employment.

In 1888, Andrew J. Braun and family came to Toledo from Wauseon, Ohio. They resided on John Street. He was an energetic and faithful confessor of the faith who came to America in 1854 on the advice of Samuel Froehlich. He first settled in Peoria. While in Europe, he endured many unpleasant experiences at the hands of governmental authorities who were not inclined toward approving his unauthorized church services. At that time the church and state were one entity, and freedom of conscience was not necessarily guaranteed. Andrew J. Braun and his followers, moved by deep conviction that they worship the true and living God, defied the state and suffered the consequences.

Records reveal that as a young boy Braun was raised in the Lutheran faith. His parents, being of different religious faiths, could not reach an accord concerning religion. Consequently, the boys in the family were raised in the Lutheran faith (that of their mother) and the girls in the Catholic faith. This arrangement never satisfied the father who thought the boys were doomed so far as their soul was concerned. It was out of these circumstances that young Andrew fortunately encountered the Froehlich movement. Andrew J. Braun served as an Elder in Germany. He was very active in evangelistic endeavors in America but served in the capacity of an Elder for only a short time in America. Here he was given duties similar to those of a deacon. He was likely a mid-Elder or in the German language, a *Miteldister.*

While living on John Street in Toledo, Andrew J. Braun held Sunday church services and Tuesday evening Bible classes in his home. Those who attended regularly were Fred Guth and members of the Schlatter, Frautschi, and Meister families. He impressed his Bible students with comments and sermons pertaining to the "beast" and the "false prophet." He also stressed the need for repentance.

In 1893, Sunday church services were held in a hall on the second floor of a building at 1666 Dorr Street. It was owned by Samuel Braun, son of Andrew J. Braun. The front part of the hall, which was used as a sanctuary, was filled with chairs, and the rear was used for serving lunch. Services were held from 10 a.m. to 4 p.m. with an intermission for a noon lunch. Among those who attended the services at this time were Henry Baer, Victor Stavenik and Sigmund Sorg. The ministers were Andrew J. Braun and his son, Samuel. The latter, some years later, wrote a treatise entitled "My Father's Conversion." This was distributed by the Apostolic Christian Church (Nazarene). Andrew J. Braun remained with the church in Toledo until his death. He and his wife are buried in Forrest Cemetery in Toledo.

In 1904, Samuel Braun took an active part in the construction of a new church at Woodland and Brown Avenues in Toledo. This church was heated by several wood-burning stoves, and gas was used to light the interior. Wooden chairs were used to seat the parishioners.

Samuel Braun and family moved to Syracuse, New York, in about 1905, a year after the new church was built. As a manufacturer of "Paradise Soap," he moved his plant to this area because of the abundance of raw materials. His moving to Syracuse was not related to the subsequent church schism that resulted in 1906-1907. At Syracuse, he aligned himself with the group known as the Apostolic Christian Church (Nazarene).

After Samuel Braun moved to Syracuse, the ministers who served the congregation at Toledo were John Snyder and William Erkert, Sr. Their tenure was short-lived, however, as they no longer associated with the church following the division of 1906-1907. The new ministers, who were installed in 1906, were Godfrey Schlatter, David Frautschi, and Jacob Frautschi. At that time church services were conducted in both the German and English languages.

In 1929, when the nation was enjoying a period of soon-to-end prosperity, the church building was remodeled. Electricity was used for lighting, and the old wooden chairs were replaced with benches. A basement was added for a Sunday School and a dining room.

In 1956, a modern new church was built at 3011 Marvin Avenue. It was dedicated in November, 1956. A brochure marking the occasion stated, "It is the sincere hope of the congregation of the Apostolic Christian Church that this new edifice will long serve as a house of worship in which the Name of God will be praised and glorified and where all can unitedly worship, and thus every heart become a temple of the Living God."

Godfrey Schlatter died in 1961. He served the church as a minister for more than fifty years and was instrumental in the building of the new church.

Elders who have served the Toledo congregation were Adam Imthurn, Archbold, Ohio; Henry Souder, Leo, Indiana; Eli Dotterer, Junction, Ohio; and Rudolph Graf, Akron, Ohio. Ben C. Maibach, Jr., Detroit, Michigan, has been the Elder since 1971.

LESTER, IOWA

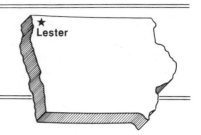

LESTER, IOWA
East side of village

The flame of faith which had swept across the Midwest for several decades soon found its way to the prairies of a remote corner of northwestern Iowa in the latter stages of the 1880's.

Lester, Iowa, is a small junction of a few hundred people located in Lyon County, Iowa. It sits only a few miles from the southern border of Minnesota and the eastern border of South Dakota. Early settlers came to the area in pursuit of less costly farm land to engage in grain and livestock farming. This means of livelihood is still prominent in the church today, but due to advancing agricultural technology, farms have grown larger, and many young people, as in other rural churches, have been forced to pursue careers in other fields. Consequently, occupations other than farming are emerging more and more among members of the church.

The roots of the Lester congregation reach back to both Germany and Elgin, Illinois. August Mogler, born September 5, 1858, at Heilbroun, Wurttemberg, Germany, became a friend of Christian and Frieda Ricka Lindoerfer.[30] The Lindoerfers, through her mother, Jacobena Schambach, earlier had become acquainted with the Froehlich movement in southern Germany. Perhaps this is where Mogler, a Lutheran, first became exposed to the dynamic doctrines of repentance, conversion, and the "new birth." In any case, when the Lindoerfers moved from Germany to Elgin, Illinois, and Frieda Ricka embraced the Apostolic Christian faith (and her husband later in 1894), they invited Mogler to attend church with them while he visited in Elgin. It was this exposure to the church that convinced him this was the "true faith," and that certain steps were necessary to get right with God.

So close was Mogler to the Lindoerfers that in 1888, when living near Lester and attending church services at West Bend, Iowa, he turned to the Lord in repentance and wrote a letter to Frieda Ricka Lindoerfer at Elgin, Illinois, informing her of his new spiritual pursuits.

August Mogler came to America in 1885 to avoid military conscription.[31] He stayed for a short time at the home of his half-brother, Adolph, in Elgin, Illinois. From there he lived for more than a year in Memphis, Tennessee, and then moved to Sioux County, Iowa, where he lived for two years. In 1888, he moved to Lyon County.

While living near Lester he attended church services in West Bend several times. He would take the train early Sunday morning and return Sunday evening. After writing a letter to Frieda Ricka Lindoerfer informing her of his conversion, she immediately notified Elder George Welk in Morton, Illinois, who in turn wrote to Elder John Anliker of West Bend. Anliker visited Mogler and became convinced he had gone through a true conversion. Some time after his baptism, he was asked to preach the gospel. This marked the beginning of the Lester, Iowa, congregation.

By 1890 the Lester "church" had four members: Ernst Nester, his wife Mary Klein Nester, Louise Wenzel, and August Mogler. Friends who met with them were the Schnepf and Klein families. They took turns hosting services and serving lunch. It was at one of these meetings that the Knobloch family, recent arrivals from Germany, tasted lemonade for the first time. This was a rare treat to them because in Germany lemons were used only to eliminate bad odors.

Wilhelm and Frieda Ricka Knobloch came to Rock Valley, Iowa, in 1890. Her brother, Ernst Nester, was already residing in the area. The Knobloch's, too, were Lutherans when they first came to America. Before leaving Germany they sold their farm and sent the money to Ernst Nester with instructions to purchase a 160-acre farm in Iowa. After meeting them at the railroad station, he took them and their few possessions by box-wagon to their new home.

After one year, Frieda Ricka Knobloch turned to the Lord. She was baptized by Elder John Anliker of West Bend. The presence of the Knobloch family gave a boost to the early Lester congregation, and by 1980 many Knobloch families attended the Lester church. In 1891, Jacob and Rosina Moser and family moved to Lester from West Bend. They were of Swiss descent and were already members of the church.

As the small church began to grow, a church building became a necessity. Accordingly, on land donated by Will Messner, a church was completed in the spring of 1893 in Cleveland Township. Jacob Moser built all the tables and benches for the new church.

The Lester congregation experienced a most unusual situation when their first church was built. It involved the horse barns located near the church. The Jacob Moser farm was located across the road from the church, and he verbally gave an acre of land on which sat the barns to house the horses during church services. Somehow, when his farm was later sold, it eventually included the acre of land where the horse barns sat. The buyer wanted that acre, too, and because the church had no deed to prove ownership, they lost the acre of land where they kept the horses. The church subsequently bought a one-half acre plot of ground from the Messner family, and the barns were moved to this location. To prevent another loss of land, a deed was secured, and Elder August Mogler announced this action to the church.

In 1907, a kitchen was built on the north side of the original building. A coal furnace was added, too. The new furnace system had just one register in each room which made it difficult to regulate the heat. Men from the church drove wagons down to Rock Valley to purchase lumber and supplies for the new addition.

A picturesque little creek which empties into Mud Creek ran along the edge of the church property. This was used for baptisms. Also, some of the early baptisms were held at the homes of converts' parents.

Because of the location of that early church, some people still refer to the area's Apostolic Christians as *Mud-creekers*.

Living conditions in those days were not easy. Yet, amid the difficulties of life, these hard-working settlers never forgot their priorities. They placed their spiritual pursuits above everything, to the honor and glory of God. As a Lester area resident once wrote, "We are and should be grateful for these pioneers who established and preserved the church for their descendants."

The Lester church grew and prospered, and by 1948 land was purchased on the northwest edge of Lester. Forty-six families united to build a $65,000 church with a seating capacity of two hundred. First services were held July 3, 1949. In 1962, when seventy families attended the church, a major renovation and addition—costing $93,000—took place. The sanctuary seating capacity was raised to six hundred. A little more than ten years later the church grew to over one hundred families and 155 members. In 1980, the church listed 135 families with 248 members.

August Mogler, the church's first Elder, was ordained in 1908 and served until his death of cancer on October 20, 1916, when he was only fifty-seven years old. This was a particularly sad occasion—as well as the end of an era—because "Father" Mogler was a charter member of the church, its first minister and Elder, and his untiring efforts on behalf of the church gave it impetus in the early days. He and his wife, Mary Ann (Banwart), raised twelve children. Over the years they hosted and cared for many persons who visited the Lester church.

From 1916 to 1963 the Lester church was served by non-resident Elders. On November 17, 1963, Leo Moser was selected as Lester's second resident Elder. During his tenure as Elder, the church has grown from 70 families to 135.

In 1983 a new 40,000-square-foot church was completed on Lester's northeast side. Its sanctuary seating capacity was near nine hundred persons.

WEINER, ARKANSAS

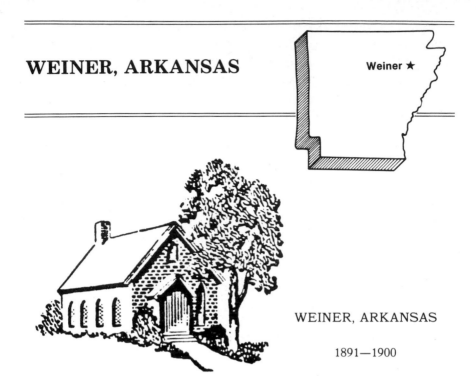

Weiner ★

WEINER, ARKANSAS

1891—1900

Early in the decade of 1890, several Apostolic Christian families—mostly from Illinois—moved to the area of Weiner, Arkansas. This spot, located approximately eighteen miles southwest of Jonesboro, appeared to have sufficient farming potential. By 1893, enough families were present to begin church services here.

Although some families migrated to Weiner as early as 1891, by 1900 they had all moved to other localities. Their farming ventures failed—were a disaster in some cases—and they were forced to move. When they left, they were poorer economically but richer for the experience. Although the land was located in the fertile Mississippi Valley, it was swampy and poorly drained. These farmers were not adept at farming under these unfamiliar conditions.

One of the first families to arrive in Weiner was that of Heinrick "Henry" Ziegenhorn who was one of the group's ministers. Other ministers were men by the name of Sinn and Reeser. Services were held only in homes. A church building was never built.

Jacob Pfister, Sr., was another farmer who took his family to Weiner, Arkansas. A native of Zurich, Switzerland, he met Sophia Rummel on a boat when coming to America and later married her. She was from Alsace-Lorraine, was raised a Lutheran, and was totally disinherited by her family when she joined the Apostolic Christian Church.[32]

The couple was married November 26, 1878, in Tremont, Illinois. It was here that a "high powered" land salesman sold Jacob Pfister, Sr., eighty acres of land and persuaded him to move to Weiner, Arkansas. They moved to Weiner by immigrant train and took all their possessions, including their horses. When they arrived in Weiner, they found it so swampy it was almost impossible to raise crops. Very likely the only ones who prospered in this venture were the land salesmen who apparently took advantage of these settlers' näiveté.

For the Pfister family and others, carving out an existence under these hopeless conditions was nearly impossible. They were driven to hunting wild hogs and scrounging for whatever food they could find to eat. Some of their children got malaria. They stayed in Weiner for two years and then moved to Indian territory near Miami, Oklahoma, before moving to Fort Scott, Kansas, in 1900.

The Ziegenhorn family returned to Cissna Park, Illinois, after a few years in Weiner. According to his grandson, Raymond Ziegenhorn of the Jonesboro Skillcare Rest Home (in a 1981 interview), Heinrick Ziegenhorn retained 160 acres despite returning to Cissna Park. Raymond and his brother, Alvin, returned to Weiner in 1912 and resumed farming operations. This land is still in the family today.

Among the other church families who lived in Weiner were the Kellars, Greiners, Knapps, and Ankers.

A church cemetery existed at Weiner at one time, but the graves were moved into a public cemetery and mingled with those of other faiths. The age of the tombstones and the fact that they are not separated from the public ones have made it nearly impossible to recognize the names of church people who might be buried in Weiner.

HARPER, KANSAS

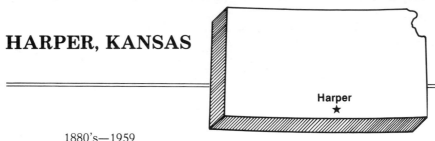

Harper
★

1880's—1959

HARPER, KANSAS
East of Highway 14

Sometime in the decade of 1880, an Apostolic Christian Church was established at Harper, Kansas, approximately fifty miles southwest of Wichita and only twenty miles north of the Oklahoma state line.

Many families came to the Harper area in pursuit of farming. By the latter stages of the 1880's, a fairly sizable congregation existed.

Serving as ministers in the early days were Gottlieb Felix Kurz, who was Elder, and Jake Meister. Kurz was born March 3, 1844, in Backnang, Wurttemberg, Germany.[33] He died in 1930. (Old-timers pronounced his name "Kortz.")

Living conditions in Kansas were difficult and primitive during the 1880's. Typical of these pioneers were John Frintz and Caroline Knapp who were married in 1885. In October of that year, they homesteaded a claim in the extreme southeast corner of Haskell County, Kansas. This was many miles from Harper. The Frintzes later moved to Illinois where they became members of the church.

The Frintzes exemplified the indomitable spirit of these undaunted pioneers. The harsh living conditions of this era were almost unbelievable. One-room homes were made of sod which formed the walls. Boards were placed across the walls to form the framework of the roof. Tar paper was laid on the boards and a layer of sod placed on the tar paper to prevent dirt and water leakage.

Water was obtained by digging a well. John Frintz once dug a 160-foot-deep well which took twenty days to complete. He did all the digging himself while two men remained on the ground above to haul up the buckets of dirt by rope. In *The Life of John Frintz,* Russell Rapp writes of his grandfather's experience:

> Three layers of quicksand were encountered during the digging; one layer was twelve feet thick. To prevent the dry pulverized quicksand from falling into the well, the men sawed the boards so that the ends formed interlocking joints which were sandproof and sturdy. Not one nail was used throughout. When the quicksand had been sealed, the digging proceeded to further depths. The walls of the well needed no reinforcing, for the soil in that region was very compact. When the depth of 160 feet was reached, Grandpa's shovel struck a hard, red, sandstone composition. He took a chisel and started chipping until he fell through the formation. Luckily, he fell into the clear, blue, cold water which was only three feet deep. The water in that well was part of an underground river which had its origin in the Rocky Mountains of Colorado.

Another couple who endured the hardships in this area were Daniel and Louisa Steiner who formerly lived in Morton, Illinois. The *Steiner Family Record, 1720 to 1978* gives a vivid account of their experiences in the Harper area:

> In 1885, enticed by the prospect of cheap land on the western frontier, Daniel sold his carpenter shop and moved his family to a farm near Harper, Kansas (located in Harper County, south central Kansas). The only building on the farm was a one-room shanty in which they lived until the erection of a four-room dwelling was completed.
>
> Their life in the new land was beset with trial and adversity. For over nine years they struggled to wrest a livelihood from the untamed prairie. There were years of drought and crop failure. One summer their hopes were shattered when a promising wheat crop, golden ripe and ready for harvest, was destroyed by hail.

The family was repeatedly plagued by diseases prevalent on the frontier, malaria and typhoid. There were times when the food supply was so depleted they wondered where the next day's meal would come from. In addition, they suffered the tragedy of losing their youngest child, Lydia, who was killed in a tornado.

Finally the two elder sons, Daniel Adam and Menno John, returned to Illinois to find employment. Daniel had no money, so he traveled as a "tramp," hopping freight trains with the advice and assistance of more experienced "knights of the road." It was a demoralizing experience for a somewhat timid young man.

After struggling along for a time with the aid of funds sent by his sons, Daniel decided to leave Harper. He packed his meager possessions in two covered wagons and, with his wife and three children, Mary, Edward Henry, and Louise Anna, struck out for Illinois.

When they reached northeast Kansas, they stopped to rest and to visit friends and acquaintances of their faith in the Bern and Sabetha communities. These kind people welcomed them and prevailed upon them to settle in this area rather than continue the long trek to Illinois.

The church at Harper continued to grow as people like Daniel and Louisa Steiner moved to the area and were willing to endure the hardships of the times. Church growth was stifled, however, when lands were opened for settlement in the Oklahoma Territory. Many families left Harper to settle on the "Cherokee Strip" lands in 1893. The church declined in membership from this migration and never recovered. It remained, however, a church of fair size for several decades and then began to dwindle considerably.

During the decade of 1910-1920, several young people became members of the church. Esther Gleichman (Ernest's daughter) remembers how disappointed her brother, Emil, was when she turned to the Lord. He told her, "You are going to break up all our fun." Her action apparently had a great impact on him because he began repenting one week later.

For many years Ernest Gleichman and Fred Domnick served as ministers. Gleichman was the Elder. He was born October 25, 1866, in Suhl, Germany, and was ordained Elder in 1933.[34] He is remembered as a man of gentleness and peace. He was formerly a Lutheran. When he came to Harper, he worked as a blacksmith. He met the Lambert and Stuckey families, and their cordial hospitality impressed him. Their kindness helped draw him to the Lord.

As the decades passed, the church declined to approximately four families. Consequently, a family would serve lunch at church every four weeks. According to Carrie Emch Gleichman, Madison, Kansas, who formerly lived in Harper, "It never made us poor" serving lunch so often.

After Ernest Gleichman's death in 1938, the small gathering in Harper met only for Sunday School classes. One Sunday evening per month the church at Burlington, Oklahoma, would travel to Harper to conduct church services. Often, the Wichita congregation would join them, and according to George Lambert, a minister at Wichita for many years, these were "very enjoyable times."

Paul Allenbach took the responsibility of teaching God's word to the few remaining members for several years. His sudden death in 1959 terminated these teaching sessions. The church was subsequently dissolved and the building sold to the city of Harper. Today it serves as a museum owned by the Harper City Historical Society.

The old Harper church building was purchased by the city and converted into a museum.

FORT SCOTT, KANSAS

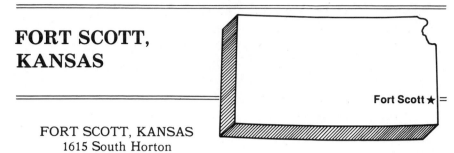

FORT SCOTT, KANSAS
1615 South Horton

When brethren and friends of the Fort Scott, Kansas, Apostolic Christian congregation gathered together on December 10, 1967, to dedicate their new church building at 1615 South Horton Street, a brochure commemorating the happy occasion accurately described the feelings and intentions of the congregation:

> *We dedicate this temple, this labor of our hands*
> *To Father, Son, and Spirit whose temple ever stands*
> *That there our hearts may worship, and here our songs ascend*
> *In loving adoration and praise that knows no end.*

Seventy-four years had transpired since the first members of the Apostolic Christian Church began holding services in the Fort Scott area. While all those first believers were farmers, today only thirty percent of the membership are tillers of the soil. The church, while always comparatively small, has nonetheless grown from a half dozen early families in 1893 to twenty-eight in 1980. Membership has remained in the forty-five to fifty range.[35] The new church, built at a cost of $85,000 on a lot donated by Mary Reber, has a sanctuary seating capacity of 144.

The Apostolic Christian Church in Fort Scott—often called the "little German church"—is located in a region considered to be very rich historically. It was here, on a flat limestone ridge overlooking the valley of the Marmaton River, the United States government located a military post—one in a series of bases stretching from Minnesota to Louisiana—to keep peace between white settlers and the Indians during frontier days. It was named for General Winfield Scott, soldier and presidential candidate.

Later, during the "Bleeding Kansas" period (1854-1861)—when free-staters and pro-slavery factions struggled for supremacy—Fort Scott was the focal point of much civil disturbance.

Four decades later (in 1893-1894) a few families of German descent began moving to farms near Fort Scott. Most came from Weiner, Arkansas, where they had previously met with terrible disappointment trying to farm the swampy Mississippi Delta land. Among the early families were those of Chris Knapp, Sr., George Knapp, Sr., John Rager, and Fred Greiner, Sr. In 1895, the George Sinn family moved here from Arkansas.[36]

The year 1900 was an encouraging one for the little congregation. After seven years of preaching, they finally realized their first convert. He was Gus Rager. During this year several more families came to Fort Scott: Charley Ehnle from Illinois, Henry Kellenberger and Jacob Pfister, Sr., from Oklahoma, and Will Bruner from Sabetha, Kansas.

Making a living off the eastern Kansas soil was both difficult and uncertain. Some of the families had a very difficult time making ends meet and were hard pressed financially. Jacob Pfister, Jr., was fourteen when his family moved to Fort Scott. He would often go hunting and later take his game to town so he could buy ammunition to kill more game. He told of how his mother used to cry because they were so poor and had very little to eat.

Despite these harsh economic conditions, a few more families continued to find residence in the Fort Scott area. Jacob Berchtold and family came from Warsaw, Missouri, in 1904. In 1917, Peter and Adam Mauer moved here from Iowa. Between 1920 and 1923, five families came to Fort Scott from Minnesota: the Joe Banwarts, Emil Banwarts, William Rebers, Tim Hohulins, and John Zauggs.

The assembly of believers at Fort Scott met together in homes from 1893 until 1921 when they began meeting in a building purchased from the Presbyterian Church. This church, located at 12th Street and Scott Avenue, cost $2,200. It was quickly repaired and made ready for services. One particularly memorable renovation was the taking down of the steeple and bell from the roof of the church. George Sinn, II, the church's oldest brother, and his son Fred climbed up and took the bell down. An instrument of this sort was considered vain and too "worldly" for those times. Also, today none of the Apostolic Christian Churches have church bells.

In 1965, the brethren in Fort Scott survived a very unnerving experience at this church—a bomb scare. One Saturday afternoon a lady called Clara Marti informing her, "Your church is going to be bombed tomorrow." Stunned, she called authorities, and the church was searched. Police were there when worship began the next morning. Despite the furor of a bomb threat, nearly all the members attended church services.

George Sinn, Sr., served the church for nearly thirty years as a minister. Jacob Pfister, Sr., preached at Fort Scott from 1923 to 1929. His son, Jacob, Jr., became a minister in 1931 and served until ill health caused his retirement in 1970. He served alone in the ministry for fifteen years.

The church's first resident Elder, Raymond Banwart, was ordained November 12, 1972. Previous to this the church was served by non-resident Elders. They were Joseph Huber, Gridley, Kansas, who as a boy in Germany was raised a Catholic; Jacob Somerhalder, also of Gridley; Emil Schubert, Peoria, Illinois, who used to travel to Fort Scott by train; Noah Schrock, Oakville, Iowa, who, according to Raymond Banwart, was at one time the only church Elder west of the Mississippi River; and Samuel Anliker, Lamont, Kansas.

A minister of the church, Jacob Pfister, Jr., wrote the following poem:[37]

> *Of all life's treasures on earth that I see,*
> *There's none so precious as Jesus to me.*
> *He left heaven's glory to ransom my soul;*
> *To serve Him and love Him shall be my life's goal.*
> *He loved me so much He shed His own blood,*
> *That I might be cleansed in that glorious flood.*
> *Tho' I can't comprehend with my finite mind*
> *What it cost God to give such a gift so divine,*
> *Yet I'll praise Him and thank Him for each day of grace,*
> *Till I see Him and meet Him at last face to face.*
> *What joy and what glory for me that will be*
> *To know the dear Saviour, who died once for me!*
> *Calv'ry beckons and calls to all who will come.*
> *Why not plunge in while day and be on your way Home?*
> *The Saviour will greet you on life's distant shore,*
> *And dwell with you alway—to part never more.*

KIOWA, KANSAS
(Formerly Burlington, Oklahoma)

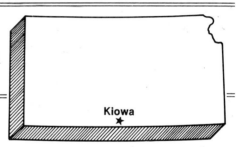

KIOWA, KANSAS
823 Holmes Street

When several families moved to the Burlington, Oklahoma, area from Harper, Kansas, in the early 1890's, it spelled the eventual decline of the Harper church but signaled the beginning of a church at Burlington.

On September 16, 1893, a vast section of northern Oklahoma Territory was opened for settlement. A major area of settlement was the famed Cherokee Strip—a strip of land 165 miles by 58 miles consisting of six million acres purchased from the Cherokee Indians in 1891 for $8.5 million.[38]

Thousands of settlers, on a signal given by federal marshals, rushed into the new territory by foot, on horseback, in buggies and wagons, and on bicycles to stake and claim quarter-section farms. The *Harper Sentinel* gave this advice to prospective settlers, "Take with you a canteen of water, three days' grub, a jack knife, a spade, a small amount of water, a Bible, a copy of the *Sentinel,* along with a good conscience."

The Homestead Act, signed May 20, 1861, declared that any United States citizen, or alien intending to become a citizen, could have 160 acres of western lands absolutely free (except for a ten dollar registration fee) provided he make certain improvements and live on the tract for five years.[39]

Many emigrants, bound for generations by a rigid class structure in their homelands and often hampered by their emigrant status in America, found the possibility of becoming independent landowners too appealing to resist. Apostolic Christians were swept along in this tide of enthusiasm to own farmland (without having to pay for it). Among those who made the "run" into Oklahoma were families with names like Kurz, Meister, Lambert, Steiger, Zehr, Kiefer, Aeschliman, Ramseyer, Stuckey, Pfister, Aberle, Schiffner, Schafer, Hinesman, Herman, Frey, Rossi, Shook, Schurter, and Hodel. They settled in or near Burlington which received its name in 1907 when Oklahoma became a state.

The 1893 run into the Cherokee Strip area of north-central Oklahoma was tabbed "The Greatest Horse Race in the World." Some of the horses used in this run were actual race horses costing from $200 to $500. Over 50,000 settlers claimed land in the six-million-acre area the first day—a sensational occurrence.

This famed race started from Kiowa's Seventh Street (a north-south street) and extended along a line east to west.

Interestingly, today's Kiowa Apostolic Christian Church is located in the zone where the race into the Cherokee Strip began in 1893.

Artist's sketch depicts settlers rushing into Oklahoma to stake their land claims.

Church members who homesteaded in Oklahoma were noted for their vigor and sturdiness which were undergirded by a deep and abiding faith in God. Many pioneering difficulties were met collectively through neighborliness and helping one another. They helped each other build homes and often purchased implements in partnership. It was only through working together that many found the courage to remain in Oklahoma amid severe privation. Many, perhaps, nurtured a deep desire to return to their former homes, but a lack of finances prevented them from doing so. At such times church fellowship and brotherly kindness were especially appreciated.

An example of one Apostolic Christian who made the trek from Harper, Kansas, was John Allenbach. He and his family rode in a covered wagon with the family cow traveling behind the wagon. They arrived in 1895 after the initial rush in 1893 and purchased a quarter-section of land by trading the cow plus $40.

The Apostolic Christian settlement was centered east of Burlington. The first church services were held in Jake Meister's sod house. Families took their own lunch to eat between the morning and afternoon church services. They would take the seats off their spring wagons, find a comfortable place in the shade, and enjoy their sandwiches prior to reassembling for the afternoon worship service.

In 1894 Gottlieb Kurz, a minister at Harper, moved to the area and donated land one-half mile east and one-quarter mile south of Burlington for a church site. A wooden structure was built, and brethren sat on planks supported by kegs until more comfortable benches could be made.

Kurz, who was quite active in the development of the Burlington church, put up a windmill and provided a small pond filled with well water to use for baptisms. This area was located north of the church. Emma Guth was the first of four persons to be baptized in this pond.

In 1900 a larger church was built and the old structure converted into a Sunday School.

In approximately 1907 an extension was made to the church's assembly room. Also, horse sheds were built to house the "teams" during the worship services.

Early in the decade of 1900-1910, several more families moved to Burlington. The continued development of railroads made travel to the area easier. Among the arrivals were the families of Gottfried Miller, Morton, Illinois, and Adolph Schupbach of Burlington, Kansas (near Gridley).

In 1907 Joseph P. Farney came from Missouri. He purchased seventeen hundred acres from a cattle baron. Featured on this farm—the former Campbell Ranch—was a large three-story barn formerly used as a racehorse stable. The second story was used for feed and the third story for hay.[40]

As the nation entered into World War I, pressure came to bear on the congregation to begin preaching in the English language instead of German. Elder Gottlieb Kurz spoke English with difficulty. John Stoll could speak English only on a limited basis. Alpha Domnick, who became a minister in 1924, would then stand in front of the pulpit after the German preaching and interpret the substance of the remarks in

English. This made the young children sit up and take notice because for the first time many of them could understand.

In 1932 Elders Ernest Graf, Sr., Akron, Ohio, and Jacob Stettner, Elgin, Illinois, made a visit to the Burlington church to make an official request that the German language no longer be used from the pulpit. Actually, the cessation of this practice had already begun.

An incident at the old Burlington church that will long be remembered occurred in the summer of 1940, a time when twelve souls were in repentance. It was described by Kathryn Miller of Kiowa, Kansas:

> One very hot summer Sunday afternoon when Noah Schrock was preaching, the sky darkened suddenly and a severe thunderstorm came up. Lightning struck so close that Brother Schrock was momentarily stunned—and there was an electrical power failure. Throughout all the storm activity the Word of God was expounded with extra effort to overcome the thundering storm, the assembly room being as dark as dusk. It was an impressive sermon, and the struggle of the elements intensified the magnanimous power of the supernatural.

In 1947 an extensive remodeling of the church took place. The enhanced structure was dedicated on October 26, 1947. Elder Noah Schrock was present for this special service.

In 1972 the congregation decided to build a new church in Kiowa, Kansas. Many of the families of the church lived in this area, and although the sentimentality associated with remaining as the only Apostolic Christian Church in the state of Oklahoma remained a strong force, it was nonetheless overcome, and the decision was made to move to Kiowa ("Kiowa" is an Indian name meaning "principal people").[41]

Sometime prior to the completion of the new church in Kiowa, an explosion occured at the old Burlington church. It resulted from air conditioning gas and caused a sticky substance to penetrate through the ducts into the church. Professional help was sought to clean up the sticky residue which enveloped the entire church. It was never understood how the church escaped being destroyed by fire.

Dedication of the new church at 823 Holmes Street in Kiowa was held March 31, 1974, with Elder Ben C. Maibach, Jr., of Detroit, Michigan, officiating.

During an electrical storm on April 29, 1977, lightning caused a fire on the roof resulting in $55,000 damage. While this was being repaired, the church assembled in the Kiowa High School auditorium.

Gottlieb Kurz and Ernest Gleichman both served as Elders at Burlington. On September 11, 1950, Roy L. Farney was elected Elder. He served until 1960 when he moved to Phoenix, Arizona. On October 22, 1978, Ronald V. Nelson was elected to serve as Elder of the congregation.

Elias Somerhalder served in the ministry for forty years at the Burlington and Kiowa churches. For a number of years he served alone.

ALTO, MICHIGAN

ALTO, MICHIGAN
Wingeier Road
2½ miles southeast of Alto

An Apostolic Christian Church presently exists in the area of Alto, Michigan, a small town a few miles southeast of Grand Rapids, Michigan. Although the seed of faith came very quietly in 1879 to this area in the heart of a devoted sister who for many years, standing alone, nurtured this "pearl of great price," a church was not established here until 1895.

Katherina Biedermann was born in 1838 in Switzerland. In 1868, at age thirty, she came to America with her husband, Samuel Wingeier, her mother-in-law, and four small sons. The family emigrated to a farm at Stone Creek, Ohio, located near New Philadelphia. Her husband began farming and making cheese. Three more sons were born to this union, giving them a total of seven. The family lived in Ohio for eight years.

It was during her stay in the Stone Creek area that Katherina Wingeier, who at this point was not familiar with the Froehlich movement, felt the call of God and experienced a religious conversion. She remained alone in her faith and quietly kept the new life deep within her heart. One day at Stone Creek she encountered two men walking north along the railroad track. She asked, "What kind of men are you?" She learned they were Elder Isaac Gehring and John Ott who were walking from the Sardis church to Rittman. She made further inquiry about their faith and invited them to her home. Her husband was very cordial to them until they began to open Scriptures and read aloud. This displeased him, and it led to the family eventually moving from the area.

While Isaac Gehring and John Ott visited with Katherina Wingeier, they learned that her religious experiences and convictions were very similar to those which they espoused. In time, she was baptized and became a member of the church.

Because of her husband's reluctance to tolerate her new religious affiliation, the family moved to far-away Michigan. In 1877, they moved to Belmont, Michigan, and in 1879 bought a farm three miles north of Lowell, Michigan. She and her husband lived there until their deaths—his in 1897 and hers in 1922.

It was on this tranquil farm that she raised her seven sons and quietly nurtured her precious faith. A descendant, Rose Wingeier, wrote in 1965:

> Here, in her spiritual life, she stood alone in a wilderness, for there were no churches and no members of her faith. But what she had was

God and the Bible and off and on, a letter from Brothers and Sisters
in Ohio and Illinois. So with an unwavering faith in God and living a
quiet and God-fearing life, she went on and on in her way until the
Lord, after hearing her many prayers, sent joy and happiness to her
starving spirit.

As the years unfolded, several of her sons and their wives
turned to the Lord. The first to repent was Mary Wingeier,
wife of Alexander, her fifth son. Elder Isaac Gehring came all
the way from Sardis, Ohio, to baptize her, and she became the
first person to be baptized at what later became known as the
Alto-Lowell church.

Later, her son Samuel Wingeier turned to the Lord and
became the first male member at Alto. He possessed the gift of
preaching and was soon placed in the ministry. This was in approximately 1897. He served alone in the ministry for thirty
years until 1927.

In 1895, church services were held in various homes.
Katherina Wingeier offered her home north of Lowell, and
church was held there for many years. Travel was difficult, but
despite snow, rain, and inclement weather, the brethren were
diligent in attending church. Sometimes it took a horse and
buggy as long as two hours to travel only fourteen miles.

As the church grew in number, converts traveled to Toledo,
Ohio, for baptism. Later, they were baptized in a small creek
which ran through the Wingeier property. Still later, baptisms
were performed in the cattle watering trough at the home of
Ferdinand and Anna Wingeier until the first church was built.
When Lydia, Mary, and Anna Wingeier were baptized
December 16, 1916, the ice on the watering trough had to be
chopped out prior to the baptismal ceremony which was conducted by Elder Gottlieb Maibach of Bay City, Michigan.

In 1921, a few months before the death of Katherina
Wingeier, a new church was built one and one-half miles east
and one mile south of Alto. It cost $3,200. About twenty
members belonged to the church at that time. Locally, it was
known as the "Swiss Church" or the "Wingeier Church." Services were conducted in the German language until 1927.
From then through 1941 both German and English were used.
From 1941 on, the services were conducted in English with the
exception of special occasions.

After Samuel Wingeier served alone in the ministry for several decades, he was joined on the pulpit by Fred Oesch (pronounced "Ersch") in 1927. A native of Switzerland, Oesch came to Alto and was employed by his future father-in-law, Ferdinand Wingeier, a member of the church. He attended church services with the Wingeiers. He remembered wearing bib-overalls to services, and he always looked forward to the noon luncheon between worship services.

At first he wanted no part of this "strange" doctrine, but later he became a believer and eventually a minister. He was very soft spoken. His messages were always the true Word of God, full of love, concern for the lost, and caution for the wayward. Often he spoke of the Christian's path as being "steep and thorny," but he always reminded his listeners of the reward ahead. He died in 1968 at age eighty.

Philip Wingeier, grandson of Katherina Wingeier, was made a minister in 1942 and served until 1979. In 1973, he moved to Sarasota, Florida, and served in the ministry there until his death in 1982.

The church building at Alto was remodeled in 1943 at an approximate cost of $2,800. Godfrey Schlatter, Toledo, Ohio, and Theo Beer, Milford, Indiana, officiated at the dedication services.

In 1966, a new church was built on the site of the old church. It cost approximately $100,000. It was constructed of brick and field stone (many stones from the surrounding fields were used), and the design was of traditional rural American architecture. The sanctuary, with a seating capacity of 220, was twice as large as the old church.

Aaron Steffen, Jr., who was selected as a minister on Mother's Day, May 14, 1967, was ordained as the church's first resident Elder on Father's Day, June 21, 1981.

When the new church was completed in 1966, many artifacts were placed in the cornerstone of the church for future generations to open and read. One paragraph on the church's history seemed to reflect the 1960's:

> We have at this time much to be thankful for as prosperity, according to things of this life, does flourish, the conveniences in our homes have never been better, and transportation to any part of the world is

readily available. Food and clothing are much in excess of our needs and all in all, our standard of living could not be better. But above all, we cherish the God-given privilege that we can worship and assemble in the way we are enlightened by the Holy Spirit and God's divine guidance. May this continue also in your time.

Katherina Wingeier, despite great odds, proved that diligence and faithfulness can eventually bear fruit. Her example of steadfastness provides much inspiration to today's churches that remain small and seem unlikely to grow and prosper. She likely felt the same way in the latter part of the nineteenth century.

EUREKA, ILLINOIS

EUREKA, ILLINOIS
700 West Cruger Avenue

Although a church building was constructed at Eureka, Illinois, as early as 1896, the congregation here remained an integral part of the Roanoke church located six miles northeast of town until 1956 when a large new church was built at Eureka. The large Roanoke church located on the vast prairie between Eureka and Roanoke and founded by Benedict Weyeneth, the first American Elder, was attended both by Eureka and Roanoke people who lived in the area. It was a common sight late in the nineteenth century to see people walking from the villages of Eureka and Roanoke to the country church.

In order to better accommodate brethren who lived in Eureka, a small meeting place was built in that village. This was primarily used for mid-week services. On Sunday, the members would go to the country church for worship services. The Eureka building was not used for Sunday services unless the roads were bad or the weather unusually inclement. A similar church was built in Roanoke for the same purpose. This little church in Eureka at 107 North Myers Street was built in 1896 on property donated by Henry B. Schumacher. Early ministers were John W. Schmidt who first occupied the pulpit; Carl Haecker, Samuel Schumacher, and Leo Grusy. Haecker's eldest son, George, remembers digging the trenches for the foundation of the first church. He assisted Albert Hinnen in this project.

With the advent of the automobile and better roads, ease of transportation prompted the virtual decline of the church at Eureka in the early 1940's. Both mid-week and Sunday services were held at the Roanoke country church, which was now easily accessible from Eureka. The old church in Eureka was vacated in 1950. The next year it was moved to 514 West Center Street and converted into a residence.

By this time, the Roanoke congregation had become very large. It had grown from approximately 350 members in 1929 to over six hundred in the early 1950's. Out of convenience, it was decided (on February 14, 1955) to build a new church in Eureka. This would alleviate the space problem at Roanoke and provide a more centrally located place of worship for the growing number of brethren in the Eureka area.

On March 21, 1956, ground was broken for the new church, a structure of brick, stone, steel and laminated wood of contemporary style. The new church, situated in the southeast corner of Eureka, sits on a three-and-one-half-acre site and has a seating capacity of seven hundred.

David Mangold of Roanoke was the first Elder to serve this church. Joe Rocke and Leroy Huber were Eureka's first ministers at this permanent church. Leroy Huber was elected Elder December 6, 1959. Joe Rocke was victim of a fatal accident November 21, 1961.

In 1966, a beautiful and spacious home for the aged was built next to the church. By 1982, the approximate number of residents in the sheltered care, infirmary, apartments, and duplexes totaled 150.

The Eureka church had 220 members by 1982.

The old "town church" in Eureka. Built in 1896 at 107 North Myers Street, its use was terminated in 1950.

LAMAR, MISSOURI

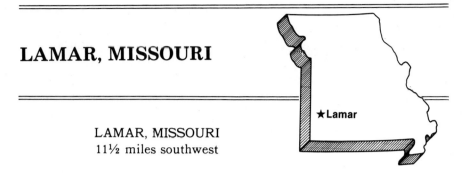

LAMAR, MISSOURI
11½ miles southwest

★Lamar

Picture in your mind a little white church serenely sitting in the quiet country, surrounded by fields and pastures. The graceful elms to the east, which provide a measure of shade, are swaying in the gentle summer breeze. A mockingbird, lustily singing its praises to the Lord, can be heard through open windows. It is a beautiful Sunday morning and the worshippers are assembling for services.

Marie Marti's vivid description makes reference to the old country church located approximately eleven miles southwest of Lamar, Missouri.

The editor of the *Lamar Democrat* used to refer to this church as "the Amish community." This term was typical of many erroneous references to the church denomination in many parts of the country.

Lamar, the birthplace of Harry S. Truman, the thirty-third President of the United States, is located in southwestern Missouri about thirty miles north of Joplin and only thirteen miles from the Kansas border.

The Apostolic Christian heritage began in this area in 1889 when a Lamar land agent, C. T. Trice, met Peter Roth in Illinois and persuaded him to visit Barton County where the price of land was far below values in Illinois. Roth traveled to Missouri and was sufficiently impressed with the land's potential. He subsequently purchased 640 acres of land one mile north and one mile west of today's church known as the "Miller section." He built a large house in the middle of the section. Many brethren who eventually moved to the area stayed at this house until they became established on their own farms. The estate had one large house and one small house. By 1981, Leonard Braker lived on the "Roth place" and Charles Marti, a minister, lived nearby.

In 1899, the Peter Roth and Henry Swing families arrived in the area to take up residence. In 1900, Sam Kahler and his family came. Also, during this time, the John, Jake, and George Kibler families moved to the area. Others who came were the families of Adolph Daetwyler, Fred Koehl (who was the group's first minister), Jake Schmit, Henry Lehman, and Andrew Obergfel (who later served as minister).

In 1902, several families came from Kansas and Iowa. Those from Kansas included the John Heinigers, William Wengers, Chris Liechties, Rudolph Lochers, Joseph Strahms, Will Cordills, John Widmers, Sr., and John Kuenzis. At about the same time, the Charley, Dan, Lou, and Will Messner families also arrived.

With so many church families settling in the area, the group incorporated as "The Apostolic Christian Church in Barton County, Missouri" in May, 1902. The first trustees were Adolph Daetwyler, Nichlaus Heiniger, and John Kibler.

On July 3, 1902, Jacob and Aline Heiniger of Iroquois County, Illinois, donated land in Barton County "to be used for church property." They also donated land for a cemetery.

During the summer of 1902, construction began on a new church with members and friends of the church donating most of the labor. The project was completed in December of that year.

In December, 1902, several families (totaling fifty people) moved from West Bend, Iowa, to Lamar. They scheduled special train cars to transport their families, furniture and livestock. Included in this group were the families of Fred, Abe, and Phillip Banwart, George Metzger, Nicholas Marti, Joshua Braker, Nathan Schlupp, and a newlywed couple, George and Minnie Frieden.

The second Sunday after the group from West Bend had arrived, the first worship services were held in the new church. A local historian described that memorable day:[42]

> There were snow-covered roads and fields on that first Sunday morning, but doors swung widely open, and there was friendly warmth inside. How good it seemed to hear Bro. Fred Koehl speaking in clear and tender tones, teaching a strong faith, deep and true.

Two events seemed to ignite a surge of emotion and joy among the members and friends of the congregation—a brand new church and almost fifty new adults and children in attendance. It was during this time that the church experienced significant growth and reached its peak membership. In 1903, thirty souls turned to the Lord in repentance. In 1904, another group responded to the Lord's call. One who turned to the Lord at this time later remarked, "What rejoicing there was in those days when so many repented and were added to the fold."[43]

As the years unfolded, crop and land conditions did not prove as promising as originally anticipated. Many families moved back to their previous homes, and membership declined considerably. Fortunately, it was not long until several young men began repenting, and the church grew again.

In 1950, the church building was remodeled and modernized. In 1980, a new church building was completed with a seating capacity of 216.

The Lamar congregation was served by non-resident Elders until Eugene Marti, Elder at Sabetha, Kansas, moved to Springfield, Missouri, and began attending church at Lamar. On September 21, 1975, he received the support of the congregation to serve as Elder, assisting their long-time Elder, Samuel Anliker of Lamont, Kansas. On February 2, 1960, Elder Anliker turned the duties over to Elder Marti.

In the earlier days of the church's existence, visiting Elders came by train and were often picked up at nearby Iantha, Missouri.

During World War II the church at Lamar served as a haven for many non-combatant brothers of the church nationally who were stationed at Camp Crowder, Fort Leonard Wood, Camp Clark, and other military posts.

Although the church at Lamar is barely eighty years old and has endured many hardships and struggles, it had evolved into a solid congregation of more than thirty-five families and approximately sixty members by December, 1981. The beautiful new church, completed in 1980, reflects a promising outlook for future generations. Yet, the past remains a strong force in the minds of the brethren as Marie Marti writes:

> The old-fashioned days have long since passed, but memory clings to those early church days. Many have walked the toilsome way, shaken hands with care, supped with pleasure. What a desolate place the world would be without the hope and faith that beckons us on to heaven. Humbly, hopefully, devotedly we journey along, with eyes uplifted, focused on that beautiful Zion, as the years are fleeting so swiftly by.

"...but they measuring themselves by themselves, and comparing themselves among themselves, are not wise."

By the turn of the century, the new church denomination had grown at a fairly rapid rate. For the most part, growth in America resulted as much from widespread immigration as from proselytizing.

Since 1847—when the first congregation had been established in Lewis County, New York—the church expanded to include activities in eleven states. Church meetings were held in New York, Ohio, Illinois, Iowa, Indiana, Kansas, Connecticut, Missouri, Oregon, Arkansas, and Michigan. Congregations (or church meetings) had sprung up in forty-five different locations. By 1900, however, services had been terminated in Partridge Prairie (Woodford County, Illinois); Archbold, Ohio; Wabaunsee County, Kansas; Diamond, Missouri; Ashtabula, Ohio; and Weiner, Arkansas.

The Apostolic Christian Church in America was established with no specific design for evangelism, no advance planning, and no central administrative headquarters. Rather, churches were established out of necessity as several families would move into a local area. Their common desire would be to organize a church. If a minister was among their group, they were fortunate, and their chance for success was greatly enhanced. If not, they would often select a suitable man among their group to minister to them. In most instances, Elders were non-resident, did not have as close a contact with the churches under their jurisdiction as today, and sometimes the span of time between their visits was quite long. Essentially, despite a strong sense of brotherhood and devotion to a common doctrine, the early churches formed a loosely-joined organization separated by primitive travel conditions, slow modes of communication, and a preoccupation with trying to eke out a living in a new and foreign land. It is obvious that these factors prevented the administrative cohesion and effective Elder oversight to the extent that existed in the early 1980's and subsequently.

By 1900, differences and attitudes among some of the brethren led to an unfortunate cleavage. This is often referred to as the "first split." Owing to the wide range of cultural backgrounds of the membership—both religious and secular—it is probably a credit to all concerned that more factions did not occur. The church was eventually divided into two groups— the Apostolic Christian Church (the one this history is about) and the Apostolic Christian Church (Nazarene). The latter, according to the perspective of the former, left to form their own congregations and today remains as the smaller of the two groups in the United States. While the split occurred mostly in 1906-1907, there was no definite point at which a total division was made. Rather, individuals departed as early as 1901 and as late as 1911. Generally, doctrine was not as much a factor in the division as were ethnic and cultural considerations.

The schism can be attributed to several reasons. Perhaps the primary causative factor was the cultural pluralism of the brotherhood which existed from 1850 to 1900. The cultural composite of the membership was quite varied, both spiritually and socially. For instance, the religious background of the members included Mennonite, Lutheran, Catholic, Swiss Protestant, "Froehlich," and American Protestant. Ethnically, members came from Switzerland, Germany, Austria, Hungary, France, and a few other countries (including America).

From a religious standpoint, one major factor stands out as a cause of the split. Two forces were subtly gathering over the years which finally resulted in a serious conflict. The first force consisted of many brethren who possessed convictions and attitudes similar to the background from which they emanated prior to embracing the Apostolic Christian Church—the Mennonite and Amish faith. It is fair to say that a sizable portion of the earliest converts in America were of Mennonite and Amish background. This was true in New York, Ohio, Indiana, Illinois, and Iowa. These brethren had a profound influence on the church and to some extent tended to dominate it during the first fifty years of its existence in America. Obviously, they brought many of their views and convictions with them when they embraced the doctrine of the Apostolic Christian Church. For them, the two appealing things about the Apostolic Christian Church were the "new birth" experience and baptism by immersion. Yet, they still held to a lifestyle which included rigid and uniform standards of dress and outward appearance.

By the time persons of Mennonite and Amish persuasion had begun to come into the Apostolic Christian Church, their previous religious heritage was more than three centuries old. Born out of the brutal persecution of the Anabaptist movement and subjected to scorn and rejection by society (due in part to their refusal to bear arms, swear oaths, and to support the state church), these people, while in Europe, had eventually settled down to quiet, rural lives centered around farming. They were noted for their talents in husbandry and were satisfied to quietly and contentedly live on their farms apart from the rest of society. They attempted to "live a quiet and peaceable life in all godliness and honesty." The Biblical doctrines of "separation from the world" and "non-conformity to the world" were taken literally and put into practice. Because they had finally found a peaceful lifestyle after suffering so much persecution over the years, many were not inclined toward evangelism and proselytization. This same attitude continued when they came to America. They were primarily interested in a peaceful life, order in the church, and an explicit, non-worldly lifestyle.

The second force consisted of many persons who did not have a Mennonite or Amish background. While in Europe, they had been exposed to the preaching of Samuel Froehlich. They came from many religious backgrounds including Lutheran, Catholic, state church, and others. They were not as deeply rooted in tradition as those with a Mennonite or Amish background. Their religious mind-set was completely different with respect to centuries-old church practices. They were more urban oriented, probably better educated, and lived more in the mainstream of society. Being directly exposed to Froehlich and his preaching colleagues—who were quite evangelistic—it is likely they were more i lined toward an aggressive program of spreading the Word and gaining new converts. Also, they were not as interested in stressing explicit standards of dress and appearance. Their background and motive were markedly different from those with Mennonite and Amish ties.

Added to differences in religious backgrounds were cultural and national differences. People who came to America and united with the Apostolic Christian Church were from many different countries. Their lifestyles were rooted in varying cultures with centuries of tradition. When they came to America as emigrants—as strangers in a foreign land—it was important to them to retain many of their former cultural practices. This caused, in some instances, misunderstanding, suspicion, and distrust—all factors which can divide and result in schism. Cultural practices which were proper and harmless to some were offensive to others. This all led to stress, strain, disunity, and lack of forebearance among the brethren.

A focal point of cultural differences seemed to center on the wearing of a mustache. This seemingly insignificant practice—which appears difficult to understand today—was favored primarily by those brothers of Eastern European (Balkan state) backgrounds.

To those brethren of Western European background (Mennonites and Amish), this was quite offensive. To them a mustache had military connotations and represented both pride and a sense of militarism. Because their heritage was so deeply rooted in non-resistance and the practice of not bearing arms—for which their forebearers suffered terribly—they were offended by those who wore mustaches. When the American Elders asked that mustaches be removed (probably because the holy kiss was practiced in the churches) and many brethren refused to do so, they were considered disobedient, and the worsening situtation was further aggravated.

In this general context, it is perhaps safe to say that a sense of pride existed on both sides because those who were opposed to mustaches still held to wearing a beard.

It is interesting to note that when Samuel Froehlich began his missionary work in Europe, he preached among and associated with Mennonite groups. He was unable to reach a satisfactory accord with them. His major religious emphasis was on the new birth experience. The emphasis he placed on outward form was not as pronounced as that practiced by the Mennonites. In this realm he wrote:[1]

> The insistence upon externals and forms is the best weapon for the destruction of the congregation of God, and what the foe cannot do by means of outward force and persecution, he succeeds in doing by such sly artifices, whereby one runs after a shadow and fights about words and loses substance.

The polarization that existed in the American churches was difficult to deal with. Travel and communications systems were quite primitive compared to today. The Elders at that time were not administratively organized to respond quickly to problems of this type.

To further understand the cleavage, one must consider the problem of communication that existed in those days which added to the already difficult situation. Because the church at that time existed on both sides of the Atlantic, Elders from Europe were involved in seeking a solution. Letters traveling by sea mail to and from Europe required several weeks to reach their destination. This added to the confusion.

Also, some of the early Elders of the church—who had worked so tirelessly in establishing the church in America—had passed away. Among them were Benedict Weyeneth, Joseph Bella, Peter Virkler, and Isaac Gehring. The force of their personality and leadership ability was now lacking, and a new group of Elders had to deal with the coming schism. Possibly as the American church grew, they did not have the grip on the church the earlier Elders had.

The schism was not a pleasant time for the church. Impatience, misunderstanding, self-will, and at times a lack of reasoning coalesced to break open an irretrievable schism. It was one of the Apostolic Christian Church's darkest hours.

The largest group of members and all the American Elders remained with the Apostolic Christian Church, and the smaller group became known as the Apostolic Christian Church (Nazarene) under the authority of the European Elders. Over the years attempts—both official and unofficial—have been made at reconciliation.

In 1947, prospects brightened, and it was hoped that an accord between the two churches could be found for unification. Elders of both churches were summoned to a special meeting at Francesville, Indiana, to explore this possibility. Extreme winter weather conditions prevented several Elders from attending this meeting. For those who did attend, hopes for union were dashed when it became apparent a final accord was impossible. Instead, the two church bodies decided to exist "side-by-side" and to "love and esteem each other."

Again, in 1959 ten Elders (five from each side) met in Mansfield, Ohio, but with no more success than the 1947 meeting. Both sides did agree, however, not to proselytize or coax members who were "on the fence."

Often when church brethren cannot be "perfectly joined together" or serve the Lord "in one accord" as stated in Scriptures, the only solution to achieve peace is to separate. This was the case already in the first century church when Paul and Barnabas contended so sharply "that they departed asunder one from the other" (Acts 15:39).

At the time of the division, the two opposing sides, although disagreeing on a few points of tradition, held many doctrines in common. The same could be said today.

PUBLIC TRIAL OF CHURCH OFFICIALS

Following close on the heels of the church schism of 1906-1907 was another unfortunate incident that seriously affected the fellowship. In 1908, six church officials in central Illinois were defendants in a lawsuit initiated by a former member of the church at Roanoke, Illinois, who had previously been disciplined.

The lawsuit asked $50,000 in damages and was directed against Elders Rudolph Witzig, Gridley; Andrew Rapp, Morton; Michael Mangold, Roanoke; and Christian Gerber, Fairbury. Also named was minister John W. Schmidt, Roanoke, and John W. Schneider, Peoria. The lawsuit charged these men with conspiracy and persecution in connection with the plaintiff's expulsion from the church at Roanoke several years earlier.

The former member moved to several states and engaged in selling farm implements. He said the mandates of church officials followed him, and it was nearly impossible for him to make a living because members of the brotherhood were prohibited from doing business with him.

Church officials vigorously denied the charges, but the matter was brought to court in Peoria. The church, against its wishes and customary practices, was forced to hire counsel (James A. Cameron and George B. Suther) and defend itself. Then, as now, there was a strongly-held belief within the church that disputes between brethren be adjudicated within the church (and not in a civil court); but since this was an accusation against it from a non-member, there was little choice but to defend itself, not only for the sake of honor, but because the amount named in the lawsuit was extremely high.

The charges against the six church officials resulted in "sensational" news coverage, particularly by the Peoria *Herald Transcript* and the *Peoria Star*. Both newspapers heralded stinging headlines telling of the trial's proceedings. Typical of these headlines were: *Law Invoked to End Relentless Rule of Czar of the New Amish Church; Accuser Tells Story of Persecution: Dramatic Statements of Plaintiff; Curious Crowds Throng Corridors;* other stories indicated speculation was rife on the eventual outcome of the trial.

The newspapers presented the Apostolic Christian Church in a very unfair light. They always referred (erroneously) to the fellowship as the "New Amish." References to the church and its officials were very negative. Describing the six brethren at the trial, a reporter wrote:

> They were all far past middle age and most of them old men, their faces lined with the marks indelibly stamped by the rigors of their years of self-repression, their shaven lips and bearded chins, dressed in plain garments, collars guiltless of cravats, unrelieved by any sign of color, they seemed men cut out of granite for whom all the pleasure and poetry of life had been denied and only the most rigorous of realities left.

Witzig, particularly, was the target of much press abuse. In one article he was referred to as a "self-appointed czar" and was also attacked viciously by the plaintiff's counsel, Joseph Weil and Frank Quinn. Witzig, Mangold, and Schmidt took the witness stand. One reporter said Mangold was a "good witness." He explained that the only printed rules of the church were in the Bible and produced a compendium of the New Testament and read from a verse in II Corinthians relating to ex-communication. He told the court the church was guided in everything by certain verses in Scriptures as they were amplified and explained by the Council of Elders.

At the conclusion of the trial, only Elders Witzig and Mangold were found guilty. They were fined a total of $1,000. They were not present when the verdict was returned and read. They never appealed the decision.

The trial generated widespread negative publicity for the church. The brotherhood was portrayed in the news media as being both very rigid and very odd. Essentially, the press mockingly described some of the church's practices and always implied that its officials were repressive.

The trial itself and the subsequent publicity only caused the brethren to recoil further and separate themselves even more from "the world." The church, generally, was still deeply devoted to German culture and customs and somewhat suspicious of the "English." The trial verdict, the recent church division, and the threat of an ever-changing society combined to set the brotherhood on a decidedly conservative course for several years to come.

REMINGTON, INDIANA

REMINGTON, INDIANA
Five miles southeast

Remington, Indiana, with its wide-open prairies and fertile soil, was a logical place for families of Apostolic Christian persuasion to eventually locate. Because land was less expensive than in Illinois, a few families moved here from Fairbury, Illinois, in the spring of 1900.

The first family to locate near Remington was that of Nicholas Nussbaum. They settled on a farm southeast of town. Later that same year (possibly in June), John Schieler located his family in Remington until he could obtain possession of a farm the following spring. He was a carpenter by trade.

The Nussbaum and Schieler families, along with the Andrew Zimmerman family, were the founders of the Remington Apostolic Christian Church. Worship services were initially held in homes with John Schieler serving as minister.

The Remington church was formed during a time when the United States was enjoying a period of general prosperity, growing industrialization, and significant social change. Although conditions were still somewhat primitive at this time, the automobile was being introduced to the nation. In 1900 the nation had only 144 miles of hard-surface roads and 13,824 motorcars.[2] Social change was coming with a fury and would eventually be felt in the church.

The prospects of buying cheaper land, together with a general mood of seeking economic improvement, led several Apostolic Christian families to take the risk of moving to Remington. In 1900 many visitors and prospective land buyers surveyed the area. In the spring of 1901, more families moved to the area including those of Conrad Beckley, Henry, Peter, and Arnold Siebenthal. In 1902 the Jacob Bahler and Fred Baier families came. The trend continued in 1903 when the Robert Bahler family came from Fairbury, the John Frey family from Cissna Park, and the Jacob Knochel family from Morton, Illinois. Also arriving were the families of Charles Wenger, John Clauss, and Phillip Knochel. During 1906-1907 the Fred Waibel, Nicholas Waibel, and Carl Kachelmuss families came to the area.

Already in 1903, increasing membership required a permanent house of worship. Jacob Von Tobel donated land to be used for building a church and also for a cemetery. The fact that John Schieler was a carpenter proved to be beneficial for the congregation because he, along with a host of volunteers, built the group's first place of assembly at a cost of $800.

The church, under the leadership of ministers John Schieler and Robert Bahler, experienced encouraging growth from 1903 to 1910; an addition to the original church was made in 1910. A new assembly room was constructed, and the original building was converted into a kitchen and Sunday School.

From 1910 to 1920, more families moved to the Remington area and attended the country church. In 1947 a larger church was needed, so the old structure was abandoned and a new one built. This brick church was still in use in 1982.

John Schieler continued in the ministry at Remington until he moved to Gridley, Illinois, in 1914. He continued in the ministry at Gridley until his death in 1927.

Robert Bahler served as Elder at Remington from 1926 until 1932. He died in 1936. Among the early ministers at Remington were Carl Baier and Nicholas Nussbaum. The latter served from 1928 to 1939.

Sam Kilgus was appointed to the ministry in 1932 and served until his retirement in 1972. In a writing for the *Silver Lining* in 1975 he commented on the "new birth." He wrote:

> The first step is to see ourselves as a lost sinner that can be saved by grace. Jesus paid a tremendous price to cleanse our sinful heart. He gave His life and blood. We go through a process of repentance and conversion, a thorough change of mind. That changes the carnal into a spiritual mind. When this change has taken place, we are baptized and promise to stay true and faithful until death. Then, we belong to a body of believers called 'the church.'

During most of its existence, the church at Remington has been served by non-resident Elders. In 1974 Alfred Bahler, Elder at the neighboring Wolcott church, assumed the oversight of the Remington congregation, also.

In 1947 the church was blessed with the addition of thirty souls who had turned to the Lord. A short time later, tragedy struck when the youngest convert, Benita Getz, lost her life in a kitchen fire.

The pretty country church south of Remington, which sits in Indiana's corn-rich Benton County, has for many years been a haven for students at nearby Purdue University at West Lafayette. Many students who are members of the church often drive the twenty-five miles up to Remington to attend Sunday and Wednesday evening worship services.

By 1981 the church had approximately one hundred members and, as one minister wrote, "We are constantly praying that we shall have an increase."

WOLCOTT, INDIANA

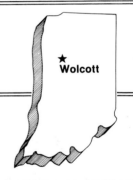

WOLCOTT, INDIANA
South side of village

The church at Wolcott, Indiana, sits on the eastern edge of a string of Apostolic Christian Churches whose towns and villages border U.S. Route 24. The line extends from Peoria, Illinois, on the west all the way to Wolcott. The eight churches located close to this highway had a combined membership of approximately eighteen hundred members or nearly twenty per cent of the denomination's total by 1980.

In approximately 1900, a few families began to move to the Wolcott, Indiana, area—the John Abersoll family being the first to come here. Because there was no Apostolic Christian Church in Wolcott at that time, they met with the few families of the faith at Remington for worship services. John Schieler served the small group as minister.

A short time later, more families began to settle in the area. Almost all of them engaged in farming. Among them were the Andrew Abersolls (parents of John Abersoll), Andrew Lehmans, Theodore Bolliers, Ben Farneys, Jacob Kellers, John Zehrs, Chris Helderles, Dan Farneys, Fred Ankers, Charles Blumes, Amos Sauders, and others. The influx of new families caused the small congregation to grow quickly. One Sunday the two groups would meet together in Remington, and the next Sunday in Wolcott. This early tradition is still being continued, as the two congregations meet together on Wednesday evenings for mid-week services, alternating churches from week to week.

By April, 1902, a permanent place of assembly was badly needed. The church selected three trustees—John Abersoll, Jacob J. Keller, and Theodore Bollier—who subsequently purchased a parcel of land in the southwestern part of town from Eben H. Wolcott for $300. A new church building was completed on this site in either 1903 or 1904.

When the new church was under construction, citizens of the village graciously invited the congregation to use a school building as a temporary place of assembly. During this time, Amos Sauder was selected as the church's first local minister, and soon Andrew Lehman was added to the ministry. Christian Gerber of Fairbury, Illinois, served as Elder at Wolcott during these formative years. The first convert, Dan Blume, was baptized in a farm pond east of town.

The spirit of optimism and adventure filled the hearts of these new "settlers." It was both a grand and unique experience for several families to pull up roots in their previous communities and come to Wolcott. Just as their fore-fathers, who had left the "old country" across the ocean and had come to a new land, these people, too, had experienced the plight of the pioneer, including much hardship, uncertainty, and discouragement as well as satisfaction and the sense of ac-complishment. One thing they felt, however—just as their emigrant fathers—was the profound sense of peace and joy to know that the Lord and His church were available in the area and they could sup on His spirit and enjoy the wonderful bonds of fellowship with brethren.

The pioneers of the church lie in a hilltop cemetery which was deeded to the church by John Lehman. The first burial was a child (name unknown) who died while the family was visiting in the area. A small marker locates the grave. This burial ground is still being used by the church.

A distinguishing feature of the Wolcott congregation has been its need to provide additional facilities for its gradual growth over the years. Following the construction of the first building after the turn of the century (which lasted until 1952), additions or new construction began in 1951, 1958, 1970, and 1974.

In May, 1951, a new church of Bedford stone was built just north of the old frame church. First services were conducted on October 12, 1952. Ministers at that time were Irvin Lehman and Will Furrer. The latter's life was claimed in a tragic automobile accident in September, 1960. George Yergler of La Crosse served as Elder until 1958.

In 1958, an addition was made to the west wing of the church along with some interior remodeling. In 1970, a new front entrance and carport were added. (In fact, most of the churches in the denomination which built or remodeled during the 1970's added carports to entrance areas.) In 1971, a Sunday School addition was added to the east wing of the church.

In early 1975, the sanctuary and fellowship areas were in-creased by a total of 1,840 square feet.

Irvin Lehman (1909-1969), a lifelong native of the Wolcott area, was installed as the church's first resident Elder on January 19, 1958. He died May 1, 1969. On April 30, 1972, Alfred Bahler became the group's second resident Elder. The church had approximately ninety-five members in 1981.

BAY CITY, MICHIGAN

BAY CITY, MICHIGAN
2791 Fraser Road
Kawkawlin, Michigan

In the late 1970's, a young lady asked Elder Joseph H. Waibel of the Bay City, Michigan, congregation what the church's doctrine was. He told her, in essence, that "Our doctrine is taken from the Holy Bible—we follow the New Testament and the teaching of the Apostles." This brief comment was an accurate generalization of the church's religious beliefs.

The church—which is located in the Bay City area and not in the city itself—is highly respected in the community. It is the denomination's most northern church in Michigan and is located a few miles northwest of Kawkawlin, Michigan, in the northern portion of the Saginaw Valley—an area of flat farmland somewhat lower in value than that found in other areas of the Midwest.

Landowners and those who wished to become landowners living in the heartland of the great Midwest—mostly in Illinois and in portions of Indiana—were anxious to purchase cheaper land during 1900 to 1910. With farms in these two states already being occupied and land values increasing, men began to look elsewhere for land that had potential but was significantly lower in price. Land in Bay County, Michigan, met their needs, and families began moving to this area in 1903.

The Bay County area was quite different at the turn of the century compared to today. Logging was still a viable industry. It was necessary for many brethren to clear the land they had purchased.

The first to locate here were Julius and Charles E. Lambert. On September 5, 1903, they came from Oklahoma where they had suffered through several years of drought. The Ben Hoffmans, in-laws to the Lambert boys, came with them. Soon others came to the area: the Ramseyers, Genzels, Clausses, Ruegseggers, Meisters, and Schlatters.

In 1904 the Karl Wieland family moved to the Kawkawlin area just west of Bay City. Also coming at this time were the August, Fred, and Adam Wielands. A very welcome benefit to the church was the arrival in 1905 of Elder Gottlieb Maibach, fifty-two, who came from Pulaski, Iowa, where he had served as Elder for ten years. Maibach's arrival ushered in the beginning of regular church services. Worship services were held in members' homes and rotated so no one particular family would have to suffer a burden. Andrew J. Braun, a minister at Toledo, visited here often in the early days.

In March, 1906, George Wackerle, Sr., moved his family to the area from Cissna Park, Illinois. He situated on a farm several miles west of Kawkawlin. Later, in 1907-1908, Wackerle gave one acre of land for a church building.

Among other early families who came between 1905 and 1908 were those of Chris Ruegsegger, John Ramseyer, George Wackerle, Carl Hacker, Albert Pfister, Henry Freidinger, George Kilgus, William Barth, Jake Kuebler, Marie Knochel (a widow), Fred Schupbach, and Joseph Waibel, Sr. Other members who came were Verena Meister, Sam Ramseyer, and William T. Stevig. Most of these brethren settled within a ten-mile radius of Kawkawlin.

The group decided to build a church in 1907. After much planning they went to a saw mill in the "back woods" of Michigan (near Crump, Michigan) to purchase materials. They hauled lumber in the rough to the building site using horses and wagons and sometimes sleighs. Often logs were dragged out of the woods with oxen.

Work on the church commenced in the fall of 1907. Because almost everyone in the church helped with the construction, it was not necessary to hire outside help. A member of the church, William Stevig, a carpenter, took charge of the project.

Continued growth necessitated additional space for worship. This was provided in 1919. In 1953 work was initiated on a new church building seating five hundred persons. It was built on the same lot just a few feet from the old church. During construction, the congregation continued to meet in the old church. In 1954 the new church was completed.

In 1982 the church was extensively remodeled. The project, which cost $360,000, included changing the entrance from the west side to the north side and adding a carport. In addition, the project included remodeling the kitchen and rest rooms and adding two new Sunday School rooms.

A cemetery is located next to the church. Land for the cemetery was donated by George Wackerle. Henry Freidinger was the first person buried in the church cemetery. In 1979 a half acre of land was donated from the Clinton Wackerle farm which added to the original cemetery.

Gottlieb Maibach served as Elder of the church from 1905 until 1922. The next resident Elder was not ordained until 1941 when Otto Ramseyer was instated into the Eldership. He served until 1955 when he retired because of ill health.

Joseph H. Waibel was chosen to bear the mantle of leadership in 1955 and was still serving in 1982. Serving along with him in this capacity was Andrew E. Virkler, formerly of Croghan, New York, who was ordained Elder on October 10, 1977.

In 1980 the church had approximately 190 members.[3]

TREMONTON, UTAH

TREMONTON, UTAH
Approximately 1901—1910

Five years after Utah was admitted to the Union, persons of Apostolic Christian background came to the area of Tremonton, Utah, located north of Salt Lake City only twenty miles from Idaho's southern border.

Brethren were lured to the area by land agents who promised cheaper land with adequate potential. One of the land agents was Alvin West of Tremont, Illinois. Many of the early families of the church who settled here were from Tremont.

Most of the families arrived here during 1901 to 1904. Among the first to make the long trek to Utah from Tremont, Illinois, were the families of Gideon Winzeler, Louis Getz, and Henry Baer. The Samuel Imthurn and Matthew Baer families were also early arrivals. In 1904 Jacob B. Meister (his wife was Lydia Imthurn) came from Archbold, Ohio, with his family. Essentially, the first families came from Ohio, Illinois, and Kansas.

These early settlers came to improve themselves financially—to participate in the "American dream"—but they met very primitive conditions when they arrived in Utah. They lived in shacks and were forced to drink canal water until springs were found. Also, they were a distinct minority in a state heavily dominated by the Mormon faith.

A congregation was quickly established with Samuel Imthurn, Henry Baer, and Gideon Winzeler serving as ministers. A very small church building was constructed on a farm near Tremonton. Later, a church was built in town and the little country church—which resembled an old-fashioned schoolhouse—was attached to the new building and used as a Sunday School. The tiny old church looked even smaller when located beside the newer church. The new church was situated on the western edge of Tremonton.

The little congregation grew to a peak of approximately fifteen to eighteen families. A sense of brotherhood and togetherness prevailed. The members used to get together for Sunday afternoon meals. In 1980 Anna Hoerr, eighty-six, of Peoria, Illinois, recalled her childhood days in Tremonton when "the crowd" (the entire church) would gather at her parents' home for supper. She remembered her mother "slaving" away at the stove preparing the meals.

One time during 1906 to 1908, baptisms were held in a ditch near the church. Those baptized were Ella Getz, Leah Winzeler, and Hannah and Martha Meister. Anna Hoerr said an Elder Gerber came to baptize. It is likely this was Christian Gerber who was an Elder at Fairbury, Illinois, during this time. Elder Christian Gerber of Rockville, Connecticut, was not ordained until 1917. Elder John Kaufman of Silverton, Oregon, also used to come to Tremonton.

Despite harsh and primitive living conditions, the people were able to make a living. Anna Hoerr said, "Those people were 'workaholics.' All they did was work, work, work!"

Although this little band of believers could manage economically, they could not manage spiritually and maintain their cohesion. The church schism—which manifested itself in the churches back east in 1906-1907 reverberated all the way to remote Utah. The brethren at Tremonton were drawn into the dispute and a new church, under the direction of ministers Gideon Winzeler and Henry Baer, was formed. Because Winzeler had donated land for the church, this group kept the church building, leaving the four remaining families, including minister Samuel Imthurn, without a place of worship.

Following this tragic division, the Samuel Imthurns moved to Sabetha, Kansas; the Jacob Meisters to Oakville, Iowa; and the Louis Getzes to Peoria, Illinois. The Apostolic Christian

Church in Tremonton was all but dissolved. In less than ten years this promising little church had been ravaged irreparably by cleavage.

Anna Hoerr remembered as a young child of the "trouble" that existed in the church. From an upstairs bedroom in her family's home she could hear (through the ceiling register) her parents and other adults talking about the unfortunate discord that existed among the brethren.

Over the years the Winzeler-Baer church would eventually fade away and be closed. Today, only descendants of these pioneers exist in Tremonton. None belong to the Apostolic Christian Church, and virtually all know little or nothing about it. The area's only link to the church's brief past is a cemetery located three and one-half miles west and one mile south of Tremonton. The Apostolic Christian Church and the Apostolic Christian Church (Nazarene) collectively provide funds for its upkeep because most of those interred there are of Apostolic Christian background. Fred and Violet Eggli of Tremonton have been retained to mow and maintain the cemetery.

A variety of names appear on the tombstones: Funk, Gassner, Eggli, Schrenk, Feucht, Weisser, Kupfer, Vierling, Meister, Imthurn, Boering, Brenkmann, Sommer, Wagenbach, Schmutz, Daininger, Storrer, Getz, Cartner, Kauber, Sorg, Kleinknecht, Trukenbrod, Woerner, Baer, and Sinn.

Cemetery plot southeast of Tremonton, Utah, contains many Apostolic Christians.

MILFORD, INDIANA

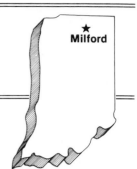

MILFORD, INDIANA
State Route 15 in Milford

Although travel conditions were still quite primitive at the turn of the century, they did not deter families from moving from one location to another. There was a lot of movement by church families in this regard.

A host of families moved to Milford, Indiana, in 1904, which was in keeping with a well-established trend among Apostolic Christian families to seek less expensive farmland. Milford is located approximately midway between South Bend and Ft. Wayne in Kosciusko County.

Through the efforts of the Neff Brothers Real Estate Company in Milford, a large number of Apostolic Christian farmers were persuaded to move to the Milford area. These two men visited many of the Apostolic Christian Churches in Illinois and were successful in selling land. Between fifty and sixty families subsequently moved to Milford. When these families were considering building a new church in 1905-1906, the Neff Brothers Real Estate Company contributed $1,000 toward the building fund. Since this was a very large amount, it gave the group courage to proceed with their building plans.

Edward Haab, who was the group's first minister, moved to Milford in 1904. A native of Zurich, Switzerland, he first landed at Morton, Illinois. Later, he moved to Claytonville, Illinois, where he worked as a blacksmith and sold farm implements. He served as minister in the church at nearby Cissna Park.

He began a German Sunday School to teach the children of the many large families that had come to Milford. Assisting him were Andy Rapp and Fred Wuthrich. Haab had a deep concern that young people find their way to the Lord. Many faithful members, who used to listen to his sermons as un-converted souls, remember the influence of his preaching. At his death, a local newspaper said he "was well and favorably known throughout the community and was very congenial. He held a prominent place in the German church and was an en-thusiastic member, commonly spoken of as one of the keystones of the church."

Just previous to Haab's arrival in Milford, the families of George Hartter, Adolph Rudin, Emil Kaiser, Henry Waldbeser, and Jake Krauter had made this their home.

Church services were held in a small house just west of town. Among the church's charter families were the Henry Rassis, John Rassis, Christ Grimms, and Matthew Weissers. Andy Rapp, his mother Anna Mary, and sister Mary, also ar-rived from Fairbury, Illinois.

Assisting Edward Haab in the ministry were Andy Rapp and George Steiglitz. Steiglitz died on June 10, 1929, and Rapp withdrew from the ministry. Sometime later in 1929, Edward Haab fell from a tree and could not attend church services for several Sundays. Previously, he had written to Elder Elias Dotterer (Elder at Junction, Ohio) regarding the need for help in the ministry at Milford. Dotterer came to Milford, polled the members, and Theo Beer, thirty-one, was chosen as the new minister. Remembering the details of this incident Beer wrote, "It was a humbling experience, but I leaned hard on His promise that where two or three are assembled in His name He would be among us. Brother Haab insisted I also speak in the German tongue. My father, being all German, also said I need to preach German."

Edward Haab passed away two years later. This created a vacancy in the pulpit. Again, Elder Elias Dotterer came and polled the church. They chose Henry Beer, thirty-one, younger brother of Theo Beer, to serve in the ministry. These two brothers served together in the ministry at Milford for several decades.

Theo Beer was ordained as Milford's first resident Elder on August 5, 1956.[4] This was twenty-seven years after he was chosen as minister. He served as Elder until November, 1980, when his nephew, Jesse Beer, was ordained as the new Elder.

In a *Silver Lining* article entitled "Repentance: God's Way of Salvation," Theo Beer wrote:

> Through faith, repentance, and confession, the new child of God is born. Only along scriptural lines should souls be added to the fold, through baptism in the name of the Father, Son, and Holy Ghost. Thus can we be adopted into the family of saints and become a new-born child of God, and a member of the church and body of Christ. Such a soul is indeed born anew of water and spirit. In a truly converted soul, it is evident that he has a new Master for he is willing to be obedient to God's teachings. Only through obedience can one become a full-grown man or woman in Christ Jesus.

The first church building in Milford was begun in 1905 and completed in 1906. It was built on a parcel of land donated by Adolph Rudin on the same site as today's church. In 1940 the church was remodeled. A new front was added and a basement put under the entire building. In 1960 a Sunday School addition was constructed as well as a nursery.

In 1972 a 40-foot by 80-foot fellowship hall was built on the west end of the church grounds.

In the winter of 1979-1980, the church benefited by an "in-gathering" of fifteen souls who had turned to the Lord in repentance.

By 1980 the church had sixty-two families on the "dinner list" and 150 members.

In 1958 Arthur Haab of the Milford congregation wrote a treatise entitled *The Apostolic Christian Church of America.* This small booklet defined many of the things for which the church stood.

*　*　*　*　*

On a humid, overcast afternoon on August 3, 1980, Henry Beer submitted to a lengthy interview concerning the things of the church. This interview was conducted both in his Christian bookstore and later under a shade tree in his beautiful garden at his home in Milford.

After serving nearly fifty years as a minister in the church, authoring several books on poetry, and playing a major part in the translation of the *Zion's Harp* hymnal from the German to the English language, his reflections provided much insight concerning the history of the church. His direct exposure to church leaders in the early part of this century together with his deep interest in the church's history and well-being allowed him to pass on a great deal of information. A general summary of the interview follows:

Samuel Froehlich was a noted reformer who was used of God to clarify the Scriptures and get people back to an apostolic foundation. His fluency in the German, French, and English languages aided him in reaching many people. He made a gallant effort to direct converts along the pathway outlined in Scriptures, particularly according to St. Matthew 28:20, "teaching them to observe all things whatsoever I have commanded you."

Froehlich was a tireless evangelist. He would fearlessly enter a Swiss or German town and inquire if there were any persons dissatisfied with the state church. If so, he would invite them to preaching services and present the truth of God's Word to them.

One time Froehlich was riding on a coach in France. He was seated up front with the driver. Officers halted the coach and shouted, "Is Samuel Froehlich in there?" Froehlich remained silent. Someone said, "No" (which was true—he was not in the coach, but up with the driver). Another account of this story has Froehlich himself repeating the question after being asked by the official; everyone remained silent, and the officials went on their way.

On another occasion, his enemies plotted to pour scalding hot water on him as he passed under a viaduct. Froehlich learned of this and traveled the route before his enemies got there.

Henry Beer came to Milford from Mansfield, Ohio, in 1912 when he was twelve years old. He was named for Henry Schwier, the first resident Elder at Mansfield. He remembers that brethren fell under the discipline of the church if they obtained lightning rods (apparently for a lack of faith and trust in God).

The church schism after the turn of the century was very bitter. One side called themselves "Believers in Christ" and the other side called themselves "Followers of Christ."

Beer's father told him that in Mansfield, brothers came from Yugoslavia and sat in the front benches of the church. They had mustaches and during the service would curl and stroke them. They were told by church leaders, who were annoyed by this, that they paid too much attention to grooming their mustaches and were asked to remove them and be more in conformity with the other brethren. When they refused, they were considered disobedient. This type of incident demonstrated the extent of the cleavage that crept into the church during that era.

One time, in either 1921 or 1922, he participated in the practice of footwashing at the home of brethren at Congerville, Illinois. This was held after a singing and was a very impressive and sobering experience to him. Occasionally, this practice was carried out in homes, but never in the churches. He said that in all his years in the church, that particular ceremony was the most memorable he had experienced. Henry Beer died on June 29, 1983, at the age of 82.

In a 1961-published booklet entitled *History, Doctrine, and Directory,* the Milford congregation listed a short doctrinal statement of their faith:

DOCTRINE OF THE APOSTOLIC CHRISTIAN CHURCH

The doctrine of the Apostolic Christian Church, as the name implies, is based on the teachings of Christ and upon the inspired teachings of the Apostles. It is the aim of the Church to retain and practice the order and discipline taught in the New Testament Churches which were founded and established by the Apostles.

The teachings found in the New Testament provide our only doctrine and creed.

The doctrine and practice of faith and repentance and remission of sin, and the baptism of faith by immersion in the name of the Father, the Son, and the Holy Ghost are required for membership.

The evidence of conversion is to be seen in conduct and speech, and by living a separated life from sin and worldliness.

Diligence in attendance and devotion to the Lord, to the Word, and to the Church is expected from all members.

Elders and ministers are chosen from the various congregations on the basis of a good report and who show forth spiritual gifts and discernment. The church does not maintain a salaried ministry. The brethren are expected to be ready unto every good work and deed and to live honorably with all men.

The practice of closed communion is observed, and its frequent observance is for the edification and strengthening of the Church body.

OAKVILLE, IOWA

OAKVILLE, IOWA
3 miles south on Iowa 99

It was soon after the turn of the century that several church families developed a great interest in purchasing land in eastern Iowa near Oakville. Three older brothers in the church from Gridley, Illinois—Jacob Rich, Engelbert Grusy, and Dan Mangold—made a survey of the Oakville-Huron bottom lands and found favorable farming prospects. On their advice six families migrated to this area. They were Otto R. Gerst and Theophil Fischer of Roanoke, Illinois; Henry K. Gerst of Gridley, Illinois; Andrew Yackley of Peoria, Illinois; Peter Glaser of Cissna Park, Illinois; and John Voelpel of Morton, Illinois.

This group of believers met initially in the one-room Williams School located on land now farmed by David Sheridan. Thereafter, they assembled in homes until 1904 when a new church was built one-half mile north of this school building.

Peter Glaser became the group's first minister. A short time later, Henry K. Gerst was chosen to assist in the ministry. The following spring Albert Reiman and Albert Rauhaus moved from New Boston, Illinois, to the area of Oakville. Reiman was a minister, and he helped Henry K. Gerst when Peter Glaser discontinued preaching.

In 1905 a number of families moved to this community. They included those of John Stoller, Fred Donner, and Chris Kuntz of Gridley, Illinois; Peter Maurer of Roanoke, Illinois; John Benninger of West Bend, Iowa; Fred Sutter of Morton, Illinois; Dan Kempf of Congerville, Illinois; and William Frank and George Wieland of Cissna Park, Illinois. Later, between 1908 and 1910, other families came from Cissna Park and Morton. Among them were the families of Paul and Joseph Reeb, Fred Siegle, and George Heinold. Several other families moved to Oakville as the years unfolded. Among them was Noah Schrock, twenty-four, who came from Congerville, Illinois, in 1916.

During World War I, when the nation was at war with Germany, the state of Iowa strongly urged that the German language be terminated in church services. In acquiescence to this wish, the church chose Noah Schrock, twenty-five, and William Rauhaus as ministers. After this "emergency" situation subsided and Henry K. Gerst became more fluent in the English language, William Rauhaus chose to resign from the ministry.

In 1935 another influx of families came to the area—this time from Minnesota. Because of this, the congregation decided to move and remodel the church building. It was relocated to its present site on State Highway 99, three miles south of Oakville. At this time the congregation numbered approximately thirty-five families.

In March of 1937 Albert Reiman—who had served as a minister for more than thirty years—was fatally wounded in a tragic automobile accident. Soon after this, John Wagenbach and Gus Scheitlin were called into the ministry. They began preaching in the fall of that year.

The church grew as families continued to move to Oakville. By the early 1940's, there were sixty families attending the Oakville church.

On Sunday morning, November 5, 1944, a roaring fire greeted many of the parishioners as they arrived for church. It was indeed a traumatic experience for members of the congregation to stand by helplessly and witness the flames devour their church building. Authorities had difficulty in establishing the cause of the fire, but generally concluded that a belt broke on the fan which distributed the air from the "hot air" furnace. As the fire raged within the furnace and the heat was not properly distributed throughout the building, fire eventually broke out. One member recalled arriving at church that morning shortly before 10 a.m. and seeing smoke and flames pouring out of the roof. The building eventually burned to the ground.

Because the nation was at war, a new building could not be erected immediately. Initially, a few services were held in a small church on Central Avenue near Smith Street in Burlington. Later, the brethren were invited to use the Oakville Presbyterian Church. Sunday School was held in the basement. This church building was used for worship until September 14, 1947.

Excavation for the new church began May 10, 1946. On September 21, 1947, the new church was opened for services.

Two years after the church fire, many Oakville brethren suffered financial setbacks due to flooding caused by an ice jam in the Iowa River near where it joins the Mississippi River. The World Relief Committee voted in Gridley, Illinois, in the summer of 1946 to accept voluntary donations to help these flood-ravaged families. The response was overwhelming.

Beginning in 1940, the Oakville congregation enjoyed an extraordinary spiritual harvest of between seventy-five to one hundred converts over a three-year period. This occurred during the first years of Noah Schrock's Eldership.

Noah Schrock, who was born August 29, 1892, near Congerville, Illinois—and later moved to Oakville in 1916—served in the ministry for fifty-nine years. He was ordained Elder at Oakville on May 10, 1940, and served until his death in April, 1976.[5] During many years of service to the church, he was known as a gifted orator. During his era, his influence was perhaps as wide as anyone's in the church. In addition to preaching and serving as Elder over many churches west of the Mississippi River, he was a meaningful force in the highest councils of the church. For several years he served in a leadership capacity in the Elder Body of the Apostolic Christian Church. He made many trips to Japan to assist the church's missionary efforts there. He also was instrumental in helping to establish a small congregation in Regina, Saskatchewan, Canada.

In addition to his church and farming duties, he served nineteen years as president of the Upper Mississippi Flood Control Association. He annually made trips to Washington, D.C., to testify before Congressional committees on requests for flood control appropriations that would help protect the area's bottom land. In 1946 he was among those who suffered flooding losses—losing 125 head of cattle and 90 hogs.

On April 8, 1976, this Christian stalwart, defender of the faith, and for many years a prominent doctrinal leader of the church, was buried in the Oakville church's cemetery plot. Twenty-seven Elders of the church from eight states converged together in his home church nestled in the bluff adjoining the Mississippi River to pay their last respects to this beloved and respected church leader.

Although striking changes in society occurred during his tenure as Elder and threatened to press in on the church, he remained resolute in standing firm for the traditional standards which the church had espoused over the years. His devotion to the Lord and to the church was unmistakable, and he was never hesitant to uphold both.

His esteem in the community was such that the *Burlington Hawkeye* sent a reporter to cover the funeral and burial services. A headline on page three of that publication's issue the next day read, "Shepherd Of The Flock Has Gone To Rest."

Noah Schrock was also noted for his interest in the history of the church. He often would make historical presentations as he traveled to the various churches he served. In his generation it is quite likely he was as knowledgeable as anyone concerning the history of the church.

Edward M. Lanz, who had been ordained one year before Noah Schrock's death, assumed the Eldership of the church.

In 1967 the church was remodeled. This added 3,500 square feet on two floors. Costing $130,000, the new addition was occupied on April 30, 1967.

By 1980 the Oakville church had approximately 215 members.[6]

NEW BOSTON, ILLINOIS

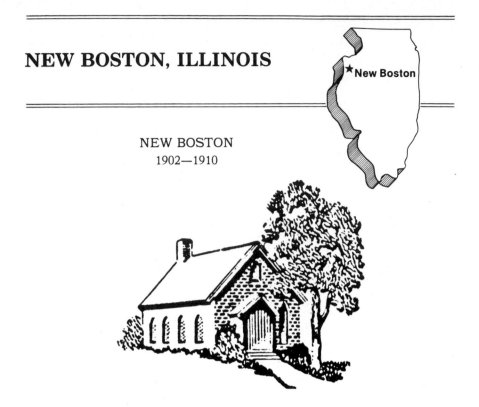

NEW BOSTON
1902—1910

From 1902 until 1910, church services were held in the vicinity of New Boston, Illinois. This area is located northeast of Oakville, Iowa, directly across the Mississippi River.

The few church families who lived here were always part of the Oakville congregation, but when weather conditions were bad and the ferry crossing was closed, worship services were held near New Boston in homes of believers. Albert Reiman usually would preach at these services.

Eventually the families who lived near New Boston moved away. The family of Joseph Getz, uncle to Elder Joe A. Getz of Morton, Illinois, returned to Morton. The Albert Reiman and Albert Rauhaus families moved across the river to the Oakville area, and the William Yoder family moved to Peoria, Illinois.

A Wieland family also lived in the New Boston area.

During the 1920's and 1930's, a few families of the Oakville congregation lived in the Muscatine, Iowa, area. These families did not hold their own church services, but traveled down to Oakville on Sunday.[7]

MORRIS, MINNESOTA

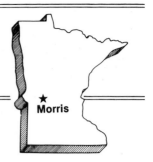

MORRIS, MINNESOTA
7 miles south on Route 59,
1 mile east

The hamlets of Morris and Hancock sit in Stevens County located in Minnesota's west central region. Over the years the question has often arisen why Apostolic Christian farmers settled in this seemingly remote section of the United States.

The answer is that young farmers wished to establish themselves in farming, and cheaper land could be procured in this area. Consequently, a good many farmers settled on the land south of Morris and west of Hancock, which still comprises the center of the church community. Despite Minnesota's "Paul Bunyan" image as the "land of 10,000 lakes," the state has a lot of productive farm land.

In the summer of 1902, the land agent at Rock Rapids, Iowa, asked Chris Moser and his son-in-law, Rudolph Tschudi, to go with him to Stevens County, Minnesota, to look at land. Moser (who died in the fall) subsequently bought a farm two miles north of Morris. Later, Christ Luthi, Sr., of West Bend, Iowa, was persuaded to look at the land in this area, too. The land agent showed him some farms north of Morris, but he was not interested. The next day the agent took him to a farm seven miles south of Morris. Impressed by the beautiful crop of wheat, Luthi purchased this farm.

Early in the spring of 1903, Chris Moser and Rudolph Tschudi of Lester, Iowa, and Christ Luthi, Sr., of West Bend, Iowa, moved with their families to Stevens County. A few months later Jacob Moser (twin brother of Chris Moser) and his two sons-in-law, William Feuchtenberger and William Reber of Lester, Iowa, bought land in this area. Also, John Zaugg of West Bend, Iowa, rented a farm purchased by August Mogler, a minister at Lester, Iowa. A nucleus of seven families formed the beginning of the Morris, Minnesota, congregation.

Jacob Moser was the group's first minister. It was not long until the preaching of the Word began to bear fruit. Rosina Luthi Moser recalls in 1904 when souls began turning to the Lord. She thought, "No, that's not for me." Soon, however, one of her friends spoke to her about salvation. She then relented and sought the Lord. A total of five souls were baptized: John and Emma Zaugg, Will Reber, and Rose Luthi and her mother.

On December 11, 1904, two Elders came to prove and baptize them. They went to the farm of John and Emma Zaugg—one-half mile east of the present church—and broke the ice in the stock tank and performed the baptism. Following this, they went into the Zaugg's living room where the laying-on-of-hands ceremony was performed. The church now had eleven members.

The establishment of the church in Morris resulted in a growing interest in the area by brethren in Illinois, Iowa, and other states. In the fall of 1905, Edward Eglin moved to the area. In 1906 Christ Luthi, Jr., and John Luthi came from West Bend, Iowa. Jacob Nohl and Timotheus "Tim" Hohulin bought farms here, and their families added to the church's growth.

Late in 1906, work began on a new church. Christ Luthi, Sr., donated two and one-half acres for this purpose. The building was completed in 1907. It measured 24 feet by 40 feet. The lumber for the building was purchased from Rumsey Reeves, owner of a local lumber yard. Reeves, in a marvelous gesture, paid for the church's pulpit which was made by a cabinet maker. The carpenters who built the church boarded at the Christ Luthi, Sr., home all that winter. The first trustees of the church were Edward Eglin, William Feuchtenberger, and Tim Hohulin.

An interesting incident—with an unfortunate ending—occurred in 1907 when Gottlieb Hohulin, a minister from Congerville, Illinois, was visiting his son Tim. He paid a visit one morning to the home of Christian and Anna Marie Luthi. Since it was raining that morning, church services were scheduled that afternoon instead of in the evening. Luthi's son, William, fifteen, was dispatched via horseback to inform all the members that church services would be held in the afternoon. He started out on his horse, but not far from home the horse slipped and fell, and William Luthi sustained a broken leg. Gottlieb Hohulin was very sorry for this unexpected turn of events and felt much pity for young William Luthi. Church services were held that evening as originally planned.

The first minister, Jacob Moser, died on October 17, 1907. His funeral and burial were the first to be held in the new church and cemetery. This was a very sad occasion for the new congregation. He was succeeded in the ministry by Edward Eglin.

Already in 1911 the growing membership—due to the arrival of eight or nine new families (including the Henry Nohl family)—necessitated larger worship accommodations. The church was moved and an auditorium (32-feet by 40-feet) was built on the north side. The foundation and cement blocks were made and tamped by Henry Nohl, Sr. The assembly room seated 170.

Families who moved to the area from 1910 to 1915 included those of Ben, Joe, and Emil Banwart; Jonathan Sommer; Eli Heininger; Charles Schambach; Fred Messerly; August Greiner; and Henry Schaefer. Other families moving here a few years later were those of Charles, John, and George Metzger; Carl Greiner; Fred and Christ Koehl; John, Henry, Fred, and Charles Schmidgall; Manny Kellerhal; Dan, William, and Henry Messner; and the William Zeltwengers who arrived as newlyweds in March, 1918.

In 1917-1918 approximately fifteen persons were baptized. Later, in 1918 a flu epidemic claimed the lives of several persons associated with the church.

In 1933-1934 a severe drought hit the Morris area, and approximately one-half of the church's families were forced to move elsewhere. While this was an extraordinarily trying time for the church, their grief was cushioned by the joy resulting from approximately forty new converts.

In 1937-1938 another "in-gathering" of souls totaled thirty. They were baptized in a metal tank outside the church. At night, car lights were used for lighting, and kerosene and gas lamps were used inside the church.

In 1948-1949 the church was enlarged and modernized. During the construction, worship services were held in a church in Hancock.

In 1962 the church was again blessed by a host of personal conversions. Approximately thirty-five persons repented for their sins and were baptized. Many of these converts came from religious backgrounds other than Apostolic Christian.

Construction of a large, new church began in the spring of 1966. On Easter Sunday, April 10, ground-breaking services were held as part of the afternoon worship service. On June 25, 1967, the congregation gathered in the new church for the first time.

The first local Elder at Morris was Jacob Stettner who was ordained in 1923. After his wife died in 1928, he moved back to Elgin, Illinois. Henry Koehl was ordained as Elder in 1941 and served until his death at age eighty-two in 1964. He was succeeded in June of that year by Paul Fehr. On October 9, 1983, Arthur H. Nohl was ordained as Elder.

FRANCESVILLE, INDIANA

FRANCESVILLE, INDIANA
U.S. 421 in Francesville

During the middle part of this century's first decade, the church's first schism was manifesting itself in many churches within the denomination. While several churches were bearing the brunt of conflict, a new church was beginning to blossom in Francesville, Indiana.

Just prior to 1906, families of the Apostolic Christian faith settled in the Francesville, Indiana, area. This fertile farming region is located in west central Indiana approximately thirty-five miles north of Lafayette, Indiana.

In 1905 Phillip Gutwein, Sr., and his wife, Louise, along with their seven sons—Phillip, Jr., Lewis, Conrad, Fred, Adam, John, and Carl—and daughter Angela left Cervenka, Hungary, where they had been involved in the flour milling business, and came to America. They came primarily so their son, Phillip, Jr., would not be forced to bear arms in the Hungarian military.

The Gutwein family first went to Fairbury, Illinois, where they were heartily welcomed by the Jacob Von Tobel family. Phillip, Sr., and two of his sons then set out to find a place to settle and buy land. They liked the flat land in the Francesville area. Because Phillip, Sr., was a minister and the few families of the faith in that area needed a minister, this was a suitable place for them to live. They moved to the Francesville area in the summer of 1906.

In 1907 the following families moved to Francesville: Jacob Boehning, Albert Gudeman, Ernest Anliker, Will Bachtold, Sam Walter, and Henry Bolliger. These families took turns hosting worship services in their homes.

Some of the families who came a little later were those of David Gudeman, Jacob Getz, Julius Honegger, Fred Yaggi, Joe Pelsy, John and Chris Wuethrich, Henry Swing, and Rudy Hauptli.

This migration continued for approximately two years with a few families being added to the congregation each year. In 1909 a house was purchased on the west edge of Francesville. It was remodeled and used for church services. The lower floor was used for a kitchen and dining area and the upper floor as a sanctuary.

In 1912 a new church was built across the street on land that was part of the Albert Gudeman farm. This is the site of today's church building. A large barn was built on the same site for horses and buggies. Before, horses and buggies were sheltered uptown in the livery stables across the street from the Methodist Church. The cost was ten cents per vehicle.

Phillip Gutwein, Sr., served as the church's first resident minister. A short time later his son, Phillip, Jr., seventeen, was appointed to the ministry before he was married. Services were conducted in the German language for several years, but during the century's second decade, the language of worship gradually evolved from German to English. Otto Norr of Leo, Indiana, preached the first English sermon at Francesville. Phillip Gutwein, Jr., was able to preach in the English language, and this was of great benefit to the younger generation.

During 1920 and 1921 the church was blessed with over forty converts. They were baptized in a horse tank just outside the church.

Also in the 1920's a fire broke out in the furnace area and caused some damage, primarily from smoke, to the church.

The church building at Francesville has undergone many additions and alterations over the years. Renovations occurred in 1942, 1953, and 1972. In 1973 construction of a new kitchen and dining area was initiated. With the cooperation of many brethren and friends, this addition was completed in June, 1974.

In 1961 the Francesville congregation endured its most trying time. Approximately fourteen families, which included three ministers, separated from the Apostolic Christian Church to worship elsewhere.

Following the sad departure of those families, the Francesville congregation began to heal. The long-established doctrines and practices of the Apostolic Christian Church proved to be a comfort and blessing to those who remained. Since that time, by the grace of God, a special spirit of love and unity has been prominent—and is very evident to visitors. Consequently, the church had grown to include 120 families and 225 members in 1980.[8] By July of 1981, nine persons had been baptized and twenty-five more were awaiting baptism.

Phillip Gutwein, Sr., was selected as the first resident Elder at Francesville in 1932. He was seventy-one years old. Phillip Gutwein, Jr., never served as Elder but was a highly respected expositor of Scriptures. He served in the ministry for many years and died in September, 1962.

Wendell Gudeman was ordained as Francesville's second resident Elder on April 13, 1969.

Francesville is the site of beautiful Parkview Haven, a retirement home sponsored by the Remington, Wolcott, La Crosse, Valparaiso, and Francesville Apostolic Christian Churches.

The Francesville congregation—during more than seventy years of existence—has proven that despite hardship, schism, and other challenges offered by the enemy of the believer's soul, a church that consists of obedience and humble attitudes can grow and prosper in the Lord.

At the dedication of the new 1974 addition, a special brochure noted:

> Those who lived during the early days of the church testified that even though the building has changed, the faith has not. Salvation is attained through faith in the shed blood of Jesus Christ and in obedience to God's word. Converts repent, make confession and restitution, and give their testimony before the believers and are baptized.

SABETHA, KANSAS

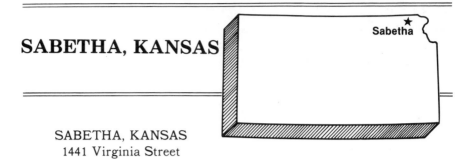

SABETHA, KANSAS
1441 Virginia Street

The Apostolic Christian Church at Sabetha, Kansas, sits in the extreme northeastern corner of the state. It is situated approximately sixty miles north of Topeka and six miles from Nebraska's southern border. Interestingly, Sabetha is only forty-five miles north of the Potawatomie Indian Reservation and fifteen miles west of the Iowa Sac and Fox Indian Reservation.

The congregation at Sabetha is essentially an outgrowth of the country church located southeast of Bern, Kansas. This country church was officially established in 1880. During the next two decades, as more and more families settled on farms in the general area, many settled in and around the Sabetha area. Everyone attended church services held near Bern.

By 1907, due to difficult travel conditions and a lack of hard-surface roads, brethren who lived in the Sabetha area decided to hold services in the village of Sabetha to provide a more convenient place of worship. In the fall of that year, a small church was built on the west edge of Sabetha.

This group of believers grew in number, and by 1914 an addition was made to the original building. A large assembly room was built, and the "old" section (seven years) was used as a dining room. Over a span of several years, improvements and modifications were made to the Sabetha church building.

Early in the decade of the 1950's, crowded conditions reflected the need for more commodious quarters. Several brothers voluntarily established a building fund which grew from unsolicited funds. On February 28, 1956, after many months of sincere and prayerful consideration, the Sabetha congregation voted to build a new house of worship.

On April 16, 1956, excavation for the new church began on the site of the old building which had been moved a short distance east of its former location. It was used as a meeting place until the new church was ready for occupancy. First services were held in the new church on December 16, 1956.

Despite unfavorable crop conditions in 1956, progress on the building project proceeded smoothly and was not hindered by financial considerations. The dedication brochure (May 12, 1957) stated, "We are thankful to God that throughout a drought-stricken adverse year He blessed the labor of the builders' hands and inspired hope and faith and courage to consummate the work."

A Prayer of Dedication

This house to thee we dedicate
And to thy service consecrate;
*   O God, grant that it be*
A temple true, a house of praise,
A sanctuary of thy grace,
*   An altar unto thee.*

O, let it be a resting place
Where weary hearts on Sabbath days
*   Find waters sweet and still;*
An Elim in the desert's heat,
Beneath whose cooling palms we meet
*   Our thirsting souls to fill.*

Lord, guard its portals, that no sin
Nor unclean thing may enter in;
   O, keep it pure and holy.
Cast out all discord, envy, pride;
Let love and peace and joy abide
   In hearts contrite and lowly.

The gifts that built this house for thee
Were first received as blessings free,
   Bestowed from heaven above—
The wealth, the skill of hands and mind,
The strength for toil, all these, we find,
   Are bounties of thy love.

Now in thy church new zeal arouse;
Build from within a Godly house
   Of lively stones, we pray.
Awaken sinners from their sleep,
Increase thy flock, watch o'er thy sheep,
   Good Shepherd, lest they stray.

This house, we know, will fall some day;
Yes, heaven and earth shall pass away;
   Thy Word alone shall stand.
O God, our faith looks up to thee
A nobler temple once to see,
   Untouched by mortal hand—

A house of heavenly design,
Of stones and workmanship divine,
   Whose light the Lamb shall be.
There with the blest, the ransomed throng,
Lord, may we join the victors' song,
   And ever worship thee.

Among the first families to attend the Sabetha church were those of "Black Joe" Strahm, Andrew Burger, Sam Baller (a song leader), Joe Meyer, Jacob Reinhart, Henry Moller, Andrew Aberle, John Aberle, Will Heise (a song leader), Sam Beyer, Jake Heiniger, Ed Steiner, Menno Steiner, Bill Brunner, George Grimm, Henry Aberle, John Aeschliman, Ed Strahm, Joseph J. Strahm, Jake Strahm, Henry Wegman, and Joe Stoller. There were also Eisering and Schurter families.

Included among the early ministers at Sabetha were Andrew Aberle, Samuel Imthurn, Joseph J. Strahm, Martin Esslinger, Menno Steiner and Rudolph Locher.

Rudolph Locher of the nearby Bern congregation emerged as a church leader and served as Elder from approximately 1934 to 1944. He was born in 1870 near Bern, Switzerland, the son of Andrew and Rose Aeschliman Locher. While a teen-ager, using funds borrowed from his father, he came to America with the Wittmer family, his neighbors in Switzerland. They were headed for Oneida, Kansas, a few miles west of Sabetha. Since Locher had no specific place to go in America, he decided to go to Oneida, too. On arriving at the depot in Oneida, the Wittmers were met by a son who had previously come to America. Young Rudolph Locher was left to fend for himself. John Wenger asked him to come with him to his house. The next day he found employment as a "hired man" with Black Joe Strahm (not to be confused with Joseph J. Strahm, a minister).

Confirmed a few years earlier as a Lutheran, Locher knew nothing of the Apostolic Christian Church, but began to assemble there on Sundays since he worked for the Strahms who were members. While attending these services, he came under conviction and felt the need of repentance. Yet, he resisted. He went to the Ozarks in Missouri to work on a farm where his sister Theresa was a "hired girl." It did not take him long to realize his calling from God. He returned to Bern, Kansas, and was soon baptized.

He married Elise Ruchti who was also a native of Switzerland. She, with her two sisters, previously drew straws to see which one was to come to America and help their sister, Louise Wenger (Mrs. William Wenger). She often commented how she had to cry most of the way across the ocean because she had to leave such a nice home and family.

Rudolph Locher served as Elder over both the Bern and Sabetha churches. He died on September 14, 1944. One of his favorite hymns was No. 146 in the *Zion's Harp,* "How Shall It Be?"

Others who served as Elders at Sabetha were Jacob Edelman and Joseph Wittmer, both of Bern. On July 11, 1963, Eugene Marti was ordained as Elder.[9] In 1975, he moved to Springfield, Missouri, and became Elder of the church at Lamar, Missouri, the area where he was born in 1930.

Sam Huber was ordained Elder in March, 1980.

Sabetha, Kansas, is the site of the beautiful Apostolic Christian Home for the Aged, located at 511 Paramount Street. Opened in 1960, it had grown to include eighty residents by 1981 with a staff of eighty-five persons.

SOUTH BEND, INDIANA
(Formerly Bremen, Indiana)

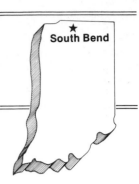

SOUTH BEND, INDIANA
15961 Madison Road
Mishawaka, Indiana

In 1911 an Apostolic Christian Church was established in the area of Bremen, Indiana. This was due, in large part, to the efforts of John and Mary Gerber who had moved here from Forrest, Illinois.

John Gerber, a minister, was born in Wayne County, Ohio, in 1849. He lived for awhile in West Bend, Iowa, where he served as a minister prior to moving south of Fairbury, Illinois in 1889.[10] He continued in the ministry at the "South Side" church.

The Gerbers eventually bought land northeast of Bremen. Two married daughters had previously moved to the area (Lydia, wife of Ed Getz and Mary, wife of Ed Hirstein). A son, Will, and family moved to the Bremen area, too. Also, another daughter, Anne, and her husband, Will Leman, moved to Bremen.

Being a minister, John Gerber was concerned that they have a place of worship. Before moving his family to Bremen, he came and prepared a dwelling place on his farm which was also used for worship services. It was built north of Bremen on Dogwood Road and was later made into a church.

The new venture of these few farm families proved to proceed smoothly. The first crop of fruits and melons was plenteous and very delicious. They were very thankful to God for the bountiful harvest of that first year in Bremen.

The congregation was stunned, however, when John Gerber, sixty-three, suddenly passed away in 1912. His wife was left with four children at home: Leah, Sam, Lou, and Jeff.

During the ensuing years, additional families came to the area. The depot at Wyatt, Indiana, a few miles north of Bremen, was the arrival place of many of the newcomers. The new arrivals often stayed in the homes of members until their future homes were ready for occupancy.

Among the early families arriving in the Bremen area were those of Abraham Schuch, Jacob Schuch, Fred Von Bergen, Christian Yackley, Edward Germann, John Laidig, Carl Von Burgen, Jacob Clauss, Christian Sinn, and Joe Unsicker.

These new families, along with other converts, necessitated larger worship accommodations. This need was met by purchasing a country school house for $100 and moving it next to the church building.[11]

An interesting occurrence is remembered from the old country church. One day some gypsies entered the church and took a large portion of silverware and dishes from the kitchen. The following Sunday rolls were served instead of bread and butter. This was because there were no utensils to use in buttering the bread. The people liked rolls, and this initiated the serving of rolls for the noon lunch at Bremen.

In 1924 a brick church was erected at 124 North Baltimore Street in Bremen. Dedication services were held November 9, 1924. Among the ministers who served Bremen following the untimely death of John Gerber were Jake Schuch, Fred Von Bergen, and Chris Zimmer. A few years after moving to Indiana, John Gerber's daughter, Leah, married Henry Souder of Grabill, Indiana. Eventually they moved to the Bremen area. He was called to the ministry in 1927 and served for many years. In 1935 Herman Hueni was appointed to the ministry. He served until his death in 1961.

In 1954 a nursery wing was added to the church. On October 26, 1969, ground-breaking ceremonies were held for another addition adjacent to the church consisting of a fellowship hall and Sunday School rooms. The cornerstone was laid

June 28, 1970. This wing was dedicated "that the youth of our church and of this community may be taught the living truths as revealed in God's Word."

The fall of 1979 proved to be a very sad time for the Bremen congregation. On October 28, 1979, a portion of the membership met together and voted to become an independent church. The counseling Elders of the church—Wendell Gudeman, Francesville, Indiana, and Loren Stoller, Latty, Ohio—were not present at this meeting. The by-laws of the local Bremen church allowed this group to retain the church's facilities. Two ministers were among the group that departed from the Apostolic Christian Church, leaving only Robert Beebe who had been placed in the ministry on December 5, 1976.

Those who remained with the Apostolic Christian Church were left without a place of worship. This group, which totaled between thirty to thirty-five persons, met in various places where it was possible to rent suitable quarters to conduct worship services. Over a period of many months, they met in Bremen, Plymouth, South Bend, Nappanee, and LaPaz, Indiana. Wednesday evening services were held in homes. This little group, unified in spirit, retained a deep affection for their heritage of faith as practiced in the Apostolic Christian Church.

With support from brethren across the land, this small band of believers soon broke ground for a new church one mile north of Woodland, Indiana. This village is located mid-way between Bremen and South Bend on Route 331. The Apostolic Christian Church here is referred to as the "South Bend" church. The new church building was occupied for services on May 31, 1981. Robert Beebe continued to serve as minister of this congregation.

The Bremen and South Bend churches have never had a local Elder. Elders who served these congregations were Barthol Rapp, Morton, Illinois; Henry Souder, Leo, Indiana; Elias Dotterer, Junction, Ohio; Sam Aeschliman, Bluffton, Indiana; Joe Waibel, Bay City, Michigan; Theo Beer, Milford, Indiana; Wendell Gudeman, Francesville, Indiana; and Loren Stoller, Latty, Ohio.

LATTY, OHIO

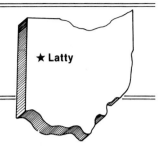

★ Latty

LATTY, OHIO
¾ mile southeast

Beginning in 1911 many families of the Apostolic Christian faith began moving to farms in the Latty, Ohio, area. On August 12, 1913, the brethren here—who previously attended worship services at Junction, Ohio—purchased thirty-four church pews from Axel White of Broughton, Ohio, for $120. He had bought them from one of Broughton's abandoned churches. These benches were used for the first Latty worship services which were held primarily in a vacant house on the John A. Stoller farm.

Latty, Ohio, is a small village located in Paulding County. It sits in the state's northwest corner only eleven and one-half miles from the Indiana border and approximately twenty-two miles southwest of Defiance, Ohio. Prior to the arrival of settlers in 1822, the area here was a dense forest consisting of giant oak, hickory, elm, maple, sycamore, ash, and cottonwood trees.

Otto Ludwig wrote of these beautiful, virgin forests, "To be out in the deep woods you had a feeling you were in a huge building and the large tree trunks were pillars supporting a green roof. The big trees would inspire and stir your emotions as a good sermon, and their benediction had no ritualism, mysticism, conformity, dogma, or creed."[12]

Much of the area was known as the Black Swamp due to poor drainage caused by ill-defined waterways which were often blocked by fallen timbers. Generally, the 1800's were spent in taming this wilderness which eventually paved the way for agricultural development early in this century. The construction of drainage ditches and tiling led to the swift emergence of a thriving commercial and agricultural community in Paulding County.

The number of families who moved to Latty from 1911 to 1920 is quite impressive. The rather large migration of farmers to this area was due, in large part, to the efforts of a land company—Straus Brothers—that specialized in promoting the sale of Paulding County land. Agents of this firm traveled extensively in Illinois and Iowa touting the purchase of lower priced land in Paulding County. Their efforts were successful, especially among Apostolic Christian people. Families moved here from several places, including Cissna Park, Roanoke, Gridley, Tremont, and Princeville, Illinois; Oakville, Iowa; and Bluffton, Remington, and Milford, Indiana.

Picking up and moving to this new area was no easy task for these farmers. Selling their property back home, packing and saying "farewell" to relatives, and pulling up their "roots" were often difficult. Most of these families loaded all their belongings on the train and traveled to their new location by this means.

One of the first families to arrive in the Latty area was that of Christian and Elizabeth Stoller of Cissna Park, Illinois. They settled on a farm north of Paulding. Because they still spoke their native German language, their children acted as interpreters for them when they went to town to purchase groceries and supplies.

In 1912 several families also moved to the area. They included: Sam and Sophia Stoller, Cissna Park, Illinois; Paul and Susan Gerber, and Theo and Julia Gerber, Oakville, Iowa (the Gerbers were brothers who worked for the Schrock family in Oakville); and John and Magdaline Sutter, Woodford County, Illinois.

John Stoller, Sr., and daughter Emma came from Gridley, Illinois. He also had three married sons and a married daughter move here: Dan and Minnie Stoller, John A. and Louisa Stoller, Albert and Rosie Stoller, and Otto and Lydia Stoller Schlatter.

The year 1912 also saw the arrival of Ben and Emma Stoller from Roanoke, Illinois. His father, Gottlieb, who had purchased several farms east of Latty, also came along with his brother Jesse. Gottlieb Stoller encouraged his sons-in-law to move on his land. They were: Emil and Percie Rocke, Peter and Emma Martin, John and Sally Greuter, and Sam and Lidy Feldman. A son, Aaron, and his wife Minnie, also came to Latty. All, except the John Greuters who were from Milford, Indiana, came from Roanoke, Illinois.

From 1913 to 1920 a host of additional families came to this almost table-top flat expanse of land around Latty. Their objective was to enhance their agricultural prospects.

Initially, these many new families attended worship services at the Apostolic Christian Church at Junction, Ohio, approximately twelve miles away. The weekly trip by horse and buggy was often difficult, especially for families with children. For some families the trip was so long the horses had to stop and be watered. Nonetheless, these families distinguished themselves by their dutiful devotion to faithful attendance at the weekly church services.

In the summer of 1913, after two years of traveling to Junction for worship, brethren in the Latty area took steps to establish their own congregation. During this year, while the Junction church was being remodeled, the Junction members met with the Latty group for worship.

On October 15, 1914, the Latty assembly bought Lot 64 in the village of Latty which contained an old church building. This was purchased from Rebecca Latty for $220. The village of Latty was named for her because of her large property holdings.

The newly-purchased building was badly in need of repair. In the fall and winter of 1914-1915 a new foundation, new roof, and new siding were completed. Also, a cloak room was built at the front, a dining area at the rear, out-buildings constructed, and general repairs made inside the building. The total cost was $1,788.15.

Sometime in 1914 six other lots were bought from Rebecca Latty. Four of these lots were used to situate a long row of sixteen stables to accommodate horses. The other two were set aside for future church expansion. These six lots cost $500. On February 21, 1915, the new church was dedicated with Elder Henry Souder, Leo, Indiana, officiating.

For more than a year, ministers from the Apostolic Christian Churches at Bluffton and Leo, Indiana, and Junction, Ohio, took turns in leading the worship services in Latty.

In the spring of 1916, Fred Rager and sixteen other families moved to the Latty area. Rager became the church's first local minister. Later the same year, Fred Oberlander was appointed to the ministry. In 1917 Dan Stoller was appointed to preach. Stoller's ordination ushered in the use of the English language during worship services. The German language, however, was taught in the Sunday School until the early 1930's.

The first trustees of the Latty church (chosen March, 1915) were Dan Stoller, Gottlieb Eisenmann and Paul Gerber.

In 1920 a raging flu epidemic claimed the lives of five people from the Latty congregation. The deaths of Emil Rocke and his son, Melvin, (who laid in his father's arms in the casket), and his wife, Percie, occurred within three days. The flu epidemic was shocking to the church and community. Also, during this year two mothers lost their lives during childbirth. The clouds of agony and despair, however, were eventually graced with a silver lining as forty-three souls were awakened from their slumber of sin and added to the congregation in 1920 and 1921.

In 1948 the congregation began pondering the need for a new church. On November 8, 1949, ground was broken on land one mile southeast of Latty across from the church's cemetery. Elias Dotterer, of Junction, who served as Latty's Elder, officiated at this ceremony. The new building was dedicated September 20, 1951. At that time the church consisted of 60 families and 150 members.

In March, 1978, a new addition was completed, costing $262,000. By July, 1980, the congregation had grown to 147 families and 251 members.

Elias Dotterer of nearby Junction served as Elder at Latty from 1923 until 1951. George Sinn served as Elder from 1951 to 1971 when he retired due to declining health. In 1916 he had come to Latty from Cissna Park, Illinois, with his parents. In 1920 he was one of thirty-four souls who had turned to the Lord in repentance, prompted to do so by the tragic flu epidemic that had swept through the area. He also served as Elder of the Alto, Michigan, and Junction, Ohio churches.

Loren Stoller was selected as Latty's second resident Elder on October 24, 1971.

LA CROSSE, INDIANA

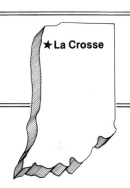

★ La Crosse

LA CROSSE, INDIANA
Vermont Street

The Apostolic Christian Church at La Crosse, Indiana, was established soon after engineers changed the course of the Kankakee River in this area. The territory south of La Crosse was formerly a large swamp that was subsequently converted into productive farmland.

La Crosse, Indiana, is located in the extreme northwestern corner of Indiana only sixty-five miles southeast of the Chicago metropolitan area. It sits in the Kankakee River Valley. The Kankakee River extends from south of Kankakee, Illinois, to the area of South Bend, Indiana. La Crosse is located near the middle of the river's course.

The original river, a few miles south of La Crosse, made a great winding course instead of flowing in a straight direction. This natural course flooded the lands as far north as La Crosse.

At the beginning of this century, the La Crosse Land Company purchased this large swamp area from the state of Indiana. They dredged a new river and bypassed the natural winding "bottleneck." A drainage system for the entire area was installed, and farms and roads were laid out in this former swamp. According to Elder Edward Frank, this area is "the main and better part of the La Crosse farming area today."[13]

This new farming area drew interest from many out-of-state buyers. Following World War I, prices of land soared, especially the more fertile lands in Illinois. This, together with effective promotion by the La Crosse Land Company, resulted in several Apostolic Christian families buying the "swamp" land and beginning farming operations.

The Joe Swing family of Fairbury, Illinois, was the first of the Apostolic Christian faith to move to La Crosse. His family settled on a farm east of La Crosse in 1914.

In 1915 the families of George Yergler and Ed Troxel came to La Crosse. Also, Edward Wittmer and his sisters, Emma and Anna, soon arrived here. The families of Andrew Heiniger, Sam Heinold, Joe Heinold, and Harvey Adams established homes in the Kouts, Indiana, area a few miles west of La Crosse.

By 1916 more families moved to La Crosse. They were those of Chris Siebenthal, David Siebenthal, Jr., Henry Meiss, John Meiss, Sam Frank, Henry Swing, Otto Fritz, and John Nuest.

During this year the number of families of the Apostolic Christian faith near La Crosse totaled approximately twenty-one. Since a church did not exist here, these families traveled to Francesville, twenty miles south of La Crosse, for worship services.

In 1924 Harry Bucher, who had come to La Crosse in 1920 from Gridley, Illinois, was added to the ministry. He is remembered as a powerful preacher with a deep and booming voice.

In 1920 another wave of families moved to the La Crosse area. Farming conditions, however, while tolerable for some, were difficult for others, and several families left by the middle of the decade and returned to their former areas. Among these were Joe and Setta Klopfenstein who returned to Gridley, Illinois. He was subsequently made a minister and Elder and served in the latter capacity from 1947 to 1965. Although the La Crosse families were always provided with adequate food and raiment, there was no flourishing era of prosperity—and this made their spiritual blessings so much more precious.

Because of their growing numbers and the inconvenience of traveling to Francesville every Sunday, this group of believers decided to build a church in La Crosse. It was located in the south end of La Crosse. They built a two-story, residential house for worship services with the idea that if membershp continued to grow, they could build a more conventional church and sell the house. Because of the uncertainty associated with production capabilities of the land they purchased at La Crosse, the brethren were not altogether confident they would remain here. If their farming plans failed and the church closed, they could sell the house. The new "church" cost $2,942 plus donated labor. The families met in homes for worship until the house church was completed.

On June 18, 1916, the first worship service was held in the new church with Edward Eglin of Morris, Minnesota, officiating. The next service was held July 2 with Dan Gerber of Bluffton, Indiana, preaching. The Francesville and Bluffton congregations provided one minister per month to preach at La Crosse until September, 1918, when George Yergler, thirty, was instated into the ministry. Elders Godfrey Rauch, Bluffton, and Henry Souder, Sr., Leo, were here and made the appointment. It was also in 1918 when the La Crosse church realized their first convert. Otto Fritz was the first person baptized at La Crosse.

In 1933 twenty-nine souls repented and were baptized. This was a tremendous boost to the congregation. Probably because of this growth spurt it became apparent that a local Elder was needed. In 1936 George Yergler was ordained as Elder. In 1938 the "long hoped-for" church building became a reality. The congregation at Cissna Park, Illinois, dismantled their old "town" church, shipped it to La Crosse (it was four days en route), and the La Crosse brethren rebuilt it. This "new" church served the congregation for twenty-eight years until a brand new church was built on the Kritch property in the southwest part of La Crosse. Dedication of this spacious and beautiful church was held November 13, 1966.

The Dedicated Church

With our new church dedicated
To our God and to His Son,
Jesus Christ its true foundation
Is its own firm cornerstone.

As the nails and glue and mortar
Hold the bricks and boards in place,
Makes the strong new house of worship
Even fiercest storms to face . . .

Let us learn the good example
How the little things on earth
Are of just as much importance
As the things of greatest worth.

Likewise love of every member
Holds the church of God secure,
Through the midst of storm and anguish
Every trial to endure.

There's a moral in this story;
Truly, there is no finer gift,
Next to serving God in Heaven,
To help another's load to lift.

Although humble seems our service
That to God and church we bring,
To some soul 'twill be essential
And will please the Heavenly King.

So let us put our soul and body
Into everything that is good;
If we love our loving Saviour,
We will love His brotherhood.

George Yergler, quiet and reserved, yet very likable and highly respected, served as Elder from 1936 to 1974. He was born December 21, 1887, in Gridley, Illinois, the son of William and Mattie Mangold Yergler. When he was eight years old, the family moved to Cissna Park, Illinois. It was at Cissna Park he married Ida Wittmer in 1913. Elder Eugene Schladenhauffen performed the wedding ceremony. After a long tour of serving the church at La Crosse as well as other congregations, Yergler wrote, "We have had many blessings, also sorrows and disappointments, but overall God has been good to us, for which we are very grateful."

On October 3, 1971, Edward Frank was ordained as La Crosse's second resident Elder.[14]

"Trust in the Lord with all thine heart; and lean not unto thine own understanding."

From 1847, when brethren first set foot on American shores, until 1917—seventy years later—churches of the Evangelical Baptist (Apostolic Christian) faith were established in many states, and the members essentially preoccupied themselves with seeking an existence in their newly-adopted country.

When the faith that was kindled anew in Europe under the guidance of Samuel Froehlich came to America, the organization of the church was patterned after that which existed in Europe. At the outset of his ministry, it was strongly felt by Froehlich and his followers that "unless these converts could be bound together in a stronger and closer union, there would be little prospect of their permanency."[1]

A Scripture that greatly impressed Froehlich and his followers was found in St. Matthew 28:20, "Teaching them to observe all things whatsoever I have commanded you." Based on these and many other Scriptures, a deep commitment was generated toward keeping the "whole counsel" of God and dwelling together, denominationally, with singleness of purpose and a devout sense of likemindedness. The strong sense of mission to establish a church based on true Christian discipleship and to live in obedience to the teachings of Christ and His disciples (which was so prominent among the followers of Froehlich in Europe) continued in the United States.

A deep sense of brotherhood was necessary in order for the fledgling European churches to prevail amid the false doctrines and often harsh persecution of the Swiss state church. The Evangelical Baptist Church's perception and understanding of God's plan of salvation did not coincide with that of the state church, particularly with respect to the important themes of repentance, conversion, baptism, and Holy Communion. In view of this, and in response to the state church's continued harassment and eventual deportation of Samuel Froehlich, the Evangelical Baptist Church developed a policy of closed communion. Closed communion was adopted and practiced in America too. The brethren in America, based largely on the unpleasant harassment suffered at the hands of governmental authorities in Europe, were glad to enjoy the benefits of religious freedom here in America. The Constitution's guarantee of the free exercise of religion was a far cry from what they had experienced in Europe where the state tried to control many aspects of their religious life.

When the brethren came to America, they were determined to do nothing that might draw the attention of the government or which might jeopardize the free exercise of their faith. Consequently, they quietly practiced their faith—mostly in rural areas. They clung to the German language and retained many of their Swiss and German cultural practices. Generally, they were somewhat suspicious of the "English" language and the effect it would have on the church. Primarily, the early church in America drew people mostly of German extraction. Language was an obvious barrier in whatever outreach attempts they might have made.

Added to their cautious attitude toward anything English or American was their deep devotion to the Biblical themes of "separation from the world" and "nonconformity to the world." These important beliefs found great reinforcement when those persons of Mennonite background were drawn into the church during its formative stages in America. Also, these people's religious ideals included the concepts of humility, simplicity, and yieldedness.

The church in America existed in relative peace and experienced continued growth—predominantly in rural areas—until 1906-1907 when a schism shattered its unity. Also, in 1908 the public trial of several church officials in central Illinois —when the church suffered much unjustified and erroneous press ridicule—only drove the church into a greater attitude of withdrawal and separation. It became more suspicious and distrustful of society and its worldly ways.

Nonetheless, following the first schism and the public trial, the church gathered itself and quietly experienced continued growth. Emigrants continued to pour into America during this time, and many brethren were among them.

So powerful was the German influence in America during this time that Congress considered a bill that would make German the official language of the United States.

The Peoria *Journal Star* wrote of the strong German influence early in this century. "German was taught in the schools here. There were lots of German newspapers. Sermons were preached in the German language."[2]

The strong German influence in America began an abrupt decline in 1917 when the United States declared war against Germany on April 6 of that year. A little more than a month later (on May 18), the Selective Service Act was passed by Congress which later registered 24,200,000 men, twenty-one through thirty years of age, and drafted nearly three million into military service.

The Apostolic Christian Church—firmly rooted in German and Swiss culture and deeply attuned to the German language—now faced, in many instances, the scorn and distrust of non-German Americans. It was a time of crisis for the church. Prejudice was very much alive in America during this era and was particularly vented, however subtle, against persons with a German heritage.

Adding to the crisis was the fact that sons—members and friends—of Apostolic Christians faced the draft, and many were conscripted into the armed forces. To comply with Scriptures, the church adopted a non-combatant position. Consequently, the young men it sent to the armed forces would not bear arms. Their stance was based largely on the clear Biblical injunctions that follow:

1. *"Thou shalt not kill." (Exodus 20:13)*

2. *"Do violence to no man." (St. Luke 3:14)*

3. *"Then said Jesus unto him, Put up again thy sword into his place: for all they that take the sword shall perish with the sword." (St. Matthew 26:52)*

4. *"Ye have heard that it hath been said, An eye for an eye, and a tooth for a tooth: But I say unto you, That ye resist not evil: but whosoever shall smite thee on thy right cheek, turn to him the other also." (St. Matthew 5:38-39)*

5. *"Love your enemies, bless them that curse you, do good to them that hate you." (St. Matthew 5:44)*

The churches at Leo and Bluffton, Indiana, wrote a statement that summarized their feelings concerning war. This document, signed by ministers Henry Souder, Gottfried Rauch, and John Aeschliman and subscribed and affirmed before Ernest A. Isch on July 18, 1918, at Bluffton, was an attempt to reflect the church's stance against bearing arms in war.[3]

Foundation and Principle of Church

First of all, a true conversion from sin to holiness, from darkness to light, and risen with Christ through baptism, and then obey His teachings, and follow Him by His Holy Spirit, which will lead us in all truth if we stay true unto Him.

The following in reference, refer to why we oppose to render such service that would be under the combatant strife of the nation.

St. Matthew the 5th chapter;

St. Matthew the 26th chapter, from the 51st and 52nd verse;

St. Luke 3rd chapter, 14th verse; the 6th chapter, from the 27th to the 32nd verse; the 9th chapter, from the 54th to the 57th verse;

Romans, the 12th chapter, from the 19th verse on.

And we believe to honor the laws of our government, as they are ordained to bear the sword not in vain, as we can find in Romans the 13th chapter.

But as to our belief, we as member and faithful attendant of the Apostolic Christian Church shall not use the sword, as we can read in the gospel. It is not our belief to serve in any combatant strife, and has always been the rule of the church according to the teaching of Christ to forbid its members to participate in war.

This record and statement is true to the best of our knowledge and ability.

Henry Souder
Gottfried Rauch
John Aeschliman

Subscribed and affirmed to before me this 18th day of July, 1918.

Ernest A. Isch,
Notary Public

Young men who entered the service as non-combatants during World War I—mostly Mennonites, Quakers, and Apostolic Christians—faced a very uncertain future due largely to the government's general inability to cope with those who refused to bear arms.

James C. Juhnke, Professor of History at Bethel College, Newton, Kansas, commented on this specific situation:

Both the American government and the Mennonite churches were quite unprepared in 1917-18 to cope with the problem of what to do with conscientious objectors in a time of wartime conscription. The government had almost no history or experience with conscription. There had been no draft for the Spanish-American War at the end of the 19th century. In the Civil War, the Union had gotten less than two per cent of its fighting men through the draft. The government had very little notion how many conscientious objectors there would be, how unyielding the COs would be in their refusal of arms, what the demoralizing effect of COs might be upon the military mobilization effort, and what policies would be workable for the punishment or the nonmilitary use of COs. As a result, the government policy for COs was formulated in confusion, without clear definitions and programs.

Secretary of War Newton D. Baker did have one clear overriding objective for handling COs as the Selective Service system was initiated in 1917. He wanted to get all the COs to report to military camps along with other conscripts. It would be decided later what would happen with them in the camps. Baker successfully persuaded the Mennonites and other COs—naive and trusting as they were—that if they only would report to camp the government would respect their consciences. The religious COs, he said, would not be forced to do anything in violation of their religious convictions. And so the Mennonites were lured into Camp Travis in Texas, Camp Funston in Kansas, Camp Dodge in Iowa, Camp Meade in Maryland, and dozens of other military camps across the country.

Baker had promised more to the COs than he could deliver. Indeed, it is fair to say that he deceived the Mennonites into sending their boys to camp. The Selective Service Law did not even allow for non-military alternative service. It allowed only for non-combatant service with the framework of military conscription. There would have to be new legislation if non-military service was the only acceptable alternative for COs. Baker could not supply such legislation—that depended upon Congress. Moreover, Baker sent secret orders to the military camp commanders across the country telling them that the COs were coming and that it was their duty to persuade these religious pacifists to take up weapons and to join the great crusade to make the world safe for democracy—the liberal democratic dream in action! The COs should be treated decently, he said, and be segregated into separate detachments. They should be kept close enough to the camp activities that they would be thrilled by the enthusiasm and idealism of the war enterprise.

Baker's strategy of duplicity and waffling was a recipe for confused confrontation. The generals running the military camps were not schooled in the techniques of friendly persuasion. Their job was to prepare an army to fight in Europe and they wanted to get on with it. And so some of the peace church draftees in military camp were subjected to humiliation, physical beatings, courts martial and to a great variety of intimidation and harassment. They would be given orders to put on the uniform, to take up weapons, or to perform other specific tasks and when they refused they would be court martialed and sentenced for 15 to 35 years in military prison. Two Hutterite Mennonites died as a result of mistreatment and ensuing illness.

It was into this kind of environment that many young Apostolic Christian men began their military training. David Meister, Peoria, Illinois (who died in 1981) spent several months in a military prison at Ft. Leavenworth, Kansas, during World War I for his refusal to bear arms.[4] Born in Harper, Kansas, he later moved with his parents to Driftwood, Oklahoma. In 1917 he went to Cherokee, Oklahoma, to register as a conscientious objector at his local draft board, but apparently to no avail.

When he arrived at Camp Travis, Texas, the camp officers were unfamiliar with the conscientious objector category. They were insensitive to those who, due to deeply-held religious convictions, were opposed to killing. Generally, camp authorities were adverse to the young men who stood firm in their resolve not to bear arms. The officers would not listen to Meister and the other conscientious objectors who were Quakers and Mennonites. They told Meister, who was converted (in the Apostolic Christian Church, Nazarene) in 1917, that he had not been a member of his church very long and he only joined it so he could enter the service as a non-combatant.

Meister recalled the terrible fear he experienced waiting for the unexpected to happen at Camp Travis. The officers did not treat the conscientious objectors very nicely. One time they were rounded up and marched out to a nearby field. They were blindfolded and told to raise their arms over their heads. Meister thought they were going to be executed. Instead, the ordeal was suddenly halted, and they were marched back to their barracks. The incident was designed to persuade, through terror, these young men to change their minds regarding their military classification.

Finally Meister, along with his fellow objectors, were court martialed and subsequently sentenced to life imprisonment for their refusal to bear arms. Then later, due to the "mercy" of the officers, the sentence was reduced to twenty-five years. Of the sentence reduction Meister said, "I was a happy boy that day." He was sent to the military prison at Ft. Leavenworth, Kansas, in the fall of 1918 and served until the spring of 1919 when he was unexpectedly released. He worked on the prison's dairy farm and actually preferred prison life to the uncertain and harsh treatment he received at Camp Travis.

Also, several young men of the church from central Illinois were sent to Camp Wheeler near Macon, Georgia, where the Thirty-First Division was training and mobilizing for eventual shipment to Germany. Among the young men were William Gramm and Harry Bucher of Gridley; Levi Sauder of Tremont; and Henry Leonhardt and Sam Zimmerman of Fairbury.

In July of 1918 Gustave Bucher of Gridley, Illinois, father of Harry Bucher, and Elder Barthol Rapp of Morton, Illinois, journeyed to Camp Wheeler to visit the young men of the church who were stationed there. On arriving they sought permission from camp authorities—from Major General Leroy S. Lyon—to conduct church services for several soldiers of the Apostolic Christian Church. These services were held on the afternoon of July 29, 1918, at Hotel Lanier in Macon. The servicemen of the church and two civilians—Gustave Bucher and Barthol Rapp—gathered in one of the hotel's rooms. They locked the door and pulled down the window shades. They passed out German language hymnals, sang from them, and Rapp conducted worship services in the German language— this at a time when the United States was involved in a war with Germany and anti-German feeling in the nation was gaining in intensity.

Both the military police and the local Macon police were evidently unaware that the worship meeting was authorized by the camp's high command. On hearing the singing and the German language, police came in and broke up the meeting, arrested the participants, and marched them down to the city jail.

On Tuesday, July 30, 1918, the following article, which appeared in *Trench and Camp,* the weekly edition printed by *The Macon Daily Telegraph* for Camp Wheeler, carried a detailed report of the incident:

GERMAN RELIGIOUS SERVICES
BROKEN UP BY THE POLICE

Twenty Soldiers Arrested in the
Raid Are Ordered Released by
Wheeler Authority.

The Meeting Is Understood to Have
Been Held With the Sanction of
Camp Headquarters.

Twenty soldiers from Camp Wheeler, most of whom are said to be of German extraction, and two civilians giving their names as Gustave Bucher and Barthol Rapp, who also were said to be of Teutonic descent, were arrested yesterday afternoon in a room at the Hotel Lanier where they were holding a religious meeting in the German language and singing German songs.

Patrolmen Whitaker and Vallette, of the city police of Macon, and two members of the city military police made the arrests. An hour later the soldiers were released by the military police upon orders from the Division Headquarters, where, it is understood, that the civilians had Saturday received permission from Major General Leroy S. Lyon to hold the meeting and had asked that certain soldiers be allowed to attend. The civilians were held in custody by the city police, but later released.

Taken to Police Station.

When the soldiers were arrested they were taken to the police station where they were detained until the order for their release. The civilians were charged with "issuing unpatriotic remarks" and were held "for safe keeping for the government," but were released after the case was further investigated.

It is understood the military police were not aware that the meeting had the sanction of camp authorities.

The two civilians came from a community in Illinois where German is about the only language spoken. Barthol Rapp is a preacher of the Apostolic Christian Church in the name of which, it is said, yesterday's services were being held. Gustave Bucher is also a member of this church and one of the soldiers arrested was a son of Bucher. Rapp said he had a son in the army in Mississippi.

Followed From Camp.

Two of the soldiers who attended the meeting were from one company in the 106th Sanitary Train and, it is said they were "shadowed" from the camp to the city and when they reached the Hotel Lanier where several other soldiers were talking with the two civilians the military police were notified by a sergeant from the 106th Sanitary Train who said he had been detailed by his commander to watch the men.

Two members of the military police were sent to the Hotel Lanier where the Germans were found in a room. The room was said to be locked and the windows and shades drawn tight. When the door was opened, the leader of the meeting, the military police claim, threw his German song book under a bed. The book is small and thick and contains German songs.

When the authorities at Camp Wheeler heard that the meeting had been broken up and the soldiers and the two Germans from Illinois had been arrested, Lieut. Miller, in charge of the city M.P. force, was notified to release the men. As the military police had arrested the soldiers only and the civilian authorities had charge of the two civilians, Lieut. Miller only released the soldiers.

Patrolmen Vallette and Whitaker made the cases against the German religious leaders.

The members of this church do not believe in fighting, it is said.

The incident at Hotel Lanier was obviously controversial, and the news spread rapidly. Word soon reached Gridley, Illinois, the home of soldiers William Gramm and Harry Bucher. Because of the war with Germany, anti-German feeling in Gridley ran high among some people. In fact, soon after the incident at Macon, vandals splashed a bold sign in yellow paint on the front of the Apostolic Christian Church at Gridley. This occurred on a Saturday night. When members arrived for worship the next morning, they saw the big yellow sign which read, "NO MORE GERMAN." This, of course, made reference to the German language which was used during worship services at the Gridley church. The sign symbolized the anti-German feeling that existed, not only in Gridley, but across the nation.

The sign stunned the congregation and deeply offended many of the brethren. Fearfully, they wondered, "What will happen next?" This unpleasant incident ultimately led to the use of the English language during worship at Gridley.

Treatment of the conscientious objectors at Camp Wheeler was often brutal. Harry Bucher, then of Gridley, Illinois, and later a minister at La Crosse and Valparaiso, Indiana, was beaten for his refusal to bear arms. One day the men of his company strapped a rifle on him and forced him to walk around all day until he was so tired he could hardly walk.[5]

Henry Leonhardt, a member of the church from Fairbury, Illinois, served at Camp Wheeler with Harry Bucher. According to William Gramm, Leonhardt was beaten until he was black and blue.[6] Because he spoke mostly German, military authorities suspected he was a spy.[7]

Sam Zimmerman of rural Fairbury also served as a conscientious objector at Camp Wheeler although he was not yet a member of the church. He was very much aware of the tension conscientious objectors experienced. In a series of letters written to his future wife, Louise Koehl, he mentioned, "a fellow sure has to be careful what he does and what he says down here." He also told her, when feeling the deep concern associated with his conscientious objector status, "I feel sorry for the whole bunch of us, but I guess we will have to bear the burden." Always anxious how his officers might treat him or where he eventually would be shipped, he described the situation as always being in "boiling hot water."

Zimmerman wrote that seven soldiers tried to force him to carry a gun. He refused. So they took a club to him and, "I'll say it was the worst beating I ever got."[8]

When Barthol Rapp and Gustave Bucher and the servicemen were arrested at Hotel Lanier in Macon, Sam Zimmerman, who was late for the scheduled church service, was sitting in a park across from the hotel. He saw the police haul them away from the hotel and speed them to the nearby police station.

Another incident dealing with the refusal to bear arms involved Elder Ernest Graf, Sr., of Akron, Ohio. In 1917 he had received a letter from some young men of the church who were stationed at Fort Dodge, Kansas. These men did not wish to bear arms despite being expected to do so by their officers. The letter sought Elder Graf's advice on how to face the dilemma.

He replied to them outlining the reasons, based on Scriptures, why opposition to war for conscience sake was justifiable. When the young men received his letter, they used the reasons he listed to explain why they could not bear arms. The officers demanded the letter be given to them. They immediately handed it over to proper investigative authorities who eventually pursued its origin.

As the weeks wore on, Elder Graf had received no response from the young servicemen in Fort Dodge. Thus, he was quite surprised while working in his field one day to be confronted by two government officers from the Attorney General's office who began to question him, item by item, concerning the advice given to the young men who had refused to take arms.

After less than an hour of conversation, the men said, "Mr. Graf, we have been sent to bring you back with us and will put you under arrest and bring you to a federal court in Cleveland, there to be heard."

To the surprise of these two agents, Elder Graf said he would not resist arrest but first wanted to go up to the house to change his clothes and to tell his wife what was taking place.

While he was changing his clothes, the two agents conferred. Obviously impressed with Elder Graf's sincere convictions and gentle disposition, they relented in their "arrest" and asked only for a promise that he would cease from advising anyone against conscription into the U.S. Army. There was, however, a subsequent hearing before a federal judge, apparently to impress upon Elder Graf that military law supercedes the Bible, at least in the view of the federal court.

The incident reflected the intervening power of the Spirit for those men who, in obedience to God, stood firm for the truth. This episode was an example of the Spirit's deliverance from fear and uncertainty on the part of many men of the church who in many other instances had suffered ridicule, persecution, and many unpleasantries by steadfastly refusing to violate a Scriptural mandate.

The refusal to bear arms, based on solid and unequivocal Biblical injunction, was a practice rooted in true Christian discipleship over many centuries. Anabaptists and their descendants placed a great emphasis on the refusal to bear arms. The peace stance was so important that it was included in the seven articles of faith that comprised the historic Schleitheim Confession, an early Anabaptist statement of faith (drawn up February 27, 1527).[9]

The Apostolic Christian position regarding the sword and bearing of arms in war, while distinctly different from that of the mass of society, also differed somewhat from the Anabaptist-Mennonite position. Apostolic Christians would register for the draft as conscientious objectors (a term which originated at the outset of the nation's entry into World War I) and then enter the service in a non-combatant capacity. Those of Mennonite extraction refused to bear arms, and also most of them refused, beginning with World War II, to even serve in the military as non-combatants. They served in civilian work camps where they performed various kinds of duties in the national interest. Those who refused to do alternative civilian service were imprisoned, usually at Ft. Leavenworth.

On the other hand, Apostolic Christians were willing to serve in the military, but would not bear weapons or kill anyone. They were willing to serve anywhere—in combat or in support groups—where they might serve the sick, wounded, and dying, and thus perform acts of mercy and compassion after the example of Christ.

The church felt it owed a debt of gratitude and appreciation to a government which guaranteed religious liberty, and so long as no killing was required, the brethren thought serving in the military was "rendering unto Caesar the things that were Caesar's."

The position of serving in a non-combatant category was likely developed early in the preaching career of Samuel Froehlich. When Froehlich was associating with Mennonites in the Emmental, Christian Gerber (who later joined his movement), a Mennonite Elder, called Froehlich's attention to the fact that his (Froehlich's) statement of faith did not cover military service. Gerber, of course, in Mennonite tradition, believed strongly in non-violence and peace. It was at this time that Froehlich gave special thought to this issue and consequently developed opposition to combatant service in the military.[10]

In America the church was never seriously confronted with its young men having to serve in the military until the time of World War I. In the Civil War the government had gotten less than two percent of its fighting men through the draft. In the Spanish-American War there was no draft. During World War I provision was made for non-combatants to serve in support units. There was no provision for alternative service. Thus, it was convenient and suitable—and in accord with the church's deeply-held conviction—for its young men to serve in the military in a non-combatant category. By doing so the church remained true to twin objectives—loyalty to God and loyalty to country. By being willing to serve as a non-combatant in a combat situation (as a medic, etc., without a weapon) they could prove their loyalty to their country and at the same time prove they were not cowards. Indeed, many young Apostolic Christian men in World War I, World War II, the Korean Conflict, and the Vietnam War distinguished themselves in the midst of grave peril on the battle lines as they dispensed aid and assistance to the wounded and dying.

Because government and military officials were not adequately schooled in the art of dealing with non-combatants during World War I, it posed a problem of no small magnitude for the brethren. Yet, the young men of the church accepted their treatment with an aplomb and dignity that reflected the Holy Spirit that was within them.

In 1972 Ronald Heiniger of Bloomington, Illinois, wrote a very convincing booklet defending conscientious objection to war entitled *Thou Shalt Not Kill*. Heiniger later was placed in the ministry at Bloomington on October 15, 1973.

CHOOSING AN OFFICIAL CHURCH NAME

It became necessary at the time of World War I—in order to properly register its young men for the draft as non-combatants—for the church to list an official name with federal authorities. Up to this point no singular, official name was adopted for the denomination. Name signs were not posted on churches, and no particular emphasis was placed on publicly conveying a denominational name. The churches at Croghan and Naumburg, New York, used the European name of "Evangelical Baptist." Some of the churches used "Christian Apostolic," and others used "Apostolic Christian." Sometimes the church was called the "German Apostolic Christian Church."

Strikingly illustrative of the inconsistency concerning a denominational name was the name on the gate to the church's cemetery plot in Queens, New York City, which read "German

Christian Congregation." In 1982 this gate still carried the same name.

Since an official name did not exist, the public often mockingly created a variety of names when referring to the church such as "Amish," "Dutch," "German Church," "New Mennonites," and "New Amish." Because of the church's strong devotion to Biblical principles, and its refusal to bend to the secular trends of the times, outsiders were often not reluctant to colloquialize when referring to their acquaintances who attended this German-like church.

It is interesting to speculate on why a specific denominational name was not chosen at the outset. In reviewing the habits of Anabaptist-related groups, and further studying the European-related mindset of those times, it gives coherence to such speculation. The early forefathers were mostly rural. Also, they were mostly reserved and tended to mind their own business and did not mind if others did the same. Preoccupation with making a living in their new land, as well as expending energies in promoting the gospel, over-shadowed the need for a universal denominational name.

One can speculate further that because of the relative diversity of the religious background of the early membership (ie. Lutheran, Swiss state church, Froehlich, Catholic, Mennonite, and Amish), church leaders might have decided to delay the choosing of an official name.

Prior to 1900 some of the local churches were known as Apostolic Christian. Titles and deeds to property indicate this. It is likely that when the first churches (aside from Croghan and Naumburg) were formed in America, the name Apostolic Christian was preferred and used on an informal basis. It is interesting to note that except for the churches at Croghan and Naumburg, the name Evangelical Baptist was not used. The reason for this is that early church leaders in America wanted the church to retain a singular and distinct identity apart from the several Baptist denominations in the United States. The church felt its doctrine was different from other Baptist churches in many respects, and it did not want to be regarded as another Baptist denomination. Thus, the name Apostolic Christian was used by many of the local churches. This name indicated they were following Christ and the Apostles.

At the time of World War I, it was necessary to list a consistent denominational name for the many young men of the church registering for the draft. This possibility was discussed informally among church leaders. Many brethren were consulted and their opinions considered. One such brother in the church who was consulted was Peter Klopfenstein of Gridley, Illinois. Because he was a businessman and familiar in dealing with a variety of people, he was consulted by the leadership of the church as to how they might proceed to list a formal name with federal authorities. Although he was not a minister, he was devout in faith, and his opinion was respected.[11]

A meeting of Elders was convened sometime in 1917-1918 to officially choose a name for the denomination nationwide. Little is known of this meeting. In those days minutes of meetings were not kept, and administrative procedures were unstructured and quite informal. Thus, data on this meeting was garnered from oral accounts passed down over the years. Elder Rudolph Graf, Akron, Ohio, indicates that older brothers in the church said his father, Elder Ernest Graf, Sr., proposed that the name—The Apostolic Christian Church—be adopted as the denomination's official name. The other Elders followed his recommendation, and an official name was chosen. Church officials from Croghan and Naumburg, New York, were unable to attend this important meeting when a denominational name was chosen. Consequently, they did not change their name and retained their original name— Evangelical Baptist. Their Elder at that time, Alpheus Virkler, felt the communities of Croghan and Naumburg recognized them as Evangelical Baptists, and it was not wise to change their name. By 1982 the church name on the front of the churches at Croghan and Naumburg, New York, read: "Evangelical Baptist Church: Affiliated with the Apostolic Christian Church of America."

When the official church name was agreed upon, it was listed with authorities in Washington, D.C. Based on oral history, it is believed Elders Mike Mangold, Roanoke, Illinois, and Barthol Rapp, Morton, Illinois, were among the group (or perhaps the only two) who traveled to the nation's capitol to meet with federal authorities. Morton, Illinois, was listed as the headquarters of the denomination because Elder Barthol Rapp, the head of the Council of Elders, resided there.

Efforts were made late in 1980 to see if any records could be found regarding the meeting between church officials and representatives of the United States Government in Washington, D.C., (in 1917-1918) during which time an official church name was listed and problems associated with the non-combatant status were discussed.

On December 4, 1980, a letter was sent to Congressman Robert H. Michel, Peoria, Illinois, who attends the Apostolic Christian Church (Nazarene). He responded on January 22, 1981:

ROBERT H. MICHEL
18TH DISTRICT, ILLINOIS

REPUBLICAN LEADER

WASHINGTON OFFICES:
H-232, U.S. CAPITOL
(202) 225-0600
2112 RAYBURN BUILDING
(202) 225-6201

RALPH VINOVICH
ADMINISTRATIVE ASSISTANT

DISTRICT OFFICE:
1007 FIRST NATIONAL BANK BUILDING
PEORIA, ILLINOIS 61602
(309) 673-6358

COUNTIES:
BROWN   MASON
BUREAU   PEORIA
CASS   SCHUYLER
KNOX   STARK
TAZEWELL

Congress of the United States
House of Representatives
Washington, D.C. 20515

January 19, 1981

Mr. Perry A. Klopfenstein
212 West Sixth Street
Gridley, Illinois 61744

Dear Mr. Klopfenstein:

I am so sorry to have taken such a long time to reply to your letter of December 4th.

I had sent a copy of your letter over to the Library of Congress and was waiting for their reply. The material they sent us does not answer your question but I am enclosing it for you to see.

I would now suggest that you write to General Services Administration, National Archives and Records Service, Washington, D.C. 20408, ATTENTION: ARCHIVIST OF THE UNITED STATES.

If we can be of any further assistance please let us know.

Sincerely yours,

Robert H. Michel
Member of Congress

RHM:JC

356

On receipt of the Michel letter, a letter was sent to the National Archives to see if their files contained any information relative to the Apostolic Christian Church:

January 22, 1981

General Services Administration
National Archives and Records Service
Washington, D.C. 20408

ATTN: Archivist of the United States

Rep. Robert H. Michel has advised me to write you regarding the following request:

I am seeking information on a meeting which took place sometime in 1917 (or subsequently) between officials of the Apostolic Christian Church of America and the federal government with respect to young men of the church entering the service during World War I as noncombatants. It is not known which department of government met with these church officials.

The purpose of the Elders of the church going to Washington was to list an official church name with the government in order for draft-age young men to register for, and enter, the armed forces as non-combatants.

The Library of Congress researched this matter and could not turn up any information. In an attached note Ann Mallory (287-8990) recommends that your organization might have a record of this meeting.

I am engaged in writing a volume on the history of the Apostolic Christian Church of America. Any efforts you can make for me will be most helpful to this project, which is very important to me and my fellow church members.

Thank you very kindly,

Perry Klopfenstein

Perry A. Klopfenstein

A response from the National Archives and Records Service was received February 11, 1981. Another was received February 24, 1981:

General Services Administration　National Archives and Records Service　Washington, DC 20408

Date February 24, 1981

Reply to Attn of: NNFJ

Subject: Apostolic Christian Church of America

To:
Perry A. Klopfenstein
212 West Sixth Street
Gridley, IL 61744

This is in further reply to your letter of January 22, 1981, a copy of which was referred to us by our Navy and Old Army Branch.

We searched the records of the Department of Justice and the Federal Bureau of Investigation but were unable to locate any information relating to the Apostolic Christian Church of America. We did locate one file (O.G. 126465) among the records of the Bureau of Investigation of the Department of Justice which related to the investigation of the Apostolic Church of Detroit for being sympathetic to the German cause. We can furnish a 16 mm. positive microfilm copy of Old German roll 257A for 13 cents a foot or a total of approximately $13.00. An exact page count will be made when the documents are reproduced. If your remittance is less than the actual cost, we will send you a bill for the difference. If your payment is more than the total cost, you will receive a refund. To order, please send a check or money order, payable to the National Archives Trust Fund (NNFJ), to the Cashier, National Archives (GSA), Washington, DC 20408.

Sincerely,

WILLIAM D. GROVER
Judicial and Fiscal Branch
Civil Archives Division

General Services Administration　National Archives and Records Service　Washington. DC 20408

Date February 11, 1981

Reply to Attn of: NNM081-1463-CAS

Subject: Apostolic Christian Church

To:
Mr. Perry A. Klopfenstein
212 West Sixth Street
Gridley, IL 61744

Examinations of the central correspondence files of the Office of the Secretary of War and The Adjutant General's Office failed to identify any documentation on the Apostolic Christian Church.

We are, therefore, forwarding copies of your letter to our Judicial and Fiscal Branch for a search of the records of the Justice Department and to our General Archives Division for an examination of the World War I Selective Service records. Both those offices will respond directly to you.

CHARLES A. SHAUGHNESSY
Navy and Old Army Branch
Military Archives Division

The only record found in federal files was in reference to a letter, dated April 3, 1918, from Ernest East, secretary to Representative Clifford Ireland, Congressman from Illinois, Sixteenth District, to Major General Enoch H. Crowder, Office of the Provost Marshal General of the War Department. In this letter Ernest East refers to correspondence received from Barthol Rapp of Morton, Illinois. East refers to Rapp as "Head of the Council of Elders of the Apostolic Christian Church" and "a man of high integrity seemingly earnest and sincere in his expressions of willingness to serve the government without violation of the doctrines of his church which are well established."

The letter from Rapp had apparently asked for a clarification of regulations associated with serving in the military as a non-combatant. Congressman Ireland directed that the letter be sent to the War Department. The response from the War Department alluded to Section 4 of the Selective Service Act which states:

> Nothing in this act shall be construed to require or compel any person to serve in any of the forces herein provided for who is found to be a member of any well-recognized religious sect or organization at present organized and existing and whose existing creed or principles forbid its members to participate in war in any form and whose religious convictions are against war or participation therein in accordance with the creed or principles of said religious organizations.

CHANGING WORSHIP LANGUAGE
TO ENGLISH

World War I and the anti-German feeling it generated in this country was largely responsible for one of the most significant and historic events in the Apostolic Christian Church history—that of changing the worship language from German to English. With few exceptions all worship services in all of the churches had been conducted in the German language. Since the membership was decidedly German and Swiss, it was only natural to do so. In fact, many well-known, larger denominations with a sizable German constituency did so as well.

Changing to the English language was a painful adjustment for many of the brethren. The emigrants who came to America and often faced bewilderment and an uncertain future could find both a sense of security and contentment in worshipping God in their native language.

To them, the change to English threatened to bring the church closer to the mainstream of society. Thus, in their view, the church might ultimately become too worldly and perhaps eventually become apostate. On the other hand, there were a few progressive brethren who actually favored the adoption of English because children and young adults (who were not proficient in the German language) could better understand the sermons and consequently become more inclined toward salvation.

The German language was cherished by the church, and many brethren thought the Word of God in the German language was a little "richer" than in English. German was taught in Sunday School. Often, special "German School" was held at many churches during the winter months. The objective was to keep the language alive so it could be passed on to future generations.

Ben Nussbaum, who formerly attended the South Side church near Fairbury, Illinois, remembered many of the older brethren praying in the German language. He said these prayers contained messages that were enlightening as well as beautiful, and no English translation faithfully reproduced them.

In 1973 he wrote the beginning of one of the prayers he remembered from his youth, *"Schoepfer unseres lebens Der Du wohnst in Himmel, Allmachtiger, Allgegenwartiger, Gnadiger, und Barmherziger Gott, Himmlische Vater..."* In 1982 Paul Klopfenstein, Normal, Illinois, translated this phrase into English: "Creator of our lives, who lives in heaven, all powerful, ever present, gracious and merciful God, Heavenly Father."[12]

The outbreak of war with Germany in 1917 brought an abrupt halt to the prospect of perpetuating the German language in the churches. The need to discontinue the German language during worship—and thus remove any trace of disloyalty to the United States—was so clear and compelling that there was little protracted debate on this issue. The church, in view of the conflict with Germany, had little choice but to begin using English, and most members realized this. Some, however, took the change with affront.

While the decision to make the change was swift, the actual changeover was slow because very few existing ministers in the church could preach in the English language. Also, a lot of members could not understand English.

Many younger men who could preach in English were thus appointed to the ministry. A major qualification for the ministry at this time was the ability to preach in this language. Noah Schrock, for instance, was appointed minister in 1918 at Oakville, Iowa, largely because he could speak English fluently. He was only twenty-five years of age. This occurred in many other churches as well.

The urgency and expediency of changing to English precluded any prolonged disagreement over this question during the time of the war. The issue did not meaningfully surface again for several years. In 1932, however, it erupted into the church's second schism.

WICHITA, KANSAS

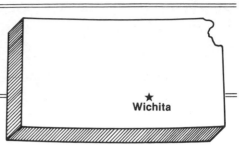

WICHITA, KANSAS
1202 Lulu Street
at Lincoln Street

In keeping with the constant movement of Apostolic Christian families to new areas and due to the gravitation toward southern Kansas and northern Oklahoma by some members of the church for several decades, an assembly of believers was established at Wichita, Kansas, late in 1916. Wichita, the state's largest city, was settled in 1864 as a trading post near the Wichita Indian Village. Later it was a terminal point for drovers on the Chisholm Trail, an early overland cattle route. It was incorporated in 1871.[13]

Situated at the confluence of the Arkansas and Little Arkansas Rivers (200 miles southwest of Kansas City), it was destined to become the leading commercial, financial, and manufacturing center for northern Oklahoma and southern Kansas. Consequently, the area drew many people, among them a few persons of Apostolic Christian extraction.

The first to move to Wichita were John and Marie Riedel. They came in 1911. In October, 1916, Alfred and Bertha Lambert and their seven children moved to Wichita from Burlington, Oklahoma, approximately one hundred miles southwest of Wichita.

It was not possible for the Riedel and Lambert families to attend the Apostolic Christian Church—either at Harper, Kansas, (forty-five miles southwest) or at Burlington, Oklahoma, because all-weather roads did not exist at that time, and the prices of automobiles were nearly prohibitive. Because of this, the devout Alfred Lambert invited the Riedels over to his house for worship and fellowship. He would gather his wife and seven children and the Riedels around him for Bible reading, prayer, and the singing of hymns. Occasionally he would read from the *Book of Martyrs*. Often tears would roll down his cheeks as he read about those who gave their lives for their faith. Although Alfred Lambert took charge of organizing and administering these meetings, he was never a minister.

In 1921 John and Rose Schrock moved to Wichita from Burlington, Oklahoma, along with their two daughters, Lydia and Louisa. Alfred Lambert used to walk the four miles to the Schrock home for visiting and fellowship. The Schrock home was noted as a stopping place for travelers who came to visit or who were en route to other places in the West.

In the 1920's more people of the faith moved to Wichita. Among them were members Joe and Katie Lorenz, and friends George and Magdaline Wohschleger, Sarah Gleichman, Valentine Barth, Herman Hohulin, Roy Yackley, and Sam Schrock, the son of John Schrock.

The growing number of families at Wichita (still without a local minister) continued to meet together for singing, prayer, and Bible reading.

On June 14, 1924, a group of approximately twenty members and friends gathered together for one of their regular meetings at the home of John Schrock. Although they had never attended the meetings previously, the three sons of Alfred Lambert—Frank, Ernest, and George—were present that evening. After an evening of singing, Alfred Lambert took the Scriptures and opened to St. Matthew, Chapter 24. He began reading, and when he came to verse 15 and got to the word "Daniel," he suddenly slumped and began falling out of his chair. His son George recalled that "we brothers caught him and gently laid him on a bed, and soon he went to sleep."[14] Because of his death, they realized if they were ever to see their father again, they must repent for their sins and be converted so they could be reunited with him in heaven. George Lambert further remembers, "It was then that the dear Lord entered into our hearts and by faith we believed." The evening must have been an unforgettable one of those present—the death of an older brother-in-faith and the spiritual awakening of his three young sons occurring in the span of a few minutes.

These young men were "taken up" at the church at Burlington, Oklahoma, in December, 1924. With the consent of the congregation, Elder Gottlieb Kurz proved all three brothers at the same time.[15]

George Lambert recalls the example his father Alfred set for his family. He said his parents were strict and demanded discipline. His father prayed and read the Bible after every meal, often explaining the meaning of what he had read. He remembers, when the family attended the Burlington church, sitting on the front bench with his brothers while his father watched closely so his sons would not be found talking, sleeping, or doing other "foolishness." He remembers the "trial" of sitting still amid stifling summer temperatures—sometimes as high as 100 degrees—with stiff, starched shirts and a hot, steaming, celluloid collar (without a tie). George Lambert later became a minister in 1952.

By 1937 the group at Wichita began discussing the possibility of building a church. In October, 1938, a new edifice was completed, and Noah Schrock of Oakville, Iowa, conducted the dedication services.

Robert Young, who had moved from Gridley, Kansas, to Wichita with his wife Dora and family in 1938, was placed in the ministry in 1939. He was the first local minister of the Wichita congregation. In 1954 they moved to a farm near Virgil, Kansas. They continued to attend services in Wichita, faithfully traveling the one hundred miles each Sunday. They moved back to Wichita in 1964.[16]

In the spring of 1973, work began on an addition to the present church. A double brick assembly building was set parallel to the old church. The old assembly room was converted into a Sunday School. The basement kitchen was totally rebuilt. Many members of the church contributed their skills to complete the building. The building committee consisted of Al Langhofer, Charley Grimm, and Max Reimschisel.

Dedication of the new quarters was held July 28, 1974, with Elders Edwin Hohulin, Goodfield, Illinois; Wendell Gudeman, Francesville, Indiana; and Samuel Anliker, Lamont, Kansas, present. A local Wichita history remembers the occasion as "a glorious meeting for all. So many came from Illinois, Indiana, Kiowa, Sabetha, Bern, and many other places."

The new facilities proved adequate for the growing little congregation which, by 1980, had approximately thirty-four families and fifty-six members.[17]

Ernest Gleichman, Harper, Kansas, served as Wichita's first Elder, but his tenure was brief due to his death on December 17, 1938. Other Elders who served at Wichita on a non-resident basis were Emil Schubert, Sr., Peoria, Illinois; Noah Schrock, Oakville, Iowa; and Roy Farney, Burlington, Oklahoma (who later moved to Phoenix, Arizona). In 1982 Samuel Anliker, Lamont, Kansas, was Wichita's Elder.

GOODFIELD, ILLINOIS

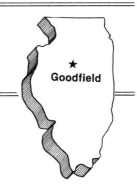

★
Goodfield

GOODFIELD, ILLINOIS
One block north of Route 150

Goodfield, Illinois, is a community of about five hundred located on U.S. 150 and Interstate 74 midway between Bloomington-Normal and Peoria. The Apostolic Christian Church is located on the western edge of the village. By 1981 the church numbered 235 members, 185 Sunday School students, and approximately 140 friends.

Several generations of growth at the Goodfield congregation have reflected the power of the Holy Spirit and the unmerited favor of God's love and mercy.

The history of the Apostolic Christian Church at Goodfield—formerly called "Guthville"—is closely tied to the Congerville church only two miles away.

Early families that came to the general vicinity settled in or near the small hamlets of Slabtown and Farnisville, as well as at Goodfield. An Apostolic Christian Church was initially established near Mackinaw Dells. Those residing in or near Goodfield attended worship services at the church in Mackinaw Dells (Congerville).

Hilly and rolling terrain made roads in the early part of this century quite narrow and winding. Consequently traveling to and from church was often difficult, especially in the winter.

The original church at Goodfield was begun in 1918 by a few families who, mainly because of transportation problems, decided to part from their brethren at the Mackinaw Dells church and establish one in Goodfield. They built a new church which was completed in 1918. It cost $20,000 together with a significant amount of volunteer labor. At this time there were less than ten families and about twenty members.

Barthol Rapp of Morton served as the church's first Elder. Samuel Hohulin, who had served as a minister at Mackinaw Dells, became the first local minister at Goodfield. Among the other men, along with their families, who were instrumental in supporting the new church at Goodfield were Peter Birkey, Joe Dreyer, Sam Goetzinger, Charlie Knapp, August Knapp, and John J. Plattner.

Samuel Hohulin was one of four sons of Gottlieb and Augustina Wenger Hohulin who emigrated to America in 1859. In early married life this couple lived in a log cabin about three miles northeast of Goodfield. Gottlieb Hohulin, ordained a minister at Mackinaw Dells, served there for many years.

Samuel Hohulin was one of only a few ministers able to articulate the gospel in the English language during the era of World War I. Because of this, he was often called to preach in the English language at surrounding Apostolic Christian Churches. At age sixty, after conducting Wednesday evening worship services, he went home and retired for the evening. He passed away unexpectedly in his sleep. This was a profound shock to the congregation.

From 1918 to 1961 the Goodfield assembly grew until an addition to the church was required. On February 28, 1961, ground was broken for a new assembly room and basement dining room. It cost $160,000. Dedication was June 17, 1962.

In 1973 a fellowship hall was built just north of the church. It was felt by brethren that such a hall was needed for singings, weddings, receptions, and other church-related activities. With a seating capacity of 300, it cost $84,000.

The biggest challenge for the Goodfield congregation came in 1980 when church facilities again proved inadequate. In less than twenty years since the 1961 renovation, larger quarters were needed. In March, 1980, ground was broken for a building and remodeling program that would more than double the size of the congregation. Many tears were shed as the wrecking crew tore down the original building of 1918, so lovingly built by those few brethren some six decades earlier. The 1961 addition was retained and used as the basis for the new structure that arose to the west and north of it. The project cost $800,000. Dedication of the renovated facility took place June 28, 1981.

Frank Woertz served as the church's first resident Elder. He was ordained April 4, 1948, and served until 1966. He died September 9, 1972.[18]

Edwin Hohulin, grandson of Gottlieb Hohulin and son of Samuel Hohulin, became the second resident Elder on November 26, 1967.[19] He was the third generation of this family to serve in the ministry in the Apostolic Christian Church. Robert Grimm became the third resident Elder on January 24, 1982.

Between the tenures of Elders Barthol Rapp and Frank Woertz, the church was served by three non-resident Elders: Elias Winzeler, Tremont; Emil Schubert, Peoria; and Carl Rassi, Morton. After Frank Woertz retired, Leroy Huber, Eureka, was Elder for one year from 1966 to 1967.

TAYLOR, MISSOURI

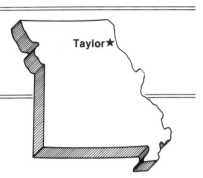

TAYLOR, MISSOURI
North on Old U.S. 61

Edward Grimm, the first minister of the Apostolic Christian Church at Taylor, Missouri, composed the lyrics to a song that succinctly captures the essence and character of the congregation which assembles in a small church on the levee of the Fabius River approximately twenty miles north of Hannibal, Missouri, and about six miles west of Quincy, Illinois, across the Mississippi River. Grimm, who used to arrive early at the church to start the furnace on Sunday morning, was moved to write these beautiful words which can be sung to the song,

"The Church in the Wildwood" (commonly called "The Little Brown Church"):

THE LITTLE WHITE CHURCH ON THE LEVEE

There's a church on the levee by the Fabby,
    No lovelier spot far around,
Where the children of God love to gather,
    In Communion with Him to be found.

It is there in that church on the levee,
    That I often find peace for my soul;
When trials and sorrows would crush me,
    And the billows of fate o'er me roll.

It is there in that church on the levee,
    That I hope to be found when He calls,
In His service I pray He will find me,
    When the curtain of life for me falls.

It is there near that church on the levee,
    That my loved ones are resting in Peace;
And 'tis near them I hope they will lay me,
    When my labors of love here shall cease.

Chorus—Oh, come, come, come, come,
Come to the church on the levee,
Oh, come to the church on the knoll:
No spot is so dear to my memory,
As the little White Church on the knoll.

The physical fortunes of the area are often tied to the behavior of the Mississippi River on the east and the Fabius River on the west. A levee system, usually secure, holds the water back and provides opportunity for farmers to cultivate the rich bottom land between the two rivers. In the spring of 1973, heavy rains filled the Mississippi River to near-flood levels, but the levees gallantly held the water back. In mid-April, unusually heavy rains of nearly thirteen inches occurring over northeast Missouri resulted in the sand levee breaking near the confluence of the Mississippi and Fabius Rivers on April 23. Uncontrolled water spilled into and heavily flooded the bottom land near Taylor and severely affected farming operations of many families, including those of Apostolic Christians. Nearly fifty families were affected, and about one-fourth of these were brethren or friends of the church.

Seven church families were driven from their homes because of the ravaging waters. Approximately $90,000 was raised by Apostolic Christian brethren across the United

States to assist the brethren at Taylor. They used $35,000. Another $35,000 was given to more than thirty neighbors in the area who were not of the church. The remaining $20,000 was returned to World Relief. The donations and assistance reflected the deep sense of brotherhood and kindred affection that exists in the Apostolic Christian Church.

In addition to financial aid, brethren from many churches drove to Taylor and helped clean up the damage caused by the flood. Approximately 225 brothers from the Midwest participated.

The quaint and picturesque little church "on the levee" at Taylor, Missouri—which had sixty-six members in 1980—had its beginning in 1918 when Andrew and Tillie Yackley and their eight sons moved from Hancock, Minnesota, to a farm southeast of Taylor. Soon, other families moved to the community; Otto and Lina Gerst and family from Oakville, Iowa, in 1919; Charlie and Rose Koelling and family from Tremont, Illinois; Ben and Carrie Wiegand and family from Oakville, Iowa; John and Dan Hoerr in 1922, and later Rudie and George Hoerr from Morton, Illinois; and Ezra Gerst and Leslie Gerst from Oakville, Iowa, in 1923. They were prompted to come because of the opportunity to purchase attractively priced Mississippi bottom land. The early privations and hardships they endured are often difficult to fathom, especially in the context of today's modern agricultural system.

In the beginning, church services were held approximately once a month in homes and occasionally at the Willow Bend School. Visiting ministers would conduct the worship services. When no minister was present, they sang hymns, prayed, and at times read sermons. Sunday School was held, too.

In February, 1926, the church received a major boost when Edward Grimm, a minister at Elgin, Iowa, (since 1913) moved with his wife Anna to the Taylor area. Others from Elgin who joined the Grimms were Fred and Rose Frieden, Will and Marie Butikofer, Eli and Elizabeth Sutter, and their families.

Only a month after these families moved to Missouri, tragedy struck when Joel Butikofer (age 1) and Edward Sutter (age 2) died from bronchial pneumonia and whooping cough on March 4, 1926. Because there was no church building here at that time, funeral services, conducted by Noah Schrock of Oakville, Iowa, were held at the LaGrange Baptist Church.

The two little boys were laid to rest in the front yard of Edward Grimm's place on the "Red Barn Farm" four miles north of Taylor.

When Edward Grimm arrived in Taylor, services were held in a large room in his home. He made a make-shift pulpit and several benches for the worship services.

In the spring of 1926, a twenty-acre plot of land just north of Taylor on U.S. Route 61 was purchased for $2,950. The four-room cottage on this property was converted into a church by removing one wall to make an assembly room accommodating fifty persons. A cemetery was located northwest of the church. The caskets of Joel Butikofer and Edward Sutter were moved from the "Red Barn Farm" to the new cemetery in the summer of 1926. The first services were held in this new church on July 4, 1926. There were fourteen members. Attendance was usually between thirty to forty people.

The first convert at Taylor was Rudie Hoerr. He was baptized in a water tank on the Otto Gerst farm.

In the spring of 1930, the church was greatly encouraged as fourteen souls turned to the Lord in repentance. Elders Elias Winzeler, Tremont, and Emil Schubert, Peoria, Illinois, conducted baptismal services on May 25, 1930. The next day (Monday) they served Holy Communion to the church.

Edward Grimm's son Fred was instated into the ministry on June 13, 1938.

In July, 1949, work began on a new church. The $40,000 structure was opened April 16, 1950, and dedication services were July 30, 1950. This new church was built just north of the old church which was subsequently sold at public auction to Eli Sutter. He moved it a short distance north where it has been used as a residence since that time.

On December 21, 1960, Fred Grimm was ordained as Taylor's first resident Elder.[20] He served until his death at age fifty-seven in 1967. He once wrote:

> In thinking of all the wonderful benefits and privileges we receive when we repent and are accepted as a member of the Apostolic Christian Church, we cannot help being impressed by the precious fellowship we have. Words can hardly express it.
>
> As often as we are privileged to have brothers and sisters visit us, or if we visit in another of our churches, we have the same reaction. The blessed fellowship overwhelms us.

We can travel from coast to coast and stop in churches of our faith where we have never been before, and yet feel at home at once.

Can we expect that this will continue? Blessed fellowship is a result of brotherly love and oneness of spirit, and of willing obedience to God's word and to the practices of the church. As long as this can be maintained to a reasonable extent, we will continue to have this wonderful fellowship, which to our knowledge is not equalled anywhere.

The church building at Taylor was extensively remodeled in 1970-1971. The building was extended to the east to provide a larger fellowship area, baby rooms, and three Sunday School rooms. The pulpit area was remodeled and the basement redecorated.

Roy Grimm, grandson of Edward Grimm, and son of Fred Grimm, became the third generation of Grimms to serve in a leadership position at the church. He became a minister October 30, 1966, and was ordained Elder January 25, 1976.[21]

The church completed a fellowship hall in 1976. It is located just southwest of the present church building.

The church at Taylor is reflective of a trend that has occurred in the church nationally—that of drawing converts from outside the realm of long-established church families. By 1982 the church listed fifteen members (out of total membership of seventy-three) who had no previous association with the Apostolic Christian Church. This amounted to twenty percent, which was probably substantially higher than other churches in the brotherhood.

WINTHROP, MINNESOTA

WINTHROP, MINNESOTA
Corner of Carver & Tenth Streets

Winthrop, Minnesota, is located seventy-five miles southwest of Minneapolis-St. Paul. In 1919 brethren of the Apostolic Christian Church began to migrate to this area when Will Messner of Morris, Minnesota, and Dan Messner and August

Fisher of West Bend, Iowa, bought farms near Winthrop. Will Messner's son and daughter-in-law, Joe and Marguerite, and Dan Messner's son and daughter-in-law, Ben and Carrie (who was a daughter of Mike Miller of Pulaski, Iowa), also moved to the area and rented land. Gust Mohrman and wife Louise (daughter of Dan Messner) moved to Winthrop at this time too.

Levi Messner, son of Dan Messner, was married to Mae Miller, daughter of Mike Miller, in December, 1920. They farmed with the Ben Messners.

This group formed the nucleus of the Winthrop group at the outset. The major thrust of church people came principally from three areas: Morris, Minnesota, and West Bend and Pulaski, Iowa. The latter area was represented initially by the daughters of Mike Miller, who in 1924, moved here with his family.

This small group of pioneers held worship services each Sunday at the home of Will Messner. During the first winter at Winthrop (1921), he died, leaving his wife Mary and family. Following his death, services were held less frequently.

During the next few years, families from several nearby Apostolic Christian Churches moved to the Winthrop area. They included those of: Henry Schmidt, Fred Messerli, Chris Grimm, Earn Frank, Dave, Nathan, and Henry Kellenberger, and Elizabeth Heiniger and her brother, Albert.

Joel A. Banwart, Sr., a minister at the church at West Bend, Iowa, became concerned that the growing number of church people at Winthrop—many who were not yet converted—did not have a minister and had worship services only on an infrequent and irregular basis. Because of this situation, he promised to visit them as often as possible.

Because of the lack of regular worship services, some of the "friends of the truth" (non-members) became discouraged and began attending churches of other faiths. Eventually, however, their early upbringing reminded them of the true way, and many returned to worship at, and embrace, the Apostolic Christian Church. One of these friends wrote to minister Edward Grimm of Elgin, Iowa, and described the pressing need for regular worship services at Winthrop, particularly in view of the growing number of people, many of whom were unconverted. Grimm, and Joel A. Banwart, Sr., of West Bend, Iowa, took this letter to heart and came to Winthrop to proclaim the message of salvation. They found "troubled waters," and sixteen souls contritely bowed to the Lord in repentance and were baptized in 1923 on Ben and Levi Messner's farm.

Due to the recent influx of souls into the church, it became obvious a permanent minister was badly needed. Mike Miller, a minister at Pulaski, Iowa, was persuaded to come to Winthrop to perform these duties. He was likely inclined to do so because some of his married daughters lived on farms in the area. Along with his wife, Ida, and sons Richard, Carl, and Noah, he moved to Winthrop in 1924. A daughter, Florence, had moved here earlier to help her sisters with housework.

The arrival of Mike Miller was a tonic for the group at Winthrop. His presence meant worship services each Sunday and the proclamation of God's Word on a regular basis. It gave a sense of cohesion and permanence that had previously been lacking because of not having a resident minister and local church leader. The gatherings now became an all-day affair— morning services, a noon lunch of bread, butter, and coffee, afternoon services, and a supper which everyone attended.

In a short time the congregation became too large to meet in homes. Consequently, a church was built in 1927 in the northern portion of Winthrop. The basement was dug with horses, and brethren of the church labored diligently to complete the new edifice. The church had no plumbing, and water was carried in pails from a neighbor's pump across the street. Coffee for the noon lunch was made in a copper wash boiler.

In the ensuing years several families left Winthrop and moved to churches of the faith in Illinois and Iowa. This gives indication of the enormous amount of moving about (among people in the denomination) which occurred in the early days of the church. This was prevalent among non-church people as well. Often, people did not have large estates, had few earthly possessions, and their roots were not deep. They were willing to move to other areas and try new experiences. Consequently, the congregation at Winthrop decreased in size. In 1938, however, a large number of souls were baptized—in a steel tank carried into the basement—and membership began to climb. By 1948 continuing growth resulted in an addition built on the church's west side.

Mike Miller, who unselfishly moved here in 1924 and served as minister for thirty-three years, passed away October 25, 1957. His son, Noah, who was instated into the ministry in 1955, moved to Minneapolis in 1965 when that small church needed a permanent minister. His move to Minneapolis was made in the same set of circumstances that existed in 1924 when his father left Pulaski to move to Winthrop and become their first resident preacher.

A beautiful new church with a seating capacity of three hundred was completed in 1968 at Winthrop.

Harold Messner was ordained as the church's first resident Elder February 2, 1977.[22]

FROM RURAL TO URBAN

Until the late 1920's most new churches of the denomination were founded in rural areas. This occurred as a result of new farming areas being opened for settlement. As these areas filled up and new farming opportunities declined, brethren of the church turned to towns and cities as places of abode.

This ushered in a new frontier for the church, and development of city churches like those at Chicago (1925) and Phoenix (1929) signaled the formation of churches in several urban areas over the ensuing few decades.

It is significant to note that the establishment of new churches of the faith in America was accomplished despite a noticeable absence of definite planning by church officials. For instance, there was no "evangelism committee" or "new church committee" within the church hierarchy to lay out a grand strategy of spreading the Word of God in the United States. Rather, the gospel seemed to follow the people. As members of the church moved to new areas for the purpose of making a living, a church, consisting mostly of already established members, would be organized. Essentially, aside from the first few decades when Elders Benedict Weyeneth and Joseph Bella appeared to be quite zealous in taking the gospel to anyone who would listen, the church did not go into a particular area of the nation to specifically seek new vistas and to "evangelize" its people.

CHICAGO, ILLINOIS

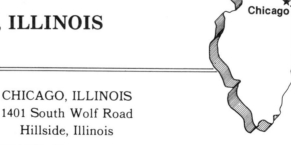

CHICAGO, ILLINOIS
1401 South Wolf Road
Hillside, Illinois

For several decades nearly all the newly-formed Apostolic Christian Churches in the United States were founded in rural areas due to opportunities associated with procuring lower priced land. In the mid-1920's it was almost a rarity when the Chicago, Illinois, congregation began to take shape. Up to this time the overwhelming number of the denomination's churches were located in or near small towns.

Although the industrial revolution and advanced farming technology, which would develop in greater intensity a few decades later and give rise to a vast migration to cities and towns, had not yet occurred to today's extent, the city of Chicago had already begun drawing some young people from outlying churches. Instead, however, of offering opportunity in industry and the professions, the overwhelming number of church-related people who came to Chicago in the 1920's were young women who were engaged in working as "domestics" for wealthy Chicagoans. The vast number of modern conveniences that would later significantly reduce the domestic workload had not yet occurred, and there was a great demand for maids and domestic workers. Young women of the church, schooled deeply in the work ethic, proved very suitable for this type work. In addition to these young women, a few married couples also came to the area to work.

The first Apostolic Christian to reside in Chicago was Caroline Gehrig who came from Peoria in 1909. She stayed until 1929. Some of the early "settlers" in the area were the Kaufmans from Princeville, Illinois, the Gottas sisters from Mansfield, Ohio, a Musselman family, and the A. F. Meyer family who was originally from Morton, Illinois. Also, Rose Mosiman, Sophie Lochler, and the Hartman girls were among the early arrivals. A short time later, Anna and Lydia Clauss from Remington, Indiana, and Clara Roth (a widow) came to Chicago. Sam and Mary Clauss of Wolcott, Indiana, were an early married couple to live in Chicago.

The group at Chicago grew rapidly and comprised fairly large numbers. There was no church of the faith here, so members and friends attended the church at Elgin, Illinois, traveling either by train or automobile. Because travel and communications were considerably slower than today, there was no apparent awareness among church officials of the potential for a church in Chicago.

George Yergler, a minister at the La Crosse, Indiana, congregation, was aware that members of the faith were living in Chicago. One day he brought some livestock to market in the city. After conducting his business he had extra time to spend since his train was not scheduled to leave until nearly midnight. He thought "he would not feel right" if he did not make contact with the brethren in Chicago before returning home.[23]

He had a general idea of where the A. F. Meyer family resided and worked. He took a streetcar to the area where he thought they might be. He knew they operated a restaurant, so he began walking around trying to find it. Walking on West Van Buren Street, he noticed a sign "Meyer Restaurant." He went inside and sat down at a table. A. F.'s two daughters, Naomi and Emily, waited on him. Naomi went back to the kitchen and told her mother (the former Caroline Baer), "I think he is one of our kind." Caroline looked through the open square window where the food was passed and said it was George Yergler. She went out and asked him to stay for the evening and hold church services. They quickly notified several of the members in Chicago, and worship services were held at the Meyer home in the 2600 block of West Jackson Boulevard later that evening.

That first service was held late in 1925 and was an enjoyable evening. Sam and Mary Clauss wrote home about the meeting which started after 9 p.m. that evening:[24] "We had such a lovely evening. We sang a few songs, and George read a chapter and preached a lovely sermon and prayed with us. He read and preached in English as there were some friends there that understood English best." This first meeting likely occurred December 29, 1925.

The A. F. Meyer home was an early "haven" for the many young people of the church at Chicago. A. F. Meyer, born in Alsace-Lorraine, came originally to Morton, Illinois. An inventor, he moved to Stevens Point, Wisconsin, to farm land for a Peoria grocer, Chris Hoerr. Later, in 1923, he and his family moved to Chicago where they operated a rooming house and restaurant.

George Yergler's visit to Chicago paved the way for worship services here on a more organized and regular basis. As a result of his visit, he realized the great need for a ministry to these souls and took a genuine interest in meeting these needs. He arranged for regular preaching services at Chicago. For a while, services were held at the Chris Siebenthal home on California Street.

In January, 1926, Andrew Lehman, a minister from Wolcott, Indiana, came to Chicago with other brethren and held the first Sunday worship service. This was held at the Sam Clauss apartment. There were about thirty-eight members and friends in attendance.

Jacob Stettner, Elgin, Illinois, became Chicago's first Elder. Churches at Elgin and Cissna Park, Illinois, and La Crosse and Leo, Indiana, took turns in furnishing ministers. Stettner was quite awed by Chicago's size. He once commented, "It's easy to get lost. You wonder if you'll ever get home."

Chicago's first converts were Robert and Margaret Haas and Louise Kettner. The Haases were baptized on Easter Sunday, 1928, at La Crosse, Indiana, by Elder Godfrey Rauch of Bluffton, Indiana, and Louise Kettner was baptized in April, 1928, in Elgin by Elder Jacob Stettner.

The growing Chicago congregation eventually became too large to gather in Sam Clauss' apartment. In 1929 a union hall was rented at Fifth and Francisco Streets on the near west side of Chicago. This proved to be an unsuitable spot for a church service. The hall, which cost $25 to rent, was cold and poorly lit.

In March, 1930, only six months after the big stock market "crash" the previous fall, a vacant church building was rented at 735 South Sacramento Street, on the west side of Chicago. Services were held each Sunday at 3 p.m. and 5 p.m. in the afternoon. They were held at these hours to accommodate the many domestic workers who did housework in River Forest, Highland Park, Wilmette, and other areas of the city. Their duties required they prepare a Sunday noon meal for their employers. There were so many of these young girls that they used to fill an entire trolly car when coming to church.

Also, at this location one of the men of the church was stationed outside the building during worship to watch the area and the cars.

On April 14, 1937, a Lutheran church, built in 1898 at 2122 Sunnyside Avenue, was purchased for $3,250. Improvements totaled $12,000. A large steeple was removed because it was regarded as too decorative and worldly. The church was obtained when Eli Winzeler, who along with Robert Haas was instated into the ministry in 1936, was in the neighborhood looking for a larger place to hold worship services. He walked into the church and inquired if it might be for sale. Since this was during a time of economic depression, the people were willing to sell their church. The first worship services were held in August, 1937. Rich Schurter wrote, "All the pews were filled." The Sunnyside church was located on the north side of Chicago.

The church had an upstairs apartment which was always occupied by someone from the church. Those who lived there over the years were Ben and Sophia Hofer, Alice Kilgus and Ethel Waibel, John and Judy Woerner, Dale and Judy Eisenmann, and Eldon and Lucille Schurter. The brethren thought it was wise, in such a large metropolitan area, to have a couple live close to the church and "keep an eye on it." This tradition was retained at the church's new location in Hillside, Illinois, where Tibor and Pearl Bozzay, who clean the church, live next door.

Midweek services were first held at the "Sunnyside" church. They were held on Thursday evening because most of the working girls in the area had Thursdays off. This was known as "maid's day out." In the 1960's the Thursday evening services were changed to Wednesday.

In 1946, Al Fisher was appointed to the ministry. In 1950, John Wagler, who later served as minister at Athens and Huntsville, Alabama, became a minister.

In 1951, the church basement was remodeled at a cost of $6,000.

On July 21, 1971, ground was broken for a new church at 1401 South Wolf Road in Hillside, Illinois. This land, across the street from Queen of Heaven Cemetery, was purchased from the Chicago Catholic Archdiocese. The signature of John Cardinal Cody, a member of the Catholic Church's College of Cardinals, appears on papers relating to the transfer of the land.

The church, located on Chicagoland's southwest side, is easily accessible via the vast freeway system in the area. Planners had this in mind when they chose the location, and this has proven beneficial for today's mobile lifestyle. First services were held June 4, 1972.

For many years Al Fisher served as the lead minister at Chicago. In December, 1954, he was appointed deacon and on February 1, 1970, ordained as Elder. It was always his sincere wish that the gospel of salvation be preached in Chicago, and that the many people of the church who came to Chicago to work or for training could find a "haven" among the brethren. He also proceeded with enthusiasm and caution as he presided over the development of a new church building. He died suddenly April 9, 1974, a few days after returning, along with his wife Margaret, from a three-month stay in Florida. His funeral, held on Good Friday, April 12, was conducted by his co-laborer in the ministry from 1958-1970, Maurice Frank of Leo, Indiana, and Dale Eisenmann, Chicago. The obituary was read by minister Lenard Meyer, a grandson of A. F. Meyer, who was a young boy of only six when Al Fisher was placed in the ministry in 1946. It was a touching moment for the closely-knit Chicago brethren.

Dale Eisenmann, a native of Cissna Park, Illinois, was ordained Elder at Chicago on January 26, 1975. He is a great-grandson of Elder John Adam Eisenmann who served as the first Elder of the Cissna Park, Illinois, congregation.

PHOENIX, ARIZONA

Phoenix
★

PHOENIX, ARIZONA
9230 North 26th Street

After the formation of a continuous series of rural churches over several decades, the Apostolic Christian denomination experienced the origins of two consecutive churches in metropolitan areas—first in Chicago, Illinois, in 1925-1926 and second in Phoenix, Arizona, in 1929.

Phoenix is the capital of Arizona and lies in the Salt River Valley 110 miles northwest of Tucson. The area was once a desert but is now a fertile agricultural region. The church building at Phoenix is one of three located in state capitals. The others are in Indianapolis and Minneapolis. On November 22, 1981, worship services were initiated at Columbus, Ohio, but the group there met in rented quarters.

Because of its dry, mild, and sunny climate and various recreational facilities, Phoenix is popular as a health and tourist region. By 1980 the Southwest—more appropriately called the "sunbelt"—emerged as the fastest-growing section in the U.S. Phoenix, which had a population of 106,818 in 1950, had grown to over 700,000 by 1981.[25]

In about 1929, Herman Nuest of Peoria, Illinois, moved to Phoenix. He was followed by the Minger and Blumenschein families. In addition, various other persons spent the winter here and returned to their homes in the spring.

As the years unfolded, more and more people spent their winters in Phoenix, and each spring fewer and fewer would return home. Church services were held in many different places—in homes, rented halls, and sometimes in the mountains surrounding the valley. Church was held occasionally in nearby Mesa, too.

Elder Ernest Graf, Sr., Akron, Ohio, was an early supporter of the church at Phoenix and visited here in the early days. Other church officials who took an interest were Edward Grimm, Taylor, Missouri; Elder Noah Schrock, Oakville, Iowa; Elder Joe A. Getz, Morton, Illinois; Elder Roy Farney, Kiowa, Kansas (who eventually moved here); and Pete Fankhauser, Lamont, Kansas.

In 1950 Clarence Yackley, a minister at Wichita, Kansas, moved to Phoenix. Also arriving were the families of Joe Heinold, La Crosse, Indiana; Joe Herbst, Peoria, Illinois; and Roy Stevig, Gridley, Illinois. A resident minister and new families gave impetus to the small group at Phoenix, and regular worship services were immediately established.

At one time this small group met for worship at South Mountain Park. They used picnic tables for seats. One attendee wrote back to Illinois that they "had a Sermon on the Mount."

In the fall of 1950, a lot was purchased for $1,800 at 2945 North 18th Place. In the spring of 1951, construction was begun, and a small church building was completed in the fall of that year. In this building, when the worship services were over, the chairs were folded so lunch could be served. A year later the church's growth already necessitated an addition.

The first Sunday in the new church—June 2—was a memorable occasion. The church's first converts—Earl and Emma Sanders—were baptized, the marriage of Floyd and Clara Banwart was solemnized, and Holy Communion was served that evening. Attendance at this time was about one hundred persons.

In 1960, when the church had approximately 105 permanent residents, a new 36-foot by 60-foot sanctuary was attached to the church. It was dedicated February 5, 1961.

In 1976 the congregation voted to build a new church. Dedication of a beautiful new edifice at 9230 North 26th Street was held February 5, 1978. It had a seating capacity of 340. Approximately eighty-three local families were attending the church in 1978.

Roy Farney, who moved to Phoenix from Kiowa, Kansas, in 1960, became the church's first resident Elder. Richard Schupbach moved to Phoenix from Kiowa, Kansas, in 1958 and was ordained Elder on December 4, 1977.[26]

Rising levels of affluence allowing greater opportunities for travel and vacations, together with the sunbelt's expanding economy, have helped the Phoenix congregation to grow at a fairly rapid rate during the last few decades.

MAYWOOD, CALIFORNIA

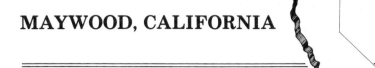

MAYWOOD, CALIFORNIA
5001 East 60th Street

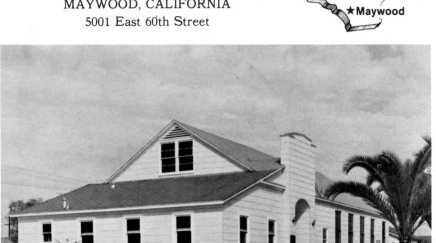

Maywood, California, is located in the heart of the Los Angeles metropolitan area. It lies ten miles southeast of downtown Los Angeles and seventeen miles south of Altadena. An Apostolic Christian Church took root here in 1929-1930.

In the 1920's a few members of the Apostolic Christian Church, along with a few friends of the truth, lived in California. In 1929 or 1930, Phillip Steer of Mansfield, Ohio, came to California. Although unordained, he held a few worship meetings in the home of Mother Emilie Imthurn, widow of Gideon Imthurn, formerly of Gridley, Illinois. He was later asked to cease his unauthorized church activities, and he subsequently moved back east.

Central to the establishment of a church in Maywood were the conversions of John and Julia Dapper in 1930. Married in Mansfield, Ohio, on October 15, 1921, they moved to California about one year later. After attending one of Phillip Steer's meetings, Julia Dapper remarked to her husband, "I don't care what you do, but I am going to repent." In a short time he followed her in this new walk of life. They returned briefly to Mansfield where they were proved and baptized by Elder Noah Hartzler of Rittman, Ohio.

The couple returned to California. At this time there were about six members who met in homes for Bible reading, hymn singing, and prayer. Among the early supporters of the church was Theopolis Schwing, formerly of Peoria, Illinois. Although not a full member of the church, he was very helpful to the group.

In 1930 John and Julia Dapper offered their home as a permanent place of worship for the Maywood congregation. For the next eight years they hosted church services in their home.

Over a period of many years, the home of John and Julia Dapper was opened to many members and friends who enjoyed their hospitality.

During the war years many soldiers and visitors found a "home away from home" as they were warmly welcomed into homes of families of the Maywood congregation.

In 1934 Elders Ernest Graf, Sr., Akron, and Eli Dotterer, Junction, Ohio, came to California. At this time the Maywood church still did not have a resident minister. John Dapper told them if he and his family stayed in California under the present circumstances (no minister and only a small group), they "would starve spiritually." Unknown to him, Graf and Dotterer canvassed the membership. The consensus was that John Dapper was qualified to minister, and if he left to go back to Ohio, the church would fall apart. The following Sunday Dapper was appointed as the group's first minister.

As the next few years transpired, the church grew. Ernest Graf, Sr., told them to begin looking for a place to build a new church. This was during the Great Depression. In time, Theopolis Schwing found two lots that were desirable for building. The asking price was $1,200. The church offered $150 down with the balance payable within ninety days, but with the provision that construction begin immediately. The seller (a Mrs. Buckley) was reluctant to agree but, due to the church's excellent credit rating, finally relented. Two sisters of the church provided the initial $150, and the project was commenced.

Theopolis Schwing erected a tent on the building site (where he lived) and worked on the new church until it was completed. John Dapper also helped with the construction. The building was designed like a house. In the event the church failed, it could be sold as a residence. Located on the corner of 60th and Alamo Streets, the $2,000 structure took four months to complete. It was dedicated in July, 1938.

An addition was made to the church in 1952 costing nearly $9,000. The new church was well attended. Prospects looked bright as membership had increased more than eight-fold from the six members in 1930. According to John Dapper, membership at Maywood peaked at fifty-two.

In 1951-1952 an Apostolic Christian Church was established at Altadena, California. Eventually, nearly half the membership (due to closer proximity) began attending this church. Because the Maywood church, up to this point, had experienced steady growth since 1930, the establishment of the new church was difficult to accept for many who remained at Maywood. The emergence of the church at Altadena, together with other factors, contributed to the decline of the church at Maywood.

In 1948 Joe Klotzle of Girard, Ohio, moved with his family to California. He served in the ministry at Maywood until he was named minister at Altadena in 1952. Albert Kaisner was later named to assist John Dapper in the ministry at Maywood.

Dapper remembers preaching three sermons on Sunday on many occasions, especially when visiting "back east." One time at Morton, Illinois, he preached three sermons on Sunday. In the afternoon, along with Elder Joe A. Getz, he made thirteen house calls to visit shut-ins. At almost every stop there was singing, reading, and prayer. Obviously, at day's end he was very exhausted.[27]

As John and Julia Dapper grew older, they moved to the Apostolic Christian Home in Eureka, Illinois. He died in February, 1983. By 1980 the Maywood church, consisting of approximately six members, was served by ministers of the church at Altadena.

THE SCHISM OF 1932

What is often referred to as the "second split" occurred in 1932. Although it was a time of turmoil and inner soul-searching, it was not nearly as far-reaching as the schism that took place soon after the turn of the century.

The two decades prior to 1932 had ushered in startling changes for the American people. For first-generation emigrants and their immediate descendants who were strongly inclined toward their Swiss and German heritage, profound change and a rapid and provocative acceleration in the pace of life proved to be very unsettling. They tended to view conventional progress as a major threat to the church. Thus, when many members of the church gradually began adopting more modern ways (although moderately so), other brethren were disturbed and unable to tolerate any significant deviation from past norms.

Probably the church's gradual change from the German to the English language (hastened by the outbreak of World War I) was the primary catalyst which initiated the cleavage that was finally resolved by a permanent separation. In an objective sense, it is easy to see how those who were especially endeared to the German language might feel a sense of loss if that language was replaced with English.

The overwhelming majority who remained with the main body of the church also felt the pangs of nostalgia when German was no longer spoken during worship, but they took a more reasonable view. They acknowledged that English was here to stay, that the German ways of the past several decades were decidedly on the wane, and that if future generations were to be brought into the church effectively, an adjustment in worship language was necessary.

In addition to language, the effects of several recent inventions—which would all be well accepted in time, but which caused dynamic change in lifestyle—tended to stir up those who wanted to stay with the old cultural ways. Mass production of the automobile, introduction of radio, and the installation of telephones—to name a few—were items that resulted in a far-reaching change in the tempo of life. Society was evolving from a rural to an urban one, and to those deeply rooted in a manner of life that had existed for more than two centuries, the abrupt changes brought about by progress were both distressing and unacceptable.

In a relative sense, the change which permeated American life in the 1920's was revolutionary. The speeding up of industry and transportation and the general acceleration of life's pace brought about by new inventions destroyed almost at once the modes and conventions of centuries. Isolation and provincialism were generally broken down, and the collective threat to the church—brought about by change—was difficult to accept. Many could not tolerate these changes and left the brotherhood to form their own group. Those who remained in the main body did not really change all that much, but were more willing to accept the gradual change to more modern ways of living.

Essentially, the major schisms took place in a few central Illinois churches, in the area of Bern and Sabetha, Kansas, and in Portland and Silverton, Oregon. The Illinois churches included Fairbury, Cissna Park, Peoria, and the area around Morton and Tremont, Illinois.

Under the general leadership of Elder Martin Steidinger, Fairbury, Illinois, and Elder Jacob Edelman, Bern, Kansas, a new denomination was formed which was later called the German Apostolic Christian Church. It remained the same in doctrine but with a stronger emphasis on several points related to dress and general manner of life. They became decidedly strict in their enforcement of church order and the maintenance of standards relating to attire and lifestyle. They also held to the German language. Over the years several groups have fragmented from this body, the largest being the Christian Apostolic Church in 1955.

The 1932 split was an obvious ordeal for the Apostolic Christian Church. Several families and individuals agonized over which route to take—to remain with the old church or follow the new one. There are two main points to make regarding this split. First, the number of persons who eventually left the church was fairly small compared to the total membership. Second, despite the separation of more conservative brethren, the main body remained decidedly conservative, both in doctrine and manner of life.

"Wherefore come out from among them, and be ye separate, saith the Lord, and touch not the unclean thing; and I will receive you, And will be a Father unto you, and ye shall be my sons and daughters, saith the Lord Almighty."

Social dynamics during the middle stages of the twentieth century resulted in the formation of many new Apostolic Christian Churches in urban areas. This was a significant change because up until this time most of the churches were formed in rural areas.

Increased industrialization and the declining demand for labor on the farms led many Apostolic Christians to seek employment in towns and cities. Consequently, churches began to spring up in metropolitan areas. This constituted a new frontier for the church.

BURLINGTON, IOWA

BURLINGTON, IOWA
North side of city west off U.S. 61

Continuing the newly-established pattern of forming churches in cities which had begun in Chicago, Illinois, ten years earlier, members and friends of the Apostolic Christian Church began meeting together at Burlington, Iowa, as early as 1935.

Burlington, a Mississippi River town, located in Iowa's extreme southeastern corner, had a population of over thirty

thousand in 1980 and was typical of larger towns where Apostolic Christians migrated to find employment.

The church at Burlington, in some respects, is an outgrowth of the large, rural church at Oakville, Iowa, twenty-two miles north. Noah Schrock and later Edward Lanz, both Elders at Oakville, have served the church at Burlington.

The first church meetings here were small and consisted of a few young sisters and friends who desired worship and fellowship during the week. Sophia Stoller opened her home for evening services once per week.[1]

In 1940 the church at Oakville enjoyed a large number of converts. Because many of these people were employed at Burlington, mid-week services took on a new importance and emphasis. The first few meetings (on a more organized basis) were held in the third floor meeting room of the Woodman of the World organization located in the Union Appliance Building on Fourth and Washington Streets. This is now the Prugh Mortuary parking lot. Later in 1940, the group met in the recreation room of the First Baptist Church on Sixth and Washington Streets and in the Williamson Presbyterian Church on Gunnison and Division Streets.

In 1958, twenty-three years after the first meetings were held in Burlington, the congregation purchased a two-story, wood-frame church building from the Concordia Lutheran Church at 1734 South Street. First services were held in

October of that year. The sanctuary seated 115 persons. There were nine families on the dinner list at this time. With a "new" church building, the Burlington congregation began to gather momentum.

With an eye on the future, the church bought a five-acre plot of ground just north of the Burlington city limits for $16,500 in April, 1970. In April, 1975, construction began on a new church, and the first Sunday worship service was held February 1, 1976, with dedication May 23, 1976. The new brick church (all on the ground floor) covered 12,000 square feet and cost $303,000. The sanctuary seated 208 persons. Twenty families were on the serving list.

Serving as minister for several years was Uriel Gehring. A native of Elgin, Iowa, he became a minister in November, 1956, at age thirty. Harvey Heiniger, who became a minister in June, 1956, at Oakville, moved to Burlington in 1978 at the invitation of the Burlington congregation.

In 1980 the Burlington church had twenty-seven families and fifty-three members.[2]

FORT WAYNE, INDIANA

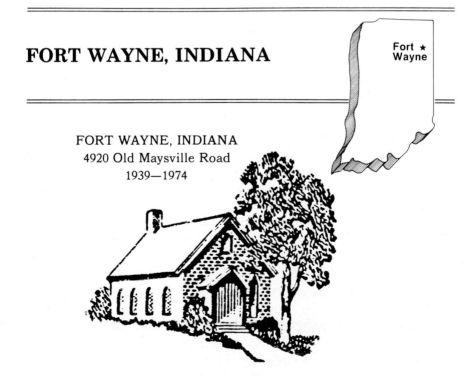

Fort ★ Wayne

FORT WAYNE, INDIANA
4920 Old Maysville Road
1939—1974

For several years prior to 1939, there were people associated with the church living in the Fort Wayne area. They desired to begin holding local worship services. After receiving permission from church Elders, plans were made to hold mid-week worship services.

On July 19, 1939, the first regular mid-week services were held (in those pre-airconditioning days) in a basement room of Philip and Lydia Schott on Spring Street. Later, in the fall and winter of 1939-1940 with cooler weather, services were held on the first floor of their home until May, 1940.

At this time a store building was rented on the corner of Tecumseh and Tennessee Avenue. Services were held there until October, 1942.

The congregation rented a large room at the Wayne Hotel on Columbia Street until 1955 when services were moved to the home of Bertha Blough on Lawton Place.

In August, 1957, a group of brethren from the Fort Wayne area met with ministers and Elders of Bluffton and Leo, Indiana, and Latty, Ohio, to explore and discuss the possibilities associated with establishing a permanent church in Fort Wayne. They drafted a letter which was sent to all the members on December 4, 1957, asking if they would be in favor of founding a permanent congregation. The majority favored such a move.

At a meeting on January 24, 1958, a building committee was organized. Later a finance committee was established. Apostolic Christian Churches throughout the nation gave financial support to the new church.

On March 30, 1959, ground-breaking services were held at 4920 Old Maysville Road, the site of the new church. On August 16, 1959, cornerstone-laying services were held with brethren from Leo, Bluffton, and Milford, Indiana, and Junction and Latty, Ohio. Elders Sam Aeschliman, Bluffton, Indiana; Theo Beer, Milford, Indiana; and George Sinn, Latty, Ohio, conducted the services.

Although the new building was not totally completed, the first worship service was held January 1, 1960. Regular Sunday services began February 14, 1960.

Until Norman Stoller was chosen as the church's first minister in October, 1961, the congregation was served by ministers from Bluffton, Milford, La Crosse, Leo, Francesville,

Bremen, and Wolcott, Indiana; Junction and Latty, Ohio; and Cissna Park, Illinois.

The church was located on the northeast outskirts of Fort Wayne. Since many church people lived in the small town of New Haven east of Fort Wayne, the new church was situated in this central location.

For several years differences in doctrine upheld by the Elders of the Apostolic Christian Church and that held by ministers serving the Fort Wayne church arose causing much concern and heartache. Many meetings were held with the ministers and finally with the entire membership. Elders visited with each family of the Fort Wayne church in an effort to effect a reconciliation.

Finally, in 1974 a majority of the congregation departed from the brotherhood to form their own congregation. Since this group retained the building facilities, the remaining members (who remained in the Apostolic Christian Church) began attending worship services in neighboring Apostolic Christian Churches.

January 31, 1974, was the last date in which members continuing to attend services here were considered as part of the Apostolic Christian Church.

ALABAMA
Athens, Hillsboro,
Landersville, Huntsville

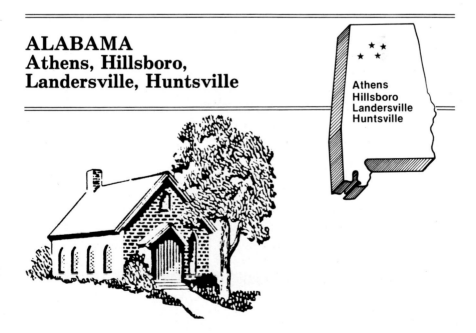

Athens
Hillsboro
Landersville
Huntsville

In the late 1930's minister Amos Hartzler of Rittman, Ohio, initiated efforts which resulted in the formation of Apostolic Christian Churches in northern Alabama.

Staunchly devout to the ways and doctrines of the church, he nonetheless was inwardly moved by the Scriptural teaching to "go ye into all the world and preach the gospel." He sincerely felt the church should do more in this realm.[3]

His method of outreach centered on placing advertisements in newspapers offering free Bibles. These advertisements appeared in newspapers in Alabama, Arkansas, and Tennessee.

The response to his advertisements was encouraging, particularly from rural areas in northern Alabama. Each person who responded to his advertisement received a free Bible and a personal letter from Amos Hartzler.

It soon became evident there was a hunger and thirst for God's word in the Lawrence and Limestone County areas in the extreme northern portion of Alabama. In connection with the interest displayed by these northern Alabamians, church officials from the north visited Alabama. The people from Alabama who were attracted to the church at that time generally lived in rural areas and were very poor. Because this area was in the middle of the "Bible Belt," many of these people had a religious background rooted in a Southern Baptist tradition which, in many instances, was decidedly different from Apostolic Christian.

Hillsboro: The first results of these "outreach" efforts appeared near Hillsboro, Alabama, twenty miles west of Decatur. The first to be converted and baptized were Mr. and Mrs. Henry Stricklin, Mr. and Mrs. Edgar Sides, Dessie Siniard, and Ruth Smith in 1940. They were baptized in a stream running through the farm where Henry Stricklin lived.

Services in the Hillsboro area were first held in the home of Henry Stricklin. When conditions became too crowded, efforts were made to build a small church. Roy Graham, who owned the land where Henry Stricklin worked, donated a plot of ground seven miles southwest of Hillsboro at an area called Mountain View. Brethren from Rittman, Ohio, led by Amos Hartzler, constructed a small church here in 1940. Amos Hartzler personally spent three weeks here working as a carpenter.

After a short time fire destroyed the new church. Worship services were then held in homes and schools until 1942 when a roof was built over the basement foundation of the burned-out church. Services were again resumed at this site.

Clara Heiniger, La Crosse, Indiana, came to the area in 1954 to work among the people. She devoted many years of her life to serving the people in this area. In 1981 she moved to Parkview Haven, a church retirement home at Francesville, Indiana.

In 1964 a new church was built here. It was dedicated November 1, 1964. B. L. "Junior" Hale, who lived across the road from the Hillsboro church, was placed in the ministry in February, 1961. He was the first native Alabamian to preach in the Apostolic Christian Church.

Athens: Soon after the establishment of worship services in the Hillsboro area, meetings were begun at Athens, Alabama, the county seat of Limestone County, only twenty miles south of the Tennessee border. The meetings were held where suitable space could be rented. For a time a Legion Hall was rented. Later, the group assembled in an empty store on Main Street using nail kegs and planks for seats and a large store box for a pulpit. The people were poor (some were illiterate), accommodations were primitive, and from the outset efforts to introduce and teach the customs and practices of the northern churches met with difficulty.

Ministers from the northern churches preached here on a rotating basis. Matt Wackerle, Bay City, Michigan, and Willis Ehnle, Princeville, Illinois (then laymen) assisted with the early work in Alabama. Later, Melvin Huber, Francesville, Indiana, worked here for a time.

In 1952 an old Baptist Church building was purchased on North Clinton Street in Athens. This facility included a small apartment north of the sanctuary.

John Wagler and family of Chicago moved to Athens in 1958. He was the first minister stationed here. When the Waglers temporarily left Alabama to work elsewhere, the Lynn Klopfenstein family of Gridley, Illinois, moved to Athens to assist with the work in Alabama. Both families, when residing in Athens, lived in the church apartment.

Athens, Alabama, church. Located on Highway 72, one mile east of I-65.

In 1976 construction began on a large brick church on the eastern edge of Athens. Dedication services were held June 26, 1977. A significant portion of the cost of this new church was contributed by the national Apostolic Christian Church.

Regarding the early worship services held in Athens, Henry Perry recalled:[4]

> My wife started going to people's homes when Otto Norr and Matt Wackerle came to Alabama around 1940. Later, some more brothers came down, and the time came when they wanted to have church at our home. Some of these brothers would come out in the fields while I plowed with an old mule. I am so glad these dear brothers kept coming to our home. They just wouldn't give up on me.

The church at Athens had grown to sixty-five families and approximately sixty-five members by 1980. Lavoyd Moore, an area native, was placed in the ministry in July, 1964. He was ordained Elder on February 10, 1980, the first resident Elder in Alabama.

Landersville (Munk City): In 1952 church meetings commenced in the small community of Landersville, approximately fifty miles southwest of Athens and four miles west of Moulton. In a year or so, the consolidation of schools in

Lawrence County left the Munk City School vacant. With the help of northern brethren, the group purchased the old schoolhouse. It was remodeled into an assembly room and four Sunday School classrooms and used for worship services, mostly on Sunday evenings.

By the mid-1960's the deteriorating condition of the church building led to a new church. In 1966 work began on a new facility just west of the old one. It was completed in 1967 with dedication services on June 4.

The Lynn Klopfenstein family moved to Decatur, Alabama, in 1969, and he served as minister at Landersville.

Huntsville: In 1971 a partially completed church was purchased at 3217 Village Drive in Huntsville, Alabama. John and Ann Wagler, who returned to Alabama after an absence of several years, were instrumental in establishing a new church in Huntsville.

* * * * * * * * * * * *

Those presiding over the missionary efforts in Alabama were Elders from the northern states. Some of the first Elders to visit here were Noah Hartzler, Rittman, Ohio, (brother of Amos Hartzler), and Ernest Graf, Sr., Akron, Ohio. Among other Elders who visited Alabama in the early days were Rudy Graf, Akron, Ohio; John Bahler, Rockville, Connecticut; and Noah Schrock, Oakville, Iowa.

At a brother meeting in Cissna Park, Illinois, November 17, 1949, Elders Noah Bauman, Rittman, Ohio, and Henry Kilgus, Forrest, Illinois, were given the oversight of the Alabama churches. [5] Kilgus served until November 3, 1962, when heart trouble forced him to relinquish his Alabama duties. During his years of service, he made sixty-five trips to Alabama. Noah Bauman died January 29, 1974.

Although he began involvement here in 1962, Elder David Bertsch, Leo, Indiana, assumed the oversight of the Alabama churches in 1966. In a twenty-year period, he made 140 trips by automobile and air travel to visit the flocks in Alabama.

Herman Norr, a layman from the Leo, Indiana, congregation, devoted much time to the Alabama churches.

In 1979 and 1980 the churches at Hillsboro, Huntsville, and Landersville withdrew from the Apostolic Christian Church. The departure of each church occurred independently. The Athens church remained a part of the Apostolic Christian Church.

In making a historical analysis of the 1979-1980 departure, much could obviously be written. Suffice it to say that the Apostolic Christian Church, with a history of rich tradition featured by a strong emphasis on church order and denominational authority, found it difficult to introduce its customs and practices in the South which had an already-established Christian tradition of its own based on the precept of local church control. In connection with this, the Apostolic Christian Church adheres to many literal Biblical exhortations which many in the South were reluctant to follow. While encouraging the Alabama churches to be in conformity with the other churches in the denomination over the years, the Elders did not forcefully impose their compliance. Consequently, the churches in Alabama did not always appear as distinctly Apostolic Christian.

The situation became strained when the churches at Landersville and Huntsville sought the church's official sanction of Christian schools established next to their churches. A special Elder committee was dispatched to Alabama in 1978 to review the schools, and if possible, to give church sanction to them. Before granting sanction the Elder committee asked the individual churches in Alabama to initiate efforts to bring their congregations into greater conformity with Apostolic Christian practices and to resolve areas of doctrinal difference. When the members did not respond, any chance for church sanction of the Christian schools was lost.

In an effort to persuade them to remain in the Apostolic Christian Church, Elder David Bertsch visited nearly every member of those churches that were contemplating leaving the fellowship. Eventually three congregations left the denomination.

It is interesting to note that the Elder committee assigned to work with the Alabama churches made a total of eight trips to the South during 1978-1980 in an effort to resolve problems in that area.

TUCSON, ARIZONA

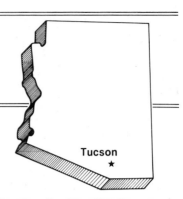

TUCSON, ARIZONA
954 South Magnolia Street

Tucson
★

More than two centuries after Jesuit priests came to this area, church services in Tucson, Arizona, were held by Apostolic Christians. In 1945 the first worship services here were conducted by Elder Ernest Graf, Sr., Akron, Ohio, in the home of Jay and Dorothy Bertsch.

Tucson, located only sixty miles north of the Mexican border, was typical of several sunbelt cities that drew thousands of people after World War II. Its mild, dry climate and almost perpetual sunshine have made it a famous winter resort. Economically, it is a trading center and shipping point of agricultural and mining products. The name "Tucson" is taken from an Indian expression, "at the foot of Black Hill."[6]

The "sunshine" of salvation—as perceived by Apostolic Christians—began to arrive in Tucson in the early 1940's when Emma Hoerr and her relatives from Peoria, Illinois, began spending winters in Tucson. Slowly, others of the faith began arriving here, and the seeds of an eventual congregation were planted. The second worship service was conducted in 1946 by Roy Farney, then of Burlington, Oklahoma. In 1947, Martha Heinold Blessman and family established their home in Tucson, and this was a welcome addition to the small group.

No significant growth took place until the 1960's when more people of the faith moved here. Ezra and Inez Sutter arrived in 1963. Germane to the ultimate growth of the Tucson congregation, however, was the arrival of Noah and Lorraine Herman, Peoria, Illinois, their daughter Laurie, and nephew Ernest Herman in 1965. In the fall of that year, a regular church was officially organized. On October 10, 1965, worship services were held at a Y.M.C.A. Following these services a special member meeting was held, and Noah Herman was called into the ministry. Previous to this, the group had met in the homes of Jay Bertsch, Martha Heinold Blessman, and Noah Herman. At this time the church consisted of seven members and eight friends of the truth.

Ezra Sutter, Tuscon's first convert, was baptized in October, 1967. A widower, his union with Esther Herman of Peoria was the congregation's first marriage. That same year the church meetings were moved from the Y.M.C.A. to the Lighthouse Y.W.C.A.

By 1968 sufficient progress was made toward building a new church. On April 9 ground was broken on a lot donated by Lorraine Herman at 954 South Magnolia Street. An "A" frame building was built at a cost of $26,500. First services were held in the new church on January 1, 1969. Elder Noah Schrock, Oakville, Iowa, dedicated the new church building to the Lord on January 26, 1969. One hundred sixty-five persons from eight states attended this ceremony as Elder Schrock exhorted, "that the Gospel be preached from this pulpit as it is given by the Holy Spirit."

On June 3, 1973, a new fellowship hall was dedicated with Elder Roy Farney, Phoenix, conducting the service. In 1980 Tucson had twenty-six families and thirty-eight members.[7] Elders Roy Farney, and later Richard Schupbach, both of Phoenix, have had the Elder oversight at Tucson.

DETROIT, MICHIGAN

DETROIT, MICHIGAN
29575 Wentworth
Livonia, Michigan

Detroit is located on the Detroit and Rouge Rivers opposite Windsor, Ontario, Canada, and eighteen miles northwest of Lake Erie. It is one of the nation's largest cities characterized by heavy industry, particularly the manufacture of automobiles. Founded in 1701 by Antoine de la Mothe Cadillac, the French military commander in the area, its name is an Anglicized version of *"d' etroit,"* meaning "of the strait."

Like an oasis in the middle of this great urban sprawl sits a beautiful little church of early American design hidden in a four and one-half acre grove of trees. The church and its surroundings comprise one of the most gorgeous settings of any church, much less in a huge metropolitan area. To be able to find a four and one-half acre plot of virgin forest in the middle of such a large city was almost a miracle. As Elder Ben C. Maibach, Jr., said, "The Lord saved this site for us."

Although the history of the Detroit Apostolic Christian Church centers on the year 1948 when the first worship services were held here, a portion of its origin traces back to 1925 when Ben C. Maibach, Sr., a son of Elder Gottlieb Maibach (Elder at Pulaski, Iowa, and Bay City, Michigan), and family moved from the Bay City area to Detroit for employment. Since there was no Apostolic Christian Church in Detroit, the family drove up to their "home" church at Bay City, a distance of one hundred miles, or to Toledo, sixty miles southwest of Detroit.

For many years it was the Maibach family's desire to have a church of their faith in Detroit. This dream did not reach fruition until 1948 when more persons associated with the church were living in the area. The first worship services were held February 9, 1948, in a basement room at the home of Ben C., Jr., and Lorene Maibach at 15655 Kinlich. Elder Otto Ramseyer and minister Henry Wackerle, Bay City, conducted these first services.

The group soon began meeting at 20911 Grand River, now known as the Redford Community War Memorial Building. Services were held once per month initially, and later twice per month. Attendance totaled twenty to thirty adults plus children.

On December 18, 1949, Elders Elias Dotterer, Junction, Ohio; Otto Ramseyer, Bay City, Michigan; and Sam Aeschliman, Bluffton, Indiana, came to visit the little flock at Detroit. A singing was held that Saturday evening. At the conclusion of the singing, Elder Dotterer took the Scriptures and opened to the place where the Lord instructed his followers to send men "two by two into every city." Unknown to the congregation, the three Elders were impressed with this Scriptural directive. Since Detroit had no resident minister, they felt the Holy Spirit and this Scripture were indicating the time was ripe to install two ministers in Detroit. After regular worship services the next day, a member meeting was called, and Floyd Wieland, thirty-six, and Ben C. Maibach, Jr. twenty-nine, son of Ben C. Maibach, Sr. (the first to arrive in Detroit), were instated into the ministry. The two were excused from beginning their preaching on the next Sunday (which was Christmas) but were told to begin their duties after the new year of 1950 began. Henry Wackerle, minister at Bay City, was very helpful in organizing a visiting minister schedule to help these two young ministers bear the load of preaching, but after two Sundays, the small flock was on its own.

In the spring of 1950, a lot was purchased at 26741 Fenkell. On May 5 construction began on a new church. Work proceeded swiftly with brethren and friends from neighboring churches joining in the building program. The first services were held July 2, 1950, less than two months after ground-breaking—perhaps one of the fastest church constructions ever. With equipment donated by the Barton-Malow construction company, members of the church built the new building at a cost of approximately $24,000. A new addition and other alterations were made in 1961 costing about $50,000.

In 1975 the church bought the beautiful four and one-half acre plot "in the wildwood" at 29575 Wentworth in Livonia on the west side of the Detroit metropolitan area. Construction on a new church did not begin on this site until March 27, 1977, when ground-breaking services were held. Similar to the 1950 church building, construction of the 250-seat facility proceeded rapidly. The cornerstone was laid on November 24 with the first services held December 18. Dedication was July 9, 1978.

The church has enjoyed converts every year since its founding and by 1980 had over eighty members.

Ben C. Maibach, Jr., was ordained as the first resident Elder at Detroit on February 2, 1969.[8]

SARASOTA, FLORIDA

SARASOTA, FLORIDA
333 Honore Avenue

An Apostolic Christian Church was founded in 1948 at Sarasota, Florida, located on Florida's west coast. This initial beginning at Sarasota coincided (during the same year) with the re-establishment of the state of Israel, considered by many to be a profound prophetic fulfillment.

Conditions leading to the formation of the sunbelt churches at Phoenix and Tucson, Arizona, also prevailed at Sarasota—mild weather, a resort area, a place to vacation, and significant post-war economic opportunity.

One of the first Apostolic Christian worship services in this area was very memorable. The meeting was held outdoors in a large wooded area. Moss-covered trees, bright sunshine, and the innocent and pure sound of chirping birds helped to draw those in attendance very close to the father heart of God. Elders Philip Beyer, Naumburg, New York, and John Bahler, Rockville, Connecticut, conducted the service. Those in attendance (about forty) took their car cushions and used them for seats.

For several years the small Sarasota group met in homes. Two who provided space were a Sister Pfister in Tampa and the Leon Virklers in St. Petersburg. An early minister who visited here was Henry Wackerle of Bay City, Michigan.

In the early 1950's more brethren began spending time in Sarasota. Those who attended services in the early days included the Chris Sauders, Peoria, and Henry Knapps, Cissna Park, Illinois; Richard Laukhufs, Latty, Ohio; Paul Von Tobel, Francesville, Indiana; and Ben Maibachs, Sr., Detroit, Michigan. Eli Farney and David Meister, Sr., were also early attendees at these Sarasota services.

Godfrey Schlatter, a long-time minister at Toledo, Ohio, became the first resident minister. Ben and Lucille Maibach were instrumental in arranging for the group to meet at the "Women's Club" building in Sarasota for worship.

The first organized regular winter services began in March, 1956. Elder John Bahler, Rockville, Connecticut, Godfrey Schlatter (who was then about eighty-five years old), Toledo, Ohio, and Ben C. Maibach, Jr., Detroit, Michigan, conducted these meetings. During the first three seasons, a small conference room was used for services. Later, as more brethren from the North spent winters in Florida, additional room was needed. Consequently, services were moved into the large auditorium. Philip Wingeier, Alto, Michigan, began visiting Sarasota as early as 1959, and in 1962 he began serving as minister of the Sarasota congregation.

In 1961 two pillars and early supporters of the church passed away. The church was saddened by the deaths of Godfrey Schlatter and Ben Maibach, Sr.

In the 1960's a host of church people came to Sarasota. Some became permanent residents, and others came to spend several months during the winter. The development of the interstate highway system, together with rising levels of affluence, were among the factors generating interest in warm and sunny Florida. This benefited the establishment of the Sarasota church.

In 1970 the Sarasota church was incorporated as a non-profit "Ecclesiastical Society." In 1971 land was purchased at 333 Honore (pronounced "onray") Avenue to eventually build a church. The need for more space occurred perhaps more swiftly than anticipated. Large crowds began to fill the Women's Club quarters, and space was no longer available at that location after May 1, 1973.

On March 25, 1973, ground-breaking services were held at 333 Honore. Under threatening skies Elder Ben C. Maibach, Jr., read from Psalms 122, and Leon Virkler, the congregation's oldest member, turned the first shovel of soil. Construction began the first week in June.

Philip Wingeier conducted the first services in the uncompleted building on December 23, 1973. The first regular, all-day worship services, together with a noon lunch, were January 27, 1974. Elders Roy Sauder, Peoria, Illinois, and Ben C. Maibach, Jr., conducted the services.

Due to the growth of the Sarasota congregation, Philip Wingeier moved from Alto, Michigan, to serve as a resident minister. He and his wife, Fern, purchased a home directly across from the new church. He retired as minister December 2, 1979.

Because winter crowds taxed the new building to capacity with numbers sometimes in excess of four hundred people in 1981, plans were formulated to add either a building to the rear of the present structure or a possible fellowship hall on the existing site.

Ben C. Maibach, Jr., Detroit, Michigan, whose parents were very helpful in establishing this congregation, has served the church as Elder. He maintains a residence in Sarasota.

In April, 1983, work began on a new addition which provided one-third more space to the church facility. It cost $300,000.

FORREST, ILLINOIS

Forrest ★

FORREST, ILLINOIS
300 West James Street

The demise of two country churches—one south of town and the other north of town—led to the establishment of a new, larger church in Forrest, Illinois, late in 1949.

Following World War II, society entered into an era of rapid change and progress. Significant advancement in modes of transportation and communication had made the world a much smaller place. Country schools, country churches, and small-town business districts all felt the effects of the great rush toward centralization.

The old North Side and South Side churches, both rich in historical lore—and possessing colloquial names which reflected their location—united in 1949 to form a larger church in Forrest, Illinois.

The country churches were deteriorating physically by the late 1940's, and rather than make repairs, both congregations, in view of bigger automobiles and better roads which allowed faster travel, acknowledged that the times demanded a larger church in Forrest. Most all the members of the North Side church and approximately one-half of the South Side members united to form the Forrest Apostolic Christian Church. The memory of these two country churches remains forever etched in the minds of those who attended those country worship services. But sadly, as time objectively marches on and "old timers" pass away, the collective memory of these churches fades, and it remains only for historians to transfer the essence of these memories onto the pages of history. In connection with this process, it can be said that while the Forrest, Illinois, congregations's history is relatively short, its historical roots, which reach deeply into the areas north and south of town, are both rich and inspiring. Ben Nussbaum's local histories on both churches bring alive the "olden days" associated with these churches.[9]

Discussions relative to the merger of the North Side and South Side churches began in the mid-1940's. Obviously, with a host of people affected by whatever decision was made as to the disposition of the congregations, conclusions were hard to reach, and progress was slow. Nevertheless, on July 11, 1947, several brethren purchased one-half of a city block in the northwest section of Forrest for $2,000 in the event a subsequent decision might be made to move the two congregations into Forrest.

entrance on the first floor. Upstairs we have four bedrooms, a complete kitchen and dining room-living room combination."

Through the years many visitors from other churches have stayed at the rooms upstairs and have enjoyed the hospitality of caretaker Elizabeth Feldman who has lived in an apartment over the church.

On February 12, 1952, Carl Kinsinger, formerly of Pulaski, Iowa, was chosen to assist Joe Klotzle in the ministry. In 1954 Kinsinger assumed the duties of deacon and on February 20, 1955, was ordained as Elder following a church vote in September, 1955. Interestingly, all his church offices—minister, deacon, and Elder—were placed on him in the month of February.

The Altadena church was never formally dedicated.

By 1980 the Altadena congregation consisted of thirty-six members.

FORT LAUDERDALE, FLORIDA

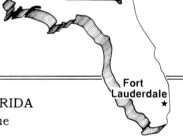

FORT LAUDERDALE, FLORIDA
750 Northwest 46th Avenue
Plantation, Florida

Services on Florida's east coast were held as early as 1950 when Elder John Bahler, Rockville, Connecticut, conducted a worship meeting in West Palm Beach.

As more and more brethren came to Florida to spend the winter months, it was decided to hold worship services in the Fort Lauderdale-Hollywood area. Church was held in the homes of George Bolliger, Andrew Betz, Walter Pfister, Godfrey Schlatter, and Ben Maibach, Sr. George Bolliger, from Forrest, Illinois, was the first member of the Apostolic Christian Church to live in the Fort Lauderdale area.

Godfrey Schlatter and the Ben Maibachs, Sr., later began spending winters in Sarasota and were instrumental in helping to establish a church in that area. Thus, these three people played a significant role in organizing two churches in Florida.

At the outset, members in the area rented a building from the Fort Lauderdale Women's Club to use for worship services in the winter. The first minister was Godfrey Schlatter. Matt Wackerle, Bay City, Michigan, served as a teacher. In the absence of a preacher or teacher, the group listened to a taped sermon.

By 1958 several families were living in the Fort Lauderdale area. In February of that year, the first organizational meeting of the church was held to put the church structure on a more formal and regular basis. Those who attended were George Bolliger, Ray Wieland, Robert Huber, Carl Bachtold, Ken Troxel, Edward Gerber, Victor Stoller, Matt Wackerle, Joe Meyer, Sam Wieland, Will Erkert, Harry Sutter, and several friends of the truth.

Matt Wackerle was selected as the first resident minister. Joe Meyer became the first Sunday School teacher. Elders Joe A. Getz, Morton, Illinois, and John Bahler were here to oversee this meeting. The former was given the duties of Elder at Fort Lauderdale.

The first baptism at Fort Lauderdale occurred in February, 1957. The church had no baptismal facility, so Elsie Bolliger, wife of George Bolliger, was baptized in the Atlantic Ocean. Elder Joe A. Getz donned hip boots to perform this impressive ceremony which was reminiscent of Bible times.

In the fall of 1961, first minister Matt Wackerle passed away after serving only three years.

In the summer of 1962, land was purchased at 750 Northwest 46th Avenue in Plantation, Florida, located on the west edge of the Fort Lauderdale metropolitan area. A new church, costing $85,000, was built on this site. It was dedicated in February, 1964, with Elder Sam Aeschliman, Bluffton, Indiana, conducting the services.

Elder Dave Mangold, Roanoke, Illinois, spent several winters in Florida due to declining health. He assisted Elder Joe A. Getz. At the demise of these two Elders, John Bahler became the church's Shepherd. In the fall of 1977, Bahler relinquished these duties to Ben C. Maibach, Jr., Detroit, Michigan, and Joe Braker, Morton, Illinois.

In 1979 a new $120,000 fellowship hall was built close to the church.

By 1981 the Fort Lauderdale congregation claimed more than forty "permanent" members. In the winter months the number swells to a much larger total. Huge crowds attend Sunday services during this time of the year. A sense of brotherly love and unity prevails at these meetings.

In 1981 Elder Joe Braker assumed the role of Shepherd, assisted by Elder Ben C. Maibach, Jr.

VALPARAISO, INDIANA

VALPARAISO, INDIANA
805 East Jefferson Street

The Apostolic Christian Church at Valparaiso, Indiana, founded February 22, 1962, was the first of ten churches to be formed during the 1960's—the most prolific decade in the Church's history in terms of beginning new churches.

Valparaiso, the county seat of Porter County with a population of 24,000, lies in Indiana's extreme northwestern corner only twelve miles from the shores of Lake Michigan, and only a few miles southeast of the Gary-Hammond metropolitan

area. It is twenty miles from La Crosse, Indiana, site of the first Apostolic Christian Church in the extreme northwestern corner of Indiana.

For several years prior to 1962, brethren who resided here desired to establish a church in Valparaiso. In January, 1962, a survey was made to determine the amount of support and interest existing among local members. The results of the survey were positive, both with respect to establishing a church and purchasing a building for worship.

The latent desire to form a new church in Valparaiso came to fruition on February 22, 1962, when members and friends gathered together and decided to proceed with plans to establish a new congregation. A week earlier, on February 13, this same group—consisting of fifteen members and six friends—held their first meeting to discuss these weighty matters.

A vacant church building—formerly occupied by the Assembly of God Church—was purchased for $13,500. A loan totaling $7,500 was taken to help finance the project. After many hours of remodeling, painting and getting the building ready for worship, the first services were held June 10, 1962. It is ironic that the joy and appreciation which resulted from the opening of this new church occurred during the same month that the U.S. Supreme Court held, by a 6-1 vote, that prayer in public schools violates the first and fourteenth Amendments to the Constitution.

The church began with sixteen members and twenty Sunday School students. Average attendance in the beginning totaled approximately sixty.

Elder Sam Aeschliman, Bluffton, Indiana, conducted dedication services at the church on September 23, 1962.

By January, 1981—just under twenty years since the church was organized—membership more than doubled to thirty-six members (plus five converts). Twenty-three souls had been baptized. Average attendance was seventy.

George Yergler, Elder at nearby La Crosse, served as the church's first Shepherd. Harry Bucher, who resided in Valparaiso and preached for many years at La Crosse, served as the first resident minister.

Rodric W. Huber, originally from Francesville, Indiana, was installed as the second minister at Valparaiso on November 1, 1975, at age thirty. Edward Frank, La Crosse, serves as the counseling Elder.

URBANA, ILLINOIS

URBANA, ILLINOIS
702 East Mumford

The first official Sunday church services in the Urbana-Champaign area were held April 7, 1963, in the Y.M.C.A. Building on the University of Illinois campus. The church here is an outgrowth of a Bible class consisting of students from the university and other young people working in the twin city area. These Bible classes began as early as 1956.

The beginning of church activities in Urbana-Champaign resulted from the proliferation of growth in the mid-1950's to the mid-1960's of land grant colleges across the nation. The rise of technology, a rapidly growing population, and an expanding economy all resulted in a demand for "higher" education. These factors were among the reasons many young people with an Apostolic Christian background began attending colleges and universities.

As these young people left home and entered the more "worldly" environment of the "intelligentsia," it was only natural that their spiritual needs would require more diligent attention.

It was not long until a local "Bible study" was requested by brethren who were students. The Elder Body, out of compassion and concern for these young people, approved the request. Edwin Hohulin, minister at the church in Goodfield, Illinois, was asked to conduct periodic Bible studies. The university offered facilities for organized groups of this type. A constitution was drawn up, an official group organized, and the first meeting was held November 7, 1956, in Room 209 of the Illinois Union Building.

After a few years the size of the meetings increased, and eventually the student group evolved into a congregation. Sunday meetings were initiated on April 7, 1963, and held twice each month. Beginning January 1, 1967, church services were held every Sunday.

In 1969 the congregation purchased a church (which resembled a residence) from the United Church of Christ. This building, located at 702 East Mumford, cost $31,650. First church services were held here February 9, 1969.

Joe A. Getz, Morton, Illinois, served as the first Elder over the activities at Urbana-Champaign. Elder Emanuel Gudeman, Cissna Park, and minister Edwin Hohulin also played a significant part in establishing these activities. The latter assumed the Eldership here in 1969. David Wiegand was installed as the church's first resident minister on March 17, 1968.

From 1965 (when record keeping began) until early 1982, the church had baptized thirteen souls. Ninety-two students who were associated with the Urbana church and Bible study activities were baptized in their home churches.

Church activities here have provided a "haven" of truth for many young people over the years. For many, away from home for the first time and sometimes lonely and disoriented, the nearby church has been a welcome comfort. To others, perhaps threatened and challenged by secular doctrines and philosophies contrary to their upbringing, the security of nearby brethren has provided a bulwark of strength in trying times.

INDIANAPOLIS, INDIANA

Indianapolis
★

INDIANAPOLIS, INDIANA
7540 East 71st Street

The church at Indianapolis demonstrates the striking change that has occurred within the denomination during the past twenty years concerning the occupational composite of its members. Whereas a good many congregations across the nation consist mainly of persons with farm-related occupations (although the proportion is steadily declining), the church at Indianapolis by 1982 was decidedly urban as the following list of occupations reflects:

Medical Doctors	2	Veterinarians	2
Medical Student	1	Insurance Person	1
Nurses	6	Factory Workers	4
CPAs	3	Accountant	1
Banker	1	Teachers	4
Consultant	1	Social Workers	2
Architect	1	Students	7
Plant Geneticist	1	Doctor's Assistant	1
Engineers	5	Grain Buyer	1
Salesmen	3	Secretaries	2
Dentist	1	Retired	1

While occupations have changed dramatically compared to a few generations ago, it is comforting to know that scriptural truths and the eternal ways of God are changeless. The sense of brotherhood in an urban setting remains as viable as that in a rural area.

Indianapolis, the state's capital city, is located in the geographical center of Indiana. It is the largest city in the Union not situated on navigable water. The town was laid out in 1821 from plans by Major Pierre Charles L'Enfant, the designer of Washington, D.C.

In the fall of 1963, a small group of brethren met in the home of John Mayer for a simple worship service. The Mayers, the Henry Zellers, and a few medical students participated in this first meeting. They also discussed the future role, if any, of the Apostolic Christian Church in Indianapolis. Bi-monthly services were initiated, first at the Mayer home, and later at the downtown Indianapolis Y.M.C.A.

For three years this small group continued to meet at the downtown Y.M.C.A. Elder Sam Aeschliman, Bluffton, Indiana, (the church's first Elder) and layman Herman Norr, Leo, Indiana, were active in providing early leadership for the group. Norr, a layman, was active for many years in World Relief work and also in helping to nurture and assist the work of the church in Alabama.

The group at Indianapolis began to increase, and in 1966 weekly services were commenced at the Krannert Westside Y.M.C.A.

On December 5, 1970, a group of brethren met at the home of Chuck Neuenschwander to discuss the purchase of land on which to eventually build a church. This possibility culminated in the purchase of a seven-acre parcel at 7540 East 71st Street costing $26,500. The church continued to meet at the Krannert Y.M.C.A.

In 1972 the Krannert Y.M.C.A. was sold to the City of Indianapolis. This forced the congregation to find other quarters. The Indiana University Union was used briefly but was inconvenient and difficult for out-of-town guests to find. From there, the church rented the basement of a Seventh Day Adventist Church.

In the fall of 1972, construction began on a new church building. John Mayer took several weeks off his regular employment to supervise the project. Church brethren from Ohio, Indiana, and Illinois donated many hours of labor to this project. When Mayer returned to his regular work, volunteer Joe Gray, Francesville, Indiana, was hired to remain as foreman of the construction crew. Donated labor kept the cost of the new church at $112,000.

Henry Beer, Milford, Indiana, who conducted the first worship service in Indianapolis several years earlier, ironically preached the last sermon to the church which was held in the Seventh Day Adventist Church.

The first Sunday in July, 1973, marked the initial worship service in the new church building with Art Gudeman, La Crosse, Indiana, preaching. The new church was dedicated on January 20, 1974, with more than two hundred present. Elder Theo Beer (the church's second Elder) acted as official host to the throng. Visiting Elders were Ben C. Maibach, Jr., Detroit, Michigan; Loren Stoller, Latty, Ohio; and Sam Aeschliman, Bluffton, Indiana.

In 1975 Elder Theo Beer stepped down and was succeeded by Elder Alfred Bahler, Wolcott, Indiana.

The church's first permanent minister was Richard Aberle who was instated in 1974. Aberle, with extraordinary devotion and zeal, drove each week to Indianapolis from his home in Cincinnati, Ohio (130 miles away), to conduct worship services. He moved to Rockville, Connecticut, in 1980. Art Ringger, a Bluffton, Indiana, native, who was selected as minister in December, 1976, continued alone in the ministry until 1981.

The church in Indianapolis grew from a handful of members in 1963 to thirty-one families and fifty-one members in 1981. Since 1963 the church has had thirteen converts.

A church brochure, in describing the new building, stated, "This comfortable and pleasant dwelling has become the permanent dwelling of the Indianapolis church. Here the love of God reigns and the heavenly sunshine radiates."

In 1982 the church at Indianapolis completed a $200,000 building project which updated their present structure and provided additional fellowship area and dining room space.

MINNEAPOLIS, MINNESOTA

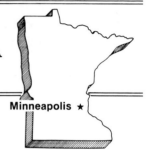

Minneapolis ★

MINNEAPOLIS, MINNESOTA
43rd Street & Wentworth Avenue South

In October, 1962, the first Apostolic Chrisitan worship service was held in the twin city area of Minneapolis-St. Paul, Minnesota. The first series of meetings here were held in the homes of believers and friends of the truth.

Among the families either attending or hosting these first church meetings were Arnold and Marjorie Gerst (he later became a minister at Chicago, Illinois, on April 21, 1968, and in 1982 moved to Taylor, Missouri), Richard and Beatrice Miller, Everett and Kathryn Olson, and Linus and Esther Lienemann.

For the first three years, ministers from congregations at Morris and Winthrop, Minnesota, and Lester and West Bend, Iowa, journeyed to Minneapolis on a rotating basis to lead the small group in worship.

In September, 1965, Noah Miller, a minister at Winthrop since 1955, moved to Minneapolis to serve the church as minister. A farmer with deep roots in Winthrop, he unselfishly availed himself to answer the call to preach regularly at Minneapolis and to nurture the permanence of the new congregation.

In February, 1963, church services were moved from the various homes of believers to the Longfellow Avenue Y.M.C.A. located at the intersection of Longfellow Avenue and Lake Street.

On December 9, 1969, a church building was purchased from the Apostolic Lutheran Church denomination (one of five denominations that use this name) at 112 West 43rd Street in Minneapolis. This church, located in the south central part of the city, cost approximately $21,000. It was remodeled for $30,000 with many brethren donating labor and assistance.

First services in the "new" church were held Sunday, May 17, 1970. Dedication services were held August 30, 1970, with Elder Noah Schrock, Oakville, Iowa, who probably delivered as many dedicatory sermons as any Elder in the denomination, preaching.

Ken Lawson was added to the ministry but later moved to Fort Lauderdale, Florida. In December, 1980, Donald Miller, forty-six, joined his father Noah as minister.

Paul Fehr, Elder at Morris, Minnesota, had the oversight of the twin city church for several years. In 1979 Harold Messner, Shepherd at Winthrop, Minnesota, assumed the duties of counseling Elder.

In the early 1980's average attendance here was fifty persons each Sunday. Membership ranged in the high twenties.

IOWA CITY, IOWA

Iowa City ★

IOWA CITY, IOWA
North George & Cherry Streets
North Liberty, Iowa

On November 5, 1978, the first regular worship services of the Apostolic Christian Church were held in North Liberty, Iowa, located five miles north of Iowa City. Since the church group essentially originated in Iowa City, the church in North Liberty is usually referred to as the "Iowa City" congregation. The church was located in this small town of 1,500 to better accommodate members of the church, several of whom live in Cedar Rapids, a short distance north.

The first services were memorable because they marked the group's first Sunday in their newly purchased building. Also, it was the first preaching service of Joseph Gerst, twenty-five, who had been ordained as minister on October 19, 1978.

421

The seeds of a future church in this section of Iowa were planted when young Apostolic Christian students began attending the University of Iowa. Prior to October, 1964, when Harvey Heiniger, Oakville, Iowa, conducted the first organized worship service at the Danforth Chapel on the University of Iowa campus, brothers and sisters of the church would often meet informally to sing hymns and listen to taped sermons. Several of these early meetings were held in the student apartment of Paul Eisenmann, Joel Banwart, and later Bill Gerst, who lived above the Donohue Mortuary. It is interesting to note that the building purchased in North Liberty was formerly the Beckman-Jones Funeral Chapel.

Meetings in Iowa City were held weekly beginning in October, 1964. The Danforth Chapel on campus was located across from the Memorial Union Building. For six years, this beautiful and peaceful setting on the banks of the Iowa River provided a tranquil respite from the rigors of university life.

As time wore on, more people of the church began moving into the area. They were either students at the University of Iowa or the Kirkwood Community College in Cedar Rapids or employees at Iowa City or Cedar Rapids industries and hospitals. Some of the first converts living in the area were Gary and Edith Anliker and Beverly Mogler. Others who were converted and lived in Iowa City during the earlier years were Joan Mogler, Joyce Eland, Andy Moser, Dan and Diane Stoller, Ed and Patty Stoller, Jack and Cathy Larson, Wayne Hermann, Vera Schaer, Jane Wiegand, and Mary Mogler.

In November, 1970, worship services were moved to the large Sunday School room of the St. Andrew's Presbyterian Church. It was here that regular Sunday services were begun. The group consisted of thirteen members and six friends. Also, several nurses from Marshalltown, Iowa, attended services. Visiting ministers from churches in Iowa, Missouri, and Illinois came to preach. Significant to the development of the church here was the ongoing support of the churches at Burlington and Oakville, Iowa.

Over the years the frequency of worship services was increased. Sunday School was initiated in 1975 with Twila Whipple serving as the first teacher.

In 1978, when the church totaled nineteen members, the congregation purchased the Beckman-Jones Funeral Home in North Liberty to use for worship. They paid $57,160. The decision to purchase this facility occurred, appropriately, during the Labor Day weekend when a special reunion was held for all persons who had attended the Iowa City "church" over the years.

In 1979, a 46-foot by 30-foot addition was placed next to the church.

Noah Schrock and Edward Lanz, Oakville, have served as Elders at the Iowa City church.

BRADFORD, ILLINOIS

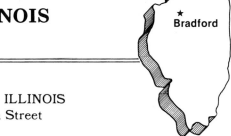

BRADFORD, ILLINOIS
East Main Street

The church at Bradford, Illinois, located thirty-five miles north of Peoria, Illinois, is an outgrowth of the congregation at Princeville. In the early 1960's the old, two-story brick church at Princeville (built in 1920-1921) became quite crowded. Since nearly thirty-five families who attended the Princeville church lived in the vicinity of Bradford, twenty-five miles north, a decision was reached to build a new church in that village.

The Bradford church was one of ten established within the denomination in the 1960's and one of only two formed in a rural area where the principal occupation of its members was related to agriculture. (Garden Grove, Iowa, was the other church.) Thus, the establishment of a church in the small farming community of Bradford marked a change in the trend established in the 1920's when subsequently most of the newly organized Apostolic Christian Churches were located in larger towns and cities.

In April, 1963, construction began on the new church located on East Main Street. The 280-seat facility, costing $265,000, was completed in the summer of 1964. First worship services were held July 5 with dedication on September 13. Initially, thirty-five families and fifty Sunday School children comprised the church. By 1980 church statistics had increased to fifty-five families, one hundred members, and ninety-nine in Sunday School.[13] Since the inception of the Bradford congregation, fifteen families have moved away over the years which indicates an even more significant growth than the above statistics reflect.

The church was served by local ministers from the beginning. Silas Leuthold, Elder at Princeville, presided over the Bradford congregation until January 12, 1972, when he retired as an active Elder. Elder David Kieser, Princeville, assumed responsibility for Bradford when he entered the Eldership on the same date.

From 1964 through 1980, sixty-four persons were baptized at Bradford.

REGINA, SASKATCHEWAN CANADA

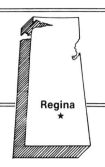

REGINA, SASKATCHEWAN, CANADA
94 Straub Crescent

Regina, capital city of the Canadian province of Saskatchewan, is the site of a very small Apostolic Christian Church. Established as the commercial center of an extensive agricultural area, Regina had a population of more than 150,000 in 1980.

The area's rich agricultural background was developed much like similar areas in the United States. Following completion of the Canadian Pacific Railway in 1885, large numbers of farmers and other settlers poured into the area. The period from 1905 to 1914 was marked by the influx of thousands of emigrants of varied origin.

Although the region found growth primarily because of agriculture, its lure found no response from Apostolic Christians, probably because of its remote location—357 miles west of Winnipeg.

In the early 1960's two area residents, Olga and Marie Simeon, came in contact with a booklet written by Joseph B. Schrock of Congerville, Illinois, entitled "God's Plan of

Salvation." Impressed with the booklet, these two sisters, one of whom was a member of the Apostolic Christian Church (Nazarene), made contact with the Schrock family. Elder Noah Schrock, along with his two brothers Joseph B. Schrock and Alvin J. Schrock, traveled to Regina to meet with the Simeon sisters. After meeting with the Simeons, it was decided to commence holding periodic services in Regina. For several years worship services were held at the Westward Motor Inn in Regina. Ministers began coming to Regina once per month. These monthly sessions were held from April to November each year. Marie Simeon, Keith and Myrna Shipley, and George and Mary Nesbitt eventually became members at Regina. In time, the Simeon sisters ceased attending services, leaving only the Shipleys and Nesbitts as members. A few other friends of the truth also attended services.

For several years Keith Shipley has served as the church's correspondent although he is not a minister. The George Nesbitt family resides approximately sixty miles northwest of Regina at Holdfast. He is a grain farmer. The Shipleys and Nesbitts are noted for their loyalty and devotion. Despite their remote location and small numbers, they have retained a close allegiance to brethren in the United States.

In October, 1979, a residence located one and one-half miles north of the airport on Regina's west side was converted into a new church building. This dwelling cost $48,000. Elder Leroy Huber, Eureka, Illinois, conducted dedication services in May, 1980.

Visiting ministers from the United States travel to Regina once per month from April to November to conduct worship services. When visiting ministers are not in attendance, the small group listens to taped sermons.

Although the Apostolic Christian Church (Nazarene) has several churches in Canada, the Apostolic Christian Church of America has only the one church in Canada at Regina. Despite its low numbers, this "outpost" church remains very loyal. Once someone asked Elder Noah Schrock why he would go so far for such a small group. He replied, "I would go to the ends of the earth for one soul."[14]

Elder Paul Butikofer, Elgin, Iowa, has served for many years as Elder at Regina.

LEXINGTON, KENTUCKY

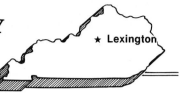

LEXINGTON, KENTUCKY
308 Locust Avenue

The Apostolic Christian Church's entry into Kentucky occurred in 1968 when the Lester Huber family of Francesville, Indiana, felt moved to locate here and establish a church. Huber had been installed as a minister at Francesville in 1955.

The venture was unlike the church's established pattern— with the exception of mission work in Alabama and Japan— whereby the church usually gravitated into an area where members of the church had already established themselves. At Lexington the Hubers moved here with the sole intent of drawing persons, as the Lord willed, into the fellowship of the church who had no previous association with the beliefs and traditions of the Apostolic Christian Church. With a plethora of Christian churches already established in Lexington (each with their own particular tradition), the project took an abundance of grace and noble motives to make it succeed.

The initial stages of the ministry in Lexington began in a third floor room of the Y.M.C.A. at 263 East High Street. In April, 1969, a house at 267 East High Street became available for rent, and services were moved to this location.

Attendance at this new "gathering of believers" was generated through home visitation and a bus ministry. Attendance sometimes reached one hundred, mostly young people. The first convert here was baptized June 6, 1971.[15]

In January, 1975, the house at 267 East High Street was sold, and the church was given a ninety-day notice to vacate the building.

Soon after this a church building at 308 Locust Avenue was purchased. The benevolence of several brethren made it possible to purchase this church building. Dedication services were held August 17, 1975, with Elders David Bertsch, Leo, Indiana, and Wendell Gudeman, Francesville, Indiana, participating. The latter Elder has the oversight of the Lexington congregation.

By 1980 the Lexington church had twenty families attending services with five listed as members. Thirty students attended Sunday School.

GARDEN GROVE, IOWA

GARDEN GROVE, IOWA
One mile south on Highway 204

In 1969 believers began to worship at Garden Grove, Iowa. Situated in the gently rolling hills of southern Iowa, Garden Grove lies 65 miles south of Des Moines, Iowa, and 120 miles north of Kansas City, Missouri. The area is well adapted to beef cow herds and is distinctly rural. The area's many timbers, flowing streams, green hills, and grazing cattle comprise a tranquil scene and engender thoughts of the Creator.

In a historical sense, Garden Grove is noted as one of three Iowa way stations where members of the Mormon faith camped during the winter of 1846-1847 en route from Nauvoo, Illinois, to Salt Lake City, Utah.[16] Many families remained in the area, and today a large Reformed Latter Day Saints Church exists at Lamoni, Iowa, thirty miles from Garden Grove.

The development of the church at Garden Grove centers largely on the efforts of William and Verle Funk. Together with their six children, they moved from Gridley, Illinois, to a farm one mile south of Garden Grove on December 27, 1967. William Funk later wrote, "It was only after much prayerful consideration and feeling directed of God that we undertook to move to Garden Grove."[17]

For a few years the Funk family journeyed each Sunday to worship at the Apostolic Christian Church in Pulaski, Iowa, eighty miles east. On April 13, 1969, William Funk was called into the ministry at Pulaski.

In July, 1969, a few friends and relatives in Garden Grove expressed to the Funks an interest in the beliefs of the Apostolic Christian Church. Because of this, church services were subsequently initiated in the Funk home and the third Sunday evening of each month. Many members and friends from the Pulaski congregation drove to Garden Grove and supported this new beginning.

In the spring of 1971, the United Church of Garden Grove was rented to hold worship services on Sunday afternoon of the first, third, and (when it occurred) fifth Sundays of the month. On the second and fourth Sundays, the group here drove to Pulaski for worship. During this phase Noah Schrock, Oakville, Iowa, served as Elder and was very supportive of the efforts to organize a church at Garden Grove.

Also in 1971 three souls turned to the Lord: Tony and Willa Funk, and Don Clark. During this time a large number of young people who attended school or worked in the Ames and Des Moines areas traveled to Garden Grove for worship.

Beginning February 3, 1974, church services were held every Sunday at Garden Grove. The parishioners gathered at the William Funk home for the morning worship service and the noon lunch and fellowship. The group then retired to the United Church building for the afternoon worship service.

On May 18, 1977, ground was broken for a new church one mile south of Garden Grove on land donated by William and Verle Funk. Brethren from many congregations contributed labor and financial help to the $71,000 project. First services were held on Christmas Day, 1977, despite the absence of pews.

Elders Wendell Gudeman of Francesville, Indiana, and Edward Lanz of Oakville, Iowa, conducted dedication services April 16, 1978. The latter succeeded Noah Schrock as Elder at Garden Grove.

In December, 1980, membership at Garden Grove totaled eight, down from the church's peak of eleven. Five persons had been baptized since the church's beginning here.

BLOOMINGTON, ILLINOIS

BLOOMINGTON, ILLINOIS
Corner of East Oakland and
Towanda-Barnes Blacktop

For several decades prior to the founding of an Apostolic Christian Church here in 1969, persons associated with the church had lived in the Bloomington-Normal area. Ideally located in the center of the state and served by key railroad lines and interstate highways, Bloomington-Normal experienced rapid growth in the 1960's and 1970's. General economic growth and the expansion of the state university system contributed to the emergence of this bustling metropolitan area. Because it is also located in the center of a host of Apostolic Christian Churches in central Illinois, it became ripe for the

establishment of a church, particularly as more and more people left the farming areas of their youth to seek careers in other
fields.

The first Apostolic Christians to move to Bloomington
were Melvin and Ann Sorg who arrived on September 1, 1941.
In 1948 Dorothy Harsh also located in the area. In November,
1954, Carl and Ann Frautschi moved to Bloomington from
Indiana. In 1957 Al and Josephine Stoller moved from Gridley,
Illinois, to Bloomington. Others who located here in the 1950's
were Ruth Lowery, Carlton and Betty Klopfenstein, and Bob
and Marilyn Hany.

In 1959 or 1960 a meeting was held among families and students living in Bloomington-Normal to determine their interest in establishing a church. The result was that not enough interest had materialized, probably because many of the
students returned to their nearby homes for weekend church
services. Nonetheless, a few members living here continued to
press for the establishment of a church in Bloomington-
Normal. In the early 1960's efforts were made, unsuccessfully,
to purchase a church building on South Fell Avenue.

By the mid-1960's the number of church families, students,
and friends of the church living in the general metropolitan
area had risen dramatically. For instance, a survey in 1965 indicated more than one hundred members of the Apostolic
Christian Church—both permanent residents and students—
lived in Bloomington-Normal, a real "nucleus" for a church.

In the fall of 1966, Elder Leroy Huber, Eureka, Illinois,
headed a committee which studied the feasibility of starting a
church here. Serving on the committee were Elders Henry
Kilgus, Forrest; Joshua Broquard, Fairbury; and George
Gramm, Gridley, Illinois. Joseph B. Schrock served as secre-
tary. Later Elders Eugene Bertschi, Roanoke, and Edwin
Hohulin, Goodfield, filled vacancies created by Elders Henry
Kilgus and George Gramm.

In April, 1967, the Elders sent survey forms to area
members to measure the interest and resolve associated with
forming a new church. On May 13, 1967, this committee of
Elders met personally with the area's sixteen permanent
Apostolic Christian families at the home of Carlton and Betty
Klopfenstein to further discuss the possibility of establishing a
church.

In 1968, a letter from the Bloomington-Normal resident members indicating their support for a local church was presented to the Elder Body at the Brotherhood Conference at Lester, Iowa, October 31, 1968.

On February 10, 1969, a meeting of the Elder committee and local families was held at the Bloomington Y.M.C.A. At this meeting official sanction was given to begin a new church in Bloomington-Normal. Arrangements were made to rent the facilities of the First Mennonite Church at 918 South University Street in Normal on Sunday afternoons. First worship services were held April 13, 1969. Ministers from fifteen Illinois churches took turns preaching at Bloomington-Normal on a rotating schedule. The church voted for Everett Hari as their first resident minister on April 18, 1970.

Also, in 1970, the church purchased a five-acre tract of land at the northwestern corner of East Oakland and the Towanda-Barnes blacktop, two and one-half miles east of Veterans Parkway.

On Sunday, April 15, 1973, ground-breaking ceremonies were held at the church plot for a new house of worship. Melvin Sorg, a Bloomington resident for more than thirty years, turned the first shovel of dirt. First services were held February 17, 1974. Dan Koch, Tremont, Illinois, who had assumed the duties of Elder here on September 24, 1972, preached the first sermon. Dedication was held June 23, 1974, with Elder Eugene Bertschi officiating.

By 1982, the Bloomington-Normal congregation had grown to over 90 families and 130 members. Forty-four persons had been baptized since services began in the new church.

*   *   *   *   *

Related to the development of a church at Bloomington-Normal, but a totally separate entity, was the emergence of a "Bible Study" at Illinois State Normal University (later named Illinois State University). Following the example set at the University of Illinois in 1956 to nurture the faith of young believers at that school, a similar project was launched in 1957 by minister Joseph B. Schrock of nearby Congerville, Illinois. A Thursday evening Bible class was held each week.

In 1959, in order to be able to use campus facilities for the Bible class, a group of forty-nine charter members complied with school regulations and became a recognized university organization. This involved drawing up a constitution, electing officers (Bill Hohulin of Goodfield was first President), and choosing a campus advisor (Dr. Kenneth A. Retzer of the Mathematics Department). Joseph B. Schrock conducted the first Thursday evening meeting of each month. On the other Thursday evenings, visiting ministers either conducted worship services or a Bible study depending on their preference.

Year after year Joseph B. Schrock dutifully drove to Normal from Congerville each Thursday evening to oversee this project. In October, 1979, Kenneth E. Hoerr, Peoria, Illinois, took over the duties of ministering to the Apostolic Christian students at Illinois State University. Elder Edwin Ringger had the oversight of this student group.

ZAPATA, TEXAS

ZAPATA, TEXAS
About 2½ miles south of
Zapata on U.S. 83

★ Zapata

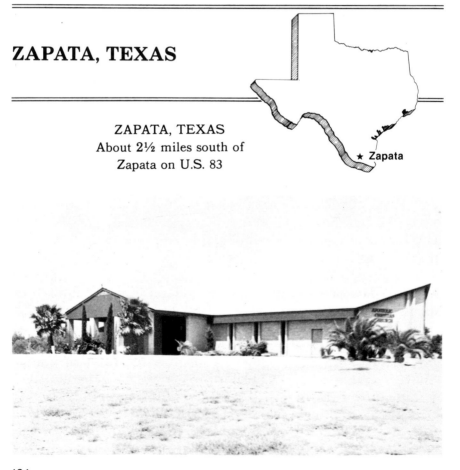

Far-away Zapata, Texas, is the site of an Apostolic Christian Church established in 1972. Situated deep in the southern section of the state, it lies 200 miles south of San Antonio and 150 miles northeast of Monterrey, Mexico. The town of Zapata (population 8,000) is located on Falcon Lake, a large man-made lake created by damming up the Rio Grande River. The dam is about thirty-five miles south of Zapata and supplies the irrigation water for the Rio Grande Valley. This area produces significant amounts of vegetables and citrus fruits for the United States. Zapata is only a few miles from the Mexican border.

Interest in the general area of south Texas was created a few decades earlier when many Apostolic Christian families journeyed to San Antonio to visit their sons who were training as non-combatants with the United States Army at Fort Sam Houston. While touring the general southern area of Texas, they became intrigued with Zapata. Its warm and dry climate in the winter months led a few older couples to spend the winter months of 1967 in Zapata for health reasons. They liked it here and continued to return each winter. In time, other couples came to escape the rigors of the cold northern winters. It was not long until the number of Apostolic Christians in the area began to increase.

The first church meeting was held in the mobile home of Ernie Anliker. Initially, worship consisted of a song service, reading from the Bible, and prayer. Sometimes a taped sermon was played. If a visiting minister was present, he would offer a meditation.

In 1972, the first official church services were held in rented quarters at the Zapata Hobby Shop with twenty-one in attendance. Another building was rented in 1973 with attendance ranging from forty to forty-five persons. In 1974 an even larger building was rented to accommodate the assembly which had again doubled to over eighty people. By the winter of 1975-1976, as many as 104 attended services. The last building rented by the church was the Siesta Shores Community Building.

As time unfolded, between forty and fifty members of the church became property owners in Zapata. This, together with the temporary residence of four Elders (Herman Kellenberger, Elgin, Illinois; Eugene Bertschi, Roanoke, Illinois; Edwin

Hohulin, Goodfield, Illinois; and Paul Fehr, Morris, Minnesota), prompted the church to officially organize. In 1976, a charter of incorporation was applied for and granted to the "Apostolic Christian Church at Zapata, Texas." Earlier, a brother in the church had donated a parcel of land to be used for a new church building.

A $140,000 church was built two and one-half miles south of Zapata on U.S. Route 83. Dedication was held February 19, 1978.

By 1980 the "winter" church here consisted of an average of forty families with one hundred members or more.[18] After the winter season, church attendance declines sharply.

Although a host of ministers visit Zapata each year, Leland Plattner, who was instated on March 19, 1978, is the local minister. Herman Kellenberger, Elgin, Illinois, served as the first Elder. He retired in September, 1981, and was succeeded by Elder Edwin Hohulin, Goodfield, Illinois.

PHILADELPHIA, PENNSYLVANIA

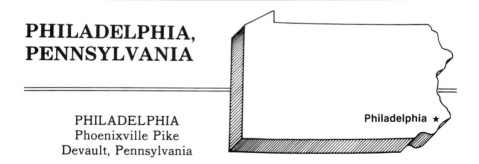

PHILADELPHIA
Phoenixville Pike
Devault, Pennsylvania

An Apostolic Christian Church was formed in January, 1974, at Devault, Pennsylvania, just a few miles off the Pennsylvania Turnpike and approximately twenty miles west of the city of Philadelphia.

It was appropriate that a church be established in this area, not only as a convenience to the few brethren living here, but also for its symbolic meaning. For centuries, prior to the founding of America, devout believers in Christ have felt the heel of oppression and religious persecution. Yet, the very essence of what America stands for is embodied in the First Amendment to the Constitution, part of which guarantees the free exercise of religion—a marvelous liberty!

It was here in the "cradle of liberty" that the fledgling American government on July 4, 1776, declared itself free from the bondage of the British Crown—an act that was to have major consequences for all persons who later associated with the Apostolic Christian Church. In connection with this "declaration" of independence, members of the Church today declare themselves "free" from the bondage of sin and unrighteousness.

It is also appropriate to have a church in this area because Philadelphia means the "City of Brotherly Love," a name personally selected in 1682 by its founder, William Penn, a Quaker.[19] In the Apostolic Christian Church, one of the greatest tenets of belief is living the Christian life within the framework of brotherhood and love.

Brethren have lived in the Philadelphia area as early as 1962. Over the years several families have lived here, but only four became permanently established. For many years those families traveled approximately 120 miles each Sunday to worship at the Apostolic Christian Church in Union City, New Jersey. Because this became a burdensome effort, and particularly because Ed Aeschleman, a minister, lived in the area (at Wilmington, Delaware), services were initiated once per month in January, 1974, at Devault, Pennsylvania (population two hundred). Worship services were held in a Grange Hall. Later the meetings were expanded to twice per month and in 1978 to three times. On the fourth Sunday, the group traveled to Union City.

In September, 1977, when Elder John Bahler, Rockville, Connecticut, came to serve Holy Communion, he suggested the group here search for an area where a church might be built some day.

In a miraculous development, the Grange organization, from whom the church had been renting a building, donated a three-acre plot of ground to the church. This was an answer to prayer, and the church felt the "door was opened" to begin proceeding with plans for a new church. It took thirteen months to resolve zoning and deed considerations.

Plans were drawn up, cost figures obtained, and the project moved to the fund-raising stage. It was at this point that a major obstacle was encountered which proved very disheartening to the group. The contractor, after presenting a cost figure in April, 1979, called in October of that year to say his estimates were in error, and the new cost was twenty-five percent higher than his original bid. This posed a major dilemma for the congregation. Temporarily, their hopes for a new church were dashed.

A solution was found when Paul Emch, a member of the church at Phoenix, Arizona, (and a builder) drew up a set of new, more practical building plans and personally visited the building site in Devault. In April, 1980, when Paul Emch was in Philadelphia, ground-breaking ceremonies were held.

Donated labor and overall assistance in building the new church were astounding. More than sixty volunteers from five states were among those who came to work on the church. Minister Edwin Bahler, a builder from Remington, Indiana, arranged for building supplies to be purchased at the lowest price possible. Roger Gasser, Akron, Ohio, spent six weeks in the summer of 1980 working on the building and coordinating the contractors, etc. In June, 1980, Orin Rufener, Rittman, Ohio, supervised a crew of workers who made substantial progress during a four-day work stint. The church was built in six months. Dedication was held May 3, 1981.

The church, of colonial design, sits on a hill overlooking the Pennsylvania Turnpike in a beautiful rural setting. It is six miles from Valley Forge.

John Bahler, Rockville, Connecticut, served the church as Elder, but was succeeded by his son Corbin in 1981.

KANSAS CITY, MISSOURI

KANSAS CITY, MISSOURI
301 West Blue Ridge Boulevard

The commercially important city of Kansas City, Missouri—located at the confluence of the Kansas and Missouri Rivers—became another site in a growing list of metropolitan Apostolic Christian Churches.

By the middle of the 1970's, enough members and friends lived in this area—known as a major convention center and the "gateway to the Southwest"—to begin worship services.

Initial efforts to establish a church in Kansas City were featured by a letter on December 10, 1974, complete with a questionnaire, mailed to members and friends in the Kansas City area by Elder Eugene Marti (then of Sabetha, Kansas) and minister Sam Huber, also of Sabetha. It was sent to measure the interest and support local persons had relative to a new church.

439

Another letter, dated January 20, 1975, was mailed which reflected that the response to the letter of December 10 was favorable. A portion of the letter read, "At this time we have twenty-five persons that have indicated they would attend these services. After prayerful consideration, we have concluded that the Lord is directing us to begin services in Kansas City and then see what He may provide for the future."

The first worship service in the area was held February 16, 1975, in the clubhouse of the Greenbrier Apartment Complex, 85th Street and Antioch Road, Overland Park, Kansas. There were seventy-three present including twenty-one visitors from out of town. Initially, church services were held twice per month with only one preaching service. Average attendance at these services was fifty. By 1977 those who were able began meeting on Thursday evening in each other's homes for singing or listening to taped sermons.

On March 23, 1975, a Sunday School was started. In either April or May, two services were held with a lunch served after the first service.

By June 22, 1975, just when momentum was gathering, the Greenbrier clubhouse was no longer available to rent. Services were temporarily discontinued until new quarters could be found. On November 9, 1975, services were resumed at the Y.W.C.A. at 9110 East 63rd Street in Raytown, Missouri. On December 7, 1975, services were moved to the Capital Federal Savings Association, 5700 Neiman Road, Shawnee, Kansas. Services were held in that location until March 21, 1976, when the group moved to the Capital Federal Savings Association building at State Line Road at 75th Street in Shawnee Mission, Kansas. Services were held on a twice-monthly basis.

In November, 1979, the congregation purchased six acres at the corner of Wornall Road and Blue Ridge Boulevard in Kansas City. Plans were initiated for constructing a 110-seat-capacity church, beginning in 1981. The first worship services were held in this new building on December 20, 1981. It is interesting to note that on this first Sunday in the new church, a baptismal service was conducted.

Since 1975 the church has been served by ministers from the church at Lamar, Missouri, and the Kansas churches of Bern, Fort Scott, Lamont, Gridley, Sabetha, and Wichita. In 1982 Eugene Marti was serving as counseling Elder.

WASHINGTON, ILLINOIS

WASHINGTON, ILLINOIS
East Cruger Road

Two hundred years after the founding of the United States—
a nation which is noted for guaranteeing religious liberty—an
Apostolic Christian Church was founded, appropriately during
this "bi-centennial" year, at Washington, Illinois, a few miles
across the Illinois River from Peoria. September 12, 1976,
marked the first worship service in Washington.

Although by 1982 the new Washington congregation had
more than one hundred members and met in a beautiful, brick
church complete with modern conveniences and a comfortable
interior, more than a century ago those of the same faith did
not enjoy the luxuries of air-conditioning, carpeting, padded
seats and all the "essentials" found in almost all Apostolic
Christian Churches today.

In the early 1850's Apostolic Christians in this area met in
homes and in the Engel Barn between Washington and
Metamora on Partridge Prairie. The Engel Barn was about
one-quarter mile south of the former A. & W. Restaurant in
Metamora (on the west side of the road).

The physical circumstances surrounding services then were a far cry from today. During services at the Engel barn, chickens would wander in and out, and if they became too noisy, they were chased out. People sat on planks and listened to long sermons preached in the German language. Many traveled by horse and wagon as far as twenty-five miles to attend services, often arising at 2 a.m. in order to arrive in time for worship.

The contrast of conditions then compared to today is almost unbelievable, yet its impact reflects the prosperity and material blessings which have fallen on today's members. Equally poignant is the fact that despite the great contrast social conditions have dictated relative to worship services, the same gospel of salvation that was preached more than a century ago at the Partridge Prairie church is still boldly and humbly proclaimed from the pulpit at Washington. A ringing testimony to the Washington church—and to all the Apostolic Christian Churches—is that the gospel message, the sacred hymns, the sincere prayers, and the simple, dignified worship liturgy have not become "modern." Those who sit in today's modern churches hear the same message, which is prompted by the Holy Spirit, that brothers and sisters heard in the 1850's as they sat in a barn on hard, wooden seats.

In the early 1970's conditions had become ripe to establish a church in Washington. A decade earlier various church officials were aware that eventually this might be a prime spot to locate a church. Washington is located in the center of a hub of surrounding Apostolic Christian Churches at Roanoke, Peoria, Morton, and Eureka. Members from the latter three churches who resided in or near Washington comprised the Washington congregation at the outset. In 1974 Peoria had 515 members, Morton 655, and Eureka 298.[20] The formation of the church at Washington, to some extent, relieved the crowded conditions at these churches.

In 1975-1976 a poll taken among Apostolic Christian families living in the Washington vicinity reflected substantial interest in establishing a new congregation. Several subsequent organizational meetings were held at the Lincoln Grade School in Washington. The first "singing" was held Sunday,

April 25, 1976. That summer (the nation's bi-centennial summer) saw these families here hold three "get-acquainted" picnics. The first worship services were held in September.

The first year of worship meetings resulted in four baptisms which gave significant encouragement to the new congregation.

On October 2, 1977, Carl Wyss, who formerly attended the Morton church, was selected as Washington's first minister.

A new church building, built mostly by volunteer labor, was completed in early 1978. First worship services were held March 12, 1978. Dedication was June 25, 1978.

Roy Sauder, Elder at the nearby Peoria church, became the first Shepherd of the Washington flock.

NORTH FORT MYERS, FLORIDA
(Formerly Port Charlotte)

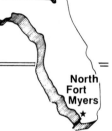

NORTH FORT MYERS, FLORIDA
North on U.S. 41

To accommodate families living in the area south of Sarasota as well as a host of winter visitors who came to the area each year, church services were initiated in Port Charlotte, Florida, on December 1, 1979. Located on the edge of Charlotte Harbor on Florida's west coast, Port Charlotte sits approximately midway between Sarasota and Fort Myers.

After considerable investigation, Rolland Keller and other brethren found a suitable place for the church to worship in Port Charlotte. Quarters were rented from the Punta Gorda-Port Charlotte Board of Realtors on Harper Avenue, just off U.S. Route 41.

Services the first year—from December 1, 1979, to April 6, 1980—drew 1,141 persons. Attendance on Easter Sunday, 1980, drew a crowd of 140. Average attendance in 1979-1980 was 70 to 75.

Because of the throng of winter visitors, the church "season" here extends from December to the early part of

April. By 1981 a year-long church schedule had not yet materialized although long-range plans include the possibility that a church with services each Sunday will be established.

The church has been served primarily by the Sarasota ministers. Ben C. Maibach, Jr., serves as Elder.

Arthur Gudeman, minister at La Crosse, Indiana, spends winters here and also serves as minister. A farmer, he comes to Port Charlotte after harvest is completed and returns home in the spring to begin planting.

Also, during the winter, ministers at the Sarasota church take turns conducting worship services at Port Charlotte.

By early 1982 the future plans of the Port Charlotte church remained uncertain. Elder Ben C. Maibach, Jr., made the following comments which reflected what eventualities might unfold.[21]

> Accommodations rented for services were remodeled by the Board of Realtors, and the area available to hold services was greatly reduced so that during the '81-'82 winter season when the attendance exceeded one hundred, the facilities were cramped, and the audience did reach as high as one hundred and thirty souls.
>
> The on-going search for suitable property on which sometime in the future to construct our own building continued. Several parcels of land were located and reviewed by the brethren, but zoning and parking restrictions caused some problem. After analyzing several interesting plots, the Lord opened the way, and a beautiful site was found just north of North Ft. Myers on U.S. Highway 41. The proposition to purchase this property was laid before the brethren on April 11, 1982, and the vote was unanimously in support of the recommendation of the brethren who had made the investigation.
>
> This three and one-half acre parcel should serve as a focal point for the many brethren and friends who are wondering where to locate so as to be reasonably close to the proposed church site. This property is quite ideal and even more centrally located than the facility we are now using at Port Charlotte, it being twenty-one miles further south than the existing meeting place.
>
> In the interim it is the intention of the brethren to continue scheduled Sunday services in Port Charlotte during the winter season 1982-83 and until conditions would justify the building of our own edifice on the property purchased.

In 1983 an additional 1.34 acres next to this property was given to the congregation, thus enlarging the site to nearly five acres. Projected plans called for constructing a 60-foot by 40-foot, one-story worship facility, costing approximately $70,000 (exclusive of furnishings, land, or paving).

DENVER, COLORADO

Denver ★

DENVER, COLORADO
280 South Revere
Aurora, Colorado

Because of its location in one of the nation's most beautiful tourist areas, the "mile high" city of Denver, Colorado, became the site of worship services beginning June 8, 1980. Since many Apostolic Christians toured the Rocky Mountain area in the summer, and because a number of people with roots in the church lived here, it was decided to begin worship services in this area. The minister at the first service was Charles Sauder, Tremont, Illinois. Of the twelve in attendance, only two were from Colorado. During that first summer, services continued each Sunday until August 31 when services were held once per month. During the summer of 1980, average attendance was twenty-three with the largest crowd numbering fifty-one.

Beginning in September, worship was held once per month during the fall, winter, and spring months.

Weekly summer services in 1981 saw average attendance increase to thirty. The largest crowd was ninety-four. Winter services were increased to twice monthly.

Providing a substantial boost to the Denver meetings was the Tom Leman family of Elgin, Illinois, who spent the summer of 1981 in Denver. As a minister, his presence at Denver every Sunday helped give a greater sense of continuity and organization to the meetings. He helped coordinate the schedule of visiting ministers, and his wife Marlene was very helpful in assisting with the noon lunches and afternoon meals. The Lemans moved to Denver permanently in 1982.

Services were held at the Victory Grange Hall in Aurora, Colorado. Elder Nathan Steffen, Elgin, Illinois, served as counseling Elder of the Denver assembly.

On February 28, 1983, a church building was purchased from the Christian Missionary Alliance at 280 South Revere in Aurora. The first worship services were held on March 6, 1983. By August, 1983, the congregation had thirteen members.

SATELLITE CHURCHES

At the outset of the 1980's, church meetings were held in various outlying areas of the United States where no established congregations of the faith existed. These services were usually held in homes, and attendance was small. They were held for the benefit of persons living in remote places who wanted to attend Apostolic Christian services.

SAN ANTONIO, TEXAS

In the winter of 1979-1980, three worship services were held. Hosting these meetings held in homes were the Elmer "Bud" Sauder and Everett Martin families. Minister Leland Plattner of Zapata, Texas, and formerly of Bern, Kansas, officiated at these meetings.

From the late 1940's through the end of the Vietnam conflict, young men of the church, serving at Fort Sam Houston in San Antonio, held church services on an organized basis.

Elder Samuel Anliker, Lamont, Kansas, was in charge of these services, and ministers from all over America traveled to San Antonio to conduct worship services.

At one time the church rented a large house where brethren and friends could assemble for worship or for listening to taped sermons, singing, and fellowship.

BELVIDERE, ILLINOIS

Beginning in the summer of 1980, worship services were held each Thursday evening in Belvidere, Illinois. Ministers from the Elgin congregation conducted these services at the home of William and Esther Troyke. Average attendance the first summer was ten to fifteen members. Belvidere is located approximately forty miles northwest of Elgin on Interstate 90.

In 1981 services here were held only periodically due to the illness of a man from Wisconsin who attended the Thursday evening meetings. Plans were made to resume services in the fall of 1981 if possible.

Belvidere's location, just east of Rockford (Illinois' second largest city) and near the Marengo and Hampshire areas where several members and friends of the Elgin congregation reside, made it a prime spot for an eventual church.

McALLEN, TEXAS

Church services were begun here on January 25, 1981, at the home of Lloyd and Joyce Nohl, 1501 Wisteria Street. Services at this location accommodated winter visitors and were discontinued on April 1 when many residing here returned to their homes in the North. Those who remained attended church at Zapata. Average attendance in 1981 was twenty-five.

ATLANTA, GEORGIA

This historic city of the old Confederacy, which was virtually destroyed in 1864 during General William Tecumseh Sherman's "march to the sea" at the time of the Civil War, became the site of Apostolic Christian Church worship services on February 1, 1981, one week following initial services at McAllen, Texas.

A major city of the southeastern section of the nation featuring stunning population growth (19.1% annually during the 1970's) and expanding commercial opportunities, Atlanta was a suitable area for church development.

Worship services were started on an experimental basis and were held only when a "northern" minister was passing through the area. On July 12, 1981, services were officially begun on the second and fourth Sundays of each month. Space was rented at the Ramada Inn in suburban Marietta, Georgia. In 1981 average attendance was twenty.

Three members attended services along with many interested friends of the truth who reside in the Atlanta metropolitan area.

Wendell Gudeman, Francesville, Indiana, and Alfred Bahler, Wolcott, Indiana, served as counseling Elders.

EMPORIA, KANSAS

The first worship service was held here on a Sunday evening on October 12, 1980. Services on a regular basis were begun in the spring of 1981. By 1982 services were held every third Sunday evening. Emporia is located in the east central portion of Kansas.

Elder Samuel Anliker, Lamont, Kansas, had the oversight of this assembly in 1982. Many members from the nearby Gridley and Lamont congregations attended these Emporia meetings.

TAMPA, FLORIDA

In the summer of 1981 periodic mid-week services were held in Tampa at the home of Gordon and Marilyn Bryant.

COLUMBUS, OHIO

On November 22, 1981, the first worship services were held in Columbus at the Holiday Inn, North. Twenty-seven adults and seven children attended the services conducted by Elders Rudy Graf, Akron, Ohio, and John Bahler, Rockville, Connecticut.

In 1982 the "congregation" moved to larger quarters at the Seventh Day Adventist Church building, 860 Griswold Avenue, in Worthington, Ohio.

DES MOINES, IOWA

Worship services in the Des Moines metropolitan area were preceded by church meetings at Ames, Iowa, twenty-five miles north.

In the mid-1960's, several students from various Apostolic Christian churches were attending college in central Iowa. Many were students at Iowa State University in Ames. First church activities in Ames occurred on April 9, 1967, when Bible classes were commenced in Room 205 at Iowa State University's Memorial Union. These classes were held once per month during the academic year.

The first regular worship service at Ames was held February 11, 1968, in a room at the First Christian Church on Sixth and Clark Streets. Approximately fifty persons attended this service conducted by Elders Paul Banwart, West Bend, and Noah Schrock, Oakville.

Because several students were living in the Des Moines and Ankeny area, worship services were moved to Johnston, Iowa (population 4,500), a small town on the northwestern edge of the Des Moines metropolitan area.

By 1982 worship services were held the second Sunday of each month at the Lion's Club in Johnston. They were conducted alternately by church ministers from West Bend, Oakville, and Lester, Iowa. Noah Gerber, a minister at West Bend, served as the church's correspondent.

KITCHENER, ONTARIO

Worship services began here in July, 1981. They were held once per month with visiting ministers conducting the services. Initially, one family with several children comprised the majority of attendance.

ST. LOUIS, MISSOURI

November 22, 1981, marked the first Sunday that worship services were held in the St. Louis metropolitan area. Brethren gathered at the Harley Hotel, 13440 Riverglen Drive, to worship God. Elder Roy Grimm, Taylor, Missouri, conducted the first services. Attendance was twenty-five. In April, 1982, services were moved to the Ben Franklin Motel, 4645 N. Lindbergh Boulevard, just west of the St. Louis International Airport.

Elder Stephen C. Rinkenberger, Cissna Park, assisted Elder Grimm in overseeing this small gathering.

CHAPTER X

"...Verily I say unto you, Inasmuch as ye have done it unto one of the least of these my brethren, ye have done it unto me."

The Apostolic Christian Church in America has been very active in the service of Christ, particularly in preaching and teaching the gospel. In addition, it has become quite involved in a host of other Christian activities which result in alleviating hunger and suffering as well as enriching the kingdom of God.

Apostolic Christian people have always been very charitable and hospitable. At the outset, when the forefathers of faith reached American shores and settled themselves on farms and in villages and towns, they mostly practiced the virtue of individual giving. Social circumstances were such, however, that their lives were preoccupied with maintaining an existence. Families were usually large, income was sparse and uncertain, and there were few cash surpluses to share with others. Also, primitive farming methods left little time to assist the poor and needy. If there was surplus time, travel was slow and inconvenient. Thus, nearly all acts of charity were unilateral and local. A unified, coordinated program of charitable outreach was seemingly far beyond the scope and realm of those hard-working pioneers.

While a few of the brethren prospered over the years, many remained confined by the harsh economic realities of war and depression which had a major impact on the United States in the first half of the twentieth century. A broadly-based and

451

sustained economic upswing never occurred until the end of World War II. It was then that organized charitable work began to increase and build on the efforts of the church's European assistance of the 1930's.

Prior to World War II, charitable activities on an organized basis were largely channeled through the Apostolic Christian Church (Nazarene) with specific emphasis on assisting conditions in Eastern Europe. Following World War I, the process of reconstruction and worldwide economic depression saw many people left homeless. Consequently many families filtered into neutral Switzerland. Because of this, the church in Switzerland organized an association named Hilfe, A.G. (meaning Help, Inc.) at Zurich in 1921. During the 1930's the "Hilfe" organization solicited help from the Apostolic Christian Church in the United States. Ed Kambly of Cissna Park, Illinois, a Swiss emigrant through whom the initial solicitations were made, served in an active capacity in these charitable endeavors.

In 1934 the church appointed Elder Joe A. Getz, Morton, Illinois, to head the "Hilfe" work, and Ed Kambly was officially assigned to receive the contributions. Elder Rudolph Graf of Akron, Ohio, worked with Ed Kambly in areas east of Illinois and Indiana. During the 1930's and 1940's, letters from "Brother Kambly" pertaining to "European Relief" were often read to the congregations.

During most of World War II (1942-1945), due to the chaotic upheaval in Europe, no funds were sent to that area. The total monies appropriated to the "Hilfe" amounted to more than $600,000. In addition, thousands of packages of clothing and non-perishable foods were sent to that continent.

Following World War II, charitable efforts on a denominational basis were largely uncoordinated. There was no centralized direction or policy-making board. As the nation prospered financially during the tranquil 1950's, so did many Apostolic Christians. The economic boom of the 1960's further added to the church's general affluence.

Soon after mid-century, when income and affluence levels rose dramatically and labor-saving devices reduced working hours and granted believers large blocks of leisure time, the door was opened for the church to purposely encourage greater efforts in many areas of service, both with respect to charitable endeavors and other soul-enriching activities.

CHURCH ELDERS

The doctrinal responsibility of the denomination rests with a council of Elders who preside over the church. Although no central church headquarters or administrative staff exists, the Elders have gathered periodically over the years to address problems that confront the church. Aside from overall doctrine and specific local projects of significant magnitude, local churches generally administer the operation of their local facilities.

Due to the church's administrative informality, it is difficult to categorize, in an ecclesiastical sense, the "government" of the church. It is neither solely episcopal, presbyterian, or congregational. Essentially, it is a combination of all three. Spiritually, the true head of the church is Christ. While earthly administrative authority must exist for the church to function in a practical sense, no one man rules over the church. Even though Elders are accorded "double honor" (I Timothy 5:17) and are to be obeyed, the church looks to Christ and the Apostles through Scriptures for final guidance in all matters of doctrine and practice.

The ordaining of Elders in the various churches reaches as far back as the early first-century church. Scriptures in Acts 14:23 and I Timothy 5:17 provide historical reference to this. Also, Acts 16:4 tells about the Apostle Paul delivering the decrees to keep that were written by the Elders in Jerusalem.

The words "Elder" and "Bishop" are so closely connected that historians have generally used the terms interchangeably. The Greek word for "Bishop" is "Overseer" which is the proper definition of an Apostolic Christian Elder's responsibility.

In the Apostolic Christian Church, Elders are also referred to as Shepherds. In the spirit of Christ—lovingly and gently— they watch over their flocks and attempt to keep them in safe pastures and by still waters in a spiritual sense. If any members stray from the flock and encounter harm and evil, the Shepherd makes an effort to draw them back to the flock.

The first clear trace of Christian Elders is at Jerusalem. In Acts 11:30 (A.D. 44) they received the offerings from Barnabas and Saul; in Acts 15:6 (A.D. 50) they took part in the conference; in Acts 21:18 (A.D. 58) they joined in the welcome of the Apostle Paul. In the post-apostolic period, reference to Elders is in James 5:14.[1]

In Anabaptist circles the terms Elder *(Aeltester, Oudste)* and Bishop were used interchangeably. Gradually, the term *Oudste* or *Aeltester* became predominant until the usage of "Bishop" disappeared from most of Europe.

Because Samuel Froehlich was influenced by the Scriptures and by the Swiss Brethren (Mennonites) when he left the state church of Switzerland, he included the office of Elder in his church's mode of operation. The churches in America followed this practice.

The early Anabaptist Elders did not receive a fixed salary partly because they were opposed to practices which prevailed in the state church. This was the situation also with the early Evangelical Baptists (the church Froehlich founded which in America became known as Apostolic Christian) and the church in America. Today, American Elders receive no salary for their untiring services to the church. In some instances, however, expense money is provided in special situations.

The first American Elder was Benedict Weyeneth. He was ordained in Europe in 1847 specifically to come to America following an invitation to come and address some spiritual problems experienced by a group of Mennonites in Lewis County, New York. By 1860 Weyeneth was listed as an Elder in America along with Joseph Virkler of Lewis County, and Michael Reuter, Tremont, Illinois. Joseph Bella, a Hungarian who was an early American Elder, may have served briefly in America during the decade of the 1860's, but his exact arrival in America is unknown.

Subsequent to these few early Elders, approximately 152 men have served as Elders in the church in America through the end of 1983. The Elder Body (also called the Council of Elders), the highest council of the church, reached its highest number to date in 1982 when fifty active Elders were serving in this body at the time of the annual conference in August.

Rudolph Witzig of Gridley, Illinois, holds the longest tenure as Elder, having served as a Shepherd for fifty-three years. Ordained an Elder in 1859 at Zurich, Switzerland, he came to America in 1883 and served as Elder until his death in 1912.

In the early days in America, the churches were scattered across several states. Although deeply united in the spirit of brotherhood and likemindedness, difficult travel conditions and comparatively less-developed modes of communication resulted in a lesser degree of administrative cohesion than exists in the latter decades of the twentieth century. Meetings among Elders were called only when the severity of church problems dictated a council meeting. Also, due to a lack of pluralism in those days, society was more accustomed to following authority, and problems that vex and confuse today's church were not as prevalent then—problems which often arise because of the pluralism fostered by today's educational system.

Life back then revolved mostly around farming, and hence was simpler and free of many of the problems encountered by today's post-rural society. Consequently, the frequency of church councils was considerably less than today.

Special convocations of brethren were held occasionally in Switzerland during the time of Samuel Froehlich. Problems of the church were discussed at these councils. The threats and subtle persecution of the state church were real, and solutions needed to be found for these problems.

The earliest known "brother meeting" in the United States occurred on August 20, 1866, at Leo, Indiana. Henry Geistlich, a visiting Elder from Meilen, Switzerland, noted the occasion: "Brothers were assembled from far and near. We opened our assembly with singing and prayer. We talked about many important things concerning the welfare of the church. On the whole, this was a blessed day."[2]

Subsequent meetings of Elders were called periodically to address specific problems. Eventually, as travel and communications improved and the church grew larger, church officials began to meet annually. On October 11, 1944, at Elgin, Illinois, lay brethren convened for the first time with the Elders following the former's earlier meetings.[3]

The Elder conference held January 14 and 15, 1942, at Rittman, Ohio, was an important one in that the Elders issued their first written report based on the precedent found in

Acts 15. This "memorandum" to the churches summarized the conclusions of the Elders relative to worldly threats faced by the membership. The first two paragraphs read:[4]

> All true Christians and members of the body of Christ feel most grateful for their adoption as the sons and daughters of the Most High God, realize that they are saved by grace and out of love, and that their service and devotion to their Lord must also proceed out of a heart of love. Therefore such service, devotion and obedience is not compulsory, but voluntary.
>
> Yet at the same time they realize that their liberty may not be used as an occasion to the flesh, and that the Spirit must rule, and the flesh be held in subjection. The separation from the world must continue if we are to continue as God's people, and we cannot have fellowship with the world if we would have fellowship with God.

The Elders adopted a planned agenda for their meeting in 1969 at Morris, Minnesota.[5] As the personal occupations of the Elders included more businessmen and administrators, their meetings became more organized and structured.

Each year, following their summer meeting, a report is drafted into letter form and read in each church by two or more Shepherds. Such a letter, following the example of Acts 15:23, fosters cohesion, likemindedness, and a deep sense of brotherhood among the various churches.

In 1970 the Elders began holding mid-year meetings on an annual basis. These winter meetings were in addition to their meetings held each summer. The site of the first meeting was Elgin, Illinois.

The "general conference" has always been a grand experience. With all church Elders together in attendance with brethren from nearly every congregation, this one-day conclave, following the two-day Elder meetings, is one of inspirational speaking and outstanding general exhortation. The beliefs and traditions of the church are unreservedly promoted, and strong encouragement is given to the present generation to pass on to the next generation what the church's forefathers have preserved from the past.

For many the annual conference is one of the spiritual highlights of the year. It is a great "coming together" to reflect on the beliefs and pathways of the church. It serves to stir up the spirit, to fortify and reinforce the doctrinal stand of the church, and to define and promote the cause of unity among the brotherhood.

The "general conference" at Bluffton, Indiana, on August 23, 1974, was one of the largest in the church's history. Over fifteen hundred persons were in attendance. The beautiful singing, inspirational exhortations, and deep sense of camaraderie were very prevalent and prompted Arthur Foote of Rockville, Connecticut, who with his brother Paul was attending his first conference, to exclaim, "This is overwhelming!"

It is a memorable and deeply moving experience to hear more than one thousand men at these annual conferences blend their voices in singing such moving hymns as "Lord Jesus Thou Art King" and "The Watchmen's Call." Another special moment comes at the end of the conference when brethren often join together in the beautiful song, "Unity":

237. UNITY
(From the *Zion's Harp*)

1. Thus u-nit-ed And in con-cord Let us walk the path of life; Hand in hand, O may love bind us For each oth-er's wel-fare strive.
2. Thus it is our Sav-iour's pleas-ure, As His foot-prints plain-ly show. May God's love, our great-est treas-ure, Rich-ly ev-'ry heart be-stow.
3. On-ly He is called a broth-er Whom the tie of love does bind; And the love of God, the Fa-ther, Fill-eth soul and heart and mind.
4. With the love of God in-spi-red, There is joy for us on earth; May the Spir-it, we've ac-qui-red, Grant us bless-ing, peace and mirth.

The 1983 Brotherhood Meeting was held at Gridley, Illinois. This aerial photo shows the parking lot filled to capacity. These annual meetings are very inspirational and serve to promote the cause of unity among the brethren.

Men Who Have Served as Elders in the Apostolic Christian Church of America

A

Philemon Aeschliman,
    Cissna Park, Illinois
Samuel Aeschliman,
    Bluffton, Indiana

John Anliker, West Bend, Iowa
Samuel Anliker, Lamont, Kansas
Heinrich Arlt,
    Union City, New Jersey

B

Peter Bach,
    North Side (Forrest), Illinois
Alfred Bahler, Wolcott, Indiana
Arthur Bahler, Fairbury, Illinois
Corbin Bahler,
    Rockville, Connecticut
John Bahler, Rockville, Connecticut
Robert Bahler, Remington, Indiana
Joel A. Banwart, Sr., West Bend, Iowa
Paul Banwart, West Bend, Iowa
Raymond Banwart,
    Fort Scott, Kansas

Noah Bauman, Rittman, Ohio
Jesse Beer, Milford, Indiana
Theo Beer, Milford, Indiana
Joseph Bella, Sardis, Ohio
David Bertsch, Leo, Indiana
Eugene Bertschi, Roanoke, Illinois
Philip Beyer, Naumburg, New York
Robert Beyer, Naumburg, New York
Joe J. Braker, Morton, Illinois
Andrew J. Braun, Toledo, Ohio
Joshua Broquard, Fairbury, Illinois
Paul Butikofer, Elgin, Iowa

D

Elias Dotterer, Junction, Ohio

Henry Dotterer, Junction, Ohio

E

Jacob Edelman, Bern, Kansas
Willis Ehnle, Shioda, Japan
Dale Eisenmann, Chicago, Illinois

John Eisenmann,
    Cissna Park, Illinois
Samuel Engwiller, Mansfield, Ohio

F

Roy Farney, Phoenix, Arizona
Conrad Fehr, Roanoke, Illinois
Paul Fehr, Morris, Minnesota
Wayne Fehr, West Bend, Iowa

Ezra Feller, Cissna Park, Illinois
Albert Fisher, Chicago, Illinois
Edward Frank, La Crosse, Indiana

G

Isaac Gehring, Sardis, Ohio
Christian Gerber, Fairbury, Illinois
Christian Gerber,
    Rockville, Connecticut
Joe A. Getz, Morton, Illinois
Ludwig Getz, Tremont, Illinois
Ernest Gleichman, Harper, Kansas
Ernest Graf, Sr., Akron, Ohio
Rudolph Graf, Akron, Ohio

George M. Gramm, Gridley, Illinois
Fred Grimm, Taylor, Missouri
Robert Grimm, Goodfield, Illinois
Roy Grimm, Taylor, Missouri
Emanuel Gudeman,
    Cissna Park, Illinois
Wendell Gudeman,
    Francesville, Indiana
Phillip Gutwein, Sr.,
    Francesville, Indiana

H

Adam Hartman, Bluffton, Indiana
Lester Hartter, Bern, Kansas
Noah Hartzler, Rittman, Ohio
Edwin Hohulin, Goodfield, Illinois

Jacob Honegger, North Side
    (Forrest), Illinois
Joseph Huber, Gridley, Kansas
Leroy Huber, Eureka, Illinois
Sam Huber, Sabetha, Kansas

I

Adam Imthurn, Archbold, Ohio
Joseph Ingold, Sardis, Ohio

Akito Inoue, Tokyo, Japan
Urs Isch, Rockville, Connecticut

K

William Kaufman,
    Silverton, Oregon
Herman Kellenberger, Elgin, Illinois
David Kieser, Princeville, Illinois
Henry Kilgus, Forrest, Illinois
Carl Kinsinger, Altadena, California

  Joseph Klopfenstein
    Gridley, Illinois
Carl Knapp, Tremont, Illinois
Daniel Koch, Tremont, Illinois
Henry Koehl, Morris, Minnesota
Christian Kropf, Pulaski, Iowa
Gottlieb Kurz, Harper, Kansas

L

Edward Lanz, Oakville, Iowa
John Laubscher,
    Cissna Park, Illinois
Irvin Lehman, Wolcott, Indiana

Rudolph Leuthold, North Side
    (Forrest), Illinois
Silas Leuthold, Princeville, Illinois
Rudolph Locher, Sabetha, Kansas

M

Ben C. Maibach, Jr., Detroit,
    Michigan
Gottlieb Maibach, Bay City,
    Michigan
David Mangold, Roanoke, Illinois
G. M. Mangold, Roanoke, Illinois
Michael Mangold, Roanoke, Illinois

Eugene Marti, Lamar, Missouri
Wilhelm Matthes, Mansfield, Ohio
Harold Messner, Winthrop, Minnesota
August Mogler, Lester, Iowa
Lavoyd Moore, Athens, Alabama
Leo Moser, Lester, Iowa

N

Ronald V. Nelson, Kiowa, Kansas

Arthur H. Nohl, Morris, Minnesota

P

Eugene Pamer, Akron, Ohio

John Plattner, Sabetha, Kansas

R

Otto Ramseyer, Bay City, Michigan
Joseph Ramsier, Rittman, Ohio
Andrew Rapp, Morton, Illinois
Barthol Rapp, Morton, Illinois
Russell Rapp, Morton, Illinois
Carl Rassi, Morton, Illinois
Gottfried Rauch, Bluffton, Indiana

John Adam Reeb, Cissna Park, Illinois
Michael Reuter, Tremont, Illinois
Edwin Ringger, Gridley, Illinois
Orville Ringger, Bluffton, Indiana
Stephen C. Rinkenberger,
    Cissna Park, Illinois
Daniel Roth, Fairbury, Illinois

S

Donald F. Sauder, Roanoke, Illinois
Roy Sauder, Peoria, Illinois
George Schambach, Elgin, Illinois
Eugene Schladenhauffen,
    Cissna Park, Illinois
John W. Schmidt, Peoria Illinois*
Noah Schrock, Oakville, Iowa
Emil Schubert, Peoria, Illinois
Richard Schupbach,
    Phoenix, Arizona
Henry Schwier, Mansfield, Ohio
George Sinn, Latty, Ohio

Jacob Somerhalder, Gridley, Kansas
Sigmund Sorg, Mansfield, Ohio
Henry Souder, Sr., Leo, Indiana
Aaron Steffen, Alto, Michigan
Nathan Steffen, Elgin, Illinois
John Steidinger, Fairbury, Illinois
Martin Steidinger, Fairbury, Illinois
Norbert Steiner, Croghan, New York
Jacob Stettner, Elgin, Illinois
William Stettner, Elgin, Illinois
Loren Stoller, Latty, Ohio

---

*John W. Schmidt served mostly as an assistant Elder. His daughter's diary indicated he was made an Elder at Peoria, Illinois, but church records were unable to confirm this.

T

John Trittenbach,
   Rockville, Connecticut

V

Alpheus Virkler,
   Croghan, New York
Andrew E. Virkler,
   Bay City, Michigan**
Joseph Virkler,
   Lewis County, New York

Peter Virkler,
   Lewis County, New York
Solomon Virkler,
   Lewis County, New York

W

Joseph Waibel, Bay City, Michigan
Robert Walder, Congerville, Illinois
George Welk, Morton, Illinois
Benedict Weyeneth, Roanoke, Illinois
John Widrick, Croghan, New York

Elias Winzeler, Tremont, Illinois
Joseph Wittmer, Bern, Kansas
Rudolph Witzig, Gridley, Illinois
Frank Woertz, Goodfield, Illinois

Y

George Yergler, La Crosse, Indiana   John Yergler, Bluffton, Indiana

Z

Michael Zimmerman,
   Congerville, Illinois

Perry Zimmerman, Forrest, Illinois

**Another Andrew Virkler of Croghan, New York, served as an ordained deacon for 50 years.

HISTORY OF WORSHIP AND LITURGY

Since the church's beginning in Europe in the 1830's the worship service has always been characterized by simplicity, dignity, reverence, and spirit-filled preaching. Ceremony, ritual, and detailed liturgy, which can often detract the parishioner from the truth of the gospel, have always been noticeably absent from Apostolic Christian worship. A dual principle deeply associated with worship is that the Lord is an unseen guest at every service and nothing should be done that might draw attention away from Him. Rather, all emphasis is meant to glorify His high and holy name.

The order of worship has remained essentially unchanged down through the years (and in the various countries). This has occurred despite the fact that no written liturgy has ever been prescribed by the church. The worship pattern followed for more than 150 years reflects both depth and simplicity:

---

1. Congregational singing before service begins (call to worship).

2. A moment of silent prayer after ministers take their places on the pulpit.

3. First Scripture reading (referred to as the "forereading").

4. Hymn, announced by minister.

5. Prayer, offered by minister.

6. Second Scripture reading (referred to as the "text" for ensuing sermon).

7. Sermon, spoken as led by the Holy Spirit.

8. Second minister confirms and supports essence of first minister's sermon.

9. Hymn, announced by second minister or lay brother.

10. Prayer, offered by second (or other) minister, or lay brother.

11. Announcements, worship service adjourns.

When a minister announces a song from the pulpit, he often reads a few verses before the congregation sings it. This is a tradition that comes from the Mennonites. Wenger, in *The Mennonite Church in America,* describes this practice as it took place in Pennsylvania: "In the nineteenth century the minister would announce a hymn after entering the pulpit, and then 'line' it, that is, he would read about two lines, which the church then sang, then read two more lines, and the singing would resume—thus through four or six stanzas. This was probably done in the eighteenth century due to a scarcity of hymn books."[6]

Preaching is conducted only by ministers of the church who are selected by the local congregations. Delivery of sermons is extemporaneous as revealed by the Holy Spirit. Although sermons are not prepared beforehand, ministers give themselves daily to much prayer and the studying of God's Word.

Singing during worship is "a capella" which adds further dignity to the service. Male "leaders," using "pitch-pipes" or "tuning forks," begin the songs and lead the congregation until several verses are completed. Singing during worship is from the *Zion's Harp* hymnal.

All women members of the church, as well as recently converted women who have not yet been baptized, wear a head covering during regular services. This is a black open net veil draped over the head. This practice is based on Scripture found in I Corinthians 11.

The church has always used the King James Version of the Bible for English language services. The language of the liturgy in prayer has always been consistent with the elegance of the King James Version in that God is referred to as "Thee, Thou, Thy, and Thine." Hymnals, too, refer to God in this manner. It is felt that this form of English shows a deeper reverence for God and a greater respect for the Creator-creature relationship than everyday language such as "You and Your." It is also much more coordinate with the church's intent to collectively come prostrate before God to make oblation and petition.

During prayer in the sanctuary, parishioners kneel forward, resting their arms on the back of the benches in front of them. In former days many members would turn around, kneel, and rest their arms on their own bench. In the latter stages of the twentieth century, during weddings and funerals, the congregation stands during prayer.

Men and women sit separately during worship. This is a centuries-old tradition reaching back to early Christianity. It was also practiced in Jewish worship in the Temple where men and women were separated by a partition or a form of lattice-work. It was universally practiced in Christianity until approximately a century ago.

Following the Sunday morning worship service, a "noon lunch" is served consisting of coffee and doughnuts (sometimes sandwiches are included), and a time of enjoyable fellowship ensues for an hour or so. An afternoon worship service is held using the same format as the morning service. A different minister usually conducts the afternoon service unless a visiting minister is present. Members are expected to attend both worship services, and except for illness or unusual circumstances, nearly all members do.

The worship service, conducted with a distinct tone of dignity and godly reverence, is void of flourish, special entertainments, choirs, guitarists, or scheduled "events" to draw people into the assembly. Rather, the opening of Scriptures which are "quick, and powerful, and sharper than any two-edged sword" and the preaching of the gospel of salvation provide a comforting appeal to the truly converted as well as a stirring reminder to the unconverted to seek the Lord. There are no "altar calls" even though strong appeal is made for repentance and conversion of the sinner.

Offerings are not made by passing a collection plate as in most other protestant churches. Instead, "charity boxes" are attached to walls in the churches' hallways, and individuals may place money or checks in these boxes after the service. All giving is done on a "free-will" basis as the giver feels led by the Holy Spirit.

Although the principle of "plainness" has prevailed in the construction of church buildings, the churches' assembly rooms are comfortable and convenient (and by the latter stages of the twentieth century, quite expensive); they are, however, bare of relics, images, elaborate artwork, and other eye-appealing detractions which were a major feature of many churches in the pre-Reformation era.

To fully understand the worship service of the Apostolic Christian Church, one must view it in the context of worship of the first century Christian church and during the time of the Reformation.

At the time of the early church, pagans criticized the Christians for their lack of "temples" and "images." Mostly, believers met in homes. In Rome, they sometimes worshipped in burial caves under the city called catacombs in order to escape the wrath and persecution of civil and religious authorities. Services were simple and centered on the pure Word of God.

As Christianity grew and eventually became international in scope, the church in many places became apostate. Large cathedrals and intricate liturgies began to overshadow the true meaning of worship. It seemed that liturgy was deemed more important than life. In addition, images, relics, statues, etc. became prevalent in many of these churches. Finally, the sad and deplorable spiritual state of the church resulted in the Reformation of 1517 which jolted all of Europe for several years, and whose influence is still felt today through the Christian world.

A major change brought about by the Reformation was found in the form of worship. It centered on the Word of God. Anabaptist concepts of worship, which eventually influenced Samuel Froehlich early in the nineteenth century, later found their way into the Apostolic Christian Church. The *Mennonite Encyclopedia* vividly summarizes these worship concepts:[7]

> In contrast to the general Reformation doctrine that the church comes to expression when the Word is preached and the sacraments properly observed, the Anabaptists believed that the "true church is raised up" where "faith, spirit, and power" result in "repentance and change of life" and obedience to the truth. Hence the Anabaptists placed little emphasis in formal public worship or ceremonies, and rejected all liturgy. Persecution, which made meetings difficult and often dangerous, gave added support to this basic attitude. The Anabaptists did not come from a week of irreligious, worldly living and expect a beautiful building and attractive liturgy to draw them to God. They insisted that the Christian walks with God constantly in holy obedience and expected their daily life to come naturally to a climax in the fellowship of the gathered community of disciples, where a major concern was to seek the will of God from His Word and to help one another to higher levels of discipleship.

In such worship a common searching of life was involved, and discipline naturally resulted, often carried through as a supplement to the regular worship. The fact that several ministers served the group in Bible reading, admonition, and prayer, and that services were not held in large church buildings but in homes or barns, in forest retreats, or even caves, in addition to the understanding that every member was a responsible adult who had chosen to follow Christ and shared fully in the life of the brotherhood, added to the intense sense of participation by all. Hence, Anabaptist congregations were not "audiences" in attendance upon a worship service furnished by a clergyman in a building belonging to the state and used for nothing else, but a genuine brotherhood sharing in Bible study, prayer, and mutual admonition. The high authority of the Bible, of course, placed it in the very center of the service, and the reading and exposition of it, or admonition from it, was the most important element. In a sense, life was more important than worship.

Because the Lord is viewed as the ultimate in holiness and righteousness and Scriptures exhort the believer to "Be ye holy; for I am holy,"[8] worship is conducted with a high degree of sobriety and rectitude. This is intended to both symbolize and reflect the church's deep respect for God's holiness.

HYMNALS AND SINGING

Singing has always played an important part in the liturgy of the church. From its inception, the church has always included sacred hymns—sung in "a capella" fashion—in its worship services. To maintain a dignified reverence while making melody to the Lord through song, the church has retained a tradition that is a credit to its liturgy—that of using only what they consider sacred and holy music.

Because church music is sung without instrumental accompaniment, an atmosphere of holiness, calmness and richness is created. The absence of a piano or organ results in greater personal participation during hymnsinging. Consequently, the Apostolic Christian Church is a "church of singers." In connection with this, singing is not necessarily intended to be artistic, but a testimony to the praise and glory of God.

The *Zion's Harp* hymnal is the official hymnal of the Apostolic Christian Church. Its songs are vivid confessions of faith and relate to a variety of themes experienced by the believer. The depth of the songs' lyrics provides moving spiritual enrichment for the parishioners. The hymnal has a very interesting history.

The *Zion's Harp* hymnal has cut through a wide swath of time. While it is true that distribution of the official, bound copies of the book we now recognize commenced only in the middle of the nineteenth century in Europe, fragments of the hymnal's contents, both the hymns and the musical compositions, date as far back as the fifteenth century before the inception of the Protestant Reformation which began in 1517.

The *Zion's Harp,* as known today, was first printed during the years 1853-1854 on the request of Samuel Froehlich in Switzerland.[9] Up until this time, various booklets and compilations of hymns had been used in one form or another in the meetings of the Evangelical Baptists.

To obtain a more general understanding of the actual beginning of this beloved and cherished hymnal, one must go back to the early stages of the nineteenth century.

On November 11, 1764, a little baby girl was born in the Russian town of Riga.[10] This Latvian city today has a population of over 600,000. The girl's name was Juliane von Vietinghoff. She was the daughter of Herman von Vietinghoff, a Russian imperial privy councilor, a man of rationalistic views and a leading freemason, and of his wife, Anna Ulrica, a strict Lutheran.

After a fashionable education she was married at age seventeen to Baron von Kruedener on September 23, 1782. He was then the first Russian minister at the court of Courland. The marriage proved to be an unhappy one since the husband was conscientious and retiring while the wife was restless, flirtatious, and given to frequenting the cosmopolitan fashion centers of the world.

Her husband died on June 11, 1802. Meanwhile, the baroness took to the task of writing a novel. It took her two years to complete. It was published in 1804 and was highly regarded. This tended to confirm that she was a very capable individual, well-educated, and talented in the art of communication. Her personality, too, was such that people were easily attracted to her.

She lived a free lifestyle and eventually found herself far from God. During a sojourn in Riga in the summer of 1804, Juliane experienced conversion, an occurrence which nothing in her past life seemed to make probable. Her experience was deep, the change in her life profound. In language we can readily understand, she experienced a "true repentance."

Yet, from this time forth, a seemingly unwholesome, nervous "religiosity" came to be the dominant element in her character, and through its extravagance, reflected a cloudy mysticism like that of the Chiliasts of Baden, Alsace, and Wurttemberg with whom she cultivated relations of intimacy.

An interesting footnote to the history of Baroness Juliane von Kruedener is that she attempted to convert the czar of Russia. In 1815 she was granted an audience with Czar Alexander which lasted for three hours at Heilbronn. So captivating was this woman that he became a constant "guest" at her Bible classes in Heidelberg and Paris. Before long, however, Alexander turned away from his new friend whose persisting associations with unsalutory elements rendered him distrustful.

Her repentance, having occurred at the outset of the nineteenth century came about at a time in which much theological change and maneuvering still lingered in Europe. It was a time when the Reformed churches were continuing to be threatened by "pietistic" and "Anabaptist" groups who were opposed to a dead orthodoxy. Essentially, the authority and influence of the protestant state churches were on the wane—they had been since the early seventeenth century.

Replacing them, to a degree, was the further development of the "free church," which among other things challenged the concept of the union of church and state. The free church also encouraged the doctrines of sanctity, repentance, adult baptism, coming out from the world and living a life of holiness, and a literal interpretation of the Bible.

In any event, Frau Kruedener's conversion and subsequent experiences were such that she felt the need to be an active worker in the Lord's vineyard. As a matter of fact, she became an "evangelist," at least according to her view of what she felt an evangelist was.

Obviously, in nineteenth century Europe, the fact of a woman evangelist carried with it quite a social stigma. Indeed today, and justifiably so, the notion of a woman minister carries with it the same stigma. Even so, Frau Kruedener was actively engaged in the work of an "evangelist," social stigma notwithstanding. In this realm, she faced two-fold opposition because of her actions. First, she conducted religious meetings outside the legally sanctioned Reformed Church. Second, she presented herself as a woman minister. Both were an anathema at that time. In spite of this she had many devout followers, not only among the peasantry, but in the intellectual community as well. One influential supporter was Friedrich Lachenal, Professor of Logic and Metaphysics at the University of Basel.

Frau Kruedener traveled extensively throughout Switzerland conducting Bible study sessions and worship meetings. She personally financed many projects to aid this work. One such project was the collection and printing of hymns to be used in her church and Bible meetings.

Why was it necessary to collect new hymns? First, in the context of religion in those days, the relationship between the established and legally sanctioned protestant state churches and those outside this church (i.e., the "free churches") was a partisan and combative one, and blatant disobedience to the will of the state church was often met with force and persecution, and if not, at least harassment was prevalent. This situation was nothing new in Europe, for a similar dispute arose three hundred years earlier between Ulrich Zwingli, an avowed Protestant and a leader of the original Protestant Reformation (but a firm supporter of the state-church concept) and Conrad Grebel, a noted leader of the often ill-fated Anabaptist movement.

Several public debates took place between these men who held to differing religious views. In fact, these differing views still lingered centuries later in the time of Frau Kruedener, and in large part still exist today.

Thus, in this context of strife and conflict, the use of a hymnal of the established state church outside one of their official services was prohibited. As a result, it became necessary for those holding their own "independent" religious meetings to print hymns to be used in these meetings, which in essence were considered outside the official sanction of the state church and consequently illegal. Frau Kruedener saw this need, and along with her followers, acted accordingly. So, the gathering of special hymns began, and these then eventually found their way into the *Zion's Harp.*

By 1817, the great need for songs to be used in "outside" religious meetings led Frau Kruedener to publish a small hymnal. It was small indeed and could hardly be considered a hymnal according to today's standards. Three songs were chosen at the outset.[11] They were printed on two sheets, and 500 copies of this "hymnal" were made.[12] The collection bore no title. Frau Kruedener financed the effort with help on the initial project by Johann Jacob Vetter (1789-1871).

From this first effort, Vetter later compiled some hymns into a publication entitled *Begginger Buchlein*. It was named for the Swiss village of Begginger. The exact publishing date is not known.

In time, a hymnal called the *Christliche Harmonika* was completed by Johann Vetter. This extended version of the *Begginger Buchlein* was the first to contain melodies. It is assumed that Vetter wrote some of the songs included in this hymnal. The exact publication date is not known, but records indicate that by 1828, D. F. Spitteler printed the fifth edition.

The fifth edition of the *Harmonika* (1828) was published together with a group of hymns collected and admired by S. H. Froehlich. Further, at this time, Froehlich made another collection of hymns that he later published along with those already bound with the *Harmonika*. This volume bore no title. According to the late author Herman Ruegger, it was simply called a collection of "hymns for meetings of believers." This volume was printed in four editions between 1828 and 1853 by Karl Weuterich-Guardard in Zurich, Switzerland.

During 1852-1853, a new version of this hymnal was printed and named *Neue Zionsharfe*. It was printed separately from the *Harmonika,* but 182 hymns from the latter were included. G. M. Mangold, a member of Froehlich's Evangelical Baptist Church, had been commissioned to compile this edition of the hymnal. Sources indicate that Froehlich himself gave the commission.

Since 1854, several editions of the *Zion's Harp* have been published both in Europe and the United States.

In the decade of the 1920's, the *Zion's Harp* was translated from the German to the English language. This was somewhat controversial at that time because a large share of the membership was either from Europe or had close ties to that continent. Nonetheless, the monumental task of translation took place.

Henry Beer, an Apostolic Christian minister from Milford, Indiana, played an instrumental role in this effort. As a young brother-in-faith in 1921, he thought it would be beneficial to translate these songs into English. After translating a few songs on his own, he sought and received encouragement from some of the older brethren to continue on. Ernest Graf, Sr., of Akron, Ohio, especially encouraged translation into English according to Beer.

Among the first hymns that Beer translated were No. 47, "Strive Aright;" No. 164, "The Image of Christ;" and No. 89, "The Seven Words of Jesus on the Cross."

On completing the translation of these hymns, Beer officially sought and received the sanction of the church leadership to translate the remaining hymns into English. Several other brothers were assigned to help with this herculean task. They included:

> Ernest Graf, Sr., Akron, Ohio
> Edward Grimm, Elgin, Iowa
> Amos Hartzler, Rittman, Ohio
> Noah Hartzler, Rittman, Ohio
> Will Stettner, Elgin, Illinois
> Jake Stettner, Elgin, Illinois

This was a huge task and took considerable time. Each brother was given approximately fifty songs to work on. The two Stettners worked as a team. The *Zion's Harp* was thus published in the English language in 1924.

Because the songs of the German *Zion's Harp* had such profound meaning, it was felt English-speaking people should not be deprived of this benefit.

The *Zion's Harp* is printed in many other languages: Serbian, Hungarian, Rumanian, and Spanish. A sister in the church in Japan is translating the hymnal into Japanese.

In the 1920's, when translation into English was initiated, three hundred stanzas were eliminated. They were reinstated in the 1958 revision because many members of the church use the hymnal as a devotional book for inspirational reading as well as for singing. The three hundred stanzas were obtained in 1958 from the Apostolic Christian Church (Nazarene) because they were already translated into English.

Henry Beer, who labored diligently on the translation of the *Zion's Harp,* commented, "The *Zion's Harp* is not the oldest hymnal in the world, but it is by far the most doctrinal. A hymnal reflects a church's soundness of faith." [13]

In 1958, the *Zion's Harp* was revised to include music with every text, thus eliminating leafing back and forth between the text and the music.

In order to set in motion a plan to revise the *Zion's Harp* hymnal, a somewhat lengthy and deliberative process took place. In the late 1940's and early 1950's there existed feeling among certain brethren that a revision was needed to improve the hymnal and make it more practical.

By 1954, Raymond Gerber, a song leader of the Bluffton, Indiana, congregation, and others favored the idea of placing music to each song, thus making it easier for the song leaders to lead the congregation. This idea was representative of many brethren across the land.

As a first move, Gerber posed the suggestion to Elder Sam Aeschliman of Bluffton who immediately concurred. His favorable response gave much courage to those brethren concerned with the need for a revision and ultimately provided the momentum to initiate the project.

Gerber then discussed the proposed project with his close associate, John H. Baumgartner, also a song leader in the large Bluffton congregation. On the basis of their visits and their discussions with other brethren, they decided it might be well to call a meeting of song leaders from various congregations for the purpose of discussing the need and plausibility of a revision. Invited along with many other song leaders was minister Henry Beer of Milford, Indiana. Although the latter was a minister, it was felt he was well qualified in the field of music. Also, his enthusiasm and poetic credentials would be helpful.

Word was thus sent to many song leaders to attend a conclave in Cissna Park, Illinois, on September 10, 1954. They were advised to bring their ministers or any other brethren they wished. Cissna Park was chosen because of its central location. Approximately 110 brethren attended the meeting.

A presentation was made regarding a proposed hymnal revision. This was followed by a lengthy discussion. About ninety-nine percent of those in attendance favored a revision.

This left only the question as to "how to proceed." Sam Wieland of Bay City, Michigan, made a motion that John H. Baumgartner, Elias Souder, Eli Gerber, and Raymond Gerber transmit the consensus of the meeting to the Elders. The motion was seconded by Henry Rapp of Morton, Illinois. The motion carried.

The proposal for a major revision of the *Zion's Harp* was presented to the Elder Body at the annual conference in October, 1954, at Elgin, Illinois. At this meeting, the Elders requested that a more in-depth proposal be submitted at the following year's conference.

At the 1955 Annual Conference, it was advised that further work and review were needed, and that consideration of proposed changes would be deferred to a future date.

The revision committee met with the Elder Body at the 1956 Annual Conference in Morton, Illinois. Subsequently, the matter of a revision was permitted to be brought before the plenary session of the conference. On hearing the basic concepts of a revision, the general conference favored improvements in the hymnal.

A committee of Elders was appointed to oversee the developments of a revision: Philip Beyer of Croghan, New York; William Stettner of Elgin, Illinois; and Rudolph Graf of Akron, Ohio. Elders Sam Aeschliman of Bluffton and Theo Beer of Milford, Indiana, also served in an advisory capacity.

A church-wide referendum was held, and the brotherhood voted in favor of the revision.

Serving on the songbook committee (or revision committee) were Raymond Gerber, Eli Gerber, and John Baumgartner, Bluffton; Fred Gutwein, Francesville; and Henry Beer, Milford, Indiana; and Jesse Gerber, Latty, Ohio. With the exception of Henry Beer, who was a minister, all were song leaders in their local congregations.

The task of supplying melodies for all the hymn texts was long and arduous. These brethren applied themselves with diligence and often toiled at night, many times burning the "midnight oil." Prior to publication, the revision committee met with the aforementioned Elders regarding the approval or disapproval of each song. In 1958, editions of the revised hymnal were distributed to the churches.

By 1976, several new faces appeared on the songbook committee: Daryl Stoller, Latty, Ohio; Henry Souder, Leo; and Jay Kipfer, Bluffton, Indiana, replaced Jesse Gerber, Eli Souder, and John H. Baumgartner, all of whom had passed on to their reward.

This committee continues to meet several times each year—usually in Fort Wayne, Indiana—to discuss matters relevant to the *Zion's Harp*.

The *Silver Lining* (Vol. 9, No. 1) described the 1958 revised hymnal, "The new book will have a melody with every song, and every song will be on a single opening to eliminate leafing over. The first three or four stanzas will be placed in the staff. There will be some 50 new melodies.

"The book will be 5½ x 7½ inches in size with rounded corners, covered with black sturdite, printed on 40 pound paper. The price will be $1.75 for white edge, and $2.20 for gold edge."

The printing of the new hymnal was done by the Berne Witness Company of Berne, Indiana.

Since 1958, one revision has taken place.

In the church's early days it was customary for members to carry their *Zion's Harp* hymnal to church. Often their name would be engraved on the front. This practice lasted well into the twentieth century. It generally ceased when church benches were constructed to provide bookholders.

Another important hymnal used in the Apostolic Christian Church in the early days was the *Heftli* or "long book" (*Heftli* means "little booklet"). This auxiliary hymnal was used mostly in Sunday School and in the home. The hymns from this book were translated into the English language by Elder Ernest Graf. Initially, it contained fifty-five hymns in the German language. The English version contained seventy-five hymns.

The *Heftli* was succeeded by the *Hymns of Zion* for use in Sunday School. The former hymnal has remained in the hands of many brethren, mostly as a relic. It is, however, a delight to sing occasionally (in the home) from the old "long books."

The *Hymns of Zion* consists of songs from the *Heftli,* from other European devotional hymnals, from other American Protestant traditional hymnals, and a few poems from Henry Beer's *My Garden of Verse* which were set to music. Because he was instrumental in compiling the *Hymns of Zion,* it is often referred to as the "Henry Beer book." Fred Gutwein of Francesville, Indiana, helped Beer select songs to be added to the *Hymns of Zion*.

Henry Beer authored the hymn, "The Babe of Bethlehem" (page 36, *Hymns of Zion*) in the 1950's. As a florist, he noted how worldly people put up nativity displays at Christmas. To them the displays apparently had little meaning, and there was no representation of the Cross of Christ. So he wrote a song about it. This is one of the most popular "Christmas carols" in the Apostolic Christian Church.

THE BABE OF BETHLEHEM

H. B.　　　　　M. Y. R.

1. The bless - ed sto - ry of the Christ, The babe of Beth - le - hem,
2. Our sav - ing hope is all in vain, If here our love should cease,
3. Be not con - tent this babe to know, Nor stay at Beth - le - hem,

Is wor - thy of our song and praise. And stirs the hearts of men.
For in the man of Gal - i - lee. We find the gift of peace.
But go with Christ to Cal - vary's brow, Be - yond Je - ru - sa - lem.

The full - ness of God's love di - vine, sur - rounds the Christ so mild
'Tis not the babe, but Christ, the man Who walked in Gal - i - lee;
'Tis there men learn to know the Christ, For there He bore man's sin.

A - las how man - y on - ly know The Sav - iour as a child.
'Tis not the man - ger, but the cross, That sets the spir - it free.
Then o - pen wide the door of heart. And let the Sav - iour in.

The first edition of the *Hymns of Zion* was published with ninety songs. The second edition had 192 songs. The third edition in 1958 contained 301 songs. Up until 1977 Henry Beer sold 35,000 copies of this hymnal. In the late 1970's Apostolic Christian Publishing took over distribution of the *Hymns of Zion* and *Heftli* songbooks.

A few other hymnals have been used by members of the church. *Tabernacle Hymns* has been used by some of the churches for Sunday School and noon hour singing. It is published by the Tabernacle Publishing Company, Wheaton, Illinois.

The *Gospel Hymns,* an 841-page hymnal published by the Gospel Hymn Publishing Company, Grabill, Indiana, has often been used for special "singings," especially by young people.

The *Melodies of Praise* and *Heavenly Highways* hymns have also been used during "singings."

* * * * *

Singing has always been a special form of worship in the Apostolic Christian Church. The brotherhood's deep reverence for God and its strongly held doctrinal beliefs have always been reflected in their hymns. By the 1970's and 1980's, the church could readily recognize the vast difference in the sacred and reverent hymns found in their hymnals compared to the more "modern" and "contemporary" church music that swept across the country with undue popularity.

"SINGINGS"

In keeping with its image as a "singing church," the Apostolic Christian Church has retained a tradition over the years in which various members assemble (usually in homes) and sing hymns. In the German language, it was called a *"Singstunde"* (hour of singing). In English it is referred to as a "singing."

A singing, as it is practiced in the Apostolic Christian Church, is quite unique. The form and procedure are almost exclusively considered to be vintage Apostolic Christian. A search among Christian groups which existed during the Middle Ages, the Reformation, and in modern times reveals that virtually no similarity to the Apostolic Christian style has existed. There is, however, one exception. John Hostetler in *Amish Society* refers to "singings" among Amish groups, especially among young people.[14] For the Amish, this serves not only as a social outlet, but as a foremost means of matching up young people for marriage. The Mennonite Encyclopedia further substantiates that historically, the Amish people have engaged in singings also.[15]

A "singing" as practiced by members of the church is described in the following essay:

"SINGINGS" IN THE APOSTOLIC CHRISTIAN CHURCH

The anticipation, warmth, and spontaneity of a singing all combine to make it a wonderful event, and a treasured blessing for young people (and others) in the church. All the older brothers and sisters can sentimentally look back to their youth when they attended many singings. They can recall with pleasure the pleased feelings they experienced when they heard the welcome news, either by phone or in person, that they were invited to a singing. Such an invitation assured the invited guest of an upcoming blessing among God's elect. It would help to fill in unused blocks of spare time and provide a spiritual alternative, perhaps, to many carnal beckonings. It is no different today. Singings provide a clean and wholesome activity for young believers in Christ.

A great thrill over the years, and one that is truly humbling, has been for a person to attend his first singing after he has begun his repentance. For a person who has trod through the mire of sin, who has groped in the arena of darkness, and who has borne the burden of sin for a long time to participate in a singing for the first time is like walking into a green and verdant valley. This can truly be likened to a pasture greened by the Holy Spirit of God. The peace and inspiration, prompted by the truths of God as revealed in song, are a needed and timely balm for the sinsick heart. And a singing is indeed a part of that inn where the sinner can find shelter and warmth. One is truly brought close to the heart of God—"a place where sin cannot molest." It is a marked contrast to worldly endeavors and the unfruitful works of darkness.

Singings are usually held in the homes of believers with the young believer of the home acting as host or hostess. All young, single people are invited, not just "favorites" or a "select few." Often some married adults are present as well. A beautiful point regarding these singings is the fact that unmarried believers all the way up to forty years of age or more participate, and age really is of no consequence. As believers unite in the love of God, the secular limitations of age, which often can result in cruel exclusion, are obliterated.

The singing usually begins between 7:30 and 8:00 p.m. when a brother announces the first hymn. By this time most everyone is seated and ready to begin singing, although a few are almost always a few minutes late. Brothers and sisters are seated apart as space and conditions permit. This is done to prevent distraction. This, then, results in more joyful and meaningful singing.

As the singing begins, God's presence is truly felt in a warm, tranquil, peaceful, and reverent way, for what converted soul can resist feeling peace upon hearing the beauty and substance of such phrases as: "Mercy there was great and grace was free, pardon there was multiplied to me;" "When I survey the wondrous cross;" "I am going to a city, where the roses never fade;" "When the roll is called up yonder, I'll be there;" "I'm filled with trust and confidence;" "Watch and pray that when the Master cometh;" and on and on?

The joyous singing continues for nearly an hour or more. Songs are spontaneously announced by both brothers and sisters. Usually, at mid-point, glasses of water are passed around. Mints are also sometimes passed several times during the singing.

After an hour or more, the pace slackens somewhat and a "farewell" song is announced. This is usually announced by an older brother of the young group, or by a brother from a visiting church. Favorite songs of farewell are the "Doxology," "God Be With You Till We Meet Again," and "Blest Be The Tie That Binds."

When the farewell song is concluded, the group quickly evolves into complete silence. At this time, the host brother or the father of the host sister requests that a brother read from the Bible. As the Spirit leads, it is decided who will do so. Visiting brothers are accorded first preference, but if none are present, a local brother takes the initiative. Usually only one chapter is read.

Following the reading, a request is made for a brother to lead in a closing prayer. Again, as the Spirit leads, a young brother usually says, "Let us pray," or some similar phrase, and the entire group stands for prayer.

Sisters do not participate in the act of reading aloud from the Bible, nor do they lead the group in prayer. The Church abides by the Biblical commandment that women are to be silent in church. Also, the sisters wear small headcoverings at singings which is in compliance with another New Testament teaching.

As soon as the Scripture reading and prayer are completed, a lunch may be served. Usually during the latter stages of the singing, several ladies are busy preparing the lunch in order that it might be served when the singing is completed. Fellowship and visiting occur during and after the lunch.

Singings are not held exclusively for young single people, but for other adults and all brethren as well. In these cases, the format is just about the same, save for the fact that the participants are mostly married.

Essay by Perry A. Klopfenstein

SUNDAY SCHOOL

*"Train up a child in the way he should go: and when
he is old, he will not depart from it."   Proverbs 22:6*

The above proverb serves as a motivating force for believers to teach their youth the ways of the Lord. While the church has always encouraged parents to instruct their children at home, the Christian education of the child is supplemented by classes at church each Sunday.

The Sunday School is regarded as one of the most characteristic and influential institutions in American Christianity, and this is true in the Apostolic Christian Church as well. Although classes are quietly and undramatically held Sunday after Sunday, year after year, their impact is felt and vividly manifested when souls turn to the Lord in repentance after reaching the age of accountability.

The idea of Sunday School reaches as far back as the early history of the Jewish nation. During the time of the Judges, the nation of Israel failed in properly teaching their children. The consequence was a new generation "who did not know the Lord, nor yet the work he had done for Israel. Then the sons of Israel did evil in the sight of the Lord, and they served Baalim" (Judges 2:10-11).

After their return from captivity, the nation of Israel concluded that spiritual instruction needed to be reinforced by groups outside the home. More than five hundred years before the time of Christ, synagogues were established to supplement temple worship. As these synagogues grew in influence, religious instruction continued as a primary function.[16]

The "Sunday School," generally, was instituted in Christendom by Robert Raikes in Gloucester, England, in 1780, and the idea reached Virginia as early as 1786.[17]

In the early nineteenth century, many American denominations were opposed to missions and Sunday Schools. The *Mennonite Encyclopedia* states that in 1830 a large share of the Baptists of the Middle West were anti-mission and anti-Sunday School.[18] Also, many of the more conservative elements of Mennonites have never accepted the idea of Sunday Schools.

In the Apostolic Christian Church, the idea of Sunday School has always existed and been well accepted. That it has never been a source of controversy is largely because Samuel

Froehlich and his followers in Europe embraced the idea of instruction for youth. From England the idea of Sunday School likely spread to other parts of Europe and was an accepted practice by the time of Froehlich's initial preaching. In *Apostolic Christian Church History, Volume I,* author Herman Ruegger refers to teachers in the European churches. Teaching was particularly important to them in order that the doctrine of the church (Evangelical Baptist) be clearly articulated, understood, and differentiated from the doctrine of the state church. This was also true in the United States due to the religious diversity that has always existed here.

In America the idea of spiritual instruction for children was continued by Apostolic Christians. Until about 1950, teachers—particularly Bible class teachers—served for lengthy and open-ended terms. A sizable percentage of the members were less educated than today, and many were not inclined to teach. Thus, anyone with a talent in pedagogy was kept in office for several years. For instance, William Gramm of Gridley, Illinois, taught Bible class for thirty continuous years. He tried to receive help in teaching, but was unable to do so. He retired from teaching in 1950.

As educational levels increased dramatically during the post-war period, more and more brethren were qualified and willing to teach Sunday School. In most churches during the early 1980's, teachers were voted into office and served specified terms. This resulted in a greater number of brethren serving in Sunday School.

At one time the German language and music were also taught in Sunday School in varying degrees. As the German language subsided in America during World War I, it was no longer necessary to teach it in Sunday School. As public schools began to include music in their curriculum, musical instruction was terminated in Sunday School.

Essentially, in the past few decades, the Apostolic Christian Churches have used teaching materials distributed by the Apostolic Christian Church Publishing Company in Eureka, Illinois. The Bible classes (high school students) are mostly taught from the King James Version of the Bible.

During the middle of the twentieth century, Vacation Bible School was introduced into many churches. This is a one or two-week instructional period held each summer. In connection with this, several churches include lectures on specific topics, usually given by visiting ministers. These topics are most often associated with the doctrine and traditions of the Apostolic Christian Church.

Special Sunday School programs at Christmas and Easter are presented at many of the churches.

WORLD RELIEF

In the early 1960's the increase in individual charitable activities generated much discussion within the church concerning the central coordination of these efforts. General affluence, as well as a raised consciousness relative to starvation, malnutrition and similar conditions around the world, caused many brethren to seek stronger and more organized administrative efforts to serve the poor and needy.

The matter was placed on the agenda of the Brotherhood Conference at Bluffton, Indiana, in October, 1963. A committee was subsequently formed to investigate and recommend how the church might most effectively serve in this respect. It was named the Committee on World Relief. Later, it came to be known as the World Relief Committee. Those serving on the new committee were Elder Herman Kellenberger, Elgin, Illinois, minister Henry Beer, Milford, Indiana, and layman Herman Norr, Leo, Indiana. Their immediate task was to study the feasibility of the church becoming more officially involved in direct help to the poor and needy. Early in the study it became evident to the committee that initially it would be best to give financial support to existing organizations rather than organizing a structure within the church. Accordingly, the committee chose three organizations to support financially: Heifer Project, Inc., because of its "self-help" emphasis; CARE, Inc. (Cooperative American Relief Everywhere) because of its broad geographical and non-doctrinal outreach; and the Mennonite Central Committee because of the church's general acquaintance with Mennonites. A major consideration in granting funds to these organizations was their low administrative costs and trained personnel on site to insure that contributions went to the truly needy.

Giving money to these groups was officially approved at the annual Brotherhood Conference at Tremont, Illinois, in September, 1964. Further elaboration and explanation of

World Relief policies were made to Elders, ministers, and local church representatives at a meeting on January 9, 1965, at Francesville, Indiana.

Hermann Norr, Leo, Indiana, son of minister Otto Norr (often referred to as "Father Norr"), was the one who provided the major impetus and motivation to initiate World Relief activities. According to minister James Hoerr, Peoria, Illinois, who served on the World Relief Committee for many years, Herman Norr was very instrumental in helping to establish this organization. He was creative, energetic, and patient. He worked very well with the Elder Body and was willing to receive a "no" answer to some of his proposals. It was Norr's idea to establish an Eastern and Western Division of World Relief. Arthur Gasser of Rittman, Ohio, was also an early and effective supporter of World Relief.

The World Relief Committee was soon expanded from the three original brothers to ten. These brethren were chosen to represent a broad cross-section of the entire brotherhood. By 1970, the committee consisted of the following men:

> Herman Kellenberger, Elgin, Illinois, Treasurer
> Wendell Gudeman, Francesville, Indiana
> Henry Beer, Milford, Indiana
> Arthur Gudeman, La Crosse, Indiana
> Arthur Gasser, Rittman, Ohio
> Francis Rother, Morton, Illinois
> Arthur Leuthold, Lester, Iowa
> James Hoerr, Peoria, Illinois
> Sidney Leman, Forrest, Illinois
> Herman Norr, Leo, Indiana, Secretary

By 1976, the World Relief Committee was expanded and comprised of the following:

> Herman Kellenberger, Elgin, Illinois, Chairman
> Wendell Gudeman, Francesville, Indiana,
>   Assistant Chairman
> Arthur Gudeman, La Crosse, Indiana
> Francis Rother, Morton, Illinois
> Arthur Leuthold, Lester, Iowa
> Albert Schneider, Rockville, Connecticut
> Sidney Leman, Forrest, Illinois
> John G. Klotzle, Altadena, California
> Leon Graf, Akron, Ohio
> Loren Strahm, Gridley, Kansas
> William Moser, Sr., Bluffton, Indiana

Floyd Wieland, Detroit, Michigan
Vernon Leman, Eureka, Illinois
James Hoerr, Peoria, Illinois

The church has been engaged in providing funds and assistance for a variety of groups and organizations. The World Relief organization has no paid staff and no "official" office. All personnel efforts are voluntary. From 1964 to 1970 the World Relief organization disbursed $360,000. Disbursements were made to seven categorical areas; 3.1% of the disbursements went to a "miscellaneous" category. The following chart indicates the areas receiving church funds:

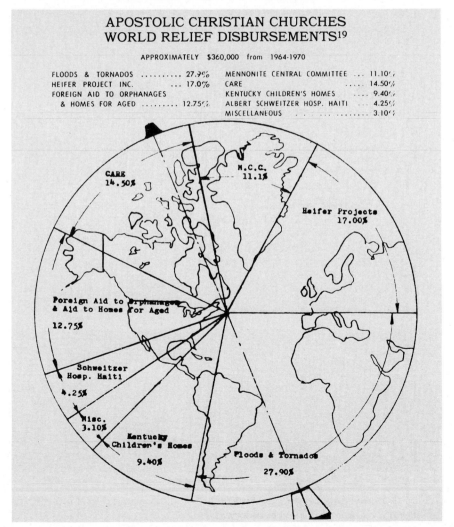

APOSTOLIC CHRISTIAN CHURCHES
WORLD RELIEF DISBURSEMENTS[19]

APPROXIMATELY $360,000 from 1964-1970

FLOODS & TORNADOS 27.9%	MENNONITE CENTRAL COMMITTEE ... 11.10%	
HEIFER PROJECT INC. ... 17.0%	CARE 14.50%	
FOREIGN AID TO ORPHANAGES	KENTUCKY CHILDREN'S HOMES 9.40%	
& HOMES FOR AGED 12.75%	ALBERT SCHWEITZER HOSP. HAITI ... 4.25%	
	MISCELLANEOUS 3.10%	

CARE
14.50%

M.C.C.
11.1%

Heifer Projects
17.00%

Foreign Aid to Orphanages
& Aid to Homes for Aged
12.75%

Schweitzer
Hosp. Haiti
4.25%

Misc.
3.10%

Kentucky
Children's Homes
9.40%

Floods & Tornados
27.90%

Activities increased sharply during the ensuing six years from 1971 to 1976. A total of $1,033,070 was distributed:[20]

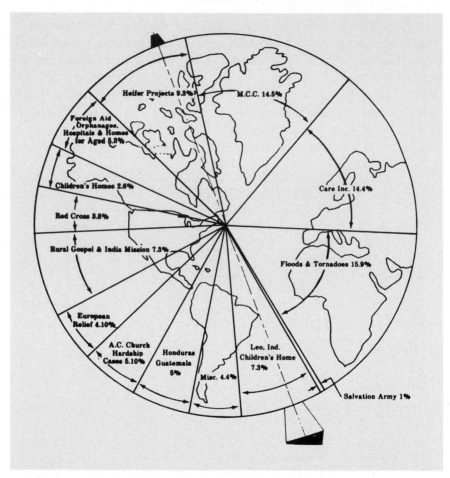

Left: Church at Balhana built with World Relief funds.
Right: Orphans outside the church at Khardi. This was the first church and orphanage established by the Bhagwats.

484

The list of those receiving aid from the Apostolic Christian Church increased and reflected the growing outreach of World Relief. The following list shows the specific areas receiving funds:

**WORLD RELIEF DISBURSEMENTS
APPROXIMATELY $1,033,000 FROM 1971-1976**[21]

1.	CARE, INC.	$ 148,305	14.40%
2.	HEIFER PROJECT INC.	96,052	9.30%
3.	MENNONITE CENTRAL COMMITTEE	149,630	14.50%
4.	FOREIGN AID TO ORPHANAGES HOSPITALS & HOMES FOR AGED	54,650	5.30%
5.	UNITED STATES TORNADO, FLOOD, STORM, EARTHQUAKE	164,891	15.90%
6.	UNITED STATES CHILDREN'S HOMES & HOSPITALS	27,186	2.60%
7.	RED CROSS	39,400	3.80%
8.	SALVATION ARMY	10,000	1.00%
9.	RURAL GOSPEL & MEDICAL MISSION OF INDIA	75,910	7.30%
10.	EUROPEAN RELIEF	41,820	4.10%
11.	APOSTOLIC CHRISTIAN CHURCH HARDSHIP CASES	52,750	5.10%
12.	PAN AMERICAN HEALTH SERVICE HONDURAS, GUATEMALA	51,764	5.00%
13.	LEO, IND. CHILDREN'S HOME	75,000	7.30%
14.	MISCELLANEOUS	45,612	4.40%
		$1,033,070	100.00%

MISCELLANEOUS – 4.40%

1. HEALTH, ACCIDENT & LIABILITY INSURANCE OF DISASTER WORKERS		$ 110.00 54.00
2. PRINTING EXPENSE (FOR SERMONS TO SERVICE MEN)		50.00
3. CHIAPOS MEX. COMMUNITY SELF-HELP PROJECT		500.00
4. TRANSPORTATION CONTINGENCY		5,000.00
5. APOSTOLIC CHRISTIAN MISSION FUND		800.00
6. WIDOW FROM PHILLIPINES LEPROSY PATIENT		100.00
7. INDIA FELLOWSHIP 3000 2000 5000 2000 2372		12,000.00
8. A.C. MATERIAL AID CENTER-WING, ILL. 3000		5,978.00
9. MAP INTERNATIONAL 2000 2000 6000 606		10,000.00
10. MIGRANT WORKER RELIEF		1,000.00
11. CHILD CARE FOUNDATION 3000 1500		4,500.00
12. EUROPEAN SOLDIERS SUPPORT		5,020.00
13. WORLD VISION		500.00
		$45,612.00

World Relief disbursements increased once more during the five years from 1976 to 1981. The total reached $1,397,958, and the following list indicates the recipients of the church's charity:[22]

Apostolic Christian Church
WORLD RELIEF DISBURSEMENTS
$1,397,958 from August 1, 1956, to August 1, 1981

1.	U.S. Hardship Cases (Brethren & Friends)	$229,350	16.35 %
2.	CARE, Inc.	185,000	13.25
3.	Mennonite Central Committee	182,030	13.00
4.	Heifer Project, Inc.	125,113	8.96
5.	Rural Gospel & Medical Mission of India	75,455	5.4
6.	European Relief	84,220	6.04
7.	Leo, Indiana, Children's Home	40,500	2.98
8.	Pan American Health Services, Honduras & Guatemala	80,203	5.73
9.	Foreign Aid to Orphanages, Korea & Jamaica	87,676	6.28
10.	Red Cross	51,000	3.65
11.	U.S. Children's Homes	38,285	2.74
12.	Haiti, Grant Foundation	37,144	2.66
13.	MAP International	37,000	2.64
14.	India Fellowship	28,200	2.02
15.	Salvation Army	29,000	2.08
16.	World Vision	22,900	1.64
17.	International Child Care	18,000	1.29
18.	A.C. Material Aid Center-Wing, Illinois	12,244	.888
19.	Disaster Aid, Tornado, Flood, etc.	11,500	.822
20.	Miscellaneous	23,138	1.65
		$1,397,958	100.00 %

Miscellaneous

1.	Insurance, Travel Expenses, Fisher Memorial	$ 4,038
2.	International Institute for Refugees	4,200
3.	Underground Evangelism	1,000
4.	Home for Handicapped	500
5.	Bags for future grain shipments	10,000
6.	South Side Mission	1,000
7.	West Side Mission	400
8.	Grace Hospital	2,000
		$23,138

Outdoor church services in rural village.

Then he said unto them, Go your way, eat the fat, and drink the sweet, and send portions unto them for whom nothing is prepared: for this day is holy unto our Lord: Neither be ye sorry: for the joy of the Lord is your strength.
Nehemiah 8:10

Because the church has no paid staff or no official public relations capability, it is often perceived as doing very little in terms of outreach, both with respect to preaching and alleviating suffering. Regarding the latter, the facts reflected a multifaceted program as the years unfolded. Not only have funds been distributed continuously to the three organizations approved by the World Relief Committee in 1964, but the church's outreach has subsequently expanded to include aid to a host of areas including orphanages, storm and flood victims, and homes for the aged. In the 1970's the church's endeavors became international in scope with aid and materials sent to such remote places as Haiti, Guatemala, Honduras, India, and Korea.

HONDURAS

Indicative of the church's growing efforts in alleviating hunger was the shipment of grain to the Pan American Health Clinic, ninety miles from San Pedro Sula, Honduras. The clinic serves as an orphanage and nutrition center in the middle of an area of abject poverty.

On November 19-21, 1974, sixty volunteers gathered at the Secor, Illinois, grain elevator and transferred 3,388 bushels of corn and 1,600 bushels of soybeans into fifty-pound bags. They loaded them onto six semi-trailer trucks and prepared them for departure to New Orleans where the cargo was loaded on a boat. The shipment, including 2,150 Spanish New Testaments, was valued at $22,631.77. A convoy of six trucks left on Monday, November 25, for the port of New Orleans. A carload of six brethren traveled along to assist in unloading the grain at the port. The bags were put on a boat and shipped to Honduras. The United Brands Company of New Orleans transported the grain, freight-free. On December 3, several men of the church flew to San Pedro Sula to assist in distributing the grain and Scriptures. Those making the trip were:

Urban Bauer and Walter Laubscher—Cissna Park, Illinois
Dean Nussbaum and Leonard Rieger—Forrest, Illinois
Ralph Klopfenstein, Ray Ringger, and Ralph Schlipf—
    Gridley, Illinois
Brad Bahler—Remington, Indiana
Ed Haas and Chuck Kellenberger—Elgin, Illinois
Bruce Hodel, Tim Sauder, Ben Sauder, and
    Chuck Sauder—Roanoke, Illinois

Richard Barth, Vernon Kaiser, and Paul Schmidgall—
   Morton, Illinois
Byron Zuercher and Milton Zuercher—Tremont, Illinois
Joe Thomas, Jr.—Peoria, Illinois
Jerry Kieser—Bradford, Illinois
Dick Graham and Jim Elsasser—Princeville, Illinois
Bill Kupferschmid—Bloomington-Normal, Illinois

As one of the shipments reached a village, some of the corn was leaking from the railroad boxcar. As the villagers crowded around the arriving grain, one of the men from the church noticed a young child, a hog, and a dog scratching around underneath the boxcar competing for the grain. Such was the extent of poverty in this area.

Subsequent shipments of grain were shipped to Honduras as the needs arose.

GUATEMALA

A devastating earthquake here on February 4, 1976, brought a quick response from the World Relief Committee. A variety of tools and blankets along with 625 bushels of corn and 35,000 pounds of pinto and black turtle beans were loaded onto two semi-trailer trucks near Wyoming, Illinois, and driven to Miami, Florida, where the items were flown to earthquake-ravished Guatemala. The shipment included 3,500 Spanish New Testaments. Brethren of the Fort Lauderdale congregation helped coordinate loading at the airport in Miami.

INDIA

The Apostolic Christian Church became involved with the Rural Gospel and Medical Mission of India when its founder, Bhagwant B. Bhagwat, was visiting among Mennonites near Rittman, Ohio, in 1968. During this time he happened to meet some brethren from the Apostolic Christian Church in that area and became impressed with their God-fearing ways. When it became apparent his religious views were reasonably common to Apostolic Christians, the church began providing assistance to his India mission which consisted of several congregations, medical clinics, and orphanages in the rural areas of western India. A former Hindu, he had embraced the Christian faith as a young man. For this, he was disinherited by his parents who later fasted themselves to death because their son left the Hindu religion and supposedly disgraced them. He died January 5, 1980.

In a report to the World Relief Committee dated June, 1980, John G. Klotzle, a minister of the church at Altadena, California, wrote, "Mr. Bhagwat's will has been filed in the United States and India and is in the process of probate. Mrs. Bhagwat is the heir to the estate in the United States and all of the real property in India. As it stands today, upon her demise, the United States and India estate will go into a United States Trust to be administered by brothers from the Apostolic Christian Churches in America." (Mrs. Bhagwat died in 1981.)

The confidence the Bhagwats placed in the Apostolic Christian Church has necessitated church officials making several trips to India to review the mission's projects. Distance and vast cultural differences posed a significant challenge to the church in the early 1980's.

MATERIAL AID CENTER

On December 7, 1974, the World Relief Committee voted unanimously in favor of purchasing the old Wing Elementary School five miles north of Forrest, Illinois. This building

The Apostolic Christian Material Aid Center is located north of Forrest at Wing, Illinois. The building is a former elementary school.

became the site of the Material Aid Center for storing clothing and other supplies to be used in case of disasters or hardships. The building cost $16,000.

Ideas for the administration and function of the center were gathered from a similar project operated by the Mennonite Central Committee at Newton, Kansas.

By 1976 seventeen churches were participating in bringing items to the center. A report from a World Relief meeting on April 10, 1976, at Francesville, Indiana, indicated items from the center had been shipped to orphanages in Bloomington, Peoria, and Chicago, as well as to individuals. Also, a truckload of clothing had been shipped to an Indian reservation in Montana. Exhortation at this meeting was made that items shipped should be of good quality to be given "in the name of Christ."

SEWING GROUPS

"The sisters and friends of the church should get together once a week and sew for the poor." These were the words of Samuel Froehlich more than 140 years ago. This admonition was heeded by the church in America, especially following World Wars I and II when clothing and blankets were sent to European refugees.

The organizing of sewing groups as a part of World Relief began in 1965. By 1980 a host of local churches participated in this effort. In fact, the church at Taylor, Missouri, has a special room designated for World Relief sewing activities. The majority of the items made by the various sewing groups are distributed by the Mennonite Central Committee.

Sewing efforts were promoted enthusiastically for several years by Ruth, Mildred, and Mary Ann Fischer of Roanoke, Illinois. They were mortally wounded in an automobile accident in July, 1976, at Vinita, Oklahoma. Their deaths were a tremendous loss to World Relief efforts.

*   *   *   *   *

The above comments were intended to show the expanded scope of World Relief and did not include other important activities. The following agenda of a meeting held at Fairbury, Illinois, on August 16, 1979, demonstrates the growing involvement of the World Relief organization:

The growth of World Relief activities resulted in the design of this logo. This windshield symbol assists World Relief workers in obtaining admittance to disaster areas.

APOSTOLIC CHRISTIAN WORLD RELIEF ANNUAL MEETING
FAIRBURY APOSTOLIC CHRISTIAN CHURCH
FAIRBURY, ILLINOIS
THURSDAY, AUGUST 16, 1979[23]
AGENDA

Welcome
1. Opening prayer
2. Minutes of April 7, 1979, meeting held at Eureka, Illinois
3. Treasurer's report—Vernon Leman
4. Unfinished and old business
5. European Relief—report prepared by Leon Graf
6. Mennonite Central Committee
7. CARE—Francis Rother
8. Heifer Project—Bruce Leman, Nick Knobloch
9. Rural Gospel & Medical Mission of India—John Klotzle
10. Sisters Sewing Groups and regional Relief meetings—
    Noah Herrmann, Eli Manz
11. Grain shipments to Honduras—Nick Knobloch, Norman Haerr
12. Haiti, Hospital Albert Schweitzer and Child Care Hospital—
    report prepared by Elaine Norr
13. Local hardship cases—Arthur Leuthold
14. Disaster assistance—floods, tornados—Art Gudeman
15. Apostolic Christian Children's Home—Sid Leman
16. Korean Babies Home—Vernon Leman
17. Red Cross, Salvation Army, MAP International
18. Kentucky Children's Homes—Bill Moser
19. Guatemala, Jamaica—Ortie Rocke, Harold Massner
20. Apostolic Christian Home for the Handicapped—Richard Kilgus
21. India Fellowship—Bill Moser
22. Sermon Letters—Homer & Virginia Blunier
23. New projects, suggestions for future consideration
24. A.C. Material Aid Center—Sid Leman
    (visit to site for interested brethren)
25. Thanks to Fairbury congregation for hosting the meeting
26. Closing prayer

BIBLE CONTRIBUTIONS

An interesting aspect to the charitable activities of the church has been its diligent contributions to the American Bible Society. For many years, the church has given money to this group to assist with the distribution of Bibles on a world-wide basis. The church has requested that this organization use their specific donations only for the distribution of the King James Version of the Bible.

It is not uncommon for the Apostolic Christian Church to be the largest denominational contributor (on a per capita basis) to the American Bible Society. The following chart was published in the May, 1977, issue of the *American Bible Society Record:*

GIFTS FROM CHURCHES

More than 80 denominations, churches, and agencies contributed a total of $1,739,194.34 to the American Bible Society in 1976. Contributions were received from the following sources:

Denominations	Contributions	Membership*	Per Member
Advent Christian Church	$ 2,280.17	31,057	$ .073
Adventists, Seventh-day	45,165.45	479,799	.094
Apostolic Christian Church of America	14,327.87	9,500	1.508
Assemblies of God	25,943.99	785,348	.033
Baptist Association of America, Conservative	1,344.26	300,000	.004
Baptist Churches in U.S.A., American	56,248.18	1,579,029	.036
Baptist Convention of America, National	88.52	2,668,799	—
Baptist Convention, Inc., Progressive National	1,491.68	521,692	.003
Baptist Convention, Southern	275,630.65	12,513,378	.022
Baptist Convention, U.S.A., Inc., National	540.44	5,500,000	—
Baptists, Free Will	126.00	215,000	—
Baptists, General Association of General	502.84	70,000	.007
Baptist General Conference	1,525.75	111,093	.014
Baptist General Conference, North America	814.18	41,437	.020
Baptist General Conference, Seventh Day	449.05	5,230	.086
Baptist, Miscellaneous	2,153.04	—	—
Bethany Fellowship	300.00	n.a.	—
Brethren Church (Ashland, Ohio)	253.03	16,279	.016
Brethren, Church of the	2,297.27	199,387	.013
Brethren, Plymouth	480.20	40,000	.012
Brethren in Christ Church	25.00	10,255	.002
Christian and Missionary Alliance	947.27	80,412	.012
Christian Church (Disciples of Christ)	37,255.91	854,844	.043
Christian Reformed Church	12,446.60	122,600	.102
Church of Christ, Scientist	20,200.00	n.a.	—
Churches of Christ	482.18	2,400,000	—
Church of God (Anderson)	253.03	161,401	.011
Church of God (Cleveland)	5,222.36	328,892	.016
Church of God Prophecy	62.56	62,743	.001
Churches of God, General Conference	526.86	37,040	.014
Community Churches, National Council of	1,290.61	n.a.	—
Congregational Christian Churches, National Association of	1,254.24	90,000	.014
Congregational Christian Conference, Conserv.	1,970.29	21,975	.090
Episcopal Church	5,177.08	2,056,254	.003
Evangelical Congregational Church	6,424.43	29,636	.217
Evangelical Covenant Church of America	1,458.86	69,960	.021
Evangelical Free Church of America	488.00	70,490	.007
Friends	615.72	96,000	.006
Greek Orthodox Archdiocese of N. & S. America	360.00	1,950,000	—
International Church of the Foursquare Gospel	1,053.00	89,215	.012
Lutheran Brethren of America, Church of the	192.00	9,000	.021
Lutheran Church, The American	343,626.87	1,764,186	.195
Lutheran Church in America	72,444.84	2,166,615	.033
Lutheran Church—Missouri Synod	96,606.63	2,010,456	.048
Lutheran Synod, Evangelical	48.52	13,097	.004
Lutheran Synod, Wisconsin Evangelical	402.23	286,858	.001
Lutheran, Miscellaneous	1,967.36	—	—
Mennonite Church	32,481.60	140,000	.232
Methodist Episcopal Church, African	106.85	1,166,301	—
Methodist Episcopal Church, Christian	2,550.00	466,718	.005
Methodist Episcopal Zion Church, African	2,986.00	1,024,974	.003
Methodist Church of North America, Free	1,050.67	65,210	.016
Methodist Church, U.S.A., Primitive	4,723.02	7,497	.630
Methodist Church, United	143,404.52	10,063,046	.014
Missionary Church	34.25	20,078	.002
Moravian Church in America, Northern Province	3,334.10	25,583	.130
Moravian Church in America, Southern Province	1,100.00	16,983	.065
Nazarene, Church of the	48,337.29	430,128	.112
Pentecostal Church of God of America	11.28	110,000	—
Pentecostal Faith, Inc., Christians of Evangelical	0	n.a.	—
Pentecostal Holiness Church	239.00	74,108	.003
Presbyterian Church, Associate Reformed	5,679.80	28,570	.199
Presbyterian Church, Cumberland	4,611.93	55,577	.083
Presbyterian Church in America	1,067.08	41,232	.026
Presbyterian Church in the U.S.	27,166.71	896,203	.030
Presbyterian Church in the U.S.A., United	38,707.36	2,723,565	.014
Presbyterian Church of N.A., Reformed	1,898.70	4,287	.443
Presbyterian, Miscellaneous	13,854.23	—	—
Reformed Church in America	27,929.09	211,470	.132
Roman Catholic Church	1,281.79	48,701,835	—
Salvation Army	1,691.25	118,400	.014
Schwenkfelder Church, The	630.00	2,520	.250
United Brethren in Christ	786.50	24,454	.032
United Church of Christ	21,750.98	1,841,312	.012
Unity of the Brethren	702.50	6,142	.114
Wesleyan Church, The	12,908.15	80,907	.160
Auxiliaries, Bible Society	9,553.79	—	—
Bible-a-Month Club (church and church group membership)	134,110.25	5,008**	—
Chaplains	92,802.61	—	—
Community-United-Federated Churches	7,388.86	—	—
Ministerial Associations	2,548.44	—	—
Union Services	14,118.16	—	—
Women's Groups, Misc.	3,609.68	—	—
Miscellaneous	27,809.51	—	—
TOTAL	$1,739,194.34		

*Membership figures are those for "full, communicant, and confirmed members," as listed in the 1976 Yearbook of American and Canadian Churches. Where this figure is not available, the "inclusive membership" figure is given.

**Number of churches and church groups enrolled, as of December 31, 1976.

Photocopy of page 38 & 39 of the May, 1977, issue of *American Bible Society Record.*

JAPAN

The Oriental islands of Japan, the "land of the rising sun," became the site of a missionary project of the Apostolic Christian Church in the early 1950's.

Japan consists of more than a thousand islands that cover an area one twenty-fifth the size of the United States. More than seventy percent of the land is comprised of mountains. Consequently, most of the population is squeezed onto the remaining thirty percent situated mainly on four major islands. Its population of 115 million makes it the sixth largest in the world.

In large measure Oriental people are known for their allegiance to ancient traditions and often to idol worship. Japan is no exception. Also, their general concept of God is totally different from that of Christians, Jews, or Muslims. This fact, together with an Oriental inclination to observe and worship "gods of stone," has been one of the obstacles the Christian message has faced as it has sought penetration into the masses of Japan.

One of the greatest obstacles Christianity faces in Japan, however, is the general rise in prosperity in the post-war era. Affluence and all its related distractions has hindered the work of the gospel.

Following World War II Japanese society placed great emphasis on technical and scientific educational programs. Youth were rushed into these programs with great intensity. As such, young people directed their energies in ways that would most efficiently prepare them for a successful career. Their diligence occupied them so overwhelmingly that they had little time or inclination to take an interest in religion. If they were approached with the message of Christianity, they would casually categorize it along with several other "gods." They became very indifferent toward religion and directed very little interest toward spiritual matters.

Despite the pressure of family and friends toward prospective believers—based on centuries of deep-seated tradition—the light of the gospel was able to penetrate, however slightly, through this wall of darkness. In nearly thirty years of Apostolic Christian endeavors in Japan (up to 1981), forty-eight Japanese had been taken into the fellowship. Of those, two had passed away. Of the forty-six living, twenty-six remained a part of the fellowship, the balance having either fallen prey to the force of local custom or a lack of proper faith and conviction. Of these twenty-six, three never attend church because of distance or personal circumstances. Therefore, about half of those taken into the fellowship remained as active, participating believers.[24]

Initial activities of the church in Japan find root in the life and work of Willis Ehnle, formerly of the Princeville, Illinois, congregation. In 1950 he was in Alabama teaching Bible classes in homes of believers. The outbreak of the Korean War in June of that year resulted in his being called into the United States Army. On January 9, 1951, he was sent on a troop ship, the *Marine Lynx,* to Tokyo, Japan, where he worked at St. Luke's Hospital, a United States Army facility.

Immediately after World War II, when Japan was crushed by the allied forces and virtually devastated and demoralized by the atomic bombs dropped on Hiroshima and Nagasaki (and emperor worship began to decline), the United States' occupation leader General Douglas MacArthur asked for one thousand Christian missionaries to come to Japan to distribute Bibles and disseminate its teachings. He felt this was essential if the Japanese people were to embrace democracy.

By 1951 the populace continued to be hungry for Scriptures. Reading materials were scarce, and many were willing to read virtually anything. It was in this context that Willis Ehnle, still a serviceman, felt moved to distribute Scriptures. He made a sign about one meter high and eighty centimeters wide which read, "Christ Gives Peace In Your Heart." He took the sign and Scriptures to the Shinjuku train station in Tokyo and began handing out materials to persons getting on and off the train.

One day a young man came up to him on the platform and said, "I want to help you work for God." Ehnle tried to decifer his broken English. He replied, "That's fine!"[25] The man

Passing out Scriptures at a crowded train station in Japan. The sign says, "Christ Gives Peace In Your Heart."

began helping pass out literature. Ehnle tried to make sure he did so reverently because they were dealing with the Word of God. The young man's name was Toshiaki Asakawa. His mother eventually became a member of the church.

One time when Ehnle was unloading soldiers who had been wounded in Korea, he noticed the Japanese guard at the hospital was very friendly and spoke English. He told him that Jesus is the Son of God. The guard replied, "I don't believe it!" Ehnle said whether he believes it or not, it is true. The young man was Hajime Utsuki.

The Utsuki family helped the Ehnle family considerably during the early phases of the missionary project in Japan. When Willis Ehnle (after going back to America and claiming his new bride) returned to Japan, he and his wife lived near the Utsuki home for a few weeks before purchasing a home of their own.

Ehnle was married to Lois Beer, Milford, Indiana, in 1953. She is the daughter of Henry Beer who labored in the ministry at Milford for forty-seven years and who played a major role in the translation of the *Zion's Harp* hymnal from the German language to the English.

Willis Ehnle entered the International Christian University at Mitaka under the G.I. Bill of Rights. It was at this time that

The Elders were very impressed with the nearly two hundred children in Sunday Schools in the area. Financing came from the American churches, but the Japanese were otherwise very involved in the project. The land and new church cost $10,000. A $2,000 dwelling was built next to the church. Dedication was held in July, 1956, with Willis Ehnle speaking on the parable of the sower. Joseph Yamamura of the Japan Bible Society translated the message. The Shioda church is eighty miles west of Tokyo and forty-five minutes by auto from Mount Fuji.

The Tokyo church was built three years later in 1959. It is located in the suburbs just outside Tokyo in an area called Kaneko. This was later changed to Tsutsujiga-Oka or "Azalea Hill" in English. It is one hour by train from downtown Tokyo. The church and land cost $9,000, and the dwelling beside the church cost $4,000. The value of the land in 1982 was $500,000. The Ehnles lived here until June, 1966, when they moved to Shioda.

The Apostolic Christian Church in the suburban "Azalea Hill" area, one hour from downtown Tokyo. It was built in 1959.

The Tamahata church was built in 1962. It is twelve miles west of the Shioda church. It cost $9,300 for the land and church. Tamahata is the family home of the Inoue family. Because the Inoue family lived next to the church, no residence was built here like those built next to the churches at Tokyo and Shioda. By the fall of 1973, the Tamahata church was closed, although the building was still used for singings once every two months in 1982.

The church at Tamahata was closed for regular worship services in 1973, but by 1982 was still used for bi-monthly singings.

Yoshito Inoue was placed in the ministry at Shioda during the church's formative years. He was Ehnle's great hope for this church. Sadly, though, he expired from cancer of the chest at age twenty-four. This was a major setback. The day before he died he begged his brother, Akito, to take him to the church, which was nearby. It seemed he wanted to die there, but he was too weak to be moved. His last words were spoken to his brother, "Please speak out more and more about the true joy." In one of Elder Noah Schrock's last visits with him prior to his illness, Yoshito said, "Brother Schrock, you are our Elder and we want you to tell us whatever you see as needful, so we can maintain a true church."[27]

Later, in 1966, Yoshito's younger brother, Akito, was placed into the ministry. On July 31, 1977, he became the first native Japanese Elder of the Apostolic Christian Church.[28]

Toshio Uchida served as a minister for a number of years at Shioda. Yoshio Yamazaki has served since 1963 at Tokyo. By 1982 Willis Ehnle, Akito Inoue, and Yoshio Yamazaki served as ministers.

Several teachers have given two years of their life to serve the Lord in Japan. Nancy Roth Pfeifer was the first to come to Japan. The second to serve, Marie Neihouser, Francesville, Indiana, eventually added Inoue to her name when she married Akito Inoue who later became an Elder. The teachers, in order of their terms of service, were:

> Nancy Roth Pfeifer, Fairbury, Illinois (now of Chicago, Illinois)
> Marie Neihouser Inoue, Francesville, Indiana, (now of
> Tokyo, Japan)
> Nancy Schrock, Congerville, Illinois
> Carol Schrenk Troxel, Chicago, Illinois (now of Remington,
> Indiana)
> Judy Bauer, Cissna Park, Illinois
> Sue Schock Kellenberger, Elgin, Illinois (now of Leo,
> Indiana)
> Betsy Eriksen Haney, Rockville, Connecticut
> Linda Morrison, Mansfield, Ohio
> Kathie Huber Inoue, Francesville, Indiana
> Sally Gramm Kaufman, Gridley, Illinois (now of
> Karuizawa, Japan)
> Libby Meyer Leman, Sabetha, Kansas (now of Elgin,
> Illinois)
> Jane Weiss Stieglitz, Bay City, Michigan (now of Leo, Indiana)
> Sally Beutel Koch, Tremont, Illinois
> Evelyn Blunier, Eureka, Illinois
> Kathy Klotzle, Altadena, California
> Vicki (Viola Mae) Ramseyer, Bay City, Michigan
> Judy Luginbuhl, Rockville, Connecticut

Concerning her stay in Japan, Sally Beutel commented, "During my stay in Japan several improvements were made in our church and in the kindergarten. We started wearing long veils during worship services, and our beautiful *Zion's Harp* hymns were translated into Japanese. Both are precious to our faith."[30]

Jane Weiss wrote of her Japan experiences, "To anyone who might be considering this labor, or perhaps if this is the first time you've heard much about the churches in Japan, I'll tell you that I don't consider it a labor in the least, but a deep privilege to share the Word with those who perhaps have never heard it before."[31]

*   *   *   *   *

There are many interesting aspects to the mission work in Japan. The following few pages will highlight some of the facts of interest associated with the church in Japan.

The *Zion's Harp* hymnal is used in the Japanese churches. Reiko Furuya, a sister in the church at Shioda, has translated 125 hymns from the German language into the Japanese. She is very dedicated to this work and hopes to complete the translation of the entire hymnal. She teaches food chemistry at her family's university. Hisato Inoue, who married Kathie Huber of Francesville, Indiana, translated No. 212, "The Lord is my Shepherd."

* * * * *

During the early 1970's the church in Japan began printing a small publication similar to the *Silver Lining*. It was called *The Voice of the Vineyard*. Approximately four issues were printed, but the project failed due to a lack of support and interest.

* * * * *

The account of how Yoshio Yamazaki, minister at Tokyo, met Willis Ehnle is quite interesting. One time Ehnle had completed a mailing to several people in the United States. For lack of postage the postmaster rejected the letters. Then, they were mistakenly returned to Yoshio Yamazaki who at that time was involved in church work with the Church of the Brethren. Yamazaki brought them to Willis Ehnle, and a long relationship began between these two men.

Yamazaki, a single man who lives alone, is conversant in the English language, is very outgoing, and loves Westerners. He is an English teacher.

* * * * *

Each year the churches in Japan hold a retreat in the mountains. The purpose is to reflect more deeply on the Christian walk of life and to learn more of Christ and His Church. Hiking in the mountains, fellowship and relaxation are also a part of this special time. The meeting—*Shuyokai*—formerly was held three times per year, but in 1982 was held twice, in July and October.

* * * * *

There are many obstacles faced by the church in Japan. The nation is rooted in tradition and idol worship, although economic recovery and general affluence have resulted in a religious lukewarmness.

The decline in attachment to an ancient religious tradition made some Japanese more prone to display interest in Christianity, but great obstacles to the furtherance of the gospel still remained due largely to the Japanese concept of God, which differed from that of Westerners.

Japanese who embraced Christianity faced great peer pressure and in some cases rebuke from their families. Yet, due to the growing religious indifference of Japanese society, they were not subject to the disapproval of a generation ago. In this context, it must be said, however, that Christian believers are admired in Japan for their honesty, moral uprightness, and high ethical standards.

There are several problem areas for those trying to promote the Christian faith in Japan, particularly among Apostolic Christians. First, it is often difficult to separate Christianity from other religions. For instance, it is not unusual for a Japanese, however casually, to believe in several different religions at once.

Two other problems center around (1) the profound pressure to conform to society and (2) marriage in the Lord. Regarding marriage, it has been a tradition in Japan (in varying degrees) for family and relatives to assist in selecting the partners in a marriage. This custom is ancient. Consequently, the concept, as practiced in the Apostolic Christian Church of a brother and sister uniting in holy matrimony as prompted by faith and sincere prayer, is a foreign one and has caused problems in the churches, particularly at Shioda. The Japanese, generally, have not objected so much to the concept of God leading two young people together, but to the fact that a young person would have to remain single because there are no eligible members in the church fellowship to marry.

Because Japan is highly industrialized, society is trained from youth on to conform to group order and behavior so the small nation (regarding land and natural resources) can reach optimum production levels and compete with the nations of the world. As a result, the pressure to conform to societal norms is immense and makes the Christian life somewhat difficult. This is particularly true since Scriptures place a great deal of emphasis on the principles of non-conformity to the world and separation from the world.

Similar to any missionary projects—including those of the Apostle Paul—the work in Japan has been prone to setbacks and discouragements. In the 1960's a disruption occurred at the Shioda church. Eventually, the Tamahata church was closed down except for singings. Added to this has been the constant influence of peer pressure and tradition emanating from the Japanese society.

Yet, a church, however small, is rising up in Japan. The American Elders have given solid support to this mission. Elder Noah Schrock made several trips to Japan. Elder Ben C. Maibach, Jr., Detroit, Michigan, has made more than ten trips to the Orient on behalf of this work.

A native Japanese has been ordained as Elder. His periodic presence at the church's annual brotherhood conference gives evidence of the success of the mission work in Japan.

Kathie Huber Inoue, Francesville, Indiana, formerly a teacher in the Shioda American Kindergarten, wrote, "May we in America continue to strengthen and uphold our Church as we have known and loved it, that the Japanese Churches may have a perfect pattern to follow."[32]

*   *   *   *

Marie Inoue, wife of Elder Akito Inoue who has lived in Japan for many years, listed her thoughts of the church work in Japan (June, 1982):

Thoughts About Going to Japan

While I was in college I first became interested in teaching in a foreign country through a math teacher. She told of many interesting traveling episodes while teaching at a U.S. Army base school in Germany. I thought this might be an interesting way to travel, rather than spending three weeks touring fifteen countries with a tour group, and at the same time enjoy my teaching career. But since our faith had no established churches there, I did not pursue the matter. Then in May, 1966, Elder Noah Schrock visited our home and said there may be an opening for a teacher in connection with our Japanese church and wondered if I might be interested and seek the Lord's guidance if I might be available to go. This offer had some appealing aspects, but it was not easy to decide to leave my family, the local brotherhood, a fine job—all with whom I daily associated. But I also wanted to observe our faith in a foreign country and culture and be helpful if I could to our brotherhood who imparted to me the loving faith on a "silver spoon" so to speak.

The First Years of Teaching at the Shioda School

I spent several years teaching in the Shioda school. The first year I was there was the first experience of a foreign family or teachers establishing somewhat of a permanent residence in the country village of Shioda as the Ehnles had just moved from their home in Tokyo to Shioda. So folks of all ages came to learn English through Bible lessons and other materials with classes being taught after hours of the local school system and evenings. During the day Nancy (Roth) Pfeifer taught elementary school subjects to the Ehnle children and several other American children in the area. I taught kindergarten several days a week and quite a few English classes in the late afternoons and evenings. The brotherhood was quite small, and we enjoyed each brother and sister and knowing how each one came to know of Christ's love. We found that many obstacles confronted their pathways never experienced by believers in the U.S. We often encouraged our students and neighbors to attend church, and some of them did. Others had school, social, or other activities that kept their interests.

Our living quarters were not so handy especially space-wise, but we lacked for nothing. Give Nancy Pfeifer or Nancy Schrock a hammer, nail, screen, and a sewing machine, and they could put together about anything. It was also a special joy to know and be with the Ehnle family. In 1971 I accepted the marriage proposal of Akito Inoue and decided to make my home in Japan. This decision was naturally more difficult than the first as it requires a lifetime—so with much prayer and seeking God's guidance in His Word and also through the counsel of those over me in the Lord I received the faith and peace from God to share my life with Akito and his home. We were married August 15, 1971, in the U.S. and soon returned to Japan.

The Beginning of the Tokyo Church

The Tokyo Church has its beginnings in 1959. The country church in Shioda had already been built, and Bro. Saburo Utsuki thought we ought to have a church in Tokyo. At this time he was not yet our brother in faith. The American Elders approved, so they looked for some land, and the Ehnles inquired of Mr. Kobayashi who had sold them their small home, and he mentioned that the site of the now-present church was available.

Before the Tokyo Church was built, most of the regular church meetings were held at the home of Willis and Lois Ehnle. Children's meetings and adult meetings were also held at the home of Saburo Utsuki, and for a time adult Bible classes were held in a bank building. Meetings for children were also held in the Akabane orphanage in northern Tokyo, which was often visited. Those who have served in the ministry have been Willis Ehnle, Hajime and Akira Utsuki, Yoshio Yamazaki, John Klaus, and Akito Inoue.

An unusual incident in connection with the beginning of the Tokyo Church took place in the Utsuki home nearly thirty years ago at one of their home meetings. One of the Utsuki children who knew some English helped with telling the Easter story because Willis Ehnle's ability in Japanese was nil. Mrs. Utsuki was present and made some comments after the flannelgraph story was finished. One of the Utsuki children told Ehnle their mother had commented, "That's a nice story for children, but you cannot expect adults to believe it." Today Mrs. Utsuki is our sister in Christ. She was baptized in the Tokyo Church on April 2, 1978.

A Few Notes on the Tokyo Church Today (1982)

Today the church is served by Elder Akito Inoue who was ordained by Elders Ben Maibach and Wendell Gudeman in July, 1974, and Yoshio Yamazaki serving since April, 1963. Though our congregation is still quite small in number, we feel the blessings have been large in number from our Heavenly Father. Yamazaki teaches an early Sunday School class on Sunday morning at 9:15 a.m. This class used to be large, but due to recent extracurricular school activities and special children's programs on Japanese television, the number of neighborhood children is usually under ten or so. Another class beginning at 10:30 a.m. for those children whose parents attend the morning worship service is taught by our sisters on a rotating basis. Lunch is served followed by a short fellowship, and another worship service.

Most fellowship activities are held with the Shioda Church. These consist of visiting back and forth, *Zion's Harp* translation meetings, singings, and especially our Summer Fellowship Meetings (three days near Mt. Fuji) where many joys and blessings are shared. Holy Communion services, Christmas and Easter children's programs are some of the activities held within our local church. Visitors from the United States also provide us with much fellowship and many blessings.

A few comments from Yoshio Yamazaki, a minister at Tokyo, concerning his conversation with a neighbor (Yoshio's legs are crippled because of polio.):

Near our Tokyo Church is an older Japanese home which is the meeting place for the local believers of the Tenri-kyo religion. *Ten* means "the heaven" and *ri* means "the truth." It is said that this religion began one hundred years ago when a daughter of a fisherman in Nara prefecture heard a voice of heaven. This is not Buddhism but a kind of Shintoism. I met a lady of the Tenri-kyo religion on the street several years ago and she said, "Mr. Yamazaki, you believe in Christianity and you still have crippled legs. If you change your beliefs, you will be able to have new legs." I replied, "Thank you for your kindness in trying to advise me, but I believe in the true and living God, and I believe if it's the Lord's will, He will always give us everything which we need. Even I can say that for my legs." Then I gave her some Bible answers: Philippians 3:18-24, and Revelation 21:5-8. The lady said, "When I was young I was in the university, and I read the Bible many times because the school was a 'mission' school, but I never knew about the words which you mention to me today."

APOSTOLIC CHRISTIAN HOME FOR THE HANDICAPPED MORTON, ILLINOIS

Heaven's Very Special Child

A meeting was held quite far from earth
"It's time again for another birth,"
Said the Angels to the Lord above,
"This special child will need much love."

His progress may seem very slow,
Accomplishments he may not show,
And he'll require extra care
From the folks he meets way down there.

He may not run, or laugh, or play
His thoughts may seem quite far away,
In many ways he won't adapt,
And he'll be known as handicapped.

So let's be careful where he's sent
We want his life to be content,
Please, Lord, find the home who
Will do a special job for You.

They will not realize right away
The leading role they're asked to play,
But with this child sent from above
Comes stronger faith and richer love.

And soon they'll know the privilege given
In caring for this gift from Heaven,
Their precious charge so meek and mild
Is Heaven's very special child.

by Edna Massimilla

October 1, 1971, marked perhaps one of the finest hours of the church's entire history. On this date the doors were opened to the first residents at the Apostolic Christian Home for the Handicapped in Morton, Illinois. This intermediate care facility was built to serve the physical and mental needs of handicapped persons regardless of their faith. First preference, however, was given to persons of the church.

The beautiful, sprawling, one-floor complex, bordered by a manicured lawn and a stately grove of trees brushed by gently blowing breezes, cost $800,000, and when completed comprised one of the finest facilities of its kind in the United States and perhaps in the entire world. A 1.1 million dollar addition in 1978 further enriched the facility.

Its completion symbolized the church's deep sensitivity and tender compassion for handicapped and mentally disabled persons. Also, the church's entry into caring for the phsically weak and mentally handicapped reflected its deep commitment to the teachings of Christ. Those who were the real beneficiaries of this project, instead of the residents, were those who gave of their time, talents, and resources in making the "Home for the Handicapped" a reality. The Lord's teaching, "it is more blessed to give than to receive," rang true amid the initial and continuing efforts in providing for the home's residents.

Apostolic Christian Home for the Handicapped, Morton, Illinois

The idea to explore the feasibility of establishing a home for the handicapped was prompted by concerns harbored by brethren of the church who had physically or mentally handicapped children. They often pondered the question, "What will happen to my child when I am gone?" These concerns were voiced to the Elders of the church. At a brotherhood conference in September, 1964, at Tremont, Illinois, a committee was named to make preliminary surveys concerning a possible home for the handicapped. Serving on this committee were Elder Sam Anliker, Lamont, Kansas, minister Harvey Grimm (Bern church), Sabetha, Kansas, and layman Phil Mogler, Lester, Iowa. On May 28, 1965, this committee mailed a questionnaire comprised of thirty-one questions to families in the church who had physically or mentally handicapped children. These were to be mailed back to Sam Anliker by July 15, 1965.

In the meantime, a subsequent committee of brothers was selected to investigate further the possibility of establishing a home. It consisted of Sam Anliker, Harvey Grimm, and Phil Mogler, who had served on the previous committee; added to the committee were Earl Feller, Cissna Park, Illinois; Andrew E. Virkler, Bay City, Michigan; Eugene Stoller (Latty church), Paulding, Ohio; and Elmer Bucher (Francesville church), Medaryville, Indiana. This committee met April 6, 1966, at Francesville, Indiana. At this meeting it was decided to send out another questionnaire in order to obtain more detailed information. The first did not yield sufficient information.

A second committee meeting was convened Saturday, July 16, 1966, at Cissna Park, Illinois. It was noted that approximately seventy handicapped persons, who may eventually be candidates for special institutional care, lived in homes of church people. Nearly fifty percent were in Illinois, fifteen percent in Indiana, and the remainder scattered in various states.

During the ensuing years this committee sent out pledge cards to determine how much money could be raised for a new facility. Members and friends of the church pledged over $550,000, which was an overwhelming amount, and signaled that broadly-based support was evident in the church for this type of project. These results were presented to the Elder Body at the 1967 Brotherhood Conference at Eureka, Illinois. In view of this generous support, the project was endorsed.

Three guiding Elders were chosen to associate with the project: Russell Rapp, Morton, Illinois; Emanuel Gudeman, Cissna Park, Illinois; and Roy Sauder, Peoria, Illinois. They selected a board of directors consisting of nine members from various areas which constituted a geographical balance. The first board of directors was comprised of the following men:

President: Carl Frautschi; Chairman, Planning Committee
Vice President: Herman Menold; Assistant Chairman,
    Planning Committee
Treasurer: Frank Honegger; Chairman, Finance
    Committee
Assistant Treasurer: George Bauer; Assistant Treasurer,
    Finance Committee
Secretary: Al Hunziker; Assistant Chairman, Operating
    Committee
Assistant Secretary: Elmer Bucher; Secretary Original
    Committee
Director: Harvey Grimm, Member Original Committee
Director: Phil Mogler; Member of Original Committee
Director: Harold Krantz; Chairman, Operating Committee

Five committees were chosen to assist with planning and development:

SITE	PLANNING	BUILDING
Earl Feller (Cissna Park)	Carl Frautschi (Bloomington)	Dick Haefli (Peoria)
John Hoerr (Peoria)	Herman Menold (Morton)	Jack Krantz (Morton)
Chris Hohulin (Goodfield)	Bruce Schafer (Peoria)	James Leman (Roanoke)
Aldon Nussbaum (Forrest)	Sam Wegman (Tremont)	Arnold Rassi (Tremont)
Harry Rocke (Eureka)	Joe Witzig (Morton)	A. J. Schrock (Congerville)

FINANCE	OPERATING
George Bauer (Cissna Park)	Al Hunziker (Morton)
Frank Honegger (Forrest)	Harold Krantz (Morton)
Adolph Roecker (Peoria)	Ray Moser (Tremont)
Carl Schieber (Congerville)	Harlan Thomas (Peoria)
John Wiedman (Fairbury)	Karl Schuon (Morton)

The purpose of the home, according to a letter sent to all the churches May 27, 1968, was "to establish and operate a home which will be church-sponsored and controlled by the Apostolic Christian Church for the benefit of handicapped people of families who regard the Apostolic Christian Church as their church home. Galatians 6:10 (As we have therefore opportunity, let us do good to all men, especially to them who are of the household of faith)."

The first general meeting of the guiding Elders, the board of directors, and the five standing committees was held February 24, 1968, at the Morton church. On June 8, 1968, an architect was chosen. It was decided to build the facility near Morton, Illinois, for the following general reasons:

1. Central location.
2. Largest concentration of churches in this general area.
3. Access to schools and workshops in area for handicapped persons.
4. Access to number of large hospitals and professional help.
5. Interstate highway nearby plus air transportation available.

Thus, after a long stretch of study and deliberate examination, seemingly endless meetings, and almost infinite patience, the tireless efforts and admirable diligence of many brethren were culminated in a ground-breaking service at a forty-acre site one and one-half miles northwest of Morton on Sunday, June 7, 1970. An estimated 250 persons from a number of surrounding churches gathered for the ceremony. Scriptures were read from John 9:1-4 and Galatians 6:2. Treasurer Frank Honegger, Forrest, Illinois, turned the first spade of dirt. Elder Roy Sauder, Peoria, Illinois, in a closing prayer, asked for God's blessing in this important undertaking. Earth-moving equipment was moved in, and work began the next morning.

Koehl Construction Company, Washington, Illinois, was the general contractor. Meister Brothers, Peoria, completed the plumbing and heating. The construction phase of the project lasted from June, 1970, to October, 1971, when the first residents began arriving. Harold Miller, Portland, Oregon, and Marlene Moser, Fairbury, Illinois, were the home's first occupants. Miller was the son of Guy Miller who ministered at Pulaski, Iowa; Gridley, Illinois; and Portland, Oregon.

On September 26, 1971, open house was held for the general public. In spite of inclement weather, nearly three thousand persons toured the facility. Each was served a snack before leaving.

October 17, 1971, was a very memorable and historic day. About three hundred persons gathered under sunny, autumn skies in the Biblical garden in front of the home. This area, featuring plantings with a Biblical connotation (sycamore trees, crown of thorns, olives, roses of Sharon, and grape vines), was a very appropriate place to dedicate the facility to Almighty God. Elders Noah Schrock, Oakville, Iowa, Herman Kellenberger, Elgin, Illinois, Roy Sauder, Peoria, Illinois, and Russell Rapp, Morton, were present. Elder Noah Schrock emphasized that the home could not remove the burden that exists in the hearts of parents of handicapped persons, but it was built to share the burden.

Robert Knobloch, formerly a farmer near Bradford, Illinois, was hired as the home's administrator. He began his duties July 1, 1971. He recalls events associated with his being hired as administrator:

> My involvement in the Home came about due to our interest in this type of a facility for many years because of our mentally handicapped son. After the letter was read in our local church at Bradford, Illinois, in the fall of 1970 asking for applicants, my wife and I discussed the thought of quitting farming, which we had enjoyed for nineteen years, and applying for the position of Administrator. After much fervent prayer, we felt led to send in my application just before the deadline. I was subsequently hired in April of 1971, to begin fulfillment July 1, 1971.

In 1980 he listed his duties at the home:

> My primary responsibility is to direct, coordinate, and be responsible for operating the Home in such a manner as to assure that our residents receive the best possible care and to see that their health, safety, social, religious, domiciliary and all other needs fall within the scope of the policies of the Home.

The new facility eventually filled with residents to the extent that by early 1976 more space was required. In March of that year construction of a large, new wing costing $1,115,000 (plus $200,000 of donated labor) was begun. It was opened in May, 1978. The growth of the facility was underscored by the fact that the institution's operating budget in 1981 was $925,000 compared to $155,100 in 1972.

The following statistics show the resident population year by year:

Year	Number of Residents
1971	6
1972	27
1973	39
1974	48
1975	51
1976	51
1977	52
1978	65
1979	67
1980	74

By 1980 statistics revealed that seventy-five percent of the residents were from the Apostolic Christian Church. Of all the residents, eighty-eight percent were state sponsored. The home has been funded on a continuous basis by contributions, private payments, Medicaid, and DMHDD.

In 1980 a staff of eighty-one employees equivalent to fifty-two full-time persons worked at the home. Statistics showed that eighteen residents were members of the Apostolic Christian Church; twenty-four were from out-of-state, and there were thirty-one males and forty-three females.

Thousands visit the home each year, and hundreds of hours each year are expended by volunteers. An annual charity bazaar was begun in November, 1971. In 1979 it grossed $30,000 during the one-day affair. A gift shop inside the front entrance provides additional income for the home.

In May, 1972, the staff and residents of the home began a monthly periodical entitled *Apostolic Christian Handicapped Times.*

Residents have been kept busy through a variety of activities. Those who are able go to the PARC training center in Peoria, others go to workshops, and some work at local jobs on a part-time basis.

A brochure describing the home's program includes the following poem on the last page:

The Gift of Understanding

Oh please—
turn not your face and hide me in the dark.
Shed not a quiet tear or lower your eyes in shame.
I am flesh and blood with heart and soul.
I need your love and understanding, too.
Accept me as He put me here
—a child to love, no more, no less.

APOSTOLIC CHRISTIAN CHILDREN'S HOME, INC. LEO, INDIANA

"A work of faith, a labor of love" is a phrase often associated with the Apostolic Christian Children's Home at Leo, Indiana. Established in 1976, it has provided a home for boys and girls from six to eighteen years of age. In 1981, it housed fourteen young people.

The idea for establishing an orphanage was born in the hearts of several brethren of the church who had assisted with construction of a new building at the Dessie Scott Children's Home in Pine Ridge, Kentucky. Warmed by their experience of associating with young boys and girls at the Dessie Scott Home, they were prompted to explore the feasibility of an orphanage that might be sponsored by the Apostolic Christian Church.

At the brotherhood conference at Roanoke, Illinois, in 1969, permission was granted to form a committee to investigate the need for a home for orphaned, unwanted, or neglected children.[33] The committee found a great need for a home for such unfortunate children. At a subsequent brotherhood conference at Princeville, Illinois, church Elders advised that no action would be taken to build a children's home until the church's "home for the handicapped" in Morton, Illinois, was completed. It recommended, however, that further studies and surveys be conducted concerning a possible site.

At the 1973 brotherhood conference at Morton, church Elders endorsed building a new children's home. This was a happy day for several brethren who had nurtured this possibility in their hearts for several years. They had worked—and patiently waited—until the "way was open" to begin this important, charitable work.

The site for construction of a home was narrowed to two areas— Francesville and Leo, Indiana. At a committee meeting at Remington, Indiana, on November 30, 1973, a vote was taken to decide between these two suitable sites. It was a tie vote. To resolve the matter, two ballots were placed in a Bible. After prayer was offered, a brother drew Leo as the Lord's choice. Following this, a site was obtained, and work began on the first buildings. By 1982, the facility included two houses and two support buildings with future plans to add four more houses as the need arises. Up to 1982, the facility had cared for more than thirty-six children.

On October 24, 1976, a crowd of 250 gathered for the dedication of the "children's home."[34] Services were conducted by Elders David Bertsch, Leo, Indiana, and Wendell Gudeman, Francesville, Indiana. The facility, located on a seventy-three-acre site one mile east of the Leo Apostolic Christian Church, was built at a total cost of $350,000. Before the first child was accepted in December, 1976, the facility was paid for due to the overwhelming benevolence of the church nationwide. The total operating budget in 1981 was $192,000.

The home centers largely around two cottages which are residential in style and designed to resemble a conventional home. First houseparents in 1976 were Terry and Mary Farney of Wichita, Kansas, and Doug and Sue Kellenberger of Elgin, Illinois. Terry Farney served as the facility's first administrator.

He was succeeded in March, 1979, by Robert Cockburn of Milford, Indiana. Bill Klopfenstein, Leo, served as an "acting director" for several months before Cockburn assumed his duties.

In 1981, Brace and Brenda Wieland, Bay City, Michigan, and Paul and Leanne Fischer, Roanoke, Illinois, were serving as houseparents along with Doug and Sue Kellenberger.

The project at Leo is sponsored by World Relief and is supported by all the churches in the denomination. A brochure published by the World Relief organization in the early 1980's included the following information:

> The Apostolic Christian Children's Home is a joint effort of the Apostolic Christian Churches of America, and as such, we derive financial and spiritual support from all who would choose to help in this important work. We are blessed with a large number of volunteers, especially in the summer months, who come and spend time with us and accomplish tasks that would otherwise not get done. We also have many brethren and friends who spend countless hours preparing items for our annual auction and sale. The hand-made quilts, comforters, craft items, etc. that are sold during our auction provide some of the financial help required to continue providing Christian homes to unfortunate children. We do not keep track of the donated hours, but we are sure that God does, and He is blessing those who give of themselves so unselfishly.
>
> We are also aided financially by many individuals and church congregations who wish to help in this labor of love. Because of the willingness of our brethren and friends, we are able to reach many children who might otherwise never have the opportunity to learn of God and experience His love. The Home is able to provide for these children because of the moral, physical, and financial support of our churches.

The institution's publication, *Children's Home News*, is printed every other month.

NURSING AND RETIREMENT HOMES

Care for elderly citizens began among Apostolic Christians as early as 1912 when the church at Peoria, Illinois, purchased a home at 711 North Monroe and called it the Apostolic Christian Home. It was used to care for older sisters of the congregation.

In 1937 a home for aged women was established in Mansfield, Ohio. The church purchased a dwelling from Elmer Young on Wooster Road for this purpose. It was completely remodeled to accommodate twelve persons. Ladies of several faiths resided at the home. This facility was closed in 1972 after thirty-five years of operation. It was comparatively small, and a host of governmental regulations ushered in the home's demise. Because it lacked nursing personnel and medical facilities, it was decided to close the home. Another reason for closing the facility was the retirement of Francelia Beer who served as matron of the home for twenty-five years. During her tenure, more than one hundred different women lived at the home. When she retired in 1972, and the home ceased operations, the nine women residents were all reluctant to leave.

The denomination did not realize any more activity in this realm of endeavor until 1960 when the congregation at Sabetha, Kansas, built a nursing home costing $115,000. During this decade churches at Fairbury (1962) and Eureka, Illinois, (1966) also built new sheltered care facilities. The church at Peoria built a new facility in 1966.

To meet the needs of the nation's fastest growing segment of the population, the trend of constructing or purchasing existing senior citizen facilities continued and accelerated during the 1970's. During this decade homes appeared in Roanoke, Illinois (1975); Rittman, Ohio (1976); Morton, Illinois (1978); and Francesville, Indiana (1978). In 1972 the congregation at Elgin, Illinois, began operation of the Apostolic Christian Rest Haven nursing home.

By 1982 exploratory studies were being conducted at Leo, Indiana; Detroit, Michigan; and Burlington, Iowa. The purpose was to determine the need for retirement homes in these various areas.

All facilities were initiated unilaterally by the local congregations and were not part of any grand design by the higher councils of the church. Care facilities were generally located on a regional basis to provide for members in those immediate areas. Some facilities were sponsored by a cluster of nearby churches, while others were sponsored solely by individual churches.

Capital expenditures from 1960 to 1980 totaled $5.7 million for newly constructed or purchased facilities. Various additions over the years brought the total to $9.4 million including a $750,000 twenty-two unit retirement apartment complex (1980) at Rockville, Connecticut. These figures do not account for annual inflation which would sharply increase the totals.

During 1981 the operating budgets of the church's nine nursing care homes totaled $5.9 million. Large staffs and impressive care were features of these pleasant facilities.

In addition to its nine nursing homes, the church had also displayed its compassion during the 1970's by building a large home for handicapped persons in Morton, Illinois, in 1971. Their 1981 operating budget totaled $925,000. Also, an orphanage at Leo, Indiana, completed in 1976, cost $350,000. Its operating budget in 1981 was $192,000.

By 1981 the approximate number of people being cared for in the church's institutional care facilities came to 660. This was likely much higher, on a percentage basis, than any denomination in the United States.

The church's accelerated pace in providing institutional care for orphans, the elderly, and the handicapped can generally be attributed to the membership's growing awareness of need. Prompted by a desire to exercise suitable stewardship for rising levels of affluence, the church became sensitive to the growing needs emanating from a longer life expectancy. Due to the strong financial base of its membership, the church was willing and felt led of God to reach out and more aggressively help those in need. By doing so it was enriched by the Lord's teaching, "It is more blessed to give than to receive." (Acts 20:35)

APOSTOLIC CHRISTIAN REST HAVEN
971 Bode Road
Elgin, Illinois 60120

Opened: May, 1972

Cost: $400,000
Capacity: 31
1981 Occupancy: 31

Status: Sheltered Care

Staff: 12

Administrator: Bill Strackany
Former Administrators:
 Nancy Kerber
 Karen Heiniger
 LeRoy Rocke
 Helen Broyles
Supporting Church: Elgin

1981 Operating Budget:
 $250,000

Institutional Publication:
 Apostolic Christian Rest Haven Newsletter

EUREKA APOSTOLIC CHRISTIAN HOME
610 W. Cruger Street
Eureka, Illinois 61530

Opened: January, 1966

Cost: $425,000

Capacity: 100

1981 Occupancy: 100

Licensing Status:
 Sheltered and
 Intermediate Care
Staff: 63 Full Time Positions

Administrator: Joel Banwart

Former Administrators:
 Mary Ann Fischer
 Kores Knapp
 LeRoy Rocke

Supporting Churches:
 Eureka
 Congerville
 Goodfield
 Princeville

Additions:
1970: 11 Apartments, $295,000
1975: 40 Beds, $642,000
1981 Operating Budget:
 $890,000

Institutional Publication:
 Silver Threads (Bi-Monthly)

FAIRVIEW HAVEN, INC.
605-609 N. Fourth Street
Fairbury, Illinois 61739

Opened: 1962

Cost: $225,000

Capacity: 47

1981 Occupancy: 47

Licensing Status:
　Intermediate Care

Staff: 63

Administrator: Wayne Drayer

Former Administrators:
　Eli Leman
　Edith Huette
　Rosy Mowery

Supporting Churches:
　Fairbury
　Forrest
　Cissna Park
　Gridley

Additions:

1971: Activity room, etc., $20,000

1978-1979: 5 Apartments, $125,000

1981-1982:
　11 Condominiums,　$480,000

1981 Operating Budget:　$525,000

Institutional Publication:
　Fairview Haven Newsletter
　(Monthly)

APOSTOLIC CHRISTIAN RETIREMENT HOME
PARKVIEW HAVEN
Brook and Ada Streets
Francesville, Indiana 47946

Opened: May, 1978

Cost: $2,000,000

Capacity: 24 Apartments
　　　　　26 Health Care Beds

1981 Occupancy: 47

Licensing Status: Residential
　and Intermediate Care

Staff: 42

Administrator: Elmer Bucher

Supporting Churches:
　Francesville
　Wolcott
　Remington
　La Crosse
　Valparaiso

Institutional Publication:
　*News and Views of
　Parkview Haven*　(Monthly)

1981 Operating Budget: $482,000

APOSTOLIC CHRISTIAN HOME FOR THE AGED
511 Paramount Street
Sabetha, Kansas 66534

Opened: 1960

Cost: $115,000

Capacity: 80

1981 Occupancy: 80

Licensing Status: Intermediate
 Care

Staff: 85

Administrator: John Lehman
Former Administrators:
 Eva Hohulin
 Pearl Meyer

Supporting Churches:
 Sabetha
 Bern
 Fort Scott
 Wichita
 Kiowa
 Lamont
 Gridley
 Lamar, Missouri

Additions:
1966: 10 beds, $30,000
1972: 4 Apartments, $64,000
1979: 44 beds, chapel, library,
 recreational area, lounge
 and personal care facilities
 Cost: $700,000

1981 Operating Budget: $689,000

Institutitional Publication: none

Construction began March, 1982
 (Planned addition to be
 completed December, 1982;
 22 congregate living units, $1,150,000)

APOSTOLIC CHRISTIAN HOME
7023 N. Skyline Drive
Peoria, Illinois 61614

Opened: 1966

Cost: $420,000

Capacity: 54

1981 Occupancy: 54

Licensing Status: Sheltered
and Intermediate Care

Staff: 40

Administrator: Roger Herman

Former Administrators:
Marie Kieser
Lydia Meyers
Bill Cottrell

Supporting Church: Peoria

Additions:
1970: Nursing Wing, $400,000
1978: Eight Apartments, $500,000
1979 through 1981:
Four duplexes financed
privately at a cost of $500,000
1981 Operating Budget: $400,000

Institutional Publication:
Skyline News (Monthly)

Apostolic Christian Church complex, Rittman. A beautiful home for the elderly sits across the road from the church. The first church building, erected in 1874, is located in the upper right-hand corner of picture.

APOSTOLIC CHRISTIAN HOME, INC.
10680 Steiner Road
Rittman, Ohio 44270

Opened: 1976

Cost: $800,000

Capacity: 51

1981 Occupancy: 51

Licensing Status: Nursing
   Home Intermediate Care

Staff: 58

Administrator: Robert Ramsier

Supporting Churches:
   Rittman
   Akron
   Mansfield

Additions:
1979: 4 apartments, $80,000

1981 Operating Budget:
   $575,000

Institutional Publication:
   Newsletter (Quarterly)

Apostolic Christian Home, Rittman, Ohio

LONGVIEW VILLAGE
34 Middle Butcher Road
Rockville, Connecticut 06066

Retirement Apartment Complex

Opened: September, 1980

Cost: $750,000

Capacity: 22 Apartments

1981 Occupancy: 21 Apartments filled;
25 persons

Licensing Status: None

Staff: 3

Administrator: Administered by
five trustees.*

Clarence and Martha Mangold serve as
caretaker and cook.

Supporting Church: Rockville

*They are independent of the church.

APOSTOLIC CHRISTIAN RESTMOR, INC.
935 E. Jefferson Street
Morton, Illinois 61550

Purchased: April 1, 1978

Cost: $1.5 million

Capacity: 142

1981 Occupancy: 132

Licensing Status: Skilled Care

Staff: 125 (part and full time)

Administrator: Jim Metzger

Supporting Church: Morton

1981 Operating Budget:
$1.56 million

Institutional Publication:
Restmor Reports
(Quarterly)

APOSTOLIC CHRISTIAN HOME
1102 W. Randolph
Roanoke, Illinois 61561

Opened: May, 1975

Cost: $368,320

Capacity: 55

1981 Occupancy: 55

Staff: 37 full time equivalent
Licensing Status: Intermediate Care

Administrator: Frank Crawford

Former Administrator:
Stan Hodel

Supporting Church: Roanoke

1981 Operating Budget:
$578,000

Institutional Publication:
Lines From Home

MILITARY SERVICE: WORLD WAR II

The Apostolic Christian Church did not escape the turmoil that engulfed the entire world during World War II. Most of the church's young men who entered the armed forces did so as conscientious objectors, and all who were members served in this capacity.

By this time the government was organized to the point where men could enter the service with a clear indication they would not have to bear arms. This was a change from World War I when many military officials were unfamiliar with the status of those who refused to bear arms. This sometimes resulted in physical abuse of many young men who, because of conscience, would not take a weapon. During World War II many men entering the service as conscientious objectors mostly suffered only mental abuse at the hands of those who did not understand the concept of non-resistance.

During World War II the Apostolic Christian Church's position against war differed somewhat from those denominations with an Anabaptist and "peace church" heritage. In most instances, young men from the latter groups refused entirely to enter the military, instead serving in the Civilian Public Service system of World War II.

Apostolic Christians, on the other hand, felt a deep sense of commitment to a government that guaranteed religious freedom, and young men of the church were willing to serve the nation in nearly any capacity short of bearing arms and killing. Rather, they felt by serving in the Medical Corps as conscientious objectors (in a non-combatant role) they could serve the Lord by caring for the sick, wounded, and dying.

World War II was a time of great national mobilization. The security of the nation was at stake. For parents of young men leaving for service in the armed forces, it was a time of great sadness and near despair. Due to the intensity of the conflict across the seas, parents had no assurance they would ever see their sons again.

It was under these circumstances that young men of the church entered military service as conscientious objectors during World War II. Although they left home with a naive innocence and felt somewhat fainthearted, they departed with mountains of ongoing prayers behind them.

Although largely unnoticed by the public—or by historians for that matter—these courageous young men served with a distinction rarely matched in the halls of valor. Armed only with a small Testament and a cloak of impenetrable faith and riding the wave of heartfelt prayers of their brethren and loved ones back home, they accompanied their units—unarmed— into battle to face the enemy. Their lot was not an easy one as they endured firefights, ambushes, artillery, bombs, enemy mines, and a host of other nuances of war. Their mission was to administer aid to the bleeding and dying. In the true spirit of Christ, they patched up the wounds of those ravaged by the unChrist-like tactics of war.

Their faith and raw courage—though mostly unheralded— was a ringing testimony of faith and reflected their deeply-held commitment to the ways of the Lord; one of the foremost principles taught by the Son of God was that men should seek reconciliation and love rather than division and hatred. Killing, according to Scriptures, is forbidden.

To enter a combat zone takes courage above and beyond that which man can muster alone. Even those who are armed tremble before and during engagement with the enemy. Yet, to enter combat unarmed requires a world of faith and an infinite amount of grace. These ingredients allowed young Apostolic Christians to do this in many of the nation's conflicts.

The number of boys associated with the church who served in the military during World War II totaled more than twelve hundred. Nearly all of these were conscientious objectors. Elder David Mangold, Roanoke, Illinois, published the *Service Men's Newsletter* which contained a sermon along with the names and addresses of boys associated with the church who were serving in the armed forces. Issue No. 18 listed the names and addresses of more than twelve hundred men.

Several young men serving as conscientious objectors were injured in battle. It is believed that only one man who was a member of the church was killed during battle. He was Dale Aeschliman, son of Elder Sam Aeschliman of Bluffton, Indiana, who lost his life in late January, 1945, on the island of Luzon in the Philippine Islands. A friend since boyhood, Homer Reineck, from Bluffton, Indiana, (now a minister at Toledo, Ohio) was serving on Luzon at the time and listed the series of events associated with the death of Dale Aeschliman:

In late January, 1945, the 38th Infantry Division was scheduled to make a beachhead assault in Mariveles Province on the west coast of the island of Luzon in the Philippine Islands. Among the men who were to go ashore that day were S/Sgt. Dale Aeschliman, S/Sgt. Sam Schladenhauffen, Sgt. Everett Geisel, and myself, S/Sgt. Homer Reineck, all from the Bluffton church.

It was welcome news when we heard that the Japanese were not going to make a stand at the beach, and we all went into the L.S.T.'s and on the shore with thankful hearts that the usual beachhead battle did not have to be fought. Instead we were met by jubilant people of the island who were thankful to see the forces of liberation.

Since there was no opposition, all the soldiers moved toward our objectives as quickly as possible. In the confusion our ambulance company apparently got a little ahead of the infantry and stopped along the road to let the foot soldiers catch up. It was there that I saw Dale march by and the last time I saw him alive. He gave me a wave of his hand and disappeared out of sight around the shoulder of a hill.

Our objective was a road which ran across the base of the Bataan Peninsula. On the evening of the third day we met the first enemy opposition. It was in the foothills of the mountains which make up the backbone of Bataan. Since it was late in the day, everyone dug in quickly for the night. The Japanese began to harass the American soldiers with mortar and small arms fire. At just about dark someone started to call for a medic. Dale started to respond but was advised by his comrades to not go out so late. He did go anyhow and gave the man first-aid and made him comfortable for the night. On the way back to his own foxhole, one of our own soldiers saw him crawling in the near dark and shot him, killing him instantly. He was one of three Americans who met death that first day of combat.

The next day one of our ambulances took the three dead men to a cemetery site which Graves Registration had selected at the beachhead. After returning from the trip, the driver told me the sad news that my buddy was dead. By this time the battle arena had moved inland a considerable distance, so they chose a burial site at Olongapo closer to the battle. Since there were only three people in the first cemetery, it was decided to move them to the second site. I heard of this impending move and, when they laid Dale in the grave, was there to utter a prayer of faith to God on his behalf.

The Olongapo cemetery was a rice paddy, and after the area was secure, all the bodies were exhumed and taken to the high lands east of Manila. From there those who desired could have their sons returned home, so finally Dale could go to his last resting place by the church where he came to faith and learned to know of the mercy of our great God.

Dale Aeschliman wrote the following poem which appeared in the April 15, 1944, issue of *The Silver Lining*.[35]

"SOMEWHERE AT SEA"

We are now many days at sea—
    Our destination is unknown to me—
But whether I'm on sea or land,
    I'll put my trust in Jesus' hand.

I've left the home I love so well
    And more dear friends than I could tell.
But even though I'm far away,
    My thoughts will be with you alway.

Some times I sigh at all this strife
    That's come to pass in my young life.
Then I think how many more
    Have borne a heavier cross before.

Oh, our dear Saviour suffered great pain,
    But did He murmur or complain?
He bore His cross and victory won;
    He said, "Not mine, thy will be done."

At night when I lie down to sleep,
    I ask in prayer that He will keep
Us from all evil and from harm
    And protect us with His mighty arm.

I ask that He will safely bring
    Us to our friends and home again,
Back to the harbor we left before
    Where we'll see lights along the shore.

There is another harbor though
    Where we will all wish to go.
And oh, what glorious joy 'twill be
    To anchor there so safe and free.

               Dale Aeschliman
               Bluffton, Indiana

The men of the church who served during World War II received basic training at various camps in the United States. Several later served for many years overseas in a variety of dangerous situations.

MILITARY SERVICE:
KOREA AND VIETNAM

Not only did young Apostolic Christian men distinguish themselves as non-combatants during both of this century's world wars but also during the Korean Conflict and the Vietnam War.

Following the pattern established by brethren during World Wars I and II, the brethren and many friends of the church, based on deeply-held convictions that killing and violence are inconsistent with the teachings of Christ, served in the military in a non-combatant capacity. Like their forebears, they served with diligence (although unarmed) in any jobs they were asked to perform. Primarily, they served as medics.

During the Korean Conflict a young brother in the church from Ohio served as an ambulance driver. Among his responsibilities was to gather in the wounded or dead following battles and skirmishes. One time he received a package of delicious dainties from home. While sharing these goodies with his buddies, he over-indulged himself and awoke the next morning feeling sick. As he arose and prepared to make his regular ambulance rounds, a buddy said to him, "You look sick to me. Let me go for you today." He did, and he lost his life in a heavy barrage of machine gunfire which completely ruined the ambulance as well.

The young soldier from Ohio always kept a Testament in the ambulance. It was placed in a small toolbox. When he went out to retrieve his fallen buddy, he noted that the ambulance and the body were riddled with hundreds of bullets. Also, the small toolbox and its contents were riddled as well. But to his surprise, he noticed the Testament did not have one bullet hole—a marvelous coincidence.

Edwin Lee Stoller, a member of the church at Fort Wayne, Indiana, was killed in a helicopter crash on March 16, 1969. This occurred during the era of the Vietnam War, but took place near the Demilitarized Zone (DMZ) in Korea.

One of the brothers from the church who served in the military under dangerous and grueling conditions in Vietnam was with the 9th Infantry Division in Vietnam's Mekong Delta.

He was the subject of a feature story in the December 26, 1967, issue of *Look* magazine entitled "Pacifist on the Killing Ground."

The article described the life of a non-combatant soldier serving in war during very dangerous conditions. It described in detail the horrors of war and the duties associated with non-combatants who served as medics caring for and treating the wounded and dying.

The brother involved was quoted, "Too many people think a conscientious objector is trying to get out of serving. I'll do anything short of bearing arms and killing. I'm no better than anyone else."

Over forty young men from the church served in Vietnam. Two who were injured were Charles Sinn, Fort Scott, Kansas, and Ronald Koehl, Forrest, Illinois. Sinn later was placed in the ministry at Fort Scott, Kansas, on June 11, 1978.

During the Korean Conflict young men of the church serving in the military as conscientious objectors were trained at Camp Pickett, Virginia. Most of the men served here for three to five months. Worship services were held twice a month. During the summer, services were sometimes held in wooded areas near the camp. Families of the service boys co-operated in bringing ministers to the area.

In the late 1940's, the U.S. Army began training conscientious objectors at Fort Sam Houston in San Antonio, Texas. With many members and friends of the church coming to this base for training, church services were held here for many years. Services were conducted by visiting ministers under the jurisdiction of Elder Sam Anliker of Lamont, Kansas.

Over the years hundreds of the church's young men passed through "Fort Sam." A deep sense of brotherhood and fellowship prevailed at this camp as the young men took their basic and medical training.

Today, years later, several "Fort Sam" reunions are held and attended by men who served at this camp.

The chapel shown above was one of several where young Apostolic Christian men met for worship at Fort Sam Houston, Texas.

Even though the young men of the church have not taken arms to kill others, their record of medical service in the armed forces has won them the respect of their peers and of others who witnessed their service.

Many who engage in warfare often find it difficult to understand the position of those whose conscience, based on New Testament teaching, will not allow them to bear arms for the purpose of killing. The discourse written by the Apostle Paul in Romans 12:17-21 articulates very clearly the Scriptural direction for the redeemed child of God:

17. *Recompense to no man evil for evil. Provide things honest in the sight of all men.*

18. *If it be possible, as much as lieth in you, live peaceably with all men.*

19. *Dearly beloved, avenge not yourselves, but rather give place unto wrath: for it is written, Vengeance is mine; I will repay, saith the Lord.*

20. *Therefore if thine enemy hunger, feed him; if he thirst, give him drink: for in so doing thou shalt heap coals of fire on his head.*

21. *Be not overcome of evil, but overcome evil with good.*

APOSTOLIC CHRISTIAN PUBLICATIONS

The publishing of books has never been a high priority in the Apostolic Christian Church. This is because the church has viewed the world's greatest collection of books—the sixty-six books of the Bible's Old and New Testaments—as generally sufficient for godly living, and that a sincere believer, led by the Holy Spirit, can be adequately fed spiritually from these divinely inspired books.

There has never been any inclination on the part of members of the church to follow theology or theologians. There is a strongly-held feeling among members to order their faith, their life, and their church by the plain and simple Word of God.

Apostolic Christian Publications is not a denominational publishing house in the traditional sense. Rather, it was officially formed in 1968, according to Article I of its by-laws, to "create, develop, print, publish, disseminate, sell and distribute religious material, publications, and the like relating to the needs, purposes, and function of the Apostolic Christian Church; to obtain, receive, and disburse the funds by gifts, collections, requests and otherwise incident to such operations; with all the activities of this not-for-profit corporation to promote the spiritual growth and religious training of the church."

Essentially, Apostolic Christian Publications develops and distributes instructional materials for Sunday School and Vacation Bible School, distributes church hymnals, and in the late 1970's engaged in publishing a set of ten books by Samuel Froehlich. It has never, nor is it likely it ever will, involve itself in publishing religious manuscripts on various theological topics.

During the church's first one hundred years in America, its people were mostly preoccupied with earning a living and making ends meet. Life was simple and orderly. Yet, as the latter stages of the twentieth century began to unfold, dynamic change in society occurred in which many traditional values were threatened, and false religious doctrines began to proliferate. The church quietly moved to provide organized and uniform instructional materials for its Sunday Schools. Other materials published were for the purpose of promulgating the church's interpretation of salvation.

Concern about the need for a publishing capability surfaced in the late 1950's and eventually came up for discussion at the 1961 Brotherhood Conference. At the following year's conference, the Elder Body assigned ministers Eugene Bertschi, Roanoke; David Kieser, Princeville; and Joseph B. Schrock, Congerville, Illinois, to study the feasibility of publishing and to determine the initial needs of the church. At the 1963 conference this committee reported that the church was in need of a more suitable program of instruction. This committee prepared Old and New Testament commentaries to be used with Hurlbut's "Story of the Bible" in the fifth and sixth grades. They could also be used by the seventh and eighth grade teachers.

At the 1964 conference the Elder Body named a Primary Grades Program Development Committee to further research the needs of the church. Named to this committee were ministers Walter Anliker, Eureka; Robert Grimm, Morton; and LeRoy Hartman, Peoria, Illinois. A questionnaire was sent to each church to obtain a "grass roots" reflection of the church's needs.

From 1964 to 1967 these brothers and a few others began to develop a series of teaching materials to be used in the Sunday School (for kindergarten through second grade). A total of fifty-one sisters from various churches developed 208 lessons. In the fall of 1966, the Elder Body approved these lessons. By July, 1967, these booklets were put on sale at the home of LeRoy Hartman in Peoria.

In 1967 the Elder Body named a Vacation Bible School Committee to determine church needs in this realm of instruction. More and more churches were conducting these summer teaching sessions, and the church was generally without any structured teaching materials. Serving on this committee initially were Perry Zimmerman, Forrest; Edmund Kloter, Fairbury; and Edwin Ringger, Gridley, Illinois. At about this time requests for teaching materials began to increase. Until this time teaching aids were primarily purchased from non-Apostolic Christian sources.

Because of the pressing need for Sunday School teaching materials, the Elder Body granted the authority to establish Apostolic Christian Publications in 1968. According to a memo sent to all the churches, "it was a necessity born out of the need to preserve and plant the true faith in the hearts and minds of our Sunday School children, because many of the Bible story books and teaching aids through regular bookstores contain teachings and doctrines contrary to, and not in harmony with, God's plan of salvation as revealed in His Word."

The first meeting of the initial board of directors of Apostolic Christian Publications (a not-for-profit corporation) was held May 31, 1968, at the home of minister Edwin Ringger, Gridley, Illinois. The following members of the board were present: Leroy Huber and Walter Anliker, Eureka; Silas Leuthold, Princeville; Perry Zimmerman, Forrest; Edmund Kloter, Fairbury; Robert Grimm, Goodfield; and LeRoy Hartman, Peoria, Illinois. Officers chosen for the following duties were:

> President: LeRoy Hartman
> Vice-President: Edmund Kloter
> Secretary: Walter Anliker
> Treasurer: Robert Grimm

The Articles of Incorporation were certified by the State of Illinois on November 25, 1968.

Apostolic Christian Publications' initial materials inventory totaled only $400 (net cost). By 1981 this figure had reached $147,000. At the outset books and pamphlets were housed in the Peoria church with samples shown in the home of LeRoy Hartman.

In 1967 a small building was constructed in Eureka, Illinois, just east of the Apostolic Christian Nursing Home to house the operations of the Apostolic Christian Publications. It cost $10,000. Alvina Rocke, Eureka, served as the store manager. Annual sales volume by 1981 reached $55,250.

In 1977 Apostolic Christian Publications undertook a major project. They published a set of ten books by Samuel Froehlich consisting of his sermons on various books of the New Testament.

For many years the Braun family of Syracuse, New York (of the Apostolic Christian Church, Nazarene)—direct descendants of Andrew J. Braun, an associate of Samuel Froehlich—had led efforts in preserving the Froehlich writings. They had gone to great lengths—often at their own expense—to translate and publish these writings. A small foundation was established by Phillip Braun to fund the costs associated with the translation.

Headquarters of Apostolic Christian Publications, located in this small building east of the Apostolic Christian Home in Eureka, was built in 1967.

Because it appeared the Apostolic Christian Church (Nazarene) was not sufficiently interested in committing itself to the furtherance and perpetuity of the Froehlich writings, Phillip Braun, a church Elder at Syracuse, requested that the Apostolic Christian Church of America, whom he felt might be inclined to involve itself in preserving these writings, take over the operation of publishing and distributing these materials.

On July 21, 1976, Don Sauder, Roanoke, Clarence Kachelmuss, Forrest, Arthur Baurer, Princeville, and Charles Sauder, Tremont, Illinois, along with Elders Edwin Hohulin, Goodfield, and Perry Zimmerman, Forrest, Illinois, flew to Syracuse to meet with Phillip Braun and observe his publishing operations. Elder John Bahler, Rockville, Connecticut, also attended.

On October 4, 1976, a special meeting of the board of directors was convened at the church's fellowship hall at Goodfield, Illinois. Phillip Braun made a presentation dealing with the details and intricacies associated with publishing Froehlich's writings.

On January 4, 1977, at the publishing bookstore in Eureka, the board voted unanimously to become involved, on a limited basis initially, in publishing the Froehlich works.

Edwin Hohulin, his son Bill Hohulin, and LeRoy Hartman served on a committee to oversee the publishing of the ten Froehlich books. This committee met weekly until the project became well organized.

The project cost $60,000. Initially, the set of ten books sold for $49.50. A total of 12,122 books were printed. Also, approximately fifteen hundred tapes of Froehlich materials were made by LeRoy Hartman. By 1981 nearly one hundred sets of books had been sold.

A letter from the publishing house to all the churches dated October 17, 1977, included the following comments:

> This letter brings before you a very important message. In this day when all kinds of reading materials are available, promoting almost any kind of so-called religious doctrine to snare people's minds, we are indeed fortunate to be able to offer to our people the God-inspired writings of Samuel Froehlich, the forefather of our faith.

The preface to each book provides an interesting insight on how these books were translated:

REVISED DRAFT OF PREFACE TO FROEHLICH WRITINGS
January 25, 1978

From the year 1832, the beginning of the early activity of Brother Samuel Heinrich Froehlich, through the end of this activity at the time of his death in 1857, a very great amount of his writings have been preserved in various forms: letters received from him were treasured family mementoes; discourses on subjects written by him to various churches were highly valued by whomever had them in safekeeping.

These individual writings were, to a large extent, assembled by Elder Brother Fritz Diebold, who was the son of a co-elder with Brother Froehlich in Strasbourg. Brother Fritz Diebold was visited by Elder Brother S. J. Braun from America in 1920, and, since both brethren were very deeply interested in the writings of Froehlich, they spent some time together in Strasbourg, where Brother Diebold himself also lived. Brother Diebold spent a great deal of his time copying these many hundreds of individual writings on the typewriter.

Concurrently, another source came into being. This was a four hundred eleven page book (8½"x11") which was produced by the church in the Zofingen-Zurich area of Switzerland. This book was a gathering together into a typed volume of the treasured heritage of S. H. Froehlich's writings which were in the possession of the various members. It was a selection by which a discernment of the doctrine was maintained at that time. Possession of this book came into the hands of Brother P. N. Braun in 1923. It was given to him by Brother

Theophil Hinnen, elder in Zurich, who was a brother to Theodore Hinnen, elder of the church in the Zofingen-Zurich area, from whom Brother Theophil also received his copy.

When this book arrived in Syracuse, New York, it was received with great joy by Brother S. J. Braun who had it indexed and transcribed, producing four copies by typewriter. From this there have since been made over the years upwards of two hundred copies. These copies were all German. In the course of time, however, the German book was translated into the English language, and is now available in the volume entitled *Evidence and Demonstration of the Truth of the Word of God.*

In 1926, Brother G. A. Braun made a trip to Europe, by way of London, where he visited the Baptist headquarters. They very kindly provided him with all they had in their records concerning Brother S. H. Froehlich. This consisted of letters between the English Continental Society and Froehlich, among which was his answer to their "six questions." This particular correspondence has been printed and reprinted often since the late part of the 1830's, and is also included in the above-mentioned book assembled in the Zofinger-Zurich area, *Evidence,* etc.

Principally, however, the writings of Froehlich, from the years of his activity, were kept intact by his descendants in the form of his many diaries spanning a period of some twenty-five years.

In his travels on the continent in 1926, Brother G. A. Braun made further search for any part of the legacy of Froehlich's writings which might be available beyond that which had already been published at that time. At G. A. Braun's request, Brother Henry Michel took him to the home in Switzerland of the deceased grandson of Brother Froehlich, where the grandson's widow was yet living. She had been an English governess in the home of the grandson's first marriage. After the death of his first wife, the grandson later married her. Brother G. A. Braun asked Mrs. Froehlich if she had any information about the things which Brother Froehlich had left behind. In reply she pointed to a long row of diaries covering a period of about twenty-five years. Each diary was a little larger than the old German *Zion's Harp* hymnal. In these diaries Brother Froehlich had written down his sermons and copied letters he had sent, as well as discourses on various subjects. Through the kindness of Mrs. Froehlich, one of these diaries was loaned to the church and two very dedicated and loving maiden sisters in faith, the Schoeffter sisters, spent most of their remaining years deciphering the old German script and transcribing these diaries. The diaries came one by one for a while, and the copied diary was returned. Finally, Mrs. Froehlich agreed to allow the church to have these diaries as its own possession, and they are presently stored in the church in Zurich.

These writings have always existed in what is known as German script, by hand of Brother S. H. Froehlich. German script is no longer taught. The old script has been replaced by Roman characters. The

German script was very beautiful since the slanted vertical lines were parallel. That is perhaps the reason why the different characters often appear to be alike. It required those who were taught in the old school German to do the work of transcribing, and the Schoeffter sisters were the ones who performed this valuable task.

After these had been copied by hand in Roman letters, they were stenographically typed, one copy being sent to the church in Zurich and the other to the church in Syracuse. There were a couple of diaries which were transcribed at a later date: the 1848 diary by an author in Berlin, and the 1849 diary by a German woman in Syracuse who was versed in the old German script.

Brother Froehlich's fine, somewhat faded handwriting had often to be read with great pains. Many of his notations were abbreviated. It was also necessary to use a very strong magnifying glass in order to read them. It took many years to decipher most of the diaries and to rewrite them by hand in the present German alphabet.

In his addresses, Brother S. H. Froehlich, chose, for the most part, continuous Bible texts, and thus, he spoke about complete portions of the Bible verse by verse. After a sermon, he would write a short notation about it in his diary.

A new start of translation work was made during the period of 1926 to 1945, at which time the publication of the translated work was begun, and has been continued to the present by the Apostolic Christian Publishing Company in Chicago, now located in Syracuse.

The earliest printed work was in the German language: *The Mystery of Godliness and the Mystery of Ungodliness (The Two Mysteries)* in 1838; also, at the same time, what was known in German as *Die Erretung des Menschen durch das Bad der Wiedergeburt und die Erneuerung des heiligen Geistes-Eine schriftgermaesse Eroerterung ueber die taufe in Christum,* and in English as *Baptismal Truth of the Salvation of Man Through the Baptism of Regeneration and Receiving the Holy Spirit—A Scriptural Discourse Concerning the Baptism in Christ.* (This book was also condensed to tract form and published in French.) These two books were table talk in the German language in the families of the believers from 1838 to the end of the century, and they have remained as sound spiritual nourishment for the believers to this very day, well worth being read and taken to heart. They were translated and published in Syracuse in 1904.

No one will ever be able to form a true concept of the sum total of love, diligence, and patience that was expended, first by Brother Froehlich himself, then by all the nameless fellow-servants, so that this precious treasure might be preserved for us even to this time, ripe with temptation. If one were to survey all of these efforts, he could only respond in wonderment: "Surely God is present in it!"

It should be clearly understood that the King James version of the Holy Bible is the source of spiritual truth and light. The writings and meditations contained in this book are meant to be a help and support and are a most welcome revelation by Almighty God to man in the person of Samuel Heinrich Froehlich during a very dark moment in religious history for true believers. It would behoove us to be continually thankful to God for this.

Apostolic Christian Publications also publishes and distributes the official church hymnal, the *Zion's Harp* hymnal and another hymnal used in the sanctuary and in Sunday School, the *Hymns of Zion* hymnal. It is also caretaker and sales outlet for the *Gospel Hymns* hymnal.

Only ministers serve on the board of directors. Two of the board members must be Elders. Board members serve no more than seven consecutive years.

The new Froehlich publications were advertised in the December, 1978, issue of *The Silver Lining:*

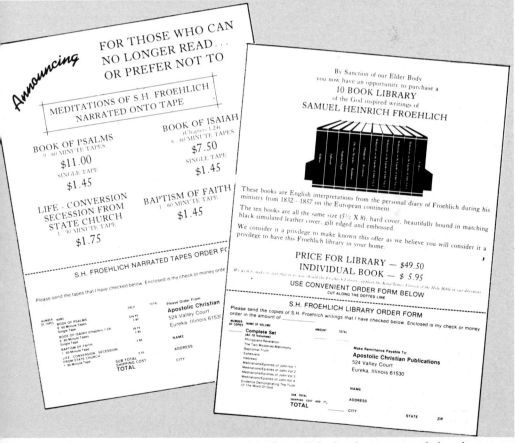

The above notice featuring the Froehlich books appeared in the December, 1978, issue of *The Silver Lining*.

THE SILVER LINING

Each month the church publishes a small periodical called *The Silver Lining*. This is a twenty-five to thirty-page publication referred to as "a light for believers." It is printed and published at Grabill, Indiana.

The Silver Lining differs markedly from most denominational publications. Instead of carrying articles on topics intended to lure readers—and using alluring graphics and layout to demand their attention—it is very simple in style and consists largely of news from the various congregations. Usually an article by a church official appears on the front page. Beginning in the late 1970's, each issue included a sermon by one of the church ministers. The publication usually has no pictures, no advertising, and is void of special graphic enhancement.

The Silver Lining was first published in October, 1943, in Grabill. It was distributed initially as a small, inspirational, four-to-six-page newspaper for men of the Leo, Indiana, area who were serving in the armed forces. It was published by the Leo Apostolic Christian Sunday School.

The first issue was well received by the servicemen. Jack Bollier, presently a minister at Leo, Indiana, wrote to *The Silver Lining* from his base in Florida,

> "I received your first issue of *The Silver Lining* and was glad to get it. I liked it and enjoyed reading it very much."

Several other complimentary letters from servicemen were printed in the December, 1943, issue (the third issue).

Minister Michael Weyeneth of Peoria, Illinois, who served in the military in Europe during World War I, wrote a letter of encouragement to the editor and indicated how much he would have appreciated such a publication when he was a soldier.[35]

The publication's general staff, listed in an issue published in the early 1980's, includes:

The Silver Lining

A LIGHT FOR BELIEVERS

VOLUME 27   NUMBER 9

Shepherd of
Bro. Noah S
viser, counselor
to rest. Noah
three years wh
neral was at t
99 south of Oak
been an ordain
years.

The funeral v
brief graveside s
etery, on the bl
the Mississippi
where Schrock f
floods.

The people wh
tives and friends
hands reflected li
the sun and soil—
loved by Schrock,
himself an ordinary

Theme of the ren
ers was this: Bro.
man of God, an exai
and community, a n
ed countless lives,
was immeasurable .
quoted Schrock, "Nc
ses me so much as
and Him crucified."

"The word of Gc
than precious to our
ther," a word that
without reservation" i
lived, and loved. He lc
believed in "labor anc
himself for others
Christ at the center o

Schrock was born n
and moved to Huron t
1915, before marryi
Lanz. He farmed for j
ed establish Huron sch(
came a church member
flood control work, Sc
extensive influence. For
he was president of t
Mississippi Flood Contr
an organization of 17
drainage districts from
berg, Iowa, to Hamburg,

Schrock annually made
Washington to testify bei

THE SILVER LINING

Grabill, Indiana 46741
USPS 496780

EDITORIAL STAFF:

Lynn Stieglitz
Robert Indermuhle
Albert Frautschi
David Bertsch
Cindy Baurer

The editorial staff wishes to acknowledge and thank all of the volunteers from the Leo Apostolic Christian Church who willingly give of their time to handle the many address changes, help mail the monthly issues and spend hours in editing. May God reward you.

Published Monthly By the Apostolic Christian Church of America.

Counselors: Theo Beer, Loren Stoller, David Bertsch.

SEND CORRESPONDENCE TO:
The Silver Lining
c/o David Bertsch
Route 2, Box 157A
Grabill, IN 46741

Second class postage paid at Grabill, IN 46741. The subscription rate is $6.00 per year. Send zip no. with address. Remember to send changes of address. Send both old and new addresses (with both zips).

IN MEMORY — EDITORS:
HENRY SOUDER
EDWARD SOUDER

rged to obedience, withheld
enings, but that we should
edient to the word of God,
simplicity that is outlined
Holy Scripture, and thus
uld remain a holy people,
it we would be able to work
salvation. We believe, be-
his was his innermost de-
iis service to his God, that
d be able to give an ac-
f his stewardship when
would come.

e was aware of the dim-
gloominess of the future,
ven saw that there would
dangerous time for those
d serve God. We believe
Mangold was well aware
his advice always was
humble. If we stay in
the Lord, be worthy of
g of God and His grace
uld be able to face the
t we would not have
nor that we would pos-
e, but that with a new
iew effort, and a new
iith, we could face the

if we hold fast to His
vord and remember
oing to be our Shep-
going to watch over
oing to supply our
s never failed in this.
e that not only here
ongregation, but else-
were many that
d find their way to
o unburden their
)elieve, that almost
on, as we are gath-
sometime or other,
of comfort to us.
of comfort in our
that were burden-
the judgment of
words of encour-
and by the Spirit
able to do this.
ies that we cher-
Jod bless us, that
ermitted to live

Although the practice was eventually discontinued, *The Silver Lining* formerly printed editorials. The January, 1944, issue carried an appropriate editorial for servicemen:

Editorial

When your thoughts turn, as they often do, to loved ones, the pleasant appreciations and familiar scenes of happier days are recalled. These memories of home—the way the sunshine streamed in on the breakfast table, father's favorite chair, the cookie jar, mother's sewing basket, the precious book, the Bible on the table—these are dear to you. Included also in your reminiscence might be the mottoes on the wall. Perhaps some of these are familiar and dear to you because they have been on the walls of your Christian homes since your childhood: "God Bless our Home," "He Careth for You," "Jesus Never Fails," "Trust and Obey," "Jesus Cares," "Prayer Changes Things," "God Answers Prayer," "The Lord Is My Shepherd," "It Pays To Serve Jesus."

Recollection and thought on these and others might be an inspiration as we start the New Year.

May God bless each of you. We would like to suggest that you make the motto, "Christ, My Guide," yours for the New Year. Then for you the dark clouds of 1944 will surely have a beautiful "Silver Lining."

As the years unfolded, *The Silver Lining* distribution increased. Eventually a few other churches began sending local news. Finally, each church began to participate. Local church reporters were chosen to submit monthly news to *The Silver Lining*.

In the beginning, circulation totaled approximately thirty-five. By 1981, it had reached 6,400.

Henry Souder, Jr., of the Leo congregation was the first editor of *The Silver Lining*. A single man, he labored diligently in preparing each month's issue. He died unexpectedly of a heart attack on September 1, 1977. He served as editor for thirty-four years. He was succeeded as editor by his brother Edward Souder. In an ironic turn of events, he, too, died suddenly of a heart attack on February 12, 1981.[36]

When Edward Souder died, the editorship evolved into a four-person editorial staff consisting of Elder David Bertsch, Lynn Stieglitz, Albert Frautschi, and Robert Cockburn—all of the Leo congregation.

A new building was erected in 1981 on the Leo church property for World Relief storage and *The Silver Lining* publishing and mailing. *The Silver Lining* room is on the right.

Almost as much as serving as a publication of inspiration and edification, *The Silver Lining* is also a vehicle for cohesion among the churches. Local church news including births, deaths, marriages, and baptisms keeps the churches well informed of each other. The abundance of local news aids in fostering familiarity among the churches. The result is the building up and reinforcing the sense of brotherhood and Christian love which runs so deep among, and is unique to, the membership.

The inspirational content of *The Silver Lining* includes sermons and writings of Samuel Froehlich, the founder of the Evangelical Baptist Church in Switzerland (which in America became known as the Apostolic Christian Church), articles on church doctrine, church history, and other writings on Bible topics. These articles, written by various church officials and other brethren, are intended to edify and strengthen the membership and to bring the truth of salvation to the many friends of the truth (those who are unconverted) who read the publication.

MINISTER'S BOOKLET

Orel Steiner of Oakville, Iowa, has completed a booklet entitled *Apostolic Christian Churches and Ministers* which lists the various Apostolic Christian Churches in the United States of America, and in Canada and Japan. Complete with names, addresses, phone numbers, and statistics regarding the number of families, members, and Sunday School students for each church, this handy booklet has proven very useful, both as a reference guide and in providing cohesion and familiarity among the churches. The 1980 edition consisted of twenty-seven pages. Six thousand copies were printed.

The first issue of this booklet was published in 1945. Two hundred copies were printed with only the churches and their ministers listed. At that time there were approximately 55 churches, 143 ministers, and 17 Elders according to the booklet. By 1980 it had been revised and updated eleven times.

The idea to publish a booklet of this type was born in 1936 when Orel Steiner, then of Morton, Illinois, and Ervin Rokey of Morton, but formerly of the Sabetha-Bern, Kansas, area, used to visit after mid-week services at the apartment of Ira and Carolyn Rokey in Morton. The idea of compiling a list of all the Apostolic Christian Churches and ministers was suggested to them. Since they were single brothers at this time, they had surplus time to devote to this project. In the winter of 1936, they began unofficially gathering data about the various churches. Minister Ben Heiniger of Morton, an uncle to Orel Steiner, helped them.

In 1939 Orel Steiner married Rose Thomas and moved to his father's farm near Oakville, Iowa. He took his notes and data on the churches with him. Getting married and moving to a new location undoubtedly diverted his attention from compiling a booklet on the churches. It was not until the fall of 1944 that he began organizing his materials and subsequently sent them to a printer in Burlington, Iowa. The various editions have been very favorably received. Over the years many brethren have offered helpful suggestions to make the book more useful and factual. Elder Joe Klopfenstein, Gridley, Illinois, was remembered by Steiner as one who was very helpful in offering suggestions for the booklet. Also, Elder Emil Schubert, Peoria, Illinois, who baptized Steiner, was appreciative of the booklet.

The booklet has been published every three years.

PRINTED SERMONS

The project of sending printed sermons to persons on a mailing list was an outgrowth of a similar project during World War II when sermons were sent to servicemen overseas.

The "Service Men's Newsletter" was prepared under the direction of Elder David Mangold, Roanoke, Illinois. Sermons were taken in shorthand and eventually typeset for printing. This was accomplished by groups of sisters from several churches who donated their stenographic talents. They also helped with stuffing envelopes and preparing the mailings.

When World War II ended and servicemen returned home, the "Service Men's Newsletter" was discontinued.

At the outbreak of the Korean conflict, the newsletter was resumed. Art Gasser, Rittman, Ohio, assumed responsibility for publishing the newsletter. He continued in this capacity until 1964 when publication once more ceased.

In 1966 publication commenced under the direction of Sidney Leman of Forrest, Illinois. Military conflict in Vietnam resulted in many young men of the church being drafted into the armed forces. Printed sermons were sent to these men. Leman served until 1974 when responsibility was given to Homer and Virginia Blunier, also of Forrest.

By the 1980's, sermons were no longer written in shorthand. Because almost every church has a tape-recording capability, sermons are tape-recorded and later transcribed. They are typed on a stencil, and a mimeograph is used to make copies.

In 1974 the mailing list numbered less than two hundred names. By 1982 it had grown to 450 names. The sermons are sent to servicemen, shut-ins, those who live far from established churches, deaf persons, and others who express an interest. Each Elder in the denomination receives a copy.

The printed sermon project is a part of World Relief. Funding usually comes from that organization, although direct contributions from individuals are accepted.

TAPED SERMONS

A fairly extensive taped sermon program has existed at Bluffton, Indiana, since the early 1960's. By 1981 more than five thousand taped sermons were sent annually to persons who requested them. Among the recipients were elderly persons, shut-ins, servicemen, persons living far from a church, and others who expressed an interest. The program has been supported by the Bluffton congregation. All tapes have been provided free of charge.

Paul and Mildred Schladenhauffen of Bluffton, Indiana, who initiated this service early in the 1960's, continued to oversee the program in the early 1980's.

The project made a notable achievement on March 31, 1982, when the one thousandth individual sermon was recorded and readied for distribution.

YOUTH ACTIVITIES

Young people are regarded as one of the church's most precious assets. Because they constitute the "future church," provision has been made, particularly in the post-World War II era, to give them proper fellowship within the framework of the church.

Programs to meet this objective have differed slightly in the various states but essentially center around special times of wholesome fellowship and singing for young people who are not members of the church.

ACYF: One of the first areas to engage young people in special activities (other than Sunday School) was central Illinois. In the late 1940's a cluster of churches initiated a program called "Christian Endeavor." In the 1970's this name was changed to Apostolic Christian Youth Fellowship (ACYF). Each church's high school Sunday School class gathered on Sunday evening at a host church. Each group made a choral presentation usually consisting of two songs. Eventually, these gatherings of young people became so large it became necessary for the host church to use two successive Sunday evenings to accommodate the large number of young people taking part. Half of the participating churches met the first Sunday and the remaining churches the second Sunday. Following the choral presentations, an inspirational talk was given with emphasis on topics of interest to young people. By 1982 these large gatherings (in Illinois) occurred four times each year during the September to May school term.

YOUTH FELLOWSHIP DAY: Out of ACYF has grown "Youth Fellowship Day," a special one-day "get-together" of several hundred young people from central Illinois churches. The Sunday Schools of the various churches sponsor this event.

Beginning in 1967, when the Bible classes of the churches at Cissna Park and Peoria met at the Three Bears area at Lake Bloomington for a picnic and evening program, Youth Fellowship Day has grown into a large, well-organized conclave held annually in the University Union at Illinois State University, Normal, Illinois. Attendance in 1975 consisted of 350 young people and nearly eight hundred who came to hear them sing at the evening program. This was considerably higher than the three hundred who attended the first gathering in 1967.

In 1968 Peoria and Cissna Park were joined by Morton and Roanoke at Lake Bloomington. Afternoon Sunday School classes were added. In subsequent years, these classes were taught only by ministers.

Although this annual event had been held at Lake Bloomington and Eureka College, in 1975 it was moved to Illinois State University where air conditioning and large food service facilities provided for ease of administration of the event.

CAMP MACK: Beginning in the late 1940's, churches in Indiana formed an annual convocation that later came to be known as "Camp Mack." This is a one-day gathering on a Sunday (usually in August) of persons from the Indiana churches with special emphasis on youth. It is held at Camp Mack, near Milford, Indiana. The campground complex is owned and operated by the Church of the Brethren. It is named for Alexander Mack who founded that church in 1708 in Germany.

The annual gathering began on a small scale. During the first few years, the Bremen, Milford, and Leo churches joined together for a picnic. Later, a few more churches joined them. This grew to the point where all the Apostolic Christian Churches in Indiana began to participate. Persons from several states often attend this event.

As the years unfolded, the project became more efficiently organized. It came to be known as the Indiana Apostolic Christian Youth Fellowship. By 1981 ministers Walter Steffen and Elmer Hartter, Milford, served as chairman and treasurer respectively. They coordinated activities with the Sunday School superintendents of the various Indiana churches.

The day-long gathering follows a schedule of Sunday School classes, preaching, singing, and fellowship. Meals are served in the camp's cafeteria. Always impressive is the afternoon hillside service on the edge of Lake Wabee. The day is climaxed by an evening service in the camp's huge auditorium. Singing by a mass choir and an inspirational message end the day.

Although average attendance generally ranges between nine and twelve hundred, as many as eighteen hundred persons have attended the Sunday evening services.

Camp Mack near Milford, Indiana

OHIO-MICHIGAN: A special day for youth of the Ohio and Michigan churches was initiated near Mansfield, Ohio, in the early 1970's. These annual sessions have been held at the Light and Life Camp on Route 39 southeast of Mansfield. This camp is owned and operated by the Free Methodist Church, although the one-day session sponsored by the Apostolic Christian Church operates independently of any affiliation with the Free Methodists.

Generally, the Mansfield church has assumed responsibility for organizing this well-attended event. The day's schedule of events is similar to that at Camp Mack.

MINNESOTA-IOWA: Each June for several years youth from churches at Minneapolis, Morris, and Winthrop, Minnesota, and Lester and West Bend, Iowa, gather together for a day of activity and fellowship. These meetings are held at the various church areas on a rotating basis, excluding Minneapolis.

MISSOURI-IOWA: Four churches hold a special day for youth each year. Participating in this event are young people from churches at Taylor, Missouri, and Pulaski, Oakville, and Burlington, Iowa.

KANSAS: Youth from the seven Kansas churches together with those of the church at Lamar, Missouri, meet each spring and fall for a weekend of fellowship. These gatherings include Sunday School children from the seventh grade through high school.

The youth groups usually meet on Saturday afternoon for registration and fellowship followed by a Saturday evening meal and special activities. On Sunday, they attend Sunday School and afternoon church and are served a delicious meal before departing to their home areas.

ARIZONA-CALIFORNIA: In 1959 the churches at Phoenix, Arizona, and Altadena, California, held their first special youth day at a public park at Blythe, California. Activities included Bible study and fellowship.

In 1974 youth from these two churches began meeting twice per year (once at each church). Later, as the Tucson congregation began to grow, youth from their church were included in these activities. By 1982, special youth meetings were held three times per year (once at each church).

UNMARRIED YOUNG ADULTS: An integral part of the life of the church consists of young adults who are members and are still single. Often referred to as the "young folks", they have remained over the years a very special part of the church.

Because single brothers and sisters do not date each other (relying instead on God to reveal their eventual mate to them), the "young folks" groups have served to provide times of rich spiritual fellowship and general social activity. Anyone who was a part of this group prior to marriage can attest to the special warmth and Christian love that exists among these young members.

A significant feature of this group is that nearly all unmarried brothers and sisters, without respect of persons, are included in their activities. For instance, some of the unmarried participants' ages may range up to forty years or more. In the true spirit of Christ, age becomes irrelevant, and because of their common repentance and conversion, all unmarried members can find comfort and a profound sense of oneness in their diligent espousal of the way of Christ.

Their major activities are "singings" which are held often. They also spend a great deal of time in visiting the aged and in other good works.

CHURCH SERVICES
IN UNIVERSITY TOWNS

As society began to change dramatically from a rural to an urban one, population shifts resulted in more Apostolic Christians living in cities and towns. Also, young people began to prepare for careers other than farming or related occupations which previously allowed them to live on farms or in farming villages.

With more and more young people attending universities, worship services were initiated on various college campuses in the Midwest. New churches at Urbana-Champaign, Illinois, and Iowa City, Iowa, emanated from these college services. The church at Bloomington, Illinois, developed independently of campus services at Illinois State University.

The first university worship services were held at the University of Illinois in 1956. Services at Illinois State University began in early 1957. In the 1960's and 1970's when state universities grew very rapidly, worship services were held in a variety of places: Purdue University, West Lafayette, Indiana; Ball State University, Muncie, Indiana; Western Illinois University, Macomb, Illinois; Michigan State University, East Lansing, Michigan; University of Michigan, Ann Arbor, Michigan; and Kansas State University, Manhattan, Kansas.

Ministers for worship services were provided by the Apostolic Christian Churches in each state where universities were located.

In the 1950's more Apostolic Christians began achieving a college education or professional training. This trend was a departure from a heritage (particularly in America) that placed little value on any formal education beyond the "three R's." In fact, the American forefathers disdained education, feeling that it was "worldly" and could pose a threat to the humble lifestyle of the believer. Although Samuel Froehlich was a man of letters and a highly polished theologian proficient in several languages, and several of his followers were in business or the professions, the church in America was decidedly rural and had "little use" for education. To them the only thing necessary to learn other than the "three R's" was hard work. The lack of efficient farming machinery resulted in the need for strong backs, and many of them. Because of this, youth remained in rural areas. There was no need for "higher" education.

As farming methods became more efficient and farms grew larger, the need for fewer farmers practically dictated that many young people leave the farms. The church has come to accept the fact that young people must prepare for professions other than farming. True to the attitude of their forefathers, however, the church has not been naive to the fact that "higher" education and its general environment can not only corrode a young person's devotion to God's Word and to the church but could uproot his faith entirely. For this reason, the church has sought to remain close to its youth who are attending colleges and universities.

COLLEGE WEEKEND

The establishment of worship services on campuses has seen the exchange of visits between young people attending the various schools.

One such special gathering of students is called "College Weekend." Held twice per year in the spring and fall, it is a meeting of Apostolic Christian college students from the various universities in the Midwest. It is not confined necessarily to students. Other young people from the church are free to attend.

"College Weekend" is the colloquial name given to these gatherings. While the church gives its sanction and support, it is not necessarily an "official" function but rather is spontaneous and organized by the students themselves with supervision from church officials. Students from several midwestern universities usually gather on a Saturday afternoon for fellowship. Often they divide into small groups and engage in discussions pertaining to matters of faith. Ministers of the church lead these discussions. Questions relevant to inquisitive young minds are answered and discussed.

Singing and fellowship are greatly enjoyed at these meetings. Church services are held on Sunday.

"College Weekend" activities began in the late 1960's.

MISSIONS

By 1982 the Apostolic Christian Church had been in America for 135 years. The church, coming from Europe, was itself an outgrowth of missionary efforts initiated by Samuel Froehlich when he sent young Benedict Weyeneth to America late in the 1840's. From such a beginning a new religious group was formed which in the 1980's totaled nearly twelve thousand persons. In more than thirteen decades, religious services had been held in more than one hundred American locations. Germane to any comments regarding the missionary activity of the Apostolic Christian Church is the fact that the church in America came about because of earlier missionary work.

In better understanding the church's missionary activity, one must first arrive at a definition of missionary work. Obviously there are many concepts in this realm. The classical definition, of course, is sending workers to spread the gospel in foreign lands, especially those considered heathen. Another definition might center on home missions, Bible distribution, or the establishment of churches in a particular area of one's native country. In fact, fulfilling a "mission" for the Lord might include things as simple as helping a neighbor, visiting a shut-in, or witnessing the Truth to an inquiring acquaintance. Thus, arriving at a true definition is difficult. At best, one might say missionary activity is multi-faceted and involves much more than conducting activities in "foreign" lands. One must take this into account when writing a history of Apostolic Christian Church missions. Also, it is well to realize that preaching the important message of salvation from an American pulpit, although perhaps not as exotic as preaching in a jungle, has just as much missionary implication—a lost soul who hears about salvation in an established American church is no less important than a lost soul who hears about salvation in a far-away land.

In its own way the Apostolic Christian Church has been active in "mission" efforts, even if seemingly less so than other "evangelical" churches. In a historical sense the church body by the floodtide of emigrants in the latter stages of the nine-general sense was evolving from being the beneficiary of missionary efforts in the mid-nineteenth century to trending toward conducting missions itself.

There are several factors which account for the activities and attitudes of the Apostolic Christian Church with respect to missions. At the outset in America, several young men of the faith from Europe were not hesitant to travel widely in the states to proclaim the gospel message. Their untiring efforts and missionary zeal resulted in the establishment of many new churches, particularly in the agriculturally-rich midwestern states. Their efforts were largely confined to farmers with a Swiss and German heritage as a common language proved very instrumental. Some of the early converts already had roots in the Evangelical Baptist Church in Europe while others were of Mennonite background. A few early converts were persons with an Anabaptist-related background. In any case, language and a common culture confined missionary activities mostly to persons with a European background. Yet, their efforts were very successful and the new churches grew, aided by the floodtide of immigrants in the latter stages of the nineteenth century.

Early missionary zeal later seemed to decline, and quite abruptly. Most of the early ministers (or "evangelists") who came from Europe were young men who had earlier been associated with Samuel Froehlich. He was a tireless evangelist, and his attitudes in this regard had a great influence on the ministers who later came to America. It is interesting to note that while Samuel Froehlich was full of missionary zeal, he was equally zealous in promoting sound doctrine and church order. He was not given to compromising his strong beliefs and convictions.

Yet, as the church in America grew and members became established on their farms, there were several factors which tended to inhibit missionary efforts, especially compared to those of earlier days. First, America was not a heathen land. By 1900, for instance, a great many religious denominations were established in America. Most people already had some sort of religious belief. Consequently, outreach activities met with competition.

Second, people of the church were preoccupied with earning a living. Ministers were not (and are not today) salaried; instead of going out and preaching, they were occupied foremost with earning a living. In addition, there was an ever-present preoccupation with adjusting from a European culture to the American one. Often this was not easy.

Third, and very significantly, a certain portion of the early American membership was not only agrarian in nature but was of Mennonite and Amish extraction. Their religious heritage was enshrouded in harsh persecution which had seen their Anabaptist forefathers' missionary zeal quelled by the heel of state authority. In response their missionary zeal was replaced by an "inner aspiration for piety and faithfulness to a more traditional type of religious life." In Europe they became known as the "Quiet of the Land," emphasizing the virtues of simplicity, honesty, and adherence to the faith of the fathers. They were content to live in peace on their farms, far from possible interference of state authorities. After several hundred years, some of these attitudes found their way into the Apostolic Christian Church and, along with the above factors, contributed significantly to the church's view of missionary activity.

Not only did Mennonites suffer persecution in Europe, but to a lesser degree Evangelical Baptists did so as well. Irritating discriminations by the state church in Switzerland, however, did not deter Samuel Froehlich from moving rapidly to establish many churches. He and his followers were very insistent, though, in their efforts to establish and maintain churches that were true to Scriptures and not patterned after the state church which they considered apostate.

The concern for doctrinal purity was very strong among Froehlich's churches, and this was a dominant value that was carried over into the newly-established American churches and is still very much alive today. Efforts aimed at protecting and defending sound doctrine, based on Scriptures, have always been very intense. Any efforts to reach out have been accompanied by concern for preserving sound doctrine and to prohibiting a watering-down process. Souls who respond to the gospel are cared for and spiritually fed within the framework of brotherhood. If a soul repents and then falls into apostasy, the Scripture says he is worse off than if he never repented.

The church over the years has felt that its primary mission in the United States has been to preach and teach the Truth and to exercise a godly stewardship over the churches established here. In this vein, one surely cannot discount or overlook the many thousands of converts who have been baptized here since 1847.

At the turn of the century, as the church grew and spread out over the Midwest and Great Plains, its overall missionary efforts were hindered by the first church schism in 1906-1907. Also the public trial of church officials in 1908 caused the church to withdraw inwardly. Added to this was the outbreak of World War I in which those with a German heritage were often disdained by other Americans. Then, both the Great Depression and later World War II proved to distract any thoughts concerning pronounced missionary activities.

Outreach activities other than forming churches basically among its own people did not materialize until the late 1930's when Amos Hartzler of Rittman, Ohio, felt moved to make exploratory efforts in northern Alabama. This was the church's first foray into an area of the United States where there were

who are devoted to the faith and who unselfishly give of themselves for the church's preservation. This alone is reason to be optimistic regarding the church's future.

The continuing dialogue of the Elder Body, through a systematic schedule of church conferences which convene to deal with divisive threats to the membership, serves as a potent, unifying, and cohesive force which serves to bind the brethren together in love and unity. Were the opposite true—no church conferences or no regularly scheduled meetings of church officials—the church denomination could easily fragment into factions. The ongoing brotherly esteem members share with one another is also a very positive force in the preservation and unity of the fellowship.

Another positive factor which bodes well for the future is the leadership's devotion to Scripture as unalterable and divine truth. Their unshakeable loyalty to God and His Word—rather than to theology and theologians—prevents a watering-down of God's ways and keeps the church on the pathways outlined in Holy Writ.

Another encouraging sign is the widespread devotion of most of the members to the godly heritage handed down from their forefathers. Basic doctrinal unity (as well as liturgy) is very strong, despite Satan's resolve to cause variance among the membership.

Even though it is possible to be optimistic regarding the future, one would be naive if he did not recognize that the church, which is decidedly on the defensive, will need to have its members stand shoulder to shoulder in order to hold its ground against the rise of evil. It must continue to be both sanctified and spiritually-minded in order to preserve itself as a pure and chaste bride that is properly adorned when her bridegroom (the Lord) comes to claim her.

The deep and enriching Biblical doctrines of submission, obedience, and yieldedness must be promulgated and maintained. So long as humility and meekness are regarded as among some of the most noble virtues of the Christian faith, the church will have a much better chance of discerning God's spirit and adhering to His ways. The Apostle James taught, "God resisteth the proud, but giveth grace unto the humble" (James 4:6). Also, the church will be wise to keep in mind a beautiful Scripture: "By humility and the fear of the Lord, are riches, and honour, and life" (Proverbs 22:4). In connection with this the doctrines of separation and nonconformity will have to be kindly but unceasingly re-enforced.

Probably one of the greatest challenges facing the church in the days ahead will be the prospect of maintaining its distinction—i.e., that of being "a peculiar people, zealous of good works" (Titus 2:14)—and of upholding godly standards in an age when moral and individual behavioral standards are on a rapid decline. These idealistic precepts can nearly become buried in today's hectic pace of life. Yet Scriptures strongly exhort God-fearing people to live in simplicity—"a quiet and peaceable life in *all* godliness and honesty" (I Timothy 2:2).

Upholding godly standards may not win the approval of an unbelieving world, but the believer's foremost obligation is to please God, not man. Brethren must realize they cannot serve two masters, and they must obediently order their lives, "Choosing rather to suffer affliction with the people of God, than to enjoy the pleasures of sin for a season" (Hebrews 11:25). It is sobering to note that the Apostle Paul exhorted Timothy, "Yea, and all that will live godly in Christ Jesus shall suffer persecution" (II Timothy 3:12).

The church will be greatly edified by appropriate and regular admonition and exhortation to strengthen among its members the truth of Scriptures, where the church came from, what it stands for, the meaning of its tradition, and where it is going. Teaching, as well as preaching, will become more and more important within the church in the days ahead.

Another important aspect of church life will be its attitude toward stewardship. In an age of abundance of material resources, the church will need to be diligent in sharing its surpluses. Each individual member's time and talent should be spent, not foolishly, but in ways that "redeem the time" and build up and further the kingdom of God. Also, the church must never lose sight of its spiritual stewardship as stated in I Peter 4:10: "As every man hath received the gift, even so minister the same one to another, as *good stewards* of the manifold grace of God."

During the culminating stages of the twentieth century, living for the Lord and fulfilling the demands of true Christian discipleship will be difficult and will require all the resources of devotion and discernment a believer can muster. Discipleship will require resolve in not yielding to the ungodly trends of society. Similar to believers in Galatia, they will do well to "Walk in the Spirit, and ye shall not fulfill the lust of the flesh" (Galatians 5:16). The battle lines between good and evil will be clearly drawn, and it will be up to the brethren to hold fast in order to make their "calling and election sure" (2 Peter 1:10). If the Lord tarries, several ironies will exist as the believer strives for righteousness on this "battlefield":

In a pluralistic society, brethren will strive to be "perfectly joined together" (I Corinthians 1:10) and to be likeminded (Romans 12:16).

Amid the tumult of a society that features frenzied activity, noise, and controversy, brethren will strive to hear "a still small voice" (I Kings 19:12) and will "study to be quiet" (I Thessalonians 4:11).

In a society that worships hedonism and self-gratification, brethren will strive to practice self-denial and service to others.

In a highly diverse and highly populated society, brethren will strive to keep themselves separated from ungodly influences and "unspotted from the world" (James 1:27).

In a society that fosters and promotes individualism and self-assertion, brethren will strive to find comfort in humility, brotherhood, and deference.

In an era that disdains authority, brethren will strive to be yielded and obedient.

In an era of "live and let live," brethren will strive to show spiritual concern for one another.

In an era of high living and outlandish consumption, brethren will strive to exercise proper stewardship of personal resources.

In an era of almost rampant divorce and family breakdown, brethren will strive to honor the concepts of fidelity and devotion within the framework of Ephesians, Chapter 5.

In an era when many modern women feel "true" fulfillment is found in pursuing a career in the work force, sisters in the Lord will strive to uphold the ideal that a much deeper and satisfying feminine fulfillment is found by being a keeper at home.

In an era when many modern women aggressively "demand" their rights, believers will strive to honor the godly order as set forth in Ephesians 5:23 and I Corinthians 11:3.

In an era when society is almost totally preoccupied with earthly and temporal matters, brethren, as pilgrims and strangers whose citizenship is in heaven, will strive to set their affection on the things that are unseen and eternal.

In an era when religious pluralism sweeps the nation, brethren will strive to appreciate and promote orthodoxy, both with respect to Scriptures and to the church.

The bride of Christ and the world must not be mixed together. The church will need to preserve its link to Scripture, to its forefathers, and to its tradition in order to maintain itself in the days ahead; to accomplish all these things and more, the church will need an abundance of God's grace and power and the "supply of the Spirit of Jesus Christ" (Philippians 1:19).

The church will be strongest, however, when its main purpose is to be about its Father's vineyard; doing the multitude of things God asks will insure a vibrant and true church. The carrying out of the noble command of preaching the gospel of salvation—repentance and conversion—will truly enrich the congregations.

Members of the church will be greatly aided in their spiritual endeavors if they can always remember the theme stated in Hebrews 13:14, "For here have we no continuing city, but we seek one to come." Moreover, brethren will have to be as "wise as serpents, and harmless as doves" (Saint Matthew 10:16).

Of great benefit to the church will be its efforts to continue in its understanding of true Christian brotherhood—members submitting one to another in the fear of God (Ephesians 5:21). Scriptures found in Saint Matthew 18, which outline how individuals and the church are to deal with erring and/or drifting members, contribute greatly to the foundation of true brotherhood. Likewise the teachings of Romans 14, instructing members of the church to have a concern for the conscience of their weaker brethren, stand out as some of the most noble precepts of love and brotherhood.

The result of devout and true discipleship is an eternal home in heaven which is reserved for the true and faithful—an abode of perfect joy and rest. Weary pilgrims, on hearing the trumpet of the Lord, will enter into that beautiful land and discover that "Eye hath not seen, nor ear heard, neither have entered into the heart of man, the things which God hath prepared for them that love him" (I Corinthians 2:9). An unknown author aptly described the tired and worn pilgrim's glimpse of heaven in the song, "At Home, 'Tis Well!" (*Zion's Harp* hymnal, No. 170, verse three):

At Home, 'tis well! There palms of peace abounding
Are gently cooling us, hot from the strife;
O'er-come now are all pains of pilgrim life;
The cries of fear give way to psalms resounding.

Thus, any earthly sacrifice, any acts of submission and self-denial, will be but a pittance when compared to the treasures and comforts reserved in heaven.

The faith of our fathers is indeed "living still." Today, however, it is not "in spite of dungeon, fire, and sword," but is exercised openly in a free land with no hindrance from without. Among the many blessings enjoyed by the Apostolic Christian Church is the tremendous opportunity to worship freely, encouraged by a marvelous government that guarantees religious liberty. In view of the past suppression that has hovered over Christianity, members of the Apostolic Christian Church should humble themselves daily at the altar of God offering thanksgiving for freedom of conscience.

*   *   *   *   *

Two verses seem to stand out regarding the conclusion of a church history:

"He hath shown thee, O man, what is good; and what doth the Lord require of thee, but to do justly, and to love mercy, and to walk humbly with thy God?"
Micah 6:8

"Let us hear the conclusion of the whole matter: Fear God, and keep his commandments: for this is the whole duty of man."
Ecclesiastes 12:13

THE END

"Let brotherly love continue."

DOWN MEMORY LANE

Akron, Ohio

Alto, Michigan

Athens, Alabama

Bay City, Michigan

Bern, Kansas

Bluffton, Indiana

Bremen, Indiana

Burlington, Iowa

Burlington, Oklahoma

Chicago, Illinois

Cissna Park, Illinois

Congerville, Illinois

Croghan, New York

Detroit, Michigan

Elgin, Illinois

Elgin, Iowa

Fairbury, Illinois

Fort Scott, Kansas

Fort Wayne, Indiana

Francesville, Indiana

Girard, Ohio

Goodfield, Illinois

Gridley, Illinois

Gridley, Kansas

Hillsboro, Alabama

Junction, Ohio

La Crosse, Indiana

Lamar, Missouri

Lamont, Kansas

Landersville, Alabama

Latty, Ohio

Leo, Indiana

Lester, Iowa

Mansfield, Ohio

Maywood, California

Milford, Indiana

Morris, Minnesota

Morton, Illinois

Naumburg, New York

Oakville, Iowa

Peoria, Illinois

Phoenix, Arizona

Portland, Oregon

Princeville, Illinois

Pulaski, Iowa

Remington, Indiana

Rittman, Ohio

594

Roanoke, Illinois

Rockville, Connecticut

Sabetha, Kansas

Sardis, Ohio

Silverton, Oregon

Taylor, Missouri

Toledo, Ohio

Tremont, Illinois

Union City, New Jersey

West Bend, Iowa

Wichita, Kansas

Winthrop, Minnesota

Wolcott, Indiana

FOOTNOTES

CHAPTER I
A New Beginning

1. Ruegger, Herman, *Apostolic Christian Church History, Volume I;* Apostolic Christian Publishing Company, 1400 Lake Shore Drive, Chicago, Illinois. 1949, page 179.
2. Ibid., page 179. There is conjecture as to which Virkler sent the summons from Lewis County, New York, to Europe. The only documented source indicates it was Joseph Virkler.
3. Bender, Arletha Zehr, *A History of the Mennonites in Lewis County, New York.* No date, no publisher, page 10.
4. Ibid., pages 11-12.
5. Ibid., page 53.
6. Farney, Mrs. Ira G., and Karcher, Mrs. Urban, *The Farney-Virkler-Zehr Families;* Willard Press, Boonville, New York. 1969, page 16.
7. Van Arnam, Lewis S., *Beaver Falls Cavalcade.* Published by Lewis S. Van Arnam, Beaver Falls, New York, 1979, page 15.
8. Bender, page 6. (John Keiffer is also referred to as Joseph Kieffer or Joseph Kaifer.)
9. Van Arnam, pages 15, 16, and 17.
10. Bender, pages 6, 7.
11. Ibid., page 7.
12. Ibid., page 7.
13. Farney and Karcher, page 474.
14. Ibid., page 474.
15. Ibid., page 474.
16. Schevill, Ferdinand, *A History of Europe from the Reformation to the Present Day.* Harcourt, Brace, and Company, 1954, pages 441-442. While this account may seem to have little relevance to Apostolic Christian Church history, it is significant in that it reflects conditions faced by young believers who served in Napoleon's army. Military conscription was a major reason for immigration to America.
17. Farney and Karcher, page 474.
18. Ibid., pages 21-22.
19. Ibid., pages 21-22.
20. Ibid., page 21.
21. Ruegger, page 179.
22. Interview with Priscilla Weyeneth Liebig, oldest daughter of Elder Benedict Weyeneth conducted by Fred Herbst, Roanoke, Illinois. Information taken from the notes of Fred Herbst, August, 1980.
23. Ruegger, page 179.
24. Getz, Joe A., and Heiniger, Arthur, *History of American Elders;* Morton, Illinois, 1972.
25. Letter from Elder Robert G. Beyer, Route 1, Castorland, New York, April 1, 1980.

26. Getz and Heiniger, page 24.
27. Ibid., page 25.
28. Steiner, Orel R., *Apostolic Christian Churches and Ministers*. Published by Orel R. Steiner, Oakville, Iowa, 1980, page 20.
29. Hough, Franklin B., *A History of Lewis County*. Munsell and Rowland, Albany, New York, 1860, page 74.
30. Farney and Karcher, page 481.
31. Ibid., page 634.
32. Information from records of Elder Robert G. Beyer, Route 1, Castorland, New York.
33. Interview with Mrs. Clara Merz, Castorland, New York, April 1, 1980.
34. Information from records of Elder Robert G. Beyer.
35. Newspaper article found in the Bible of Priscilla Farney in 1881. In possession of Mrs. Urban Karcher, Castorland, New York.
36. Linton, Calvin D., Ph.D., Editor-in-Chief, *The American Almanac*, Royal Publishers, Inc., Nashville, Tennessee, page 220.
37. Farney and Karcher, page 481.
38. Interview with Mrs. Clara Merz.
39. Farney and Karcher, page 489.
40. Notes from files of Minister Kenneth Indermuhle, Sardis, Ohio, November, 1980.
41. Baumgartner, John H., *The First One Hundred Years, 1870-1970*. 1970. No publisher, page 16.
42. Duke, Donald, Editor, *Water Trails West,* Doubleday and Company, Inc., Garden City, New York, 1978, page 44.
43. Kenneth Indermuhle notes.
44. Interview with Isaac Gehring, Sardis, Ohio, July 21, 1980.
45. Baumgartner, page 16.
46. Kenneth Indermuhle notes.
47. Getz and Heiniger, page 28.
48. Newspaper article from Sardis area describing Open House of Sardis Apostolic Christian Church, August 13, 1967.
49. *Silver Lining,* September, 1964.
50. Kenneth Indermuhle notes.
51. Getz and Heiniger, page 28.
52. From the records of Jerry Schar, Rittman, Ohio.
53. Ibid.
54. Letter from Elder Ben C. Maibach, Jr., 14726 Fox Road, Detroit, Michigan, September 18, 1980.
55. Steiner, page 23.
56. Article from *Silver Lining*.
57. Letter from Elder Rudolph Graf, 1404 Keystone Boulevard, Akron, Ohio, February 4, 1982.
58. Interview with Mrs. Minnie Barth Welz, 812 Fifth Street, New Martinsville, West Virginia, July 21, 1980.
59. Interview with Mrs. Minnie Barth Welz.
60. Interview with Mrs. Minnie Barth Welz.

CHAPTER II
Lighting A Candle

1. Kuiper, B. K., *The Church In History*. William B. Eerdmans' Publishing Company, Grand Rapids, Michigan, 1970, pages 307-308.
2. *Autobiography of Samuel H. Froehlich,* a pamphlet published by Phillip Braun, Syracuse, New York.
3. Douglas, J. D., General Editor, *The New International Dictionary of the Christian Church*. Zondervan Publishing House, Grand Rapids, Michigan, 1979, pages 295-296.
4. *Individual Letters and Meditations From The Legacy of S. H. Froehlich*. Apostolic Christian Publishing Company, Syracuse, New York, 1926, page 2.
5. Ibid., page 2.
6. Ibid., page 3.
7. Ibid., page 3.
8. Ibid., page 3.
9. Ibid., page 4.
10. Ibid., page 5.
11. Ibid., page 5.
12. Ibid., page 7.
13. Ibid., page 7.
14. Ibid., page 7.
15. Ibid., page 9.
16. Ruegger, Herman, *Apostolic Christian Church History, Volume I,* Apostolic Christian Publishing Company, 1400 Lake Shore Drive, Chicago, Illinois, 1949, page 39.
17. Douglas, J. D., page 729.
18. Ruegger, page 39.
19. Ibid., page 42.
20. *A Condensed Outline of the Life of Samuel H. Froehlich*. Author not listed. No date. Published in pamphlet form by the Apostolic Christian Publishing Company, 237 Robineau Road, Syracuse, New York, page 5.
21. Ruegger, page 43.
22. *Condensed Outline,* page 5.
23. Ephesians 4:5.
24. Ruegger, page 44.
25. Ibid., pages 46, 47, and 48.
26. Ibid., page 47.
27. *The Mennonite Encyclopedia,* Volume III, page 290.
28. Ruegger, page 95.
29. *Condensed Outline,* page 5.
30. Wenger, John Christian, *Glimpses of Mennonite History and Doctrine;* Herald Press, Scottdale, Pennsylvania, 1959, page 44.
31. Ibid., page 44.

32. *The Mennonite Encyclopedia,* Volume II, page 415.
33. Ruegger, page 61.
34. Interview conducted by Peter Weber, 522 West Westwood Drive, Peoria, Illinois, with Theodor Froehlich, grandson of Samuel H. Froehlich, on July 22, 1980, at the retirement home "Mattenhof" in Berne, Switzerland.
35. Interview with Theodor Froehlich.
36. Ruegger, pages 69-70.
37. Ibid., pages 59-60.
38. Ibid., page 72.
39. Ibid., page 93.
40. Ibid., page 94.
41. Ibid., page 131.
42. Ibid., page 139.
43. Kuiper, page 163.
44. Blanke, Fritz, *Brothers in Christ.* Herald Press, Scottdale, Pennsylvania, 1961, page 20.
45. Smith, C. Henry, *The Story of the Mennonites.* Mennonite Publication Office, Newton, Kansas, 1959, page 14.
46. Wenger, John Christian, *Separated Unto God;* Herald Press, Scottdale, Pennsylvania, 1955, page 58.
47. *The Mennonite Encyclopedia,* Volume IV, page 433.
48. Dowley, Dr. Tim, Organizing Editor; *Eerdmans' Handbook to the History of Christianity,* William B. Eerdmans' Publishing Company, Grand Rapids, Michigan, 1977, page 400.
49. *The Mennonite Encyclopedia,* Volume I, page 595.

CHAPTER III
Toward A Better Land

1. *Encyclopedia Americana, Volume XIV,* page 804.
2. Kirkham, E. Kay, *Survey of American Church Records, Volume II,* Deseret Book Company, Salt Lake City, Utah, no date, page 53.
3. Ibid., page 56.
4. Krout, John A., *U.S. History Since 1865,* Barnes and Noble, Inc., New York, 1955, page 15.
5. Ruegger, Herman, *Apostolic Christian Church History, Volume I,* Apostolic Christian Publishing Company, 1400 Lake Shore Drive, Chicago, Illinois, 1949, pages 68, 69.
6. Ibid., pages 158, 159.
7. Meiss, Roland, Editor, *Family and Descendants of John Adam Meiss,* Revised Edition, 1975, no publisher.
8. Interview with Mrs. Dena Wernli Emch, Madison, Kansas, October 12, 1980.
9. Schlipf, William O., and Schlipf, Martha, *Genealogy of the Georg Leonard Schlipf Family, 1790-1960;* no date, no publisher, pages 48-49.

10. Baumgartner, John H., *The First One Hundred Years, 1870-1970,* no publisher, 1970, page 53.
11. *Genealogy of the Jacob Wittmer Family,* pages 7, 8.
12. *Silver Lining,* February, 1963.
13. *Time Magazine,* December 15, 1980, page 14.
14. Taylor, J. Earl, *The Old Timer.* Published by The Gridley News, no date, page 7.

CHAPTER IV
Early Evangelism In America

1. Getz, Joe A., and Heiniger, Arthur, *History of American Elders;* 1972; page 12.
2. Notes from files of Fred Herbst, Roanoke, Illinois.
3. Butikofer, Gary Edward, *The Complete Life History of John Grimm, Sr., and His Wife Anna Elizabeth Eberhart,* 1968, no publisher, page 17.
4. Michel, Henry, *I Will Remember the Works of the Lord.* An address given to Apostolic Christian Camp, Lake Bloomington, Illinois, August 24, 1947. This address was later printed in pamphlet form. Page 14.
5. Ibid., page 14.
6. Notes from the files of Fred Herbst, Roanoke, Illinois.
7. *Silver Lining,* December, 1963.
8. Baumgartner, John H., *The First One Hundred Years, 1870-1970,* 1970, no publisher, page 14.
9. Ruegger, Herman, *Apostolic Christian Church History, Volume I,* Apostolic Christian Publishing Company, 1400 Lake Shore Drive, Chicago, Illinois, 1949, page 169.
10. Nussbaum, Ben, *74 Years of South Side Apostolic Christian Church History;* printed by Data Services Corp., Dayton, Ohio, 1973, page 14.
11. Ruegger, pages 166-167.
12. Michel, page 13.
13. Ibid., page 13. This incident actually took place in Budapest. The city is divided by the Danube River. Formerly, the west side of the river was called Buda and the east side Pest *(World Book Encyclopedia,* Volume II, page 554).
14. Interview with Elder Rudolph Graf, 1404 Keystone Boulevard, Akron, Ohio, July 19, 1980.
15. *Silver Lining,* December, 1963.
16. Studies in Anabaptist and Mennonite History: *Centennial History of the Mennonites of Illinois, 1829-1929* by Harry F. Weber. Mennonite Historical Society, Goshen College, Goshen, Indiana, 1931, page 101.
17. *History of the Peoria Apostolic Christian Church.* Included in Directory of the Apostolic Christian Church of Peoria, Illinois, 1978, page 1.
18. Michel, page 14.
19. *Silver Lining,* December, 1963.

20. Diary of Elder Henry Geistlich, Meilen, Switzerland. He visited America from May 28, 1866, to September 7, 1866. Diary entry June 10, 1866.
21. Interview with Albert Wuthrich, 519 Arkansas Avenue, Bloomfield, Iowa, November 8, 1980.
22. Gingerich, Melvin, *The Mennonites in Iowa*, published at Iowa City, Iowa, in 1939 by the State Historical Society of Iowa, page 62.
23. Robertson, Col. Robert S., *History of the Upper Maumee Valley*, *Volume I*, Brant and Fuller, Madison, Wisconsin, 1889, page 463.
24. Letter from Mrs. Mary Lou Klopfenstein, 5719 Tomahawk Trail, Fort Wayne, Indiana, March 23, 1982.
25. *Silver Lining*, November, 1963.
26. Baumgartner, page 31.
27. Stoller, Elma L., *1874-1974 Rittman Apostolic Christian Church*, 1974, no publisher, page 6.
28. Geistlich Diary, page 25.
29. Getz and Heiniger, page 25.
30. Farney, Mrs. Ira G., and Karcher, Mrs. Urban, *The Farney-Virkler-Zehr Families;* Willard Press, Boonville, New York, 1969, page 634.
31. Getz and Heiniger, page 25.

CHAPTER V
Decades of Promise—1850 to 1870

1. Linton, Calvin D., Ph.D., Editor-in-Chief, *The American Almanac*, Royal Publishers, Inc., Nashville, Tennessee, 1977, pages 136-138.
2. *Silver Lining*.
3. *Silver Lining*, July, 1977.
4. Moore, Roy L., A.B., *History of Woodford County*, Woodford County *Republican*, 1910, page 20.
5. Ibid., page 20.
6. Diary of Elder Henry Geistlich, Meilen, Switzerland, page 16.
7. *Des Moines Register*, February 21, 1937.
8. Fitsch, George W., *Past and Present of Fayette County, Iowa, Volume I*, 1910, page 432, 1910.
9. Ibid., page 433.
10. *Silver Lining*, December, 1963. Vol. 14, p. 26.
11. Butikofer, Gary Edward, *The Complete Life History of John Grimm, Sr., and His Wife Anna Elizabeth Eberhart*, 1968, no publisher, page 17.
12. Ibid., page 17.
13. Ibid., page 19.
14. Interview with Marie Schupbach Butikofer, 90, a lifelong resident of Elgin, Iowa, August 30, 1980.
15. Ruegger, Herman, *Apostolic Christian Church History, Volume I*, Apostolic Christian Publishing Company, 1400 Lake Shore Drive, Chicago, Illinois, 1949, page 185.

16. Koch, Hanna, *Genealogies of the Getz-Koch-Wick Families*. No date, no publisher, page 135.
17. Ibid., page 127.
18. Interview with Minister John Diggelman, 9107 Second Avenue, North Bergen, New Jersey, December 9, 1980.
19. *Silver Lining*, October, 1969.
20. Ruegger, page 181.
21. Letter from Louise Mueller Akel, 7507 Kimberly Boulevard, North Lauderdale, Florida, January, 1981.
22. Lehman, James O., *Crosswinds: From Switzerland to Crown Hill*, Crown Hill Mennonite Church, Rittman, Ohio, 1975, page 28.
23. *The Mennonite Encyclopedia*, Volume II, page 717.
24. Getz, Joe A., and Heiniger, Arthur, *History of American Elders*, 1972, page 28.
25. Stoller, Elma L., *1874-1974 Rittman Apostolic Christian Church*, no publisher, page 6.
26. *Silver Lining*, October, 1964.
27. Telephone conversation with Minister Walter Rehklau, 4905 Pine Ridge Road, Toledo, Ohio, May 22, 1981.
28. Studies in Anabaptist and Mennonite History: *Centennial History of the Mennonites of Illinois 1829-1929* by Harry F. Weber. Mennonite Historical Society, Goshen College, Goshen, Indiana, 1931, page 217.
29. Transcript of address by Elder Noah Schrock, Oakville, Iowa, presented at the Apostolic Christian Church at Phoenix, Arizona, August, 1968, page 2.
30. Perrin, W. H., and Hill, H. H., *The Past and Present of Woodford County, Illinois;* Wm. LeBaron, Jr., and Co., 186 Dearborn Street, Chicago, Illinois, 1878, pages 614-615.
31. *Genealogy of Peter Rinkenberger II,* a short family history. No author listed.
32. Geistlich Diary, August 12, 1866, page 23.
33. Interview with Elizabeth Gudeman Pfister, Roanoke, Illinois, summer, 1979.
34. *Silver Lining*.
35. Perrin, W. H., and Hill, H. H., page 337.
36. Geistlich Diary, August 12, 1866, page 23.
37. Notes from files of Fred Herbst, Roanoke, Illinois.
38. Kenyon, Franklin L., Editor, *Bridging the Years*. Published by the Roanoke Centennial Association, 1974, page 17.
39. *Silver Lining*.
40. Ruegger, page 133.
41. *Silver Lining*, April, 1969.
42. Baumgartner, John H., *The First One Hundred Years, 1870-1970*, no publisher, page 31.
43. *The Mennonite Encyclopedia*, Volume I, page 298.
44. Gratz, Delbert, *Bernese Anabaptists,* The Mennonite Historical Society, Goshen College, Goshen, Indiana, 1953, page 153.
45. *The Mennonite Encyclopedia*, Volume IV, page 646.

46. *The Mennonite Encyclopedia,* Volume III, page 178.
47. Baumgartner, page 35.
48. *History of the Peoria Apostolic Christian Church,* included in Directory of the Apostolic Christian Church of Peoria Illinois, 1978, page 1.
49. Ibid., page 1.
50. Letter from Richard D. Hartman, 4564 Olive Avenue, La Mesa, California, January 28, 1981.
51. Interview by Minister LeRoy Hartman, Peoria, Illinois, with Mary Huette, Restmor Nursing Home, Morton, Illinois, in 1977.
52. Ruegger, pages 158 and 184.
53. Peoria Church History, page 3.
54. Steiner, Orel R., *Apostolic Christian Churches and Ministers,* 1980, no publisher, page 7.
55. Notes from files of Arthur Heiniger, 109 Behrends Court, Morton, Illinois.
56. *History of Tazewell County, Illinois.* Chas. C. Chapman and Company, Chicago, Illinois, 1879, page 536.
57. Geistlich Diary, July 29, 1866, page 21.
58. *Silver Lining,* December, 1974.
59. Notes from files of Arthur Heiniger, 109 Behrends Court, Morton, Illinois.
60. Getz and Heiniger, page 10.
61. Morton Centennial Edition, published by the Tazewell Publishing Company in cooperation with R. C. Conibear and the Morton Historical Society, January, 1977, page 5.
62. Interview with Mary Getz, Morton, Illinois, September 27, 1980.
63. *The Mennonite Encyclopedia,* Volume IV, page 667.
64. *The Mennonite Quarterly Review,* April, 1976.
65. Ibid.
66. Letter from Mark Souder, Grabill, Indiana, January 8, 1981.
67. Getz and Heiniger, page 16.
68. Robertson, Col. Robert S., *History of Upper Maumee Valley, Volume I,* Brant and Fuller, Madison, Wisconsin, 1889, page 463.
69. Geistlich Diary, August 19, 1866, page 24.
70. *Silver Lining,* January, 1968.
71. *Silver Lining,* June, 1964.
72. Letter from Kathryn Beer Emch, 5637 West Liberty, Hubbard, Ohio, October 17, 1980.
73. Farney, Mrs. Ira G., and Karcher, Mrs. Urban, *The Farney-Virkler-Zehr Families;* Willard Press, Boonville, New York, 1969, page 660.
74. *Silver Lining,* May, 1970.
75. Nussbaum, Ben, *110 Years of North Side (Forrest) Apostolic Christian Church History 1864-1974;* Fairbury, Illinois, no date, no publisher, page 33.
76. Ibid., page 27.
77. *Silver Lining.*
78. Gingerich, Melvin, *The Mennonites in Iowa,* published at Iowa City, Iowa, in 1939, by the State Historical Society of Iowa, page 89.

79. Ibid., page 62.
80. *Silver Lining.*
81. Steiner, page 2.
82. Ruegger, page 120.
83. Getz, Joe A., and Heiniger, Arthur, page 4.
84. Interview with Elder John Bahler, 79, 24 Hilltop Drive, Tolland, Connecticut, March 31, 1980.
85. Steiner, page 14.
86. Nussbaum, Ben, *74 Years of South Side Apostolic Christian Church History.* Fairbury, Illinois, 1972, no publisher, page 29.
87. Ibid., pages 59-60.
88. Ibid., page 61.

CHAPTER VI
Flame Across the Prairie—1870-1900

1. Feucht, Betty Jane and Shirley, *Princeville Apostolic Christian Church, 1880 to 1976;* printed by Illinois Valley Printing, Peoria, Illinois, 1976, page 4.
2. Wahls, Mrs. R. H., and Hill, Mrs. W. H., *A Short History Of Our Community;* Gridley Centennial Book, 1956, no publisher, page 139.
3. *History of McLean County;* Wm. LeBaron, Jr., and Company, Chicago, Illinois, 1879, page 912.
4. Ibid., pages 562, 563.
5. Drury, John, *This is Livingston County, Illinois;* The Loree Company, Chicago, Illinois, 1955, page 271.
6. Lewis-James, Alma, *Stuffed Clubs and Antimacassars;* printed by Riverside Graphics, Streator, Illinois, 1977, page 31.
7. *Silver Lining,* May, 1971.
8. *Silver Lining,* March, 1967.
9. Steiner, Orel R., *Apostolic Christian Churches and Ministers,* 1980, no publisher, page 4.
10. Interviews with Leamon "Rex" Beyer, Diamond, Missouri, on October 10, 1980, and January 3, 1981.
11. Interview with Elder Sam Anliker, Madison, Kansas, October 11, 1981.
12. *Autobiography of Ernest Graf, Sr.,* Route 6, Akron, Ohio, 1941, no publisher, page 18.
13. Telephone conversation with Earl Sauder, Groveland, Illinois, May 24, 1981.
14. Steiner, page 5.
15. *Silver Lining,* February, 1963.
16. The *Fox Valley Mirror,* 104 Western Avenue, Carpentersville, Illinois, September, 1940, page 189.
17. Telephone conversation with Marie Schupbach Butikofer, Elgin, Iowa, October 31, 1981.
18. Telephone conversation with Ernestine Gudeman, Fairview Haven Nursing Home, Fairbury, Illinois, October 31, 1981.

19. Schlipf, William O., and Schlipf, Martha, *Genealogy of the Georg Leonard Schlipf Family, 1790-1960,* no date, no publisher, page 63.
20. *Silver Lining,* August, 1964.
21. Steiner, page 21.
22. Notes from files of Fred Herbst, Roanoke, Illinois.
23. Interview with Samuel Kraft, Gridley, Kansas, October 11, 1980.
24. Getz, Joe A., and Heiniger, Arthur, *History of American Elders;* 1972, page 20.
25. Emch, Bernie, *A History of the Apostolic Christian Church of Greenwood County, Kansas (Lamont) 1881-1978.* Printed by Sekan Printing, Inc., Fort Scott, Kansas, 1978, page 6.
26. Linton, Calvin D., Ph.D., Editor-in-Chief, *The American Almanac,* Royal Publishers, Inc., Nashville, Tennessee, 1977, page 220.
27. Emch, page 6.
28. Interview with Bernie Emch, Madison, Kansas, October 11, 1980.
29. Letter from Geraldine Fankhauser Beyer, Phoenix, Arizona, February 21, 1981.
30. Mogler, Charles, *Golden Memories of Yesteryear,* West Bend, Iowa, 1979, no publisher, page 3.
31. Ibid., page 3.
32. Notes of Ruth Pfister Sinn, Fort Scott, Kansas.
33. Getz and Heiniger, page 29.
34. Ibid., page 29.
35. Steiner, page 15.
36. *Silver Lining,* June, 1963.
37. *Silver Lining,* June, 1963.
38. Trager, James, *The People's Chronology,* Holt, Rinehart, and Winston. 1979, page 636.
39. Ibid., page 507.
40. Much of the history of the Burlington-Kiowa church was gathered from the recollections of John Hoffman as told to Kathryn Miller.
41. Swanson, John R., *The Indian Tribes of North America.* Smithsonian Institute Press, page 294.
42. *Silver Lining,* June, 1963.
43. *History of Lamar Church.* No author listed, page 3.

CHAPTER VII
Growth and Challenge—1900-1915

1. Ruegger, Herman, *Apostolic Christian Church History, Volume I,* Apostolic Christian Publishing Company, 1400 Lake Shore Drive, Chicago, Illinois, 1949, page 189-90.
2. Trager, James, *The People's Chronology.* Holt, Rinehart, and Winston, 1979, page 672.
3. Steiner, Orel R., *Apostolic Christian Churches and Ministers.* Oakville, Iowa, 1980, no publisher, page 18.

4. Getz, Joe A., and Heiniger, Arthur, *History of American Elders.* 1972, page 17.
5. Ibid., page 19.
6. Steiner, page 14.
7. Information on the New Boston meetings was provided by Orel R. Steiner, Oakville, Iowa.
8. Steiner, page 10.
9. Ibid., page 19.
10. Nussbaum, Ben, *74 Years of South Side Apostolic Christian Church History.* Fairbury, Illinois, 1973, no publisher, page 16.
11. Getz and Heiniger, page 14.
12. Paulding, Ohio, newspaper article.
13. Letter from Elder Edward Frank, La Crosse, Indiana, November 18, 1980.
14. Steiner, page 11.

CHAPTER VIII
Crises and Adjustments—1915-1935

1. Ruegger, Herman, *Apostolic Christian Church History, Volume I;* Apostolic Christian Church Publishing Company, 1400 Lake Shore Drive, Chicago, Illinois, 1949, page 215.
2. The Peoria *Journal Star,* Peoria, Illinois, February 1, 1980.
3. *Silver Lining,* May, 1965.
4. Interview with David Meister, Peoria, Illinois, November 1, 1980.
5. Interview with William Gramm, Gridley, Illinois, March, 1980.
6. Interview with William Gramm, March, 1980.
7. Telephone conversation with Lorene Leonhardt Clauss, Remington, Indiana, July 27, 1982.
8. Interview with Sam Zimmerman, Forrest, Illinois, July, 1981.
9. *The Mennonite Encyclopedia,* Volume I, page 447.
10. *The Mennonite Encyclopedia,* Volume I, page 138.
11. Interview with Elder Rudolph Graf, 1404 Keystone Boulevard, Akron, Ohio, July 19, 1980.
12. Nussbaum, Ben, *74 Years of South Side Apostolic Christian Church History,* 1973, Fairbury, Illinois, no publisher, page 73.
13. *Funk and Wagnalls Encyclopedia,* Volume 25, page 9196.
14. *Silver Lining,* September, 1974.
15. *Silver Lining,* September, 1974.
16. *Silver Lining,* September, 1964.
17. Steiner, Orel R., *Apostolic Christian Churches and Ministers,* published by Orel R. Steiner, Oakville, Iowa, 1980, page 17.
18. Getz, Joe A., and Heiniger, Arthur, *History of American Elders,* 1972, page 9.
19. Steiner, page 6.
20. Getz and Heiniger, page 24.
21. Steiner, page 20.
22. Ibid., page 19.

23. Letter of January 6, 1926, from Sam and Mary Clauss, Chicago, Illinois, to Andrew Lehman, Wolcott, Indiana.
24. Same letter; Sam and Mary Clauss to Andrew Lehman.
25. *Funk and Wagnalls Encyclopedia,* Volume 19, page 7037.
26. Steiner, page 1.
27. Interview with John Dapper, Apostolic Christian Church Home, Eureka, Illinois, 1981.

CHAPTER IX
A New Frontier—1935-1982

1. *Silver Lining,* page 13.
2. Steiner, Orel R., *Apostolic Christian Churches and Ministers,* published by Orel R. Steiner, Oakville, Iowa, 1980, page 13.
3. Telephone conversation with Minister Benjamin Hartzler, Marshallville, Ohio, September 2, 1981.
4. *Silver Lining,* May, 1975.
5. *Silver Lining,* July, 1975.
6. *Silver Lining,* August, 1972.
7. Steiner, page 1.
8. Ibid., page 18.
9. Ben Nussbaum, Fairbury, Illinois, wrote histories on both the North Side and the South Side churches.
10. Steiner, page 6.
11. Ibid., page 6.
12. *Silver Lining,* February, 1963.
13. Steiner, page 4.
14. *Silver Lining,* April, 1978.
15. *Silver Lining,* August, 1971.
16. Arrington, Leonard J., and Bitton, Davis, *The Mormon Experience,* published by Alfred A. Knopf, Inc., and distributed by Random House, Inc., New York, 1979, pages 97-98.
17. Letter from Minister William Funk, Garden Grove, Iowa, to Perry A. Klopfenstein, Gridley, Illinois, November 29, 1980.
18. Steiner, page 24.
19. *Funk and Wagnalls Encyclopedia,* Volume 19, page 7004.
20. Steiner, pages 5, 7.
21. Letter from Elder Ben C. Maibach, Jr., Detroit, Michigan, to Perry A. Klopfenstein, Gridley, Illinois, June 11, 1982.

CHAPTER X
Serving the Lord

1. Hastings, James, Editor, *Dictionary of the Bible.* Charles Scribner's Sons, New York, 1961, page 107.
2. Diary of Elder Henry Geistlich, Meilen, Switzerland, who traveled to America in 1866 to visit all the newly established churches, page 25.

3. Letter from Elder Roy Sauder, Peoria, Illinois, to Perry A. Klopfenstein, Gridley, Illinois, January 23, 1982.
4. *Silver Lining,* January, 1967.
5. Letter from Elder Ben C. Maibach, Jr., Detroit, Michigan, to Perry A. Klopfenstein, Gridley, Illinois, January 21, 1982.
6. Wenger, J. C., *The Mennonite Church in America,* Herald Press, Scottdale, Pennsylvania, 1966, page 76.
7. *The Mennonite Encyclopedia,* Volume IV, page 984.
8. I Peter 1:16.
9. Moser, Robert Edward, *The Origin, Content, and Development of the Zion's Harp Hymnal of the Apostolic Christian Church of America.* Master's Thesis, Illinois State University, Normal, Illinois, 1973, page 21.
10. *The New Schaff-Herzog Encyclopedia of Religious Knowledge,* Volume VI, Baker Book House, 1950, pages 383-384.
11. Moser, page 19.
12. Ibid., page 19.
13. Interview with Minister Henry Beer, Milford, Indiana, August 3, 1980.
14. Hostetler, John, *Amish Society,* the Johns Hopkins Press, Baltimore, Maryland, pages 158-159.
15. *The Mennonite Encyclopedia,* Volume IV, page 534.
16. Willis, Wesley R., *200 Years—And Still Counting!,* Victor Books, Wheaton, Illinois, 1973, page 14.
17. Ibid., page 11.
18. *The Mennonite Encyclopedia,* Volume IV, page 657.
19. World Relief Booklet. 1981.
20. World Relief Booklet, 1981.
21. World Relief Booklet, 1981.
22. World Relief Booklet, 1981.
23. World Relief minutes.
24. Information provided by Elder Willis Ehnle, Japan, 1981.
25. *Silver Lining,* July, 1975.
26. Church Elders traveling to Japan over the years kept detailed diaries of their trips. Much information regarding the Japanese mission was gleaned from these reports.
27. *Silver Lining,* May, 1964.
28. Steiner, Orel R., *Apostolic Christian Churches and Ministers,* published by Orel R. Steiner, Oakville, Iowa; 1980, page 25.
29. Ibid., page 25.
30. *Silver Lining,* April, 1980.
31. *Silver Lining,* December, 1979.
32. *Silver Lining,* December, 1974.
33. *Silver Lining,* October, 1970.
34. *Silver Lining,* November, 1976.
35. *Silver Lining,* April, 1944.
36. Letter from Mrs. Irma Souder of the Leo, Indiana, congregation to Perry A. Klopfenstein, Gridley, Illinois, October 17, 1981.

STATEMENT
OF
FAITH

Apostolic Christian Church
Of America

(Adopted by the Council of Elders at Wolcott, Indiana, in January, 1982.)

STATEMENT
OF
FAITH

1. The Bible is the inspired and infallible Word of God to man. The New Testament serves as the foundation of the doctrine of the Apostolic Christian Church. The authorized King James version is embraced. John 1:1, II Tim. 3:16, II Pet. 1:20-21, Rev. 22:18-19.

2. There is one eternal God, the Creator of all things, who exists in three persons: the Father, Son, and Holy Spirit. Gen. 1:1, Matt. 28:19, Col. 1:16-17, Rev. 1:8.

3. Jesus Christ, the Son of God, was begotten by the Holy Spirit, born of the Virgin Mary, and lived a sinless life. Is. 7:14, Matt. 1:23, Heb. 1:1-8, Heb. 7:26.

4. Man was created in God's image, but by his transgression, he became separated from God. All who reach the age of accountability become sinners in thought, word, and deed. Gen. 1:26, Gen. 3, Rom. 3:10, 12, 23.

5. Jesus Christ gave His life a ransom for all on Calvary's cross, shed His precious blood, was buried, and rose again the third day for our justification. Rom. 5:8, I Cor. 15:3-4, I Tim. 2:6, Pet. 1:18-19.

6. Both the saved and the lost will be resurrected: the saved unto eternal life and the lost unto eternal damnation. Dan. 12:2, John 3:16, John 5:28-29, II Pet. 3:7-9, Rev. 20:12-15.

7. A true Christian life begins with faith in Christ's redemptive work on Calvary and repentance. The fruits of repentance are a humble, contrite heart, prayer, godly sorrow, confession to God in the presence of man, forsaking all sin, restitution, and a forgiving spirit. Ps. 34:18, Prov. 28:13, Matt. 3:6-8, Matt. 18:21-35, Lk. 14:33, Lk. 19:8, Acts 17:30, Acts 19:18, II Cor. 7:10, Eph. 2:8-9, Heb. 11:6, I John 1:9.

8. A true conversion is evidenced by a spiritual rebirth, restoration of peace with God and man, the fruit of the Spirit, and obedience to God's Word. John 16:22, Rom. 5:1, Gal. 5:22-26, I John 2:3-6.

9. Following a testimony of faith and conversion, a covenant of faithfulness to God is made. Baptism of faith (by immersion) is administered in the name of the Father, Son, and Holy Ghost. Matt. 28:19, Rom. 6:3-4, I Pet. 3:21.

10. The Holy Spirit is confirmed and sealed in the heart. A prayer of consecration, by the laying on of hands of the Elder follows baptism. As a member of the body of Christ, the believer experiences spiritual growth and edification within the church. Rom. 12:5, Eph. 1:13, Eph. 4:15, Heb. 6:1-2.

11. The New Testament Church appears in two distinct aspects:

    a. A fellowship of converted men and women, with Christ as Head, functioning in accord with New Testament teachings. Matt. 18:20, I Cor. 1:10, Col. 1:18.

    b. The glorious Church, the Bride of Christ, including all saints of all ages, to be fully manifested at the return of Christ Jesus. I Cor. 15:52, Eph. 5:27, I Thess. 4:17.

12. Brethren sound in faith, doctrine, and example serve as elders, ministers, and teachers. They are chosen from the congregation for the furtherance of the Gospel of the grace of God to all people. Matt. 28:19-20, Eph. 4:11-12, II Tim. 2:2, Heb. 13:7,17.

13. The bread and fruit of the vine in Holy Communion symbolize the body and blood of Christ. A closed communion is observed by the church following self-examination. I Cor. 10:16, I Cor. 11:17-32, II Cor. 6:14-18.

14. The Holy Greeting of a kiss of charity is practiced among brethren as a symbol of love for one another. Rom. 16:16, I Cor. 16:20, I Pet. 5:14.

15. The veil or head covering is worn by sisters in the Lord during prayer and worship as a symbol of their submission according to God's order of Creation. I Cor. 11:1-16.

16. The believers live separated, sanctified lives and are not conformed to the world. Discipline of erring members is practiced for their spiritual welfare and for the preservation of the church. Matt. 18:15-17, John 17:14-16, Rom. 12:2, I Cor. 5:1-13, Gal. 6:1, I Thess. 5:22, II Thess, 3:6, 14-15, James 1:14-15, James 4:4, I Pet. 1:14-15, I John 2:15-17.

17. Governmental authority is respected and obeyed. Members serve in a non-combatant status in the military. Oaths are not taken, but truth is affirmed. Matt. 22:21, Luke 3:14, Rom. 13:1-10, I Tim. 2:1-2, Heb. 12:14, James 5:12, I Pet. 2:12-14.

18. Marriage is a lifelong union ordained of God in which a man and a woman of like mind, faith, and fellowship are united in the Lord in Holy Matrimony. Mk. 10:9, I Cor. 7:39, Eph. 5:21-33, Col. 3:18-19, Titus 2:2-6, I Pet. 3:1,7.

19. Although the gift of eternal life is a present possession of every true believer, it is possible for a believer of his own free will to no longer continue in faith, but instead to fall away, return to sin, and consequently forfeit eternal life with Christ. Matt. 25:24-30, John 3:36, John 15:1-7, Rom. 6:16, Rom. 8:35-39, I Cor. 9:27, I Tim. 1:18-20, I Tim. 4:1, II Pet. 2:22, I John 5:11-13, Rev. 2:10, Rev. 3:5, 16, 21.

20. Built upon the Lord Jesus Christ, the church is a closely knit body of believers, sharing each other's joys and sorrows in the true spirit of brotherhood. The church seeks to grow in the love of Christ and the understanding of His Word, always willing to extend a gracious invitation to all to come and worship in spirit and in truth. Luke 24:47, John 4:24, I Cor. 1:10, I Cor. 12:25-26, Eph. 4:16, Phil. 1:21.

APOSTOLIC CHRISTIAN CHURCH GOVERNMENT

1. Local

a. Christ is the head of the church, the Chief Shepherd, and all authority flows from Him. Eph. 1:22-23, I Pet. 5:4.

b. Direction is sought from the congregation for filling teaching and leadership offices either by vote or by personal suggestion. The final decision for appointment rests with the elder, a responsibility given to Timothy by the Apostle Paul. II Tim. 2:2.

c. The bishop or elder and deacons are selected according to the directions given in I Tim. 3 and Titus 1:5-9 and in light of the qualifications stated there. The congregation's sentiment for support of a ministering brother for such duties is obtained by ballot. The final decision for appointment rests with the national elder body for elders and ordained deacons.

d. Duties of offices
   1) Elder: spiritual administration of the church, perform the rites, (baptism, communion, laying on of hands, and weddings), counseling of converts and members, in addition to all ministerial duties. (Heb. 13:7, 17; I Pet. 5:1-5).
   2) Deacon: serves as assistant to the elder as well as all ministerial duties (Acts 6:1-6).

2. Denominational

a. Currently there are 50 active elders who meet semi-annually to handle national governance matters.

b. All doctrinal authority rests with this elder body which depends upon the inspiration of the Holy Spirit and the Word for guidance.

c. There is no hierarchy within the elder body. Each is of equal authority and responsibility except that a rotating committee of five (elected by the body) handles correspondence, making up an agenda, conducting an orderly meeting, and responding to special local congregational needs.

d. Approval of candidates for elder and ordained deacon and for establishment of major church projects rests with the elder body.

e. Extensive communication and cooperation exists among the elders with frequent interchurch visiting and assistance in carrying out duties such as communion, hearing of testimonies and many other important matters.

3. Discipline

Discipline of erring members is practiced for their spiritual welfare and for the preservation of the church (I Cor. 5:1-13, Gal. 6:1, II Thess. 3:6, 14-15). Responsibility for executing discipline rests with the elder and is carried out in the assembly of believers with the support of and for the benefit of the church (I Tim. 5:20).

REPENTANCE, CONVERSION, AND SANCTIFICATION

Faith	Conviction	Profession	Contrition	Confession
Restitution	Separation	Forgiveness	Proving	Covenant
Baptism	Laying on of Hands	Sanctification		Perseverance

Beginning a life for the Lord is a very important and significant time for a believer. Digging deep and building a solid foundation of faith serves to bolster the novice pilgrim as he begins to walk anew and follow the Saviour.

For an Apostolic Christian the intent to follow the Lord goes far deeper than "accepting Christ," "making an objective decision for the Lord," or completing confirmation classes. It involves making a complete and unconditional surrender of self-will to Christ—the putting away and "crucifying" the old man of sin and taking on the righteousness of Christ by faith. A seeking soul comes to the foot of the Cross in a broken and contrite state. This regenerating process is all made possible by the atoning work of the Lord Jesus Christ who bled and died on Calvary's cruel cross.

The experience of turning to the Lord is called "repentance." It embodies many steps and is culminated, after much prayer and supplication, by forgiveness of sin and the wonderful peace of God that "passeth all understanding."[1] This peace can only be realized and fully understood by a sinner who has had his sins forgiven by a benevolent God. Related to repentance is the process of conversion whereby the soul, after repenting toward God, subsequently experiences a dynamic change in lifestyle—from a life of sin and darkness to one of righteousness and circumspection. In this sense repentance is only viable if it is followed by conversion. Repentance without conversion is meaningless. Essentially, repentance is the beginning of a changed life which, if the believer remains faithful until life's end, will lead to eternal life in heaven.

The intention of the convert to humbly carry out the commands of God should in no way be interpreted as a form of legalism which stems from man's own strength and merit. Salvation is totally a work of God. Man, however, must order his life to live in conformity with the wishes of God as revealed in Scriptures. A believer's most sincere wish is to "serve God *acceptably* with reverence and godly fear."[2] He is created unto good works, lest any man should boast.[3]

REPENTANCE—Its Meaning

In order to begin a new life in Christ Jesus a soul must come to the Lord in a meek and childlike way. Jesus said, "Verily I say unto you, Whosoever shall not receive the kingdom of God as a little child, he shall not enter therein."[4] In connection with this the Lord said, "Except a man be born again, he cannot see the kingdom of God."[5]

The overall seriousness associated with beginning this new life stems from the exhortation by the Saviour, who said, "Enter ye in at the strait gate: for wide is the gate and broad is the way, that leadeth to destruction, and many there be which go in thereat: Because strait is the gate and narrow is the way, which leadeth unto life, and few there be that find it."[6]

Jesus also said, "If any man will come after me, let him deny himself, and take up his cross daily, and follow me. For whosoever will save his life shall lose it: but whosoever will lose his life for my sake, the same shall save it."[7]

The Apostle Paul writes in this context, "For if ye live after the flesh, ye shall die: but if ye through the Spirit do mortify the deeds of the body, ye shall live."[8]

The experience of repentance and conversion embodies the act of crucifying the old fleshly nature: "Our old man is crucified with Him, that the body of sin might be destroyed, that henceforth we should not serve sin."[9]

REPENTANCE—The Experience

While the sequence of personal experiences involved in turning to the Lord may vary slightly from individual to individual (due to the extent of previous sins), the general progress is similar among most souls who undergo a true repentance.

The first step, of course, is to have FAITH. One must first believe in the existence of God and have confidence that His Word is revealed in Holy Scriptures. Faith can exist in one's heart even though a soul does not live for the Lord. This is a dead faith, not a saving faith. However, as a person goes to church and hears sermons, attends Sunday School, and/or is taught at home from Scriptures (and by example), he may soon come under CONVICTION. This is a time when a soul becomes burdened because of sinful guilt, feels eternally lost, and can readily recognize his lost and wretched condition before God. This conviction is often compelling and unceasing. Day and night one is reminded through a "still small voice" of his need to do something about the impending doom, eternally, of his soul. His thoughts often turn toward God, toward the suffering Saviour, and toward the positive example he witnesses among members of the church. This provokes a longing in his heart to follow the Lord and live in peaceful contentment.

His desire for redemption, however, is met with another force. Satan cleverly provides a way to drive out these thoughts and to delay the day of repentance, thus reducing the strong desire for a changed life. The desire to serve the Lord may wane for awhile, but it almost always comes back. One longs for the new life—for the courage and grace to hurl oneself into the Lord's bosom—but the prince of the world still maintains a tenuous grip on him.

The time eventually comes, for many, when the sinner can no longer tolerate his sinful condition and the prospect of eternal doom. It is then that he breaks down and makes an outright PROFESSION of his desire to seek the Lord and to turn to him, unconditionally, in repentance.

It is at this time that the seeking soul is able to receive a measure of grace, however meager, to penetrate the wall of darkness that previously kept him in the clutches of Satan, to openly announce, without shame or regret, that he wants to repent and serve the Lord. This act of turning from darkness unto Light is a miracle that can only come from a merciful God.

Repentance is defined as "feeling sorry or self-reproached for what one has done, or not done, in his former life of sin." In this realm the seeking soul exhibits CONTRITION and deep sorrow. He is truly conscience-stricken. His regret and dissatisfaction concerning his fallen estate causes him to entirely abandon his old carnal-oriented life and turn in a new and positive way to God. His former direction, toward eternal doom, is turned completely around, and he now, by the grace and mercy of a loving Savior, turns to travel on the straight and narrow pathway that leads to heaven. He remembers the Scripture, "Ask, and it shall be given you; seek, and ye shall find; knock, and it shall be opened unto you."[10] He thus casts himself in humble prostration at the foot of the cross and begs the Lord Jesus to forgive him for his former sins and iniquity.

The throwing off of the old life of vanity and pride is a serious matter. Old habits are often difficult to abandon. A conflict between the flesh and the Spirit ensues, causing much internal distress. This battle, along with sorrow for sin, often causes much supplication and many tears, although the intensity of inner turmoil is often commensurate with the degree of sin in which one was formerly involved. In this realm, the soul moves ahead within the framework of yieldedness, humility, and submission to God and to the earthly authority He has graciously placed over him. The Biblical teachings of "humble yourself in the sight of God and He will lift you up" and "God resisteth the proud and giveth grace to the humble" are taken literally and put into practice. It is at this time that the seeking soul becomes totally aware of his nothingness in the sight of God. His turning from sin unto righteousness is often painful (because the old habits are cast away). The soul's estate is accurately expressed in the following verses:

"Oh, Jesus look upon My helpless situation;
My heart feels deadly fear; My spirit, condemnation.
Within me is the wish, But not the power to do,
Because my weary soul Is full of grief and woe.

Have mercy then, Oh Lord! Before Thy feet I'm bowing;
Let into my weak heart The stream of grace be flowing.
I pray I'll leave Thee not Until Thy blessing's pow'r
Can conquer death in me, And bring life's blessed shower."
Zion's Harp hymnal No. 45

The burden of sin is so heavy that it can no longer be contained inwardly. CONFESSION of sins to a church Elder is therapeutic and gives great relief to the new convert. Confession to man is done after the example found in the book of Saint Matthew when believers came for baptism to John the Baptist, *"confessing* their sins."[11] Also later at Ephesus, "many that believed came, and *confessed,* and *shewed their deeds."*[12]

Another important step in repentance is making RESTITUTION for past wrongs. In order to be an effective "light" to the world, the convert seeks to be at peace with God *and man.* Previous disagreements, offenses, and disputes are "made right." Humbly and sincerely the convert approaches all persons he has wronged to ask for forgiveness and to explain his intention to follow the Lord in newness of life. This is done according to examples found in the New Testament.[13]

It is very important in being "re-born" to come out from the world of sin and darkness and walk in newness of life. Because as Jesus stated, "they are not of the world, even as I am not of the world;" [14] the new convert takes to heart the Master's words, "Love not the world, neither the things that are in the world. If any man love the world, the love of the Father is not in him." [15] SEPARATION thus represents an adherence to the narrow way that leads to life eternal and offers protection from worldly trends and lusts which "war against the soul." A careless lifestyle could result in apostasy. Love for the things of the world which bear no spiritual fruit crowds out the Spirit, makes one weak in the things of the Lord, and blurs one's power of discernment.

Following confession and restitution, the soul soon finds FORGIVENESS from a benevolent Saviour. Joy and peace then flood his cleansed and purified heart. [16] The Lord's profound nearness and kind providence are felt with a deep impact.

When a seeking soul finds peace with God and man and becomes over-joyed and content with the solace found therein, he is not immediately baptized. A period of time is allowed to elapse in order for the soul to reflect the sustaining grace of God and to indicate his worthy intentions of living for the Saviour. If a soul is able to remain in a state of grace, can remain humble, maintains an identity with the holy church, and zealously desires to continue in faith, he then requests the sacred rite of baptism.

Prior to baptism the soul enters a state of PROVING. Actually this begins perhaps at the inception of the new life. In the ensuing weeks and months the convert proves, both to himself and to God, and also to others, that he has found the grace and stamina to live for the Lord, enduring the temptations and frustrations associated with rejecting the flesh and living devotedly for the Lord. The proving becomes official, or public, when the convert comes before a special session of the congregation to give his testimony of faith and conversion and his willingness to follow the ways of the Lord within the framework of the church. This testimony is given to the satisfaction of the church. If it is evident to the brethren that the soul is humble and sincere and has gone through a common conversion experience, he is then ready for baptism.

Immediately prior to baptism, as the candidate stands in the baptismal water, he makes a COVENANT of lifetime fidelity to God. This two-way promise between God and man will remain valid so long as the believer upholds his end of the covenant. This is a very serious promise that is striking in its impact.

The making of a covenant is immediately followed by BAPTISM. This is done by immersion, a method patterned after the Scripture found in Saint Matthew 3:13-17. Baptism represents a symbolic burial of the old sinful nature (which must be symbolically dead before it can be buried) into the death of Christ and the arising of the believer out of the baptismal waters to a new life in Christ. Since the act of baptism is a symbolic burial, water baptism by immersion is more reflective of a "burial" than sprinkling or pouring, which seemingly have no association with a burial.

Baptism also reflects the "answer of a good conscience toward God."[17] It further demonstrates a vivid expression on the part of the believer of his new life and his total commitment to God.

The LAYING ON OF HANDS rite follows baptism. This act, whereby an Elder lays his hand(s) on the believer's head and prays over him, represents God affixing His seal of the Holy Spirit in the believer's heart.[18] It also officially documents the believer's actions to date (concerning his new life) and is his official entry into the congregation of saints.

SANCTIFICATION—Set Apart As Holy

Repentance and conversion represent a vitally important beginning of a life of faith and obedience. To those who continue to overcome evil until life's end, a glorious and eternal heavenly bliss awaits. Yet, it is only reserved for those who remain true and faithful. To this end, and for the believer's benefit, God has very wisely and mercifully called him to a life of SANCTIFICATION. This aspect of faith represents one of the highest ideals of the Christian life and is an honor for the believer. To be "set apart as holy," at the Master's request, is a serious calling. Jesus, in His high priestly prayer, indicated, "They are not of the world, even as I am not of the world. Sanctify them through thy truth."[19] The term "sanctify you wholly" is used in I Thessalonians 5:23.

In this realm, then, the true believer strives to set aside all in life that is carnal, worldly, and of no benefit spiritually. His motive is to keep his eyes of discernment clear so that he may prove the perfect will of God. As one who is dead unto sin and alive unto Christ, he abhors evil and rejects anything that closely resembles the unfruitful works of darkness or the "appearance of evil."[20] His focus is on spiritual matters and on things that build up the kingdom of God.

The Apostle Peter exhorted believers to live in holiness, "As obedient children, not fashioning yourselves according to the former lusts in your ignorance: But as he who hath called you is holy, *so be ye holy in all manner of conversation;* Because it is written, Be ye holy; for I am holy."[21]

The Apostle Paul exhorted the church at Rome, "I beseech you therefore, brethren, by the mercies of God, that ye present your bodies a living sacrifice, holy, *acceptable unto God,* which is your reasonable service. And be not conformed to this world: but be ye transformed by the renewing of your mind, that ye may prove what is that good, and acceptable, and perfect, will of God."[22]

The high calling of God in Christ Jesus remains very sobering to the believer. He thus orders his life after Scriptures, striving to please his Lord and Saviour. It is imperative that his life reflects the virtues of Christ and that his friends and neighbors see this "light" in him. As an ambassador for his Lord, he does nothing that will bring reproach to the Saviour. Where he goes, how he looks outwardly, and what he says either reflects positively or negatively for the Lord. As a living epistle, known and read of all men, he is careful to walk circumspectly in order that his light will shine out to the world, to the honor and glory of God.[23] With a heart full of grace and love, his life is one of joy and peace; his days are filled with doing good and engaging in those things which reinforce and build up the kingdom of God. His foremost aim in life is to be obedient and to "redeem the time."

In the tradition of the saints of all ages, he strives diligently toward heaven, realizing he is a stranger and pilgrim in this present world, and remembering the teaching of the Apostle Paul, "I press toward the mark for the prize of the high calling of God in Christ Jesus."[24]

The doctrine of PERSEVERANCE remains as a vivid reminder to the true pilgrim. The book of Revelation teaches, "...To him that overcometh will I give to eat of the tree of life, which is in the midst of the paradise of God."[25] The themes of perseverance and overcoming are further reinforced several times in the book of Revelation.[26]

> Now therefore ye are no more strangers and foreigners, but fellow citizens with the saints, and of the household of God; And are built upon the foundation of the apostles and prophets, Jesus Christ himself being the chief corner stone; In whom all the building fitly framed together groweth unto an holy temple in the Lord: In whom ye also are builded together for an habitation of God through the Spirit.
>
> Ephesians 2:19-22

References

1. Philippians 4:7
2. Hebrews 12:28
3. Ephesians 2:9, 10
4. Mark 10:15
5. John 3:3
6. Matthew 7:13-14
7. Luke 9:23-24
8. Romans 8:13
9. Romans 6:6
10. Matthew 7:7
11. Matthew 3:6
12. Acts 19:18
13. Matthew 5:23-24 and Luke 19:8
14. John 17:14
15. I John 2:15
16. Hebrews 12:11 and Romans 5:1
17. I Peter 3:21
18. Acts 8:17-19 and Ephesians 1:13
19. John 17:16, 17
20. I Thessalonians 5:22
21. I Peter 1:14, 15, 16
22. Romans 12:1, 2
23. II Corinthians 3:2
24. Philippians 3:14
25. Revelation 2:7
26. Revelation 2:17, 26; 3:12, 21; and 21:7

THE NEW JERUSALEM

By S. H. Froehlich

1. *Oh city! new Jerusalem, from heaven now descending,*
   How precious now you are to those who are your ways attending.
   Oh King of Zion, you have built this glorious city solely.
   And when in spirit we look up, our cares of earth leave wholly.

2. *What hath my spirit now perceived, of something great attaining?*
   As through this new door now I gazed, the old no more remaining.
   So lovely in abundance now my eye is all attending,
   What caused this silence and sweet rest? I am not comprehending.

3. *My breathing is so easy now, the air is so agreeing,*
   The region is all joyful here where e'er my eyes are seeing,
   And when my eyes look toward the east I see the sunrise gleaming,
   I then am charmed because this place with holiness is streaming.

4. *I think 'tis only but a dream, or some imagination,*
   But no, so how shall I kneel down in true humiliation?
   I am so happy now within, with heav'nly jubilation,
   I am so happy now within, through pain's elimination.

5. *An escort then was sent to me, to walk with me so gently,*
   He kindly offered me his hand, and promised he would guide me.
   So calmly now he leads me with increased acceleration,
   Peace grows within, and now the day shows more illumination.

6. *The sunrays now have reached their height, My Lord, what am I seeing?*
   I asked my guide of these strange fields, who brought them into being?
   And what amazing glory here, who made these sights so pretty?
   Who has this all in order set? Who built this glorious city?

7. *My loved one dear, what sights I see in this full sunlight glowing!*
   This is the land of Canaan now with Zion's border showing.
   The city, new Jerusalem, its doors you are perceiving
   Where you shall soon in comfort dwell, and never more be leaving.

8. *Oh brother! it is now I sense a new life I'm discovering,*
   And there I see in heav'ns gleam the souls of thousands hov'ring.
   I see what I ne'er saw before and it is so astounding,
   I hear oh such a melody, I hear the trumpets sounding.

9. *Oh brother, let your courage rise, think what you will be hearing,*
   And there the watchmen are on guard, your honor they're revering.
   The heav'ns rejoice with gladness now that you have been victorious,
   For now you have eternal peace, and that will be most glorious.

10. How can I prove my righteousness, what merits this within me?
    O brother, when I see my sins, of this I am not worthy!
That door will yet be closed to me; here's my walk's termination,
    So let me in the sunlight here prepare my habitation.

11. My brother, be not now despaired, the door ajar is standing,
    No thought is giv'n to sins up here, and here, no reprimanding
About the things that hindered you, your crossing will be certain,
    Where many of your loved ones dwell, who've gone beyond death's curtain.

12. We now move upward on our way, so swiftly and so easy,
    And there I saw the pearly gate was opened wide before me.
Then as I looked upon the streets, through this door in my vision,
    I thought how pure one has to be, who makes this great decision?

13. A new thought then occurred to me, what peace throughout the ages.
    The Book of Life was opened and my name was on its pages.
My righteousness was soon declared, my wedding garb in order,
    Come servant enter into rest, within this city's border.

14. I now was fully through the door, most royally conducted,
    A robe of white was now my garb and as a prince instructed.
What singing and what shouting here upon these streets they're raising,
    I hardly understood the cause for all this thanks and praising.

15. The city's glory then I saw, its beauty it was boundless,
    Great tones of praise heard far and wide, ne'er leave the city soundless.
The sun is always shining here, its rays the clouds ne'er hiding,
    The rule of love is in control, the judge is never chiding.

16. As I saw now from whence I'd come, to join this numerous union,
    Together there in peace they live, in pleasant sweet communion.
Where each one to the other looks with lovelight fully glowing,
    Soon songs of honor, love, and thanks, unto the Lamb they're showing.

17. My leader asked that I proceed, more distance still unfolding,
    For in this city you will be much greater things beholding.
Then passing through the golden streets, my way I still was wending,
    Till I became so overloved, I was not comprehending.

18. From everywhere I heard them sing the songs with tones victorious,
    I also heard the trumpets and the harps chime oh so glorious.
Here once again we stood a bit, the victors' flags were swaying,
    The victors' crowns were given, too, their conqu'ring pow'rs displaying.

19. Then finally I moved in line, their code of honor heeding,
    A crown of righteousness I gained as I was there proceeding.
A crown of honor, too, was giv'n, while in this place of glory,
    Such as King Solomon ne'er wore as told to us in story.

20. *I now have come to the redeemed, beyond the scenes terrestrial,*
    A citizen complete within the city built celestial.
    Forevermore our joy is full, all grief from here is banished,
    And we are told all things are new, the former all have vanished.

21. *Then nearly to the ground I bowed in true humiliation,*
    What shall I do? What will they do? What is my situation?
    So I cried out, "My God and Lord, my burden you are bearing!
    Such honor you bestow on me, such values you are sharing."

22. *Then everyone who saw me there showed gladness for our meeting,*
    They welcomed me so kindly and embraced me with their greeting.
    The multitude began to praise their Lord who lives forever,
    Because another child came home, his ties no more to sever.

23. *A friend whom I had known on earth, still toward me there was pressing,*
    With loving clasp he shook my hand, then said, my name addressing,
    "Enter into your great reward, we welcome you with pleasure,
    This is true rest, delight and peace, the soul's eternal treasure."

24. *Then soon another came to me and said to me with feeling,*
    Vict'ry, redemption be to you for your true faith revealing.
    Because on earth you gave to me good counsel and example,
    Beside the grace of God in life your guidance was most ample.

25. *Still farther on along the way, these heav'nly brethren guiding,*
    We came unto another place, found other friends residing.
    What are these scenes, these lovely sights, before my eyes appearing?
    Oh yes, it is a children's choir, the sounds that I am hearing.

26. *There I could see them from afar, delight and joy was showing,*
    Also the sounds so wonderful were from their harps uprising.
    These golden harps with heav'nly tones were to God's glory ringing,
    And joined with this you heard the choir their hallelujah's singing.

27. *Respect to God and to the Lamb were central in their praising,*
    Also the sounds so wonderful were from their harps uprising.
    These golden harps with heav'nly tones were to God's glory ringing,
    And joined with this you heard the choir their hallelujah's singing.

28. *I saw their radiant innocence, almost beyond defining,*
    With tenderest humility, their cheeks were bright and shining.
    Full glory, love and happiness, enriched their jubilation,
    I felt they're mine; my friends were there, amidst this congregation.

29. *In their delight I saw them gleam, oh such a home of beauty,*
    Oh peace, true peace, but as for now they leave their choir duty.
    Then soon they're recognizing me and come without delaying,
    To greet me with their welcome and paternal honor paying.

30. *They said, "Dear father, have you come, do you appear before us?*
    Oh triumph, victory, and here, we're thine," said they in chorus.
    Embracing them with outstretched arms, they waited to receive me,
    And then they all began to think that they would never leave me.

31. No one can know just how these scenes to me bring exultation,
       We learn here the true joys of heav'n, and meaning of salvation.
     Salvation to my children, Lord, you highly recommended,
       And now you've shown me this anew, although it never ended.

32. I found my mansion there prepared so nicely and inviting,
       They took me in for on the door my name was placed in writing.
     How ornate here, what splendor, too, the room it is so spacious,
       And many mansions you have made, dear Saviour, you've been
       gracious.

33. The children's little band of love indeed was very touching,
       When there they lead me farther on as they my hand were clutching.
     They brought me to their home where they eternally are reigning,
       And as of now they think that I with them will be remaining.

34. This house of God he built himself, and true it is most surely,
       And here I see the temple, too, as farther on they lead me.
     The fount of life here issues forth, and is God's glory showing,
       In holiness and purity, it crystal clear is flowing.

35. It constantly is flowing on and new streams is creating,
       Providing all the streets up there, its volume ne'er abating.
     Its princes there are honored while the city it's supplying,
       And he who drinks shall never thirst, 'tis fully satisfying.

36. There, too, you see the trees of life, along the stream they're growing,
       How wondrously they spread their limbs, true humbleness they're
       showing.
     One sees them nearly all the time, their green leaves showing clearly,
       They're also filled with sweetest fruit that's yielded twelve times
       yearly.

37. Yet this is not just to behold or only for our knowing,
       This fruit is giv'n for our delight, its good to us bestowing,
     And here is a true paradise prepared for each one's sharing,
       When viewed with Eden's garden now its charm's beyond
       comparing.

38. All trees that grow here may be touched, their fruit's for our receiving,
       The serpent has no room up here, there is no more deceiving.
     True servants here refresh themselves, exhaustion is here never,
       The word is true as we have read, all tears are gone forever.

39. For this is that true Canaan land with milk and honey flowing,
       Tired wanderers can here enjoy heaven's breezes gently blowing.
     Affliction, strife, and sorrow past, true rest is now remaining,
       Here in this holy Zion where God with His own is reigning.

40. And there I saw from Adam on, the Patriarchs, the sages,
       In joy and brightness fully praise, the monarchs of the ages.
     The kings of earth who to the Lord their loyalty had plighted,
       To catch a glimpse of Him from earth would have been most
       delighted.

41. *The teachers and the prophets are in perfect state reclining,*
   Like heaven's stars and planets, they with brightness there are
   shining.
Through faith's light they the Saviour saw, who rescues each believer,
   And then they saw the serpent's face who is man's great deceiver.

42. *The Lord's disciples here in joy and triumph are remaining,*
   They gladly followed Him on earth, but now with Him are reigning.
With grief and trials now all past they there with Him are sharing,
   Next to Him now, they'll judge with Him when man's fate He's
   declaring.

43. *Here one can see great multitudes of holy men selected,*
   The Lamb they served through trial's hour, their strong faith not
   affected.
They stand before the glassy sea, and they God's harps are playing,
   In worship, they before Him fall, to Him full honor paying.

44. *The cherubims and seraphims are openly relating,*
   With countenance uncovered they on this great King are waiting.
One sees them there in worship as before God they are kneeling,
   And now in holiness one hears, the words "thrice holy" pealing.

45. *If I could but express myself to all, what I am seeing,*
   Made joyful by the brightness, it's enchanting all my being.
I saw there in that holy light a bliss beyond defining,
   I saw my Saviour face to face, who wore a crown so shining.

46. *He was so gentle and so mild, but I must cease to share it,*
   For oh, there is no picture that's sufficient to compare it.
A mortal can no more explain, his words are non-availing,
   I therefore now must veil my face because my words are failing.

Translated by Amos B. Hoover
Metered by Martin E. Ressler

INDEX

A

Believers in Christ 96, 100, 312

Bella, Joseph 28, 30, 37, 79, 83-86, 90, 95, 97, 120, 147, 148, 150, 168, 169, 185, 293, 376, 454, 458

Belsey, Joseph 101

Belvidere, Illinois 447

Bender, Arletha Zehr 11, 15

Benniger, John 192

Bern, Kansas 211-213

Berchtold, Jacob 272

Bertsch, David 168, 397, 398, 428, 458, 544

Bertsch, Jay & Dorothy 399-400

Bertsch, Robert 254

Bertschi, Eugene 140, 432, 433, 435, 458, 535

Betz, Andrew 411

Beutel, Sally 502

Beyer, Elizabeth Schiffer 223

Beyer, Geraldine Fankhauser 244

Beyer, Leamon "Rex" 223-225

Beyer, Martin 223

Beyer, Martin N. 223, 225

Beyer, Philip 116, 404, 458

Beyer, Philip A. 23, 412, 473

Beyer, Robert G. 23, 458

Beyer, Sam 328

Bhagwat, Bhagwant B.488, 559

Bible 302

Biedermann, Katherine 279

Birkey, Peter 366

Bishop 453

Black Swamp 124

Black, Thomas 200

Blaurock, Georg 60

Blessman, Martha 400

Bloomington, Illinois 431-434

Blough, Bertha 392

Bluffton, Indiana 84, 90, 145-151

Bluffton, Indiana, North 151-152

Blume, Charles 300

Blume, Dan 300

Blunier, Evelyn 502

Blunier, Homer & Virginia 547

Bollier, Jack 542

Bollier, Theodore 300

Bolliger, Elsie 411

Bolliger, George 411

Bolliger, Henry 323

Bollinger, Jacob 170

Bonaparte, Napoleon 17, 110

Bost, Arni 47

Bozzay, Tibor & Pearl 380

Bradford, Illinois 203, 423-424

Brake, William 33

Braker, Joe J. 164, 412, 458

Braker, Joshua 191, 287

Braker, Samuel 191

Braun, Andrew J. 21, 67, 111, 128, 155, 257, 258, 458, 536

Braun, G. A. 539

Braun, Philip 67, 536-538

Braun, Samuel or S. J. 258, 259, 538, 539

Brehm, Anna 96

Bremen, Indiana 330-332

Brigger Jacob 218

Broquard, Joshua 196, 217, 222, 432, 458

Brother Meeting 455

Brotherhood 62

Brotli, Johannes 60

Bruellman, Emil 191

Brugg, Aargau 9, 39

Bruner, Will 271

Brunschweiler, Johann Joachim & family 53

Brunschweiler, Susette 53

Bryant, Gordon & Marilyn 449

Bucher, Elmer 510, 511, 521

Bucher, Gustave 347, 348, 350

Bucher, Harry 347, 349, 350, 414

Burdick, M.V. 105

Burkert, Mrs. Christian 115

Burkhart, Della & Emma 245

Burlington, Iowa 389-391

Burlington, Oklahoma 273-278, 364

Butikofer, Eleanor 105

Butikofer, Jacob, Sr. 106

Butikofer, Marie 108, 233

Butikofer, Paul 108, 426, 458

Butikofer, Will & Marie, Joel 370

Butler County, Ohio 89

E

Froehlich, Samuel, family
39-41, 53
Fuhrer, John 99
Funk, Frank 233
Funk, George 208
Funk, Rachel Rinkenberger
211

Funk, Tony 430
Funk, Willa 430
Funk, William & Verle 429,
430
Furrer, Will 301
Furuya, Reiko 503

G

Garden Grove, Iowa 428-430
Garfield, James A. 190, 243
Gasser, Arthur 482, 547
Gasser, Roger 438
Gehrig, Caroline 377
Gehring, Isaac 27, 28, 30, 31,
33, 37, 84, 89-92, 95, 108,
118, 119, 120, 121, 147,
148, 170, 279, 280, 293, 459
Gehring, Jacob, Sr. 107
Gehring, Uriel 107, 391
Geisel, Everett 529
Geistlich, Henry 58, 86, 88,
92, 102, 109, 133, 137, 160,
168, 186, 215, 455
Gemeinde 124
Gerber, Christian 48, 49, 50,
84,
Gerber, Christian, Fairbury
186, 196, 215, 217, 222,
300, 306, 459
Gerber, Christian, Langnau
186, 352
Gerber, Christian, Rockville
116, 185, 186, 294, 306, 459
Gerber, Dan 339
Gerber, Edward 411
Gerber, Eli 473
Gerber, Fred 185
Gerber, Jesse 473, 474
Gerber, John & Mary, Forrest
330, 331
Gerber, John, West Bend 191
Gerber, Katherine 213
Gerber, Mathias 191
Gerber, Michael 106
Gerber, Noah 450
Gerber, Paul 334, 336

Gerber, Raymond 472, 473
Gerber, Susan 334
Gerber, Theo & Julia 334
Gerber, Ulrich & Elizabeth 30
German Apostolic Christian
Church 206, 217
German Baptist Church 36
German, George & Eve 99
German language 480
Germann, Edward 331
Gerst, Arnold & Marjorie 420
Gerst, Bill 422
Gerst, Ezra 370
Gerst, Henry 314, 315
Gerst, Joseph 421
Gerst, Leslie 370
Gerst, Lina 370
Gerst, Otto 314, 370, 371
Getchell, Gordon C. 187
Getz, Benita 299
Getz, Ed & Lydia 330
Getz, Ella 306
Getz, Hanna 160
Getz, Jacob 324
Getz, Joe A. 158, 163, 222,
318, 382, 386, 408, 411,
412, 415, 450, 459
Getz, Joseph 320
Getz, Louis 305, 306
Getz, Ludwig 112, 161, 459
Getz, Peter & Katherine 112,
160
Giebel 48
Girard, Ohio 169-171, 581
Girtannin Family 45
Glaser, Peter 314, 315
Glaubige 102
Gleichman, Carrie Emch 269

Gleichman, Ernest 268, 269, 365, 459
Gleichman, Esther 268
Gleichman, Sarah 363
Goetzinger, Sam 366
Goodfield, Illinois 365-368, 582
Gospel Hymns 476, 541
Gottier, Rudolph 185
grace 85
Graf, Clarence 409
Graf, Elmer 237
Graf, Ernest, Sr. 100, 140, 171, 186, 222, 227, 235, 236, 256, 277, 350, 351, 355, 385, 397, 399, 459, 471, 474
Graf, Leon 482
Graf, Rudolph 91, 171, 355, 397, 449, 452, 459, 473, 558
Graham, Dick 488
Graham, Roy 394
Gramm, George 210, 432, 459
Gramm, Sally 502
Gramm, William 347, 349, 350, 480
Grant, Ulysses 182
Gratz, Delbert 146
Gray, Joe 418
Great Depression 117
Grebel, Conrad 60, 166, 469
Green Hill, West Virginia 35, 36
greeting 187, 617
Greiner, August 321
Greiner, Carl 321
Greiner, Fred, Sr. 271
Gridley, Ashael 205, 206
Gridley, Illinois 204-211, 582
Gridley, Kansas 240-242, 583
Grimm, Charley 365

Grimm, Chris 373
Grimm, Christ 220, 309
Grimm, Edward 368, 370, 371, 372, 382
Grimm, Fred 371, 459
Grimm, George 328
Grimm, Harvey 510, 511
Grimm, Henry 145
Grimm, Robert 367, 459
Grimm, Roy 372, 450, 459, 559
Grueter, John & Sally 335
Grusy, Anna 208
Grusy, Engelburt 208, 209, 314
Grusy, Franciska 208
Grusy, Gregory 208
Grusy, Leo 208
Guatemala 488, 491
Gudeman, Albert 323, 324
Gudeman, Arthur (Art) 418, 444, 482, 491
Gudeman, David 324
Gudeman, Emanuel 222, 415, 459, 511
Gudeman, Wendell 325, 332, 428, 430, 448, 459, 482, 507
Guingerich, Melvin 179
Guingrich, J. P. 210
Guingrich, John 218
Guingrich, Joseph 173
Guingrich, Magdalena 131
Guth, Emma 276
Guth, Frederick 67
Guthville, Illinois—see Goodfield, Illinois
Gutwein, Fred 473, 475
Gutwein, Phillip, Jr. 324, 325
Gutwein, Phillip, Sr. 323, 324, 325, 459

H

Haab, Arthur 311
Haab, Edward (Ed) 220, 309, 310
Haas, Ed 492

Haas, Margaret 383
Haas, Robert 379
Habeger, Louisa 190
Habeger, Peter 191
Hacker, Carl 305

I

J

L

M

Meyers, Lydia 523
Michel, Henry 539
Michel, Robert H. 356, 357
midweek services 99
Milford, Indiana 308-313, 589
military service 64, 527-533
Miller, Beatrice 420
Miller, Donald 420
Miller, Gottfried 276
Miller, Guy 181, 254, 512
Miller, Harold 512
Miller, Henry 220
Miller, Jacob John 99
Miller, John 220
Miller, Kathryn 277
Miller, Mike 181, 373, 374, 375
Miller, Noah 375, 420
Miller, Peter 180
Miller, Richard 420
Miller, Rose Steffen 249
Minger, Fred 191
ministers 313, 546, 547
Minneapolis, Minnesota 419-421
Mirror of the Soul 61
missionary journeys 48
Miteldister 140
Mogler, August 260, 261, 262, 263, 320, 460
Mogler, Beverly 422
Mogler, Joan 422

Mogler, Mary 422
Mogler, Phil 510, 511
Mohrman, Gust 373
Moller, Henry 328
Monroe County, Ohio—see Sardis, Ohio 71
Montandon, Emma 253
Moore, Lavoyd 396, 460
Morris, Minnesota 319-322, 589
Morrison, Linda 502
Morton, Illinois 158-164, 590
Moser, Andy 422
Moser, Bill 491
Moser, Chris 319, 320
Moser, Christ 191
Moser, Jacob 220, 262, 320
Moser, Jacob (Jake) 191, 262, 320, 321
Moser, Leo 108, 263, 460
Moser, Marlene 512
Moser, Ray 511
Moser, Rosina 262, 320
Moser, William, Sr. 482
Mosiman, Rose 377
mourners bench 151
Mowery, Rosy 521
Mud-creekers 263
Mueller, August 116
Munz, Conrad 175
mustache 292

N

Naffzinger, Catherine 131
National Archives and Records Service 356-358
Naumburg, New York 9-25, 590
Needy, Oregon 251
Neihouser, Marie—see also Inoue, Marie 502
Nelson, Ronald V. 278, 460
Nesbitt, George 426
Nesbitt, Mary 426
Nester, Ernst 261, 262
Nester, Mary Klein 261
Neuenschwander, Chuck 418
Neutaufer 119

New Amish 102, 295, 354
new birth 148, 180
New Boston, Illinois 318
"New Colossus" 63
New Lighters 180
New Martinsville, West Virginia 34-38, 171
Noffzinger, Catherine 131
Nohl, Arthur H. 322, 460
Nohl, Henry, Sr. 321
Nohl, Jacob 320
Nohl, Lloyd & Joyce 448
non-combatant 346, 353, 359
non-conformity 291
non-resistance 166

O

P

Q

Quinn, Frank 295

R

Radical Reformation 59, 60
Rager, Fred 336
Rager, Gus 271
Rager, John 271
Raikes, Robert 479
Ramseyer, John 303
Ramseyer, Otto 304, 402, 460
Ramseyer, Sam 253, 304
Ramseyer, Vicki 502
Ramsier, John 191
Ramsier, Joseph 121, 460
Ramsier, Peter 218
Ramsier, Robert 524
Rapp, Andrew 156, 161, 162, 294, 460
Rapp, Andy 309
Rapp, Anna Mary 309
Rapp, Barthol 117, 134, 161, 162, 332, 347, 348, 350, 355, 359, 366, 368, 460
Rapp, Christian 162
Rapp, Christian & Mary 161
Rapp, Henry 473
Rapp, Julia 161
Rapp, Katherine 161
Rapp, Mary 309
Rapp, Russell 163, 267, 460, 511, 513
Rassi, Arnold 511
Rassi, Carl 163, 368, 460
Rassi, Henry 309
Rassi, John 309
Rauch, Godfrey 151, 339, 379
Rauch, Gottfried 344, 460
Rauhaus, Albert 315, 318
Rauhaus, William 315
Reber, Mary 271
Reber, William 272, 320
Reeb, John Adam 68, 221, 460
Reeb, Joseph 315
Reeb, Paul 315
Reeves, Rumsey 320
reformation 60

Regina, Saskatchewan 317, 425-426
Rehklau, Elizabeth Imthurn 97
Rehklau, John 124
Reiman, Albert 315, 318
Reimschisel, Max 365
Reineck, Homer 528, 529
Reineck, Joseph 176
Remington, Indiana 296-299, 594
repentance 24, 111, 310, 468, 616, 619, 620
Ressler, Martin E. 629
Rest Haven, Apostolic Christian, Elgin 520
restitution 108, 616, 621
Restmor Nursing Home 164
retirement homes 518-526
Reugg, Jacob 106
Reuter, Magdalena 110
Reuter, Michael, Jr. 110, 111, 454, 460
Rich, Jacob 206, 314
Rich, Joe 208
Richt, Rosa Christina 232
Riedel, John & Marie 363
Rieger, Leonard 487
Riggenbach, Emma 28
Riggenbach, John 36
Riggenbach, Marie 28
Riggenbach, Mildred 28
Riggenbach, Sebastian 36
Rinehard, Benjamin 192
Rinehart, Henry 191
Rinehart, Jacob 212, 328
Ringenberg, William C. 166
Ringger, Art 418
Ringger, Edwin 210, 434, 460, 535
Ringger, Jacob 115
Ringger, Orville 151, 460
Ringger, Ray 487

Rinkenberger, Lynn 496
Rinkenberger, Peter 132, 133
Rinkenberger, Stephen C. 222,
    450, 460
Rittman, Ohio 90, 91, 118-123,
    594
Roanoke, Illinois 82, 134-143,
    595
Rocke, Alvina 536
Rocke, Emil 335, 336
Rocke, Harry 511
Rocke, Joe 284
Rocke, LeRoy 520
Rocke, Melvin 336
Rocke, Ortie 491
Rocke, Percie 335
Rockville, Connecticut
    182-188, 595
Roecker, Adolph 511
Rokey, Andrew 212
Rokey, Carolyn 546
Rokey, Ervin 546

Rokey, Ira 546
Roth, Andrew 195
Roth, Christ 227
Roth, Clara 377
Roth, Daniel 460
Roth, Katherine 216
Roth, Nancy 502
Roth, Peter 286
Rother, Francis 482, 491
Rothlisberger family 71
Ruchti, Elise 329
Rudin, Adolph 309, 310
Ruegger, Herman 110, 116,
    470, 480
Ruegsegger, Chris 303
Rufener, Orin 438
Rumbold, Elvin 497
Rummel, Sophia 265
Rupp, Jacob 227, 235
Rural Gospel and Medical
    Mission 485, 486, 488, 491

S

Sabetha, Kansas 213, 326-329,
    596
Sac Bottom 105
St. Helena Cemetery,
    Strasbourg, France 51
St. Louis, Missouri 450
San Antonio, Texas 447
Sanders, Earl & Emma 383
Sarasota, Florida 403-406
Sardis, Ohio 26-33, 71, 84, 90,
    95, 96, 596
Sattler, Michael 61
Sauder, Amos 300
Sauder, Ben 487
Sauder, Charles 445, 537
Sauder, Chris 404
Sauder, Chuck 487
Sauder, Donald F. 140, 460,
    537
Sauder, Elmer (Bud) 447
Sauder, Henry & Elizabeth—
    see Souder, Henry 167
Sauder, Jacob 167

Sauder, Roy 158, 405, 443,
    460, 511, 512, 513
Sauder, Tim 487
Schaefer, Henry 321
Schaer, Vera 422
Schafer, Bruce 511
Schafer, Louis 191
Schambach, Charles 321
Schambach, Christina 228
Schambach, George 228, 233,
    460
Schambach, Jacobena 228,
    229, 260
Schambach, John 228, 229
Schar, Jacob 249
Scheitlin, Gus 315
Schieber, Carl 511
Schieler, John 216, 297, 298,
    300
schism 290-294, 387-388
Schladenhauffen, Eugene 221,
    340, 460
Schladenhauffen, Karl 170

647

T

Wolcott, Indiana 299-301, 601
World Relief 481-492
World War I 181
World War II 452, 527-530
Worship Language 360-361, 387
Wuethrich, Chris 324

Wuethrich, John 324
Wuthrich, Albert 181, 182
Wuthrich, Fred 180, 309
Wuthrich, John 180
Wuthrich, Mariana 185
Wyss, Carl 443

Y

Yackley, Andrew 314, 370
Yackley, Christian 331
Yackley, Clarence 382
Yackley, Eleanor 7
Yackley, Roy 363
Yackley, Tillie 370
Yaggi, Fred 324
Yamamura, Joseph 498
Yamazaki, Yoshio 499, 503, 507
Yergler, George 222, 301, 338, 339, 340, 377, 378, 414, 461
Yergler, John 151, 209, 461,

Yergler, William & Mattie 340
yieldedness 61
Yoder, Irene "Mimm" 96, 97, 99
Yoder, Will 175
Yoder, William 318
Yost, Andy 91
Young, Albert 145
Young, Elmer 518
Young, Lizzie 145
Young, Robert and Dora 364
Yousey, Mary Keiffer Rauhe 22
youth 548-551

Z

Zapata, Texas 434-436
Zaugg, Emma 320
Zaugg, John 192, 272, 320
Zaugg, Mary 190
Zaugg, Theophil 191
Zehr, Barbara 18
Zehr, John 300
Zeller, Henry 417
Zeltwenger, William 321
Ziegenhorn, Alvin 265
Ziegenhorn, Heinrich (Henry) 196, 218, 219, 264, 265
Ziegenhorn, Raymond 265
Zimmer, Chris 331
Zimmerman, Andrew 131, 297
Zimmerman, Annie 131
Zimmerman, David 191

Zimmerman, John 131, 172
Zimmerman, Michael 131, 133, 134, 172, 461
Zimmerman, Perry 408, 461, 535, 536, 537
Zimmerman, Sam 347, 350
Zion's Harp 33, 139, 237, 311, 463, 466-474, 495, 503, 541, 558
Zobrist, John 162
Zollinger, Albert 227
Zueg, Rudolph 188
Zuercher, Byron 488
Zuercher, Milton 488
Zurlinden, John 218
Zwingli, Ulrich 41, 60, 469

1984 Location of sites or
churches where regular
scheduled services are conducted
by ministers and elders of the
Apostolic Christian Church of America.